Fodor's 2001

The Carolinas and Georgia

The complete guide, thoroughly up-to-date

Packed with details that will make your trip

The must-see sights, off and on the beaten path

What to see, what to skip

Mix-and-match vacation itineraries

City strolls, countryside adventures, beach excursions

Smart lodging and dining options

Transportation tips, distances and directions

Key contacts, savvy travel tips

When to go, what to pack

Clear, accurate, easy-to-use maps

Excerpted from *Fodor's The South*

Fodor's The Carolinas and Georgia 2001

EDITOR: Lauren A. Myers

Editorial Contributors: Andrew Collins, Hollis Gillespie, Mary Sue Lawrence, Lisa H. Towle
Editorial Production: Tom Holton
Maps: David Lindroth, *cartographer;* Rebecca Baer, Bob Blake, *map editors*
Design: Fabrizio La Rocca, *creative director;* Guido Caroti, *art director;* Jolie Novak, *photo editor*; Melanie Marin, *photo researcher*
Cover Design: Pentagram
Production/Manufacturing: Angela L. McLean
Cover Photo (Blue Ridge Parkway, NC): Kelly Culpepper/Transparencies, Inc.

Copyright

ISBN 0-679-00581-1

ISSN 1525-5832

Important Tip

Although all prices, opening times, and other details in this book are based on information supplied to us at press time, changes occur all the time in the travel world, and Fodor's cannot accept responsibility for facts that become outdated or for inadvertent errors or omissions. So **always confirm information when it matters,** especially if you're making a detour to visit a specific place.

Special Sales

Fodor's Travel Publications are available at special discounts for bulk purchases for sales promotions or premiums. Special editions, including personalized covers, excerpts of existing guides, and corporate imprints, can be created in large quantities for special needs. For more information, contact your local bookseller or write to Special Markets, Fodor's Travel Publications, 280 Park Ave., New York, NY 10017. Inquiries from Canada should be directed to your local Canadian bookseller or sent to Random House of Canada, Ltd., Marketing Department, 2775 Matheson Boulevard East, Mississauga, Ontario L4W 4P7. Inquiries from the United Kingdom should be sent to Fodor's Travel Publications, 20 Vauxhall Bridge Road, London SW1V 2SA, England.

PRINTED IN THE UNITED STATES OF AMERICA

10 9 8 7 6 5 4 3 2 1

CONTENTS

On the Road with Fodor's v

Don't Forget to Write *v*

Smart Travel Tips A to Z x

1 Destination: The Carolinas and Georgia 1

The Incongruous South *2*
New and Noteworthy *3*
What's Where *4*
Pleasures and Pastimes *4*
Fodor's Choice *6*
Festivals and Seasonal Events *8*

2 Georgia 10

Atlanta *17*
Savannah *54*
The Coastal Isles and the Okefenokee *75*
Athens to Augusta *86*
North Georgia *95*
Elsewhere in Georgia *102*
Georgia A to Z *103*

3 North Carolina 106

Charlotte *112*
The Triad *122*
The Triangle *133*
The Sandhills *149*
The Outer Banks *154*
New Bern and the Central Coast *164*
Wilmington and the Cape Fear Coast *168*
The Mountains *175*
North Carolina A to Z *192*

4 South Carolina 195

Charleston *201*
Myrtle Beach and the Grand Strand *231*
Hilton Head and Beyond *243*
Columbia and the Heartland *255*
The Upcountry *266*
South Carolina A to Z *271*

5 *Cold Mountain* by Charles Frazier 273

Excerpts from the novel

Index 278

Maps

The Carolinas and Georgia *vi–vii*
The United States *viii–ix*
Georgia *12–13*
Downtown Atlanta and Sweet Auburn *24*
Atlanta Neighborhoods *27*
Downtown Atlanta Dining and Lodging *35*
Atlanta Neighborhoods Dining and Lodging *37*
Savannah Historic District *56*
Savannah Dining and Lodging *65*
The Coastal Isles *77*
North Carolina *108*
Charlotte *113*
Downtown Raleigh *134*
Durham *141*
The Outer Banks *155*
South Carolina *198–199*
Charleston *203*
Charleston Dining and Lodging *215*

ON THE ROAD WITH FODOR'S

EVERY TRIP is a significant trip. Acutely aware of that fact, we've pulled out all stops in preparing *Fodor's The Carolinas and Georgia 2001.* To guide you in putting together your Carolinas and Georgia experience, we've created multiday itineraries and neighborhood walks. And to direct you to the places that are truly worth your time and money, we've rallied the team of endearingly picky know-it-alls we're pleased to call our writers. Having seen all corners of the Carolinas and Georgia, they're real experts. If you knew them, you'd poll them for tips yourself.

Former Fodor's editor **Andrew Collins,** who updated and expanded the Smart Travel Tips A to Z section, writes a weekly syndicated column on gay travel for numerous newspapers as well as for the Web sites gay.com and planetout.com, and he's the travel columnist for *Fairfield County Magazine,* in Westport, Connecticut. He authored *Fodor's Gay Guide to the USA* and recently wrote the *Connecticut Handbook* for Avalon Travel Publishing; he is presently writing the *Rhode Island Handbook* and *CitySmart New Orleans* for the same publisher.

Hollis Gillespie, who updated and expanded the Georgia chapter, was born in Southern California but moved to Atlanta eleven years ago, almost immediately swapped her Valley Girl accent for a Southern drawl. A prolific travel writer and foreign language interpreter, she also regularly pens humor pieces for *Atlanta Magazine* as well as the Atlanta-based Leader publications.

Mary Sue Lawrence, who added fresh insights to the South Carolina chapter, is a freelance writer and editor whose features on travel, entertainment, health, and business have appeared in national and British magazines. She is a South Carolina native and a proud descendant of Charlestonian General William Moultrie. She lives on Sullivan's Island near Charleston, and is a frequent contributor to Fodor's guides.

Lisa H. Towle, the author of the North Carolina chapter, remains fascinated by the diversity of her home state—a place she really grew to appreciate after living away from it for many years. And because she can't decide what part of the Old North State she likes best, she lives in its central portion, thus giving herself equal access to all directions. Lisa, a long-time journalist, has written for a number of national and regional publications and contributed to *Fodor's USA* and *The South's Best Bed & Breakfasts.*

Don't Forget to Write

Keeping a travel guide fresh and up-to-date is a big job. So we love your feedback—positive and negative—and follow up on all suggestions. Contact the Carolinas and Georgia editor at editors@fodors.com or c/o Fodor's, 280 Park Avenue, New York, New York 10017. And have a wonderful trip!

Karen Cure
Editorial Director

The Carolinas and Georgia

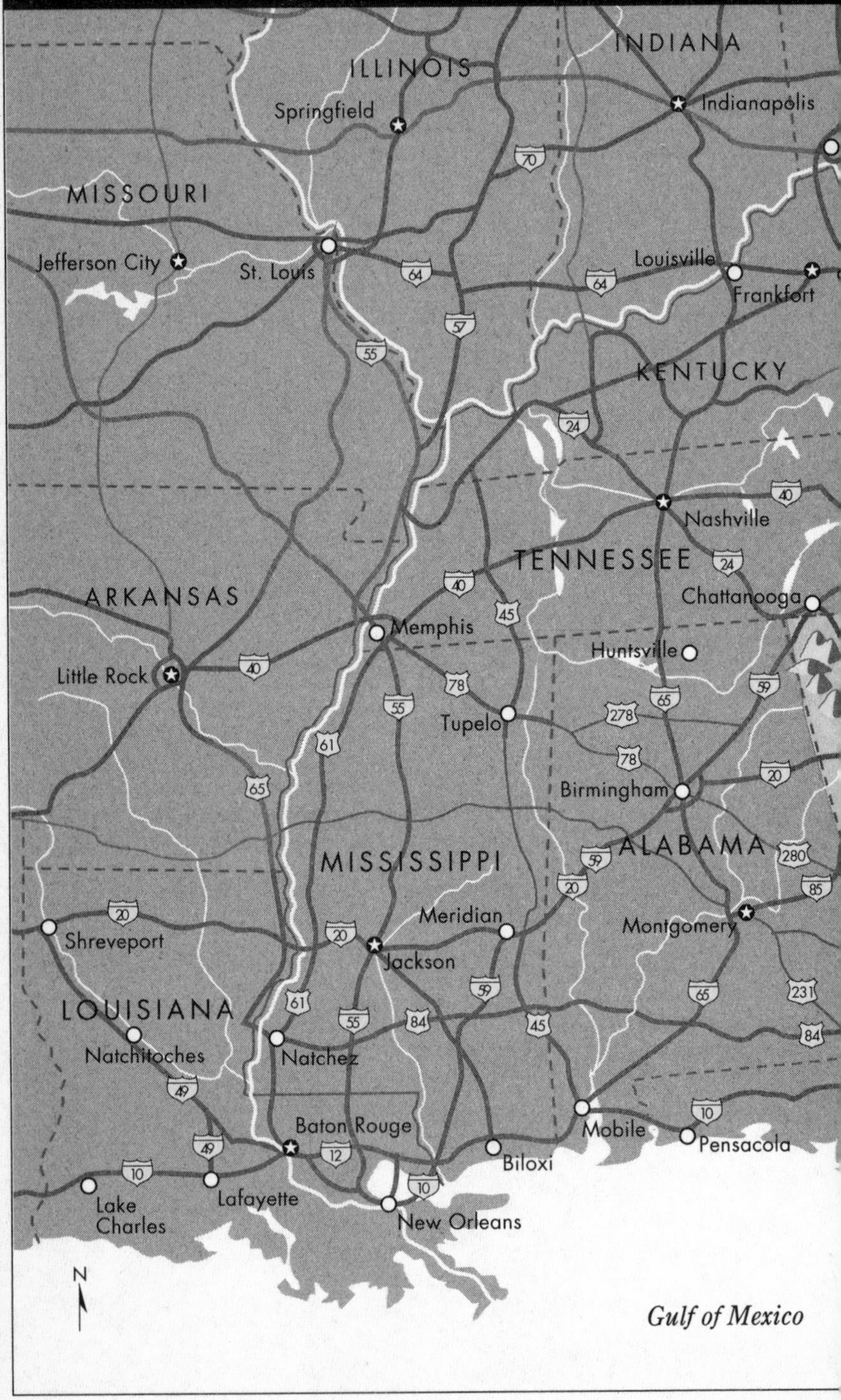

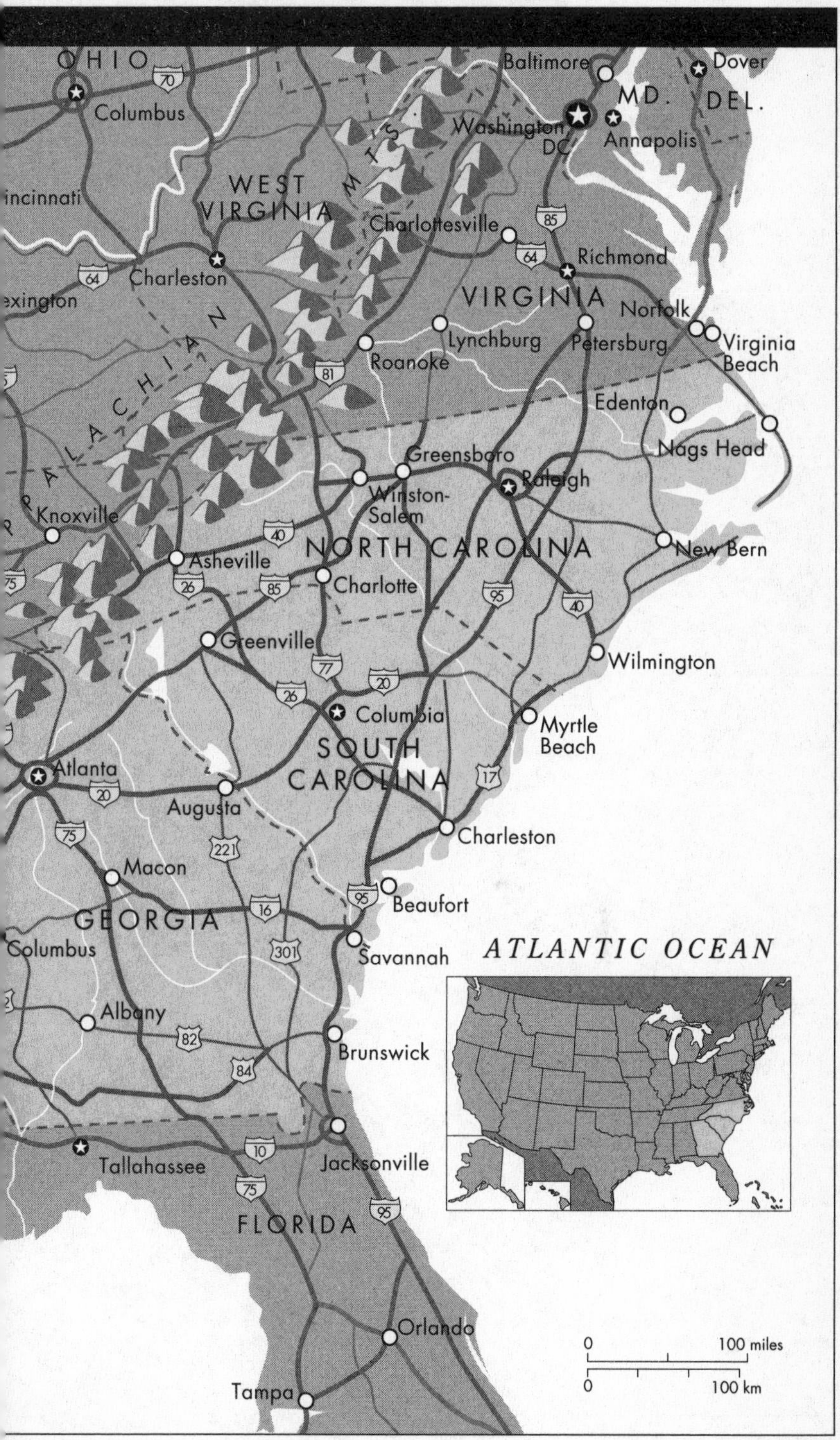
OHIO
Columbus
Cincinnati
WEST VIRGINIA
Charleston
Lexington
APPALACHIAN MTS.
Baltimore
Dover
MD.
DEL.
Washington DC
Annapolis
Charlottesville
Richmond
VIRGINIA
Norfolk
Virginia Beach
Lynchburg
Petersburg
Roanoke
Edenton
Nags Head
Greensboro
Raleigh
Winston-Salem
Knoxville
NORTH CAROLINA
New Bern
Asheville
Charlotte
Greenville
Wilmington
Columbia
Myrtle Beach
SOUTH CAROLINA
Atlanta
Augusta
Charleston
Macon
Beaufort
GEORGIA
Columbus
Savannah
ATLANTIC OCEAN
Albany
Brunswick
Tallahassee
Jacksonville
FLORIDA
Orlando
Tampa
0
100 miles
0
100 km
70
64
85
81
40
26
85
95
40
77
20
26
17
20
75
221
16
95
301
82
84
10
75
95

The United States

ONTARIO
CANADA
QUÉBEC
NEW BRUNSWICK
Fredericton
Québec
MAINE
Augusta
Montréal
Ottawa
Montpelier
VT
Concord
N.H.
Boston
MASS.
R.I.
Providence
CONN.
Hartford
Albany
Hudson R.
NEW YORK
New York
N.J.
Trenton
Philadelphia
PENNSYLVANIA
Harrisburg
Lake Superior
MINNESOTA
Duluth
WISCONSIN
MICHIGAN
Lake Huron
Lake Michigan
Lake Ontario
Toronto
Buffalo
Lake Erie
Cleveland
Green Bay
St. Paul
Minneapolis
Milwaukee
Lansing
Madison
Detroit
Chicago
IOWA
Des Moines
Omaha
ILLINOIS
INDIANA
OHIO
Pittsburgh
Columbus
Indianapolis
Springfield
Cincinnati
Charleston
WEST VIRGINIA
Baltimore
MD
Dover
DEL.
Annapolis
Washington, D.C.
Richmond
Norfolk
VIRGINIA
Topeka
Kansas City
Jefferson City
St. Louis
Mississippi R.
Louisville
Frankfort
Ohio R.
KENTUCKY
MISSOURI
Nashville
TENNESSEE
NORTH CAROLINA
Raleigh
Tulsa
ARKANSAS
Memphis
Little Rock
Mississippi R.
Tennessee R.
Columbia
SOUTH CAROLINA
Savannah R.
Birmingham
Atlanta
GEORGIA
MISSISSIPPI
ALABAMA
Montgomery
Savannah
ATLANTIC OCEAN
Jackson
Jacksonville
Mobile
Tallahassee
FLORIDA
Baton Rouge
New Orleans
Orlando
Houston
LOUISIANA
Bahama Islands
Miami
Nassau
Gulf of Mexico
N
0
500 miles
0
800 km

SMART TRAVEL TIPS A TO Z

Basic Information on Traveling in the Carolinas and Georgia, Savvy Tips to Make Your Trip a Breeze, and Companies and Organizations to Contact

AIR TRAVEL

BOOKING YOUR FLIGHT

Price is just one factor to consider when booking a flight: frequency of service and even a carrier's safety record are often just as important. Major airlines offer the greatest number of departures. Smaller airlines—including regional and no-frills airlines—usually have a limited number of flights daily. On the other hand, low-cost airlines usually are cheaper, and their fares impose fewer restrictions, such as advance-purchase requirements. Safety-wise, low-cost carriers as a group have a good history—about equal to that of major carriers.

When you book **look for nonstop flights** and **remember that "direct" flights stop at least once.** Try to avoid connecting flights, which require a change of plane.

CARRIERS

➤ MAJOR AIRLINES: **American** (☎ 800/433–7300). **Continental** (☎ 800/525–0280). **Delta** (☎ 800/221–1212). **Northwest Airlines/KLM** (☎ 800/225–2525). **TWA** (☎ 800/221–2000). **United** (☎ 800/241–6522). **US Airways** (☎ 800/428–4322).

➤ SMALLER AIRLINES: **Air Canada** (☎ 800/776–3000). **AirTran** (☎ 770/994–8258 or 800/247–8726). **American Eagle** (☎ 800/433–7300). **Atlantic Southeast/Delta Connection** (☎ 800/221–1212 or 800/282–3424). **ComAir** (☎ 800/221–1212). **Continental Express** (☎ 800/525–0280). **Eastwind** (☎ 888/327–8946). **Kiwi** (☎ 800/538–5494). **Midway** (☎ 800/446–4392). **Midwest Express** (☎ 800/452–2022). **Northwest Airlink** (☎ 800/225–2525). **Southwest** (☎ 800/435–9792). **Spirit** (☎ 800/772–7117). **TW Express** (☎ 800/221–2000).

➤ FROM THE U.K.: **American** (☎ 0345/789–789). **British Airways** (☎ 0345/222–111). **Delta** (☎ 0800/414–767).

For further information on airports and airlines serving the Carolinas and Georgia, see individual state chapters.

CHECK-IN & BOARDING

Assuming that not everyone with a ticket will show up, airlines routinely overbook planes. When everyone does, airlines ask for volunteers to give up their seats. In return, these volunteers usually get a certificate for a free flight and are rebooked on the next flight out. If there are not enough volunteers, the airline must choose who will be denied boarding. The first to get bumped are passengers who checked in late and those flying on discounted tickets, so **get to the gate and check in as early as possible,** especially during peak periods.

Always **bring a government-issued photo I.D. to the airport.** You may be asked to show it before you are allowed to check in.

CUTTING COSTS

The least expensive airfares to the Carolinas and Georgia must usually be purchased in advance and are nonrefundable. It's smart to **call a number of airlines, and when you are quoted a good price, book it on the spot**—the same fare may not be available the next day. Always **check different routings** and look into using different airports. Travel agents, especially low-fare specialists (☞ Discounts & Deals, *below*), are helpful.

Consolidators are another good source. They buy tickets for scheduled international flights at reduced rates from the airlines, then sell them at prices that beat the best fare available directly from the airlines, usually without restrictions. Sometimes you can even get your money back if you need to return the ticket. Carefully read the fine print detailing penalties for changes and cancellations, and **confirm your consolidator reservation with the airline.**

When you **fly as a courier,** you trade your checked-luggage space for a ticket deeply subsidized by a courier service. There are restrictions on when you can book and how long you can stay.

➤ CONSOLIDATORS: **Cheap Tickets** (☎ 800/377–1000). **Discount Airline Ticket Service** (☎ 800/576–1600). **Unitravel** (☎ 800/325–2222). **Up & Away Travel** (☎ 212/889–2345). **World Travel Network** (☎ 800/409–6753).

ENJOYING THE FLIGHT

For more legroom, **request an emergency-aisle seat.** Don't sit in the row in front of the emergency aisle or in front of a bulkhead, where seats may not recline. If you have dietary concerns, **ask for special meals when booking.** These can be vegetarian, low-cholesterol, or kosher, for example. On long flights, try to maintain a normal routine, to help fight jet lag. At night, **get some sleep.** By day, **eat light meals, drink water** (not alcohol), and **move around the cabin** to stretch your legs.

FLYING TIMES

Flying time to Atlanta is 2½ hours from New York, 2 hours from Chicago, 4½ hours from Los Angeles, 2 hours from Dallas, and 9 hours from London. Charlotte is an hour northeast of Atlanta, Raleigh 75 minutes northeast, Wilmington an hour and 45 minutes east, and Charleston, Hilton Head, and Savannah an hour east–southeast.

HOW TO COMPLAIN

If your baggage goes astray or your flight goes awry, complain right away. Most carriers require that you **file a claim immediately.**

➤ AIRLINE COMPLAINTS: U.S. Department of Transportation **Aviation Consumer Protection Division** (✉ C-75, Room 4107, Washington, DC 20590, ☎ 202/366–2220, airconsumer@ost.dot.gov, www.dot.gov/airconsumer). **Federal Aviation Administration Consumer Hotline** (☎ 800/322–7873).

AIRPORTS

➤ AIRPORT INFORMATION: **Hartsfield Atlanta International Airport** (✉ 6000 N. Terminal Pkwy., ☎ 404/530–6600 or 404/209–1700). **Raleigh-Durham International Airport** (✉ 1600 Terminal Blvd., ☎ 919/840–2123). **Charleston International Airport** (✉ 5500 International Blvd., ☎ 843/767–1100). **Savannah International Airport** (✉ 400 Airways Ave., ☎ 912/964–0514)).

For more information on airports serving the Carolinas and Georgia, *see* the A to Z section at the end of each regional section *in* individual state chapters.

BIKE TRAVEL

Throughout coastal Georgia, South Carolina, and North Carolina hills are few and the scenery remarkable. You'll find a number of extensive, in many cases marked, bike routes throughout North Carolina's Outer Banks, around Savannah and Georgia's coastal islands, and throughout greater Charleston and coastal South Carolina's Low Country. Serious enthusiasts, especially of mountain-biking, might take to the more precipitous parts of North Carolina and Georgia, toward the Great Smoky and north Georgia mountains, respectively.

There are dozens of local bike clubs throughout the area. To reach one of these groups, which generally welcome visitors and can provide detailed advice on local routes and rental shops, contact the local tourist board or visit the appropriate tourism Web site (☞ Web sites, *below*), many of which have information on or links to area cycling resources. Many tourist boards also distribute bike maps.

BIKES IN FLIGHT

Most airlines accommodate bikes as luggage, provided they are dismantled and boxed. For bike boxes, often free at bike shops, you'll pay about $5 from airlines (at least $100 for bike bags). International travelers can sometimes substitute a bike for a piece of checked luggage at no charge; otherwise, the cost is about $100. Domestic and Canadian airlines charge $25–$50.

BOOKS AND VIDEOS

Before your trip, you may want to read some books or watch some movies about the region, which, like the rest of the South, has given rise to a substantial literary heritage: novels, drama, and poetry, as well as short stories and songs. Its authors have many a Pulitzer, among them Georgia-born Caroline Miller for fiction (*Lamb in His Bosom*, 1934). You can choose from works by Thomas Wolfe, Reynolds Price, Pat Conroy, and Flannery O'Connor, to name just a few. Charles Frazier's 1997 novel *Cold Mountain*, about the journeys of a Confederate soldier in western North Carolina, won a National Book Award.

The area has produced writers of popular fiction as varied as Margaret Mitchell (*Gone With the Wind*), Kaye Gibbons, and Anne Rivers Siddons. The late journalist Charles Kuralt was a North Carolinian whose books included *Charles Kuralt's America*. Tom Wolfe weaves tales of success and failure in modern Atlanta in his novel *A Man in Full*. Although it's not by a Southerner, John Berendt's nonfiction *Midnight in the Garden of Good and Evil* is a tale of modern-day mayhem in sultry Savannah.

One important element in Southern culture is the region's passion for history, defined as both personal, family history and regional history. To see the importance of the Civil War period, view Ken Burns's nine-episode PBS television documentary *The Civil War*. Shelby Foote's three-volume history, *The Civil War*, is excellent, as is James McPherson's one-volume *Battle Cry of Freedom*, another history of the war.

The classic treatise on the culture of the South is W. J. Cash's groundbreaking *The Mind of the South*, published more than 50 years ago. The *Oxford Book of the American South*, edited by Edward L. Ayers and Bradley C. Mittendorf, is an outstanding collection of Southern writing about the region from the 18th century to the present.

For a clear picture of classic Southern architecture, look at Mills B. Lane's series *The Architecture of the Old South* from his Beehive Press. Each book is devoted to a single state and has black-and-white photographs that handsomely detail the richness of 19th-century Southern architecture. The definitive book on Southern food is sociologist John Egerton's *Southern Cooking: On the Road, at Home, and in History*, a veritable treatise on Southern culture that includes many fine recipes.

Alfred Uhry's *Driving Miss Daisy*, a Pulitzer Prize–winning play and award-winning film, portrays an aspect of relationships between the races in the South. Black Southern writers, of both fiction and nonfiction, now get the recognition they deserve. Although she currently lives in San Francisco, Alice Walker (from Eatonton, Georgia) made her mark with the book *The Color Purple*, later a film.

The most important resource for Southern culture produced in recent years is the work of the Center for Southern Culture at the University of Mississippi in Oxford. Its single-volume *Encyclopedia of Southern Culture* serves as a guide to all matters Southern.

Fodor's *Compass American Guides: Georgia*, *Compass American Guides: North Carolina*, and *Compass American Guides: South Carolina*, with their handsome photos and historical, cultural, and topical essays, are good companions to this guide.

BUS TRAVEL

Regional bus service, provided by Greyhound, is abundant throughout the Carolinas and Georgia. It's a handy and affordable means of getting around; if it's a simple matter of getting from one city to another, and you've got a bit of time on your hands, consider this option. Remember that buses sometimes make frequent stops, which may delay you but may also provide you the chance to see parts of the region you might not otherwise. For a comparison of different ways of getting around the region, see Transportation to and Around the Carolinas and Georgia, *below.*

CUTTING COSTS

Greyhound offers the **Ameripass,** which allows unlimited travel in the United States within any 7-, 10-, 15-, 30-, 45-, or 60-day periods ($169 to $479, depending on length of the pass), and the similar International Ameripass (for non-U.S. residents only), which offers the same 7- to 60-day passes for $149 to $429. Greyhound also has senior citizen, children's, and student discounts.

➤ BUS INFORMATION: **Greyhound** (☎ 800/231–2222) operates passenger buses connecting many towns and cities in the region.

BUSINESS HOURS

Banks are usually open weekdays 9 to 3 and some Saturday mornings, the post office from 8 to 5 weekdays and often on Saturday mornings. Shops in urban and suburban areas, particularly in indoor and strip malls, typically open at 9 or 10 daily and stay open until anywhere from 6 to 10 PM on weekdays and Saturdays, and until 5 or 6 on Sundays. Hours vary greatly, so call ahead when in doubt.

CAMERAS & PHOTOGRAPHY

➤ PHOTO HELP: **Kodak Information Center** (☎ 800/242–2424). ***Kodak Guide to Shooting Great Travel Pictures,*** available in bookstores or from Fodor's Travel Publications (☎ 800/533–6478; $16.50 plus $5.50 shipping).

CAR RENTAL

Rates vary from city to city, generally being lowest in destinations with busy airports, where there's the greatest competition. Below is a range of sample rates, for both economy and luxury car-rentals, quoted by the most popular agencies in two major cities (note that unlimited mileage is nearly always included).

In Atlanta, daily rates range from about $32 to $59 for an economy car to $65 to $100 for luxury car; weekly rates range from $170 to $285 for economy to $290 to $530 for luxury. Atlanta has an additional 7% sales tax, and at the airport location there are also a 10% "concession recoupment fee" and a 3% airport excise tax.

In Raleigh, daily rates range from about $46 to $65 for an economy car to $78 to $80 for a luxury car; weekly rates range from $209 to $265 for economy to $345 to $370 for luxury. Raleigh has an additional 8% sales tax and a 5% local transportation tax, and at the airport location there's also a 10% "concession recoupment fee."

These rates are typical of those found in larger cities in the Carolinas and Georgia, but specials and deals may be available based upon dates of travel and length of contract. It's important to **reserve a car well in advance of your expected arrival.**

➤ MAJOR AGENCIES: **Alamo** (☎ 800/327–9633; 020/8759–6200 in the U.K.). **Avis** (☎ 800/331–1212; 800/879–2847 in Canada; 02/9353–9000 in Australia; 09/525–1982 in New Zealand). **Budget** (☎ 800/527–0700; 0144/227–6266 in the U.K.). **Dollar** (☎ 800/800–4000; 020/8897–0811 in the U.K., where it is known as Eurodollar; 02/9223–1444 in Australia). **Hertz** (☎ 800/654–3131; 800/263–0600 in Canada; 020/8897–2072 in the U.K.; 02/9669–2444 in Australia; 03/358–6777 in New Zealand). **National InterRent** (☎ 800/227–7368; 0845/722–2525 in the U.K., where it is known as Europcar InterRent).

CUTTING COSTS

To get the best deal, **book through a travel agent who will shop around.** Also **price local car-rental companies,** although the service and maintenance may not be as good as those of a major player. Some off-airport locations offer lower rates, and their lots are only minutes from the terminal via complimentary shuttle. Also ask whether certain frequent-flyer, American Automobile Association (AAA), corporate, or other such promotions are accepted; and whether the rates might be lower the day before or after you had originally intended to travel. In some cases, you'll find that the same agency offers a region's cheapest luxury car rates but priciest economy cars, or that the cheapest agency in one city may have high rates in another. It pays to check around.

Also, while economy is almost always your cheapest option, agencies sometimes offer upgrade specials that cost only a dollar or two more per day. Think carefully about how much and where you'll be using the car before choosing among economy, compact, standard, luxury, or premium; it may be worth the extra few dollars per day for a more substantial vehicle if you're traveling long distances, driving up into the mountains or over rugged terrain, traveling with more than a couple passengers, or using the car extensively.

Remember to ask about required deposits, cancellation penalties, and drop-off charges if you're planning to pick up the car in one city and leave it in another. If you're traveling during a holiday period, make sure that a confirmed reservation guarantees you a car.

INSURANCE

When driving a rented car you are generally responsible for any damage to or loss of the vehicle as well as for any property damage or personal injury that you may cause. Before you rent, see what coverage your personal auto-insurance policy and credit cards already provide.

For about $15 to $20 per day, rental companies sell protection, known as a collision- or loss-damage waiver (CDW or LDW), that eliminates your liability for damage to the car.

In most states you don't need a CDW if you have personal auto insurance or other liability insurance. However, **make sure you have enough coverage to pay for the car.** If you do not have auto insurance or an umbrella policy that covers damage to third parties, purchasing liability insurance and a CDW or LDW is highly recommended.

REQUIREMENTS & RESTRICTIONS

In the Carolinas and Georgia you must be 21 to rent a car, and rates may be higher if you're under 25. You'll pay extra for child seats (about $3 per day), which are compulsory for children under five, and for additional drivers (about $2 per day). Non-U.S. residents will need a reservation voucher, a passport, a driver's license, and a travel policy that covers each driver, when picking up a car.

SURCHARGES

Before you pick up a car in one city and leave it in another, **ask about drop-off charges or one-way service fees,** which can be substantial. Note, too, that some rental agencies charge extra if you return the car before the time specified in your contract. To avoid a hefty refueling fee, **fill the tank just before you turn in the car,** but be aware that gas stations near the rental outlet may overcharge.

CAR TRAVEL

A car is your most practical and economical means of traveling around the Carolinas and Georgia. Atlanta, Savannah, Charleston, Myrtle Beach, and Asheville can also be explored fairly easily on foot or using public transit and cabs, but a car is helpful to reach many of the most intriguing museums, parks, restaurants, and lodgings nearby.

Although you'll make the best time traveling along the South's extensive network of interstate highways, keep in mind that U.S. and state highways offer some delightful scenery and the opportunity to stumble upon funky roadside diners, leafy state parks, and historic town squares. While the area is rural, it's still densely populated, so you'll rarely drive for more than 20 or 30 mi—even on local roads—without passing roadside services, such as gas stations, restaurants, and ATM machines.

Among the most scenic highways in the Carolinas and Georgia, consider **U.S. 78** across Georgia; **U.S. 25, 19, 74,** and **64** through the Great Smoky Mountains of western North Carolina; **U.S. 17** from Brunswick, GA along the coast through South Carolina and North Carolina; and the **Blue Ridge Parkway** from the eastern fringes of the Great Smoky Mountains through western North Carolina into Virginia.

Here are some common distances and approximate travel times between popular destinations: Atlanta to Myrtle Beach is 360 mi and about 5 hours; Nags Head and the Outer Banks of North Carolina to Savannah is 515 mi and 7½ hours; Columbus (GA) to the North Carolina/Virginia border on I–95 is 600 mi and 8 hours; and Asheville to Charleston is 266 mi and a little over 3 hours.

For a comparison of different ways of getting around the region, *see* Transportation to and Around the Carolinas and Georgia, *below.*

RULES OF THE ROAD

State lawmakers now set speed limits, even for federal interstate highways. Limits vary from state to state and from rural to urban areas, so **check posted speeds frequently.**

ROAD MAPS

Rand McNally and **Delorme** produce highly detailed atlases of all seven southern states, while a number of companies including Rand McNally produce foldout state, regional, and city maps that cover the Carolinas and Georgia. These are available at service stations and from bookstores throughout the region.

If you're a serious road-tripper and you have a laptop along with you that has a CD-ROM drive, definitely consider investing in CD-ROM road atlases and trip planners—these handy disks can pinpoint exact locations of virtually every address in America, highlight attractions and certain businesses, and calculate times and distances for just about any itinerary you can dream up. **Delorme** and **Expedia** both make extremely user-friendly CD-ROMs, with costs ranging from about $30 to $50; they are available at just about any store that sells computer software.

CHILDREN IN THE CAROLINAS AND GEORGIA

Most of the Carolinas and Georgia is ideal for travel with kids. This is an enjoyable part of the country for family road trips, and things are relatively affordable—you'll have no problem finding inexpensive kid-friendly hotels and family-style restaurants. Just keep in mind that a number of fine, antiques-filled B&Bs and inns punctuate the landscape, and these places are less suitable for kids—some of them flat-out refuse to accommodate children. Also, some of the quieter and more rural parts of the region—while exuding history—lack children-oriented attractions.

If you are renting a car, don't forget to **arrange for a car seat** when you reserve.

FLYING

If your children are two or older, **ask about children's airfares.** As a general rule, infants under two not occupying a seat fly at greatly reduced fares or even for free.

Experts agree that it's a good idea to use safety seats aloft for children weighing less than 40 pounds. Airlines set their own policies: U.S. carriers usually require that the child be ticketed, even if he or she is young enough to ride free, since the seats must be strapped into regular seats. Do **check your airline's policy about using safety seats during takeoff and landing.** And since safety seats are not allowed just everywhere in the plane, get your seat assignments early.

When reserving, **request children's meals or a freestanding bassinet** if you need it. But note that bulkhead seats, where you must sit to use the bassinet, may lack an overhead bin or storage space on the floor.

LODGING

Most hotels in the Carolinas and Georgia allow children under a certain age to stay in their parents' room at no extra charge, but others charge for them as extra adults; be sure to **find out the cutoff age for children's discounts.**

SIGHTS & ATTRACTIONS

Places that are especially appealing to children are indicated by a rubber duckie icon in the margin.

CONSUMER PROTECTION

Whenever shopping or buying travel services in the Carolinas and Georgia, **pay with a major credit card** so you can cancel payment or get reimbursed if there's a problem. If you're doing business with a particular company for the first time, **contact your local Better Business Bureau and the attorney general's offices** in your own state and the company's home state, as well. Have any complaints been filed? Finally, if you're buying a package or tour, always **consider travel insurance** that includes default coverage (☞ Insurance, *below*).

➤ BBBs: **Council of Better Business Bureaus** (✉ 4200 Wilson Blvd., Suite 800, Arlington, VA 22203, ☎ 703/276–0100, FAX 703/525–8277, www.bbb.org).

DINING

While certain ingredients and preparations are common in southern cooking, the genre as a whole varies greatly not only from state to state but county to county. Nevertheless, in the Carolinas and Georgia you'll often find restaurants serving black-eyed peas, catfish, chitlins (fried tripe), corn on the cob, crab claws, cole slaw, crawfish, fried chicken, hushpuppies, fried green tomatoes, grits, collared greens, chicken-fried steak, raw and fried shellfish (especially oysters and shrimp), and desserts infused with pecans, peaches, peanuts, caramelized bananas, or sweet potatoes.

A number of fast-food chain eateries are based in the South. These include the Krispy Kreme doughnut chain, Shoney's, Cracker Barrel, Waffle House, Hardee's, Popeye's, and Chick-fil-A. You'll also likely encounter hearty and filling, if at times greasy, cuisine at most of the affordable luncheonettes, diners, and family-style eateries that proliferate in rural, suburban, and urban areas.

Over the past couple of decades, most southern cities—especially boom towns like Atlanta, Charleston, Savannah, and Charlotte—have partaken of the nation's culinary revolution. In these parts you'll discover regional ingredients and time-honored recipes running head-on with inventive twists and foods and styles borrowed from myriad faraway places, from Latin America to the Mediterranean to the Pacific Rim. Some of America's finest culinary talents can be found in a surprising number of tiny, off-the-beaten-path hamlets, too.

The restaurants we list are the cream of the crop in each price category. They are indicated in the text by ✕. Properties indicated by ✕🏨 are lodging establishments whose restaurant warrants a special trip.

RESERVATIONS & DRESS

Reservations are always a good idea: we mention them only when they're essential or not accepted. Book as far ahead as you can, and reconfirm as soon as you arrive. We mention dress only when men are required to wear a jacket or a jacket and tie.

DISABILITIES & ACCESSIBILITY

The Carolinas and Georgia rank on par with the rest of America in terms of their accessibility for persons with disabilities or special needs. A drawback is the abundance of historic accommodations, restaurants, and attractions with narrow staircases, doorways, and small rooms that fail to conform to the Americans with Disabilities Act (ADA) guidelines. Increasingly, however, businesses throughout the region—especially those in densely populated areas—are changing to improve accessibility.

RESERVATIONS

When discussing accessibility with an operator or reservations agent, **ask hard questions.** Are there any stairs, inside *or* out? Are there grab bars next to the toilet *and* in the shower/tub? How wide is the doorway to the room? To the bathroom? For the most extensive facilities meeting the latest legal specifications, **opt for newer accommodations.**

TRANSPORTATION

➤ COMPLAINTS: **Disability Rights Section** (✉ U.S. Department of Justice, Civil Rights Division, Box 66738, Washington, DC 20035-6738, ☎ 202/514–0301 or 800/514–0301; TTY 202/514–0301 or 800/514–0301, FAX 202/307–1198) for general complaints. **Aviation Consumer Protection Division** (☞ Air Travel, *above*) for airline-related problems. **Civil Rights Office** (✉ U.S. Department of Transportation, Departmental Office of Civil Rights, S-30, 400 7th St. SW, Room 10215, Washington, DC 20590, ☎ 202/366–4648, FAX

202/366–9371) for problems with surface transportation.

TRAVEL AGENCIES

In the United States, the Americans with Disabilities Act requires that travel firms serve the needs of all travelers. Some agencies specialize in working with people with disabilities.

➤ TRAVELERS WITH MOBILITY PROBLEMS: **Access Adventures** (✉ 206 Chestnut Ridge Rd., Rochester, NY 14624, ☎ 716/889–9096, dltravel@prodigy.net), run by a former physical-rehabilitation counselor. **Accessible Vans of the Rockies** (✉ 2040 W. Hamilton Pl., Sheridan, CO 80110, ☎ 303/806–5047 or 888/837–0065, FAX 303/781–2329, www.access-able.com/avr/avrockies.htm). **CareVacations** (✉ 5-5110 50th Ave., Leduc, Alberta T9E 6V4, ☎ 780/986–6404 or 877/478–7827, FAX 780/986–8332, www.carevacations.com), for group tours and cruise vacations. **Flying Wheels Travel** (✉ 143 W. Bridge St., Box 382, Owatonna, MN 55060, ☎ 507/451–5005 or 800/535–6790, FAX 507/451–1685, thq@ll.net, www.flyingwheels.com).

➤ TRAVELERS WITH DEVELOPMENTAL DISABILITIES: **Sprout** (✉ 893 Amsterdam Ave., New York, NY 10025, ☎ 212/222–9575 or 888/222–9575, FAX 212/222–9768, sprout@interport.net, www.gosprout.org).

DISCOUNTS & DEALS

Be a smart shopper and **compare all your options** before making decisions. A plane ticket bought with a promotional coupon from travel clubs, coupon books, and direct-mail offers may not be cheaper than the least expensive fare from a discount ticket agency. And always keep in mind that what you get is just as important as what you save.

DISCOUNT RESERVATIONS

To save money, **look into discount reservations services** with toll-free numbers, which use their buying power to get a better price on hotels, airline tickets, even car rentals. When booking a room, always **call the hotel's local toll-free number** (if one is available) rather than the central reservations number—you'll often get a better price. Always ask about special packages or corporate rates.

➤ AIRLINE TICKETS: ☎ **800/FLY–4–LESS.**

➤ HOTEL ROOMS: **Accommodations Express** (☎ 800/444–7666, www.accommodationsexpress.com). **Central Reservation Service (CRS)** (☎ 800/548–3311). **Hotel Reservations Network** (☎ 800/964–6835, www.hoteldiscounts.com). **Quickbook** (☎ 800/789–9887, www.quickbook.com). **RMC Travel** (☎ 800/245–5738, www.rmcwebtravel.com). **Steigenberger Reservation Service** (☎ 800/223–5652, www.srs-worldhotels.com). **Turbotrip.com** (☎ 800/473–7829, www.turbotrip.com).

PACKAGE DEALS

Don't confuse packages and guided tours. When you buy a package, you travel on your own, just as though you had planned the trip yourself. Fly/drive packages, which combine airfare and car rental, are often a good deal.

FOR INTERNATIONAL TRAVELERS

CAR TRAVEL

In the Carolinas and Georgia gasoline costs $1.40–$1.75 a gallon. Stations are plentiful. Most stay open late (24 hours along large highways and in big cities), except in rural areas, where Sunday hours are limited and where you may drive long stretches without a refueling opportunity. Highways are well paved. Interstate highways—limited-access, multilane highways whose numbers are prefixed by "I–"—are the fastest routes. Interstates with three-digit numbers encircle urban areas, which may have other limited-access expressways, freeways, and parkways as well. Tolls may be levied on limited-access highways. So-called U.S. highways and state highways are not necessarily limited-access but may have several lanes.

Along larger highways, roadside stops with rest rooms, fast-food restaurants, and sundries stores are well spaced. State police and tow trucks patrol major highways and lend assistance. If your car breaks down on an interstate, pull onto the shoulder and wait for help, or have your passengers wait while you walk to an emergency phone. If you carry a cell phone, dial *55, noting your location on the small green roadside mileage markers.

Driving in the United States is on the right. Do **obey speed limits** posted along roads and highways. Watch for lower limits in small towns and on back roads. Most states require front-seat passengers to wear seat belts. On weekdays between 6 and 10 AM and again between 4 and 7 PM **expect heavy traffic.** To encourage carpooling, some freeways have special lanes for so-called high-occupancy vehicles (HOV)—cars carrying more than one passenger (☞ *above*).

For more car information, *see* Car Rental and Car Travel, *above.*

EMBASSIES

➤ AUSTRALIA: **Australian Embassy** (1601 Massachussetts Ave. NW, Washington, DC 20036, ☎ 202/797–3000).

➤ CANADA: **Canadian Embassy** (501 Pennsylvania Ave. NW, Washington, DC 20001, ☎ 202/682–1740).

➤ NEW ZEALAND: **New Zealand Embassy** (37 Observatory Circle NW, Washington, DC 20008, ☎ 202/328–4800).

➤ UNITED KINGDOM: **British Embassy** (19 Observatory Circle NW, Washington, DC 20008, ☎ 202/588–7800).

CURRENCY

The dollar is the basic unit of U.S. currency. It has 100 cents. Coins include the copper penny (1¢); the silvery nickel (5¢), dime (10¢), quarter (25¢), and half-dollar (50¢); and the golden $1 coin, replacing a now-rare silver dollar. Bills are denominated $1, $5, $10, $20, $50, and $100, all green and identical in size; designs vary. The exchange rate at press time was $1.41 per British pound, 68¢ per Canadian dollar, 54¢ per Australian dollar, and 41¢ per New Zealand dollar.

CUSTOMS & DUTIES

Australian residents who are 18 or older may bring home $A400 worth of souvenirs and gifts (including jewelry), 250 cigarettes or 250 grams of tobacco, and 1,125 ml of alcohol (including wine, beer, and spirits). Residents under 18 may bring back $A200 worth of goods. Prohibited items include meat products. Seeds, plants, and fruits need to be declared upon arrival.

Canadian residents who have been out of Canada for at least 7 days may bring home C$500 worth of goods duty-free. If you've been away less than 7 days but more than 48 hours, the duty-free allowance drops to C$200; if your trip lasts 24–48 hours, the allowance is C$50. You may not pool allowances with family members. Goods claimed under the C$500 exemption may follow you by mail; those claimed under the lesser exemptions must accompany you. Alcohol and tobacco products may be included in the 7-day and 48-hour exemptions but not in the 24-hour exemption. If you meet the age requirements of the province or territory through which you reenter Canada, you may bring in, duty-free, 1.14 liters (40 imperial ounces) of wine or liquor *or* 24 12-ounce cans or bottles of beer or ale. If you are 16 or older you may bring in, duty-free, 200 cigarettes and 50 cigars. Check ahead of time with Revenue Canada or the Department of Agriculture for policies regarding meat products, seeds, plants, and fruits. You may send an unlimited number of gifts worth up to C$60 each duty-free to Canada. Label the package UNSOLICITED GIFT—VALUE UNDER $60. Alcohol and tobacco are excluded.

Homeward-bound New Zealand residents 17 or older may bring back NZ$700 worth of souvenirs and gifts. Your duty-free allowance also includes 4.5 liters of wine or beer; one 1,125-ml bottle of spirits; and either 200 cigarettes, 250 grams of tobacco, 50 cigars, or a combination of the three up to 250 grams. Prohibited items include meat products, seeds, plants, and fruits.

From countries outside the European Union, including the United States, residents of the United Kingdom may bring home, duty-free, 200 cigarettes or 50 cigars; 1 liter of spirits or 2 liters of fortified or sparkling wine or liqueurs; 2 liters of still table wine; 60 ml of perfume; 250 ml of toilet water; plus £136 worth of other goods, including gifts and souvenirs. If returning from outside the EU, prohibited items include meat products, seeds, plants, and fruits.

➤ IN AUSTRALIA: **Australian Customs Service** (Regional Director, ✉ Box 8, Sydney, NSW 2001, Australia, ☎ 02/9213–2000, FAX 02/9213–4000, www.customs.gov.au).

➤ IN CANADA: **Revenue Canada** (✉ 2265 St. Laurent Blvd. S, Ottawa, Ontario K1G 4K3, Canada, ☎ 613/993–0534; 800/461–9999 in Canada, FAX 613/991–4126, www.ccra-adrc.gc.ca).

➤ IN NEW ZEALAND: **New Zealand Customs** (Custom House, ✉ 50 Anzac Ave., Box 29, Auckland, New Zealand, ☎ 09/300–5399, FAX 09/359–6730), www.customs.govt.nz).

➤ IN THE U.K.: **HM Customs and Excise** (✉ Dorset House, Stamford St., Bromley, Kent BR1 1XX, U.K., ☎ 020/7202–4227, www.hmce.gov.uk).

ELECTRICITY

The U.S. standard is AC, 110 volts/60 cycles. Plugs have two flat pins set parallel to each other.

EMERGENCIES

For police, fire, or ambulance, **dial 911** (0 in rural areas).

INSURANCE

Britons and Australians need extra medical coverage when traveling overseas.

➤ INSURANCE INFORMATION: In the U.K.: **Association of British Insurers** (✉ 51–55 Gresham St., London EC2V 7HQ, U.K., ☎ 020/7600–3333, FAX 020/7696–8999, info@abi.org.uk, www.abi.org.uk). In Australia: **Insurance Council of Australia** (☎ 03/9614–1077, FAX 03/9614–7924). In Canada: **Voyager Insurance** (✉ 44 Peel Center Dr., Brampton, Ontario L6T 4M8, Canada, ☎ 905/791–8700, 800/668–4342 in Canada). In New Zealand: **Insurance Council of New Zealand** (✉ Box 474, Wellington, New Zealand, ☎ 04/472–5230, FAX 04/473–3011, www.icnz.org.nz).

MAIL & SHIPPING

You can buy stamps and aerograms and send letters and parcels in post offices. Stamp-dispensing machines can occasionally be found in airports, bus and train stations, office buildings, drugstores, and the like. You can also deposit mail in the stout, dark blue, steel bins at strategic locations everywhere and in the mail chutes of large buildings; pickup schedules are posted.

For mail sent within the United States, you need a 33¢ stamp for first-class letters weighing up to 1 ounce (22¢ for each additional ounce) and 20¢ for domestic postcards. For overseas mail, you pay 60¢ for ½-ounce airmail letters, 50¢ for airmail postcards, and 35¢ for surface-rate postcards. For Canada you need a 52¢ stamp for a 1-ounce letter and 40¢ for a postcard. For 50¢ you can buy an aerogram—a single sheet of lightweight blue paper that folds into its own envelope, stamped for overseas airmail.

To receive mail on the road, have it sent c/o General Delivery at your destination's main post office (use the correct five-digit zip code). You must pick up mail in person within 30 days and show a driver's license or passport.

PASSPORTS & VISAS

When traveling internationally, **carry your passport** even if you don't need one (it's always the best form of I.D.) and **make two photocopies of the data page** (one for someone at home and another for you, carried separately from your passport). If you lose your passport, promptly call the nearest embassy or consulate and the local police.

Visitor visas are not necessary for Canadian citizens or for citizens of Australia, New Zealand, and the United Kingdom staying fewer than 90 days.

➤ AUSTRALIAN CITIZENS: **Australian Passport Office** (☎ 131–232). The

U.S. Office of Australia Affairs (✉ MLC Centre, 19-29 Martin Pl., 59th floor, Sydney NSW 2000, Australia).

➤ CANADIAN CITIZENS: **Passport Office** (☎ 819/994–3500; 800/567–6868 in Canada).

➤ NEW ZEALAND CITIZENS: **New Zealand Passport Office** (☎ 04/494–0700 for application procedures; 0800/225–050 in New Zealand for application-status updates). **U.S. Office of New Zealand Affairs** (✉ 29 Fitzherbert Terr., Thorndon, Wellington, New Zealand).

➤ U.K. CITIZENS: **London Passport Office** (☎ 0870/521–0410) for application procedures and emergency passports. **U.S. Embassy Visa Information Line** (☎ 01891/200–290). **U.S. Embassy Visa Branch** (✉ 5 Upper Grosvenor Sq., London W1A 1AE, U.K.); send a self-addressed, stamped envelope. **U.S. Consulate General** (✉ Queen's House, Queen St., Belfast BTI 6EO, Northern Ireland).

TELEPHONES

All U.S. telephone numbers consist of a three-digit area code and a seven-digit local number. Within most local calling areas, dial only the seven-digit number. Within the same area code, dial "1" first. To call between area-code regions, dial "1" then all 10 digits; the same goes for calls to numbers prefixed by "800," "888," and "877"—all toll-free. For calls to numbers preceded by "900" you must pay—usually dearly.

For international calls, dial "011" followed by the country code and the local number. For help, dial "0" and ask for an overseas operator. The country code is 61 for Australia, 64 for New Zealand, 44 for the United Kingdom. Calling Canada is the same as calling within the United States. Most local phone books list country codes and U.S. area codes. The country code for the United States is 1.

For operator assistance, dial "0". To obtain someone's phone number, call directory assistance, 555–1212 or occasionally 411 (free at public phones). To have the person you're calling foot the bill, phone collect; dial "0" instead of "1" before the 10-digit number.

At pay phones, instructions are usually posted. Usually you insert coins in a slot (10¢–35¢ for local calls) and wait for a steady tone before dialing. When you call long-distance, the operator will tell you how much to insert; prepaid phone cards, widely available in various denominations, are easier. Call the number on the back, punch in the card's personal identification number when prompted, then dial your number.

For more information on area codes and making long-distance calls, *see* Telephones, *below.*

GAY & LESBIAN TRAVEL

Attitudes about gays and lesbians tend toward disapproving throughout much of the South, especially outside urban areas. On the whole, however, despite a reputation for conservative-minded residents, this part of the country is not any more hostile or dangerous for lesbians and gays—traveling solo or together—than the rest of America. It's prudent, however, to show an awareness of your surroundings and exercise a degree of discretion whenever you're venturing into unfamiliar territory.

As for lesbian and gay resources, there are several major newspapers serving the community throughout the Carolinas and Georgia, notably *Southern Voice* in Atlanta, plus a host of smaller local papers in the Carolinas. The gay nightlife and social scenes in Atlanta rival those of virtually any comparably sized cities in the North America, and you'll also find thriving gay communities of varying sizes in Savannah, Charlotte, Charleston, Raleigh/Durham, and Columbia. With a much lower profile than most cities with large gay populations, Asheville is something of a well-kept secret; it has sizeable lesbian and gay communities and a high number of gay-friendly businesses and accommodations.

Fodor's Gay Guide to the USA, 2nd edition, by Andrew Collins, provides information on travel in Atlanta, Charleston, and Savannah (available in bookstores, or from Fodor's at ☎ 800/533–6478; $20 plus shipping). Also, the Web site (www.gay.com) has a number of valuable resources and travel articles geared toward lesbian and gay travelers.

➤ Gay- & Lesbian-Friendly Travel Agencies: **Different Roads Travel** (✉ 8383 Wilshire Blvd., Suite 902, Beverly Hills, CA 90211, ☎ 323/651–5557 or 800/429–8747, FAX 323/651–3678, leigh@west.tzell.com). **Kennedy Travel** (✉ 314 Jericho Turnpike, Floral Park, NY 11001, ☎ 516/352–4888 or 800/237–7433, FAX 516/354–8849, main@kennedytravel.com, www.kennedytravel.com). **Now Voyager** (✉ 4406 18th St., San Francisco, CA 94114, ☎ 415/626–1169 or 800/255–6951, FAX 415/626–8626, www.nowvoyager.com). **Skylink Travel and Tour** (✉ 1006 Mendocino Ave., Santa Rosa, CA 95401, ☎ 707/546–9888 or 800/225–5759, FAX 707/546–9891, skylinktvl@aol.com, www.skylinktravel.com), serving lesbian travelers.

HEALTH

PESTS & OTHER HAZARDS

Mosquitoes, seasonal black flies, and other insects known to North America proliferate in the humid and often lush southern states. **Exercise common precautions and wear lotions or sprays that keep away such pests.**

Although you might associate Lyme disease with New England, where it was first well-documented, this relatively common and potentially dangerous disease strikes frequently in the South, too. The disease is spread by bites from infinitesimal deer ticks carrying spiral-shaped bacterium called spirochete. Most victims show a red-ring-shaped rash around the bite from the deer tick, somewhat resembling a little bull's eye and appearing from a week to many weeks after the incident. Flu-like symptoms often follow—fever, achy joints, swelling, and if left untreated for more than a couple months, the chronic arthritis may set in. Lyme disease may also attack the nervous system, causing a loss or reduction of motor skills, severe headaches, paralysis of some facial muscles, and general fatigue—and in somewhat rare cases, patients have also developed heart problems. This is in no way a disease to be taken lightly. Unfortunately, testing for Lyme disease is a sketchy business at best, as no definitive method has yet been developed. Doctors typically rely on a series of blood tests and more often than that rely simply on observation of various symptoms. Research is currently underway to come up with new and more reliable tests, but in the meantime you should consult with your health care provider the very second you develop any of the symptoms outlined above—especially if you've been spending time in areas where ticks, and deer, are commonplace: wooded terrain, meadows, and coastal scrub.

When spending time in areas where tick infestation is a problem, wear long-sleeve clothing and slacks, tuck your pant-legs into your boots and/or socks, apply tick and insect repellent generously, and check yourself carefully for signs of ticks or bites. It's a good idea to don light-colored clothing, as you'll have an easier time sighting ticks, which are dark. Remember that the more commonly found wood ticks do not carry the disease, and that deer ticks are extremely small—about the size of a pinhead.

HOLIDAYS

Major national holidays include New Year's Day (Jan. 1); Martin Luther King, Jr., Day (3rd Mon. in Jan.); President's Day (3rd Mon. in Feb.); Memorial Day (last Mon. in May); Independence Day (July 4); Labor Day (1st Mon. in Sept.); Thanksgiving Day (4th Thurs. in Nov.); Christmas Eve and Christmas Day (Dec. 24 and 25); and New Year's Eve (Dec. 31).

INSURANCE

The most useful travel insurance plan is a comprehensive policy that includes coverage for trip cancellation and interruption, default, trip delay, and medical expenses (with a waiver for preexisting conditions).

Without insurance you will lose all or most of your money if you cancel your trip, regardless of the reason. Default insurance covers you if your tour operator, airline, or cruise line goes out of business. Trip-delay covers expenses that arise because of bad weather or mechanical delays. Study the fine print when comparing policies.

Always **buy travel policies directly from the insurance company**; if you buy them from a cruise line, airline, or tour operator that goes out of business you probably will not be covered for the agency or operator's default, a major risk. Before making any purchase, **review your existing health and home-owner's policies** to find what they cover away from home.

If you are traveling from outside the United States or Canada, *see* Insurance in For International Travelers, *above*.

➤ TRAVEL INSURERS: In the U.S.: **Access America** (✉ 6600 W. Broad St., Richmond, VA 23230, ☎ 804/285–3300 or 800/284–8300, FAX 804/673–1583, www.previewtravel.com), **Travel Guard International** (✉ 1145 Clark St., Stevens Point, WI 54481, ☎ 715/345–0505 or 800/826–1300, FAX 800/955–8785, www.noelgroup.com). In Canada: **Voyager Insurance** (✉ 44 Peel Center Dr., Brampton, Ontario L6T 4M8, ☎ 905/791–8700; 800/668–4342 in Canada).

LODGING

With the exception of Atlanta, Savannah, and Charleston, most lodging rates in the region fall below the national average. They do vary a great deal seasonally, however—coastal areas as well as the Great Smoky Mountains tend to have significantly higher rates in summer. All major chains are well-represented in this part of the country, both in cities and suburbs, and interstates are lined with inexpensive to moderate chains. It's not uncommon to find clean but extremely basic discount chains offering double rooms for as little as $20 to $30 nightly along the busiest highways.

In cities and some large towns you might want to forgo a modern hotel in favor of a historic property—there are dozens of fine old hotels, many of them fully restored and quite a few offering better rates than chain properties with comparable amenities and nowhere near the ambience.

The lodgings we list are the cream of the crop in each price category. They are denoted in the text by 🏨 ; lodging establishments whose restaurant warrants a special trip are denoted by ✕🏨. We always list the facilities that are available—but we don't specify whether they cost extra: When pricing accommodations, **always ask what's included and what costs extra.**

Assume that hotels operate on the **European Plan** (EP, with no meals) unless we specify that they use the **Continental Plan** (CP, with a Continental breakfast), **Breakfast Plan** (BP, with a full breakfast), **Modified American Plan** (MAP, with breakfast and dinner), or the **Full American Plan** (FAP, with all meals).

APARTMENT RENTALS

If you want a home base that's roomy enough for a family and comes with cooking facilities, **consider a furnished rental.** These can save you money, especially if you're traveling with a group. Home-exchange directories sometimes list rentals as well as exchanges.

➤ INTERNATIONAL AGENTS: **Hideaways International** (✉ 767 Islington St., Portsmouth, NH 03801, ☎ 603/430–4433 or 800/843–4433, FAX 603/430–4444 info@hideaways.com www.hideaways.com; membership $99).

Vacation Home Rentals Worldwide (✉ 235 Kensington Ave., Norwood, NJ 07648, ☎ 201/767–9393 or 800/633–3284, FAX 201/767–5510, vhrww@juno.com, www.vhrww.com).

B&BS AND INNS

Historic B&Bs and inns are found in just about every region in the Carolinas and Georgia, and include quite a few former plantation houses and lavish southern estates. In many rural or less touristy areas, B&Bs offer an affordable and homey alternative to chain properties, but in tourism-dependent destinations you can expect to pay about the same or more for a historic inn as for a full-service hotel. Many of the South's finest restaurants are also found in country inns.

CAMPING

The Carolinas and Georgia are popular for RV and tent camping, with facilities throughout the area, especially in state and national parks. For more information on parks and other campgrounds, contact the state tourism offices (☞ Visitor Information, *below*) or *see* Contacts and Resources *in* regional A to Z sections and *in* the A to Z section at the end of each state chapter.

HOME EXCHANGES

If you would like to exchange your home for someone else's, **join a home-exchange organization,** which will send you its updated listings of available exchanges for a year and will include your own listing in at least one of them. It's up to you to make specific arrangements.

➤ EXCHANGE CLUBS: **HomeLink International** (✉ Box 650, Key West, FL 33041, ☎ 305/294–7766 or 800/638–3841, FAX 305/294–1448, usa@homelink.org, www.homelink.org; $98 per year). **Intervac U.S.** (✉ Box 590504, San Francisco, CA 94159, ☎ 800/756–4663, FAX 415/435–7440, www.intervac.com; $89 per year includes two catalogues).

HOSTELS

No matter what your age, you can **save on lodging costs by staying at hostels.** In some 5,000 locations in more than 70 countries around the world, Hostelling International (HI), the umbrella group for a number of national youth-hostel associations, offers single-sex, dorm-style beds and, at many hostels, rooms for couples and family accommodations. Membership in any HI national hostel association, open to travelers of all ages, allows you to stay in HI-affiliated hostels at member rates; one-year membership is about $25 for adults (C$26.75 in Canada, £9.30 in the U.K., $30 in Australia, and $30 in New Zealand); hostels run about $10–$25 per night. Members have priority if the hostel is full; they're also eligible for discounts around the world, even on rail and bus travel in some countries.

➤ ORGANIZATIONS: **Hostelling International—American Youth Hostels** (✉ 733 15th St. NW, Suite 840, Washington, DC 20005, ☎ 202/783–6161, FAX 202/783–6171, www.hiayh.org). **Hostelling International—Canada** (✉ 400–205 Catherine St., Ottawa, Ontario K2P 1C3, ☎ 613/237–7884, FAX 613/237–7868, www.hostellingintl.ca). **Youth Hostel Association of England and Wales** (✉ Trevelyan House, 8 St. Stephen's Hill, St. Albans, Hertfordshire AL1 2DY, ☎ 01727/855215 or 01727/845047, FAX 01727/844126, www.yha.uk). **Australian Youth Hostel Association** (✉ 10 Mallett St., Camperdown, NSW 2050, ☎ 02/9565–1699, FAX 02/9565–1325, www.yha.com.au). **Youth Hostels Association of New Zealand** (✉ Box 436, Christchurch, New Zealand, ☎ 03/379–9970, FAX 03/365–4476, www.yha.org.nz).

HOTELS

All hotels listed have private bath unless otherwise noted.

➤ TOLL-FREE NUMBERS: **Adam's Mark** (☎ 800/444–2326, www.adamsmark.com). **Baymont Inns** (☎ 800/428–3438, www.baymontinns.com). **Best Western** (☎ 800/528–1234, www.bestwestern.com). **Choice** (☎ 800/221–2222, www.hotelchoice.com). **Clarion** (☎ 800/252–7466, www.choicehotels.com). **Colony** (☎ 800/777–1700. www.colony.com), **Comfort** (☎ 800/228–5150, www.comfortinn.com). **Days Inn** (☎ 800/325–2525. www.daysinn.com). **Doubletree and Red Lion Hotels** (☎ 800/222–8733, www.doubletreehotels.com). **Embassy Suites** (☎ 800/362–2779, www.embassysuites.com). **Fairfield Inn** (☎ 800/228–2800, www.marriott.com). **Four Seasons** (☎ 800/332–3442, www.fourseasons.com). **Hilton** (☎ 800/445–8667, www.hiltons.com). **Holiday Inn** (☎ 800/465–4329, www.holiday-inn.com). **Howard Johnson** (☎ 800/654–4656, www.hojo.com). **Hyatt Hotels & Resorts** (☎ 800/233–1234, www.hyatt.com). **La Quinta** (☎ 800/531–5900, www.laquinta.com). **Marriott** (☎ 800/228–9290, www.marriott.com). **Omni** (☎ 800/843–6664, www.omnihotels.com). **Quality Inn** (☎ 800/228–5151, www.qualityinn.com). **Radisson** (☎ 800/333–3333, www.radisson.com). **Ramada** (☎ 800/228–2828. www.ramada.com), **Renaissance Hotels & Resorts** (☎ 800/468–3571, www.hotels.com). **Sheraton** (☎ 800/325–3535, www.sheraton.com). **Westin Hotels & Resorts** (☎ 800/228–3000, www.starwood.com). **Wyndham Hotels & Resorts** (☎ 800/822-4200, www.wyndham.com).

MOTELS

➤ TOLL-FREE NUMBERS: **Budget Hosts Inns** (☎ 800/283–4678). **Econo Lodge** (☎ 800/553–2666). **Friendship Inns** (☎ 800/453–4511). **Motel 6** (☎ 800/466–8356). **Rodeway** (☎ 800/228–2000). **Super 8** (☎ 800/848–8888).

MEDIA

There's no major regional newspaper that serves the area, but the *Atlanta Journal-Constitution* ranks among the most influential dailies in the Carolinas and Georgia; just about every city with a population of greater than 40,000 or 50,000 also publishes its own daily paper.

Most major cities have very good alternative newsweeklies with useful Web sites and information on area dining, arts, and sightseeing—these are usually free and found in restaurants, coffeehouses, bookstores, tourism offices, hotel lobbies, and some nightclubs. Of particular note is Atlanta's *Creative Loafing*, which has separate editions for a number of additional southern cities and regions including Gwinnett County (GA), Savannah, Charlotte, and Greenville (SC). Visit its Web site (www.cln.com) to find links to each of these editions, as well as to other useful alternative newsweeklies in Athens (GA), Augusta (GA), Columbia (SC), Asheville, Charleston, Raleigh-Durham, and Wilmington (NC).

The monthly features magazine *Southern Living* gives a nice sense of travel, food, and lifestyle issues relevant to the region. Local lifestyles magazines—including *Atlanta* and *Charlotte's Best*—have colorful stories and dining and entertainment coverage; they're worth picking up prior to your visit, especially if you're planning an extended stay; virtually all of these have useful Web sites, too.

All of the major television and radio networks are well-represented throughout the Carolinas and Georgia, and Ted Turner's omnipresent CNN empire is based in Atlanta.

MONEY MATTERS

As with most of America, credit and debit cards are accepted at the vast majority of shops, sit-down restaurants, and accommodations in the Carolinas and Georgia. Common exceptions include small, independent stores and also B&Bs in more rural areas. Banks—as well as convenience stores, groceries, and even nightclubs—with ATMs are easy to find in just about every community.

While the cost of living remains fairly low in most parts of the South, travel-related costs (such as dining, lodging, museums, and transportation) have become increasingly steep in Atlanta over the years and can also be dear in resort communities throughout the Carolinas and Georgia.

Prices throughout this guide are given for adults. Substantially reduced fees are almost always available for children, students, and senior citizens. For information on taxes, *see* Taxes, *below.*

CREDIT CARDS

Throughout this guide, the following abbreviations are used: **AE,** American Express; **D,** Discover; **DC,** Diner's Club; **MC,** Master Card; and **V,** Visa.

➤ REPORTING LOST CARDS: To report lost or stolen credit cards, call the following toll-free numbers: **American Express** (☎ 800/327–2177), **Discover Card** (☎ 800/347–2683), **Diner's Club** (☎ 800/234–6377), **MasterCard** (800/307–7309).

NATIONAL AND STATE PARKS

National and state parks abound in the Carolinas and Georgia and have a broad range of visitor facilities, including campgrounds, picnic grounds, hiking trails, boating, and ranger programs. State forests are usually somewhat less developed. For more information, contact the state tourism offices (☞ Visitor Information, *below*) or parks departments (☞ Contacts and Resources, at the end of each state chapter).

NATIONAL PARK PASSES

Look into discount passes to **save money on park entrance fees.** The Golden Eagle Pass ($50) gets you and your companions free admission to all parks for one year (camping and parking are extra). Both the Golden Age Passport ($10), for those 62 and older, and the Golden Access Passport (free), for travelers with disabilities, entitle holders to free entry to all national parks, plus 50% off fees for the use of many park facilities and services. You must show proof of age and of U.S. citizenship or permanent residency (such as a U.S. passport, driver's license, or birth certificate) and, if requesting Golden Access, proof of disability. All three passes are available at all national park entrances where entrance fees are charged. Golden Eagle and Golden Access passes are available by mail.

➤ PASSES BY MAIL: **National Park Service** (✉ National Park Service National Office, 1849 C St. NW, Washington, DC 20240-0001, ☎ 202/208–4747).

OUTDOORS & SPORTS

With daytime temperatures rarely dipping below freezing and a plethora of waterways, mountains, forests, and swamps, the Carolinas and Georgia make for an ideal outdoor destination. Fans of pro and college sports will find the area rife with live athletic events, and southerners to be among the most passionate and knowledgeable of sports enthusiasts.

PARTICIPANT SPORTS AND RECREATION

It's tough to come up with an outdoor activity that isn't celebrated somewhere in this part of the country. **Golfers** will find an entire community of world-class courses in the Pinehurst region of North Carolina, the Hilton Head and Myrtle Beach regions of South Carolina, and the coastal islands off Georgia. These areas also have plenty to offer in the way of **tennis.** In the inland Appalachian regions, you'll find many excellent mountain courses. **Fishing** die-hards find plenty of freshwater action in the Carolinas and Georgia, with stocked lakes and rivers at many state and municipal parks. Deep-sea and surf fishing prevails (including crabbing and shrimping) all along the Atlantic seaboard; charter- and guided-fishing operators abound in these parts.

Other activities with a strong following in the Carolinas and Georgia include **bicycling** (☞ Bike Travel, *above*), boating and rafting, bowling, **camping and hiking** (☞ National and State Parks, *above*), hang-gliding, and hunting. Further information on these and other activities can be found under individual town listings and in the A to Z sections in each state chapter.

SPECTATOR SPORTS

Several cities have major pro sports teams. In **baseball** check out the Atlanta Braves; **basketball** fans cheer on the Atlanta Hawks and Charlotte Hornets; for **football** there are the Atlanta Falcons and Carolina Panthers; and **hockey** fans watch the Atlanta Thrashers and Carolina Hurricanes.

Among the most popular **college basketball** programs are those of Duke University (NC), University of North Carolina, and North Carolina State University, to name a few. **College football** programs include East Carolina University, University of Georgia, Georgia Institute of Technology, and Wake Forest (NC).

Other major sporting events include numerous pro **golf** tournaments, highlighted by the Bell-South Classic (Duluth, GA) and the Masters (Augusta, GA), and the MCI Classic–Heritage of Golf (Hilton Head, SC). A smattering of world **tennis** tournaments are held in the area, notably the Atlanta Tennis Challenge for men, and the Family Circle Cup (in Hilton Head, SC) for women. **Auto-racing** fans will find NASCAR events staged throughout the region.

PACKING

Much of the Carolinas and Georgia has hot, humid summers and sunny, mild winters. With a few formal exceptions, most of them in Atlanta, smart but casual attire works fine wherever you go. For colder months, pack a lightweight coat, slacks, and sweaters; you'll need heavier clothing in some mountainous areas, where cold, damp weather prevails and snow is not unusual. Keeping summer's humidity in mind, **pack absorbent natural fabrics that breathe;** bring an umbrella, but leave the plastic raincoat at home. You'll want a jacket or sweater for summer evenings and for too-cool air-conditioning. And **don't forget insect repellent.**

CHECKING LUGGAGE

How many carry-on bags you can bring with you is up to the airline. Most allow two, but not always, so make sure that everything you carry aboard will fit under your seat or in the overhead bin, and get to the gate early. Note that if you have a seat at the back of the plane, you'll probably board first, while the overhead bins are still empty.

If you are flying internationally, note that baggage allowances may be determined not by piece but by weight—generally 88 pounds (40 kilograms) in first class, 66 pounds (30 kilograms) in business class, and 44 pounds (20 kilograms) in economy.

Airline liability for baggage is limited to $1,250 per person on flights within the United States. On international flights it amounts to $9.07 per pound or $20 per kilogram for checked baggage (roughly $640 per 70-pound bag) and $400 per passenger for unchecked baggage. You can buy additional coverage at check-in for about $10 per $1,000 of coverage, but it excludes a rather extensive list of items, shown on your airline ticket.

Before departure, **itemize your bags' contents** and their worth, and label the bags with your name, address, and phone number. (If you use your home address, cover it so potential thieves can't see it readily.) Inside each bag, **pack a copy of your itinerary.** At check-in, **make sure that each bag is correctly tagged** with the destination airport's three-letter code. If your bags arrive damaged or fail to arrive at all, file a written report with the airline before leaving the airport.

SAFETY

In even the most rural and least tourism-dependent places, you have little cause to worry about theft or crime—just exercise common sense. Be wary of suspicious-looking figures and keep valuables hidden away or locked up, if possible. Especially in urban areas and along major highways, never leave valuables in your unattended car. Wherever you venture in this part of the world, folks are generally happy to offer directions and advice.

SENIOR-CITIZEN TRAVEL

To qualify for age-related discounts, **mention your senior-citizen status up front** when booking hotel reservations (not when checking out) and before you're seated in restaurants (not when paying the bill). When renting a car, ask about promotional car-rental discounts, which can be cheaper than senior-citizen rates.

➤ EDUCATIONAL PROGRAMS: **Elderhostel** (✉ 75 Federal St., 3rd floor, Boston, MA 02110, ☎ 877/426–8056, FAX 877/426–2166, www.elderhostel.org).

STUDENTS IN THE CAROLINAS AND GEORGIA

➤ I.D.S & SERVICES: **Council Travel** (CIEE; ✉ 205 E. 42nd St., 14th floor, New York, NY 10017, ☎ 212/822–2700 or 888/268–6245, FAX 212/822–2699, info@councilexchanges.org, www.councilexchanges.org) for mail orders only, in the U.S. **Travel Cuts** (✉ 187 College St., Toronto, Ontario M5T 1P7, ☎ 416/979–2406 or 800/667–2887, www.travelcuts.com) in Canada.

TAXES

Sales taxes are as follows: Georgia 4%; North Carolina 4%; and South Carolina 5%. Most municipalities also levy a lodging tax (usually exempt at small inns with only a few rooms, but rules vary regionally), and in some cases a restaurant tax. The hotel taxes in the South can be rather steep, greater than 10% in Georgia and many counties in North Carolina.

TELEPHONES

AREA & CODES

To place a long-distance call within the United States, you need to dial "1" followed by the three-digit area code, and then the seven-digit number. Over the past several years—with an influx in cellular phones, fax machines, and second lines—dozens of new area codes have been added. Some cities are now served by multiple area codes; in these places it's often necessary to dial the full 10-digit number (including area code), sometimes preceding by "1," even when placing local calls. In Atlanta, for example, you must dial an area code before dialing the local number. If in doubt, dial "0" when you arrive to check with an operator, or ask your hotel's front desk.

LONG-DISTANCE CALLS

Competitive long-distance carriers make calling within the United States relatively convenient and let you avoid hotel surcharges. By dialing an "800" number, you can get connected to the long-distance company of your choice.

If you want to charge a long-distance call to the person you're calling, you can call collect by dialing "0" instead of "1" before the 10-digit number, and an operator will come on the line to assist you (the party you're calling, however, has the right to refuse the call). It's far less costly to purchase a long-distance phone card—these are available in a wide range of denominations from convenience stores, gas stations, and newsstands and offer rates that are competitive with those set by most major long-distance carriers.

➤ LONG-DISTANCE CARRIERS: **AT&T** (☎ 800/225–5288). **MCI** (☎ 800/888–8000). **Sprint** (☎ 800/366–2255).

For information on directory and operator assistance, international calls, and public phones, *see* Telephones *in* For International Travelers, *above*.

TOURS & PACKAGES

On a prepackaged tour or independent vacation everything is prearranged so you'll spend less time planning—and often get it all at a good price.

BOOKING WITH AN AGENT

Travel agents are excellent resources. But it's a good idea to collect brochures from several agencies as some agents' suggestions may be influenced by relationships with tour and package firms that reward them for volume sales. If you have a special interest, **find an agent with expertise in that area**; ASTA (☞ Travel Agencies, *below*) has a database of specialists worldwide.

Make sure your travel agent knows the accommodations and other services of the place they're recommending. Ask about the hotel's location, room size, beds, and whether it has a pool, room service, or programs for children, if you care about these. Has your agent been there in person or sent others whom you can contact?

Do some homework on your own, too: local tourism boards can provide information about lesser-known and small-niche operators, some of which may sell only direct.

BUYER BEWARE

Each year consumers are stranded or lose their money when tour operators—even large ones with excellent reputations—go out of business. So **check out the operator.** Ask several travel agents about its reputation, and try to **book with a company that has a consumer-protection program.** (Look for information in the company's brochure.) In the United States, members of the National Tour Association and the United States Tour Operators Association are required to set aside funds to cover your payments and travel arrangements in the event that the company defaults. It's also a good idea to choose a company that participates in the American Society of Travel Agents' Tour Operator Program (TOP); ASTA will act as mediator in any disputes between you and your tour operator.

Remember that the more your package or tour includes the better you can predict the ultimate cost of your vacation. Make sure you know exactly what is covered, and **beware of hidden costs.** Are taxes, tips, and transfers included? Entertainment and excursions? These can add up.

➤ TOUR-OPERATOR RECOMMENDATIONS: **American Society of Travel Agents** (☞ Travel Agencies, *below*). **National Tour Association** (NTA; ✉ 546 E. Main St., Lexington, KY 40508, ☎ 606/226–4444 or 800/682–8886, www.ntaonline.com). **United States Tour Operators Association** (USTOA; ✉ 342 Madison Ave.,

Suite 1522, New York, NY 10173, ☎ 212/599–6599 or 800/468–7862, FAX 212/599–6744, ustoa@aol.com, www.ustoa.com).

TRAIN TRAVEL

Amtrak has a number of routes that pass through the Carolinas and Georgia; however, many areas are not served by train, and those cities that do have service usually only have one or two arrivals and departures each day. Major cities served include Atlanta, GA; Charleston, SC; Charlotte, NC; Columbia, SC; Durham, NC; Greenville, SC; Hilton Head, SC; Raleigh, NC; Savannah, GA; and Winston-Salem, NC. A number of other places—Myrtle Beach, SC—are handled by Amtrak connecting services (depending on the route, these services may be provided by train, bus, or van). For a comparison of different ways of getting around the region, *see* Transportation to and Around the Carolinas and Georgia, *below.*

➤ TRAIN INFORMATION: **Amtrak** (☎ 800/872–7245).

CUTTING COSTS

Amtrak offers different kinds of rail passes that allow for travel within certain regions, including a set number of stops, at a significant savings over the standard posted fare. They also have a **North America rail pass** that offers you unlimited travel with the United States and Canada within any 30-day period ($656 peak, $459 off-peak), and several kinds of **USA Rail passes** (for non-U.S. residents only) offering unlimited travel for 15- to 30 days. Amtrak also has senior citizen, children's, disability, and student discounts, as well as occasional deals that allow a second or third accompanying passenger travel for half-price or even free. The **Amtrak Vacations** program customizes entire vacations, including hotels, car-rentals, and tours.

TRANSPORTATION TO AND AROUND THE CAROLINAS AND GEORGIA

Although a car is your best bet for getting around the region, it's worth considering a few different strategies in terms of getting about conveniently and economically.

If you're planning to spend more than several days and visit more than a couple cities, you might consider driving your own car rather than flying in and renting one—especially if you live anywhere within 500 miles of the region (i.e., the mid-Atlantic states, the Midwest, and the Deep South), and you're traveling with three or more in your group. Even if you have to spend a night at a motel on your way there and back, you'll save a considerable amount of money on airfare and car-rentals this way. If, however, you lease your car rather than own it outright, you might factor in the number of miles you're planning to burn up before deciding which strategy works best. Obviously, if time is tight, flying is your best bet.

If coming by plane, plan to fly into one of the region's major airports, to which fares tend to be considerably lower than to smaller regional facilities. The sheer competition and wealth of connections at Atlanta's busy Hartsfield Airport make it an excellent choice—car-rental rates here are also highly competitive, and Atlanta is within 300 mi of Savannah, Charleston, Charlotte, and Asheville. Charlotte-Douglas International Airport in North Carolina is probably the second-best choice as far as centrality goes.

It's difficult to find direct flights to most of the other airports in the Carolinas and Georgia, especially if flying from outside of the region. However, within the area, check to see what airfares are between some smaller cities—very often airlines offer specials for popular shorter routes like Atlanta to Savannah or Charlotte to Hilton Head.

If you're trying to save money, you have a fair amount of time, and you're interested taking in the landscape without having to drive, consider getting around via bus—Greyhound (☞ Bus Travel, *above*) has frequent and regular service to virtually every city in the region. Some of the routes, near the coastal areas and over the mountainous interior section, can be quite breathtaking. And if you book at least a couple days ahead, you'll find the rates quite reasonable. A bit less practical is relying on train travel (☞ Train Travel, *above*), as Amtrak's coverage within the region is a bit spotty, and round-trip fares are sometimes quite a bit higher than comparable bus fares—occasionally even more than corresponding air fares. However, if you were planning a one-way or multi-segment trip, you'd likely find that train travel offers a better value with more flexibility and fewer restrictions than attempting such an endeavor by plane. And you'd generally find the ride more comfortable and pleasant by train than by bus.

TRAVEL AGENCIES

A good travel agent puts your needs first. Look for an agency that has been in business at least five years, emphasizes customer service, and has someone on staff who specializes in your destination. In addition, **make sure the agency belongs to a professional trade organization.** The American Society of Travel Agents (ASTA), with 27,000 agents in some 170 countries, is the largest and most influential in the field. Operating under the motto ìIntegrity in Travel,î it maintains and enforces a strict code of ethics and will step in to help mediate any agent-client disputes if necessary. ASTA also maintains a Web site that includes a directory of agents. (If a travel agency is also acting as your tour operator, *see* Buyer Beware *in* Tours & Packages, *above.*)

➤ LOCAL AGENT REFERRALS: **American Society of Travel Agents** (ASTA; ☎ 800/965–2782 24-hr hot line, FAX 703/684–8319, www.astanet.com). **Association of British Travel Agents** (✉ 68–71 Newman St., London W1P 4AH, ☎ 020/7637–2444, FAX 020/7637–0713, abta.co.uk, www.abtanet.com). **Association of Canadian Travel Agents** (✉ 1729 Bank St., Suite 201, Ottawa, Ontario K1V 7Z5, ☎ 613/521–0474, FAX 613/521–0805, acta.ntl@sympatico.ca). **Australian Federation of Travel Agents** (✉ Level 3, 309 Pitt St., Sydney 2000, ☎ 02/9264–3299, FAX 02/9264–1085, www.afta.com.au). **Travel Agents' Association of New Zealand** (✉ Box 1888, Wellington 10033, ☎ 04/499–0104, FAX 04/499–0827, taanz@tiasnet.co.nz).

VISITOR INFORMATION

For general information and brochures before you go, contact the state tourism bureaus below.

➤ TOURIST INFORMATION: **Georgia Department of Industry, Trade and Tourism** (✉ Box 1776, Atlanta, GA 30301, ☎ 404/656–3590 or 800/847–4842, FAX 404/651–9063, www.georgia.org). **North Carolina Travel and Tourism Division** (✉ 301 N. Wilmington St., Raleigh, NC 27601, ☎ 800/847–4862, FAX 919/733–8582, www.visitnc.com). **South Carolina Department of Parks, Recreation, and Tourism** (✉ 1205 Pendleton St., Suite 106, Columbia, SC 29201, ☎ 803/734–1700 or 800/872–3505, FAX 803/734–0133, www.travelsc.com).

WEB SITES

Check out the World Wide Web when you're planning. You'll find everything from up-to-date weather forecasts to virtual tours of famous cities. Fodor's Web site, www.fodors.com, is a great place to start your online travels. When you see a 🖱 in this book, go to www.fodors.com/urls for an up-to-date link to that destination's site. For more information on events in the Carolinas and Georgia, try visiting the Web sites of major newspapers and alternative newsweeklies in the area (☞ Media, *above*). Also take a look at the following Web sites, many of which contain copious information and links to regional attractions, tours, history, dining, lodging, and other useful categories: for Georgia, check out www.acvb.com, the Atlanta Convention and Visitors Bureau; www.bgivb.com, the Brunswick and the Golden Isles of Georgia Visitors Bureau; and www.savcvb.com, the Savannah Area Convention and Visitors Bureau; for North Carolina, check out www.ashevillechamber.org, Asheville Convention and Visitors Bureau; www.cape-fear.nc.us, Cape Fear Coast and Wilmington Convention and Visitors Bureau; www.charlottecvb.org, Charlotte Convention and Visitors Bureau; www.durham-nc.com, Durham Convention and Visitors Bureau; www.raleighcvb.org, Greater Raleigh Convention and

Visitors Bureau; and www.wscvb.com, Winston-Salem Convention and Visitors Bureau; for South Carolina, check out www.charlestoncvb.com, Charleston Convention and Visitors Bureau; www.columbiasc.net, Columbia Metro Convention and Visitors Bureau; www.hiltonheadisland.org, Hilton Head Island Chamber of Commerce; and www.myrtlebeach-live.com, Myrtle Beach Area Chamber of Commerce.

WHEN TO GO

Spring is probably the most attractive season in this part of the United States. Throughout the region, cherry blossoms are followed by azaleas, dogwood, and camellias from April into May, and by apple blossoms in May. Summer can be hot and humid in many areas, but temperatures will be cooler along the coasts or in the mountains. Folk, craft, art, and music festivals tend to take place in summer, as do sports events. State and local fairs are held mainly in August and September, though there are a few in early July and into October. Fall can be a delight, with spectacular foliage, particularly in the mountains. The region is large and conditions vary; see the individual state chapters for more information.

CLIMATE

In winter, temperatures generally average in the low 40s inland, in the 60s by the shore. Summer temperatures, modified by mountains in some areas, by water in others, range from the high 70s to the mid-80s and now and then the low 90s.

The following are average daily maximum and minimum temperatures for key cities.

ATLANTA, GEORGIA

Jan.	52F	11C	May	79F	26C	Sept.	83F	28C
	36	2		61	16		65	18
Feb.	54F	12C	June	86F	30C	Oct.	72F	22C
	38	3		67	19		54	12
Mar.	63F	17C	July	88F	31C	Nov.	61F	16C
	43	6		70	21		43	6
Apr.	72F	22C	Aug.	86F	30C	Dec.	52F	11C
	52	11		70	21		38	3

RALEIGH, NORTH CAROLINA

Jan.	50F	10C	May	78F	26C	Sept.	81F	27C
	29	− 2		55	13		60	16
Feb.	52F	11C	June	85F	29C	Oct.	71F	22C
	30	− 1		62	17		47	8
Mar.	61F	16C	July	88F	31C	Nov.	61F	16C
	37	3		67	19		38	3
Apr.	72F	22C	Aug.	87F	31C	Dec.	52F	11C
	46	8		66	18		30	−1

CHARLESTON, SOUTH CAROLINA

Jan.	59F	15C	May	81F	27C	Sept.	84F	29C
	41	6		64	18		69	21
Feb.	60F	16C	June	86F	30C	Oct.	76F	24C
	43	7		71	22		59	15
Mar.	66F	19C	July	88F	31C	Nov.	67F	19C
	49	9		74	23		49	9
Apr.	73F	23C	Aug.	88F	31C	Dec.	59F	11C
	56	13		73	23		42	6

➤ FORECASTS: **Weather Channel Connection** (☎ 900/932–8437), 95¢ per minute from a Touch-Tone phone.

1 DESTINATION: THE CAROLINAS AND GEORGIA

THE INCONGRUOUS SOUTH

By Lisa H. Towle

THE FOLKS AT THE Center for the Study of the American South are valiant in their attempts to help people understand a region that has five centuries of recorded history. In their literature they propose many ways to take stock of the South. There's the census: it's the most populous and fastest-growing region in the United States. There's the culture: it increasingly directs the national agenda. And there's the change: an area of deep roots, its rate of change is accelerating and, at times, dislocating.

In the triumvirate of North Carolina, South Carolina, and Georgia, past and present shimmer with equal energy. Eighteenth-century inns and joints serving the standard Southern plate lunch of "meat and three" (meat with three side dishes) nestle at crossroads or in towns the size of a parking lot. In metropolitan hubs the high-rise headquarters of Bank of America, CNN, and Coca-Cola—monuments to Southern enterprise—stand tinted glass panel to tinted glass panel with sleek luxury hotels.

It all surpasses what Henry Grady envisioned when he popularized the term New South. In a speech delivered to the New England Club of New York in 1886, the longtime editor of the *Atlanta Constitution* made the case that the South was an ideal area for industrial investment. The growth and progress of Atlanta would serve, he said, as an example for the rest of the region. They did. And today, the convergence of Old South and New South is nowhere more evident than in these three states.

Atlanta is a sprawling city in the heart of a spaghetti knot of interstate highways. Underground, however, beneath the viaducts that cover the original streets and railroad yards of old Atlanta, is an entertainment capital and Heritage Row, a historic district that recalls the city's different stages, from the wilderness years to the days of King Cotton, from the Civil War siege to present day.

The South has a history of controversy—of slavery and civil strife—but it also has a history of beauty and warmth. In South Carolina, the Gullah rhythms of African-Americans who have saved and made sacred the language, music, and traditions of ancestors who were brought to the Sea Islands as slaves are part of the cadence of life. Now, German accents join the chorus. In upstate Spartanburg County, BMW has opened Zentrum, a 28,000-square-ft visitor center, with a museum for the automaker's collection of vintage and current automobiles, motorcycles, racing cars, and aero engines.

Everything from Astroturf to Zantac has come from North Carolina's Research Triangle area (Raleigh–Durham–Chapel Hill), where gleaming research and medical centers, set on lush campuses, employ tens of thousands of people who believe in the power and promise of technology. Every year for nearly a century those who believe in another kind of promise have made their way to the Blue Ridge Mountains and the Southern gospel music festival at Grandfather Mountain's McRae Meadow. Here, thousands of participants are reminded of a time when "the Word" was delivered outdoors in oratory and song.

To really experience the Carolinas and Georgia, you must let go of stereotypes; this is not a one-dimensional place. In the classic South, valued assets are stately old homes, rich recreational resources, and scenery that shifts effortlessly from tropical palms and sandy beaches to meandering roads and mountainsides. The states are home to many notable firsts: South Carolina's Beth Elohim Reform Temple was the birthplace of Reform Judaism in America, and the University of North Carolina at Chapel Hill was founded more than three centuries ago as the nation's first state institution of higher education.

The temperate weather draws people like moths to a flame. But if climate is king, then construction is queen in the New South, leaving her mark on even the sleepiest backwaters. Consider Brunswick, North Carolina's southernmost coastal county, whose reputation was built around its pristine beaches, golf courses, and historic sites. Now, the number of building permits issued in Brunswick each year is rivaled only by that of Las Vegas.

Take what you want from these notions. The South, after all, writes Shannon Ravenel, cofounder of Algonquin Books in Chapel Hill, is a "state of mind." And should that state seem incongruous at times, well, that's all right. So what if a profusion of Atlanta road names include the word "Peachtree" (63 at last count)? Don't mind that Georgia calls itself the Peach State though South Carolina is actually the nation's largest producer of fresh-market peaches. And when North Carolinians call their town of Beaufort "bow-furt," while South Carolinians pronounce their Beaufort "bew-fert," just say no problem, and chalk it up to the South.

In the center of the changing landscape, growing population, and increasingly influential culture, the rock of the South is the Southerner. As T. S. Eliot explained, "culture is not merely the sum of several activities, but a way of life." Southerners perpetuate the culture of the Carolinas and Georgia, the way of life that still calls for civility. Here, people know there's a proper way of doing things, they believe in manners, and their world immediately lets you know you're in a different place when you step out of the car or off the plane.

NEW AND NOTEWORTHY

Georgia

The sparkling, two-year-old **Philips Arena** continues to be a dazzling sports and entertainment venue, hosting the games of the NBA's Atlanta Hawks and the NHL's Atlanta Thrashers as well as the massive rock and pop concerts of Bruce Springsteen and Elton John, among other artists.

Atlanta maintains its reputation for fine restaurants with the recent addition of establishments like **Sotto Sotto,** renowned for its exquisite Italian entrées, and **Zocalo,** a breezy and colorful café serving Mexican haute cuisine. **Bacchanalia,** a favorite among food critics, continues to dazzle the city with its menu, only now it does so from a spectacular new location in West Atlanta.

And there's plenty of scrumptious food in Georgia to be found outside Atlanta as well. In Savannah, new restaurant sensations like the elegant **Sapphire Grill,** under the helm of chef Chris Nason, keep company with old-time mainstays like **Johnny Harris,** which started as a small roadside stand in 1924 and has since grown into a favorite Savannah eatery.

In 2000 all **exit numbers** on Georgia's interstate highways were changed to bring them into line with those of other states. Nationwide, exits on interstates are numbered based on their distance from the nearest state line; Georgia's were previously numbered consecutively from the time you entered the state. We refer to many exit names, and provide their corresponding number, in order to enable you to better negotiate Georgia's interstates. For more information, consult the Georgia Department of Transportation Web site: www.dot.state.ga.us.

North Carolina

In spring 2000, the transformation of the **North Carolina Museum of Natural Sciences** in Raleigh was completed. Now the largest museum of its kind in the Southeast, the building is an architectural and technological showplace for exhibits that include a two-story mountain waterfall, the world's only display of a 110-million-year-old skeleton of an Acrocanthosaurus, as well as the only known dinosaur heart.

The **North Carolina Aquarium at Roanoke Island** has reopened, at twice its former size, after a two-year renovation. Animals found in the diverse aquatic environment of the Outer Banks are at home in the aquarium, whose centerpieces are a 285,000-gallon ocean tank with reef fish and the skeletal remains of a re-created Civil War ironclad.

The state has produced a 52-page book, *The Rich Heritage of African Americans in North Carolina*. The free publication offers a plethora of historic, cultural, and educational information starting with the well-founded theory that the state's first permanent African-American inhabitants arrived as early as the 1500s.

South Carolina

The new **African American Trail,** outlined in a brochure put out by South Carolina Department of Parks, Recreation and

Tourism, highlights African and African-American sites in three Lowcountry counties. Divided into two parts—the Coastal Trail, which winds along the coast, and the Folkways & Communities Trail, which travels through rural and urban centers—it familiarizes visitors with the lifestyle, culture, and achievements of formerly enslaved Africans and African-Americans in the counties of Charleston, Dorchester, and Colleton.

In April 2001, the **Family Circle Magazine Cup Tennis Tournament,** in which top women professionals compete, will be held on Daniel Island, a few miles out from downtown Charleston. The tournament was formerly held on Hilton Head Island.

In **Myrtle Beach,** the Conway Bypass is scheduled to open fully at the end of 2001 (sections of it opened at the end of 2000).

In **Chesnee,** about 15 minutes from Spartanburg, the Carolina Foothills Artisan Center opened in fall 2000; it showcases and sells the work of local artists.

WHAT'S WHERE

Georgia

Georgia has contrasting landscapes and varied cities and towns, each reflecting its own version of Southern charm. The northern part of the state has the Appalachian Mountains and their waterfalls; Dahlonega, the site of an early gold rush; and Alpine Helen, a re-created Bavarian village in the Blue Ridge Mountains. Also in the north are Atlanta, a fast-growing city that serves as a banking center, and Macon, an antebellum town with thousands of cherry trees. If you drive some five hours southeast from Atlanta, you'll reach Savannah, which has the nation's largest historic district, filled with restored colonial and 19th-century buildings. From Savannah, the state's 100-mi Atlantic coast runs south to the Florida border. Along this stretch is a string of lush, subtropical barrier islands including historic Sapelo Island and the Golden Isles, the elegant seaside communities of Jekyll, Sea, and St. Simons islands. Farther south is Cumberland Island National Seashore, a sanctuary of marshes, beaches, forests, lakes, and ponds. Much of southern Georgia consists of gator-infested swampland, including the mysterious rivers and lakes of the Okefenokee.

North Carolina

Historic sights and natural wonders abound in North Carolina, from Old Salem, where the 1700s spring to life in modern-day Winston-Salem, to the Great Smoky and Blue Ridge mountains in the west, where waterfalls cascade over high cliffs into gorges thick with evergreens. On the Cape Hatteras and Cape Lookout national seashores, tides wash over the wooden skeletons of ancient shipwrecks, and lighthouses stand as they have for 200 years. Here, too, you'll find sophisticated cities such as Charlotte and Raleigh, world-class golf in the Pinehurst Sandhills, and the rich soil of the gently rolling Piedmont, which has supported generations of farmers and potters alike.

South Carolina

South Carolina's scenic Lowcountry shoreline is punctuated by the lively port city of Charleston, decked out with fine museums (several in restored antebellum homes), and is anchored by the recreational resorts of Myrtle Beach and Hilton Head at either end of the coast. The state capital, Columbia, is set in the fertile interior, and the Blue Ridge Mountains form the western border of the state. Also to the west are the rolling fields of Thoroughbred Country, noted for top racehorses and sprawling mansions, and Upcountry, at the state's northwestern tip, with incredible mountain scenery and white-water rafting.

PLEASURES AND PASTIMES

Dining

Time was when "dinner" in the South meant the midday meal—the principal meal of the day—and the lighter evening meal was known as "supper." But no more. Now, dinner is the last meal of the day, and grits aren't just for breakfast anymore. In fact, dishes such as chili grits and shrimp with cheese grits are popping up as entrées on the states' most sophisticated menus. And it's not just in major cities that you'll find upscale cuisine. In Blowing Rock, a small resort town in the mountains of North Carolina, one chef regularly whips up creations such as grilled ostrich with vegetable tortilla lasagna and smoked apple ketchup. Purists can take heart, however, as there's still plenty of down-home cookin' (country ham and fried chicken, biscuits and corn bread, collard and turnip greens) to be had, and South Carolina's Lowcountry kitchens continue to ooze with she-crab soup, stuffed oysters, and pecan pie. Barbecue, which in the South is used as a noun, not a verb, is served in a stunning variety of ways, the meat (usually pork) dressed in everything from vinegar and red pepper to sweet mustard.

History

Long before 16th-century explorers Giovanni de Verrazano and Hernando de Soto came calling on what is today the Carolinas and Georgia, tribe after tribe of Native Americans occupied the land. The history of one of the mightiest, the Cherokee, is chronicled in the state-of-the-art Museum of the Cherokee Indian in Cherokee, North Carolina, beneath the shadow of the Great Smoky Mountains. Farther south, the Charleston Museum, founded in 1773 as the first public museum in the United States, still welcomes visitors. Across the region, colonial history comes alive at Revolutionary War sites—at Kings Mountain National Military Park in Upcountry South Carolina for example, and Guilford Courthouse National Military Park in Greensboro, North Carolina. In 1799, America's first gold rush got its start east of Charlotte; the Reed Gold Mine State Historic Site marks the spot. In Georgia meanwhile, Savannah stands as testimony to the antebellum era, as do many of the towns lining U.S. 441, such as Madison and Milledgeville and, just to the south, Macon. The entire Confederate treasury, last seen at Chennault Plantation in Lincolnton, Georgia, is nowhere to be found, though rumor has it the gold is hidden somewhere on the grounds. A century after the Civil War, the South was the center of another wrenching conflict: the civil rights movement. Landmarks and memorials of the campaign, including Martin Luther King Jr.'s Ebenezer Baptist Church in Atlanta, are found across the region.

Music

Travel along the coast of the Carolinas and Georgia during the summer months and you'll hear the strains of beach music, sanctified oldies such as "Under the Boardwalk" by the Drifters. The focal point of this music is a dance ritual, the shag. South Carolina's Myrtle Beach, site of a huge annual festival celebrating beach music and the shag, also has a large number of country venues. Out of clubs and bars in the region's college towns have come scores of alternative rock bands and many national headliners such as R.E.M. and Hootie and the Blowfish. For bluegrass head to the mountains of North Carolina; for classical try Charleston's Spoleto Festival USA; and if you want a little of everything sidle up to the listening stations in the Georgia Music Hall of Fame in Macon. It honors the amazing array of music industry leaders and artists who hail from the state, everybody from Toni Braxton, James Brown, and Ray Charles to Al Green, Isaac Hayes, and Lena Horne.

Outdoor Activities and Sports

Though the Carolinas and Georgia have professional baseball, basketball, football, and hockey teams, college sports—especially football and basketball—elicit the most fiery loyalty. School colors don't matter when it comes to fishing and boating, though, and Southerners do a lot of both. There are huge bays and sounds here, natural and man-made lakes, the Atlantic Ocean and Intracoastal Waterway, as well as rivers for white-water rafting and flat-water canoeing. If beaches are your passion, take your pick: the windswept shores of North Carolina's Outer Banks, the bustling resorts at South Carolina's Myrtle Beach, or Georgia's lush barrier islands. The myriad courses of Southern Pines and Pinehurst in North Carolina's Sandhills are a golfer's paradise. The region's mountains, from the Blue Ridge to the Great Smokies, have well-marked hiking trails, including parts of the Appalachian Trail, to take you away from everyday bustle. But if it's sound and motion you crave, then that most Southern of sports, stock car racing (NASCAR), is just the ticket.

FODOR'S CHOICE

No two people will agree on what makes a perfect vacation, but it's fun and helpful to know what others think. We hope you'll have a chance to experience some of Fodor's Choices yourself in the Carolinas and Georgia. For detailed information about each entry, refer to the appropriate chapter.

Special Moments

Historic District, Savannah, Georgia. Architecture buffs will have a field day strolling by the hundreds of restored buildings within a 2½-square-mi area.

Okefenokee National Wildlife Refuge, southeastern Georgia. Savor nature at its most primeval as alligators and frogs bellow their respective mating calls in spring.

Martin Luther King Jr. Center, Atlanta, Georgia. The eternal flame burning at Martin Luther King Jr.'s tomb in front of the downtown center inspires reflection.

Cape Hatteras National Seashore, North Carolina. Stretching from Oregon Inlet to Ocracoke Island, this scenic coastline is dotted with beach communities, wildlife refuges, and beaches cluttered only by wild sea oats.

Old Salem, Winston-Salem, North Carolina. A 1700s village of brick-and-wood structures peopled by tradesmen and gentlewomen in period costume provides a slice of living history.

Cypress Gardens, Moncks Corner, South Carolina. A boat tour among the spring blossoms reflecting in the black waters of the gardens is a visual dazzler.

Dining

Bacchanalia, Atlanta, Georgia. Mediterranean cuisine with Asian influences is served in a new, stunning location that matches its exquisite menu. *$$$–$$$$*

Elizabeth on 37th, Savannah, Georgia. In an elegant early 20th-century mansion in the city's Victorian district, the emphasis is on regional specialties. *$$$–$$$$*

The 1838 Langston House at Henderson Village, Perry, Georgia. You'll dine on French-based fare and interpretations of regional dishes in a restored early 19th-century Greek Revival house outside of Macon. *$$$*

Mrs. Wilkes Dining Room, Savannah, Georgia. Expect long lines waiting to devour the reasonably priced, well-prepared Southern food, served family style at big tables. *$*

Gabrielle's at Richmond Hill, Asheville, North Carolina. The fabulous dinners at this Victorian inn are not to be missed—held by some to be the most imaginative (wild boar sausage and grilled antelope medallions) and delicious food in the state. *$$$$*

Second Empire, Raleigh, North Carolina. Elegance and epicurean innovation are the bywords at this renovated Victorian-era mansion just blocks from the capital building. *$$$$*

Lamplighter, Charlotte, North Carolina. Fine contemporary cuisine served in the softly lighted interior of an old Dilworth home is the hallmark of this favorite. *$$$–$$$$*

Peninsula Grill, Charleston, South Carolina. Superb, elegant dining makes the restaurant at Planters Inn a favorite with Charleston's jet set. *$$$–$$$$*

Woodlands Inn, Summerville, South Carolina. The restaurant at this luxurious inn continues to be the most sophisticated in the Charleston area. *$$$–$$$$*

Collectors Cafe, Myrtle Beach, South Carolina. This pleasantly arty spot includes a gallery, so you can shop after you try the barbecued duck or veal-stuffed ravioli. *$$–$$$*

Magnolias, Charleston, South Carolina. Lots of Lowcountry dishes and a magnolia theme infuse this refurbished warehouse with Southern charm. *$$–$$$*

Lodging

Ritz-Carlton, Buckhead, Atlanta, Georgia. The Ritz's signature 18th- and 19th-century furnishings grace this discreetly elegant gem close to Lenox Square mall and Phipps Plaza shopping. *$$$$*

Kehoe House, Savannah, Georgia. Elegance, refinement, and Victorian opulence make a stay at this inn a grand experience in every way. *$$$–$$$$*

Henderson Village, Perry, Georgia. An elegant, rustic cluster of farmhouses with a fine restaurant, it's the perfect base for your visit to Macon. *$$$*

Jekyll Island Club Hotel, Jekyll Island, Georgia. This former private hunting retreat for the wealthy now has luxurious guest rooms and an excellent restaurant. *$$$*

Fearrington House, Chapel Hill, North Carolina. This French-style country inn was once a working farm and looks like an English country village. You'll get top-notch service in a genteel atmosphere. *$$$$*

Grove Park Inn, Asheville, North Carolina. The city's premier resort, Grove Park Inn has Arts and Crafts furnishings. It has been the haunt of guests such as Thomas Edison and F. Scott Fitzgerald since its opening in 1913. *$$$$*

First Colony Inn, Nags Head, North Carolina. Four-poster beds, English antiques, and whirlpool tubs lend an air of romance to this inn by the ocean, reminiscent of the beach hotels of years past. *$$$–$$$$*

Pinehurst Resort & Country Club, Pinehurst, North Carolina. Thanks to its serene atmosphere, attentive service, round-the-calendar blooming flora, and recreational opportunities including tennis and bicycling, the world's largest golf resort attracts more than golfers. *$$$–$$$$*

Charleston Place, Charleston, South Carolina. The upscale address of Charleston, this full-service hotel is conveniently in the historic district. *$$$$*

John Rutledge House Inn, Charleston, South Carolina. The elegant John Rutledge House has ornate ironwork on its facade and is impeccably furnished and maintained. *$$$$*

Kingston Plantation, Myrtle Beach, South Carolina. This self-contained resort, loaded with facilities such as a spa and a marina, has a great location on a broad beach well removed from the bustle of the pavilion area. *$$$–$$$$*

Westin Resort, Hilton Head Island, South Carolina. Top of the line for Hilton Head, the Westin concentrates on luxury and service. *$$$–$$$$*

Historic Houses and Gardens

Callaway Gardens, Pine Mountain, Georgia. This is one of the country's biggest, with 2,500 acres and a butterfly center. Also on the grounds are four renowned golf courses, a lakefront beach, bicycling trails, and tennis courts.

Japanese Garden at the Carter Presidential Center Library, Atlanta, Georgia. Built as a legacy to President Jimmy Carter's administration, the Carter Center is a splendid, landscaped estate with meticulously tended Japanese gardens that provide a tranquil vantage point of Atlanta's cityscape.

Robert Toombs House, Washington, Georgia. The former home of U.S. Senator Robert Toombs, who served as secretary of state during the Civil War, this Greek Revival mansion is furnished with 19th-century antiques and other personal items from Toombs' estate.

Biltmore Estate, Asheville, North Carolina. This castle is part of an 8,000-acre estate masterminded by premier landscape architect Frederick Law Olmsted and contains an Italian garden, a walled garden, a conservatory, the Biltmore Forest, and meandering woodland trails.

Orton Plantation Gardens, Winnabow, North Carolina. Aside the Cape Fear River, these gardens were established in 1725, and descendants of the original owners continue to maintain the 20 lush acres of trails, informal gardens, and sculpted formal gardens filled with azaleas, camellias, and other ornamentals.

Sarah P. Duke Gardens, Durham, North Carolina. The gardens occupy 55 acres of Duke University's West Campus. They include native plants, an Asiatic garden, a rock garden and fish pond, a circular rose garden, and an enormous wisteria-covered pergola offering a grand view of the core of the landscaped gardens, the Terraces.

Drayton Hall, Charleston, South Carolina. Unfurnished and unrestored, this mid-18th-century National Historic Landmark is considered the nation's finest example of unspoiled Georgian-Palladian architecture.

Magnolia Plantation and Gardens, Charleston, South Carolina. The 50-acre informal garden was begun in 1685; here and in the Audubon Swamp Garden, flowers bloom year-round. The Manor House offers a look at plantation life.

Middleton Place, Charleston, South Carolina. These are the nation's oldest landscaped gardens, dating to 1741, with terraced lawns, ornamental lakes (including the famous Butterfly Lakes), and floral allées.

FESTIVALS AND SEASONAL EVENTS

The Carolinas and Georgia hold a wide variety of festivals and special events throughout the year. Call local or state visitor information offices for further information.

WINTER

➤ DECEMBER: **Christmas** is celebrated all over the South, with events in almost every city. Highlights include Old Salem Christmas, which recreates a Moravian Christmas in Winston-Salem, North Carolina. The annual Festival of Trees in Atlanta highlights specially decorated trees, and Savannah glows with candlelight tours of the Historic District. **New Year's** events include the Peach Bowl, played in Atlanta, and First Night festivals held in the downtown areas of Charlotte and Raleigh, North Carolina.

➤ JANUARY: In South Carolina, Orangeburg invites the country's finest coon dogs to compete in the **Grand American Coon Hunt.** Regional **runners race** in the Savannah Marathon and Half Marathon in Savannah, Georgia, and the *Charlotte Observer* Marathon and Runners' Expo in Charlotte, North Carolina. **Martin Luther King Jr. Week** is celebrated in Atlanta.

➤ FEBRUARY: In North Carolina, Asheville welcomes visitors to its annual **Winterfest Arts and Crafts Show.** Wilmington stages the **North Carolina Jazz Festival.**

SPRING

➤ MARCH: The Old South comes alive: **Antebellum mansion and garden tours** are given in Charleston and Beaufort, South Carolina. A **Revolutionary War battle** is reenacted on the anniversary of the Battle of Guilford Courthouse in Greensboro, North Carolina. **Spring** is celebrated with a Cherry Blossom Festival in Macon, Georgia, and Springfest on Hilton Head Island, South Carolina. **St. Patrick's Day** in Savannah is one of the nation's largest celebrations of the day. Aiken, South Carolina, has its own horse-racing **Triple Crown,** including Thoroughbred trials, harness races, and steeplechases.

➤ APRIL: **Spring festivals** abound, including dogwood festivals in Atlanta, Georgia, and Fayetteville, North Carolina. Also consider the Okefenokee Spring Fling in Waycross, Georgia. The **World Grits Festival** is held in St. George, South Carolina. In Wilkesboro, North Carolina, the **Merle Watson Memorial Festival** features Doc Watson's renowned bluegrass picking. The Biltmore Estate in Asheville, North Carolina hosts the **Festival of Flowers,** a breathtaking display with more than 50,000 tulips, hundreds of varieties of azaleas, and dogwood and cherry trees. The **Masters Golf Tournament** in Augusta, Georgia, attracts top pros and thousands of spectators. More than 40,000 participate in the **Cooper River Bridge Run and Walk** in Charleston, South Carolina.

➤ MAY: Festivals take to the air this month with the annual **Hang Gliding Spectacular** in Nags Head, North Carolina. Over Memorial Day weekend, Greenville, South Carolina, hosts **Freedom Weekend Aloft,** the second-largest balloon rally in the country. **Spoleto Festival USA,** in Charleston, South Carolina, is one of the world's biggest arts festivals; **Piccolo Spoleto,** running concurrently, showcases local and regional talent. In South Carolina, Beaufort's **Gullah Festival** highlights the fine arts, customs, language, and dress of Lowcountry African-Americans.

SUMMER

➤ JUNE: Popular arts festivals, such as the juried **Virginia-Highland Summerfest,** flourish throughout Atlanta. June is the time for Durham, North Carolina's, renowned **American Dance Festival.** Summer gets under way at the **Sun Fun Festival** on Myrtle Beach's Grand Strand on the South Carolina coast.

➤ JULY: **Independence Day** celebrations are annual traditions around the South. Clog and figure dancing are part of the **Shindig-on-the-Green** in Asheville, North Carolina. The annual **Highland Games & Gathering of the Scottish Clans** is held on Grandfather Mountain near Linville, North Carolina.

➤ AUGUST: The **Georgia Mountain Fair,** a mountain crafts and music extravaganza, is held in Hiawassee. North Carolina holds an **Apple Festival** in Hendersonville. August **music festivals** include a Beach Music Festival on Jekyll Island, Georgia, and the annual Mountain Dance and Folk Festival in Asheville, North Carolina.

AUTUMN

➤ SEPTEMBER: Truly a **festival month,** September welcomes local events throughout the South. In **Georgia,** Stone Mountain Park is the site of the Yellow Daisy Festival, celebrating this flower and also arts and crafts. The annual **Woolly Worm Festival** takes place in Banner Elk, North Carolina. The **Candlelight Tour of Houses and Gardens** is held in Charleston during this month and October.

➤ OCTOBER: Autumn brings more celebrations of food, including the **Big Pig Jig** in Vienna, Georgia, celebrating the glories of authentic Southern barbecue. The annual **Highland Games,** a celebration of Scottish heritage, is held at Stone Mountain Park in Georgia. A barbecue and parade of pigs guarantee fun at the **Lexington Barbecue Festival** in North Carolina. The **South Carolina State Fair** is a Columbia highlight. **Oktoberfest** is celebrated in Helen, Georgia, and in Myrtle Beach and Walhalla, South Carolina. The "ghost capital of the world"—Georgetown, South Carolina—stages a **Ghost Tour.**

➤ NOVEMBER: **Christmas preparations** include the Mistletoe Market in Albany, Georgia. Autumn **food festivals** include the Catfish Festival in Society Hill, South Carolina, and the Chitlin' Strut in Salley, South Carolina.

2 GEORGIA

Georgia is geographically the largest state east of the Mississippi River. Its varied terrain ranges from the foothills of the Appalachian Mountains in the north to the great coastal plain running from the state's center toward the shore to the beaches of the Golden Isles and the delicate ecology of the Okefenokee in the southeast. From progressive Atlanta to antebellum Macon and colonial Savannah, each of Georgia's cities and towns has its own special charm.

Updated by Hollis Gillespie

GEORGIA IS LIKE A CLEVERLY MADE PATCHWORK quilt. Its landscape encompasses the hazy blue foothills of the Appalachian Mountains in the north, the coastal plain connecting the heartland to the unspoiled beaches of the Atlantic, and the mysterious black-water swamps of the state's southern portion. Most visitors travel its interstate highways (I–75, I–85, I–95, and I–16), but the adventurous traveler who decides to explore the state's byways will be rewarded with pristine vistas and detours through charming towns.

Within the landscape lies a rich diversity of unusual flora, including mountain laurel, rhododendrons, azaleas, and camellias. Spanish moss drapes live oak trees in the southern and coastal areas, and flat fields of white puffy cotton line the horizon through the middle of the state. Known for its peaches, Georgia is also proud of its apples, and the fruit trees' soft blooms create splendid sights in spring. Hiking in the north Georgia mountains could reveal their wealth of deer charging through the forest. Along the coast, alligators, egrets, and herons take the visitor in stride.

As varied as its landscape, Georgia's citizens reflect the diversity of early settlers, native peoples, and new arrivals. During the 18th century, not only English and Scottish immigrants but also Jewish settlers, both Sephardic and Ashkenazic, and German religious refugees (the Salzburgers) arrived to take up positions of importance and prominence in the Georgia colony. Africans and native peoples—chiefly Cherokee and Creek—added their cultural spice to the mix, creating a state that is richer in ethnic character than is often recognized. Irish immigrants arriving throughout the 19th century and Greeks, Middle Easterners, and Asians during the late 19th and early 20th centuries contributed to the state's diversity. Georgians speak with accents that vary from the classic, slightly nasal mountain "twang" to the distinctive, soft coastal lilt of upper-crust Savannahians.

Georgia's towns each define in their own way that famous Southern charm of fable and film. Bustling Atlanta, the state capital since the Civil War ended in 1865, has been compared with Margaret Mitchell's heroine, Scarlett O'Hara, the classic Steel Magnolia: gentle in form but brash and tough in substance. Colonial Savannah, with the nation's largest Historic District, lures visitors to its 21 cobblestone squares, giant parterre gardens, waterfront gift shops, jazz bars, and parks. Dahlonega, site of the nation's early gold rush in 1828, is a typical example of the small Georgia town, with its central square dominated by a county courthouse. Macon, full of flowering Japanese cherry trees and images of both the antebellum and Victorian South, celebrates its heritage as home to poet and flutist Sidney Lanier. A few small towns are named for glittering foreign capitals that they resemble not in the slightest: Vienna (pronounced vy-*en*-ah), Madrid (may-*drid*), Rome, Athens, Cairo (*cay*-row), and so forth.

Georgia's 100-mi coast runs from the mouth of the Savannah River south to the mouth of the St. Marys River. The seaside resort communities blend Southern elegance with a casual sensibility. St. Simons Island, about 70 mi south of Savannah, attracts a laid-back crowd of anglers, beachgoers, golfers, and tennis players. On nearby Jekyll Island, the lavish lifestyle of America's early 19th-century rich and famous is still evident in their stately Victorian "cottages." Cumberland Island's protected forests and miles of sandy coastline, the rustically beautiful Sapelo Island, the isolated solitude of Little St. Simons Island, and the dark waters of the Okefenokee are favorite haunts of nature lovers.

Georgia

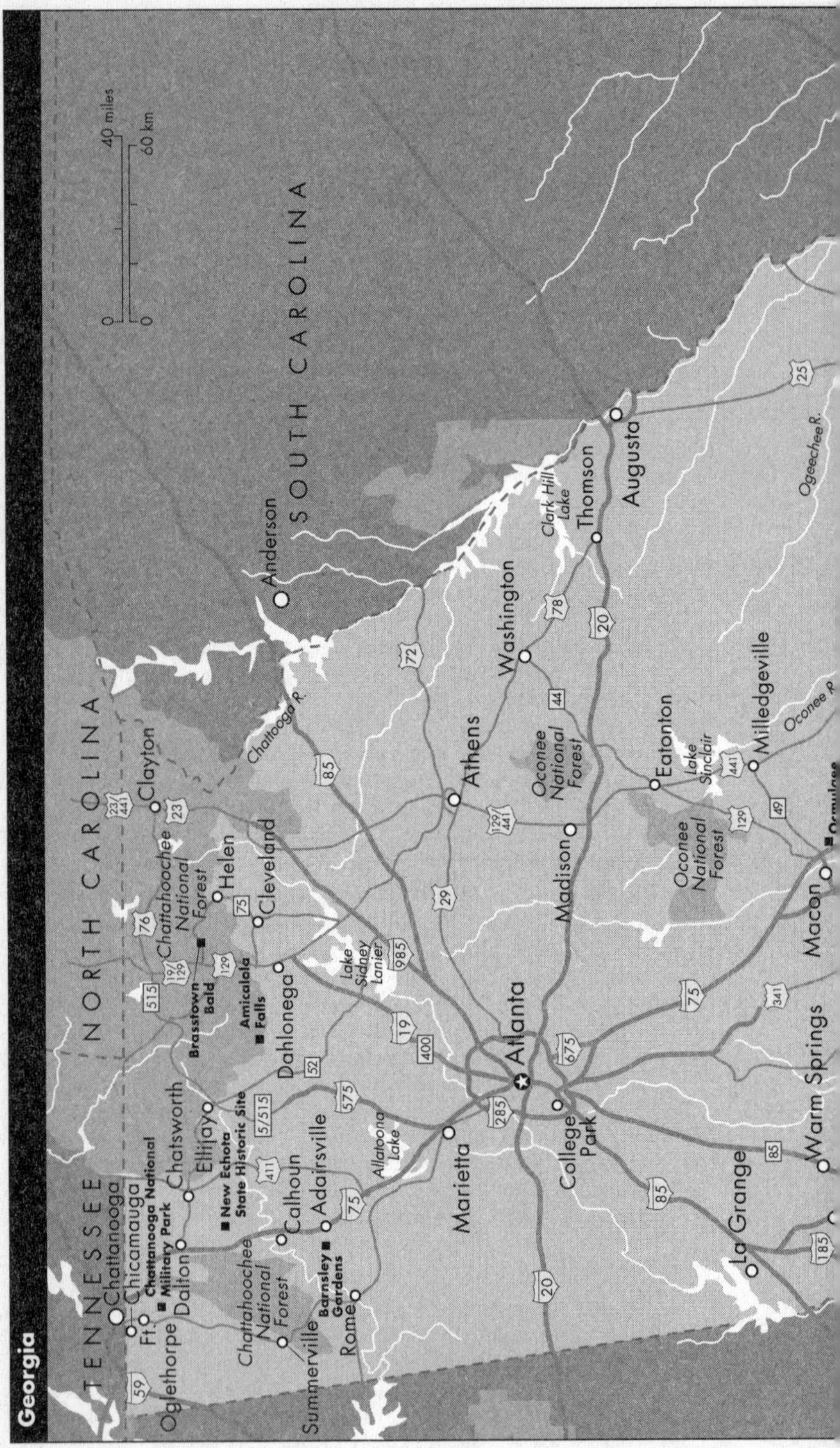

NORTH CAROLINA
SOUTH CAROLINA
TENNESSEE
0 40 miles
0 60 km
Chattanooga
Chicamauga
Ft. Oglethorpe
Chattanooga National Military Park
Dalton
Chatsworth
Chattahoochee National Forest
Summerville
New Echota State Historic Site
Calhoun
Adairsville
Barnsley Gardens
Rome
Ellijay
Dahlonega
Brasstown Bald
Amicalola Falls
Chattahoochee National Forest
Helen
Cleveland
Clayton
Chattooga R.
Anderson
Lake Sidney Lanier
Allatoona Lake
Marietta
Atlanta
College Park
Athens
Washington
Clark Hill Lake
Thomson
Augusta
Oconee National Forest
Madison
Eatonton
Lake Sinclair
Milledgeville
Oconee R.
Ogeechee R.
Macon
Warm Springs
La Grange
59
515
76
23/441
23
19/129
129
75
52
5/515
411
575
19
400
985
85
72
29
129/441
44
78
20
25
285
675
341
185
441
49

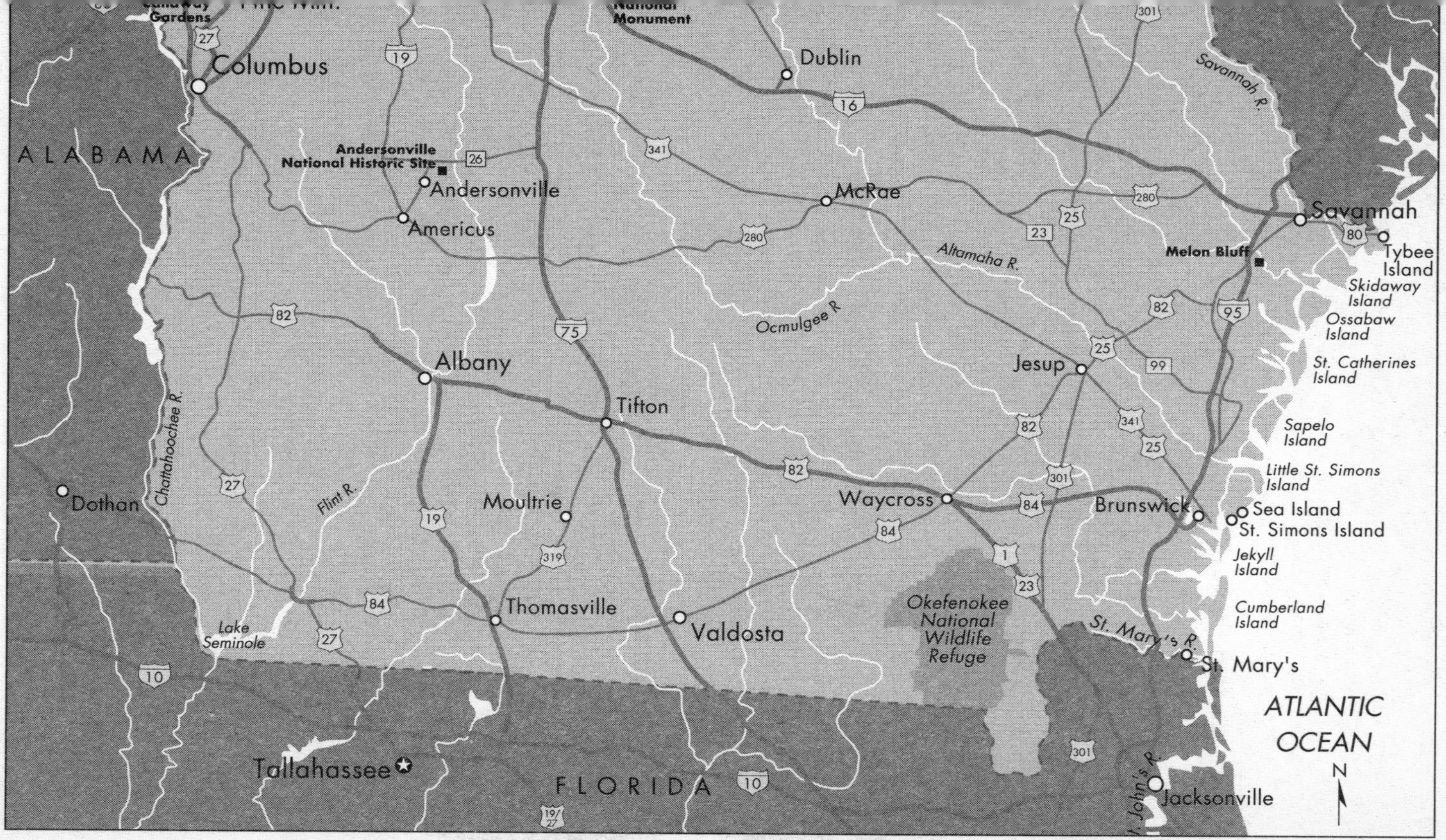
Gardens
Monument
Columbus
Dublin
Savannah R.
ALABAMA
Andersonville National Historic Site
Andersonville
Americus
McRae
Savannah
Tybee Island
Melon Bluff
Skidaway Island
Ossabaw Island
Altamaha R.
Ocmulgee R.
Albany
Jesup
St. Catherines Island
Tifton
Sapelo Island
Little St. Simons Island
Chattahoochee R.
Dothan
Flint R.
Moultrie
Waycross
Brunswick
Sea Island
St. Simons Island
Jekyll Island
Thomasville
Valdosta
Okefenokee National Wildlife Refuge
Cumberland Island
Lake Seminole
St. Mary's R.
St. Mary's
ATLANTIC OCEAN
Tallahassee
FLORIDA
Jacksonville
N
27
19
16
301
341
26
280
25
23
80
82
95
75
99
27
84
1
319
10
19/27

Other historical riches include thousand-year-old Native American homesites and burial mounds, antebellum mansions, war heroes' memorials, and intriguing monuments built by eccentric folk artists and obsessive gardeners. Georgia's many state parks have superb facilities for white-water rafting, canoeing, fishing, golf, and tennis; and nature trails wind through mountain forests delicately laced with wild rhododendrons, dogwoods, and azaleas.

Pleasures and Pastimes

Dining

Dining in Georgia has its ups and downs. Areas that have attracted substantial tourism have respectable to downright outstanding restaurants. Others lag far behind, their best offerings the chain restaurants, or the local barbecue joint. When dining in a small town, you might ask the fire department; firefighters often know which are the best local restaurants.

Atlanta sets the culinary pace, of course, with cutting-edge fare from outstanding chefs. Dress in Atlanta—and elsewhere in the state—is casual unless otherwise noted. Classic meat-and-threes—diners serving meat with three side dishes—are found throughout Georgia. On the byways of Georgia, barbecue stands and restaurants still cook the whole pig, serving customers its meat pulled off the bone for sandwiches or its tender ribs, both bathed in tangy sauce. Brunswick stew, a hunter's stew that traditionally contained the day's catch, is the standard accompaniment. Some of these places are full-fledged restaurants; others have no place to sit at all. If you're off the beaten path, these establishments offer your best chance for decent food.

CATEGORY	COST*
$$$$	over $50
$$$	$35–$50
$$	$25–$35
$	under $25

**per person for a three-course meal, excluding drinks, service, and 7% tax*

Historic Sites

You may want to plan your trip with Georgia's historic sites in mind. From the moment you enter the state along the interstate highways, brown markers with white lettering alert you to the locations of the state's principal historical sights along those routes. Georgia's towns constitute a special glimpse into the past. Savannah, founded in 1733, can be viewed from carriage or bus via specialty tours, by private car, or on foot; it's an excellent walking city. Augusta, founded in 1736, has a fine Riverwalk, a restored downtown, and the 19th- and 20th-century houses of Olde Town and Summerville. Macon, founded in 1823, is known for its wealth of fine antebellum and Victorian mansions that may be viewed by private car or on specialty tours. You'll find more than a fair share of battlefields to explore, including the dark woods and open fields of Chickamauga and unusual historic sites such as New Echota, the lost capital of the Cherokee Nation.

Lodging

Most national and some international hotel and motel chains have establishments in Georgia. Within the past decade, bed-and-breakfast inns have arisen throughout the state, some providing exquisite lodging, others doing a perfunctory job. Campsites are marked along the interstate highways, and the state has a fine network of parks, some of which offer campsites and overnight facilities. Always telephone ahead to bed-and-breakfast inns and campsites for reservations, as these are popular accommodations.

CATEGORY	ATLANTA AND SAVANNAH*	OTHER AREAS*
$$$$	over $230	over $170
$$$	$170–$230	$120–$170
$$	$100–$170	$75–$120
$	under $100	under $75

All prices are for a standard double room, excluding 13% tax and service.

🖰 following the text of a review is your signal that the property has a Web site, where you will find details and, usually, images; for a link, visit www.fodors.com/urls.

Nightlife

No night in Georgia need ever be boring. Clubs, music venues, theater, film, symphony, and comedy revues all make nightlife hum. Blues and jazz, country and western and gospel, and rock and roll are all part of this region's—and Georgia's—homegrown musical tradition. Local composers and performers who made their marks on the national music scene include Savannah's Johnny Mercer; Macon's Otis Redding and the Allman Brothers; and Augusta's James Brown, the godfather of soul. Macon's Little Richard and Albany's Ray Charles still perform. Local groups that have gained national and international fame include R.E.M. and the B-52's from Athens, Indigo Girls from Decatur, and Black Crowes from Marietta. In country-and-western music, Travis Tritt started out in Marietta and Trisha Yearwood in Monticello. To hear rising new stars, call local radio stations for information about venues.

In the classical department, opera diva Jessye Norman is from Augusta, and violinist Robert McDuffie is from Macon. The state abounds in symphony orchestras, chamber groups, and classical and jazz ensembles, many of which perform on college campuses. For details, contact a local college campus or consult the local newspaper.

Theater is vital not only in Atlanta but also throughout the state, home to thespians Joanne Woodward (Thomasville), Julia and Eric Roberts (Smyrna), Holly Hunter (Conyers), Melvin Douglas (Macon), Pernell Roberts (Waycross), and playwright Alfred Uhry (Atlanta). If you can catch a performance of *Swamp Gravy,* by residents of Colquitt, Georgia, or *Reach of Song,* based on the poetry of mountain poet Byron Herbert Reece, you'll enjoy traditional local subject matter and music.

Outdoor Activities and Sports

For the sports enthusiast, Georgia has a full plate of activities—fishing, camping, golf and tennis, sailing and rowing. There's also a beloved baseball team, the Atlanta Braves. Hiking opportunities abound: At the Chattahoochee Nature Center outside Atlanta, you can see birds and other woodland animals in their natural habitat while hiking through 124 acres of lush forests and wetlands. Another outdoor favorite is Stone Mountain Park and its Walk Up Trail, an atmospheric jaunt up the west side of the mountain culminated by a rigorous 825-ft climb to the peak. It's well worth the challenge, as the ensuing panoramic view of Atlanta is stunning.

Exploring Georgia

Georgia has several distinct touring areas; the state is large, and you'd need more than a week to hit even some of the highlights. The Foothills of the Appalachian Mountains run from west to east in north Georgia, making this a popular destination for tourists, especially in spring and fall. Atlanta alone warrants serious exploration. The coast offers other opportunities, especially for the history aficionado; it's a good place to start if you have just a few days. From Savannah, Georgia's oldest city, to Augusta, its third oldest, colonial and Civil War history awaits at every turn. It's in east Georgia where you'll see most of the columned antebellum homes visitors have come to expect. The coastal islands have fine beaches and opportunities for nature-focused expeditions. The best spot for would-be naturalists, of course, is the Okefenokee Natural Wildlife Refuge.

Great Itineraries

IF YOU HAVE 3 DAYS

Explore the coast to get a true taste of what early Georgia was all about. Spend a day and night in **Augusta,** being sure to visit Meadow Garden, home of George Walton, youngest signer (at age 26) of the Declaration of Independence. Exhibits at the Morris Museum of Southern Art range from luminous 19th-century landscapes to folk art and the challenging abstracts of Augusta native Jasper Johns. Give the remaining two days over to an exploration of **Savannah.** Stay at a bed-and-breakfast inn (be sure to have reservations, especially for weekends) and view any of the fine restored homes the city offers. Spend some time along Riverfront Plaza, enjoying the waterfront, dining in restaurants, and just plain kicking back. Other must-see sights include the 1815 Isaiah Davenport House and the Colonial Park Cemetery, the final resting place for some of America's founders. Spring and fall are the best times to visit both these cities; in spring you may be able to catch a tour of Savannah's glorious private gardens.

IF YOU HAVE 7 DAYS

Add a trip to **Atlanta** to the three-day itinerary. History enthusiasts will want to visit the Atlanta History Center and its gardens, viewing those exhibits that focus on the history of the city and touring its two house museums. A fine small museum, the African-American Panoramic Experience, chronicles the history of blacks in America. In Grant Park, the Atlanta Cyclorama has a huge painting of the 1864 Battle of Atlanta. The Chattahoochee National Recreational Area is a great spot for joggers, walkers, hikers, and nature lovers. At Stone Mountain Park, you can see the Confederate Memorial (the world's largest sculpture), two Civil War museums, and the Road to Tara Museum. Atlanta is famous for its springtime, and no doubt this is a glorious time to visit. But fall is exquisite, too, as the hardwoods change color, beginning about early October.

IF YOU HAVE 10 DAYS

Follow the seven-day itinerary (☞ *above*). Then take a run up to the north Georgia mountains, visiting **Clayton,** with its many art and antiques shops; **Dahlonega,** where you can pan for gold in "them thar hills"; or **Chickamauga,** site of one of the Civil War's most important conflicts. The north Georgia mountains are glorious from spring through fall. A second option is to turn south and visit the heart of the state, taking in **Macon,** with its antebellum and Victorian homes and museums. Spring in middle Georgia is splendid, with azaleas and other flowers in full bloom. Many garden and historic home tours are scheduled at this time.

When to Tour Georgia

Spring is the best time to visit, although autumn, especially beginning in early October, is another glorious season.

ATLANTA

Founded in 1837 as the end of the Western & Atlantic railroad line and thus named Terminus, Atlanta today is a transportation hub, not just for the country but for the world: Hartsfield Atlanta International Airport is one of the nation's busiest in daily passenger flights. Direct flights to Europe, South America, and Asia have made Atlanta easily accessible to the more than 1,000 international businesses that operate here and the nearly 50 countries that have representation in the city through consulates, trade offices, and chambers of commerce. The city has emerged as a banking center and is the world headquarters for such Fortune 500 companies as CNN, Coca-Cola, Delta Airlines, Holiday Inn Worldwide, and United Parcel Service.

Atlanta's character has evolved from a mix of peoples: Transplanted Northerners and those from elsewhere account for 50% of the population and have undeniably affected the mood and character of the city. Irish immigrants had a major role in the city's early history, along with Germans and Austrians; the Hungarian-born Rich brothers founded Atlanta's principal department store. And the immigrants keep coming. In the past two decades, Atlanta has seen spirited growth in its Asian and Latin-American communities. Their restaurants, shops, and institutions have become part of the city's texture.

For more than four decades, Atlanta has been linked to the civil rights movement. Among the many accomplishments of Atlanta's African-American community is the Nobel Peace Prize that Martin Luther King Jr. won in 1964. Dr. King's widow, Coretta Scott King, continues to operate the King Center, which she founded after her husband's assassination in 1968. In 1972 Andrew Young was elected the first black congressman from the South since Reconstruction. After serving as ambassador to the United Nations during President Jimmy Carter's administration, Young was elected mayor of Atlanta. He is now a consultant with an international firm.

The traditional South—which in romantic versions consists of lacy moss dangling from tree limbs; thick, sugary Southern drawls; a leisurely pace; and luxurious antebellum mansions—is rarely found here. Even before the Civil War, the columned house was a rarity. The frenetic pace of construction that characterized the period after the Civil War continues unabated. Still viewed by die-hard Southerners as the heart of the Old Confederacy, Atlanta has become the best example of the New South, a fast-paced modern city proud of its heritage.

In the past two decades, Atlanta has experienced unprecedented growth. A good measure of that is its ever-changing downtown skyline, along with skyscrapers constructed in the Midtown, Buckhead, and outer perimeter (set by I–285) business districts. Since the late 1970s, dozens of dazzling skyscrapers designed by such luminaries as Philip Johnson, I. M. Pei, and Marcel Breuer have reshaped the city's profile. Residents, however, are less likely to measure the city's growth by skyscrapers than by increasing traffic jams, crowds, higher prices, and the ever-burgeoning subdivisions that continue to push urban sprawl farther and farther into surrounding rural areas. Although the Chamber of Commerce advertises Atlanta as a 20-county metropolitan area, the core of Atlanta revolves around five counties. The city of Atlanta is primarily in Fulton and DeKalb counties, with the southern part and the airport in Clayton County. Outside I–285, Cobb and Gwinnett counties on the northwest and northeast corners of the city, respectively, are experiencing much of Atlanta's population increase.

Atlanta's lack of grid system in most parts of the city will confuse some drivers. Some streets change their names along the same stretch of road, including the city's most famous thoroughfare, Peachtree Street, which follows a mountain ridge from downtown to suburban Norcross outside I–285N: It becomes Peachtree Road after crossing I–85 and then splits into Peachtree Industrial Boulevard beyond the Buckhead neighborhood and the original Peachtree Road, which heads into Chamblee. Adding to the confusion, 60 other streets in the metropolitan area use the word Peachtree in their names. Before setting out anywhere, get the complete street address of your destination, including landmarks, cross streets, or other guideposts, as street numbers and even street signs often are difficult to find.

Downtown Atlanta

Downtown Atlanta clusters around the hub known as Five Points. Here is the MARTA station that intersects north–south and east–west transit lines. On the surface, Five Points is formed by the intersection of Peachtree Street with Marietta, Broad, and Forsyth streets.

Numbers in the text correspond to numbers in the margin and on the Downtown Atlanta and Sweet Auburn map.

A Good Walk

This walk branches in three directions, which are most efficiently managed by taking MARTA trains to get quickly from one spot to the next. The valiant will, of course, prefer to go it on foot. Begin at **Woodruff Park** ①, and then proceed north on Peachtree Street, noting Atlanta's **Flatiron Building** ② on the west side of Peachtree and the **Candler Building** ③ on the east side of the street. Nearby on Peachtree Street at John Wesley Dobbs Avenue is the modern **Georgia-Pacific Center** ④, and across from it are **Margaret Mitchell Park** ⑤ and the **Atlanta-Fulton Public Library** ⑥. Continuing north up Peachtree Street, note the modern hotel **Ritz-Carlton, Atlanta** ⑦, the neo-Gothic **One-Ninety-One Peachtree Tower** ⑧, and **Peachtree Center** ⑨, which includes the small but worthwhile **Atlanta International Museum of Art and Design** ⑩. Walk east on Baker Street one block to Courtland Street; head north on Courtland until you reach Ralph McGill Boulevard. Here you'll find an open-air folk art exhibition known as the **Folk Art Park** ⑪.

Return to Peachtree Center and take the subway back one stop to the **Five Points MARTA station** ⑫, from which you can walk north on Peachtree Street to the **William-Oliver Building** ⑬, an award-winning restoration. (From Folk Art Park you can also follow Ralph McGill Boulevard west to Peachtree and then head south down to the William-Oliver Building.) From here, go east on Edgewood Avenue and just ahead you'll see the **Hurt Building** ⑭, a rare Atlanta example of Chicago-style architecture. Around the corner on Marietta Street at Broad Street is the handsome **Bank of America Building** ⑮, and nearby is the **Statue of Henry Grady** ⑯, right across from the building now housing the newspaper he founded, the ***Atlanta Journal-Constitution*** ⑰. A block west on Marietta Street is the **Federal Reserve Bank** ⑱, with its monetary museum. At Marietta Street and Techwood Drive, **Centennial Olympic Park** ⑲ hosts concerts and special events. Adjacent to the park is **CNN Center** ⑳, which you may tour if you make a reservation. At the rear of the center is the **Georgia Dome** ㉑.

At the CNN Center/Georgia Dome station, take MARTA one station back to the Five Points station and exit at the sign for **Underground Atlanta** ㉒. After taking a rest and a restorative snack in its food court, wander the maze of subterranean streets here and exit the doors of Underground

Atlanta, bearing slightly left toward the **Georgia Railroad Freight Depot** ㉓. Across the plaza from the depot is the **World of Coca-Cola** ㉔, with fun memorabilia on display. Across Martin Luther King Jr. Drive at Central Avenue is the historic **Shrine of the Immaculate Conception** ㉕, one of many historic churches still operating in downtown. Just south of the shrine are the neo-Gothic **City Hall** ㉖, with a modern addition housing a permanent art collection, which is on Mitchell Street, and the Renaissance-style **Georgia State Capitol** ㉗ on Washington Street.

TIMING

This walk requires at least a day, assuming you don't spend much time at any one location. If you plan to walk at a more leisurely pace, finish the first day at the Folk Art Park, and allow another half day for the rest of the walk. If you plan tours of CNN Center, the Georgia Dome, and World of Coca-Cola, you'll need an additional half day. If you tour these sights at length, it will probably take two full days to cover the territory. The terrain is fairly level and not too taxing, with sidewalks the entire distance.

Sights to See

OFF THE BEATEN PATH

★ **ATLANTA CYCLORAMA & CIVIL WAR MUSEUM** – In Grant Park (named for a New England–born Confederate colonel, not the U.S. president), you'll find a huge circular painting, completed by a team of expert European panorama artists shortly after the Civil War, depicting the 1864 Battle of Atlanta. The museum has one of the best Civil War bookstores anywhere. To reach the Cyclorama by car, take I–20 east to Exit 59A, turn right onto Boulevard, and then take a right at the next traffic light into Grant Park; follow signs to the Cyclorama. ✉ *Grant Park, 800 Cherokee Ave.,* ☎ *404/624–1071 information.* 🎟 *$5.* ⏲ *June–Labor Day, daily 9:20–5:30; Labor Day–May, daily 9:20–4:30.*

❻ **Atlanta-Fulton Public Library.** The Marcel Breuer–designed building houses on its fourth floor a large collection of *Gone With the Wind* memorabilia and newspapers from most major cities in the United States and elsewhere. ✉ *1 Margaret Mitchell Sq.,* ☎ *404/730–1700.* ⏲ *Mon. and Fri.–Sat. 9–6, Tues.–Thurs. 9–8, Sun. 2–6.*

★ ❿ **Atlanta International Museum of Art and Design.** In the Peachtree Center in the Marriott Marquis Two Tower, this museum has mounted more than 30 major international exhibitions covering such subjects as textiles, puzzles, boxes, masks, and baskets. Exhibits focus on arts and crafts, design, and culture from around the globe. ✉ *285 Peachtree Center Ave.,* ☎ *404/688–2467.* 🎟 *$3.* ⏲ *Weekdays 11–5.*

⓱ ***Atlanta Journal-Constitution.*** The building containing the business offices and printing plant for the city's—and the state's—dominant newspaper has a lobby that displays front-page news of historic events, an old printing press, and photographs of famous former employees. Tours must be scheduled at least two weeks in advance and are not open to children under six. ✉ *72 Marietta St.,* ☎ *404/614–2688.* ⏲ *Tours of plant available by prior arrangement, weekdays at 11:30 and 12:30.*

⓯ **Bank of America Building.** Originally known as the Chicago-style Empire Building and, more recently, as the NationsBank Building, this handsome 1901 classic was designed by Atlanta architect Phillip Trammel Shutze. In 1929 Shutze refashioned the first three floors, bestowing upon them a decidedly Renaissance look. This is one of the city's first steel-frame structures, and at 14 stories one of its tallest, but during the renovation Shutze resheathed the base with masonry. ✉ *35 Broad St.*

3 **Candler Building.** Asa G. Candler, founder of the Coca-Cola Company, engaged the local firm of Murphy and Stewart to design this splendid terra-cotta and marble building in 1906. The ornate bronze and marble lobby shouldn't be missed. ✉ *84 Peachtree St.* ⏲ *Daily 9–5.*

19 **Centennial Olympic Park.** This 21-acre urban landscape, the largest urban park to be developed in this country in more than two decades, was the central venue for Olympics entertainment in the summer of 1996. The park's Fountain of Rings (the world's largest using the Olympic symbol) centers a court of 24 flags, each of them representing the Olympic Games as well as the host countries of the modern Games. Seating in the fountain amphitheater allows you to enjoy the water and music spectacle (five tunes are programmed and timed to coincide with water displays). The park has a 6-acre great lawn and pathways formed by commemorative brick paving stones. ✉ *Marietta St. and Techwood Dr.,* ☏ *404/223–4412; 404/223–4636 information.* ⏲ *Daily 8:30 AM–9 PM.*

26 **City Hall.** When the 14-story neo-Gothic building, designed by Atlanta architect G. Lloyd Preacher, was erected in 1929 critics dubbed it the Painted Lady of Mitchell Street. The newer wing, with its five-story glass atrium and beautiful marble entryway, houses a splendid permanent collection of art. ✉ *68 Mitchell St.,* ☏ *404/330–6000.* ⏲ *Weekdays 8:15–5.*

20 **CNN Center.** The home of Ted Turner's Cable News Network occupies all 14 floors of this dramatic structure on the edge of downtown. The 40-minute CNN studio tour begins with a ride up the world's longest escalator to an eighth-floor exhibit about Turner's global broadcasting empire. Tours are not open to children under age six. ✉ *1 CNN Center,* ☏ *404/827–2300. Reservations must be made at least 1 day in advance using credit card (AE, MC, V); walk-up tickets for same day only, if available, go on sale at 8:30 AM.* 🎟 *45-min tour $7; 1¼-hr VIP tour $24.50.* ⏲ *Daily 9–5:30.*

18 **Federal Reserve Bank.** This bank sits on the site once occupied by Thrasherville, a settlement that predates the 1837 establishment of Atlanta. An exhibit explains the story of money as a medium of exchange and the history of the U.S. banking system. Items displayed include rare coins, uncut sheets of money, and a gold bar. There's a tour and a video, *Inside the Fed.* ✉ *104 Marietta St.,* ☏ *404/521–8764.* ⏲ *Weekdays 9–4.*

12 **Five Points MARTA Station.** This MARTA station serves Underground Atlanta and nearby Woodruff Park, Georgia State University, and numerous businesses; the station is at the crossroads of MARTA's east–west and north–south lines. Stand on the corner of Peachtree and Alabama streets, outside the station, and notice the old-fashioned gas streetlight, with its historic marker proclaiming it the **Eternal Flame of the Confederacy.** ✉ *Corner of Peachtree and Alabama Sts.*

2 **Flatiron Building.** The English-American Building, as it was originally known, was designed by Bradford Gilbert. Similar to the famous New York City Flatiron Building, built after the turn of the 20th century, this one dates from 1897 and is the city's oldest high-rise. Its distinguishing features include a knife-sharp point that looks proudly up Peachtree Street. The rounded facade gazes toward Woodruff Park, and interesting bays within protrude out of the facade about 3 ft. ✉ *74 Peachtree St.* ⏲ *Weekdays 8:15–5:30.*

11 **Folk Art Park.** Revitalizing an ignored part of the city, the park pays homage to an important American art form by gathering works that reflect the diverse styles of American (especially Southern) folk art. Work by more than a dozen different artists is on display, among them Harold Rittenberry, Howard Finster, and Eddie Owens Martin. Mar-

tin's brightly painted totems and snake-topped walls replicate portions of *Pasaquan* (the legendary visionary environment that Martin created at his farm near Columbus, Georgia). ✉ *Ralph McGill Blvd. at Courtland St., Baker St., and Piedmont Ave.*

21 **Georgia Dome.** This arena accommodates 71,500 spectators with good visibility no matter where the seat is; it is the site of Atlanta Falcons football games, major rock concerts, conventions, and trade shows. The white, plum, and turquoise 1-million-square-ft facility is crowned with the world's largest cable-supported oval, giving the roof a circus-tent top. ✉ *1 Georgia Dome Dr.,* ☎ *404/223–8687.* *Tour $2 (groups only).* *Tours Wed.–Fri. every hr 10–4.*

4 **Georgia-Pacific Center.** The towering, 52-story structure occupies the site of the old Loew's Grand Theatre, where *Gone With the Wind* premiered in 1939. From certain angles, the red-marble high-rise appears to be flat against the sky. The **High Museum of Art, Folk Art and Photography Galleries** is inside the building. ✉ *133 Peachtree St., at John Wesley Dobbs Ave. Museum:* ✉ *30 John Wesley Dobbs Ave.,* ☎ *404/577–6940.* *Mon.–Sat. 10–5.*

23 **Georgia Railroad Freight Depot.** After downtown's oldest extant building was constructed in 1869 to replace the one torched by Sherman's troops in 1864, it burned again in 1935 and was rebuilt in its present form. It is now used by several downtown companies as a banquet hall and for special events. It may be viewed only by appointment. ✉ *65 Martin Luther King Jr. Dr.,* ☎ *404/656–3850.*

★ 27 **Georgia State Capitol.** A Renaissance-style edifice, the capitol was dedicated on July 4, 1889. The gold leaf on its dome was mined in nearby Dahlonega. Inside, the **Georgia Capitol Museum** houses exhibits on the history of the Capitol Building. On the grounds, state historical markers commemorate the 1864 Battle of Atlanta, which destroyed 90% of the city. Statues memorialize a 19th-century Georgia governor and his wife (Joseph and Elizabeth Brown), a Confederate general (John B. Gordon), and a former senator (Richard B. Russell). Former governor and president Jimmy Carter is depicted with his sleeves rolled up, a man at work. ✉ *Capitol Square,* ☎ *404/656–2844.* *Guided tours weekdays at 10, 11, 1, and 2.*

OFF THE BEATEN PATH

HAMMONDS HOUSE GALLERIES AND RESOURCE CENTER – Dr. Otis Thrash Hammonds donated his handsome Eastlake Victorian house and his fine collection of Victorian furniture and paintings to the city of Atlanta as an art gallery and resource center. The permanent and visiting exhibitions are devoted chiefly to work by African-American artists, although art from anywhere in the African-influenced world can be a focus. ✉ *503 Peeples St.,* ☎ *404/752–8730.* *$2.* *Tues.–Fri. 10–6, weekends 1–5.*

HERNDON HOME – Alonzo Herndon, a former slave, emerged from slavery and founded both a chain of successful barber shops and the **Atlanta Life Insurance Company.** He traveled extensively and influenced the cultural life around Atlanta's traditionally black colleges. Alonzo's son, Norris, created a foundation to preserve the handsome Beaux Arts home as a museum and heritage center. ✉ *587 University Pl., near Morris Brown College,* ☎ *404/581–9813.* *Donation.* *Tues.–Sat. 10–4; tours every hr.*

14 **Hurt Building.** Named for Atlanta developer Joel Hurt, this restored 1913 Chicago-style high-rise, with its intricate grillwork and sweeping marble staircase, has a lower level of shops and art galleries. The

excellent City Grill (☞ Dining, *below*) restaurant is at the top of the sweeping staircase. ✉ *50 Hurt Plaza.*

❺ **Margaret Mitchell Park.** A cascading waterfall and columned sculpture are highlights of this park named for Atlanta's most famous author, whose masterpiece and only novel is *Gone With the Wind.* ✉ *Margaret Mitchell Sq.*

❽ **One-Ninety-One Peachtree Tower.** Designed by John Burgee with Philip Johnson as a consultant, the 50-story neo-Gothic skyscraper, built in 1990, has a dazzling lobby with a seven-story-high atrium. ✉ *191 Peachtree St.*

❾ **Peachtree Center.** John Portman designed this skyscraper complex, built between 1960 and 1992, which contains shops, offices, and a variety of restaurants. Across the street, connected to Peachtree Center by skywalks, is the massive **Atlanta Market Center.** Two additional Portman creations, the **Atlanta Marriott Marquis** and the **Hyatt Regency Hotel,** are also connected to the center by skywalks. A MARTA stop is available at Peachtree Center. ✉ *225 Peachtree St.,* ☎ *404/654–1255.*

❼ **Ritz-Carlton, Atlanta.** The hotel (☞ Lodging, *below*) has a fabulous collection of hunting art, both paintings and sculptures, in the restaurant and the bar. ✉ *181 Peachtree St.,* ☎ *404/659–0400.*

㉕ **Shrine of the Immaculate Conception.** During the Battle of Atlanta, Thomas O'Reilly, the church's pastor, persuaded Union forces to spare his church and several others around the city. That 1848 structure was then replaced by this much grander building, whose cornerstone was laid in 1869. O'Reilly, a native of Ireland, was interred in the basement of the church. Now on the National Register, the church was nearly lost to fire in 1982 but has been exquisitely restored. The vestibule is always open, allowing visitors to view the interior, or you may contact the rectory for an appointment. ✉ *48 Martin Luther King Jr. Dr., at Central Ave.,* ☎ *404/521–1866.* ⏲ *Weekdays 8:30–5, Sat. 9–7, Sun. 7–3.*

⓰ **Statue of Henry Grady.** New York artist Alexander Doyle's bronze sculpture honors the post–Civil War editor of the *Atlanta Constitution* and early advocate of the so-called New South. Much about Grady reminds one of Ted Turner, contemporary Atlanta media mogul. Among other things, Grady was an early booster of baseball. The memorial was raised in 1891, after Grady's untimely death at age 39. ✉ *Corner of Marietta and Forsyth Sts.*

㉒ **Underground Atlanta.** This six-block entertainment and shopping district, dotted with historic markers, was created from the web of underground brick streets, ornamental building facades, and tunnels that fell into disuse in 1929, when the city built viaducts over the train tracks. Merchants moved their storefronts to the new viaduct level, leaving the original street level for storage. Today it houses restaurants, clubs, art galleries, shopping emporiums, and a food court, making it a good stop on a walking tour. ✉ *50 Upper Alabama St.,* ☎ *404/523–2311.*

⓭ **William-Oliver Building.** Walk through the lobby of this Art Deco gem and admire the ceiling mural, brass grills, and elevator doors. Formerly an office building, it has been renovated for luxury downtown residences and won a 1997 award for historic preservation from the Atlanta Urban Design Commission. ✉ *32 Peachtree St.*

❶ **Woodruff Park.** Named for the city's great philanthropist Robert W. Woodruff, the late Coca-Cola magnate, the triangular park fills during lunchtime on weekdays with executives, street preachers, politicians,

Georgia State University students, and homeless people. ✉ *Bordered by Pryor, Houston, and Peachtree Sts.*

24 **World of Coca-Cola.** At this three-story, $15 million special-exhibit facility, you can sip samples of 38 Coca-Cola Company products from around the world and study memorabilia from more than a century's worth of corporate archives. Everything Coca-Cola, the renovated gift shop, sells everything from refrigerator magnets to evening bags. ✉ *55 Martin Luther King Jr. Dr.,* ☎ *404/676–5151.* *$6.* *June–Aug., Mon.–Sat. 9–6, Sun. 11–6; Sept.–May, Mon.–Sat. 9–5, Sun. noon–6.*

OFF THE BEATEN PATH

ZOO ATLANTA – This zoo has nearly 1,000 animals living in naturalistic habitats, such as the Ford African Rain Forest, Flamingo Lagoon, Masai Mara (re-created plains of Kenya), and Sumatran Tiger exhibits. Sibling gorillas Kudzoo and Olympia are always hits. To reach the zoo by car, take I–20 east to Exit 59A, turn right on Boulevard, then right again at the next light into Grant Park. Follow signs to the zoo. ✉ *Grant Park, 800 Cherokee Ave.,* ☎ *404/624–5600.* *$10.* *Daily 9:30–4:30.*

Sweet Auburn

Between 1890 and 1930 the historic Sweet Auburn district was Atlanta's most active and prosperous center of black business, entertainment, and political life. Following the Depression, the area went into an economic decline that lasted until the 1980s, when the residential area where civil rights leader Rev. Martin Luther King Jr. was born, raised, and later lived was declared a National Historic District.

Numbers in the text correspond to numbers in the margin and on the Downtown Atlanta and Sweet Auburn map.

A Good Walk

Start your walk in the Martin Luther King Jr. National Historic District, the heart of Sweet Auburn, where you may get a sense of what the civil rights movement and its principal leader were all about. Here, first visit the **Martin Luther King Jr. Birth Home** ㉘ on Auburn Avenue, and on the next block west, the **Martin Luther King Jr. Center for Nonviolent Social Change** ㉙, where Dr. King is entombed. Next stop at the nearby **Ebenezer Baptist Church** ㉚, where Dr. King preached along with his grandfather, father, and brother. Proceed a few blocks west near the I–75/85 overpass to enjoy the **John Wesley Dobbs Plaza** ㉛, a good place to take a breather. The **Odd Fellows Building** ㉜, on the other side of Auburn Avenue just after you walk under the expressway, is a handsome structure not to be missed. At this point, go south on Bell Street and walk one block to Edgewood Avenue to visit the **Sweet Auburn Curb Market** ㉝. Walk three blocks west on Edgewood Avenue, and you'll reach the **Baptist Student Center** ㉞, a fine example of Victorian architecture. Returning north to Auburn Avenue, you'll see the **Atlanta Daily World Building** ㉟, and next to it the **African-American Panoramic Experience (APEX)** ㊱. Continue down Auburn Avenue just a few steps and enter the lobby of the **Atlanta Life Insurance Company** ㊲ to view its fabulous art collection. Now, proceed across the street and finish your walk with a stop at the **Auburn Avenue Research Library on African-American Culture and History** ㊳.

TIMING

This is a leisurely walk along level sidewalks, with shops and historic sites along the way. If you stop for tours, you'll fill an entire day. If you simply stroll and look, the walk should take an hour or two.

Downtown Atlanta and Sweet Auburn

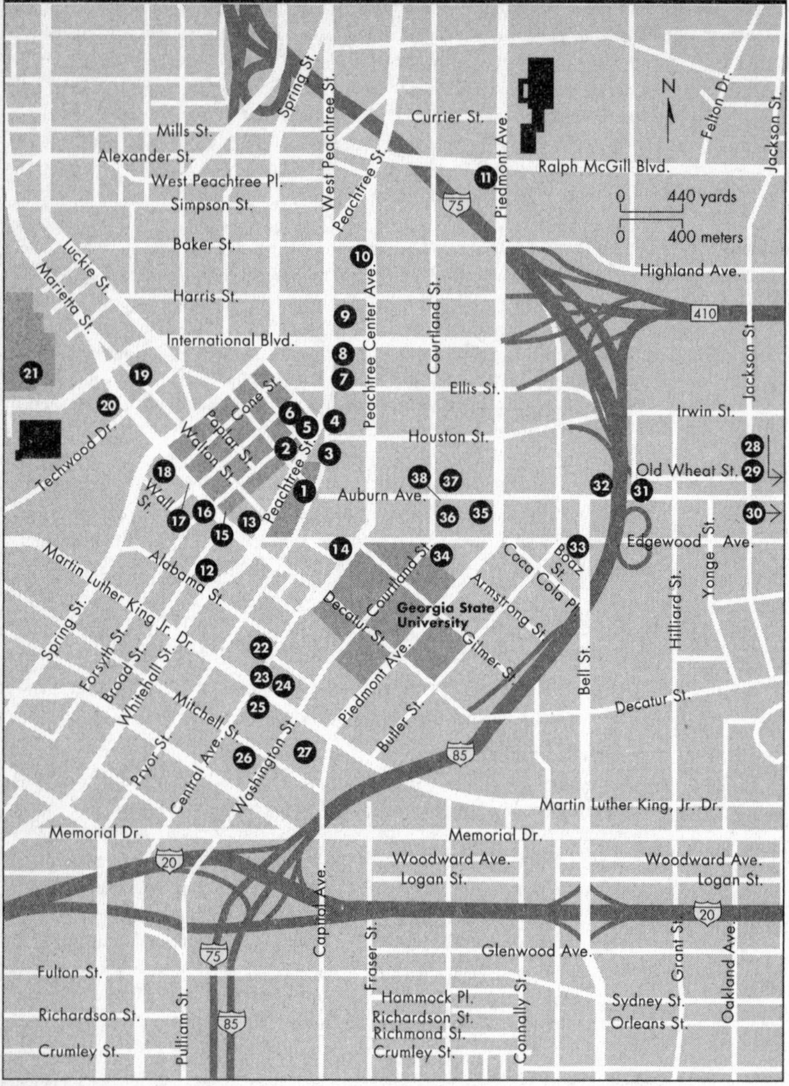

African-American Panoramic Experience (APEX) **36**
Atlanta Daily World Building **35**
Atlanta-Fulton Public Library **6**
Atlanta International Museum of Art and Design **10**
Atlanta Journal–Constitution **17**
Atlanta Life Insurance Company **37**
Auburn Avenue Research Library on African-American Culture and History **38**
Bank of America Building **15**
Baptist Student Center **34**
Candler Building **3**
Centennial Olympic Park **19**
City Hall **26**
CNN Center **20**
Ebenezer Baptist Church **30**
Federal Reserve Bank **18**
Five Points MARTA Station **12**
Flatiron Building **2**
Folk Art Park **11**
Georgia Dome **21**
Georgia-Pacific Center **4**
Georgia Railroad Freight Depot **23**
Georgia State Capitol **27**
Hurt Building **14**
John Wesley Dobbs Plaza **31**
Margaret Mitchell Park **5**
Martin Luther King Jr. Birth Home **28**
Martin Luther King Jr. Center for Nonviolent Social Change **29**
Odd Fellows Building **32**
One-Ninety-One Peachtree Tower **8**
Peachtree Center **9**
Ritz-Carlton, Atlanta **7**
Shrine of the Immaculate Conception **25**
Statue of Henry Grady **16**
Sweet Auburn Curb Market **33**
Underground Atlanta **22**
William-Oliver Building **13**
Woodruff Park **1**
World of Coca-Cola **24**

Sights to See

★ 36 **African-American Panoramic Experience (APEX).** The museum's quarterly exhibits chronicle the history of black people in America. Videos illustrate the history of Sweet Auburn, the name bestowed upon Auburn Avenue by businessman John Wesley Dobbs, who fostered business development for African-Americans on this street. ✉ *135 Auburn Ave.,* ☎ *404/521–2739.* *$3.* *June–Aug., Tues.–Sat. 10–5, Sun. 1–5; Sept.–May, Tues.–Sat. 10–5.*

35 **Atlanta Daily World Building.** This simple two-story brick building, banded with a white frieze of lion's heads, was constructed in the early 1900s; since 1945 it has housed one of the nation's oldest black newspapers. Despite its title, the publication is no longer a daily, although it was in the past. Alexis Reeves, publisher and CEO, is the granddaughter of William A. Scott II, who founded the paper as a weekly in 1928. ✉ *145 Auburn Ave.,* ☎ *404/659–1110.*

37 **Atlanta Life Insurance Company.** The landmark enterprise founded by Alonzo Herndon, a former slave, was in modest quarters at 148 Auburn Avenue until the modern complex at No. 100 was opened in 1980. The lobby holds an exhibition of art by black artists from the United States and Africa. ✉ *100 Auburn Ave.,* ☎ *404/659–2100.* *Weekdays 8:30–5.*

38 **Auburn Avenue Research Library on African-American Culture and History.** This unit, added to the **Atlanta-Fulton Public Library** system (☞ *above*) in 1994, is a noncirculating library housing about 35,000 volumes devoted to African-American subjects. Special exhibits, programs, and tours are free and open to the public. The archives division contains art and artifacts, ephemera, oral histories, pamphlets, prints, rare periodicals, rare books, manuscript collections, photographs, and memorabilia. ✉ *101 Auburn Ave.,* ☎ *404/730–4001.* *Mon. and Wed. 10–8, Tues. and Thurs. noon–8, Fri. 1–5, weekends 2–6.*

34 **Baptist Student Center.** Adjacent to the Georgia State University campus, this restored Victorian building once contained the Coca-Cola Company's first bottling plant. ✉ *125 Edgewood Ave.,* ☎ *404/659–8726.*

30 **Ebenezer Baptist Church.** A Gothic Revival–style building completed in 1922, the church became known as the spiritual center for the civil rights movement after Martin Luther King Jr. won the Nobel Peace Prize in 1964. Members of the King family have preached at the church for three generations; Dr. King's funeral was held here. A tour of the church includes an audiotape outlining the history of the building. Since 1999 the congregation has occupied the building across the street. ✉ *407 Auburn Ave.,* ☎ *404/688–7263.* *Tours free.* *Tours Mon.–Sat. 9–5.*

31 **John Wesley Dobbs Plaza.** John Wesley Dobbs was an important civic leader whose legacy includes coining the name Sweet Auburn for Atlanta's black business and residential neighborhood. The plaza, which was built for the 1996 Olympic Games, has a life mask of Dobbs himself; children playing in the plaza may view the street through the mask's eyes. ✉ *Auburn Ave. adjacent to I–75/85 overpass.*

★ 28 **Martin Luther King Jr. Birth Home.** This modest Queen Anne–style historic home is managed by the National Park Service, which also has a visitor center across the street from the **Martin Luther King Jr. Center for Nonviolent Social Change** (☞ *below*). The visitor center contains a multimedia exhibit focused on the civil rights movement and Dr. King's role in it. To sign up for tours, go to the **fire station** (✉ 39 Boulevard).

✉ *501 Auburn Ave.,* ☎ *404/331–6922.* *Tours free.* *Daily guided ½-hr tours every hr 10–5.*

29 **Martin Luther King Jr. Center for Nonviolent Social Change.** The Martin Luther King Jr. National Historic District occupies several blocks on Auburn Avenue, a few blocks east of Peachtree Street in the black business and residential community of Sweet Auburn. The neighborhood was the birthplace of Martin Luther King Jr. in 1929. After King's assassination in 1968, his widow, Coretta Scott King, established the center, which exhibits personal items, such as King's Nobel Peace Prize, Bible, and tape recorder, along with memorabilia and photos chronicling the civil rights movement. In the courtyard in front of Freedom Hall, on a circular brick pad in the middle of the rectangular Meditation Pool, is King's white marble tomb; the inscription reads FREE AT LAST! Nearby, an eternal flame burns. A chapel of all faiths sits at one end of the reflecting pool. ✉ *449 Auburn Ave.,* ☎ *404/524–1956.* *Daily 9–5.*

32 **Odd Fellows Building.** The Georgia Chapter of the Grand United Order of Odd Fellows was a trade and social organization for African-Americans. In 1912 the membership erected this handsome Romanesque Revival–style building housing meeting rooms, a theater, commercial spaces, and a community center. African-featured terra-cotta figures adorn the splendid entrance. Now handsomely restored, the building houses offices. ✉ *250 Auburn Ave.*

33 **Sweet Auburn Curb Market.** The market, an institution on Edgewood Avenue since 1923, sells vegetables, fish, flowers, prepared foods, and meat. Individual stalls are operated by separate owners, making this a true public market. Don't miss the splendid totemic sculptures by young Atlanta artist Carl Joe Williams. The pieces were placed as part of Atlanta's Olympic art program. ✉ *209 Edgewood Ave.,* ☎ *404/659–1665.* *Mon.–Thurs. 8–5, Fri.–Sat. 8–7.*

Midtown

Just north of downtown lies this thriving area, a hippie hangout in the late '60s and '70s and now home to a large segment of the city's gay population, along with young families, young professionals, artists, and musicians. Formerly in decline, Midtown has evolved into one of the city's most interesting neighborhoods. Its gleaming new office towers give it a skyline to rival downtown's, and the renovated mansions and bungalows in its residential section have made it a city showcase.

Numbers in the text correspond to numbers in the margin and on the Atlanta Neighborhoods map.

A Good Drive

From downtown, take Piedmont Avenue about ½ mi to **SciTrek** (39), a science museum all ages will enjoy. Turn left from Piedmont Avenue onto Ponce de Leon Avenue and drive two blocks to Peachtree Street; then turn right and find the 1929 **Fox Theatre** (40) and, across the street, the **Georgian Terrace** (41), a luxury suites hotel. From Peachtree Street, circle around the block, turning right on 3rd Street to Juniper Street; then turn right on Juniper Street, continue two blocks, and turn right onto North Avenue. Turn right again onto Peachtree Street to view the **Bank of America Plaza Tower** (42). Continuing up Peachtree Street to Peachtree Place (one block south of 10th Street), you'll find the **Margaret Mitchell House** (43), the restored building where the Pulitzer Prize–winning author lived while completing *Gone With the Wind.* Continue one block up Peachtree Street and turn left onto 10th Street for four blocks to its intersection with 14th Street, where you'll find **One At-**

Atlanta Neighborhoods

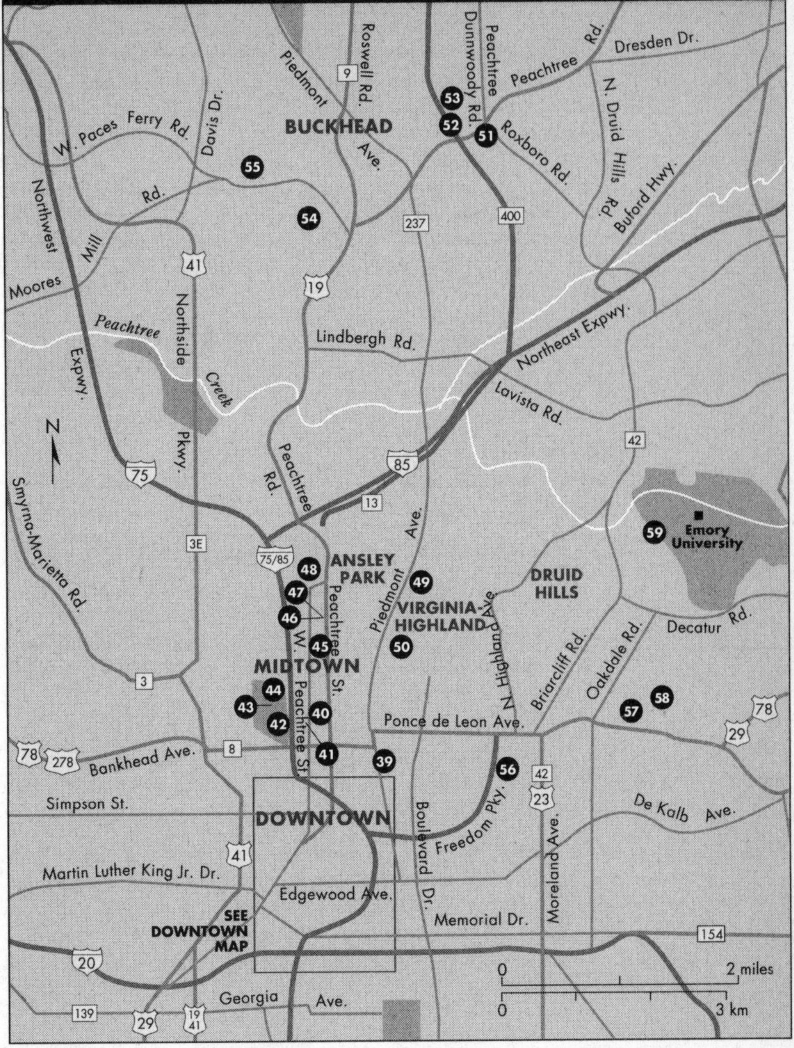

- Atlanta Botanical Garden . . . 49
- Atlanta History Center . . . 54
- Bank of America Plaza Tower . . . 42
- Carter Presidential Center . . . 56
- Center for Puppetry Arts . . . 45
- Fernbank Museum of Natural History . . . 57
- Fernbank Science Center . . . 58
- Fox Theatre . . . 40
- Georgia Governor's Mansion . . . 55
- Georgian Terrace . . . 41
- High Museum of Art . . . 47
- Lenox Square . . . 51
- Margaret Mitchell House . . . 43
- Michael C. Carlos Museum . . . 59
- One Atlantic Center . . . 44
- Phipps Plaza . . . 53
- Piedmont Park . . . 50
- Rhodes Memorial Hall . . . 48
- Ritz-Carlton, Buckhead . . . 52
- SciTrek . . . 39
- Woodruff Arts Center . . . 46

lantic Center ㊹, built for IBM. Turn left onto 18th Street to reach the **Center for Puppetry Arts** ㊺. Take 18th Street east back to Peachtree Street, turn left, and continue on to the **Woodruff Arts Center** ㊻, which includes the modern structure of the **High Museum of Art** ㊼. From this point, travel two blocks north on Peachtree Street to **Rhodes Memorial Hall** ㊽. From here, take Beverly Road east off Peachtree Street for about ¼ mi to Montgomery Ferry Drive; turn a quick dogleg left, then right, continuing on Beverly to Park Lane, and then turn right on Park Lane and drive about ¼ mi to where it intersects the Prado. Here, these two streets dead-end onto Piedmont Avenue, where you'll enter the **Atlanta Botanical Garden** ㊾, which adjoins **Piedmont Park** ㊿, bounded by Piedmont Avenue, 10th Street, and Westminster Drive.

TIMING

This drive is best accomplished between midmorning (about 9:30) and midafternoon (3:30) to avoid rush hour traffic. Give yourself between four and five hours to visit all the sights. Each place has parking no more than a few steps away, and often it's free.

Sights to See

49 **Atlanta Botanical Garden.** Occupying 30 acres inside **Piedmont Park** (☞ *below*), the grounds contain 15 acres of display gardens, including a serene Japanese garden, a 15-acre hardwood forest with walking trails, and the Fuqua Conservatory, which has unusual and threatened flora from tropical and desert climates. A permanent Fuqua Conservatory exhibit of tiny, brightly colored poison dart frogs is popular, especially with children. ✉ *1345 Piedmont Ave., at the Prado,* ☎ *404/876–5859.* *$6; free Thurs. after 3.* ⊙ *Mar.–Sept., Tues.–Sun. 9–7; Oct.–Feb., Tues.–Sun. 9–6.*

42 **Bank of America Plaza Tower.** Built in 1992, the skyscraper has a graceful birdcage roof easily visible from the interstate and is the South's tallest building, at 1,023 ft. Its elegant marble central lobby is worth seeing. ✉ *600 Peachtree St.*

★ 45 **Center for Puppetry Arts.** At this interactive museum, you can see puppets from around the world and attend puppet-making workshops. Performances, which include original dramatic works and classics adapted for the museum theater, are presented by professional puppeteers who leave youngsters and adults alike spellbound. ✉ *1404 Spring St., at 18th St.,* ☎ *404/873–3391.* *$5; special exhibits and programs extra.* ⊙ *Mon.–Sat. 9–5.*

40 **Fox Theatre.** One of a handful of remaining classic movie palaces in the nation, the Fox was built in 1929 in a fabulous Moorish-Egyptian style to be the headquarters of the Shriners Club. The interior's crowning glory is its skylike ceiling—complete with clouds and stars above Alhambra-like minarets. Threatened by demolition in the 1970s, the Fox was saved from the wrecker's ball by concerted civic action and is still a prime venue for musicals, rock concerts, dance performances, and film festivals. ✉ *660 Peachtree St.,* ☎ *404/881–2100; 404/876–2041 Atlanta Preservation Center.* *Tour conducted by Atlanta Preservation Center $5.* ⊙ *Tours Mon., Wed., and Thurs. at 10, Sat. at 10 and 11.*

41 **Georgian Terrace.** Originally built in 1911 as a fine Beaux Arts–style hotel, the Georgian Terrace, designed by William L. Stoddart, housed the stars of the film *Gone With the Wind* when it premiered at the nearby Loew's Theater (now demolished) in 1939. President Calvin Coolidge also slept here. Stars of the Metropolitan Opera stayed at the hotel when the Met used to make its annual trek to Atlanta, and according to locals, Enrico Caruso routinely serenaded passersby from its balconies.

Renovated with style and historic sensitivity, the building is now a luxury hotel (☞ Lodging, *below*). ✉ *459 Peachtree St.,* ☎ *404/897–1991.*

47 **High Museum of Art.** The permanent holdings of this high-tech museum built in 1983 focus on American decorative arts and African art. The Uhry Print Collection contains works by French Impressionists and other European artists. In 1991 the American Institute of Architects listed the sleek structure, designed by Richard Meier, among the 10 best works of American architecture in the 1980s. ✉ *Woodruff Arts Center, 1280 Peachtree St., MARTA Arts Center station,* ☎ *404/733–4444 recorded information.* *$6.* ⏲ *Tues.–Thurs. and Sat. 10–5, Fri. 10–9, Sun. noon–5.*

43 **Margaret Mitchell House.** Although the author of *Gone With the Wind* detested the turn-of-the-20th-century house (she called it "the Dump") where she lived when she wrote her masterpiece, determined volunteers got backing to restore the house and open it to the public. The visitor center exhibits photographs, archival material, and personal possessions, including her original typewriter. ✉ *990 Peachtree St., at the corner of Peachtree Pl.,* ☎ *404/249–7012.* *$10.* ⏲ *Daily 9–4.*

44 **One Atlantic Center.** You can see the unique profile of this pyramid-top office building, also known as the **IBM Tower,** from many parts of the city. It was designed by Philip Johnson and built in 1987. ✉ *1201 W. Peachtree St.* ⏲ *Weekdays 9–5.*

50 **Piedmont Park.** The city's outdoor recreation center, this park is a major venue for special events. Tennis courts, a swimming pool, and paths for walking, jogging, and rollerblading are part of the attraction, but many retreat to the park's great lawn for picnics with a smashing view of the Midtown skyline. Each April the park hosts the popular Dogwood Festival (☞ Festivals and Seasonal Events *in* Chapter 1). ✉ *Piedmont Ave. between 10th St. and the Prado.*

48 **Rhodes Memorial Hall.** Headquarters of the **Georgia Trust for Historic Preservation,** this former residence is one of the finest works of Atlanta architect Willis F. Denny II. Built at the northern edge of the city in 1904 for Amos Giles Rhodes, the wealthy founder of a Southern furniture chain, the hall has stained-glass windows that depict the heroes of the Confederacy. ✉ *1516 Peachtree St.,* ☎ *404/881–9980.* *$5.* ⏲ *Weekdays 11–4, Sun. noon–3.*

★ 39 **SciTrek.** The Science and Technology Museum of Atlanta covers 96,000 square ft and has rotating exhibitions and daily science demonstrations at the Coca-Cola Science Show Theater. About 150 hands-on exhibits occupy four environments: Simple Machines; Light, Color, and Perception; Electricity and Magnetism; and Kidspace, for children ages two–seven. The Information Petting Zoo exhibits "cybercritters." ✉ *395 Piedmont Ave.,* ☎ *404/522–5500.* *$7.50.* ⏲ *Mon.–Sat. 10–5, Sun. noon–5.*

46 **Woodruff Arts Center.** The center is home to the world-renowned **Atlanta Symphony Orchestra,** the **High Museum of Art** (☞ *above*), the **Alliance Theatre,** and the intimate **Studio Theater.** Both theaters present contemporary dramas, classics, and frequent world premieres. ✉ *1280 Peachtree St.,* ☎ *404/733–4200.*

Buckhead

Atlanta's sprawl doesn't lend itself to walking between major neighborhoods, so take a car or MARTA to reach Buckhead. Many of Atlanta's trendy restaurants, music clubs, chic shops, and hip art galleries are concentrated in this neighborhood. Finding a parking spot on the weekends and at night can be a real headache, and waits of two hours or more are common in the hottest restaurants.

Numbers in the text correspond to numbers in the margin and on the Atlanta Neighborhoods map.

A Good Drive

Although the adventurous and high spirited may elect to walk this tour, most will prefer to drive. For one thing, the distance between the Atlanta History Center and the Georgia Governor's Mansion, while not great, entails walking where there are no sidewalks, a tricky proposition with traffic zooming just inches away. So begin the drive at the intersection of two splendid shopping malls. The older and larger of the two, **Lenox Square** ⑤①, sprawls from Peachtree Road down Lenox Road to East Paces Ferry Road. Across the street from Lenox Square is the **Ritz-Carlton, Buckhead** ⑤②, one of two Ritz hotels in Atlanta; across the Buckhead Loop from the hotel, you'll find the elegant shops of **Phipps Plaza** ⑤③. Leaving Phipps Plaza, exit onto Peachtree Road and turn right (south), traveling about ⅓ mi to West Paces Ferry Road. At this intersection, turn right and proceed about ¼ mi to Andrews Drive. Turn left, and the entrance to the **Atlanta History Center** ⑤④ is almost immediately on the left. Leaving the center, turn right from the entrance back to West Paces Ferry Road, and then turn left, driving about ½ mi to reach the **Georgia Governor's Mansion** ⑤⑤.

TIMING

As with other driving tours in this busy part of town, you are well advised to stick to the midmorning to midafternoon hours, or from about 9:30 to 3:30. In Buckhead, an additional wrinkle is the lunchtime traffic, which lasts from about 11:30 to 1:30. Simply driving the distance around the five sights, looking briefly at each one, will consume, generally, no more than 30 minutes. Allot several hours if you want to shop or tour the History Center and Governor's Mansion.

Sights to See

★ 54 **Atlanta History Center.** The museum highlights materials native to Georgia, with a floor of heart pine and polished Stone Mountain granite. Displays are provocative, juxtaposing *Gone With the Wind* romanticism with the grim reality of Ku Klux Klan racism. Also on the 33-acre site are the elegant 1928 **Swan House**; the **Tullie Smith Farm,** with a two-story plantation plain house (1840s); and **McElreath Hall,** an exhibition space for artifacts from Atlanta's history. ✉ *130 W. Paces Ferry Rd.,* ☎ *404/814–4000.* 🎫 *$7.* ⏲ *Mon.–Sat. 10–5:30, Sun. noon–5:30.*

55 **Georgia Governor's Mansion.** Built in 1967, this 24,000-square-ft Greek Revival mansion contains 30 rooms and sits on 18 acres originally belonging to the Robert Maddox family (no relation to Georgia governor Lester Maddox, who was its first occupant). American Federal-period antiques fill the public rooms. ✉ *391 W. Paces Ferry Rd.,* ☎ *404/261–1858.* ⏲ *Free guided tours Tues.–Thurs. 10 AM–11:30 AM.*

51 **Lenox Square.** Local shoppers come for the more than 250 stores and several good restaurants at this mall (☞ Shopping, *below*). ✉ *3393 Peachtree Rd.,* ☎ *404/233–6767.*

53 **Phipps Plaza.** The mall is one of Atlanta's premier shopping areas, with upscale chain stores, specialty shops, and restaurants. It also includes a 14-screen movie theater (☞ Shopping, *below*). ✉ *3500 Peachtree Rd.,* ☎ *404/262–0992 or 800/810–7700.*

52 **Ritz-Carlton, Buckhead.** Among the finest hotels in the country, the Ritz contains one of the South's most valuable private art collections, pri-

marily 18th- and 19th-century American and European painting, sculpture, and porcelain. It's also home to the renowned **Dining Room** (☞ Dining, *below*). ✉ *3434 Peachtree Rd.*, ☎ *404/237–2700.*

Virginia-Highland and the Emory Area

Restaurants and art galleries are the backbone of Virginia-Highland/Morningside, northeast of Midtown. Like Midtown, this residential area was down-at-the-heels only 25 years ago. Reclaimed by writers, artists, and a few visionary developers, Virginia-Highland today offers intriguing shopping and delightful walking. Nightlife hums here as well.

Numbers in the text correspond to numbers in the margin and on the Atlanta Neighborhoods map.

A Good Drive

This tour meanders through some residential areas, such as Druid Hills, the location for the film *Driving Miss Daisy,* by local playwright Alfred Uhry. The neighborhood was designed by the firm of Frederick Law Olmsted, which also designed New York's Central Park. Begin at the **Carter Presidential Center** ⑤⑥, the central attraction in a subneighborhood called Poncey Highlands, because it lies south of Ponce de Leon Avenue and south of Virginia-Highland. The former president's center is bounded by Freedom Parkway, which splits and encircles the facility. To reach it from downtown, drive on Ralph McGill Boulevard about 1 mi east of I–75/85 (Exit 248C) to where the boulevard intersects with Freedom Parkway. Alternately, you can take North Avenue east from downtown about 1 mi to its intersection with North Highland Avenue, then turn right after a short distance and follow the signs.

From the center, take a left and drive only one short block on Highland Avenue to Ponce de Leon Avenue, and turn right (east), continuing for 1 mi to Clifton Road; next take a left onto Clifton and almost immediately enter the driveway for **Fernbank Museum of Natural History** ⑤⑦. On the east end of this extensive forest and recreational-educational preserve lies **Fernbank Science Center** ⑤⑧. To reach it, return via Clifton Road to Ponce de Leon Avenue and take a left. Drive east on Ponce de Leon Avenue about ½ mi and then turn left onto Artwood Road, which turns into Heaton Road. The center is on the left side of Heaton Road about ¼ mi from Ponce de Leon Avenue. Leaving the center, turn left and take Heaton a short way to Coventry Road, where you should go left again until you see East Clifton Road. Turn right on East Clifton and follow it around to Clifton Road, and continue north ¼ mi to North Decatur Road. The entrance to Emory University is directly in front of you. Enter the campus, bear right, and park in the lot if you wish to visit the **Michael C. Carlos Museum** ⑤⑨, an exquisite contemporary structure.

TIMING

You can drive this tour in about 15 minutes without stops. If you spend a few hours at each sight, it can easily take a full day.

Sights to See

★ 56 **Carter Presidential Center.** This complex occupies the site where Union general William T. Sherman orchestrated the Battle of Atlanta (1864). The museum and archives detail the political career of former president Jimmy Carter. The center itself, which is not open to the public, focuses on conflict resolution and human rights issues. It sponsors foreign-affairs conferences and projects on such matters as world food supply. Outside, the Japanese-style garden is a serene spot to unwind. ✉ *1 Copenhill Ave.*, ☎ *404/331–3942.* *$5.* ⏲ *Mon.–Sat. 9–4:45, Sun. noon–4:45.*

57 **Fernbank Museum of Natural History.** The largest natural history museum south of the Smithsonian Institution in Washington, D.C., holds a permanent exhibit, *A Walk Through Time in Georgia*. Visitors meander through 15 galleries to explore the earth's natural history. The museum's IMAX theater shows films about the natural world. The café, with an exquisite view overlooking the forest, serves great food. ✉ *767 Clifton Rd.*, ☎ *404/370–0960; 404/370–0019 IMAX; 404/370–0850 directions hot line.* *Museum $8.95, IMAX $6.95, both $13.95.* ⊙ *Mon.–Sat. 10–5, Sun. noon–5, IMAX Fri. 6:30–10.*

58 **Fernbank Science Center.** The museum focuses on geology, space exploration, and ecology; it's best for younger children. Special seasonal programs for children under five, priced at 50¢, are offered weekends at 1:30 from October through November, early December through the first week of January, the end of January to March 15, and during the summer. ✉ *156 Heaton Park Dr.*, ☎ *404/378–4311.* *Museum free, planetarium shows $2.* ⊙ *Mon. 8:30–5, Tues.–Fri. 8:30 AM–10 PM, Sat. 10–5, Sun. 1–5; planetarium shows Tues.–Fri. at 3:30 and 8, weekends at 3:30.*

★ 59 **Michael C. Carlos Museum.** Housing a permanent collection that embraces more than 16,000 objects, this excellent museum designed by renowned American architect Michael Graves exhibits artifacts from Egypt, Greece, Rome, the Near East, the Americas, and Africa. European and American prints and drawings cover the Middle Ages through the 20th century. The gift shop has rare art books, jewelry, and art-focused items for children. The museum's Caffé Antico is a good lunch spot. ✉ *Emory University, 571 S. Kilgo St.*, ☎ *404/727–4282.* *Suggested donation $3.* ⊙ *Mon.–Sat. 10–5, Sun. noon–5.*

Other Area Attractions

Atlanta's suburbs have excellent entertainment options. It is essential to drive to these venues, so plan your visits with Atlanta's notorious rush hours in mind.

★ **Château Élan.** A 16th-century-style French château has Georgia's best-known winery, set in 2,400 rolling acres about an hour north of downtown Atlanta. Winery tours and tastings are free. Château Élan is also a complete resort: European luxury blends with Southern hospitality at the 274-room inn and spa with private villas, golf courses, and an equestrian center. ✉ *100 Rue Charlemagne, Braselton, I–85 to GA 211, Exit 126 (Chestnut Mountain/Winder)*, ☎ *770/932–0900 or 800/233–9463*, FAX *770/271–6005.* ⊙ *Wine market weekdays 11–3:30, weekends 11–4. Tours weekdays at 11, 12:15, 1:30, 2:45, and 4; Sat. hourly 11–5; Sun. at 12:30 and hourly 1–5.*

Chattahoochee Nature Center. Birds and animals in their natural habitats may be seen from nature trails and a boardwalk winding through 124 acres of woodlands and wetlands. A gift shop, indoor exhibits, birds-of-prey aviaries, and a picnic area are on the property. Naturalist guides accompany evening canoe floats from May through August. ✉ *9135 Willeo Rd., Roswell*, ☎ *770/992–2055.* *$5.* ⊙ *Mon.–Sat. 9–5, Sun. noon–5.*

Kennesaw Mountain National Battlefield. A must for Civil War buffs, this 2,884-acre park with 16 mi of hiking trails was the site of several crucial battles in June 1864. The visitor center contains a small museum with exhibits of Civil War weapons, uniforms, and other items recovered from the battlefield. A 10-minute slide presentation explains the battles. ✉ *Old U.S. 41 and Stilesboro Rd. (look for signs on I–75N), Kennesaw*, ☎ *770/427–4686.* *Free.* ⊙ *Daily 7:30–dusk.*

Six Flags over Georgia. Atlanta's major theme park, with eight theme sections, heart-stopping roller coasters, and water rides (best saved for last to prevent being damp all day), is a child's ideal playground. The new Georgia Scorcher, a roller coaster that you ride standing up, moves at 54 mph. The park also has well-staged musical revues, concerts by top-name artists, and other performances. Take MARTA's west line to Hightower station and then the Six Flags bus. ✉ *I–20W at 7561 Six Flags Pkwy., Austell,* ☎ *770/739–3400.* *All-inclusive 1-day pass $37, parking $6.* ⏲ *June–Aug., daily 10 AM–11 PM; Mar.–May and Sept.–Oct., weekends from 10, closing times vary.*

Stone Mountain Park. This 3,200-acre state park has the largest exposed granite outcropping on earth. The Confederate Memorial on the north face of the 825-ft-high domed mountain is the world's largest sculpture, measuring 90 ft by 190 ft. The park has a skylift to the mountaintop, a steam locomotive ride around the mountain's base, an antebellum plantation, a swimming beach, a campground, a hotel, a resort, a wildlife preserve, restaurants, and two Civil War museums. Summer nights are capped with a laser light show, and annual events such as the Yellow Daisy Festival and the Scottish Highland Games draw visitors in the fall. ✉ *U.S. 78E, Stone Mountain Pkwy.,* ☎ *770/498–5600.* *Per car $6; annual pass $30; day pass to all attractions $12.85 Georgia residents, $17.10 out-of-state residents; additional fees for special events.* ⏲ *Daily 6 AM–midnight.*

Dining

Atlanta has sophisticated kitchens run by world-class chefs, myriad ethnic restaurants, and classic Southern establishments serving such regional favorites as fried chicken, Brunswick stew, fried catfish, and hush puppies. There's no shortage of urban chic in the dining scene, but traditional Southern fare—including Cajun and Creole, country-style and plantation cuisine, coastal and mountain dishes—continues to thrive.

The local taste for things sweet and fried holds true for restaurants serving traditional Southern food. Tea in the South comes iced and sweet; if you want hot tea, specify hot. Desserts in the region are legendary. Catch the flavor of the South at breakfast and lunch in modest establishments that serve only these meals. Reserve evenings for culinary exploration, including some of the new restaurants that present traditional ingredients and dishes in fresh ways. The influx of Asian immigrants makes Atlanta the perfect city to sample Thai, Vietnamese, Japanese, and authentic Chinese cuisines.

Downtown

$$$–$$$$ ★ ✕ **Bacchanalia.** A favorite among dining critics, this swank restaurant is newly situated in an impressive former industrial space. Dazzling dishes inspired by Mediterranean and occasionally regional cuisines fill the four-course prix-fixe menu. The plentiful options may include sautéed foie gras, Georgia white shrimp, veal sweetbreads, or American farmstead cheeses. Desserts are incredible—as are most items on the menu. ✉ *1198 Howell Mill Rd.,* ☎ *404/365–0410. Reservations essential. AE, DC, MC, V. Closed Sun.–Mon. No lunch.*

$$–$$$$ ★ ✕ **The Abbey.** Established in 1968, the restaurant is housed in a former church. Stained-glass windows and celestial music played by a harpist in the former choir loft reinforce the ambience. Dishes range from the dramatic lobster claw salad with mâche, mango, and apple to a grilled elk chop with dauphinoise potatoes and turnips. Desserts, such as the white chocolate and roasted banana napoleon, finish a meal with sweet abandon. ✉ *163 Ponce de Leon Ave.,* ☎ *404/876–8532. Reservations essential. AE, D, DC, MC, V. No lunch.*

$$–$$$$ ✕ **Atlanta Grill.** With an outdoor veranda overlooking Peachtree Street, this restaurant in the Ritz-Carlton, Atlanta (☞ *below*), has taken dining in the hotel from formal to casual. Chef Peter Zampaglione focuses on regional Southern ingredients and specializes in grilled seafood and game. Sweet corn beignets are a nod to Creole cooking, while sweet-potato spoon bread acknowledges Southeastern traditions. ✉ *181 Peachtree St.,* ☎ *404/659–0403. AE, D, DC, MC, V.*

$$–$$$$ ★ ✕ **City Grill.** This posh, breezy restaurant has made the most of its grand location in the elegantly renovated historic Hurt Building. An impressive wine list accompanies the equally impressive menu. City Grill is a top Atlanta power-lunch spot. ✉ *50 Hurt Plaza,* ☎ *404/524–2489. AE, D, DC, MC, V. Closed Sun. No lunch Sat.*

$$–$$$ ★ ✕ **Food Studio.** A piece of a former plow factory, this stylish restaurant gleams with high-tech and industrial touches. From the same group that made South City Kitchen (☞ Midtown Dining, *below*) a success, the Studio is known for innovative American food, but has added a few more traditional dishes. The grilled veal chop with broccoli and spaghetti squash is a prime example. Desserts range from the parfaitlike frozen lemon basil bombe to chocolate gold mousse cake. ✉ *887 W. Marietta St., Studio K-102, King Plow Arts Center,* ☎ *404/815–6677. Reservations essential. AE, DC, MC, V. No lunch weekends.*

$$–$$$ ★ ✕ **Mumbo Jumbo.** A long bar skirts the left side of the establishment, guiding the eye to the rear dining room. Sleek young staffers conduct guests to tables. The menu emphasizes game in cool weather, fish and shellfish in summer, and regional ingredients and locally grown produce all year round. Dishes that tempt include heirloom tomatoes with milk-sweet buffalo mozzarella, rabbit, and the famous Mumbo Gumbo, a light seafood gumbo. ✉ *89 Park Pl.,* ☎ *404/523–0330. Reservations essential. AE, D, DC, MC, V. No lunch weekends.*

$–$$$ ✕ **Max Lager's American Grill & Brewery.** Line up a tasting of the house brews—the pale ale and brown ale are tops—and then order the Gulf Coast gumbo, the excellent fish-and-chips, or for lunch the vegetarian pita pocket. This lively brewpub near the city's major high-rise buildings is hopping after business hours. It brews its own root and ginger beers. ✉ *320 Peachtree St.,* ☎ *404/525–4400. AE, D, DC, MC, V.*

$ ✕ **ACE Barbecue Barn.** This slightly worn, down-home restaurant is right near the Martin Luther King Jr. Center (☞ Sweet Auburn, *above*). Delicious ribs and chopped rib tips, baked chicken and dressing, and sweet-potato pie are the draws. ✉ *30 Bell St. NE,* ☎ *404/659–6630. No credit cards. Closed Tues.*

$ ✕ **Thelma's Kitchen.** After losing her original location to the Centennial Olympic Park (☞ *above*), Thelma Grundy moved her operation down the road to the street level of the somewhat renovated Roxy Hotel. Brighter, spiffier, and more cheerful than the earlier spot, it has okra pancakes, fried catfish, "cold" slaw, and macaroni and cheese that are among the best in town. Thelma's desserts are stellar. *768 Marietta St. NW,* ☎ *404/688–5855. Reservations not accepted. No credit cards. Closed weekends. No dinner.*

Midtown

$$$–$$$$ ✕ **Le Saint Amour.** Bright colors—warm pink, orange, and teal—decorate this charming, intimate bistro. Young staff members, many still struggling with English, offer friendly service. The food is straight out of Provence, with such dishes as duck confit with sautéed truffles and coquilles St. Jacques (scallops) in wine sauce. ✉ *1620 Piedmont Ave.,* ☎ *404/881–0300. Reservations essential. AE, MC, V. Closed Sun. No lunch Sat.*

Dining

The Abbey **2**
ACE Barbecue Barn . . **8**
Atlanta Grill **6**
Bacchanalia **1**
City Grill **9**
Food Studio **13**
Max Lager's American Grill & Brewery **3**
Mumbo Jumbo **7**
Thelma's Kitchen . . . **12**

Lodging

Atlanta Marriott Marquis **4**
Hyatt Regency, Atlanta **5**
Omni Hotel at CNN Center **10**
Quality Hotel Downtown **11**
Ritz-Carlton, Atlanta **6**

Downtown Atlanta Dining and Lodging

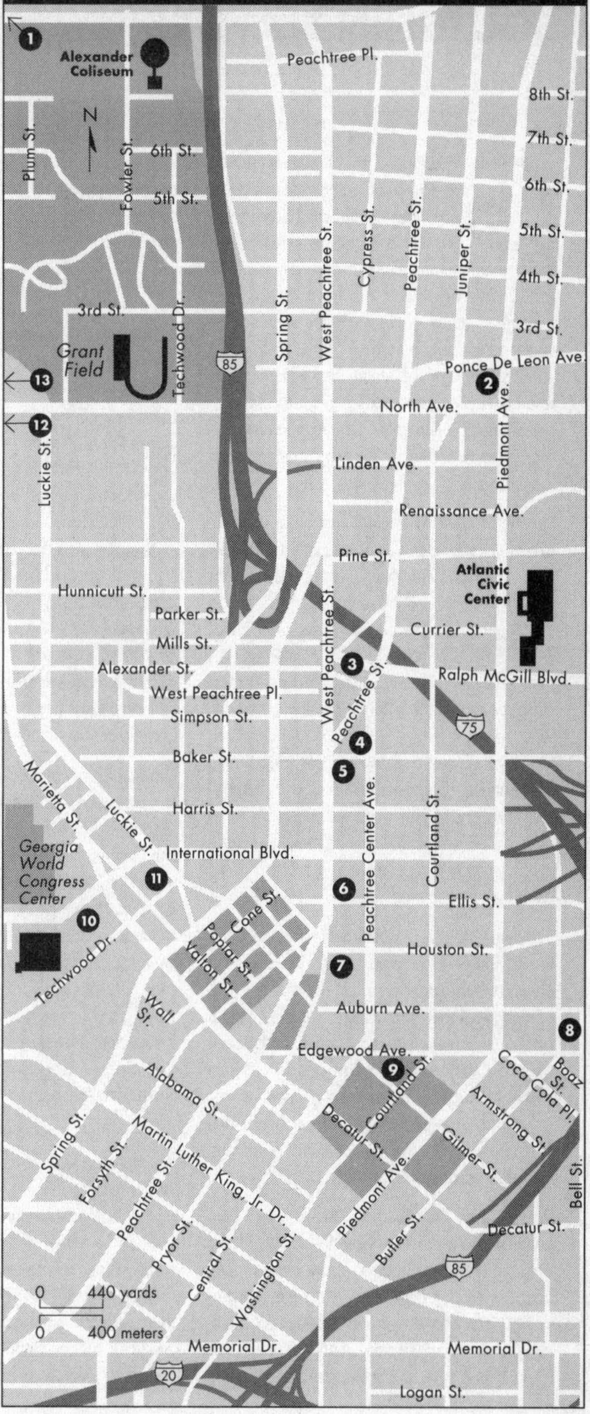

Close-Up

SOUTHERN FLAVORS

GEORGIA IS AN EXCELLENT PLACE to sample Southern food; cities such as Atlanta and Savannah have restaurants that serve the finest traditional fare as well as more innovative cooking. It helps to know that Southern food varies widely across the region and even within states. Nothing reflects this more than barbecue, and few culinary differences produce as many passionate opinions. Do your own tasting as you travel, and you can add to the debate.

Locals in Georgia and Mississippi generally prefer tomato-based sauces on ribs or chopped meat, although plenty of variations may be found. In North Carolina, barbecue is chopped pork piled on a bun with hand-cut coleslaw on top. The sauces range from vinegar and pepper (and little else) to Lexington style, with some tomato in the mix. And North Carolinians serve hush puppies (deep-fried ball-shape cornmeal fritters) with barbecue, which, for them, does not generally include ribs. For the rest of the South, the hush puppy is reserved for fried fish, whether fin or shell.

In South Carolina, mustard-based barbecue sauces are widely savored, whether on chopped meat or on ribs. In eastern Alabama (and the Florida Panhandle), you'll find a unique white sauce for barbecue. Memphis-style 'cue is famous for its dry rub, although there is also a "wet" style, in which the same spices, moistened, are rubbed on the ribs. In parts of Tennessee, barbecued mutton is traditional.

Prior to the Depression, there were two sorts of cooking in the South—country food and the elegant plantation fare drawn from French and English models. In recent years, country cooking, blending European, African, and Native American fare, has come to be the defining Southern cuisine in most people's minds. But many an elegant table was set with European-based dishes, especially along the coasts.

Gumbo, the spicy soup that is so clearly from this region, is a more apt metaphor for the South's demographics than the term *melting pot* because the word *gumbo* reflects all that comes to the Southern table (and to Southern culture) from its people. The term is West African, from *ngombo,* which meant okra in that part of the world. And what would gumbo be without okra? But gumbo is also European: A proper gumbo is based on a *roux,* a sauté of fat and flour cooked to the color of peanut butter. The cook might sauté vegetables for a gumbo, making a kind of *sofrito,* a legacy from the Spanish settlers in the lower part of Louisiana. Using sassafras or filé powder to thicken gumbo is a legacy of Southern Native Americans.

One defining ingredient in Southern cooking is corn, another Native American legacy. Parch the corn with lye, which swells the grains, and you make hominy. Grind the corn, white or yellow, and you have grits. Sift the grits, and you have cornmeal for making corn bread, fluffy spoon bread, cornpone, hoecakes, hush puppies, johnnycake (or Native American "journey" cake). Ferment the grain, and you have corn whiskey, also known as white lightning or moonshine (and arguably like Southern grappa).

In traveling Georgia and the rest of the South, you will find the area's diversity on its tables. Many of the region's chefs use the traditional ingredients to craft "new" Southern dishes as a way of restoring that sense of elegant dining to the region's cuisine. Others wouldn't get near that sort of fare, preferring to do the original dishes proud. Take your pick: Either way, you'll dine divinely.

Atlanta Neighborhoods Dining and Lodging

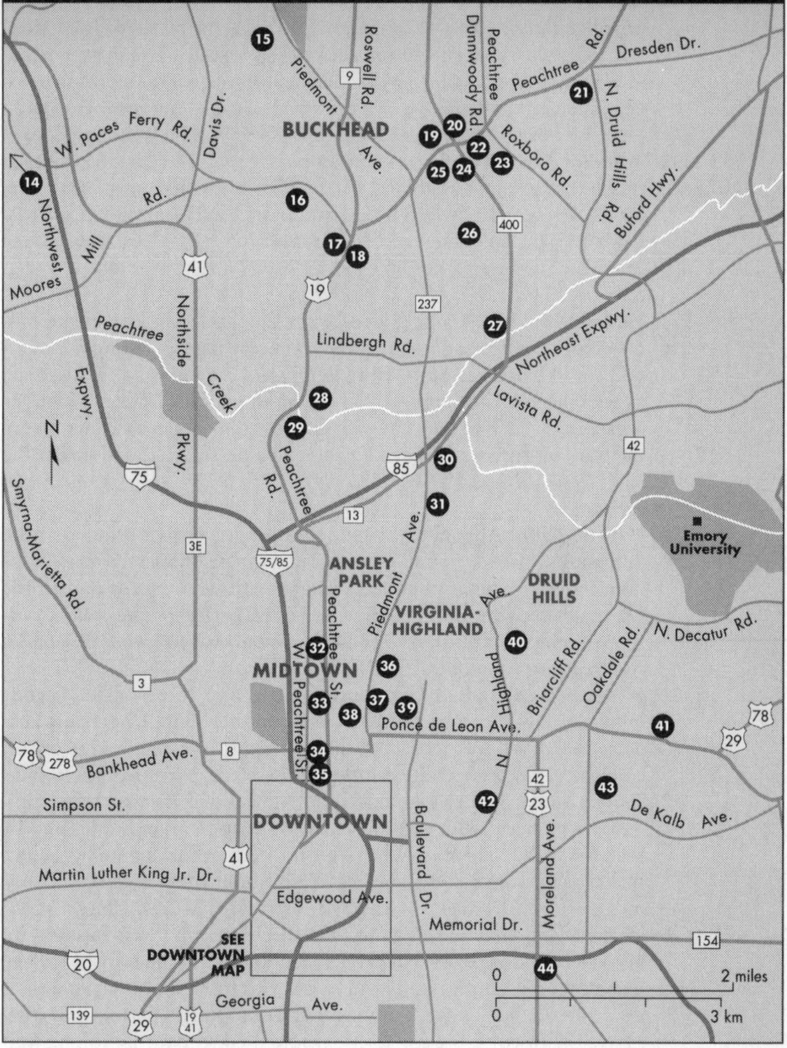

Dining

- Aria **26**
- Brasserie Le Coze . . . **22**
- Canoe. **14**
- Colonnade Restaurant **30**
- Dining Room, The Ritz-Carlton, Buckhead **20**
- Eclipse di Luna **27**
- The Flying Biscuit . . . **43**
- Heaping Bowl and Brew **44**
- Horseradish Grill . . . **15**
- Indigo Coastal Grill **40**
- La Grotta **18**
- Le Saint Amor. **31**
- Luna Sí **29**
- Mary Mac's Tea Room **39**
- Seeger's **16**
- Sotto Sotto **42**
- South City Kitchen. . . **33**
- Toulouse **28**
- Veni Vidi Vici **34**
- Vino! **17**
- Watershed **41**
- Zocalo **37**

Lodging

- Doubletree Hotel. . . . **19**
- Embassy Suites Hotel. **25**
- Four Seasons Hotel. **32**
- Georgian Terrace **35**
- Ritz-Carlton, Buckhead **20**
- Shellmont. **36**
- Sheraton at Colony Square Hotel **38**
- Sheraton Buckhead **23**
- Sierra Suites Atlanta Brookhaven **21**
- Swissôtel **24**

$$–$$$ ★ ✕ **South City Kitchen.** The culinary traditions of South Carolina's Low-country inspire the cooking at this bright restaurant. The clean, spare, art-filled interior attracts a hip crowd. This is the place for fried green tomatoes with goat cheese and she-crab soup. Catfish comes prepared in a variety of intriguing ways. The crab hash, served with poached eggs and chive hollandaise, is a classic. Don't miss the chocolate pecan pie. ✉ *1144 Crescent Ave.,* ☎ *404/873–7358. AE, MC, V.*

$–$$$ ✕ **Indigo Coastal Grill.** You can sample the world's coastal cuisines at this lively Virginia-Highland eatery. The menu has sushi and Thai food along with fresh deep-fried seafood, such as cornmeal-crusted oysters with jalapeño tartar sauce. For Sunday brunch there's jalapeño cheese grits, and for dessert, key lime pie. ✉ *1397 N. Highland Ave.,* ☎ *404/876–0676. AE, DC, MC, V. No lunch.*

$–$$$ ★ ✕ **Veni Vidi Vici.** Gleaming woods, contemporary styling, and an outdoor boccie court and dining patio create the perfect setting for an indulgent Italian meal. Start with *Piatti piccoli,* savory small dishes such as veal meatballs or herbed goat cheese in marinara sauce. Then, try a pasta dish such as gnocchi with Gorgonzola cheese, or order one of the fragrant rotisserie meats. Finish with a dessert that will soothe the soul. ✉ *41 14th St.,* ☎ *404/875–8424. AE, D, DC, MC, V. No lunch weekends.*

$–$$ ★ ✕ **Sotto Sotto.** Atlanta's hot spot close to downtown brings a fresh, authentic approach to Italian food. The former commercial space hops with patrons dining on grilled scallops with white beans and truffle oil, spaghetti with sun-dried mullet roe, and perfect *panna cotta* (a custard of cooked cream). ✉ *313 N. Highland Ave.,* ☎ *404/523–6678. Reservations essential. AE, MC, V. No lunch.*

$–$$ ✕ **Watershed.** Indigo Girl Emily Saliers and three of her friends launched this casual restaurant–cum–gourmet shop. Chef Scott Peacock makes the planet's best shrimp salad, homemade flat bread, chicken salad with white truffles, homemade pimento cheese with sharp cheddar and egg, and desserts (these alone are worth the trip). Also an enoteca (wine bar), it sells wine both retail in bottles and by the glass at the comfy bar. When she's not in the recording studio, Saliers makes a fine sommelier and loves to talk about wine. ✉ *406 W. Ponce de Leon Ave., Decatur,* ☎ *404/378–4900. AE, MC, V. Closed Mon.*

$ ✕ **The Flying Biscuit.** This garage-sale-decorated spot was formerly an all-day breakfast café. Now open for dinner, its huge hits are egg dishes, turkey sausage and bean cakes with tomatilla salsa, as well as a side item called Pudge, a dense mound of mashed potatoes and rosemary. The biscuits, big and fluffy, are credited with the hour-long wait on weekends. ✉ *1655 McLendon Ave.,* ☎ *404/687–8888. Reservations not accepted. AE, D, MC, V. Closed Mon.*

$ ✕ **Heaping Bowl and Brew.** This eatery in the newly established, ultrahip East Atlanta Village has become a favorite. Meals are served in big, comfortable bowls, be it noodles, seared salmon, mashed potatoes, or Southwestern chicken. Specials often depend on what's growing fresh in the garden that day. ✉ *469 Flat Shoals Ave.,* ☎ *404/523–8030. AE, D, MC, V.*

$ ✕ **Mary Mac's Tea Room.** Local celebrities and ordinary folk line up for the country-fried steak, fried chicken, and fresh vegetables. Here, in the Southern tradition, lunch is called "dinner," and the evening meal is referred to as "supper." Waitresses will call you "honey" and pat your arm to assure you that everything's all right. It's a great way to plunge into Southern food and hospitality all at once. ✉ *224 Ponce de Leon Ave.,* ☎ *404/876–1800. No credit cards. No dinner Sun.*

$ ★ ✕ **Zocalo.** A unique open-air patio restaurant (which manages to stay warm in the frigid winter months with pillar-size heaters), it offers some of the best Mexican fare to be found in the city. Spicy chipotle-pepper shrimp and creamy poblano pepper soup are just a sampling of the chef's culinary artworks. The bar has an excellent selection of epicurean tequilas. ✉ *187 10th St.,* ☎ *404/249–7576. Reservations not accepted. AE, D, MC, V.*

Buckhead

$$$$ ✕ **Dining Room, The Ritz-Carlton, Buckhead.** This elegant, restrained dining room, with formal hunt scenes on the walls, romantic lighting, and generously spaced tables, comes across like an old gentlemen's club. Having worked in Bangkok, chef Joel Antunes brings an Asian touch to French fare. Lately though, such regional dishes as squab with collard greens have appeared on the menu. ✉ *3434 Peachtree Rd.,* ☎ *404/237–2700. Reservations essential. Jacket and tie. AE, D, DC, MC, V. Closed Sun. No lunch.*

$$$$ ★ ✕ **Seeger's.** Celebrated chef Guenter Seeger, formerly at the Dining Room in the Ritz-Carlton (☞ *above*), presides over this sophisticated place. Some find the sleek space a bit noisy, but you'll forget about the volume after the first fragrant, flavorful bite. Dishes such as a roulade of foie gras and smoked salmon are outstanding. Local ingredients appear, as in grilled lamb chops with Vidalia onions. Prix fixes include a vegetable menu and, in season, an entire menu based on truffles. ✉ *111 W. Paces Ferry Rd.,* ☎ *404/846–9779. Reservations essential. Jacket and tie. AE, D, DC, MC, V. Closed Sun. No lunch.*

$$$–$$$$ ★ ✕ **Aria.** Formerly known as the ultraformal Hedgerose, this restaurant was recently reinvented with a contemporary flair. Delectable entrées by chef Gerry Klaskala include pan-roasted salmon and lobster noodle soup. Don't miss the mouthwatering dessert menu created by renowned pastry chef Kathryn King. ✉ *490 E. Paces Ferry Rd.,* ☎ *404/233–7673. Reservations essential. Jacket and tie. AE, D, DC, MC, V. Closed Sun. No lunch.*

$$–$$$$ ✕ **La Grotta.** Overlook the location in the ground level of a posh condominium: This is one of the best-managed dining rooms in town. The interior is elegant and sophisticated, with a burgundy and cream decor. Old northern Italian favorites are the core of the menu. Savor prosciutto with grilled pears and mascarpone cheese, then try roast quail stuffed with Italian sausage, and finish with zabaglione. ✉ *2637 Peachtree Rd.,* ☎ *404/231–1368. Reservations essential. Jacket required. AE, D, DC, MC, V. Closed Sun., last wk in June, and first wk in July. No lunch.*

$$–$$$ ★ ✕ **Horseradish Grill.** Once a red horse barn, this establishment is now painted gray with white trim and has arched windows across the front that brighten the space. Some find it a bit noisy, but this place is a must for upscale Southern dishes that retain authenticity. Autumn venison stew and Carolina-style barbecue topped with coleslaw are examples from the seasonal menu. ✉ *4320 Powers Ferry Rd.,* ☎ *404/255–7277. Reservations not accepted. AE, D, DC, MC, V.*

$–$$$ ★ ✕ **Brasserie Le Coze.** Shoppers stream into this glowing, wood-paneled space with comfortable banquettes and comforting bistro-style fare. Traditional dishes include quiche, onion tart, mussels, coq au vin, and warm chocolate soufflé cake. *Vacherin* (meringue rings placed on a pastry base) filled with ice cream is just one of many extravagant desserts. ✉ *3393 Peachtree Rd., Lenox Sq., near Neiman Marcus, Buckhead,* ☎ *404/266–1440. AE, DC, MC, V. Closed Sun.*

$–$$$ ★ ✕ **Canoe.** This popular spot on the banks of the Chattahoochee River brims with appreciative patrons nearly all day. In nice weather, the outdoor dining spaces allow the best view of the river. The restaurant's national reputation is based on such dishes as sea scallops with asparagus risotto, mushroom risotto with quail, and ravioli of roast rabbit. Sunday brunch is superb. ✉ *4199 Paces Ferry Rd. NW,* ☎ *770/432–2663. AE, D, DC, MC, V.*

$–$$$ ✕ **Luna Sí.** The emphasis is on fun at this New York loft–style restaurant, where Latin music blares and customers are encouraged to write on the walls. The menu, which changes weekly, is dominated by seafood. Signature items include salmon with a ginger crust, roast chicken and mashed potatoes, excellent foie gras, and homemade biscotti. ✉ *1931 Peachtree Rd.,* ☎ *404/355–5993. Reservations essential. AE, D, DC, MC, V. Closed Sun. No lunch.*

$–$$ ★ ✕ **Colonnade Restaurant.** For traditional Southern food such as oyster stew, ham steak, and turkey and dressing, insiders head for the Colonnade, an Atlanta institution since 1927. The interior, with patterned carpeting, feels like a stylish version of a classic 1950s restaurant. ✉ *1879 Cheshire Bridge Rd.,* ☎ *404/874–5642. Reservations not accepted. No credit cards.*

$–$$ ✕ **Toulouse.** Open spaces enclosed by warm, rough-brick walls characterize this attractive dining spot. The food is inspired in theory by the cooking of southwestern France but seems more American in execution. The country potato soup is a perfect cold weather meal. Especially wonderful are the roast chicken, duck confit with blueberry vinaigrette, and crème brûlée. ✉ *2293B Peachtree Rd., Peachtree Walk,* ☎ *404/351–9533. AE, D, DC, MC, V. No lunch.*

$–$$ ✕ **Vino!** Mediterranean colors create a warm, intimate atmosphere. The focus is on tapas and wines by the glass, but you can eat a full meal here, too. Tapas ($5–$6) are traditional; among the best are the meat-stuffed pastries called empanadas, and Serrano ham, a Spanish meat similar to prosciutto. ✉ *2900 Peachtree Rd.,* ☎ *404/816–0511. AE, DC, MC, V. Closed Sun.*

$ ★ ✕ **Eclipse di Luna.** Tucked at the very end of Miami Circle, a "trade-only" design center, this hot spot has captured the fancy of twenty-somethings, who flock here on weekends. Lunch is sandwiches and salads, and evening fare is tapas ($3) and wine by the glass. *Patatas bravas* (potatoes with olive oil and spicy sauce), tender braised chicken with saffron and garlic, and flan will take you to Castile. ✉ *764 Miami Circle,* ☎ *404/846–0449. AE, DC, MC, V. Closed Mon.*

Lodging

One of America's three most popular convention destinations, Atlanta offers a broad range of lodgings. More than 12,000 rooms are in the compact downtown area, close to the Georgia World Congress Center, Atlanta Civic Center, Atlanta Merchandise Mart, and Omni Coliseum. Other clusters are in Buckhead, in the north I–285 perimeter, and around Hartsfield Atlanta International Airport.

Downtown

$$$$ ★ 🏨 **Ritz-Carlton, Atlanta.** The mood here is set by traditional afternoon tea served in the intimate, sunken lobby beneath an 18th-century chandelier. Notice the 17th-century Flemish tapestry when you enter from Peachtree Street. Some guest rooms are luxuriously decorated with marble writing tables, plump sofas, four-poster beds, and white-marble bathrooms. The Atlanta Grill (☞ Dining, *above*) is one of downtown's only outdoor dining spots. ✉ *181 Peachtree St. (entrance to MARTA's Peachtree Center rail station is across the street), 30303,* ☎ *404/659–0400 or 800/241–3333,* FAX *404/688–0400. 425 rooms, 22 suites. Restaurant, bar, laundry service, business services, parking (fee). AE, D, DC, MC, V.*

$$$–$$$$ 🏨 **Hyatt Regency, Atlanta.** This Hyatt was John Portman's first atrium-centered building, and it became the model for other Portman-designed hotels, including the San Francisco Embarcadero and the Atlanta Marriott Marquis (☞ *below*). The blue-bubble top stands out against the Atlanta skyline. Expect the careful service and quality facilities typ-

ical of Hyatt hotels. ✉ *265 Peachtree St. (connected by skywalk to Peachtree Center), 30303,* ☎ *404/577–1234 or 800/233–1234,* FAX *404/588–4137. 1,206 rooms, 58 suites. 3 restaurants, bar, pool, health club, business services, parking (fee). AE, D, DC, MC, V.*

$$$–$$$$ **Omni Hotel at CNN Center.** The hotel is adjacent to the home of Ted Turner's Cable News Network. The lobby combines old-world and modern accents, with marble floors, Oriental rugs, and exotic floral and plant arrangements. Rooms have large windows and contemporary-style furniture, including a sofa. Guests have access to the Downtown Athletic Club and two small meeting rooms. ✉ *100 CNN Center (MARTA's Omni rail station is adjacent to CNN Center), 30305,* ☎ *404/659–0000 or 800/843–6664,* FAX *404/525–5050. 455 rooms, 4 suites. 2 restaurants, lobby lounge, business services, parking (fee). AE, D, DC, MC, V.*

$$$ **Atlanta Marriott Marquis.** Immense and coolly contemporary, the Marquis seems to go on forever as you stand under the lobby's huge fabric sculpture that hangs from the skylighted roof 47 stories above. Guest rooms, which open onto this atrium, are decorated in dark greens and neutral shades. Major suites have live plants and fresh flowers; two suites have grand pianos and ornamental fireplaces. ✉ *265 Peachtree Center Ave., 30303,* ☎ *404/521–0000,* FAX *404/586–6299. 1,671 rooms, 60 suites. 5 restaurants, 2 bars, indoor-outdoor pool, health club, business services, parking (fee). AE, D, DC, MC, V.*

$–$$ **Quality Hotel Downtown.** This quiet, older downtown hotel, two blocks off Peachtree Street, has a marble lobby with sofas and a grand piano that guests sometimes play. Modest-size rooms in teal and navy make the hotel inviting. The place is popular for conventions due to its proximity to the World Congress Center and the show marts; prices go up when conventions are in town. ✉ *89 Luckie St., 30303,* ☎ *404/524–7991,* FAX *404/524–0672. 70 rooms, 5 suites. Pool. AE, D, DC, MC, V.*

Midtown

$$$$ **Four Seasons Hotel.** A sweeping staircase leads up to a welcoming, refined bar and Park 75, the hotel's fine dining establishment. Rose-hue marble creates a warm feeling in the public spaces. Marble bathrooms, pale lemon or celadon color schemes, and polished brass chandeliers are among the guest room appointments. ✉ *75 14th St., 30309,* ☎ *404/881–9898,* FAX *404/873–4692. 226 rooms, 18 suites. Restaurant, bar, pool, health club, business services. AE, D, DC, MC, V.*

$$$–$$$$ **Georgian Terrace.** Spend a night where Enrico Caruso and the Metropolitan Opera stars once lodged. This fine old hotel across the street from the Fox Theatre (☞ Midtown, *above*) is on the National Register of Historic Places and housed the rich and famous in its heyday. Now restored, and with an added matching tower, all units are suites with kitchenettes or full kitchens. ✉ *659 Peachtree St., 30308,* ☎ *404/897–1991 or 800/651–2316,* FAX *404/724–0642. 320 suites. Restaurant, pool, convention center, meeting rooms, parking (fee). AE, D, DC, MC, V.*

$$–$$$ **Sheraton at Colony Square Hotel.** Theatricality and opulence are epitomized by the dimly lighted lobby with overhanging balconies, piano music, and fresh flowers. Rooms are modern, with muted tones; those on higher floors have city views. The hotel is two blocks from MARTA's Arts Center station and two blocks from the Woodruff Arts Center and the High Museum of Art (☞ Midtown, *above*); it anchors the Colony Square complex of office, residential, and retail buildings. ✉ *188 14th St., 30361,* ☎ *404/892–6000 or 800/422–7895,* FAX *404/872–9192. 436 rooms, 31 suites. Restaurant, lobby lounge, pool, parking (fee). AE, D, DC, MC, V.*

INNS AND GUEST HOUSES

$$ **Shellmont.** The Shellmont is named for the shell motif that adorns the house. Designed in 1891 by Massachusetts-born, Atlanta-reared architect Walter T. Downing for Dr. William Perrin Nicholson, the house has classical architectural elements, detailed stained-glass windows, and a reproduction of the original Victorian stenciling on the walls. Guest rooms have American Victorian antiques and CD players. ✉ *821 Piedmont Ave., 30306,* ☎ *404/872–9290 or 404/872–5379. 2 rooms, 2 suites, 1 carriage house. AE, D, DC, MC, V. BP.*

Buckhead

$$$$ ★ **Ritz-Carlton, Buckhead.** Decorated with the Ritz's signature 18th- and 19th-century antiques and art, this elegant gem bids a discreet welcome. Shoppers from nearby Lenox Square mall and Phipps Plaza often revive here over afternoon tea or cocktails in the richly paneled Lobby Lounge. The **Dining Room** (☞ Dining, *above*) is one of the city's finest restaurants. The spacious rooms are furnished with traditional reproductions and have luxurious white-marble baths. From the hotel's club floors you get a view of Buckhead and an understanding of why Atlanta is known as a city of trees. Weekend musical performances are a delight. ✉ *3434 Peachtree Rd., 30326,* ☎ *404/237–2700 or 800/241–3333,* FAX *404/239–0078. 524 rooms, 29 suites. 2 restaurants, bar, pool, hot tub, health club, parking (fee). AE, D, DC, MC, V.*

$$–$$$$ **Swissôtel.** Sleek and efficient, this stunner boasts a chic, modern glass and white-tile exterior with curved walls and Biedermeier-style interiors. Convenient to Lenox Square mall, a prime location for shopping and dining, the hotel is a favorite with business travelers. The restaurant, the Palm, is noted for its steaks. The full-service fitness center has everything from facials to fitness trainers. ✉ *3391 Peachtree Rd., 30326,* ☎ *404/365–0065 or 800/253–1397,* FAX *404/365–8787. 364 rooms, 16 suites. Restaurant, bar, pool, health club, business services, parking (fee). AE, D, DC, MC, V.*

$$–$$$ **Embassy Suites Hotel.** This modern high-rise is just blocks from the Phipps Plaza and Lenox Square malls. A variety of suites ranging from deluxe presidential (with wet bars) to more basic sleeping- and sitting-room combinations are available. Rates include afternoon cocktails. ✉ *3285 Peachtree Rd., 30305,* ☎ *404/261–7733 or 800/362–2779,* FAX *404/261–6857. 313 suites. Restaurant, indoor pool, outdoor pool, exercise room, parking (fee). AE, D, DC, MC, V. BP.*

$$–$$$ **Sheraton Buckhead.** This modern, eight-floor hotel has the advantage of being right across from Lenox Square mall. Rooms have contemporary furnishings; some have a desk and chair, others sofas. ✉ *3405 Lenox Rd., 30326,* ☎ *404/261–9250,* FAX *404/848–7391. 355 rooms, 7 suites. Restaurant, bar, pool. AE, D, DC, MC, V.*

$$ **Doubletree Hotel.** It has spacious rooms and reasonable rates given the excellent location. Guests have access to a health club. The hotel offers complimentary transportation within 2 mi of the hotel and is adjacent to the Buckhead MARTA station. ✉ *3340 Peachtree Rd., 30326,* ☎ *404/231–1234 or 800/222–8733,* FAX *404/231–5236. 217 rooms, 4 suites. Restaurant, free parking. AE, D, DC, MC, V.*

$–$$ **Sierra Suites Atlanta Brookhaven.** The feel is modern Southwestern at this comfortable hotel, just north of Lenox Square. Cream and green color schemes decorate the one-bedroom studio suites with kitchenettes (no ovens). ✉ *3967 Peachtree Rd.,* ☎ *404/237–9100,* FAX *404/237–0055. 92 suites. Pool, exercise room, laundry service. AE, D, DC, MC, V.*

Nightlife and the Arts

The Arts

For the most complete schedule of **cultural events,** check the *Atlanta Journal-Constitution*'s Friday "Weekend Preview" and Saturday "Leisure" sections. Also available for cultural and entertainment listings are two lively community weeklies, *Creative Loafing* and *Atlanta Press,* each distributed free at Atlanta restaurants, bars, and stores. You can also call the 24-hour **Arts Hotline** (☎ 404/853–3278).

Tickets for the Fox Theatre, Atlanta Civic Center, and other locations are handled by **TicketMaster** (☎ 404/249–6400 or 800/326–4000) and **Ticket-X-Press, Inc.** (☎ 404/231–5888). Some companies only sell tickets through their own box offices.

CONCERTS

The **Atlanta Symphony Orchestra (ASO),** under the new musical direction of Robert Spano, is now more than a half century old, with 14 Grammy Awards to its credit. It performs the fall–spring subscription series in the 1,800-seat Symphony Hall at Woodruff Arts Center (✉ 1280 Peachtree St., ☎ 404/733–5000). During the summer, the orchestra regularly plays with big-name popular and country artists in Chastain Park's outdoor amphitheater (✉ 4469 Stella Dr., ☎ 404/733–4800).

Emory University (✉ N. Decatur Rd. at Clifton Rd., ☎ 404/727–6187, FAX 404/727–6421), an idyllic suburban campus, has four venues where both internationally renowned guest artists and faculty and student groups perform. Expect quality music from a variety of ensembles, including woodwinds, brass, jazz, and vocal.

Georgia State University (✉ Art and Music Bldg., Peachtree Center Ave. and Gilmer St., ☎ 404/651–4636 or 404/651–3676), with the entrance on Gilmer Street and free parking at the corner of Edgewood and Peachtree Center avenues, sponsors many concerts (about 80%) that are free and open to the public. Performances by faculty, student, and local groups and guest artists focus on jazz and classical. There are also performances at the Rialto Center for the Performing Arts (☞ *below*), an old movie theater the university turned into a performance venue.

DANCE

The country's oldest continuously operating ballet company (founded in 1929), the **Atlanta Ballet** (✉ 1400 W. Peachtree St., ☎ 404/873–5811) has received international recognition for its productions of classical and contemporary works. Performances are usually at the Fox Theatre (☞ *below*) but sometimes take place elsewhere. Artistic director John McFall, only the third in the company's history, brings new ideas and vision to the group.

FESTIVALS

The **Atlanta Jazz Festival,** held Memorial Day weekend, gathers the best local, national, and international musicians to give mostly free concerts at Atlanta's Piedmont Park. For information, contact the Atlanta Bureau of Cultural Affairs (☎ 404/817–6815, FAX 404/817–6827).

The **Montreux/Atlanta International Music Festival** began in 1988, when Atlanta joined with Montreux, Switzerland, to cohost a music festival featuring a variety of styles: jazz, blues, gospel, reggae, and classical. The festival typically starts during Labor Day weekend, with performances in Piedmont Park (free) and Chastain Park (expensive). For information, contact the Atlanta Bureau of Cultural Affairs (☎ 404/817–6815, FAX 404/817–6827).

OPERA

The **Atlanta Opera** (✉ 728 W. Peachtree St., ☎ 404/881–8801 or 800/356–7372) usually mounts four main-stage productions each year from spring through fall at the Fox Theatre (☞ *below*). Major roles are performed by national and international guest artists, while the chorus and orchestra come from the local community. Call TicketMaster (☎ 404/817–8700) for information.

PERFORMANCE VENUES

Atlanta Civic Center (✉ 395 Piedmont Ave., ☎ 404/523–6275) presents touring Broadway musicals, pop music, and dance concerts.

Fox Theatre (✉ 660 Peachtree St., ☎ 404/881–2100), a fine faux-Moorish theater (☞ Midtown, *above*), is the principal venue for touring Broadway shows and national productions, as well as the home of the Atlanta Opera (☞ *above*) and the Atlanta Ballet (☞ *above*).

Georgia Tech Center for the Performing Arts (✉ 349 Ferst Dr., ☎ 404/894–9600), at the Georgia Institute of Technology, offers performances that run the gamut, from classical to jazz, from dance to theater. The highly regarded student-operated theater, DramaTech, is in the James E. Dull Theatre. There's ample free parking on site.

Rialto Center for the Performing Arts (✉ 80 Forsyth St., ☎ 404/651–4727), developed by Georgia State University in a beautifully renovated and restructured former movie theater, features film, theater, and dance, as well as musical performances by local and international performers.

Spivey Hall (campus: ✉ 5900 N. Lee St., ☎ 770/961–3683) is a gleaming, modern, acoustically magnificent performance center at Clayton College and State University, 15 mi south of Atlanta in Morrow. The hall is considered one of the country's finest concert venues. Internationally renowned musicians perform everything from chamber music to jazz.

Variety Playhouse (✉ 1099 Euclid Ave., ☎ 404/524–7354), a former movie theater, is one of the cultural anchors of the hip Little Five Points neighborhood. Its denizens don't don fancy frocks to listen to rock, bluegrass and country, blues, reggae, folk, jazz, and pop.

Woodruff Arts Center (✉ 1280 Peachtree St., ☎ 404/733–4200) is home to the Alliance Theatre and the Atlanta Symphony Orchestra (☞ *above*).

THEATER

Check local newspaper listings for information on the outstanding companies in Atlanta and its suburbs. Consult *Creative Loafing* and the *Atlanta Journal-Constitution* for performance information.

Actor's Express (✉ 887 W. Marietta St., ☎ 404/607–7469), an award-winning theater, presents an eclectic selection of classic and cutting-edge productions in the 150-seat theater of the King Plow Arts Center, a stylish artists' complex hailed by local critics as a showplace of industrial chic. For an evening of dining and theater, plan on dinner at the Food Studio (☞ Dining, *above*), at the King Plow Arts Center.

Alliance Theatre (✉ 1280 Peachtree St., ☎ 404/733–4200), Atlanta's premier professional theater, presents everything from Shakespeare to the latest Broadway and off-Broadway shows in the Woodruff Arts Center (☞ Midtown, *above*).

Atlanta Shakespeare Tavern (✉ 499 Peachtree St., ☎ 404/874–5299) produces plays by the Bard, his peers, and more contemporary dramatists. Performances vary in quality but are always fun. The Elizabethan-style playhouse is a tavern, so alcohol and pub-style food are available. It's also home to the Kaleidoscope Children's Theater, which presents classics, such as *The New Adventures of the Three Musketeers,* on most weekends during the day.

14th Street Playhouse (✉ 175 14th St., ☎ 404/733–4750 or 404/733–4754) is part of the Woodruff Arts Center (☞ Midtown, *above*). The house has three theaters, a 400-seat main stage, a 200-seat second stage, and an 80-seat stage, which are rented for special productions. There is no resident company. Musicals, plays, and sometimes opera are presented.

Horizon Theatre Co. (✉ 1083 Austin Ave., Little Five Points, ☎ 404/584–7450) is a professional troupe that was established in 1983; it produces premieres of provocative and entertaining contemporary plays in its 185-seat theater.

Nightlife

The pursuit of entertainment—from Midtown to Buckhead—is known as the "Peachtree Shuffle." Atlanta's vibrant nightlife includes everything from coffee bars to sports bars, from country line dancing to high-energy dance clubs. Atlanta has long been known for having more bars than churches, and in the South, that's an oddity.

Most bars and clubs are open seven nights, until 2–4 AM. Those with live entertainment usually have a cover charge. Consult *Creative Loafing* and the *Atlanta Journal-Constitution* for information.

ACOUSTIC

Eddie's Attic (✉ 515B N. McDonough St., Decatur, ☎ 404/377–4976) is a good spot for catching local and some national acoustic, folk, pop, and country-music acts. It has a full bar and restaurant and is right near the Decatur MARTA station. Covers range from $6 to $12.

BARS

The **Beluga Martini Bar** (✉ 3115 Piedmont Rd., ☎ 404/869–1090) has caviar, smoked salmon, champagne by the glass, and other light fare in an intimate, comfortable space with live music.

For Irish atmosphere, food, beer, and music (both live and on CD), head straight over to **Fadó** (✉ 3035 Peachtree Rd., ☎ 404/841–0066). The food ranges from *boxty* (potato pancakes with savory fillings) to Irish stew made with lamb, cottage pie, and whiskey trifle.

Limerick Junction (✉ 822 N. Highland Ave., ☎ 404/874–7147), a lively Irish pub, features singers from the large Atlanta community that ably render traditional Irish music, as well as performers from the Old Sod itself. It has a rollicking, good-time atmosphere. Parking is dreadful, so consider a cab. A small cover may be charged.

Manuel's Tavern (✉ 602 N. Highland Ave., ☎ 404/525–3447) is a neighborhood saloon where families, politicians, writers, students, and professionals gather for drinks, beer-steamed hot dogs, veggie soy burgers, and the like. When the Atlanta Braves play, the crowd gathers around the wide-screen TVs.

Mike n' Angelo's (✉ 312 E. Paces Ferry Rd., ☎ 404/237–0949), with a friendly atmosphere, knowledgeable bartenders, live bands, and hearty pub fare, is a local favorite.

To make it through the door at **Tongue & Groove** (✉ 3055 Peachtree Rd., ☎ 404/261–2325), you must dress up: long dresses for ladies and jackets for men. Live music—sometimes rock, sometimes salsa—alternates with recorded tunes. The light-fare menu is as chic as the atmosphere. Covers range from $5 to $10, depending on the program.

COMEDY

The **Punchline** (✉ 280 Hilderbrand Dr., Sandy Springs, Balconies Shopping Center, ☎ 404/252–5233), Atlanta's oldest comedy club, books major national acts, among them Henry Cho, Craig Shoemaker, Tom Rhodes, and Judy Tenuta. The small club is popular, so you need a reservation. Cover charges vary and can be upwards of $20 for some acts, but it's usually worth it. The menu has light fare and sandwiches, and there's a one-item minimum, either food or beverage. To enter, you must be 21.

COUNTRY

Buckboard Country Music Showcase (✉ 2080 Cobb Pkwy., Windy Hill Plaza, ☎ 770/955–7340), a 425-seat house, has a large dance floor, pool tables, and two full bars; it serves food of the hamburgers, nachos, and chicken fingers variety. The house band is the Buckboard Bandits, and Nashville-based bands play on Thursday night. The cover charge is $5–$10.

Cowboys Concert Hall (✉ 1750 N. Roberts Rd., Kennesaw, ☎ 770/426–5006) attracts national talent twice monthly on Friday. On Wednesday, Thursday, Friday, and Sunday, line-dancing classes and couple-dancing lessons are taught. This 44,000-square-ft venue is north of the city. The cover is $5, unless an unusually high-profile act is slated.

DANCE

Cajun dancing is rapidly gaining favor as a weekend frolic. The **Atlanta Cajun Dance Association** (✉ 2704 Laurelwood Rd., ☎ 770/451–6611) offers a one-hour lesson before the party, called a *fais do-do*. Although two local Cajun bands frequent the stage, nationally known bands from Louisiana often take over. Weekend dances usually take place at the Knights of Columbus Hall (✉ 2620 Buford Hwy.).

Backstreet (✉ 845 Peachtree St., ☎ 404/873–1986), drawing both men and women, has been Midtown's mainstay gay club for nearly two decades, but straight people enjoy the place, too. Downstairs is the dance floor with recorded music, and upstairs is Charlie Brown's Cabaret, with female impersonators. As the club is open 24 hours, membership is required; quarterly memberships cost $10, entitling cardholders to free admission Sunday through Thursday and $5 covers Friday and Saturday.

JAZZ AND BLUES

Blind Willie's (✉ 828 N. Highland Ave., ☎ 404/873–2583) showcases New Orleans– and Chicago-style blues that sends crowds into a frenzy. The name honors Blind Willie McTell, a native of Thomson, Georgia, whose original compositions include "Statesboro Blues," made popular by the Macon, Georgia–based Allman Brothers. Cajun and zydeco are also on the agenda from time to time. Cover charges run in the $10 range.

Dante's Down the Hatch (✉ 3380 Peachtree Rd., Buckhead, ☎ 404/266–1600) is popular for its music and sultry atmosphere. Regular entertainers include the Paul Mitchell Trio, which conjures silky-smooth jazz in the "hold" of a make-believe sailing ship.

Fuzzy's Place (✉ 2015 N. Druid Hills Rd., ☎ 404/321–6166), a crowded and smoke-filled neighborhood bar, begins the day by serving lunch to the denizens of nearby office buildings. By night, it's a restaurant with a surprisingly sophisticated menu, sports bar, and blues room. The finest local talent holds forth on the stage, including the venerable Francine Reed, one of Atlanta's favorite entertainers. There's usually no cover.

Sambuca Jazz Cafe (✉ 3102 Piedmont Rd., ☎ 404/237–5299), with decent dining, a lively bar, and good live jazz, attracts a trendy young set.

Whiskers (✉ 8371 Roswell Rd., in shopping center at Roswell and Northridge Rds., ☎ 770/992–7445) hosts blues and rock groups, with some of the best local talent. There's no cover.

ROCK

Masquerade (✉ 695 North Ave., ☎ 404/577–8178) is a grunge hangout with music, from disco to techno, from industrial rock to swing. Basic bar food is available. The mix of people reflects the club's three separate spaces, dubbed Heaven, Hell, and Purgatory. The cover is $2–$8.

Smith's Olde Bar (✉ 1578 Piedmont Ave., ☎ 404/875–1522) schedules a wide variety of talent, both local and regional, in its acoustically fine performance space. Food is available in the downstairs restaurant. Covers vary depending on the act but are usually in the $5–$10 range.

Star Community Bar (✉ 437 Moreland Ave., ☎ 404/681–9018) is highly recommended for those who enjoy garage bands and rockabilly. Bands are featured almost nightly, with covers varying depending on the act. The bar is fully equipped, with an all-Elvis jukebox and an Elvis shrine that must be seen to be believed.

Outdoor Activities and Sports

Participant Sports

At almost any time of the year, in parks, private clubs, and neighborhoods throughout the city, you'll find Atlantans pursuing everything from tennis to soccer to rollerblading. ***Atlanta Sports & Fitness*** magazine (☎ 404/843–2257), available free at many health clubs and sports and outdoors stores, is a good link to Atlanta's athletic community. At the same locations, you can pick up ***Georgia Athlete,*** a guide to individual sporting events.

AEROBICS

Jeanne's Body Tech (✉ 334 E. Paces Ferry Rd., ☎ 404/261–0227) has a variety of exercise equipment and classes including step and spinning. The drop-in fee is $10.

BIKING AND ROLLERBLADING

Piedmont Park (✉ Piedmont Ave. between 10th St. and the Prado) is closed to traffic and popular for rollerblading and other recreational activities. **Skate Escape** (✉ 1086 Piedmont Ave., across from the park, ☎ 404/892–1292) rents bikes and skates.

GOLF

Golf is enormously popular here, as the large number of courses attest. The only public course within sight of downtown Atlanta is the **Bobby Jones Golf Course** (✉ 384 Woodward Way, ☎ 404/355–1009), named after the famed golfer and Atlanta native and located on a portion of the site of the Battle of Peachtree Creek. Despite having some of the city's worst fairways and greens, the immensely popular 18-hole, par-71 course is always crowded. At Chastain Park, the 18-hole, par-71 **North Fulton Golf Course** (✉ 216 W. Wieuca Rd., ☎ 404/255–0723) has one of the best layouts and lies within the I–285 perimeter.

Stone Mountain Park (✉ U.S. 78, ☎ 770/498–5715) has two courses. Stonemont, an 18-hole, par-72 course with several challenging and scenic holes, is the better of the two. The other course, Lakemont, is also 18 holes and par 72.

HEALTH CLUBS

Crunch Fitness (✉ 3340 Peachtree Rd., ☎ 404/262–2120), with six other locations, has equipment and amenities that vary from one location to another. The Cobb location (✉ 1775 Water Pl., ☎ 770/952–2120), for instance, has indoor and outdoor tennis courts. Single visits cost $16. Select hotels, such as the Doubletree (☞ Lodging, *above*), offer complimentary visits to guests.

JOGGING AND RUNNING

Chattahoochee National Recreation Area contains different parcels of land that lie in 15 separate units spread along the banks of the Chattahoochee River, much of which has been protected from development. The area is crisscrossed by 70 mi of trails. ✉ *1978 Island Ford Pkwy.,* ☎ *770/399–8070.* ⏲ *Daily 7–7.*

SWIMMING

Dynamo Community Swim Center (✉ 3119 Shallowford Rd., Chamblee, ☎ 770/451–3272) has an eight-lane, 165-ft outdoor pool; a 10-lane, 25-yard pool; and a five-lane, 25-yard pool. Locker facilities and a weight room are on site. The cost is $4 per visit. Take I–85 to Exit 93.

TENNIS

Bitsy Grant Tennis Center (✉ 2125 Northside Dr., ☎ 404/609–7193), named for one of Atlanta's best-known players, is the area's best public facility, with 13 clay courts (6 of which are lighted) and 10 lighted hard courts. Charges are $2 per person per hour for the hard courts during the day and $2.50 at night (courts close around 10 PM), $2.25–$2.75 for the clay courts, which close around 7 PM. The clubhouse closes at 8 PM.

Piedmont Park, Atlanta's most popular park, has 12 lighted hard courts. Access the tennis center from Park Drive off Monroe Drive; even though the sign says DO NOT ENTER, the security guard will show you the parking lot. Courts are always open, but personnel keep specific hours. Costs are $1.50 per person per hour before 6 PM and $1.75 after 6. ✉ *Piedmont Ave. between 10th St. and the Prado.* ☎ FAX *404/853-3461.* ⏲ *Weekdays 9–9, weekends 9:30–6.*

Spectator Sports

BASEBALL

The **Atlanta Braves** (✉ Turner Field, I–75/85, Exit 246 [Fulton St.]; I–20, westbound Exit 58A [Capitol Ave.]; eastbound Exit 56B [Windsor St./Spring St.], ☎ 404/522–7630) play in Turner Field, formerly the 1996 Olympic Stadium.

BASKETBALL

The **Atlanta Hawks** (✉ Philips Arena, 1 CNN Center, ☎ 404/827–3800) had a proud Olympics moment when Coach Lenny Wilkenson was selected to coach the U.S. Olympic men's basketball team in Atlanta.

FOOTBALL

Under coach Dan Reeves, the **Atlanta Falcons** (✉ Georgia Dome, 1 Georgia Dome Dr., ☎ 404/223–9200) have brought on board many impressive new personnel, both on the coaching staff and on the team. The Falcons have made the playoffs seven times, most recently in 1995.

HOCKEY

The 1999–2000 season was the first for the NHL's **Atlanta Thrashers** (✉ Philips Arena, 1 CNN Center, ☎ 404/827–5300). Named for the state bird, the brown thrasher, the team is backed by Atlanta's sports and media guru Ted Turner.

Shopping

Atlanta's department stores, specialty shops, large enclosed malls, and antiques markets draw shoppers from across the Southeast. Most stores are open Monday–Saturday 10–9, Sunday noon–6. Many downtown stores close Sunday. Sales tax is 7% in the city of Atlanta and Fulton County and 6%–7% in the suburbs.

Shopping Centers

Brookwood Square (✉ 2140 Peachtree Rd.) is an arrangement of unusual shops, including the Vespermann Gallery (☞ Art Galleries, *below*) and the Piano Gallery, Atlanta's Steinway dealership.

Buckhead has many specialty and strip malls. At Peachtree Plaza, at the intersection of Peachtree Road and Mathieson Drive, you'll find Beverly Bremer's Silver Shop, devoted to fine antique silver, and Irish Crystal Co., offering fine cut glass and linens. Down Maple Drive off Peachtree Road you'll find Yesteryear, dealing in antique books (☞ Books, *below*), next to the Atlanta Guitar Center. A raft of boutiques and gift shops, along with some fine restaurants, lines Grandview Avenue (off Peachtree Road), and another similar collection runs down East Shadowlawn Avenue. East Village Square (✉ Buckhead Ave. and Bolling Way) has art galleries and restaurants. Across from Lenox Square, the Around Lenox Shopping Center includes Tower Records–Video–Books. Andrews Square, on East Andrews Drive, is a treasure trove of shops, eateries, nightspots, and galleries. Next to it, Cates Center has similar stores.

Lenox Square mall (✉ 3393 Peachtree Rd., ☎ 404/233–6767), one of Atlanta's oldest and most popular shopping centers, has branches of Neiman Marcus, Rich's (the local department store), Crate & Barrel, and Macy's looming next to specialty shops such as Geode (fine art jewelry) and Mori's (luggage and travel gifts). You'll fare better at one of the several good restaurants here—even for a quick meal—than at the food court.

Peachtree Center Mall (✉ 231 Peachtree St., ☎ 404/524–3787), downtown, does steady business. Stores here are chiefly specialty shops, such as International Records and Tapes, the Architectural Book Center, and the Atlanta International Museum gift shop.

Perimeter Mall (✉ 4400 Ashford-Dunwoody Rd.), known for upscale family shopping, has stores such as Nordstrom, the High Museum of Art Gift Shop, Gap Kids, and the Nature Company, as well as branches of Rich's, Sears, and JCPenney, and a good food court.

Phipps Plaza (✉ 3500 Peachtree Rd., ☎ 404/262–0992 or 800/810–7700) has branches of Tiffany & Co., Saks Fifth Avenue, Birmingham-based Parisian, Lord & Taylor, and Abercrombie & Fitch alongside such shops as Skippy Musket (unique jewelry, collectibles, and decorative items for the home).

Underground (✉ 50 Upper Alabama St., ☎ 404/523–2311) has galleries such as African Pride, with objets d'art from Africa; specialty shops such as Hats Under Atlanta; and Habersham Vineyard & Winery, a tasting room for Georgia wines. The classic chicory-laced New Orleans coffee and beignets at Café du Monde are the perfect way to refuel.

Outlets

The interstate highways leading to Atlanta have discount malls similar to those found throughout the country. Worth noting is the huge cluster around both sides of Exit 149 off I–85, 60 mi north of the city. The **North Georgia Premium Outlets** mall (✉ GA 400 at Dawson Forest Rd.) is worth the 45 minutes it takes to get there from Atlanta's northern perimeter. This shopping center has more than 70 stores, including Williams-Sonoma for cookware; OshKosh B'gosh, a clothing store for children; Music for a Song, dealing in discount CDs and tapes; Stone Mountain Handbags, specializing in quality leather goods; a Barneys New York; and numerous designer outlet shops not found in most malls.

Specialty Shops

ANTIQUES

Buckhead has several antiques shops, most of them along or near Peachtree Road; expect rare goods and high prices here. Venture into Virginia-Highland and the city's suburban towns to find treasures galore.

Bennett Street (✉ 116 Bennett St., ☎ 404/352–4430) has art galleries such as Out of the Woods; antiques shops such as Kelim; and a good restaurant, Fratelli di Napoli (✉ 2101B Tula St., ☎ 404/351–1533), making it easy to spend a whole day here. The Stalls is a fine antiques market.

Chamblee Antique Row, at the intersection of Peachtree Road and Broad Street in the suburban town of Chamblee just north of Buckhead and about 10 mi north of downtown, is a browser's delight. For information, contact the Chamblee Antique Dealers Association (☎ 770/458–1614).

Little Five Points (✉ intersection of Moreland and Euclid Aves.) attracts "junking" addicts who find nirvana in Atlanta's version of Greenwich Village, characterized by vintage clothing stores, art galleries, used-record and -book shops, and some stores that defy description.

Miami Circle, off Piedmont Road, is an upscale enclave for antiques and decorative arts lovers. Drop in for a snack at Eclipse di Luna (✉ Miami Circle, ☎ 404/846–0449).

Stone Mountain Village (✉ Main St., Stone Mountain, ☎ 770/879–4971 visitor center) is a 19th-century village beside a railroad track at the foot of Stone Mountain (☞ Other Area Attractions, *above*). Storefronts are exquisitely decorated at holiday time. Shops of note include Stone Mountain Handbags Factory Store (☎ 770/498–1316) and the Stone Mountain General Store (☎ 770/469–9331). The village is 17 mi from downtown. For a quick snack, have a coffee milk shake at Continental Park Café (✉ 941 Main St., ☎ 770/413–6448).

2300 Peachtree Road, one of Buckhead's most stylish complexes, has more than 25 antiques shops, art galleries, and enough home furnishing stores to fill multiple mansions.

Virginia-Highland is one of the city's gentrified areas, full of art galleries, restaurants, fashionable boutiques, antiques shops, and bookstores. Atlanta designer Bill Hallman (✉ 792 N. Highland Ave., ☎ 404/876–6055) showcases his own designs at his eponymous boutique. There's a wide array of memorabilia from 20th Century Antiques (✉ 1044 N. Highland Ave., ☎ 404/892–2065).

ART GALLERIES

The city bursts with art galleries, some well established, others new, some conservative, others cutting edge. For more information on the Atlanta art gallery scene, including openings and location maps, consult ***Museums & Galleries*** (☎ 770/992–7808), a magazine distributed free at welcome centers and select area galleries. **Fay Gold Gallery** (✉ 247 Buckhead Ave., East Village Sq., ☎ 404/233–3843) displays works by nationally renowned contemporary artists. **Jackson Fine Art Gallery**

(✉ 3115 E. Shadowlawn Ave., ☎ 404/233–3739) exhibits fine art photography. **Modern Primitive** (✉ 1393 N. Highland Ave., Virginia-Highland, ☎ 404/892–0556) has a fascinating assembly of folk and visionary art from around the state and the region. **Ray's Indian Originals** (✉ 90 N. Avondale Rd., Avondale Estates, ☎ 404/292–4999) shows exquisite original work by Native American artists. **Vespermann Gallery** (✉ 2140 Peachtree Rd., Brookwood Sq., ☎ 404/350–9698) has lovely handblown glass objects.

BOOKS

Chapter 11 (✉ 6237 Roswell Rd., ☎ 404/256–5518) is a great place to find recently published titles at good prices. **Yesteryear** (✉ 3201 Maple Dr., ☎ 404/237–0163) is the destination of choice for antiquarians. Its strengths include military history, Georgiana, and old cookbooks.

FOOD

DeKalb Farmers Market (✉ 3000 E. Ponce de Leon Ave., Decatur, ☎ 404/377–6400) has 175,000 square ft of exotic fruits, cheeses, seafood, sausages, breads, and delicacies from around the world. **East 48th St. Market** (✉ 2462 Jett Ferry Rd., at Mt. Vernon Rd., Williams at Dunwoody Shopping Center, ☎ 770/392–1499) sells Italian deli meats, fabulous breads, cheeses, and Italian prepared foods. Shop at **Eatzi's Market & Bakery** (✉ 3221 Peachtree Rd., ☎ 404/237–2266) for prepared foods, imported cheeses, great breads, and fine wines. **Harry's Farmers Markets** (✉ 1180 Upper Hembree Rd., Roswell, ☎ 770/664–6300; 2025 Satellite Pointe, Duluth, ☎ 770/416–6900; 70 Powers Ferry Rd., Marietta, ☎ 770/578–4400) consists of three markets north of the city, spun off from the original (☞ DeKalb Farmers Market, *above*) by the owner's brother; they sell quality fish, cheese, wine, produce, ethnic foods, meats, and deli items. To grab a quick picnic basket before a concert, find one of several **Harry's in a Hurry** shops (three locations are ✉ 1061 Ponce de Leon Ave., ☎ 404/439–1100; 1875 Peachtree St., ☎ 404/352–7800; and 2804 Roswell Rd., ☎ 404/266–0800). Homesick Parisians take comfort at **Paris Market** (✉ 1833 Peachtree Rd., ☎ 404/351–4212), with fresh pâté, imported cheese and wine, and great bread. For health food, go to **Whole Foods Market** (✉ 2111 Briarcliff Rd., at LaVista Rd., ☎ 404/634–7800).

Atlanta A to Z

Arriving and Departing

BY BUS

Greyhound Bus Lines (✉ 232 Forsyth St., ☎ 404/584–1731 or 800/231–2222) provides transportation to downtown Atlanta.

Amtrak (✉ 1688 Peachtree St., ☎ 404/881–3060 or 800/872–7245) operates its Thru-Way bus service daily from Birmingham and Mobile, Alabama, to Atlanta's Brookwood station. Another bus goes daily from the station to Macon.

BY CAR

The city is encircled by I–285. Three interstates—I–85, running northeast–southwest from Virginia to Alabama; I–75, north–south from Michigan to Florida; and I–20, east–west from South Carolina to Texas—also crisscross Atlanta.

BY PLANE

Hartsfield Atlanta International Airport (✉ 6000 N. Terminal Pkwy, ☎ 404/530–6600), 13 mi south of downtown, is served by Atlantic Southeast Airlines, America West, American, Continental, Delta, GP Express, Markair, Midwest Express, National, Northwest, TWA,

United, and US Airways, as well as many international carriers (☞ Air Travel *in* Smart Travel Tips A to Z for airline telephone numbers).

Atlanta Airport Shuttle (☎ 404/766–5312) operates vans every half hour between 7 AM and 11 PM daily. The downtown trip, $12 one-way, $20 round-trip, takes about 20 minutes and stops at major hotels. Vans also go to Emory University and the Lenox area; $18 one-way, $28 round-trip.

If your luggage is light, take **MARTA** (Metropolitan Atlanta Rapid Transit Authority; ☎ 404/848–4711) high-speed trains between the airport and downtown and other locations. Trains operate 5 AM–1 AM weekdays and 6 AM–12:30 AM weekends. The trip downtown takes about 15 minutes to the Five Points station, and the fare is $1.50.

From the airport to downtown, the **taxi** fare is $20 for one person, $22 for two, and $25 for three or more, including tax. From the airport to Buckhead, the fare is $30 for one and $32 for two or more. With a reasonable advance reservation, **Carey-Executive Limousine** (☎ 404/223–2000) will provide 24-hour service. **Buckhead Safety Cab** (☎ 404/233–1152) and **Checker Cab** (☎ 404/351–1111) offer 24-hour service.

BY TRAIN

Amtrak (✉ 1688 Peachtree St., ☎ 404/881–3060 or 800/872–7245) operates the *Crescent* train, with daily service to Atlanta's Brookwood station from New York; Philadelphia; Washington, D.C.; Baltimore; Charlotte; and Greenville. It also goes daily from New Orleans to New York through Atlanta.

Getting Around

BY BUS

The **Metropolitan Atlanta Rapid Transit Authority** (MARTA; ☎ 404/848–4711), with a fleet of 667 buses, operates 150 routes covering 1,500 mi. The fare is $1.50, and exact change is required. Weekly and monthly TransCards give you a slight discount. Service is very limited outside the perimeter set by I–285, except for a few areas in Clayton, DeKalb, and Fulton counties.

BY CAR

Some refer to Atlanta as the Los Angeles of the South, because driving is virtually the only way to get to most parts of the city. Although the congestion isn't comparable to that in Los Angeles yet, Atlantans have grown accustomed to frequent delays at rush hour. Beware: The South as a whole may be laid back, but Atlanta drivers are not; they tend to drive faster than drivers in other Southern cities. Drive with vigilance.

BY SUBWAY

MARTA (☎ 404/848–4711) has clean and safe rapid-rail subway trains with somewhat limited routes that link downtown with many major landmarks. The rail system's two main lines cross at the Five Points station downtown. Trains run 5 AM–1 AM, and large parking lots (free) are at most stations beyond downtown. Tokens ($1.50 each) can be bought from machines outside the station entrance. TransCards and information on public transportation are available at Rides Stores, open weekdays 7–7 and Saturday 8:30–5; Rides Stores are at the airport, the Five Points station, the headquarters building by the Lindbergh station, and the Lenox station. You can also buy TransCards at Kroger and Publix grocery stores. Free transfers, needed for some bus routes, are available by pressing a button on the subway turnstile or requesting one from the bus driver.

BY TAXI

Taxi service in Atlanta can be a mixed experience. Drivers often do not have correct change even for a small bill, so be prepared either to charge your fare (many accept credit cards) or insist that the driver obtain change. Drivers also appear as befuddled as visitors by Atlanta's notoriously winding and hilly streets, so if your destination is something other than a major hotel or popular sight, come armed with directions.

Taxi fares start at $1.60 for the first mile, with 20¢ for each additional ⅐ mile, 50¢ per extra passenger, and $12 per hour waiting time. Each additional person is charged another $1. Within the Downtown Convention Zone a flat rate of $5 for one person or $1 for each additional passenger will be charged for any destination. **Buckhead Safety Cab** (☎ 404/233–1152) and **Checker Cab** (☎ 404/351–1111) offer 24-hour service.

Contacts and Resources

B&B RESERVATIONS

Great Inns of Georgia (✉ 541 Londonberry Rd., 30327, ☎ 404/843–0471 or 800/501–7328, FAX 404/252–8886) can provide brochures on inns in Atlanta.

EMERGENCIES

Emergency assistance (☎ 911). For **24-hour emergency rooms,** contact **Georgia Baptist Medical Center** (✉ 303 Parkway Dr., ☎ 404/265–4000), **Grady Memorial Hospital** (✉ 80 Butler St., ☎ 404/616–4307), **Northside Hospital** (✉ 1000 Johnson Ferry Rd., ☎ 404/851–8000), and **Piedmont Hospital** (✉ 1968 Peachtree Rd., ☎ 404/605–5000).

GUIDED TOURS

The **Atlanta Preservation Center** (✉ 156 7th St., Suite 3, ☎ 404/876–2041, 404/876–2040 tour hot line) offers 10 walking tours of historic areas and neighborhoods for $5 each. Especially noteworthy are tours of Sweet Auburn, the neighborhood associated with Martin Luther King Jr. and other leaders in Atlanta's African-American community; Druid Hills, the verdant, genteel neighborhood where *Driving Miss Daisy* was filmed; and the Fox Theatre, the elaborate 1920s picture palace.

Gray Line of Atlanta (✉ 705 Lively Ave., Norcross 30071, ☎ 770/449–1806 or 800/593–1818, FAX 770/249–9397) has tours of downtown, Midtown, Buckhead, and the King Center. Stone Mountain may be included on some tours.

RADIO STATIONS

AM: WGST 640, news/talk; WSB 750, news/talk; WQXI 790, sports/talk. **FM:** WABE 90.1, National Public Radio/classical; WCLK 91.9, jazz/soul; WZGC 92.9, classic rock; WPCH 94.9, light rock; WNNX 99.7, modern rock; WKHX 101.5, country; WVEE 103.3, urban contemporary.

24-HOUR PHARMACIES

CVS (✉ 1943 Peachtree Rd., ☎ 404/351–7629; 1554 North Decatur Rd., ☎ 404/373–4192; 2350 Cheshire Bridge Rd., ☎ 404/486–7289).

VISITOR INFORMATION

The **Atlanta Convention & Visitors Bureau** (ACVB; ✉ 233 Peachtree St., Suite 2000, 30303, ☎ 404/222–6688 or 800/285–2682, FAX 404/584–6331) has information on Atlanta only. The ACVB has several visitor information centers in Atlanta: Hartsfield Atlanta International Airport, in north terminal at west crossover; Underground Atlanta (✉ 65 Upper Alabama St.); Georgia World Congress Center (✉ 285 International Blvd.); and Lenox Square mall (✉ 3393 Peachtree Rd.). Write to the **Georgia Department of Industry, Trade, and Tourism** (✉ Box 1776, 30301, ☎ 404/656–3590 or 800/847–4842, FAX 404/651–9063).

SAVANNAH

The very sound of the name Savannah conjures up misty images of mint juleps, handsome mansions, and a somewhat decadent city moving at a lazy Southern pace. It's hard even to say "Savannah" without drawling. Well, brace yourself. The mint juleps are there all right, along with the moss and the mansions and the easygoing pace, but this Southern belle rings with surprises. Take, for example, St. Patrick's Day: Savannah has a St. Patrick's Day celebration second only to New York's. The greening of Savannah began more than 164 years ago and everybody in town talks a blue (green) streak about St. Patrick's Day. Everything turns green on March 17, including the faces of startled visitors when green scrambled eggs and green grits are put before them.

Savannah's beginning was February 12, 1733, when English general James Edward Oglethorpe and 120 colonists arrived at Yamacraw Bluff on the Savannah River to found the 13th and last colony in the New World. As the port city grew, people from England and Ireland, Scottish Highlanders, French Huguenots, Germans, Austrian Salzburgers, Sephardic and Ashkenazic Jews, Moravians, Italians, Swiss, Welsh, and Greeks all arrived to create what could be called a rich gumbo.

In 1793 Eli Whitney of Connecticut, who was tutoring on a plantation near Savannah, invented a mechanized means of "ginning" seeds from cotton bolls. Cotton soon became king, and Savannah, already a busy seaport, flourished under its reign. Waterfront warehouses were filled with "white gold," and brokers trading in the Savannah Cotton Exchange set world prices. The white gold brought in solid gold, and fine mansions were built in the prospering city.

In 1864 Savannahians surrendered their city to Union general Sherman rather than see it torched. Following World War I and the decline of the cotton market, the city's economy virtually collapsed, and its historic buildings languished for more than 30 years. Elegant mansions were razed or allowed to decay, and cobwebs replaced cotton in the dilapidated riverfront warehouses.

In 1955, Savannah's spirits rose again. News that the exquisite Isaiah Davenport House (⊠ 324 E. State St.) was to be destroyed prompted seven outraged ladies to raise money to buy the house. They saved it the day before the wrecking ball was to swing. Thus was born the Historic Savannah Foundation, the organization responsible for the restoration of downtown Savannah, where more than 1,000 restored buildings form the 2½-square-mi Historic District, the nation's largest. Many of these buildings are open to the public during the annual tour of homes, and today Savannah is one of the country's top 10 cities for walking tours.

John Berendt's wildly popular *Midnight in the Garden of Good and Evil,* published in 1994, has lured many new visitors to Savannah. A nonfiction account of a notorious 1980s shooting, the book brings to life such Savannah sites as Monterey Square, Mercer House, and Bonaventure Cemetery. Clint Eastwood's 1997 film version was not a box-office hit, but visitor interest in Savannah has remained intense, to the consternation of old-timers who find the story's characters less than savory and the nosy Northerners a nuisance. Other Savannahians have rolled out the welcome mat, while still others have hiked prices, profiting from the tourist dollars.

Georgia's founder, General James Oglethorpe, designed the original town of Savannah and laid it out in a perfect grid. The Historic District is neatly hemmed in by the Savannah River, Gaston Street, East Street, and Martin Luther King Jr. Boulevard. Streets are arrow-straight, public squares of varying sizes are tucked into the grid at precise intervals, and each block is sliced in half by narrow, often unpaved streets. Bull Street, anchored on the north by City Hall and the south by Forsyth Park, charges down the center of the grid and lunges around the five public squares that stand in its way.

Numbers in the text correspond to numbers in the margin and on the Savannah Historic District map.

The Historic District

A Good Walk and Drive

You can cover Historic Savannah on foot, but to save time and energy, you might want to drive part of this tour. Start at the **Savannah Visitors Center** ⑥⓪, on Martin Luther King Jr. Boulevard. In the same building, the **Savannah History Museum** ⑥① is an ideal introduction to the city's history. There is public parking next to the center and museum.

Exit the parking lot and turn left (north), walking or driving two short and one very long blocks on Martin Luther King Jr. Boulevard to the **Scarborough House** ⑥②, which contains the Ships of the Sea Museum. Cross Martin Luther King Jr. Boulevard and continue two blocks east on West Congress Street, past Franklin Square to **City Market** ⑥③. Skirting around Franklin Square north on Montgomery Street, go two blocks to West Bay Street and turn right.

From this point, continue east on West Bay Street four blocks to Bull Street. On your left, you'll see **City Hall** ⑥④. Continue east down West Bay Street (which now becomes East Bay Street) to **Factors Walk** ⑥⑤, which lies south of River Street and the Savannah River. If you're driving, leave your car here to continue on foot (be sure to park in long-term parking, as the short-term meters are carefully watched and tickets dispensed expeditiously). Step down from Factors Walk toward the river and visit **Riverfront Plaza** ⑥⑥, which is best seen on foot.

At this point, if you're driving, you'll probably want to get back in your car to continue the tour. Return to East Bay Street and head west two long blocks back to Bull Street. Walk or drive four blocks south on Bull Street to **Wright Square** ⑥⑦; then turn right (west) and go two blocks to Telfair Square, where you can stop at the **Telfair Mansion and Art Museum** ⑥⑧. Stroll around Telfair Square and then continue east on West York Street back toward Wright Square, and turn right on Bull Street, heading two blocks south to the **Juliette Gordon Low Birthplace/Girl Scout National Center** ⑥⑨. Two more short blocks south from the Low House on Bull Street, and you'll reach **Chippewa Square** ⑦⓪. Continue south on Bull Street to the Gothic Revival **Green-Meldrim House** ⑦①. Next, walk four blocks south on Bull Street to **Monterey Square** ⑦②. Proceed two blocks farther south from Monterey Square to **Forsyth Park** ⑦③, the divide between East and West Gaston streets.

From the park, walk east on East Gaston Street and go one block to Abercorn Street; then turn left (north) on Abercorn, to Calhoun Square, and note the **Wesley Monumental Church** ⑦④. Continue north on Abercorn four blocks to Lafayette Square and view the **Andrew Low House** ⑦⑤. Northeast of Lafayette Square looms the **Cathedral of St. John the Baptist** ⑦⑥ on East Harris Street. Two blocks north at the intersection of Abercorn and East Oglethorpe streets is the huge **Colonial Park Cemetery** ⑦⑦. Proceeding two blocks north on Abercorn from the cemetery takes you to Oglethorpe Square; across from the square is the **Owens-Thomas House and Museum** ⑦⑧. From the house, walk east on East President Street two blocks to Columbia Square. Northwest of the square

Andrew Low House . . 75
Armstrong House 82
Bonaventure Cemetery 89
Cathedral of St. John the Baptist 76
Chatham County Courthouse 88
Chippewa Square . . . 70
City Hall 64
City Market 63
Colonial Park Cemetery 77
Emmet Park 80
Factors Walk 65
Forsyth Park 73
Forsyth Park Apartments 83
Green-Meldrim House 71
Hamilton-Turner House 87
Isaiah Davenport House 79
Joe Odom's First House 86
Juliette Gordon Low Birthplace/Girl Scout National Center 69
Lee Adler's Home 85
Mercer House 81
Monterey Square 72
Owens Thomas House and Museum 78
Riverfront Plaza 66
Savannah History Museum 61
Savannah Visitors Center 60
Scarborough House . . 62
Serena Dawes's House 84
Telfair Mansion and Art Museum 68
Wesley Monumental Church 74
Wright Square 67

on East State Street stands the **Isaiah Davenport House** ⑲. From here, continue north up Habersham Street to **Emmet Park** ⑳, a splendid park to relax in at the end of your tour.

TIMING

This is a long but comfortable walk, as Savannah has no taxing hills. Allow a full day to see everything along this route, especially if you plan to read all the historic markers and explore the sights thoroughly, stopping for tours. Driving around the squares can be slow—but you can drive the entire route in two hours, a pace that allows for some stopping along the way. Allow extra time if you want to linger in Riverfront Plaza for a half hour or so.

Sights to See

75 **Andrew Low House.** This residence was built in 1848 for Andrew Low, a native of Scotland and one of Savannah's merchant princes. The home later belonged to his son William, who married Juliette Gordon. After her husband's death, she founded the Girl Scouts in this house

on March 12, 1912. The house has 19th-century antiques, stunning silver, and some of the finest ornamental ironwork in Savannah. ✉ *329 Abercorn St.,* ☎ *912/233–6854.* *$7.* ⏲ *Mon.–Sat. 10:30–4, Sun. noon–4; last tour at 3:30.*

Beach Institute African-American Cultural Center. It's in the building that housed the first school for African-American children in Savannah, established after emancipation (1867). The center exhibits work by African-American artists from the Savannah area and around the country. ✉ *502 E. Harris St.,* ☎ *912/234–8000.* *$3.50.* ⏲ *Tues.–Sat. noon–5.*

76 **Cathedral of St. John the Baptist.** Soaring over the city, the French Gothic–style cathedral, with pointed arches and free-flowing traceries, is the seat of the Diocese of Savannah. It was founded in 1799 by the first French colonists to arrive in Savannah. Fire destroyed the early structures; the present cathedral dates from 1874. Most of the cathedral's impressive stained-glass windows were made by Austrian glassmakers and imported around the turn of the 20th century. The high altar is of Italian marble, and the stations of the cross were imported from Munich. ✉ *222 E. Harris St.,* ☎ *912/233–4709.* ⏲ *Daily 9–5.*

70 **Chippewa Square.** Daniel Chester French's imposing bronze statue of General James Edward Oglethorpe, founder of Savannah and Georgia, anchors the square. Also note the **Savannah Theatre** on Bull Street, which claims to be the oldest continuously operated theater site in North America. ✉ *Bull St. between Hull and Perry Sts.*

64 **City Hall.** Built in 1905 on the site of the Old City Exchange (1799–1904), this imposing structure anchors Bay Street. Notice the bench commemorating Oglethorpe's landing on February 12, 1733. ✉ *1 Bay St.,* ☎ *912/651–6444.* ⏲ *Weekdays 8:15–5.*

63 **City Market.** This popular pedestrian-only area encompasses galleries, nightclubs, restaurants, and shops. ✉ *Between Franklin Sq. and Johnson Sq. on W. St. Julian St.*

★ 77 **Colonial Park Cemetery.** The park is the final resting place for Savannahians who died between 1750 and 1853. You may want to stroll the shaded pathways and read some of the old tombstone inscriptions. There are several historical plaques, one of which marks the grave of Button Gwinnett, a signer of the Declaration of Independence. ✉ *Oglethorpe and Abercorn Sts.*

Columbia Square. When Savannah was a walled city (1757–1790), Bethesda Gate (one of six) was here. The square was laid out in 1799. ✉ *Habersham St. between E. State and E. York Sts.*

80 **Emmet Park.** The lovely tree-shaded park is named for Robert Emmet, a late-18th-century Irish patriot and orator. ✉ *Borders Bay St.*

65 **Factors Walk.** A network of iron walkways connects Bay Street with the multistory buildings that rise up from the river level, and iron stairways descend from Bay Street to Factors Walk. Cobblestone ramps lead pedestrians down to River Street. (These are serious cobblestones, so wear comfortable shoes.)

73 **Forsyth Park.** The park forms the southern border of Bull Street. On its 20 acres it has a glorious white fountain dating from 1858, Confederate and Spanish-American War memorials, and the Fragrant Garden for the Blind, a project of Savannah garden clubs. There are tennis courts and a tree-shaded jogging path. Outdoor plays and concerts often take place here. At the northwest corner of the park, in **Hodgson Hall,** a 19th-century Italianate–Greek Revival building, you'll find the **Geor-**

gia Historical Society, which shows selections from its collection of artifacts and manuscripts. ✉ *501 Whitaker St.*, ☎ *912/651–2128.* ⏲ *Tues.–Sat. 10–5.*

★ 71 **Green-Meldrim House.** Designed by New York architect John Norris and built in 1850 for cotton merchant Charles Green, this Gothic Revival mansion cost $90,000 to build—a princely sum back then. The house was bought in 1892 by Judge Peter Meldrim, whose heirs sold it to **St. John's Episcopal Church** to use as a parish house. General Sherman lived here after taking the city in 1864. Sitting on **Madison Square** (☞ *below*), the house has such Gothic features as a crenellated roof, oriels, and an external gallery with filigree ironwork. Inside are mantels of Carrara marble, carved black-walnut woodwork, and doorknobs and hinges of either silver plate or porcelain. The house is furnished with donated 16th-, 17th-, and 18th-century antiques, although some original pieces have been reacquired. ✉ *1 W. Macon St.*, ☎ *912/233–3845.* 🎟 *$5.* ⏲ *Tues., Thurs., and Fri. 10–4; Sat. 10–4. Closed last 2 wks of Jan. and 2 wks before Easter.*

★ 79 **Isaiah Davenport House.** The proposed demolition of this historic Savannah structure galvanized the city's residents into action to save their treasured buildings. Semicircular stairs with wrought-iron trim lead to the recessed doorway of the redbrick Federal mansion that master builder Isaiah Davenport built for himself between 1815 and 1820. Three dormered windows poke through the sloping roof of the stately house, and the interior has polished hardwood floors, fine woodwork and plasterwork, and a soaring elliptical staircase. Furnishings, from the 1820s, are Hepplewhite, Chippendale, and Sheraton. ✉ *324 E. State St.*, ☎ *912/236–8097.* 🎟 *$6.* ⏲ *Mon.–Sat. 10–4, Sun. 1–4.*

Johnson Square. The oldest of James Oglethorpe's original 24 squares was laid out in 1733 and named for South Carolina governor Robert Johnson. A monument marks the grave of Nathanael Greene, a hero of the Revolutionary War. The square was once a popular gathering place: Savannahians came here to welcome President Monroe in 1819, to greet the Marquis de Lafayette in 1825, and to cheer for Georgia's secession in 1861. ✉ *Bull St. between Bryan and Congress Sts.*

69 **Juliette Gordon Low Birthplace/Girl Scout National Center.** This majestic Regency town house, attributed to William Jay (built 1818–1821), was designated in 1965 as Savannah's first National Historic Landmark. "Daisy" Low, founder of the Girl Scouts, was born here in 1860, and the house is now owned and operated by the Girl Scouts of America. Mrs. Low's paintings and other artwork are on display in the house, restored to the style of 1886, the year of Mrs. Low's marriage. ✉ *142 Bull St.*, ☎ *912/233–4501.* 🎟 *$6.* ⏲ *Mon.–Tues. and Thurs.–Sat. 10–4, Sun. 12:30–4:30.*

OFF THE BEATEN PATH

KING-TISDELL COTTAGE – Tucked behind a picket fence is this museum dedicated to the preservation of African-American history and culture. The Negro Heritage Trail Tour (☞ Beach Institute *in* Savannah A to Z, *below*) visits this little Victorian house. Broad steps lead to a porch, and dormered windows pop up through a steep roof. The interior is furnished to resemble a middle-class African-American coastal home of the 1890s. To reach the cottage by car, go east on East Bay Street to Price Street, and turn south (right) on this street; continue for about 30 blocks to East Huntington Street, and take a left (east). The building is in the middle of the block. ✉ *514 E. Huntington St.*, ☎ *912/234–8000.* 🎟 *$3.* ⏲ *By appointment only.*

Lafayette Square. Named for the Marquis de Lafayette, the square contains a graceful three-tier fountain donated by the Georgia chapter of the Colonial Dames of America. ✉ *Abercorn St. between E. Harris and E. Charlton Sts.*

Madison Square. A statue on the square, laid out in 1839 and named for President James Madison, depicts Sergeant William Jasper hoisting a flag and is a tribute to his bravery during the Siege of Savannah. Though mortally wounded, Jasper rescued the colors of his regiment in the assault on the British lines. ✉ *Bull St. between W. Harris and W. Charlton Sts.*

72 **Monterey Square.** Commemorating the victory of General Zachary Taylor's forces in Monterrey, Mexico, in 1846, this is the fifth and southernmost of Bull Street's squares. A monument honors General Casimir Pulaski, the Polish nobleman who lost his life in the Siege of Savannah during the Revolutionary War. Also on the square is **Temple Mickve Israel** (☞ *below*). ✉ *Bull St. between Taylor and Gordon Sts.*

★ 78 **Owens-Thomas House and Museum.** English architect William Jay's first Regency mansion in Savannah is the city's finest example of that architectural style. Built in 1816–1819, the English house was constructed mostly with local materials. Of particular note are the curving walls of the house, Greek-inspired ornamental molding, half-moon arches, stained-glass panels, and Duncan Phyfe furniture. In 1825, the Marquis de Lafayette bade a two-hour au revoir from a wrought-iron balcony to a crowd below. ✉ *124 Abercorn St.,* ☎ *912/233–9743.* *$8.* ⏲ *Mon. noon–5, Tues.–Sat. 10–5, Sun. 2–5.*

OFF THE BEATEN PATH

RALPH MARK GILBERT CIVIL RIGHTS MUSEUM – In Savannah's Historic District, this history museum has a series of 15 exhibits on segregation, from emancipation through the civil rights movement. The role of black and white Savannahians in ending segregation in their city is detailed in these exhibits, largely derived from archival photographs. The museum also has touring exhibits. ✉ *460 Martin Luther King Jr. Blvd.,* ☎ *912/231–8900,* FAX *912/234–2577.* *$4.* ⏲ *Mon.–Sat. 9–5.*

Reynolds Square. John Wesley, who preached in Savannah and wrote the first English hymnal in Savannah in 1736, is remembered here. A monument to the founder of the Methodist Church is shaded by greenery and surrounded by park benches. The **Olde Pink House** (✉ 23 Abercorn St.), built in 1771, is one of the oldest buildings in town. Now a restaurant (☞ Dining, *below*), the porticoed pink-stucco Georgian mansion has been a private home, a bank, and headquarters for a Yankee general during the Civil War. ✉ *Abercorn St. between E. Bryant and E. Congress Sts.*

66 **Riverfront Plaza.** Here you can watch a parade of freighters and pugnose tugs; youngsters can play in the tugboat-shape sandboxes. River Street is the main venue for many of the city's celebrations, including the First Saturday festivals when flea marketeers, artists, and artisans display their wares and musicians entertain the crowds.

61 **Savannah History Museum.** In a restored railway station, the museum is an excellent introduction to the city. Exhibits range from old locomotives to a tribute to Savannah-born songwriter Johnny Mercer. Situated on top of the **site of the Siege of Savannah,** it marks the spot where in 1779 the colonial forces, led by Polish count Casimir Pulaski, laid siege to Savannah in an attempt to retake the city from the Redcoats. They were beaten back, and Pulaski was killed while leading a cavalry charge against the British. The dead lie underneath the building. ✉ *303*

Martin Luther King Jr. Blvd., ☎ *912/238–1779.* 🎫 *$3.* ⏲ *Weekdays 8:30–5, weekends 9–5.*

60 **Savannah Visitors Center.** Come here for free maps and brochures, friendly advice, and an audiovisual overview of the city. The starting point for a number of guided tours, the center is in a big 1860 red-brick building with high ceilings and sweeping arches. It was the old Central of Georgia railway station. The parking lot is a good spot to leave your car while you explore the nearby Historic District. ⊠ *301 Martin Luther King Jr. Blvd.,* ☎ *912/944–0455.* ⏲ *Weekdays 8:30–5, weekends 9–5.*

62 **Scarborough House.** This exuberant Greek Revival mansion, built during the 1819 cotton boom for Savannah merchant prince William Scarborough, was designed by English architect William Jay. Scarborough was a major investor in the steamship *Savannah.* The house has a Doric portico capped by one of Jay's characteristic half-moon windows. Four massive Doric columns form a peristyle in the atrium entrance hall. Inside is the **Ships of the Sea Museum,** with displays of ship models, including steamships, a nuclear-powered ship (the *Savannah*), China clippers with their sails unfurled, and Columbus's vessels. ⊠ *41 Martin Luther King Jr. Blvd.,* ☎ *912/232–1511.* 🎫 *$5.* ⏲ *Tues.–Sun. 10–5.*

68 **Telfair Mansion and Art Museum.** The oldest public art museum in the Southeast was designed by William Jay in 1819 for Alexander Telfair and sits across the street from **Telfair Square.** Within its marble rooms are American, French, and Dutch Impressionist paintings; German tonalist paintings; a large collection of works by Kahlil Gibran; plaster casts of the Elgin Marbles, the Venus de Milo, and the Laocoön, among other classical sculptures; and some of the Telfair family furnishings, including a Duncan Phyfe sideboard and Savannah-made silver. ⊠ *121 Barnard St.,* ☎ *912/232–1177.* 🎫 *$6; free Sun.* ⏲ *Mon. noon–5, Tues.–Sat. 10–5, Sun. 1–5.*

Temple Mickve Israel. A Gothic Revival synagogue on Monterey Square is home to the third-oldest Jewish congregation in the United States; its founding members settled in town five months after the establishment of Savannah in 1733. The synagogue's collection includes documents and letters (some from George Washington, James Madison, and Thomas Jefferson) pertaining to early Jewish life in Savannah and Georgia. ⊠ *20 E. Gordon St.,* ☎ *912/233–1547.* ⏲ *Weekdays 10–noon and 2–4.*

74 **Wesley Monumental Church.** This Gothic Revival–style church memorializing the founders of Methodism is patterned after Queen's Kirk in Amsterdam. Noted for its magnificent stained-glass windows, the church celebrated a century of service in 1968. ⊠ *429 Abercorn St.,* ☎ *912/232–0191.* ⏲ *By appointment only.*

67 **Wright Square.** Named for James Wright, Georgia's last colonial governor, the square has an elaborate monument in its center that honors William Washington Gordon, founder of the Central of Georgia Railroad. A slab of granite from Stone Mountain (☞ *above*) adorns the grave of Tomo-Chi-Chi, the Yamacraw chief who befriended General Oglethorpe and the colonists. ⊠ *Bull St. between W. State and W. York Sts.*

Midnight in the Garden of Good and Evil

Town gossips can give you the best introduction to a city, and as author John Berendt discovered, Savannah's not short on them. In his 1994 best-seller, *Midnight in the Garden of Good and Evil,* Berendt shares the juiciest of tales imparted to him during the eight years he spent here wining and dining with Savannah's high society and dancing with her Grand Empress, drag queen the Lady Chablis, among others. By the time he left, there had been a scandalous homicide and several trials: The wealthy Jim Williams was accused of killing his assistant, Danny Hansford.

Before you set out, find a copy of the book, pour yourself a cool drink, and enter an eccentric world of cutthroat killers and society backstabbers, voodoo witches, and garden-club ladies. Then, slip on a pair of comfortable shoes and head over to the Historic District to follow the characters' steps to their homes and haunts. By the end of this walking tour, you'll be hard-pressed to find the line between Berendt's creative nonfiction and Savannah's reality. Note: Unless otherwise indicated, the sights on this tour are not open to the public.

A Good Walk and Drive

Begin at the southwest corner of Monterey Square, site of the **Mercer House** ⑧①, whose construction was begun by songwriter Johnny Mercer's great-grandfather just before the Civil War. Two blocks south on Bull Street is the **Armstrong House** ⑧②, an earlier residence of Jim Williams, the main character in the book. Walk south through Forsyth Park to the corner of Park Avenue and Whitaker streets (or, if driving, turn right on East Gaston to West Gaston Street, then left onto Whitaker). The **Forsyth Park Apartments** ⑧③, where author John Berendt lived, are on the southwest corner of Forsyth Park. Then, if you're walking, turn back north through the park (if driving, turn left onto Park Avenue, left onto Drayton Street at the park's southeast corner, then left again onto East Gaston Street). At the midpoint of the park's northern edge, turn north up Bull Street in the direction of Monterey Square. Turn left on West Gordon Street off Bull Street and walk toward the corner of West Gordon Street and Whitaker Street, where you'll reach **Serena Dawes's House** ⑧④. Next, cross West Gordon Street, walk north on Bull Street in front of Mercer House, cross Wayne Street, and the first house on the left facing Bull Street at Wayne Street is **Lee Adler's Home** ⑧⑤, which sits across from Monterey Square's northwest corner. (If you're driving, proceed around Monterey Square to West Taylor Street, and at its intersection with Whitaker Street, take a left and go two blocks to West Gordon Street. Take a left onto West Gordon Street; the house is on the left.)

Continue walking north on Bull Street and take a right (east) on East Jones Street. **Joe Odom's first house** ⑧⑥ is the third house on the left before Drayton Street. (If you're driving, go around the square again onto Bull Street, and go north on Bull Street to East Jones Street. Take a right, and the house will be on the left.)

Continue on East Jones Street to Abercorn Street and turn left (north), walking two blocks on Abercorn Street to East Charlton Street and the **Hamilton-Turner House** ⑧⑦, now a bed-and-breakfast inn. Then, swing around Lafayette Square to East Harris Street, and take it about six blocks west to Pulaski Square at Barnard Street; turn right (north) on Barnard Street through Orleans Square and continue north to Telfair Square. On foot, you may elect to head west down West York Street on the south side of Telfair Square to find the **Chatham County Courthouse** ⑧⑧, scene of all those trials, two blocks away. Drivers will have to continue around the square to take a left (west) onto West State Street, two blocks from the courthouse. Finally, take either Whitaker Street or Abercorn Street south to Victory Drive and turn left. Go through Thunderbolt to Whatley Avenue, and turn left again. Whatley Avenue leads directly to Bonaventure Road, which curves in both directions;

bear left, and on your right about a quarter mile up the road is **Bonaventure Cemetery** (89).

TIMING

Allow a leisurely two hours to walk the main points of the tour, plus another hour to visit the cemetery. If driving, you'll easily complete the tour in an hour, but remember to add time to meander around Bonaventure Cemetery.

Sights to See

(82) **Armstrong House.** Antiques dealer Jim Williams lived and worked in this residence before purchasing the Mercer House. On a late-afternoon walk past the mansion, Berendt met Mr. Simon Glover, an 86-year-old singer and porter for the law firm of Bouhan, Williams, and Levy, occupants of the building. Glover confided that he earned a weekly $10 for walking one of the firm's former partner's deceased dogs up and down Bull Street. Baffled? So was the author. Behind the house's cast-iron gates are the offices of Frank Siler, Jim Williams's attorney, who doubles as keeper of Uga, the Georgia Bulldog mascot. ✉ *447 Bull St.*

(89) **Bonaventure Cemetery.** A cemetery east of downtown is the final resting place for Danny Hansford. The haunting female tombstone figure from the book's cover has been removed to protect surrounding graves from sightseers. Now you can view the figure at the Telfair Mansion (☞ The Historic District, *above*). ✉ *330 Bonaventure Rd.,* ☎ *912/651–6843.*

(88) **Chatham County Courthouse.** The courthouse was the scene of three of Williams's murder trials, which took place over the course of about eight years. An underground tunnel leads from the courthouse to the jail where Williams was held in a cell that was modified to allow him to conduct his antiques business. ✉ *133 Montgomery St.*

(83) **Forsyth Park Apartments.** Here was Berendt's second home in Savannah; from his fourth-floor rooms he pieced together the majority of the book. While parking his newly acquired 1973 Pontiac Grand Prix outside these apartments, Berendt met the Lady Chablis coming out of her nearby doctor's office, freshly feminine from a new round of hormone shots. ✉ *Whitaker and Gwinnett Sts.*

(87) **Hamilton-Turner House.** After one too many of Joe Odom's deals went sour, Mandy Nichols, his fourth fiancée-in-waiting, left him and took over his third residence, a Second Empire–style mansion dating from 1873. Mandy filled it with 17th- and 18th-century antiques and transformed it into a successful museum through which she led tour groups. The elegant towering hulk is at the southeast corner of Lafayette Square. Hillis sold the house in 1997, and the new owners turned it into a bed-and-breakfast inn (☞ Hamilton-Turner Inn *in* Lodging, *below*). ✉ *330 Abercorn St.*

(86) **Joe Odom's First House.** At this stucco town house, Odom, a combination tax lawyer, real-estate broker, and piano player, hosted a 24-hour stream of visitors. The author met Odom through Mandy Nichols, a former Miss Big Beautiful Woman, who stopped by to borrow ice when the power had been cut off, a frequent occurrence. ✉ *16 E. Jones St.*

(85) **Lee Adler's Home.** Just north of the Mercer House, in half of the double town house facing West Wayne Street, Lee Adler, the adversary of Jim Williams, runs his business of restoring historic Savannah properties. Adler's howling dogs drove Williams to his pipe organ, where he churned out a deafening version of César Franck's *Pièce Heroïque.*

Later, Adler stuck reelection signs in his front lawn, showing his support for the district attorney who prosecuted Williams three times before he was finally found not guilty. ✉ *425 Bull St.*

81 **Mercer House.** This redbrick Italianate mansion on the southwest corner of Monterey Square became Jim Williams's Taj Mahal; here he ran a world-class antiques dealership and held *the* Christmas party of the season; here also his sometime house partner Danny Hansford was shot and died. Williams himself died here in 1990, near the very spot where Hansford fell. Today, his sister lives quietly among the remnants of his Fabergé collection and his Joshua Reynolds paintings, in rooms lighted by Waterford crystal chandeliers. ✉ *429 Bull St.*

84 **Serena Dawes's House.** Near the intersection of West Gordon and Bull streets, this house was owned by Helen Driscoll, also known as Serena Dawes. A high-profile beauty in the 1930s and '40s, she married into a Pennsylvania steel family. After her husband accidentally and fatally shot himself in the head, she retired here, in her hometown. Dawes, Berendt writes, "spent most of her day in bed, holding court, drinking martinis and pink ladies, playing with her white toy poodle, Lulu." Chief among Serena's gentlemen callers was Luther Driggers, rumored to possess a poison strong enough to wipe out the entire city. ✉ *17 W. Gordon St.*

Other Area Attractions

Ebenezer. When the Salzburgers arrived in Savannah in 1734, Oglethorpe sent them up the Savannah River to establish a settlement. The first effort was assailed by disease, and they sought his permission to move to better ground. Denied, they moved anyway and established Ebenezer. Here, they engaged in silkworm production and, in 1769, built the Jerusalem Church, which still stands. After the Revolution, the silkworm operation never resumed, and the town faded into history. Descendants of these Protestant religious refugees have preserved the church and assembled a few of the remaining buildings, moving them to this site from other locations. Be sure to follow GA 275 to its end and see Ebenezer Landing, where the Salzburgers came ashore. ✉ *Ebenezer Rd., U.S. 21 to GA 275, Rincon.*

Fort Jackson. About a mile outside Savannah via President Street, you'll see a sign for the fort, which is 3 mi from the city. Purchased in 1808 by the federal government, this is the oldest standing fort in Georgia. It was garrisoned in 1812 and was the Confederate headquarters of the river batteries. The brick edifice is surrounded by a tidal moat, and there are 13 exhibit areas. Battle reenactments, blacksmithing demonstrations, and programs of 19th-century music are among the fort's activities for tour groups. ✉ *1 Ft. Jackson Rd.,* ☎ *912/232–3945.* *$3.50.* ⏲ *Daily 9–5.*

★ **Fort Pulaski National Monument.** Named for Casimir Pulaski, a Polish count and Revolutionary War hero, this must-see sight for Civil War buffs was built on Cockspur Island between 1829 and 1847. Robert E. Lee's first assignment after graduating from West Point was as an engineer here. During the Civil War the fort fell on April 11, 1862, after a mere 30 hours of bombardment by newfangled rifled cannons. The restored fortification, operated by the National Park Service, has moats, drawbridges, massive ramparts, and towering walls. The park has trails and picnic areas. It's 14 mi east of downtown Savannah; you'll see the entrance on your left just before U.S. 80E reaches Tybee Island. ✉ *U.S. 80,* ☎ *912/786–5787.* *$2.* ⏲ *Sept.–May, daily 9–5; June–Aug., daily 9–6.*

Melon Bluff. On a centuries-old 3,000-acre plantation that has been in one family since 1735, Melon Bluff includes a nature center, facilities for canoeing, kayaking, bird-watching, hiking, and other outdoor activities. You can camp here or stay at one of the three bed-and-breakfast inns ($$–$$$): Palmyra Plantation, an 1850s cottage; the Ripley Farmhouse, a classic rural house with a tin-covered roof; and an old barn, renovated to contain nine guest rooms. From Melon Bluff you can visit nearby **Seabrook Village,** a small but growing cluster of rural buildings from an African-American historic community; **Old Sunbury,** whose port made it a viable competitor to Savannah until the Revolutionary War ended its heyday; **Fort Morris,** which protected Savannah during the Revolution; and **Midway,** an 18th-century village with a house museum and period cemetery. To get here, take I–95 south from Savannah (about 30 mi) to Exit 76 (Midway/Sunbury), turn left, and go east for 3 mi. ✉ *2999 Islands Hwy., Midway, 31320,* ☎ *912/884–5779 or 888/246–8188,* FAX *912/884–3046.*

Mighty Eighth Air Force Heritage Museum. The famous World War II squadron the Mighty Eighth Air Force was formed in Savannah in January 1942 and shipped out to the United Kingdom. Flying Royal Air Force aircraft, the Mighty Eighth became the largest air force of the period, with some 200,000 combat crew personnel. Many lost their lives during raids on enemy factories or were interned as prisoners of war. Exhibits begin with the prelude to World War II and the rise of Adolf Hitler and continue through Desert Storm. ✉ *I–95 and U.S. 80, 175 Bourne Ave., Exit 102, Pooler,* ☎ *912/748–8888.* 🎫 *$7.50.* ⏲ *Daily 9–6.*

Skidaway Marine Science Complex. On the grounds of the former Modena Plantation, it has a 14-panel, 12,000-gallon aquarium with marine and plant life of the continental shelf. Other exhibits highlight coastal archaeology and fossils of the Georgia coast. Nature trails overlook marsh and water. ✉ *30 Ocean Science Circle, Skidaway Island,* ☎ *912/598–2496.* 🎫 *$1.* ⏲ *Weekdays 9–4, Sat. noon–5.*

Tybee Island. *Tybee* is an Indian word meaning "salt." The Yamacraw Indians came to this island in the Atlantic Ocean to hunt and fish, and legend has it that pirates buried their treasure here. The island is about 5 mi long and 2 mi wide, with seafood restaurants, chain motels, condos, and shops—most of which sprang up during the 1950s and haven't changed much since. The entire expanse of white sand is divided into a number of public beaches, where visitors shell and crab, charter fishing boats, and swim. It's 18 mi east of Savannah; take Victory Drive (U.S. 80), sometimes called Tybee Road, onto the island. On your way here, stop by Fort Jackson and Fort Pulaski National Monument (☞ *above*). Nearby, the misnamed Little Tybee Island, actually larger than Tybee Island, is entirely undeveloped. Contact **Tybee Island Beach Visitor Information** (✉ Box 491, Tybee Island 31328, ☎ 800/868–2322).

Dining

Savannah has excellent seafood restaurants, and locals have a passion for spicy barbecue. The Historic District yields culinary treasures, especially along River Street. Several of the city's restaurants—such as Elizabeth on 37th, 45 South, the Olde Pink House, and Il Pasticcio—can easily compete with Atlanta's best dining establishments. Savannahians often drive to restaurants in Thunderbolt, and on Skidaway, Tybee, and Wilmington islands.

Savannah Dining and Lodging

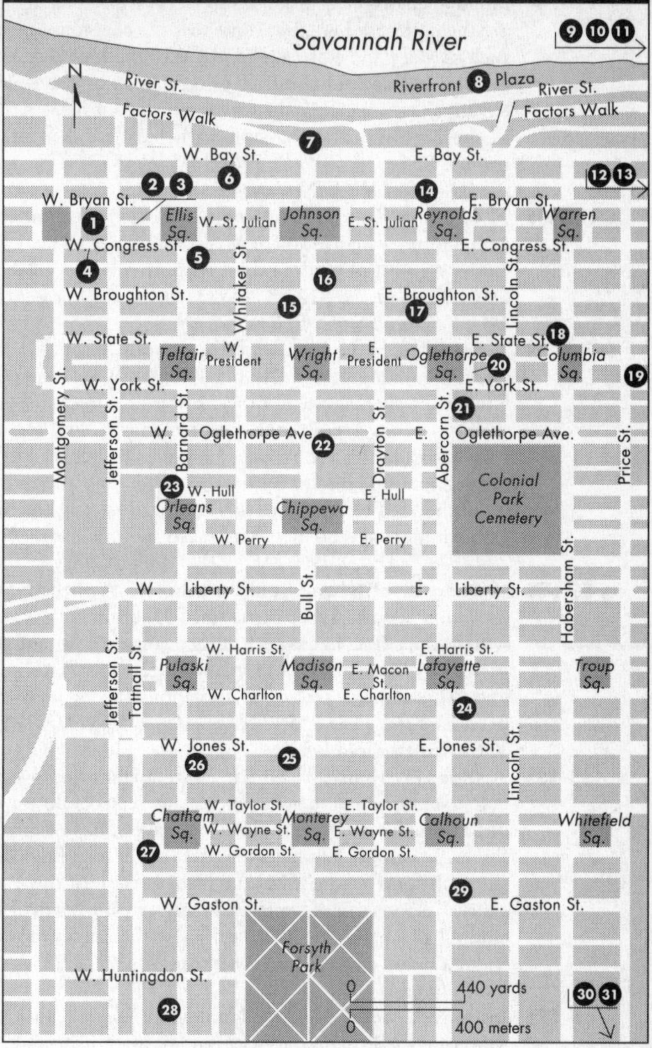

Dining

- Bistro Savannah 1
- Elizabeth on 37th 30
- 45 South 13
- Georges' of Tybee 10
- Il Pasticcio 15
- Johnny Harris 31
- The Lady & Sons 4
- Mrs. Wilkes Dining Room . . . 26
- Nita's Place 21
- North Beach Grill 9
- Olde Pink House 14
- Sapphire Grill 2
- Seasons 3
- So' Soleil 16
- Trattoria Rivazza 5
- Wall's Bar-B-Q 19

Lodging

- Ballastone Inn 22
- Bed & Breakfast Inn 27
- Eliza Thompson House 25
- Foley House Inn 23
- Gastonian 29
- The Grande Toots Inn 28
- Hamilton-Turner Inn 24
- Hyatt Regency Savannah 7
- Kehoe House 18
- Marshall House 17
- Mulberry Inn 12
- The President's Quarters 20
- Quality Inn Heart of Savannah 6
- River Streeet Inn 8
- 17th Streeet Inn 11

$$$–$$$$ ★ ✕ **Elizabeth on 37th.** There's something ingratiating about a restaurant that credits local produce suppliers on its menu. Regional specialties are the hallmark here, but somehow the chef manages to make dishes such as Maryland crab cakes and a Vermont blue cheese tamale sit comfortably beside Southern fried grits and country ham. The extravagant Savannah cream cake is the way to finish your meal in this elegant turn-of-the-20th-century mansion with hardwood floors and spacious rooms. ✉ *105 E. 37th St.,* ☏ *912/236–5547. Reservations essential. AE, D, DC, MC, V. No lunch.*

$$$–$$$$ ★ ✕ **45 South.** This popular south-side eatery is small and stylish, with contemporary mauve and green decor. The game-heavy menu often includes a confit of tender rabbit with morels and mashed potatoes. ✉ *20 E. Broad St.,* ☏ *912/233–1881. Reservations essential. AE, D, DC, MC, V. Closed Sun. No lunch.*

$$$–$$$$ ✕ **So' Soleil.** In the interior of a beautifully renovated downtown commercial building, former Atlanta chef Ian Winslade and partners have launched a slick, contemporary restaurant. Local ingredients, such as shrimp, get an Asian touch with lemongrass and ginger; the chicken with herbs and black olive sauce conjures Provence; and the crispy calamari in tomato rémoulade (dressing with mustard and herbs) brings a bit of the Mediterranean to this Southern establishment. The chef amicably honors special dietary requests. ✉ *1 W. Broughton St.,* ☏ *912/234–1212. AE, D, DC, MC, V. No dinner Sun.*

$$–$$$ ✕ **Georges' of Tybee.** From the proprietors of the North Beach Grill (☞ *below*) comes Tybee's first fine restaurant. The warmly lit interior, with its appealing bar, is perfect for a romantic evening. Duck liver and frissee salad, roasted beets in sherry-ginger vinaigrette, and venison short loin in a cranberry reduction are among the dishes that delight diners here. ✉ *1105 E. U.S. 80, Tybee Island,* ☏ *912/786–9730. AE, MC, V. Closed Sun. No lunch.*

$$–$$$ ✕ **Olde Pink House.** The brick Georgian mansion was built for James Habersham, one of the wealthiest Americans of his time, in 1771. One of Savannah's oldest buildings, the tavern has original Georgia pine floors, Venetian chandeliers, and 18th-century English antiques. The she-crab soup is a light but flavorful version of this Lowcountry specialty. Regional ingredients find their way into many of the dishes, including the black grouper stuffed with blue crab and served with Vidalia onion sauce. ✉ *23 Abercorn St.,* ☏ *912/232–4286. AE, MC, V. No lunch.*

$–$$$ **Trattoria Rivazza.** Good for families with small children, it's the place for pastas made in myriad ways and hardier dishes, such as grilled veal chop with a vegetable stew, salmon braised in a fresh tomato broth, and grilled tuna steak with risotto. Fragrant coffee and decadent desserts round meals out nicely here. ✉ *116 W. Congress St.,* ☏ *912/234–7300. AE, D, MC, V.*

$$ ★ ✕ **Bistro Savannah.** High ceilings, burnished heart-pine floors, and gray-brick walls lined with artwork by local artists all contribute to the bistro atmosphere. The menu has such regional specialties as bouillabaisse of local seafood, crab cakes with lemon-caper aioli and chowchow, and shrimp and *tasso* (seasoned cured pork) on stone-ground grits. More cosmopolitan tastes are represented, too, in such treats as crispy roasted duck. The restaurant is near City Market. ✉ *309 W. Congress St.,* ☏ *912/233–6266. AE, MC, V. No lunch.*

$$ ✕ **Il Pasticcio.** Sicilian Pino Venetico turned this former department store into his dream restaurant. The bistro-style spot gleams with steel, glass, and tile and attracts a lively, hip, young crowd. The menu changes frequently, but fresh pastas and sauces are a constant. Don't miss the second-floor art gallery. Excellent desserts, including a superior tiramisu, make this one worth seeking out. ✉ *2 E. Broughton St.,* ☎ *912/231–8888. AE, D, DC, MC, V. No lunch.*

$$ ★ ✕ **Sapphire Grill.** Savannah's young and restless pack this popular bistro every night. Chef Chris Nason focuses his seasonal menus on local ingredients, such as Georgia white shrimp, crab, and fish. Vegetarians will delight in his elegant vegetable presentations, such as a seasonal vegetable tart. The chocolate flan takes chocolate lovers to a new level of ecstasy. ✉ *110 W. Congress St.,* ☎ *912/443–9962. Reservations essential. AE, D, DC, MC, V. No lunch.*

$$ ✕ **Seasons.** In the heart of City Market, Seasons is great for Sunday brunch, when so many of the downtown venues are closed. A complimentary glass of sparkling wine arrives at your table when you place your order. Brunch entrées include egg dishes, such as eggs Florentine with crabmeat. The lunch and dinner menus focus on seafood, including Georgia pecan grouper and Lowcountry shrimp and grits. ✉ *315 W. St. Julian St.,* ☎ *912/233–2626. AE, D, DC, MC, V.*

$–$$ ✕ **Johnny Harris.** What started as a small roadside stand in 1924 has grown into one of the city's mainstays, with a menu that includes steaks, fried chicken, seafood, and a variety of meats spiced with the restaurant's famous tomato-and-mustard sauce. The lamb barbecue is a treat. There's live music Friday and Saturday night, except on the first Saturday night of the month, when there's dancing. ✉ *1651 E. Victory Dr.,* ☎ *912/354–7810. AE, D, DC, MC, V. Closed Sun.*

$–$$ ✕ **North Beach Grill.** The tiny kitchen of this casual beachfront locale serves up a taste of the Caribbean. Diners will be tempted by dishes such as jerk-rubbed fish tacos with fruit salsa, grilled okra, and sea bass topped with caramelized onions and feta cream sauce. Come in a swimsuit for lunch but a bit more covered for dinner. ✉ *41A Meddin Dr., Tybee Island,* ☎ *912/786–9003. Reservations not accepted. D, MC, V. Closed weekdays Dec.–Jan.*

$ ✕ **The Lady & Sons.** Visitors and locals stand in line at this eatery, patiently waiting to attack the buffet, laden at both lunch and dinner with such specials as moist, crispy fried chicken; the best baked spaghetti in the South; green beans cooked with ham and potatoes; tender sweet creamed corn; and homemade lemonade. The interior of this 1870s-era building, painted pale pink with faux ivy tendrils draped along its perimeter, is bright, cheerful, and busy. Owner Paula H. Deen's book, *The Lady & Sons: Savannah Country Cookbook,* includes recipes for many of the most popular dishes. Sons Bobby and Jamie work here with her. ✉ *311 W. Congress St.,* ☎ *912/233–2600. AE, D, MC, V. No dinner Sun.*

$ ★ ✕ **Mrs. Wilkes Dining Room.** Folks line up for a culinary orgy of fine Southern food, served family style at big tables. For breakfast there are eggs, sausage, piping hot biscuits, and grits. At lunch, try fried or roast chicken, collard greens, okra, mashed potatoes, corn bread—the dishes just keep coming. ✉ *107 W. Jones St.,* ☎ *912/232–5997. Reservations not accepted. No credit cards. Closed Jan. and weekends. No dinner.*

$ ★ ✕ **Nita's Place.** Juanita Dixon has a reputation for perfectly preparing down-home Southern cooking at this little steam-table operation. People come for salmon patties, baked chicken, perfectly cooked okra, outstanding squash casserole, and homemade desserts. The fresh vegetables alone are worth the trip. ✉ *140 Abercorn St.,* ☎ *912/238–8233. Reservations not accepted. MC, V. Closed Sun. No dinner.*

$ ✕ **Wall's Bar-B-Q.** It's a bit hard to find this little hole in the wall, but the barbecue (get the tangy hot-but-not-too-hot mustard-and-tomato sauce), deviled crab, red rice, greens, sour cream pound cake, and layered red velvet cake are all worth the search. The perfect quick bite is the rib snack. ✉ *515 E. York La.,* ☎ *912/232–9754. Reservations not accepted. No credit cards. Closed Sun.–Tues.*

Lodging

Although Savannah has its share of chain hotels and motels, the city's most distinctive lodgings are the more than two dozen historic inns, guest houses, and bed-and-breakfasts gracing the Historic District.

If "historic inn" brings to mind images of roughing it in shabby genteel mansions with antiquated plumbing, you're in for a surprise. Most inns are in mansions with the requisite high ceilings, spacious rooms, and ornate carved millwork. Most have canopy, four-poster, or Victorian brass beds. And amid antique surroundings, there is modern luxury: enormous baths, many with whirlpools or hot tubs; film libraries for in-room VCRs; and turndown service with a chocolate, praline, or even a discreet brandy on your nightstand. Continental breakfast and afternoon refreshments are often included in the rate. Prices have risen since the filming of *Midnight in the Garden of Good and Evil.* Special seasons and holidays, such as St. Patrick's Day, push prices up a bit as well. On the other hand, weekdays and the off-season can yield excellent bargains.

Inns and Guest Houses

$$$–$$$$ ★ **Ballastone Inn.** This sumptuous inn occupies an 1838 mansion that once served as a bordello. Rooms are handsomely furnished, with luxurious linens on canopy beds, antiques and fine reproductions, and a collection of original framed prints from *Harper's* scattered throughout. On the garden level, rooms are small and cozy, with exposed brick walls, beam ceilings, and, in some cases, windows at eye level with the lush courtyard. Most rooms have working gas fireplaces, and three have whirlpool tubs. ✉ *14 E. Oglethorpe Ave., 31401,* ☎ *912/236–1484 or 800/822–4553,* FAX *912/236–4626. 13 rooms, 3 suites. In-room VCRs, concierge. AE, MC, V. BP.*

$$$–$$$$ ★ **Gastonian.** Guest rooms at this inn, built in 1868, have working fireplaces and antiques from the Georgian and Regency periods; most also have whirlpool tubs or Japanese soak tubs. The Caracalla Suite is named for the oversize whirlpool tub built in front of the fireplace. Breakfast features such specialty items as ginger pancakes. Afternoon tea, evening cordials, and complimentary wine are other treats. ✉ *220 E. Gaston St., 31401,* ☎ *912/232–2869 or 800/671–0716,* FAX *912/232–0710. 14 rooms, 3 suites. Outdoor hot tub, concierge. AE, D, MC, V. BP.*

$$$–$$$$ **Kehoe House.** A fabulously appointed bed-and-breakfast inn, the Victorian-style Kehoe House has brass-and-marble chandeliers, a courtyard garden, and a music room. On the main floor, a double parlor holds two fireplaces and sweeps the eye upward with its 14-ft ceilings. Turndown service includes chocolates, wine, and bottled water. Rates include access to the Downtown Athletic Club. ✉ *123 Habersham St., 31401,* ☎ *912/232–1020 or 800/820–1020,* FAX *912/231–0208. 15 rooms. Concierge, meeting rooms. AE, D, DC, MC, V. BP.*

$$$ ★ **Foley House Inn.** Two town houses, built 50 years apart, form this elegant inn. Named for an Irish immigrant who made a fortune in Savannah, the original house was built by his widow for her five grandchildren, whose parents had died, leaving them in her care. Most rooms have antiques and reproductions; five rooms have whirlpool tubs. A carriage house to the rear of the property has less-expensive rooms. ✉ *14 W. Hull St., 31401,* ☎ *912/232–6622 or 800/647–3708,* FAX *912/231–1218. 17 rooms, 2 suites. Lounge, in-room VCRs, concierge. AE, MC, V. BP.*

$$–$$$ **The Grande Toots Inn.** Delores Ellis, Savannah's only African-American innkeeper, spent six years refurbishing this fine old Victorian house, built in 1890. On the edge of Forsyth Park (☞ The Historic Dis-

trict, *above*), the neighborhood, inspired by her diligence, is slowly making a comeback. A grandmother, Ellis fusses over guests as if they were her own offspring. Amenities range from gas-log fireplaces to a whirlpool tub. ✉ *212 W. Hall St., 31401,* ☎ *912/236–2911 or 800/835–6831,* FAX *912/236–4010. 4 rooms, 1 carriage house. D, MC, V. BP.*

$$–$$$ **Hamilton-Turner Inn.** Experience *Midnight in the Garden of Good and Evil* with a stay in this 1873 mansion built by wealthy Savannah jeweler Samuel Hamilton. Until recently, the house belonged to Mandy Nichols, one of the principal figures in the book. It's furnished with fine Second Empire, Eastlake, and Renaissance antiques. Four rooms have large whirlpools, two have fireplaces, and two have both plus a balcony. Complimentary afternoon tea, robes, and a film library are among the amenities. ✉ *330 Abercorn St., 31401,* ☎ *912/233–1833 or 888/448–8849,* FAX *912/233–0291. 15 rooms. In-room data ports. AE, D, DC, MC, V. BP.*

$–$$$ **Eliza Thompson House.** Eliza Thompson was a socially prominent widow when she built her fine town house around 1847. In 1995 Carol and Steve Day purchased the house and repainted, refinished, and refurnished it in period style. Marble baths have been added. Continental breakfast and complimentary afternoon wine and cheese are served in the parlor or on the patio, with its fine Ivan Bailey sculpture. ✉ *5 W. Jones St., 31401,* ☎ *912/236–3620 or 800/348–9378,* FAX *912/238–1920. 25 rooms. Concierge. MC, V. CP.*

$$ ★ **The President's Quarters.** Each room in the classic Savannah inn is named for an American president. Guests are greeted with wine and fruit, and the complimentary afternoon tea tempts with sweet cakes. Turndown service includes a glass of port or sherry. There are also rooms in an adjacent town house. ✉ *225 E. President St., 31401,* ☎ *912/233–1600 or 800/233–1776,* FAX *912/238–0849. 11 rooms, 8 suites. Concierge, free parking. D, DC, MC, V. BP.*

$$ **17th Street Inn.** The inn's deck, adorned with plants, palms, and swings, is a gathering place for visitors to chat, sip wine, and enjoy breakfast with their hosts, Susie Morris and her spouse, Stuart Liles. Steps away from the beach, it has two-story porches and rooms with generous kitchenettes, double iron beds, and bright colors. ✉ *12 17th St., Box 114, Tybee Island 31328,* ☎ *912/786–0607 or 888/909–0607,* FAX *912/786–0601. 7 rooms. D, MC, V. CP.*

$–$$ **Bed & Breakfast Inn.** So called, the owner claims, because it was the first such property to open in Savannah more than 20 years ago, the inn is a restored 1853 Federal-style row house on historic Gordon Row near Chatham Square. The courtyard garden is an oasis from a day's hectic events. Although much of the furniture suggests the period, the dining room is not as elegant as those of more expensive inns. One room has a private deck. Afternoon pastries, lemonade, coffee, and tea are served. ✉ *117 W. Gordon St., 31401,* ☎ *912/238–0518,* FAX *912/233–2537. 15 rooms. Kitchenettes (some). AE, D, MC, V. BP.*

Hotels and Motels

$$$–$$$$ **Hyatt Regency Savannah.** When this riverfront hotel was built in 1981, preservationists opposed the construction of the seven-story modern structure in the Historic District. The main architectural features are the towering atrium and glass elevators. Rooms have modern furnishings, marble baths, and balconies overlooking either the atrium or the Savannah River. MD's Lounge is the ideal spot to have a drink and watch the river traffic drift by. Windows, the hotel's restaurant, serves a great Sunday buffet. ✉ *2 W. Bay St., 31401,* ☎ *912/238–1234 or 800/233–1234,* FAX *912/944–3673. 325 rooms, 21 suites. Indoor pool, concierge, business services. AE, D, MC, V.*

$$$ ★ 🏨 **Mulberry Inn.** This Holiday Inn is ensconced in an 1860s livery stable that later became a cotton warehouse and then a Coca-Cola bottling plant. Gleaming heart-pine floors and antiques, including a handsome English grandfather clock and an exquisitely carved Victorian mantel, make it unique. Guest rooms are traditionally decorated, and suites have king-size beds and wet bars. The café is a notch nicer than most other Holiday Inn restaurants. ✉ *601 E. Bay St., 31401,* ☎ *912/238–1200 or 800/465–4329,* FAX *912/236–2184. 96 rooms, 26 suites. Bar, pool, outdoor hot tub. AE, D, DC, MC, V.*

$$–$$$ 🏨 **Marshall House.** This restored hotel, with original pine floors, woodwork, and bricks, caters to business needs while providing the intimacy of a bed-and-breakfast inn. Different spaces reflect different parts of Savannah's history, from its founding to the Civil War. Artwork is mostly by local artists. You can listen to live jazz on weekends in the hotel lounge. Café M specializes in local cuisine such as Southern pot-au-feu, a seafood-rich Lowcountry dish with okra and greens, and Georgia smoked quail. ✉ *123 E. Broughton St., 31401,* ☎ *912/644–7896 or 800/589–6304,* FAX *912/234–3334. 65 rooms, 3 suites. Café, lounge, in-room data ports, meeting rooms. AE, D, MC, V.*

$$–$$$ 🏨 **River Street Inn.** The interior is so lavish that it's hard to believe the building was once a vacant warehouse. Today, the structure, which dates to 1817, houses guest rooms with antiques and reproductions from the era of King Cotton. One floor has charming shops and a New Orleans–style restaurant. ✉ *115 E. River St., 31401,* ☎ *912/234–6400 or 800/678–8946,* FAX *912/234–1478. 86 rooms. 3 restaurants, 3 bars, concierge, business services. AE, D, DC, MC, V. BP.*

$ 🏨 **Quality Inn Heart of Savannah.** This basic, quality motel-style lodging is clean and very popular with the older budget-minded set. In the Historic District, it offers convenience, a friendly staff, complimentary coffee, and on-site parking at rock-bottom prices. ✉ *300 W. Bay St.,* ☎ *912/236–6321 or 800/221–2222,* FAX *912/234–5317. 53 rooms. Free parking. AE, D, DC, MC, V. CP.*

Nightlife and the Arts

Savannah's nightlife reflects its laid-back personality. Some clubs have live reggae, hard rock, and other contemporary music, but most stick to traditional blues, jazz, and piano-bar vocalists. After-dark merrymakers usually head for watering holes on Riverfront Plaza or the south side.

Bars and Nightclubs

The **Bar Bar** (✉ 219 W. St. Julian St., ☎ 912/231–1910), a neighborhood hangout, has pool tables, games, and a varied beer selection. Once a month at **Club One Jefferson** (✉ 1 Jefferson St., ☎ 912/232–0200), a gay bar, the Lady Chablis (☞ *Midnight in the Garden of Good and Evil, above*) bumps and grinds her way down the catwalk, lip-synching disco tunes in a shimmer of sequin and satin gowns; the cover is $5. **Kevin Barry's Irish Pub** (✉ 117 W. River St., ☎ 912/233–9626) has a friendly atmosphere, a full menu until 1:45 AM, and traditional Irish music Wednesday to Sunday; it's *the* place to be on St. Patrick's Day. The rest of the year there's a mix of tourists and locals, young and old. **Malone's** (✉ 27 Barnard St., ☎ 912/234–3059 or 912/237–9862), a sports bar, has 13 TV screens and monitors. Pool tables and a bar are downstairs, and a dance floor with live entertainment is upstairs. **Stogies** (✉ 112 W. Congress St., ☎ 912/233–4277) has its own humidor where patrons buy expensive cigars. It's a fun spot if you can take the smoke.

Coffeehouses

Thanks to a substantial student population, the city has sprouted coffeehouses as if they were spring flowers. The **Savannah Coffee House and Café** (✉ 102 W. Congress St., ☎ 912/233–5311) serves locally made bagels, croissants, and muffins and good coffee. Students cluster around tables and play chess or draw. **Ex Libris** (✉ 228 Martin Luther King Jr. Blvd., ☎ 912/238–2427) is a handsome space where you can browse through new books over a sandwich, soup, salad, or an espresso. It's student managed and operated by the Savannah College of Art and Design (☞ Art Galleries *in* Shopping, *below*).

Jazz and Blues Clubs

Bayou Café and Blues Bar (✉ 14 N. Abercorn St., at River St., ☎ 912/233–6414) has acoustic music during the week and the Bayou Blues Band on the weekend. The food has a Cajun flavor. **Cafe Loco** (✉ 1 Old Hwy. 80, Tybee Island, ☎ 912/786–7810), a few miles outside Savannah, showcases local blues and acoustics acts. You can rollick with Emma Kelly, the undisputed "Lady of 6,000 Songs," at **Hard Hearted Hannah's East** (✉ 20 E. Broad St., ☎ 912/233–2225) from Tuesday through Saturday.

Outdoor Activities and Sports

Boating

At the **Bull River Yacht Club Marina** (✉ 8005 Old Tybee Rd., ☎ 912/897–7300), you can arrange a dolphin tour, a deep-sea fishing expedition, or a jaunt through the coastal islands. **Lake Mayer Park** (✉ Montgomery Crossroads Rd. and Sallie Mood Dr., ☎ 912/652–6780) has paddleboats, sailing, canoeing, and an in-line skating and hockey facility. **Saltwater Charters** (✉ 111 Wickersham Dr., ☎ 912/598–1814) provides packages ranging from 2-hour sightseeing tours to 13-hour deep-sea fishing expeditions. Water taxis to the coastal islands are also available. **Public boat ramps** are found at **Bell's Landing** (✉ Apache Ave. off Abercorn St.) on the Forest River, **Islands Expressway** (✉ Islands Expressway adjacent to Frank W. Spencer Park) on the Wilmington River, and **Savannah Marina** on the Wilmington River in the town of Thunderbolt.

Golf

Bacon Park (✉ 1 Shorty Cooper Dr., ☎ 912/354–2625), a public course with 27 holes, is par 72 for 18 holes and has a lighted driving range. **Henderson Golf Club** (✉ 1 Al Henderson Dr., at I–95 and GA 204 [Exit 94], ☎ 912/920–4653) is an 18-hole, par-71 course about 15 mi from downtown Savannah. **Mary Calder** (✉ W. Lathrop Ave., ☎ 912/238–7100) is par 35 for its 9 holes.

Health Clubs

The **Jewish Educational Alliance** has racquetball courts, a gymnasium, weight room, sauna, whirlpool, outdoor pool, and aerobic dance classes. Call ahead to arrange admission. ✉ *5111 Abercorn St.,* ☎ *912/355–8111.* 🎫 *Guest fee $10.*

Savannah Downtown Athletic Club has an exercise room, free-weight equipment, sauna, swimming pool, aerobics, tanning beds, and tae kwon do classes. ✉ *7 E. Congress St.,* ☎ *912/236–4874.* 🎫 *Guest fee $7 daily, $25 weekly, $50 monthly.*

YMCA Family Center has a gymnasium, aerobics, racquetball, and a pool. ✉ *6400 Habersham St.,* ☎ *912/354–6223.* 🎫 *Guest fee $10.*

Jogging and Running

Low-lying coastal terrain is ideal for jogging. **Forsyth Park** (☒ Bull St. between Whitaker and Drayton Sts.) is a flat, pleasant place to walk, jog, or run. **Tybee Island** (☞ *above*) has a white-sand beach that is hard packed and relatively debris free, making it a favorite with runners. For **suburban jogging trails,** head for **Daffin Park** (☒ 1500 E. Victory Dr.), with level sidewalks available during daylight hours, and **Lake Mayer Park** (☒ Montgomery Crossroads Rd. and Sallie Mood Dr.), with 1½ mi of level asphalt available 24 hours a day.

Tennis

Bacon Park (☒ 6262 Skidaway Rd., ☎ 912/351–3850) has 16 lighted asphalt courts. Fees are $1.75 per hour during the day and $2.25 after dark. **Forsyth Park** (☒ Drayton St. and Park Ave., ☎ 912/351–3850) contains four lighted courts available until about 10 PM for free. **Lake Mayer Park** (☒ Montgomery Crossroads Rd. and Sallie Mood Dr., ☎ 912/652–6780) has eight asphalt lighted courts available at no charge and open 8 AM–10 PM (until 11 PM May–Sept.).

Shopping

Find your own Lowcountry treasures among a bevy of handcrafted wares—handmade quilts and baskets; wreaths made from Chinese tallow trees and Spanish moss; preserves, jams, and jellies. The favorite Savannah snack, and a popular gift item, is the benne wafer. It's about the size of a quarter and comes in a variety of flavors. As once-empty downtown storefronts begin to fill with new businesses, a period of stagnation gives way to revitalization. Antiques malls and junk emporiums are still part of the scenario—but that's Savannah.

Shopping Districts

City Market, on West Saint Julian Street between Ellis and Franklin squares, has sidewalk cafés, jazz haunts, shops, and art galleries. **Riverfront Plaza/River Street** is nine blocks of shops in the renovated waterfront warehouses, where you can find everything from popcorn to pottery.

Specialty Shops

ANTIQUES

Alexandra's Antique Gallery (☒ 320 W. Broughton St., ☎ 912/233–3999) is a four-level extravaganza of items from kitsch to fine antiques. **Arthur Smith Antiques** (☒ 1 W. Jones St., ☎ 912/236–9701) has four floors showcasing 18th- and 19th-century European furniture, porcelain, rugs, and paintings.

ART GALLERIES

Compass Prints, Inc./Ray Ellis Gallery (☒ 205 W. Congress St., ☎ 912/234–3537) sells original artwork, prints, and books by internationally acclaimed artist Ray Ellis. **Gallery Espresso** (☒ 6 E. Liberty St., ☎ 912/233–5348) has a new show every two weeks focusing on work by local artists. A true coffeehouse, it stays open until the wee hours. **Gallery 209** (☒ 209 E. River St., ☎ 912/236–4583) is a co-op gallery, with paintings, watercolors, pottery, jewelry, batik, stained glass, weavings, and sculpture by local artists. **Off the Wall** (☒ 412 Whitaker St., ☎ 912/233–8840) exhibits artists from everywhere but Savannah. **Southern Images** (☒ 132 E. Oglethorpe Ave., ☎ 912/234–6449) displays the work of Jack Leigh, whose photograph of Bonaventure Cemetery graces the cover of *Midnight in the Garden of Good and Evil.*

Savannah College of Art and Design (☒ 26 W. Harris St., ☎ 912/525–5200), a privately owned school, has restored at least 40 historic buildings in the city, including 12 galleries. Work by faculty and students is often for sale, and touring exhibitions are frequently in the on-campus galleries. Stop by Exhibit A, Pinnacle Gallery, and the West Bank Gallery, and ask about other student galleries. Garden for the Arts has an amphitheater and shows performance art.

BENNE WAFERS

Byrd Cookie Company (✉ 6700 Waters Ave., ☎ 912/355–1716), founded in 1924, is the best place to get the popular cookies that are also sold in numerous gift shops around town.

BOOKS

For regional to general Southern subjects and Americana, visit the **Book Lady** (✉ 17 W. York St., ☎ 912/233–3628), in a two-centuries-old house for more than two decades. The shop also has a search service. **E. Shaver Booksellers** (✉ 326 Bull St., ☎ 912/234–7257) is the source for 17th- and 18th-century maps and new books on regional subjects; the shop covers 12 rooms. **V. & J. Duncan** (✉ 12 E. Taylor St., ☎ 912/232–0338) specializes in antique maps, prints, and books.

COUNTRY CRAFTS

Charlotte's Corner (✉ 1 W. Liberty St., ☎ 912/233–8061) carries expensive and moderately priced Savannah souvenirs, children's clothes and toys, and beach wear.

Savannah A to Z

Arriving and Departing

BY BUS

Greyhound/Trailways (✉ 610 W. Oglethorpe Ave., ☎ 912/233–8186 or 800/231–2222).

BY CAR

I–95 slices north–south along the eastern seaboard, intersecting 10 mi west of town with east–west I–16, which dead-ends in downtown Savannah. U.S. 17, the Coastal Highway, also runs north–south through town. U.S. 80, which connects the Atlantic to the Pacific, is another east–west route through Savannah.

BY PLANE

Savannah International Airport (✉ 400 Airways Ave., ☎ 912/964–0514), 18 mi west of downtown, is served by Delta, US Airways, AirTran, and Continental Express for domestic flights (☞ Air Travel *in* Smart Travel Tips A to Z for telephone numbers). Despite the name, international flights are nonexistent. The foreign trade zone, a locus for importing, constitutes the "international" aspect.

Vans operated by **McCall's Limousine Service** (☎ 912/966–5364 or 800/673–9365) leave the airport daily for downtown locations. The trip takes 15 minutes, and the one-way fare is $15 for one person, $25 round-trip for one person; two-person rate is $10 per person one-way. Routes can include other destinations in addition to downtown. Advance reservation is required.

Taxi fare from the airport to downtown is $18 for one person, $5 for each additional person.

By car, take I–95 south to I–16 east into downtown Savannah.

BY TRAIN

Amtrak has regular service along the eastern seaboard, with daily stops in Savannah. The Amtrak station (✉ 2611 Seaboard Coastline Dr., ☎ 912/234–2611 or 800/872–7245) is 4 mi southwest of downtown. Cab fare into the city is $5–$10, depending on the number of passengers.

Getting Around

Despite its size, much of the downtown Historic District can easily be explored on foot. Its grid shape makes getting around a breeze, and you'll find any number of places to stop and rest.

BY BUS

Chatham Area Transit (CAT; ☎ 912/233–5767) operates buses in Savannah and Chatham County Monday through Saturday from 6 AM to 11 PM, Sunday from 7 to 7. Some lines may stop running earlier or may not run on Sunday. The CAT Shuttle operates throughout the Historic District; the cost is 75¢ one-way. Buses require 75¢ in exact change.

BY TAXI

Adam Cab Co. (☎ 912/927–7466) is a reliable, 24-hour taxi service. Calling ahead for reservations could yield a flat rate. Taxis start at 60¢ and cost $1.20 for each mile.

Contacts and Resources

BED-AND-BREAKFAST RESERVATIONS

Great Inns of Georgia (✉ 541 Londonberry Rd., Atlanta 30327, ☎ 404/843–0471 or 800/501–7328, FAX 404/252–8886) can help you choose one of Savannah's many inns.

EMERGENCIES

Ambulance, police (☎ 911).

GUIDED TOURS

Carriage Tours of Savannah (✉ Box 2402, 31402, ☎ 912/236–6756) takes you through the Historic District by day or by night at a 19th-century clip-clop pace, with coachmen spinning tales and telling ghost stories along the way. A romantic evening tour in a private carriage costs $65 ($85 on Friday and Saturday evenings), and although champagne can no longer be included, guests may bring whatever refreshment they wish; regular tours are a more modest $17 per person.

Gray Line (✉ 215 W. Boundary St., 31401, ☎ 912/234–8687 or 800/426–2318) conducts a four-hour tour to Isle of Hope and the Lowcountry, including Thunderbolt (a shrimping community) and Wormsloe Plantation Site. Options include walking tours, minibus tours, and trolley tours. The cost ranges from $16 to $24.

Historic Savannah Foundation (✉ 117 W. Perry St., 31401, ☎ 912/234–4088 or 800/627–5030), a preservation organization, leads tours of the Historic District and the Lowcountry. Preservation, *Midnight in the Garden of Good and Evil,* the Golden Isles, group, and private tours also are available. In addition, the foundation leads excursions to the fishing village of Thunderbolt; the Isle of Hope, with stately mansions lining Bluff Drive; the much-photographed Bonaventure Cemetery on the banks of the Wilmington River; and Wormsloe Plantation Site, with its mile-long avenue of arching oaks. The cost depends on the number of people on the tour and its length.

Old Town Trolley Tours (☎ 912/233–0083) has narrated 90-minute tours traversing the Historic District. Trolleys go by 13 designated stops every half hour daily 9–4:30; you can hop on and off as you please. The cost ranges from $16 to $20.

HOSPITALS

Candler Hospital (✉ 5353 Reynolds St., ☎ 912/692–6000) and **Memorial Medical Center** (✉ 4700 Waters Ave., ☎ 912/350–8000) are area hospitals with 24-hour emergency rooms.

SPECIAL-INTEREST TOURS

Beach Institute African-American Cultural Center (☞ The Historic District, *above*) is headquarters for the Negro Heritage Trail Tour. A knowledgeable guide traces the city's more than 250 years of black history. Tours, which begin at the Savannah Visitors Center (☞ The Historic District, *above*), are at 1 and 3 and cost $15.

Garden Club of Savannah (✉ Box 13892, 31416, ☎ 912/238–0248) runs spring tours of private gardens tucked behind old brick walls and wrought-iron gates. It costs $20 and finishes with tea at the Green-Meldrim House (☞ The Historic District, *above*).

A Ghost Talk Ghost Walk Tour (✉ 127 E. Congress St., ☎ 912/233–3896) should send chills down your spine during an easy 1-mi jaunt through the old colonial city. Tours, lasting an hour and a half, leave from Reynolds Square (✉ Congress and Abercorn Sts.) at the John Wesley Memorial, in the middle of the square. Call for dates, times, and reservations; cost is $10.

Square Routes (✉ 60 E. Broad St., Suite 11, ☎ 912/232–6866 or 800/868–6867) provides customized strolls and private driving tours that wend through the Historic District and other parts of the Lowcountry. In-town tours focus on the city's architecture and gardens, and specialized tours include the *Midnight in the Garden of Good and Evil* Walk. Tours usually last two hours and cost from $20 to $30.

24-HOUR PHARMACY

CVS Pharmacy (✉ Medical Arts Shopping Center, 4725 Waters Ave., ☎ 912/355–7111).

VISITOR INFORMATION

Savannah Area Convention & Visitors Bureau (✉ 222 W. Oglethorpe Ave., 31401, ☎ 912/644–6401 or 877/728–2662, FAX 912/944–0468) provides maps and brochures about Savannah.

THE COASTAL ISLES AND THE OKEFENOKEE

Jekyll, St. Simons, and Sea Islands

The coastal isles are a string of lush, subtropical barrier islands meandering lazily down Georgia's Atlantic coast from Savannah to the Florida border. The islands have a long history of human habitation; Native American relics have been found here that date from about 2500 BC. The four designated Golden Isles—Little St. Simons, Sea, St. Simons, and Jekyll islands—are great vacation spots. The best way to appreciate the barrier islands' rare ecology is to visit Sapelo and Cumberland islands or take a guided tour.

Each coastal isle has a distinct personality, shaped by its history and ecology. All the Golden Isles but Little St. Simons are connected to the mainland by bridges in the vicinity of Brunswick; these are the only coastal isles accessible by automobile. Little St. Simons Island, a privately owned retreat with guest accommodations, is reached by a launch from St. Simons. Sapelo Island is accessible by ferry from the visitor center just north of Darien. The Cumberland Island National Seashore is reached by ferry from St. Marys. About 50 mi inland is the Okefenokee National Wildlife Refuge, which has a character all its own.

Lodging prices quoted here may be much lower during nonpeak seasons, and specials are often available during the week in high season. All Georgia beaches are in the public domain.

Numbers in the margin correspond to points of interest on the Coastal Isles map.

Sapelo Island

90 *8 mi from Darien.*

In Sapelo's fields, you'll find chips of Guale Indian pottery dating as far back as 2000 BC and shards of Spanish ceramics from the 16th century. On the northern end, remains of the Chocolate Plantation reveal the island's French heritage and role during the plantation days of the 19th century. Today, researchers occupy the southern sector of the island, studying ecology at the Sapelo Island National Estuarine Research Reserve and evaluating the marshland at the Marine Institute. The organizations' studies are instrumental to the preservation of Sapelo's delicate ecosystem and others like it throughout the world.

You can explore many historical periods and natural environments here, but facilities on the island are limited, for the most part, to drinking fountains and rest rooms. Bring insect repellent, especially in summer, and leave your pets at home.

Start your visit at the **Sapelo Island Visitors Center** (✉ Rte. 1, Box 1500, Darien 31305, ☎ 912/437–3224, 912/485–2300 group tours, 912/485–2299 camping reservations), where you'll see an exhibition on the island's history, culture, and ecology. Here you can purchase a ticket good for a round-trip ferry ride and bus tour of the island. The bus tour views different sights on different days of the week but always includes the marsh, the sand dune ecosystem, and the wildlife management area. On Saturday, the tour views the 80-ft **Sapelo Lighthouse,** built in 1820, a symbol of the cotton and lumber industry once based out of Darien's port. To see the island's **Reynolds Mansion,** schedule your tour for Wednesday. Reservations are required for tours. If you wish to stay overnight on Sapelo, you can either camp or choose from several bed-and-breakfast inns. If you stay overnight (and only if you do), you may visit the beach and the **Hog Hammock Community,** one of the few remaining sites where ethnic African-American culture has been preserved on the south Atlantic coast. Hog Hammock's 65 residents are descendants of slaves who worked the island's plantations during the 19th century. You can rent a bicycle to tour the area but may not bring one on the ferry.

Dining and Lodging

$–$$ ✕ **Mudcat Charlie's.** It's plastic forks and plates all the way at this casual eatery. Local seafood—crab stew, fried oysters, and shrimp—is the specialty. The steaks, burgers, and pork chops are good, too. Peach and apple pies are made on the premises. It's between Brunswick and Darien on U.S. 17. ✉ *250 Ricefield Way,* ☎ *912/261–0055. AE, D, DC, MC, V.*

$ 🏨 **Open Gates.** This comfortable white frame Victorian house dates from 1876. Fine antiques fill the public spaces and guest rooms. Breakfast specialties include fresh fig preserves, plantation pancakes (puffed pancakes), and Hunter's casserole (a baked egg strata). Innkeeper Carolyn Hodges guides guests on tours of the Altamaha River. ✉ *Vernon Sq., Box 1526, Darien 31305,* ☎ *912/437–6985,* FAX *912/882–9427. 4 rooms, 2 with bath. Pool. No credit cards. BP.*

Little St. Simons Island

91 *10–15 mins by ferry from the Hampton River Club Marina on St. Simons Island.*

The Coastal Isles

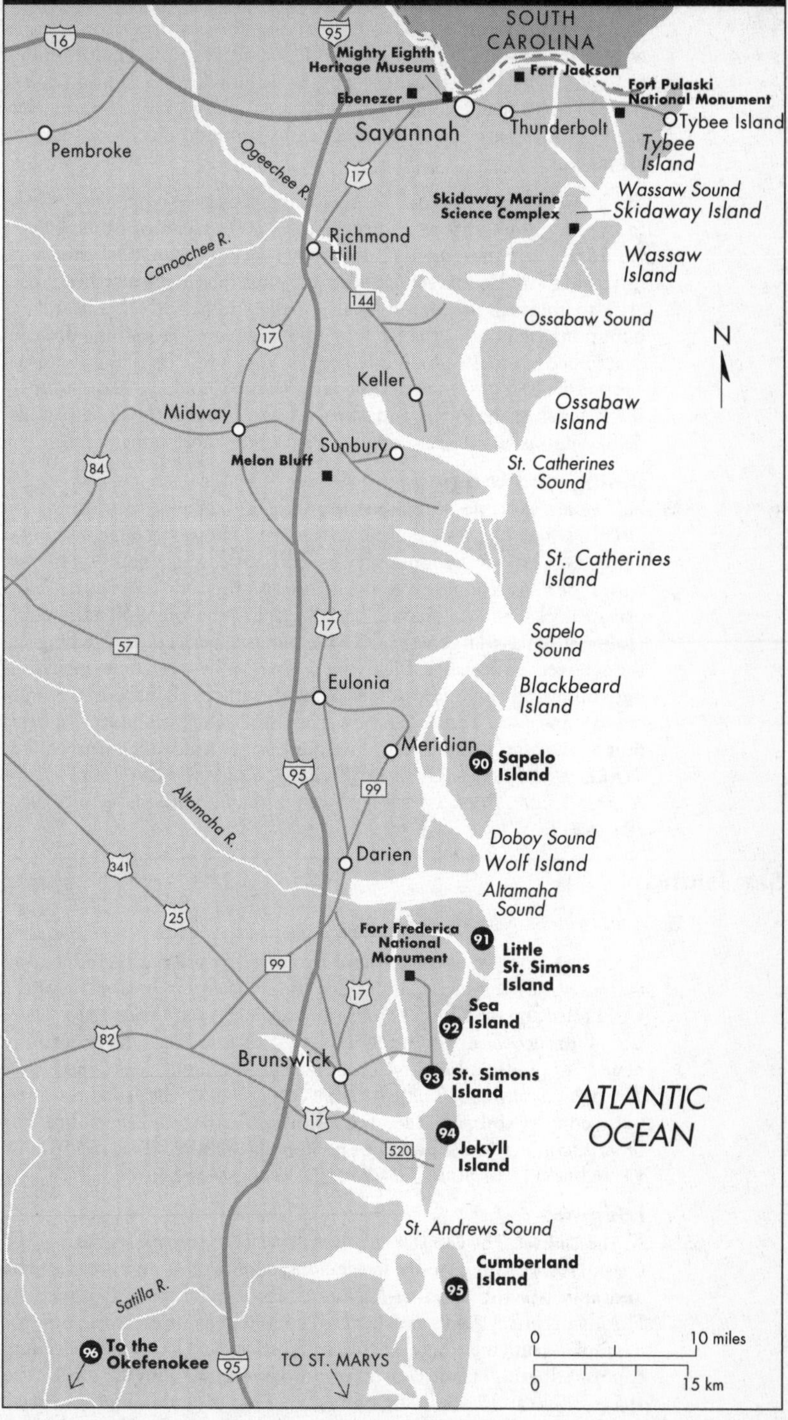

Six miles long, 2–3 mi wide, skirted by Atlantic beaches and salt marshes teeming with birds and wildlife, this privately owned resort is custom-made for Robinson Crusoe–style getaways. The island's only development is a rustic but comfortable guest compound. Guided tours, horseback rides, canoe trips, fly-fishing lessons, and other extras can be arranged, some for no additional charge. Inquire about children, as there are some limitations. In summer, day tours may be arranged.

The island's forests and marshes are inhabited by deer, armadillos, horses, raccoons, gators, otters, and more than 200 species of birds. Guests are free to walk the 6 mi of undisturbed beaches, swim in the mild surf, fish from the dock, and seine for shrimp and crabs in the marshes. There are also horses to ride, nature walks with experts, and other island explorations via boat or the back of a pickup truck. From June through September, up to 10 nonguests per day may visit the island by reservation; the $75 cost includes the ferry to the island, an island tour by truck, lunch at the lodge, and a beach walk. Contact the Lodge on Little St. Simons Island (☞ Lodging, *below*) for more information.

Dining and Lodging

$$$$ ✕🏨 **Lodge on Little St. Simons Island.** The spacious, airy rooms are distributed among four buildings: the 1917 Hunting Lodge, with two antiques-filled guest rooms; a two-bedroom cottage; and two houses with four guest rooms each. In the houses, the four rooms each have private decks, and each house has a large living room with a fireplace. Houses also have large screened back porches, perfect for watching the sun set over the marshes. Meals are served family style in the main dining room and include platters heaped with fresh fish, homemade breads, and pies. Transportation from St. Simons Island, transportation on the island, and interpretive guides are included. ✉ *Box 21078, 31522,* ☎ *912/638–7472 or 888/733–5774,* FAX *912/634–1811. 14 rooms, 1 suite. Pool, horseback riding, beach, boating, fishing, bicycles. AE, D, MC, V. FAP.*

Sea Island

92 *5 mi from St. Simons Island.*

Separated from St. Simons Island by a narrow waterway and a good many steps up the social ladder, Sea Island has been the domain of the well-heeled and the Cloister Hotel (☞ Lodging, *below*) since 1928. There is no entrance gate, and nonguests are free to admire the beautifully planted grounds and to drive past the mansions lining Sea Island Drive. The owners of the 180 or so private cottages and villas treat the hotel like a country club, and their tenants may use the hotel's facilities. For rentals, contact **Sea Island Cottage Rentals** (✉ Box 30351, 31561, ☎ 912/638–5112 or 800/732–4752, FAX 912/638–5824).

Lodging

$$$$ 🏨 **The Cloister.** The Cloister still lives up to its celebrity status as a grand coastal resort. Guests lodge in spacious, comfortably appointed rooms and suites in the Spanish Mediterranean–style hotel, designed by Florida architect Addison Mizner. The hotel has its eccentricities; for example, gentlemen may not wear short-sleeved shirts in the dining rooms. Still, this classic coastal resort has kept up with the times. The spa is in a beautiful building of its own. Guests (and nonguests, space permitting) can play at the Sea Island Golf Course (on St. Simons). Other recreational options are skeet shooting, horseback riding, sailing, playing lawn games, and surf and deep-sea fishing. After dinner, you can dance to live music in the lounge. ✉ *Sea Island 31561,* ☎ *912/638–*

3611, 800/732–4752 reservations, FAX 912/638–5823. 254 rooms, 32 suites. 4 restaurants, 2 pools, spa, 54-hole golf course, 18 tennis courts, health club, bicycles, children's programs, concierge, business services, airport shuttle. AE, D, DC, MC, V. FAP.

St. Simons Island

93 *6 mi from Brunswick.*

As large as Manhattan, with more than 14,000 year-round residents, St. Simons is the Golden Isles' most complete resort destination. Fortunately, accelerated development in recent years has failed to spoil the natural beauty of the island's regal live oaks, beaches, and salt marshes. Visits are highlighted by swimming and sunning, golfing, biking, hiking, fishing, horseback riding, touring historic sites, and feasting on fresh local seafood at more than 50 restaurants.

Many sights and activities are in the **village** area along Mallery Street at the more developed south end of the island, where there are shops, several restaurants, pubs, and a popular public pier. A quaint "trolley" takes visitors on a 1½-hour guided tour of the island, leaving from near the pier several times a day in high season, less frequently in winter; cost is $10.

Neptune Park (✉ 550 Beachview Dr., ☎ 912/638–2393), on the island's south end, has picnic tables, a children's play park, miniature golf, and beach access. A swimming pool ($2 per person), with showers and rest rooms, is open each summer in the **Neptune Park Casino.**

St. Simons Lighthouse, a beacon since 1872, is virtually the symbol of St. Simons. The **Museum of Coastal History** in the lightkeeper's cottage has a permanent exhibit of coastal history. ✉ *101 12th St.,* ☎ *912/638–4666.* *$3, including lighthouse.* *Mon.–Sat. 10–5, Sun. 1:30–5.*

At the burgeoning north end of the island there's a marina, a golf club, and a housing development, as well as **Fort Frederica National Monument,** the ruins of a fort built by English troops in the mid-1730s as a bulwark against a Spanish invasion from Florida. Around the fort are the foundations of homes and shops. Start at the **National Park Service Visitors Center,** which has a film and displays. ✉ *Off Frederica Rd. just past Christ Episcopal Church,* ☎ *912/638–3639.* *$4 per car.* *Daily 9–5.*

Consecrated in 1886 following an earlier structure's desecration by Union troops, the white-frame Gothic-style **Christ Episcopal Church** is surrounded by live oaks, dogwoods, and azaleas. The interior has beautiful stained-glass windows. ✉ *6329 Frederica Rd.,* ☎ *912/638–8683.* *Donations welcome.*

Dining and Lodging

$$ ✕ **The Redfern Café.** A popular spot with locals, the Redfern features 8–10 specials each night in addition to the regular menu. Fried oysters in a light cornmeal coating, shrimp and crab bisque with corn fritters, and the crab cakes are specialties. ✉ *200 Redfern Village,* ☎ *912/634–1344. Reservations essential. MC, V. Closed Sun. No lunch.*

$–$$ ✕ **Blanche's Courtyard.** In the village, this lively restaurant and nightclub has a "Bayou Victorian" style, with lots of antiques and memorabilia. The menu features seafood as well as basic steak and chicken dishes. Blue crab soup is a local favorite, and the huge seafood platter could easily feed two. Be sure to taste the popular apple fritters, known as "sweet puppies." ✉ *440 King's Way,* ☎ *912/638–3030. AE, DC, MC, V. Closed Mon. No lunch.*

$-$$ ✕ **Georgia Sea Grill.** This tiny and very popular place does a wide variety of fare, from such local dishes as the blue crab melt and key lime pie to pastas such as farfalle with spinach and feta cheese. ✉ *310B Mallory St., behind the kiosks,* ☎ *912/638–1197. MC, V. Closed Sun.–Mon. Oct.–Apr., Mon. June–Aug. No lunch.*

$$$ **Sea Palms Golf and Tennis Resort.** Given the resort's emphasis on golf and tennis, it's an ideal location for the sports-minded visitor. It is a contemporary complex with fully furnished villas, most with kitchens, nestled on an 800-acre site. Guests also enjoy Beach Club privileges. ✉ *5445 Frederica Rd., 31522,* ☎ *912/638–3351 or 800/841–6268,* FAX *912/634–8029. 117 rooms, 37 suites. 2 restaurants, lounge, 2 pools, 27-hole golf course, 12 tennis courts, health club, volleyball, bicycles, children's programs, convention center. AE, DC, MC, V.*

$$-$$$ **King and Prince Beach and Golf Resort.** It's worth the trouble to get a room with easy beach access. Guest rooms are spacious, and villas have two or three bedrooms. The villas are owned by private individuals, so the total number available for rent varies from time to time. ✉ *201 Arnold Rd., Box 20798, 31522,* ☎ *912/638–3631 or 800/342–0212,* FAX *912/634–1720. 130 rooms, 10 suites, 43 villas. 2 restaurants, lounge, 1 indoor and 4 outdoor pools, hot tub, golf privileges, 4 tennis courts, bicycles, concierge. AE, D, MC, V.*

$$ **Holiday Inn Express.** With brightly decorated rooms at great prices, this nonsmoking facility is an excellent choice for the budget traveler. The six king executive rooms have sofas and desks. ✉ *Plantation Village, 299 Main St., 31522,* ☎ *912/634–2175 or 800/787–4666,* FAX *912/634–2174. 60 rooms. Pool, bicycles, coin laundry, meeting rooms. AE, D, MC, V. CP.*

RENTALS

For St. Simons condo and cottage rentals, contact **Golden Isles Realty** (✉ 330 Mallory St., 31522, ☎ 912/638–8623 or 800/337–3106, FAX 912/638–6925) and **Trupp-Hodnett Enterprises** (✉ 520 Ocean Blvd., 31522, ☎ 912/638–5450 or 800/627–6850, FAX 912/638–2983).

Jekyll Island

94 *90 mi from Savannah, 10 mi from Brunswick.*

For 56 winters, between 1886 and 1942, America's rich and famous faithfully came south to Jekyll Island. Through the Gilded Age, the Great War, the Roaring '20s, and the Great Depression, Vanderbilts and Rockefellers, Morgans and Astors, Macys, Pulitzers, and Goodyears shuttered their 5th Avenue castles and retreated to the serenity of their wild Georgia island. Here they built elegant "cottages," played golf and tennis, and socialized. Early in World War II, the millionaires departed for the last time. In 1947 the state of Georgia purchased the entire island for the bargain price of $675,000.

Jekyll Island is still a 7½-mi playground but no longer restricted to the rich and famous. The golf, tennis, fishing, biking, jogging, water park, and picnic grounds are open to all. One side of the island is lined by nearly 10 mi of hard-packed Atlantic beaches; the other, by the Intracoastal Waterway and picturesque salt marshes. Deer and wild turkeys inhabit interior forests of pine, magnolia, and moss-veiled live oaks. Egrets, pelicans, herons, and sandpipers skim the gentle surf. Jekyll's clean, mostly uncommercialized public beaches are free and open year-round. Bathhouses with rest rooms, changing areas, and showers are open at regular intervals along the beach. Beachwear, suntan lotion, rafts, snacks, and drinks are available at the **Jekyll Shopping Center,** facing the beach at Beachview Drive.

Jekyll Island Museum Visitor Center gives tram tours of the Jekyll Island National Historic Landmark District. Tours originate at the Museum Visitor Center on Stable Road and include several millionaires' residences in the 240-acre historic district. Faith Chapel, illuminated by Tiffany stained-glass windows, is open for meditation daily 2–4. ✉ *I–95 to Exit 29, 375 Riverview Dr.,* ☎ *912/635–2119 group tours, 912/635–2762 daily tours, 800/841–6586,* FAX *912/635–4004.* *$10.* ⏲ *Daily 9–5, tours daily 10–3.*

Dining and Lodging

$$–$$$ ★ ✕ **Grand Dining Room.** In the Jekyll Island Club Hotel (☞ *below*), the dining room sparkles with silver and crystal. The cuisine reflects the elegance of the private hunting club that flourished from the late 19th century to the World War II era and boasted a fine chef and staff brought in from New York's Delmonico's. Today, enjoy blue crab cakes, Georgia white shrimp, and other local fare. The restaurant has its own label pinot noir and chardonnay, made by Mountain View Vineyards. ✉ *371 Riverview Dr.,* ☎ *912/635–2600. Reservations essential. Jacket required at dinner. AE, D, DC, MC, V.*

$$$–$$$$ ★ **The Beachview Club.** They literally raised the roof on an old motel to build this luxury all-suites lodging in 1998. Stucco walls are painted light yellow, and big old oak trees shade the grounds. Efficiencies have either one king or two queen beds, a desk, and a kitchenette. More luxurious suites have full kitchens. ✉ *721 N. Beachview Dr., 31527,* ☎ *912/635–2256 or 800/299–2228,* FAX *912/635–3770. 26 efficiencies, 12 suites. Kitchenettes (some), pool, hot tub, meeting room. AE, D, DC, MC, V.*

$$$ ★ **Jekyll Island Club Hotel.** Built in 1886, the four-story clubhouse with wraparound verandas and Queen Anne–style towers and turrets once served as the winter hunting retreat for wealthy financiers. In 1985 a group of Georgia businessmen spent $17 million restoring it. The guest rooms and suites are custom-decorated with mahogany beds, armoires, and plush sofas and chairs. The nearby Sans Souci Apartments, built in 1896 by a group of club members, have been converted into spacious guest rooms. The hotel operates a free shuttle to area beaches. The bed-and-breakfast packages are a great deal. ✉ *371 Riverview Dr., 31527,* ☎ *912/635–2600 or 800/535–9547,* FAX *912/635–2818. 113 rooms, 21 suites. 2 restaurants, pool, 9 tennis courts, croquet, bicycles, meeting rooms. AE, D, DC, MC, V.*

$$–$$$ **Holiday Inn Beach Resort.** Nestled amid natural dunes and oaks in a secluded oceanfront setting, this hotel has a private beach, but its rooms with balconies don't have an ocean view. The boardwalk out to the beach meanders through a lovely regional landscape, thick with palm trees and other native flora. ✉ *200 S. Beachview Dr., 31527,* ☎ *912/635–3311 or 800/753–5955,* FAX *912/635–2901. 200 rooms. Restaurant, lobby lounge, pool, 2 tennis courts, bicycles, playground. AE, D, DC, MC, V.*

$$ **Jekyll Inn.** Much of this popular oceanfront complex has been upgraded with modern conveniences like computer hookups in some rooms. The 15 acres of grounds space the buildings generously apart. Popular with families, the inn accommodates children under 17 free when they stay with parents or grandparents. Packages include summer family-focused arrangements and romantic getaways. The restaurant has an Italian theme. ✉ *975 N. Beachview Dr., 31527,* ☎ *912/635–2531 or 800/431–5190,* FAX *912/635–2332. 188 rooms, 76 villas. Restaurant, lobby lounge, in-room data ports, pool, volleyball, playground, coin laundry, meeting rooms. AE, D, DC, MC, V.*

RENTALS

Jekyll's more than 200 rental cottages and condos are handled by **Jekyll Realty** (✉ Box 13096, 31527, ☎ 912/635–3301 or 888/333–5055, FAX 912/635–3303) and **Parker-Kaufman Realty** (✉ Box 13126, 31527, ☎ 912/635–2512 or 888/453–5955, FAX 912/635–2190).

Outdoor Activities and Sports

GOLF

The **Jekyll Island Golf Course** has 63 holes, including three 18-hole, par-72 courses with a main clubhouse (✉ 322 Capt. Wylly Rd., ☎ 912/635–2368) and a 9-hole, par-36 course known as the Historic Oceanside Nine (✉ N. Beachview Dr., ☎ 912/635–2170), where the millionaires used to play. Greens fees are $26, good all day, and carts are $13.50 per person plus tax.

NATURE CENTER

The **Coastal Encounters Nature Center** runs summer programs for children and families on the ecology of the coastal islands. Programs and excursions are individually priced. At the center are exhibits about the fauna of the region. ✉ *100 S. Riverview Dr.,* ☎ *912/635–9102.* *$2.*

TENNIS

The **Jekyll Island Tennis Center** (✉ 400 Capt. Wylly Rd., ☎ 912/638–0221) has 13 clay courts, with 7 lighted for nighttime play; it hosts eight USTA-sanctioned tournaments throughout the year. Costs are $12 per hour daily 9–6 and $14 per hour for lighted courts; reservations for lighted courts are required and must be made prior to 6 PM on the day of reservation. Lighted courts are available until 10 PM.

WATER PARK

Summer Waves, an 11-acre water park, has an 18,000-square-ft wave pool, water slides, a children's activity pool with two slides, and a circular river for tubing and rafting. Guests are not permitted to bring their own equipment. ✉ *210 S. Riverview Dr.,* ☎ *912/635–2074.* *$14.95.* *Memorial Day–Labor Day, plus select weekends in May and Sept., Sun.–Fri. 10–6, Sat. 10–8 (hrs vary at beginning and end of season).*

Cumberland Island

95 *100 mi from Savannah to St. Marys via I–95, 45 mins by ferry from St. Marys.*

The largest, most southerly, and most accessible of Georgia's primitive coastal islands is Cumberland, a 16- by 3-mi sanctuary of marshes, dunes, beaches, forests, lakes and ponds, estuaries, and inlets. Waterways are home to gators, sea turtles, otters, snowy egrets, great blue herons, ibis, wood storks, and more than 300 other species of birds. In the forests are armadillos, wild horses, deer, raccoons, and an assortment of reptiles.

After the ancient Guale Indians came 16th-century Spanish missionaries, 18th-century English soldiers, and 19th-century planters. During the 1880s, the Thomas Carnegie family (he was the brother of industrialist Andrew) of Pittsburgh built several lavish homes here, but the island remained largely as nature created it. In the early 1970s, the federal government established the **Cumberland Island National Seashore** and opened this natural treasure to the public. There is no transportation on the island itself, and the only public access to the island is on the *Cumberland Queen,* a reservations-only, 146-passenger ferry based near the National Park Service Information Center at St. Marys. Ferry bookings are heavy in summer, but cancellations and no-shows often make last-minute space available. Reservations may be made up to 11 months in advance.

From the park-service docks at the island's south end, you can follow wooded nature trails, swim and sun on 18 mi of undeveloped beaches, go fishing and bird-watching, and view the ruins of Andrew Carnegie's great estate, **Dungeness.** You can also join history and nature walks led by park-service rangers. Bear in mind that summers are hot and humid and that you must bring everything you need, including your own food, soft drinks, sunscreen, and a reliable insect repellent. All trash must be transported back to the mainland. ✉ *Cumberland Island National Seashore, Box 806, 31558,* ☎ *912/882–4335,* FAX *912/673–7747.* *Round-trip ferry $10.17, day pass $4, annual pass $20.* *Mid-May–Sept., ferry departure from St. Marys daily at 9 AM and 11:45 AM, from Cumberland at 10:15 AM and 4:45 PM. No ferry service Oct.–May 14, Tues.–Wed.*

Dining and Lodging

ISLAND

$$$$ **Greyfield Inn.** Cumberland Island's only accommodations are in a turn-of-the-20th-century Carnegie family home. Greyfield's public areas are filled with family mementos, furnishings, and portraits (you may feel as though you've stepped into one of Agatha Christie's mysterious Cornwall manors). Prices include all meals, transportation, tours led by a naturalist, and bike rentals. ✉ *8 N. 2nd St., Box 900, Fernandina Beach, FL 32035,* ☎ *904/261–6408,* FAX *904/321–0666. 13 rooms, 4 suites. AE, D, MC, V. FAP.*

$ **Camping.** The island has three primitive camping sites in a National Wilderness Area. Reservations are required for all camping at these sites, and the rate is $2 per person per day. To reach the sites (Hickory Hill, Yankee Paradise, and Brickhill Bluff), start north of Sea Camp dock, and then hike (with all equipment) from 4 to 10 mi. Equipment must include rope to suspend provisions from trees for critter control. Nonwilderness Stafford Beach is good for novice backpackers. A half mi from the dock, with rest rooms and showers adjacent to campsites, Sea Camp is the ideal spot for first-time campers ($4 per person per day). A maximum of 16 campsites for 60 persons is available. Reservations are required (recommended at least two months in advance); no pets or fires are allowed; and a seven-day stay is the limit. Bring all required equipment. The beach is just beyond the dunes. To make a reservation, contact the Cumberland Island National Seashore (☞ *above*).

MAINLAND

$–$$ **Greek Mediterranean Grill.** It's a block from the St. Marys River, but the sky-blue murals and Greek proprietors make it seem more like the Mediterranean than the South. Traditional Greek dishes, such as *pastitso* (pasta and ground beef baked with cinnamon and white cream sauce) and moussaka, are the mainstay. ✉ *122 Osborne St., St. Marys 31558,* ☎ *912/576–2000. No credit cards.*

$$–$$$ **Spencer House Inn.** This comfortable Victorian inn dates from 1872 and is named for the sea captain who built it as a hotel. Innkeepers Mike and Mary Neff reside here and will prepare picnic lunches if you ask. The inn makes a perfect base for a tour of historic St. Marys and the waterfront and is convenient to the *Cumberland Queen* ferry. ✉ *200 Osborne St., St. Marys 31558,* ☎ *912/882–1872,* FAX *912/882–9427. 13 rooms, 1 suite. AE, D, MC, V. BP.*

Okefenokee National Wildlife Refuge

40 mi from Brunswick, 38 mi from St. Marys.

Covering 730 square mi of southeast Georgia and spilling over into ★ 96 northeast Florida, the **Okefenokee,** with its mysterious rivers and lakes, bristles with seen and unseen life. Scientists agree that the Okefenokee, the largest intact freshwater wetlands in the contiguous United States, is not duplicated anywhere else on earth. The impenetrable Pinhook Swamp to the south, part of the same ecosystem, adds another 100 square mi. If the term *swamp* denotes a dark, dank place, the Okefenokee is never that. Instead, it is a vast peat bog with numerous and varied landscapes, including aquatic prairies, towering virgin cypress, sandy pine islands, and lush subtropical hammocks. During the last Ice Age 10,000 years ago, it was part of the ocean flow. Peat began building up 7,000 years ago atop a mound of clay, now 120 ft above sea level. Two rivers, the St. Marys and the Suwanee, flow out of the refuge, and it provides at least a part-time habitat for myriad species of birds, mammals, reptiles, amphibians, and fish.

As you travel by canoe or speedboat among the water lilies and the great stands of live oaks and cypress, be on the lookout for, among many others, alligators, otters, bobcats, raccoons, opossums, white-tailed deer, turtles, bald eagles, red-tailed hawks, egrets, muskrats, herons, cranes, and red-cockaded woodpeckers. The black bears tend to be more reclusive.

The Seminole people, in their migrations south toward Florida's Everglades, once took refuge in the Okefenokee. The last Native Americans to occupy the area, they were evicted by the army and Georgia's militia in the 1830s. When the Okefenokee acquired its present status of federal preserve (1937), the white homesteaders on its fringe were forced out.

Noting the many floating islands, the Seminole named this unique combination of land and water "Land of the Quivering Earth." If you have the rare fortune to walk one of these bogs, you will find the earth does indeed quiver, rather like fruit gelatin in a bowl.

The Okefenokee Swamp Park (☞ *below*), 8 mi south of Waycross, is a nonprofit development. The northern entrance to the refuge is here. There are two other gateways to the swamp: an eastern entrance at U.S. Fish & Wildlife Service Headquarters in the Suwanee Canal Recreation Area (☞ *below*), near Folkston; and a western entrance at Stephen C. Foster State Park (☞ *below*), outside the town of Fargo. You may take an overnight canoeing-camping trip into the interior, but the Okefenokee is a wildlife refuge and designated national wilderness, not a park. Access is restricted by permit. The best way to see the Okefenokee up close is to take a day trip at one of the three gateways. Plan your visit between September and April to avoid the biting insects that emerge in May, especially in the dense interior.

South of Waycross, via U.S. 1, **Okefenokee Swamp Park** has orientation programs, exhibits, a 1⅓-mi nature trail, observation areas, wilderness walkways, an outdoor museum of pioneer life, and boat tours into the swamp that reveal its unique ecology. A boardwalk and 90-ft tower are excellent places to glimpse cruising gators and a variety of birds. You may arrange for guided boat tours at an additional cost. A 1½-mi train tour passes by a Seminole village and stops at Pioneer Island, a re-created pioneer homestead, for a 30-minute walking tour. ✉ *5700 Swamp Park Rd., Waycross 31501,* ☎ *912/283–0583,* FAX *912/283–0023.* 💳 *$10, additional costs for tour packages.* ⏲ *Daily 9–5:30.*

Stephen C. Foster State Park, 18 mi from Fargo via Route 177, is an 80-acre island park within the Okefenokee National Wildlife Refuge. The park encompasses a large cypress and black gum forest, a majestic backdrop for one of the thickest growths of vegetation in the southeastern United States. Park naturalists leading boat tours will spill out a wealth of Okefenokee lore while you observe alligators, birds, and native trees and plants. You may also take a self-guided excursion in rental canoes and a motorized, flat-bottom boat. Campsites and cabins are available (☞ Lodging, *below*). ✉ *Rte. 1, Box 131, Fargo 31631,* ☎ *912/637–5274.* *$5 per vehicle to National Wildlife Refuge.*

Suwanee Canal Recreation Area, 8 mi south of Folkston via GA 121/23, is administered by the U.S. Fish and Wildlife Service. Stop first at the visitor center, with exhibits on the Okefenokee's flora and fauna. A boardwalk takes you over the water to a 50-ft observation tower. The concession has equipment rentals and daily food service; you may sign up here for one- or two-hour guided boat tours. Hikers, bicyclists, and private motor vehicles are welcome on the Swamp Island Drive; several interpretive walking trails may be taken along the way. Picnicking is allowed. Wilderness canoeing and camping in the Okefenokee's interior are by reserved fee permit only. Permits are hard to get, especially in cool weather. Call refuge headquarters (☎ 912/496–3331) when it opens at 7 AM *exactly* two months in advance of the desired starting date. Guided overnight canoe trips can be arranged by refuge concessionaire Carl E. Glenn Jr. ✉ *Rte. 2, Box 3325, Folkston 31537,* ☎ *912/496–7156. Refuge headquarters:* ✉ *Rte. 2, Box 3330, Folkston 31537,* ☎ *912/496–7836.* *$5 per car; 1-hr tours $10.50; 2-hr tours $19.* ⏲ *Refuge Mar.–Sept. 10, daily 6:30 AM–7:30 PM; Sept. 11–Feb., daily 8–6.*

Lodging

$$–$$$ **The Inn at Folkston.** This craftsman-style inn has a huge front veranda and four working gas-log fireplaces. The inn is just 7 mi from the refuge, and guest rooms are individually decorated. The Garden Room has a king-size bed and whirlpool tub. ✉ *509 W. Main St., Folkston 31537,* ☎ *912/496–6256 or 888/509–6246. 4 rooms. AE, MC, V. BP.*

$ **Laura S. Walker State Park.** Named for a Waycross teacher who championed conservation, the park, 9 mi from Okefenokee Swamp Park, has campsites with electrical and water hookups. Be sure to pick up food and supplies on the way to the park. Boating and skiing are permitted on the 120-acre lake, and there's an 18-hole championship golf course, with all amenities. The cost is $20; carts are $10. ✉ *5500 Laura Walker Rd., Waycross 31503,* ☎ *912/287–4900 or 800/864–7275. Picnic areas, pool, fishing, playground.*

$ **Stephen C. Foster State Park.** The park has two-room furnished cottages, each capable of sleeping eight, and campsites with water, electricity, rest rooms, and showers. Because of roaming wildlife and poachers and because of the park's location inside the refuge, the gates close between sunset and sunrise. If you're staying overnight, stop for groceries before you get here. ✉ *Fargo 31631,* ☎ *912/637–5274 or 800/864–7275.*

The Coastal Isles and the Okefenokee A to Z

Arriving, Departing, and Getting Around

BY CAR

From Brunswick, take the Jekyll Island Causeway ($2 per car) to Jekyll Island, and the Torras Causeway to St. Simons and Sea Island. You can get by without a car on Jekyll Island and Sea Island, but you'll need one on St. Simons. You cannot bring a car to Cumberland Island or Little St. Simons. To reach the Sapelo Island Visitors Center, take U.S. 17 north to Darien. At the courthouse, turn right onto GA 99 and take it for 8 mi. Then, make a right on Landing Road and follow the signs for the Sapelo Island National Estuarine Research Reserve.

BY FERRY

Cumberland Island and Little St. Simons are accessible only by ferry or private launch (☞ *above*). You can also get to Sapelo Island by ferry (☞ *above*).

BY PLANE

The coastal isles are served by Glynco Jetport, 6 mi north of Brunswick, which is served in turn by Delta affiliate **Atlantic Southeast Airlines** (ASA; ☎ 800/282–3424), with flights from Atlanta.

Visitor Information

The **Brunswick and the Golden Isles Visitors Center** (✉ 2000 Glynn Ave., Brunswick 31520, ☎ 912/264–5337 or 800/933–2627) provides helpful information on all of the Golden Isles. Georgia has centralized park reservations (Reservation Resource) for the state's **Department of Natural Resources** parks. For reservations, call ☎ 800/864–7275. In metropolitan Atlanta, the reservation number is ☎ 770/398–7275. For general park information, call ☎ 404/656–3530.

ATHENS TO AUGUSTA

If it's traces of the old South you crave, you'll want to take in Georgia's Antebellum Trail, a former stagecoach route that is now a highway, U.S. 441. It is dotted with small towns, like Madison, Eatonton, and Milledgeville, saturated in historic architecture: you'll find an abundance of white-columned mansions, shaded verandas, and magnolia gardens reminiscent of pre–Civil War days. Try to plan a visit in April or October, when these towns host community tours of their homes and gardens.

We begin in Athens—with its historic homes, thriving music and entertainment scene, and the University of Georgia—following the Antebellum Trail south to Macon. A visit to Washington and Augusta necessitates a side trip east along U.S. 78 and I–20, but both are well worth the detour, as they are steeped in history and tradition.

Athens

90 mi from Atlanta via I–85 north to GA 316.

Athens, the artistic jewel of the American South, is known as a breeding ground for such famed rock groups as the B-52's and R.E.M. Because of this distinction, creative types from all over the country flock to its trendy streets in hopes of becoming, or catching a glimpse of, the next big act to take the world by storm. At the center of this artistic melee is the University of Georgia (UGA). With more than 28,000 students, UGA lends its influential ingredient into the Athens mix, giving the quaint but compact city a distinct flavor that falls somewhere between a misty Southern enclave, a rollicking college town, and a smoky, jazz-club studded alleyway. It truly is a fascinating blend of Mayberry R.F.D. and MTV. The effect is as irresistible as it is authentic.

While the streets bustle at night with students taking in the coffee-house and concert life, Athens's quieter side also flourishes. The streets are lined with many gorgeous old homes, some of which are open to the public. Most prominent among them is the **Athens Welcome Center** (✉ 280 E. Dougherty St., ☎ 706/353–1820) in the town's oldest surviving residence, the 1820 Church-Waddel-Brumby House. Athens also has several splendid Greek Revival buildings, including, on campus, the University Chapel, built in 1832, and the **university president's house** (✉ 570 Prince Ave.), built in the late 1850s. The **Taylor-Grady House** (✉ 634 Prince Ave.) was constructed in 1844. The 1844 **Franklin House** (✉ 480 E. Broad St.) has been restored and reopened as an office building.

Just outside the Athens city limits is the **State Botanical Gardens of Georgia,** a tranquil, 313-acre wonderland of aromatic gardens and woodland paths. It has a massive conservatory overlooking the International Garden that functions as a welcome foyer and houses an art gallery, gift shop, and café. ✉ *2450 S. Milledge Ave., off U.S. 129/441,* ☎ *706/542–1244.* *Free.* *Grounds: Apr.–Sept. weekdays 8–8, Oct.–Mar. weekdays 8–6; visitor center: Tues.–Sat. 9–4:30, Sun. 11:30–4:30.*

Dining and Lodging

$–$$ ✕ **East West Bistro.** This popular bistro, one of the busiest spots in downtown Athens, has a bar, formal upstairs dining, and casual dining downstairs. The most interesting selections downstairs are the small plates that allow you to sample cuisines from around the world—from vegetable tempura to salmon bruschetta. The quieter upstairs dining room serves a more expensive classic Italian menu. ✉ *351 E. Broad St.,* ☎ *706/546–4240. AE, D, MC, V.*

$–$$ ✕ **Harry Bissett's.** One of the best restaurants in Athens, it serves sumptuous Cajun recipes straight from the streets of New Orleans. Wait for your table at the oyster bar, where they charge you by the shell. ✉ *279 E. Broad St.,* ☎ *706/353–7065. AE, D, MC, V. No lunch Mon.*

$ ✕ **Last Resort Grill.** It's a pleasant place to unwind with its cheery sidewalk café section. The cuisine is a cross between Tex-Mex and California, with items such as salmon and black bean quesadillas, roasted eggplant sandwiches, and grilled shiitake mushrooms and feta cheese tossed with pasta. ✉ *174 W. Clayton St.,* ☎ *706/549–0810. AE, D, MC, V.*

$ ✕ **Weaver D's Fine Foods.** This place not only serves some of the best soul food in Athens-Clarke County, it's also a piece of musical history; R.E.M. was so inspired by Weaver D's service motto, "Automatic for the People," that the band named its 1992 album after it. ✉ *247 E. Washington St.,* ☎ *706/353–7797. No credit cards.*

$$–$$$ **Magnolia Terrace.** This bed-and-breakfast is housed in a 1912 mansion right in the middle of the historic district. Each room is decorated with a mishmash of antiques. It's within walking distance of the Grit, a popular vegetarian restaurant founded by one of Athens's musical prodigies, Michael Stipe of R.E.M., who himself lives close by in a house marked by big, opulent gates. ✉ *288 Hill St., 30601,* ☎ *706/548–3860,* FAX *706/369–3439. 8 rooms, 1 suite. AE, D, MC, V. BP.*

$$ **Nicholson House.** This 19th-century house, set on 6 acres of an 18th-century land grant originally deeded to William Few, one of Georgia's two signers of the U.S. Constitution, is, at its core, a two-over-two log house. Later additions and changes hide this original structure beneath a 1947 Colonial Revival exterior. The inn has a wide front veranda with rocking chairs. Rooms are decorated in rich colors, and furnishings are a mix of antiques and good reproductions. ✉ *6295 Jefferson Rd., 30607,* ☎ *706/353–2200,* FAX *706/353–7799. 6 rooms, 3 suites. AE, D, MC, V. BP.*

$ **Best Western Colonial Inn.** Just ½ mi from the UGA campus, it's a favorite among visiting relatives in town to attend graduation. Some rooms come with a microwave and refrigerator, and all rooms are equipped with a coffeemaker. Directly across the street is the Varsity Drive-In, where hungry students have been feasting on smothered hot dogs and heaps of fries for years. ✉ *170 N. Milledge Ave., 30607,* ☎ *706/546–7311 or 800/528–1234,* FAX *706/546–7959. 69 rooms. Refrigerators (some), pool. AE, D, DC, MC, V.*

Nightlife and the Arts

THE ARTS

The **Classic Center** (✉ 300 N. Thomas St., ☎ 706/357–4444) features a splendid array of plays and other theatrical performances. The ultramod **Georgia Theater** (✉ 215 N. Lumpkin St., ☎ 706/549–9918) doubles as a movie house and concert hall, showcasing edgy cinema and booking local bands. **UGA's Performing Arts Center** (✉ South Campus on River Rd., ☎ 706/542–4400) routinely has world-class music recitals—by the Atlanta Symphony orchestra, for example—and modern dance shows.

NIGHTLIFE

For some boisterous rock-a-billy tunes, check out **Bumpers** (✉ 1720 Commerce Dr., ☎ 706/369–7625). **40 Watt Club** (✉ 285 W. Washington St., ☎ 706/549–7871) is the launching pad of numerous rock groups, such as R.E.M., that later went on to superstar status. Famed greats such as Bessie Smith and Cab Calloway regularly performed at **Morton Theatre** (✉ 195 W. Washington St., ☎ 706/613–3770), listed on the National Register of Historic Places; it is now a performing arts center with musicals, concerts, and modern dance.

Madison

30 mi south of Athens via U.S. 129/441, 60 mi east of Atlanta via I–20 to U.S. 129/441.

Directly south of Athens is this small treasure filled with plenty of restaurants and irresistible antiques shops and gift boutiques. The town is a virtual odyssey of well-preserved examples of antebellum and Victorian architecture, a treat since so few buildings in Atlanta escaped the torches of the Union troops. Madison's homes are well preserved largely because of a curious stroke of luck: when Major General William Tecumseh Sherman (1820–91) burned a path through Georgia during the Civil War, he left Madison intact because of his friendship with U.S. Senator Joshua Hill, a Madison resident and Union sympathizer. That's how Madison earned the moniker "The Town that Sherman refused to burn." Hill's former home (not open to the public) is now one of Madison's most cherished mansions.

The **Madison-Morgan Cultural Center,** housed in an early 20th-century schoolhouse built in Romanesque Revival style, has tools and furniture from the late 19th century and a restored classroom of the period, plus information and printed guides on the Joshua Hill house and other historic sites in town. ✉ *434 S. Main St.,* ☎ *706/342–4743.* *$3.* *Tues.–Sat. 10–5.*

At **Heritage Hall** (✉ 277 S. Main St., ☎ 706/342–9627), you can take a guided tour of a preserved 1833 Greek Revival home and learn about aspects of antebellum high-brow society life.

The **welcome center** (✉ 115 E. Jefferson St., ☎ 706/342–4454) provides maps for walking tours of historic neighborhoods and three house museums as well as information regarding annual events and celebrations.

Dining and Lodging

$ ✕ **Ye Olde Colonial Restaurant.** Housed in a renovated bank building (complete with seating accommodations in the former vault), this cafeteria-style restaurant is a must for hungry patrons passing through Madison. The buffet is a complete cornucopia of Southern faves: butterbeans, country-fried steak, sweet-potato casserole, fried chicken, corn bread, cobbler and, of course, iced tea. ✉ *108 W. Washington St.,* ☎ *706/342–2211. AE, D, MC, V. Closed Sun.*

$ ✕ **Yesterday Cafe.** The brick walls of this former pharmacy are lined with archival black-and-white photographs. Drawing patrons from Atlanta to Eatonton and Athens, Teri Bragg has developed a following for her traditional but updated Southern fare: country fried steak with mashed red-skin potatoes, fresh vegetables, and buttermilk pie from an old recipe. The full Southern breakfast, served Tuesday through Sunday, is outstanding. It is 8 mi west of Madison. ✉ *120 Fairplay St., Rutledge,* ☎ *706/557–9337. AE, MC, V. No dinner Sun.–Wed.*

$$ **Burnett Place.** This charming bed-and-breakfast, right in the heart of town, is housed in a gorgeous Federal-style home built in the early 1800s. The guest rooms are spacious and inviting, and the proprietors are friendly and knowledgeable about the history of the region. ✉ *317 Old Post Rd., 30650,* ☎ *706/342–4034. 3 rooms. MC, V. BP.*

$$ **The Farmhouse Inn.** It is on a farm that has been in Melinda Hartney's family for generations. Guests have private entrances to their rooms, which are off a common area where they enjoy breakfast and late-afternoon gatherings. Over the barn is an apartment suite. The inn is 6 mi east of Madison. ✉ *1051 Meadow La., Madison, 30650,* ☎ *706/342–7933. 5 rooms, 1 suite. AE, MC, V. BP.*

Eatonton

26 mi south of Madison on U.S. 129/441.

It's not your imagination—that really is a giant rabbit on the Eatonton courthouse lawn. This small town is the birthplace of celebrated novelist Joel Chandler Harris of Br'er Rabbit and Uncle Remus fame. The **Uncle Remus Museum,** built from authentic slave cabins, houses countless carvings, paintings, and other artwork depicting the characters made famous by the imaginative author. It's on the grounds of a park. ✉ *Turner Park, U.S. 441,* ☎ *706/485–6856.* *50¢.* *June–Aug., Mon.–Sat. 10–noon, Sun. 1–5; Sept.–May, Wed.–Mon. 10–noon, Sun. 1–5.*

The **Eatonton-Putnam Chamber of Commerce** (✉ 105 Sumter St., ☎ 706/485–7701) provides printed maps detailing landmarks from the upbringing of Eatonton native Alice Walker, who won the Pulitzer Prize for her novel *The Color Purple.* It also has information on the many fine examples of antebellum architecture in Eatonton, including descriptions and photographs of the town's prize antebellum mansions, and a walking tour of homes.

Lodging

$$ **Crockett House.** With its aromatic gardens, majestic wraparound porch, and in-room fireplaces, this bed-and-breakfast nestled in a restored 1895 Victorian home is perfect for a romantic getaway. Make sure to get a room with an old-fashioned, claw-foot bathtub. All rooms have working fireplaces. ✉ *671 Madison Rd., 31024,* ☎ *706/485–2248. 6 rooms. AE, MC, V. BP.*

Milledgeville

17 mi south of Eatonton on U.S. 441.

Locals believe ghosts haunt what remains of the antebellum homes in Milledgeville. Formerly the state capital of Georgia (a title held for 64 years), the town was not as fortunate as Madison in terms of torch exposure. Sherman's troops stormed through with a vengeance after the general heard hardship stories from Union soldiers who had escaped from a prisoner-of-war camp in nearby Andersonville. The 1838 Greek Revival **Old Governor's Mansion** became Sherman's headquarters during the war. His soldiers are said to have tossed government documents out of the windows and fueled their fires with Confederate money. Guided tours of the building, now a museum home, are given daily. ✉ *120 S. Clark St.,* ☎ *912/453–4545.* 🎫 *$5.* ⏲ *Tues.–Sat. 10–4, Sun. 2–4.*

On West Hancock Street is the Georgia College and State University campus. One of its most famous students was prolific Southern novelist Flannery O'Connor, author of such acclaimed novels as *Wise Blood* and *The Violent Bear It Away.* O'Connor did most of her writing at the family farm, Andalusia, just north of Milledgeville on U.S. 441. The **Flannery O'Connor Room,** inside the **Ina Russell Library,** has many of the author's hand-written manuscripts on display. It also contains O'Connor's typewriter and some of her furniture. ✉ *231 West Hancock St.,* ☎ *912/445–4047.* 🎫 *Free.* ⏲ *Weekdays 9–4.*

Dining and Lodging

$ ✕ **The Brick.** This bar-restaurant has a comfortable, worn-at-the-elbows appeal, and comfort is important when you're about to consume massive pizzas with epicurean toppings like feta cheese and spinach. The menu also has salads and calzones. ✉ *136 W. Hancock St.,* ☎ *912/452–0089. AE, D, MC, V. Closed Sun.*

$–$$ 🏨 **Antebellum Inn.** Each room of this pre–Civil War mansion is beautifully appointed with period antiques. Fabulous full Southern breakfasts are included in the rate. ✉ *200 N. Columbia St., 31061,* ☎ *912/453–3993. 5 rooms. Pool. AE, MC, V. BP.* 🚭

Macon

30 mi southwest of Milledgeville via U.S. 441 to GA 49, 90 mi southeast of Atlanta via I–75.

At the state's geographic center, Macon, founded in 1823, has more than 100,000 flowering cherry trees, which it celebrates each March with a knockout festival. Its antebellum and Victorian homes are among the state's best preserved. Famous artists who have called Macon home include flutist and pre–Civil War poet laureate of the United States Sidney Lanier, violinist Robert McDuffie, Little Richard, the Allman Brothers, and Otis Redding.

To enjoy Macon at night, get a copy of the brochure *Lights on Macon* from the **Macon Convention and Visitors Bureau** (✉ 200 Cherry St., ☎ 912/743–3401 or 800/768–3401) in the old train station.

★ Among the city's many sites to see is the **Georgia Music Hall of Fame,** appropriately located in Macon as a tribute to the city's extensive contribution to American music. The museum is a joint effort of state and private resources and is dedicated to Georgians who have helped define America's musical culture. Among the honorees are Ray Charles, James Brown, the Allman Brothers Band, Chet Atkins, R.E.M., and the B-52's. Exhibits pay homage to classical musicians including Robert Shaw, the late director emeritus of the Atlanta Symphony Orchestra;

opera singers Jessye Norman and James Melton; and violinist Robert McDuffie. ✉ *200 Martin Luther King Jr. Blvd.,* ☎ *912/750–8555.* 🎫 *$8.* ⏲ *Mon.–Sat. 9–4:30, Sun. 1–4:30.*

The **Georgia Sports Hall of Fame,** with its old-style ticket booths, has the look and feel of an old ballpark. Exhibits honor sports at all levels, from prep and college teams to professional. ✉ *301 Cherry St.,* ☎ *912/752–1585.* 🎫 *$6.* ⏲ *Mon.–Sat. 9–5, Sun. 1–5.*

★ The unique **Hay House,** designed by the New York firm T. Thomas & Son, is a virtual study in fine Italianate architecture prior to the Civil War. The marvelous stained-glass windows and many technological advances, including indoor plumbing, make a tour worthwhile. ✉ *934 Georgia Ave.,* ☎ *912/742–8155.* 🎫 *$6.* ⏲ *Mon.–Sat. 10–4:30, Sun. 1–4:30.*

African-American entrepreneur Charles H. Douglass built the **Douglass Theatre** in 1921. Great American musicians have performed here, among them Bessie Smith, Ma Rainey, Cab Calloway, Duke Ellington, and locals Little Richard and Otis Redding. It is currently a venue for movies, plays, and other performances. You can take a guided tour of the building. ✉ *355 Martin Luther King Jr. Blvd.,* ☎ *912/742–2000.* 🎫 *$2.* ⏲ *Tues.–Sat. 9–5.*

The **Macon Museum of Arts and Sciences and Mark Smith Planetarium** displays everything from a whale skeleton to fine art. Discovery House, an interactive exhibit for children, is modeled after an artist's garret. ✉ *4182 Forsyth Rd.,* ☎ *912/477–3232.* 🎫 *$5.* ⏲ *Mon.–Thurs. and Sat. 9–5, Fri. 9–9, Sun. 1–5.*

Just 3 mi east of the city limits, the **Ocmulgee National Monument,** a significant archaeological site, was occupied for more than 10,000 years and was at its peak under the Mississippian peoples who lived here between AD 900 and 1100. There are a reconstructed earth lodge and displays of pottery, effigies, and jewelry of copper and shells discovered in the burial mound. ✉ *U.S. 80 east of Macon, 1207 Emery Hwy.,* ☎ *912/752–8257,* FAX *912/752–8259.* 🎫 *Free.* ⏲ *Daily 9–5.*

The **Tubman African American Museum** honors the former slave who led more than 300 people to freedom as one of the conductors on the Underground Railroad. A mural depicts several centuries of black history and culture. The museum also has an African artifacts gallery. ✉ *340 Walnut St.,* ☎ *912/743–8544.* 🎫 *$3.* ⏲ *Weekdays 9–5, Sat. 10–5, Sun. 2–5.*

OFF THE BEATEN PATH

MUSEUM OF AVIATION – This museum at Robins Air Force Base has an extraordinary collection of 90 vintage aircraft including a MIG, an SR-71 (Blackbird), a U-2, and assorted other flying machines from past campaigns. From Macon, take I–75 south to Exit 146 (Centerville/Warner Robins), and turn left onto Watson Boulevard, 7 mi to GA 247, then right for 2 mi. ✉ *GA 247 at Russell Pkwy., Warner Robins, 20 mi south of Macon,* ☎ *912/926–6870.* 🎫 *Free; film $2.* ⏲ *Daily 9–5.*

Dining and Lodging

$ ✕ **The Cherry Corner.** This taste of Italy is the perfect spot for lunch, a quick snack of pizza or soup, or coffee and a pastry. Dine at one of the sidewalk tables for a view of Macon's 19th-century buildings and blooming flowers. ✉ *502 Cherry St.,* ☎ *912/741–9525. MC, V. Closed Sun. No dinner Mon.–Thurs.*

$$$ ★ ✕ 🏨 **Henderson Village.** Stunning 19th- and early 20th-century farm buildings, some original to the site, are clustered around a green. Guest rooms are rustic, but suites are more elegant, with fireplaces and whirlpool tubs. Buttermilk-yellow walls give the fine 1838 Langston House restaurant a warm atmosphere, perfect for a meal of squab and foie gras on a potato haystack or wild game on buckwheat polenta. Perry is 30 mi south of Macon, 1 mi off I–75. ✉ *125 S. Langston Circle, Perry 31069,* ☎ *912/988–8696 or 888/615–9722,* FAX *912/988–9009. 19 rooms, 5 suites. Restaurant, pool, in-room VCRs, hot tubs, convention center. AE, MC, V. BP.*

$$$–$$$$ 🏨 **1842 Inn.** With its grand, white-pillared front porch and period antiques, this inn offers a taste of antebellum Macon. You can eat breakfast in your room, in one of the parlors, or in the courtyard. It's an easy walk to downtown and the historic district. ✉ *353 College St.,* ☎ *912/741–1842 or 800/336–1842,* FAX *912/741–1842. 21 rooms. In-room data ports, hot tubs. AE, MC, V. BP.*

Washington

38 mi east of Athens via U.S. 78, 100 mi east of Atlanta via I–20 to Exit 154.

Washington, the first city chartered in honor of the country's first president, is a living museum of Southern culture. Brick buildings, some of which date back to the American Revolution, line the lively downtown area, which bustles with shops, cafés, and antiques shops. People live and work downtown, giving Washington a little-city appeal that separates it from most other small Southern towns. The Confederate treasury was moved here from Richmond in 1865, and soon afterward the half-million dollars in gold vanished. This mysterious event has been the inspiration for many a treasure hunt, since many like to believe the gold is still buried somewhere in Wilkes County.

The **Washington-Wilkes Chamber of Commerce** (✉ 104 E. Liberty St., ☎ 706/678–2013) is a good starting point for exploring the town. It has information about antebellum life and architecture. The **Washington Historical Museum** (✉ 308 E. Robert Toombs Ave., ☎ 706/678–2105) houses a collection of Civil War relics, including the camp chest of Jefferson Davis. The **Robert Toombs House** (216 E. Robert Toombs Ave., ☎ 706/678–2226) is furnished with 19th-century antiques, some of which are the personal items of former U.S. Senator Robert Toombs, who served as secretary of state during the Civil War.

Be sure to stop by historic **Callaway Plantation.** Here you can experience the closest thing to an operating plantation, dating back to 1785. Among a cluster of buildings on the estate you'll find a blacksmith's house, school house, and weaving house. An ancient family cemetery is also fun to explore. During the second week of April and October the estate comes alive with Civil-War reenactments and activities such as butter-churning and quilting demonstrations. ✉ *U.S. 78,* ☎ *706/678–7060.* 🎟 *$4.* ⏲ *Tues.–Sat. 10–5, Sun. 2–5.*

Dining and Lodging

$ ✕ **Another Thyme Cafe.** This café on the square in downtown Washington makes excellent salads and sandwiches. Try the grilled vegetables on focaccia. Dinner goes upscale but stays regional with fried green tomatoes, sweet-potato chips, and fried seafood. Homemade breads and desserts (pecan pie) are worth the trip. ✉ *5 East Public Sq.,* ☎ *706/678–1672. AE, D, MC, V. Closed Sun. No dinner Mon., Oct.–Mar.*

$$ 🏨 **Maynard's Manor.** This Classical Revival structure, originally built in 1820, was transformed into a B&B in 1998. Fireplaces in the main house warm the public spaces. Guests can gather in the library and parlor for conversation and light refreshments. The day begins with coffee, tea, and juice in the main hall at 7 AM, followed by a full breakfast in the morning rooms. ✉ *219 E. Robert Toombs Ave., 30673,* ☎ *706/678–4303. 6 rooms, 1 guesthouse suite. MC, V. BP.*

Augusta

60 mi east of Washington via U.S. 78 to I–20, 151 mi east of Atlanta via I–20.

Although Augusta escaped the ravages of Union troops during the Civil War, nature herself was not so kind. Situated on a river crossing along the Savannah River, the town was flooded many times before modern-day city planning redirected the water into a collection of small lakes and creeks. Now the current is so mild that citizens gather to send bathtub toys downstream every year in the annual Rubber Duck Race.

Augusta is Georgia's third-oldest city, founded in 1736 by James Edward Oglethorpe, who founded Savannah in 1733. The city was named for Augusta, Princess of Wales, wife of the future Frederick Louis, Prince of Wales. Augusta served as Georgia's capital from 1785 to 1795. The well-maintained paths of **Riverwalk** (✉ between 5th and 10th Sts.) curve along the Savannah River and are the perfect place for a leisurely stroll. **Olde Town,** lying along Telfair and Greene streets, is a restored neighborhood of Victorian homes. The 1845 tree-lined **Augusta Canal** is another pleasant place for a walk.

Many antebellum and Victorian homes of interest are spread throughout the city. The **Ezekiel Harris House** dates from the late 18th century and is notable for its exterior staircase, a space-saving feature, and its gambrel roof. ✉ *1840 Broad St.,* ☎ *706/737–2820.* 🎟 *$2.* ⏲ *Sat. 10–1 or by appointment.*

Meadow Garden was the home of George Walton, one of Georgia's three signers of the Declaration of Independence and its youngest signer, at age 26. It is documented as Augusta's oldest extant residence. ✉ *1320 Independence Dr.,* ☎ *706/724–4174.* 🎟 *$3.* ⏲ *Weekdays 10–4.*

The **Morris Museum of Southern Art** has a splendid collection of Southern art, from early landscapes and portraits through neo-Impressionism and native and modern art. ✉ *Riverfront Center, 1 10th St., 2nd floor,* ☎ *706/724–7501.* 🎟 *$3.* ⏲ *Tues.–Sat. 10–5:30, Sun. noon–5:30.*

Children love the National Science Center's **Fort Discovery,** an interactive museum with a moonwalk simulator, a bike on square wheels, a hot-air balloon, and a little car propelled by magnets. ✉ *1 7th St.,* ☎ *706/821–0200 or 800/325–5445.* 🎟 *$8.* ⏲ *Mon.–Sat. 10–5, Sun. noon–5.*

Dining and Lodging

$$–$$$$ ✕ **La Maison on Telfair.** Augusta's best entry in the fine dining category, from owner and chef Heinz Sowinski, presents a classic menu of game, sweetbreads, and, with a nod to the chef's heritage, Wiener schnitzel. The experience is enhanced by the quiet and elegant atmosphere. ✉ *404 Telfair St.,* ☎ *706/722–4805. AE, D, DC, MC, V. No lunch.*

$$–$$$ 🏨 **The Partridge Inn.** A National Trust Historic hotel, the restored inn sits at the gateway to Summerville, a hilltop neighborhood of summer homes dating to 1800. There's a splendid view of downtown Augusta from the rooftop concierge floor. Rooms are simple and sparsely decorated. Suites and some studios have full kitchens. ✉ *2110 Walton Way,*

30904, ☎ 706/737–8888 or 800/476–6888, FAX 706/731–0826. 129 rooms, 27 suites. Restaurant, bar, lounge, pool, exercise room. AE, D, DC, MC, V. BP.

Athens to Augusta A to Z

Arriving and Departing

BY BUS

Greyhound Bus Lines (✉ 220 W. Broad St., Washington, ☎ 706/678–4479 or 800/231–2222) serves the entire area.

BY CAR

U.S. 441, known as the Antebellum Trail, runs north–south, merging with U.S. 129 for a stretch and connecting Athens, Madison, Eatonton, and Milledgeville. Macon is on GA 49, which splits off of U.S. 441 at Milledgeville. The total distance from Athens to Macon is approximately 98 mi. Washington lies at the intersection of U.S. 78, running east from Athens to Thomson, and GA 44, running south to Eatonton. I–20 runs east from Atlanta to Augusta, which is about 93 mi east of U.S. 441.

BY PLANE

Athens-Clarke Airport (✉ 1501 Aviation Way, ☎ 706/613–3420) is served by US Airways for domestic flights. **Augusta Ben Epps Airport** (✉ 1010 Ben Epps Ave., ☎ 706/798–3236) is served by both Delta and US Airways for domestic flights. (For airline telephone numbers, *see* Air Travel *in* Smart Travel Tips A to Z.)

Getting Around

BY BUS

Athens Transit (☎ 706/613–3430) operates buses throughout Athens-Clarke County from 6 AM to 6:45 PM Monday through Saturday, with no service on Sunday. The fare is $1 with free transfers; exact change is required.

The **Augusta Public Transit** (☎ 706/821–1719) runs bus service throughout Augusta-Richmond County from 6:30 AM to 8:30 PM Monday though Saturday, with no bus service on Sunday. The fare is 75¢, with an additional 35¢ for a transfer; exact change is required.

The **Macon Transit Authority** (☎ 912/746–1318) provides public transportation throughout the city from 5:30 AM to 6:45 PM Monday through Saturday, with no bus service on Sunday. The fare is 75¢; transfers cost 25¢.

BY TAXI

Augusta Cab Company (☎ 706/724–3543) provides transportation throughout Augusta-Richmond County. There is a $1.75 initial charge, plus $1.50 per mile. The fare from the airport to downtown Augusta, a distance of approximately 11 mi, is around $18.

Your Cab Company (☎ 706/546–5844) is a reliable, 24-hour taxi service in Athens. Calling ahead for reservations could yield a flat rate. Rates are determined by a grid of designated zones throughout the area, starting at $3. A trip from the airport to downtown costs $6.

Contacts and Resources

BED-AND-BREAKFAST RESERVATIONS

Great Inns of Georgia (✉ 541 Londonberry Rd., Atlanta 30327, ☎ 404/843–0471 or 800/501–7328, FAX 404/252–8886) can help you choose one of this area's many inns.

EMERGENCIES

Ambulance, police (☎ 911). **Doctors Hospital** (✉ 3651 Wheeler Rd., Augusta, ☎ 706/651–3232). **Macon Northside Hospital** (✉ 400 Charter Blvd., Macon, ☎ 912/757–8200). **Medical Center** (✉ 1199 Prince Ave., Athens, ☎ 706/549–9977).

GUIDED TOURS

Augusta Cotton Exchange (✉ 32 8th St., ☎ 706/724–4067) conducts free tours of its historic brick building, with exhibits from its past as an arbiter of cotton prices. It also has Saturday van tours throughout the historic district of Augusta with a fee of $10 per person.

Classic City Tours (✉ 280 E. Dougherty Way, ☎ 706/353–1820) conducts daily tours starting from the steps of the Athens Welcome Center (☞ Visitor Information, *below*) at 2 PM. The 1½-hour tour takes participants through the city's antebellum neighborhoods. The fee is $10 per person ($8 per person for groups of 10 or more).

24-HOUR PHARMACY

CVS (✉ 1520 Walton Way, Augusta, ☎ 706/724–0598; 1271 Gray Hwy., Macon, ☎ 912/743–6979 or 912/743–8936).

VISITOR INFORMATION

Athens Convention and Visitors Bureau (✉ 300 N. Thomas St., 30601, ☎ 706/357–4430 or 800/653–0603, FAX 706/549–5636). **Eatonton-Putnam Chamber of Commerce** (✉ 105 Sumter St., Eatonton 31024, ☎ 706/485–7701). **Macon Convention and Visitors Bureau** (✉ 200 Cherry St., 31201, ☎ 912/743–3401 or 800/768–3401). **Madison/Morgan County Chamber of Commerce** (✉ 115 E. Jefferson St., Madison 30605, ☎ 706/342–4454). **Milledgeville Convention and Visitors Bureau** (✉ 200 W. Hancock St., 31061, ☎ 912/452–4687). **Washington-Wilkes Chamber of Commerce** (✉ 104 E. Liberty St., Box 661, Washington 30673, ☎ 706/678–2013).

Georgia Welcome Center (✉ Box 211090, Martinez 30917, ☎ 706/737–1446) provides maps and brochures about prominent historical and recreational sites around the state.

NORTH GEORGIA

As an antidote to the congestion of city life, nothing beats the clear skies, cascading waterfalls, and tranquil town squares to be found in north Georgia. Within a half-day's drive from Atlanta, you'll find yourself in the middle of a refreshing cluster of old Southern towns and nature sites that pepper the northern region of the state, comprising the heart of Appalachia.

Dahlonega, Cleveland, Helen, Clayton, and Ellijay, directly to the north and northeast of Atlanta, abound in shops selling such Southern finds as handmade quilts, folk-art pottery, antiques, and loads of Grandma's chowchow in gingham-capped mason jars. They also offer a range of unusual experiences, from descending into a gold mine to exploring a re-created Alpine village to picking apples. To the northwest are two of Georgia's most important historic sites: New Echota State Historic Site and Chickamauga and Chattanooga National Military Park. And whether your preference is rustic or romantic, there are plenty of bed-and-breakfast inns and campgrounds to accommodate your sensibilities.

Dahlonega

60 mi north of Atlanta on GA 400/U.S. 19.

Hoards of fortune-seekers stormed the town of Dahlonega (named after the Cherokee word for "precious yellow metal") in the early 1800s in response to the discovery of gold in the hills nearby, but by 1849 miners were seeking riches elsewhere. In fact, the famous call, "There's gold in them thar hills!" originated as an enticement to miners in the Georgia mountains to keep their minds away from the lure of the gold rush in the West. It worked for a while, but government price fixing eventually made gold mining unprofitable, and by the early 1920s Dahlonega's mining operations had halted completely.

After that most mining villages would have become ghost towns, but not Dahlonega. Today it thrives as a rustic country outpost with an irresistible town square rife with country stores, art galleries, coffee houses, gem shops, old small-town businesses, and even a sophisticated restaurant or two. The gold mines are still there but are open mainly for show. **Consolidated Gold Mine** is open to the public for guided tours. You enter the mine, which has been reconstructed for safety, go through a breathtaking stone passage, and then begin a descent down 120 ft into the mine's depths to gaze at the geological wonders all around. Tour guides expound on historical mining techniques and tools, such as the "widowmaker," a drill that kicks up mining dust and caused disease among many of the miners. Before you leave you are invited to pan for gold prospector-style from a long wooden sluice. ✉ *185 Consolidated Rd.,* ☎ *706/864–8473.* 🎟 *$10.* ⏲ *Daily 10–4.*

A U.S. mint operated in this modest boomtown from 1838 to 1861. The **Gold Museum,** in the present-day courthouse on the square, has coins, tools, and a 5½-ounce nugget. The building is the oldest in north Georgia, and if you look closely at the bricks that form the building's foundation you'll notice a sprinkling of gold dust in their formation. Along with the exhibits, the museum shows a short film celebrating the region's history through interviews with Appalachian old-timers. ✉ *Public Sq.,* ☎ *706/864–2257.* 🎟 *$2.50.* ⏲ *Daily 10–5.*

OFF THE BEATEN PATH

AMICALOLA FALLS – Rushing waters will tumble your troubles away here in no time. This is the highest waterfall east of the Mississippi, with waters plunging an eye-popping 729 ft through a cluster of seven cascades. The surrounding state park is dotted with scenic campsites and cottages strategically situated near a network of nature trails, picnic sites, and fishing streams. ✉ *Off GA 52, 18 mi west of Dahlonega,* ☎ *706/265–4703.* 🎟 *Parking $2.* ⏲ *Daily 7–10.*

Dining and Lodging

$$ ✕ **Renée's Café & Wine Bar.** This fine, casual restaurant in a 19th-century restored residence is within walking distance of the village square. The contemporary cuisine has regional and Mediterranean accents, such as crawfish tails with spinach tortellini and Gorgonzola Alfredo sauce. Upstairs, patient patrons wait for their tables in a warmly lit bar or attend one of the monthly wine tastings hosted at the restaurant. ✉ *136 N. Chestatee St.,* ☎ *706/864–6829. Reservations not accepted. MC, V. Closed Sun.–Mon. No lunch.*

$ ✕ **Smith House.** One of the most popular dining destinations in the north Georgia mountains, it has all-you-can-eat family-style meals that'll have the tables groaning under the weight of the heaping plates. Potatoes, fried chicken, peas, cobbler—you name a Southern dish and it's probably offered here. ✉ *84 S. Chestatee St.,* ☎ *706/864–2348. Reservations not accepted. AE, D, MC, V. Closed Mon.*

$$ **Worley Homestead.** This pristine bed-and-breakfast is housed in an 1845 mansion with two garden courtyards. Rates include a full country breakfast, and often on weekend evenings the proprietors arrange a wine table with cheese and crackers in the entry foyer. Each beautifully furnished room comes with a small TV. ✉ *410 W. Main St., 30533,* ☎ *706/864–7002. 7 rooms. MC, V. BP.*

$–$$ **Blueberry Inn & Gardens.** The inn, which crowns the crest of a low hill, takes its name from the wild blueberries growing on its 55 acres. Porch rocking chairs welcome guests at the end of a busy day of touring. Gracious hosts Phyllis and Harry Charnley have built a structure reminiscent of a 1920s farmhouse. Rooms are decorated with antiques and family pieces. On the grounds are mountain laurel, oaks, and dogwoods, along with flowering plants of all kinds. ✉ *400 Blueberry Hill, 30533,* ☎ *706/219–4024 or 877/219–4024,* FAX *706/219–4793. 12 rooms. MC, V. BP.*

Outdoor Activities and Sports

Appalachian Outfitters (✉ Box 793, Dahlonega 30533, ☎ 800/426–7177) provide equipment and maps for self-guided canoeing and kayaking expeditions on the Chestatee River. River trails begin at their outpost in town and extend to GA 400.

Shopping

Golden Memories Antiques (✉ 121 S. Public Sq., ☎ 706/864–7222) has an impressive array of local rocks and minerals as well as Coca-Cola collectibles for sale. **Pottery Plus** (✉ 1127-B Hwy. 52E, ☎ 706/864–8362) has Southern folk art and traditional folk-art pottery; many pieces are one-of-a-kind. **Quigley's Antiques and Books** (✉ 170-B North Public Sq., ☎ 706/864–0161) sells old and rare books, Blue Ridge china, vintage trunks, and old toys.

Cleveland

19 mi northeast of Dahlonega via U.S. 19 to U.S. 129, 60 mi northeast of Atlanta via I–985 and U.S. 129.

Cleveland's tiny town square has a number of antiques shops with some dusty steals. In the center of the square, look for the **Old White County Courthouse,** which was constructed by slaves in the mid-1800s and resembles Philadelphia's Independence Hall. ✉ *1 Cleveland Sq.,* ☎ *706/865–3225.* *Free.* *Thurs.–Sat. 10–6.*

By far Cleveland's biggest claim to fame is **Babyland General Hospital,** best known for starting the pandemoniac craze for Cabbage Patch Kids in the late 1970s; it was here that the dolls were first produced. The makeshift "hospital" is actually housed in a former clinic, and the dolls are displayed in a fake cabbage field. ✉ *19 Underwood St.,* ☎ *706/865–5164.* *Free.* *Mon.–Sat. 9–6, Sun. 1–6.*

Shopping

Mary T's Auction and Antique (✉ 233 Friendship Rd., ☎ 706/865–0575) has antique furniture, china and crystal, as well as Waverly fabrics and Sedgefield lamps. **Mount Yonah Gifts** (✉ 3745 Helen Hwy., ☎ 706/865–5003) abounds in colorful curios such as pottery, birdhouses, ornamental concrete statuaries, and fountains. **Rocks Relics and Beads** (✉ 5419 Hwy. 129N, ☎ 706/865–5003) sells minerals and rocks from local mines and from all over the world. It also has one of the best selections of antique and ornamental beads in the state.

Helen

13 mi north of Cleveland on GA 75, 85 mi northeast of Atlanta via I–985 and U.S. 129 to GA 75.

When Helen was founded at the turn of the 20th century, it was a simple little lumber outpost. By the 1960s it was in danger of turning into a ghost town because of a logging bust. Local business leaders came up with a plan to save the town: they transformed the tiny village of 300 into a virtual theme town, and "Alpine Helen" was born. Today all the businesses along Helen's central streets sport a distinctive German (as well as Swiss, Belgian, Danish, Dutch, and Scandinavian) facade, giving visitors the impression that they've stumbled upon a Bavarian vista in the middle of Appalachia. Everywhere you look are beer halls, steepled roofs, flowering window boxes, and billboards written in Renaissance script. As phony as it all is, the effect is contagious and makes you feel as if you've walked into a fairy tale.

The entrance to the village is particularly picturesque, with a narrow bridge traversing a pretty section of the Chattahoochee River. Along Main Street are a multitude of patio cafés lushly shaded by trees. A network of cobblestone walkways and plazas span a thicket of bakeries and little shops selling Bavarian-theme souvenirs. Costumed shop workers add to the charade. Housed in a faux castle that can't be missed is the **Museum of the Hills,** with an exhibit of "artifacts" that tell the tale of Helen's transformation. ✉ *Main St.,* ☎ *706/878–3140.* 🎫 *$5.* ⏲ *Daily 10 AM–10 PM.*

OFF THE BEATEN PATH

BRASSTOWN BALD – This is the highest mountain in Georgia, at 4,784 ft. In the heart of the Chattahoochee National Forest, it has a dramatic vantage from which you can view four different states (Tennessee, North Carolina, South Carolina, and Georgia). And sight is not the only sense that gets an aesthetic pick-me-up at Brasstown Bald: bushels of wildflowers in the spring and autumn give a boost to the nose as well. ✉ *Off GA 180, 15 mi west of Helen,* ☎ *706/896–2556.* 🎫 *Parking $3.* ⏲ *Daily 9:30–5:30.*

Dining and Lodging

$ ✕ **Hofbrauhaus Inn.** This beer hall has the same name as Hitler's favorite hangout in Munich, but thankfully the patrons are decidedly more friendly here. The menu is saturated with hearty German fare, such as schnitzel, *bratkartoffeln* (fried potatoes), and wurst. ✉ *Main St.,* ☎ *706/878–2248. AE, D, DC, MC, V.*

$$$ 🏨 **Brasstown Valley Resort.** This resort has lodge-style accommodations, plus a full line of sports activities: tennis, golf, hiking trails, and a fitness center. The rooms are comfortable and spacious with an elegant but rustic decor, and some come with fireplaces and balconies overlooking the breathtaking valley. It's 32 mi west of Helen. ✉ *6321 U.S. 76, Young Harris 30582,* ☎ *800/201–3205,* FAX *706/379–4615. Restaurant; bar. 129 rooms, 5 suites. AE, D, DC, MC, V. BP.*

$$–$$$ 🏨 **Fieldstone Inn.** Many of the beautifully appointed rooms, decorated with cherry-wood furniture, have a gorgeous view of Lake Chatuge. A nearby marina has a full array of boat rentals, including pontoons, paddle boats, sailboats, and kayaks. Sizable discounts are available in the winter months. It's 25 mi north of Helen. ✉ *3499 U.S. 76, Hiawassi 30546,* ☎ *800/545–3408,* FAX *706/896–4128. 66 rooms. Restaurant, pool, tennis court. AE, D, DC, MC, V. BP.*

Shopping

Gift World of Helen (✉ 8614 Main St., ☎ 706/878–2504) sells a variety of candles, ceramics, knives, and T-shirts among other items. **Jolly's Toys** (✉ 8800 Main St., ☎ 706/878–2262) is a wonderland of wooden American and European toys. **Kaiser Bill's II** (✉ 8635 Main St., ☎ 706/878–2057) is the place to go for collectible beer steins. It also sells figurines.

Clayton

27 mi northeast of Helen on U.S. 23/441, 100 mi northeast of Atlanta via I–85 and I–985 to U.S. 23.

An unassuming mountain town, Clayton is near spectacular Tallulah Gorge, the deepest canyon in the United States after the Grand Canyon, and was a popular early 20th-century destination for Atlantans. The state of Georgia recently acquired the gorge for a state park and has created walking and mountain biking trails. Clayton is rich in art galleries, flea markets, and antiques shops; the **Main Street Gallery** (⊠ 641 Main St., ☎ 706/782–2440, FAX 706/782–2815), one of the state's best sources for folk art, features works by regional artists such as Sarah Rakes, O. L. Samuels, Jay Schuette, and Rudy Bostick. The nearby **Dillard House** (☞ *below*) is famous for its reasonably priced country food served family style. Be forewarned: as much as a two-hour wait can make getting in a bit of a chore.

Dining and Lodging

$$–$$$$ ★ ✕🏨 **Glen-Ella Springs Country Inn.** This restored old hotel draws from far and wide with its rustic charm, restful setting, and fine food emphasizing regional specialties, such as trout pecan, pickled shrimp, and Lowcountry shrimp on grits. Rooms have no TVs but plenty of reading material, and the splendid grounds invite hiking and exploring. The restaurant ($–$$$) does not serve alcohol, but you may bring your own (corkage $2.50). It is 15 mi south of Clayton. ⊠ *1789 Bear Gap Rd., Rte. 3 Box 3304, Clarkesville 30523,* ☎ *706/754–7295 or 877/456–7527,* FAX *706/754–1560. 14 rooms, 2 suites. Restaurant, pool, conference center. AE, MC, V. BP.*

$–$$$ ★ ✕🏨 **Dillard House.** Consisting of an inviting cluster of cottages and motel-style rooms, this establishment sits on a plateau in the Little Tennessee River valley. Some rooms and the glass-walled Dillard House Restaurant ($) have vistas of the Blue Ridge Mountains. The restaurant serves all-you-can-eat, family-style platters overflowing with Southern favorites such as country ham, fried chicken, barbecue, corn on the cob, acorn squash, lima beans, and cabbage casserole. Breakfast is a gut buster: fresh muffins, piping hot biscuits, fresh eggs, and cottage fried potatoes are just the beginning. It is 7 mi north of Clayton. ⊠ *768 Franklin St., Box 10, Dillard 30537,* ☎ *706/746–5348 or 800/541–0671,* FAX *706/746–3680. 51 rooms, 6 suites. Restaurant, kitchenettes (some), hot tubs. AE, D, DC, MC, V.*

Ellijay

73 mi west of Clayton via U.S. 76 to GA 5/515, 80 mi north of Atlanta via I–75, I–575, and GA 5/515 to GA 52.

Billed as "Georgia's Apple Capital," Ellijay is popular with antiques aficionados as well. The town, founded by Cherokee Indians, is home to a colorful cluster of crafts shops, antiques markets, and art galleries.

The most popular time to visit Ellijay is in the fall, when roadside stands brimming with delicious ripe apples dot the landscape. The annual **Georgia Apple Festival** takes place here in mid-October. In addition to showcasing the many manifestations of the crisp fruit—apple butter, apple pie, apple cider, and so on—the festival offers a host of arts and crafts shows. For more information, contact the **Gilmer County Chamber of Commerce** (☎ 706/635–7400).

During the apple festival, you can tour rows upon rows of ripening apple trees at **Hillcrest Orchards** (⊠ 9696 Hwy. 52E, ☎ 706/273–3838). Pick your own apples and then feast on homemade jellies, jams, breads, and doughnuts. Also on the orchard's premises are a petting zoo and picnic area.

Lodging

$$-$$$ **Whitepath Lodge.** Set amid the tranquil scenery of the north Georgia mountains, this lodge has panoramic vistas from every room. The main lodge has seven suites, each with two bedrooms, three baths, and a fully-equipped kitchen. The Shenandoah Lodge has six two-floor suites that come with a fireplace and multilevel decks overlooking the woods. *⊠ 987 Shenandoah Dr., 30540, ☎ 706/276–7199 or 888/271–7199. 13 suites. AE, D, DC, MC, V.*

Outdoor Activities and Sports

There are plenty of fishing, canoeing, and kayaking opportunities on the Cartecay River, which runs through town. **Mountaintown Expeditions** (⊠ GA Hwy. 52E, ☎ 706/273–3838) arranges outdoor adventures for people of all skill levels.

Shopping

Antiques & More (⊠ 6 River St., ☎ 706/365–7738) is a colorful collective of 45 dealers who sell everything from antique dolls and furniture to stained-glass windows and English china. **Crafts in the Cohuttas Pottery** (⊠ 1444 Zion Hill Rd., ☎ 706/636–2233) sells works by husband-and-wife team William Boerner and Ann Hofstadter; they host the Cohuttas Arts Studio Tour every fourth weekend in October.

New Echota State Historic Site

60 mi northwest of Atlanta via I–75 north to GA 225, 25 mi west of Ellijay.

From 1825 to 1838, New Echota was the capital of the Cherokee Nation, whose constitution was patterned after that of the United States. There was a council house, a printing office, a Supreme Court building, and the *Cherokee Phoenix,* a newspaper that utilized the Cherokee alphabet developed by Sequoyah. Some buildings have been reconstructed. *⊠ GA 225, 1 mi east of I–75N, near Calhoun, ☎ 706/624–1321. $3. Tues.–Sat. 9–5, Sun. 2–5:30.*

Just a few miles north of New Echota, the beautifully restored two-story brick **Chief Vann House,** with its intricately carved interior, was commissioned in 1805 by a leader of the Cherokee Nation, who hired Moravian artisans to construct it. Of mixed Scottish and Cherokee parentage, Chief James Vann owned numerous slaves who worked on the construction of the house. *⊠ GA 52A west of Chatsworth, 82 Hwy. 225N, Chatsworth, ☎ 706/695–2598. $3. Tues.–Sat. 9–5, Sun. 2–5:30.*

Dining and Lodging

$-$$ ✕ **La Scala.** Piero Barba from Capri, Italy, established this outpost of Italian cooking in 1996. The menu is dominated by classic dishes such as osso buco, braciola, and seafood and pasta. The wine list, which Barba claims is the largest in north Georgia, includes French, American, and Italian wines. The lunch buffet is a bargain. *⊠ 413 Broad St., Rome, ☎ 706/238–9000. AE, D, DC, MC, V. Closed Sun. No lunch Sat.*

$$ **Claremont House.** Jeff and Linda Williams's beautifully restored 1890s Victorian inn has huge rooms furnished with period antiques. Breakfast is sumptuous, with stuffed French toast and the like. Claremont House is about 30 minutes south of New Echota State Historic Site and the Chief Vann House. *⊠ 906 E. 2nd Ave., Rome 30161, ☎ 706/291–0900 or 800/254–4797, FAX 706/802–0551. 5 rooms, 1 suite. AE, D, MC, V. BP.*

Chickamauga and Chattanooga National Military Park

93 mi northwest of Atlanta via I–75 to Hwy. 2 west to Fort Oglethorpe, 33 mi north of New Echota State Historic Site.

This site, established in 1890 as the nation's first military park, was the scene of one of the Civil War's bloodiest battles (30,000 casualties), which ended in the Union Capture of Chattanooga. The normally thick cedar groves and foliage covering Chickamauga were supposedly so trampled that the area resembled an open field, and so shot up were the trees that a sweet cedar smell mingled with the blood of fallen soldiers. The trees grew back in abundance, though, and today the park hosts battle-scene reenactments for spectators.

Monuments, battlements, and weapons adorn the road that traverses the 8,000-acre park, with markers explaining the action. An excellent visitor center has reproduction memorabilia, books, and a film on the battle. The center also provides trail maps and guides through the more than 80 mi of hiking trails. ✉ *U.S. 27 off I–75, 12 mi south of Chattanooga,* ☎ *706/866–9241.* *Free.* ⏲ *Mid-Aug.–mid-June, daily 8–4:45; mid-June–mid-Aug., daily 8–5:45.*

Lodging

$$–$$$ **Gordon-Lee Mansion.** To capture the feeling of the Civil War era, stay overnight at this antebellum mansion, which served as a field hospital during the battle. Guests in the log house, formerly Congressman Gordon Lee's office, have the run of two bedrooms, a living room with fireplace, and a full kitchen, where they prepare their own breakfast. ✉ *217 Cove Rd., Chickamauga 30707,* ☎ *706/375–4728 or 800/487–4728,* FAX *706/375–9499. 4 rooms, 1 cottage. MC, V. BP.*

North Georgia A to Z

Arriving, Departing, and Getting Around

BY BUS

Greyhound Bus Lines (☎ 706/678-4479 or 800/231–2222) serves select cities and towns around the area. It has connections to Atlanta, Savannah, Athens, Augusta, and Macon.

BY CAR

U.S. 19 runs north–south, passing through Dahlonega and up into the north Georgia mountains. U.S. 129 runs northwest from Athens, passing through Cleveland and subsequently merging with U.S. 19. GA 75 stems off U.S. 129 and goes through Helen and up into the mountains. U.S. 23/441 runs north through Clayton; U.S. 76 runs west from Clayton to Dalton, merging for a stretch with GA 5/515. GA 52 runs along the edge of the Blue Ridge Mountains, passing through Ellijay. I–75 is the major artery in the northwesternmost part of the state and passes near the New Echota State Historic Site and Chickamauga and Chattanooga National Military Park.

BY TAXI

All of the small towns and villages in north Georgia can easily be explored by foot, but to get from town to town, call **A Rainbow Taxi** (☎ 706/219–3275), which is based in Cleveland and services the surrounding region.

Contacts and Resources

B&B RESERVATIONS

Great Inns of Georgia (✉ 541 Londonberry Rd., Atlanta 30327, ☎ 404/843–0471 or 800/501–7328, FAX 404/252–8886) can help you choose one of the region's many inns.

EMERGENCIES

Ambulance, police (☎ 911). **Laurelwood/Blairsville Hospital** (✉ 214 Hospital Circle, Blairsville, ☎ 706/745–8641).

GUIDED TOURS

Upper Hi Fly Fishing and Outfitters (✉ 257 Big Sky Dr., Hiawassee 30546, ☎ 706/896–9075) offer personalized guided trout and fly fishing trips in the Southern Appalachian Mountains. They also operate a full-service fly-fishing shop with state-of-the-art equipment.

OUTDOOR ACTIVITIES AND SPORTS

Fort Mountain State Park (✉ 181 Fort Mountain Park Rd., Chatsworth 30705, ☎ 706/695–2621) has campgrounds amid prehistoric rock formations, plus hiking, mountain biking, horseback riding, miniature golf, fishing, boating, and swimming. It is 8 mi east of Chatsworth via GA 52. For more information, contact the Gilmer County Chamber of Commerce (☞ Visitor Information, *below*).

Trackrock Campground and Cabins (✉ 4887 Trackrock Campground Rd., Blairsville 30512, ☎ 706/745–2420) offers camping accommodations throughout a network of hiking trails filled with ancient Indian carvings and historical markers. It also has fishing and horseback riding. It is 9 mi east of Blairsville via Hwy. 180E. For more information, contact the Blairsville/Union County Chamber of Commerce (☞ Visitor Information, *below*).

RADIO STATIONS

AM: WDGR 1210, country and gospel music, news, sports, and weather; WZCM 770, country. **FM**: WKHC 104.3, classical and country music, news, sports, and weather.

24-HOUR PHARMACIES

Kroger store pharmacies, select locations.

VISITOR INFORMATION

Alpine Helen–White County Convention and Visitors Bureau (✉ Box 730, Helen 30545, ☎ 706/878–2181 or 800/858–8027). **Blairsville/Union County Chamber of Commerce** (✉ 385 Blue Ridge Hwy., Blairsville 30512, ☎ 706/745–5789). **Clayton Chamber of Commerce** (✉ Box 702, 30525-0702, ☎ 706/782–4512, FAX 706/782–4596). **Dahlonega-Lumpkin Chamber of Commerce** (✉ 13 Park St. South, Dahlonega 30533, ☎ 706/864–3513 or 800/231–5543, FAX 706/864–7917). **Gilmer County Chamber of Commerce** (✉ 5 Westside Sq., Ellijay 30540, ☎ 706/635–7400). **Helen Welcome Center** (✉ 726 Bruckenstrasse, Box 730, 30545, ☎ 706/878–2181 or 800/858–8027, FAX 706/878–4032). **White County Chamber of Commerce** (✉ 122 N. Main St., Cleveland 30528, ☎ 706/865–5356).

ELSEWHERE IN GEORGIA

Andersonville National Historic Site

110 mi south of Atlanta via I–75 to GA 49.

Andersonville, which opened in 1864, was the Civil War's most notorious prisoner-of-war site: 13,000 prisoners died here, and at war's end the Swiss-born commandant Captain Henry Wirz was tried, convicted, and hanged when he refused to exculpate himself by blaming Confederate president Jefferson Davis for the brutal treatment of the prisoners. Each state that had prisoners at Andersonville has a monument to their memory, and it is a place of active burial for U.S. veterans and their spouses. The National Prisoner of War Museum is also on the grounds. *Andersonville Welcome Center:* ✉ *114 Church St.,* ☎ *912/924–2558; Andersonville National Historic Site:* ✉ *Box 800, Andersonville 31711,* ☎ *912/924–0343.* *Free.* *Daily 8–5.*

Dining and Lodging

$$ **Windsor Hotel.** Just 10 mi from Andersonville, Americus is one of Georgia's most attractive regional towns. In its downtown lies a jewel of a National Trust Historic hotel, a veritable monument to Victorian architecture. All rooms have 12-ft ceilings and ceiling fans. The menu in this elegant white-and-eggplant-scheme dining room focuses on Southern fare, with such dishes as corn chowder, barbecued shrimp on linguine, crab cakes, and pecan-crusted salmon. ✉ *125 W. Lamar St., Americus 31709,* ☎ *912/924–1555 or 888/297–9567,* FAX *912/928–0533. 40 rooms, 5 suites. Restaurant. AE, D, MC, V. No dinner Sun.*

Callaway Gardens

70 mi south of Atlanta via I–85 to U.S. 27S.

This 14,000-acre family-style golf and tennis resort (you can also visit for the day) is best known for its impressive gardens developed in the 1930s by a couple determined to breathe new life into the area's dormant cotton fields. On the grounds are four nationally recognized golf courses, 17 tennis courts, bicycling trails, and a lakefront beach. The **Day Butterfly Center** has more than 1,000 varieties flying free. **Creek Lake** is well stocked with largemouth bass and bream. Dining and lodging are available at the gardens, as well as in nearby towns. ✉ *U.S. 27S, Pine Mountain 31822,* ☎ *706/663–2281 or 800/282–8181.* *Day visit $12.* *Mar.–Aug., daily 7–7; Sept.–Feb., daily 8–5.*

For a nearby bed-and-breakfast inn, *see* Magnolia Hall *in* Warm Springs, *below.*

Warm Springs

63 mi south of Atlanta via I–85 to exit 41.

The **Little White House Historic Site** is the restored home of President Franklin Delano Roosevelt, who first visited Warm Springs in 1924 to take the therapeutic hot waters. In 1932 he built what became known as the Little White House, a simple three-bedroom cottage. It contains his personal effects and looks much as it did the day he died here. The pools where Roosevelt took his therapy are now open for tours. ✉ *401 Little White House Rd.,* ☎ *706/655–5870.* *$5.* *Daily 9–4.*

Lodging

$$ **Magnolia Hall.** Painted green with taupe shutters, this handsome Victorian cottage 20 mi southwest of Warm Springs has gingerbread trim and a wraparound porch. Rooms are soundproof, and each has a thermostat. Breakfast, with such dishes as stuffed French toast, bacon pie, and lemon biscuits, is served in the formal dining room. ✉ *127 Barnes Mill Rd., Hamilton 31811,* ☎ *706/628–4566. 3 rooms, 2 suites. No credit cards. BP.*

GEORGIA A TO Z

Arriving and Departing

By Bus

Greyhound Bus Lines (✉ 232 Forsyth St., Atlanta, ☎ 404/584–1731 or 800/231–2222) serves Atlanta and towns across the state, large and small.

By Car

Georgia is traversed east and west by several interstate highways. North and south are covered by I–75, running from northwest through the center of the state to the Florida line; I–85 runs from the northeastern part of the state through the west to Alabama; I–95 runs along the Georgia coast from South Carolina to Florida. I–85 and I–75 converge in Atlanta near its downtown; this nexus is called the Connector. Running east and west, I–20 stretches from Birmingham, Alabama, to Augusta, Georgia, running through the center of downtown Atlanta on its way. From Macon, I–16 leads directly east to Savannah, where it ends; along its route lie several interesting towns, including Vidalia (home of the famous onion). Scenic routes include U.S. 76, a good highway running east–west through the north Georgia mountains, and U.S. 441, running north–south from the mountains to the Florida line. Along the way, U.S. 441 links numerous charming small towns and is lined with barbecue joints of worth. On the west side of the state, various pleasant small towns are connected by U.S. 19, the north–south route of choice prior to development of the interstate and still a good option if I–75 comes to a standstill, as it routinely does. I–75 also runs through a number of quaint small towns.

By Plane

Numerous international and domestic airlines serve **Hartsfield Atlanta International Airport** (✉ 6000 N. Terminal Pkwy., ☎ 404/530–6600), 13 mi south of downtown (☞ Atlanta A to Z, *above*).

By Train

Amtrak serves Atlanta and the state from the Brookwood station (✉ 1688 Peachtree St., ☎ 404/881–3060 or 800/872–7245). The *Crescent* operates daily to Atlanta from New York; Philadelphia; Washington, D.C.; Baltimore; Charlotte; and Greenville; and daily from New Orleans to New York through Atlanta. Its Thru-Way bus service operates daily from Birmingham and Mobile, Alabama, to Atlanta's Brookwood station. Another bus goes from the train station to Macon.

Getting Around

By Bus

Greyhound (☎ 800/231–2222) serves select cities and towns around the state.

By Car

The speed limit on interstates is 50 mph in metropolitan areas and 70 mph elsewhere. Right turns on red lights are permitted unless otherwise indicated. Contact the **Georgia Department of Industry, Trade, and Tourism** (☞ Visitor Information, *below*) for brochures and maps, including the annual guide "Georgia on My Mind."

By Plane

Numerous regional airports serve the state. For airline telephone numbers, *see* Air Travel *in* Smart Travel Tips A to Z. **Glynco Jetport** (✉ 500 Connole St., ☎ 912/265–2070), 6 mi north of Brunswick near the coastal isles, is served by Atlantic Southeast Airlines, with flights from Atlanta. The **Macon Municipal Airport** (✉ 4000 Terminal Dr., GA 247 and I–75, ☎ 912/788–3760) is served by Atlantic Southeast Airlines. Eighteen miles west of downtown, **Savannah International Airport** (✉ 400 Airways Ave., ☎ 912/964–0514) is served by Delta, US Airways, and AirTran.

By Train

Amtrak has regular service along the eastern seaboard, with daily stops in Savannah (✉ 2611 Seaboard Coastline Dr., ☎ 912/234–2611 or 800/872–7245), where a station is 4 mi southwest of downtown.

Contacts and Resources

B&B Reservations

For home stays, **Bed & Breakfast Atlanta** (✉ 1608 Briarcliff Rd., Suite 5, Atlanta 30306, ☎ 404/875–0525 or 800/967–3224, FAX 404/875–8198) represents 80–100 homes and can find lodging in carriage houses, apartments, and bed-and-breakfast inns. **Great Inns of Georgia** (✉ 541 Londonberry Rd., Atlanta 30327, ☎ 404/843–0471 or 800/501–7328, FAX 404/252–8886) can provide information on inns throughout the state.

Biking

With a membership of about 3,000, the **Southern Bicycle League** (✉ Box 870387, Stone Mountain 30087, ☎ 770/594–8350) has promoted bicycling across Georgia and the South for more than 20 years. The **Bicycle Ride Across Georgia** (BRAG; ☎ 770/921–6166) is an annual event, and the same organization holds numerous shorter bicycling events throughout the year. Advance application is required.

Emergencies

For **ambulance and fire emergencies statewide,** call ☎ 911.

Fishing

The **Georgia Department of Natural Resources, Game and Fish Division** (✉ 2070 U.S. 278, Social Circle 30025, ☎ 770/918–6400) has free pamphlets covering Georgia's regulations and maps suggesting good fishing spots.

Road Conditions

For road information, call the **Georgia Department of Transportation** (☎ 404/656–1267).

State Parks

Housed under the Georgia Department of Natural Resources, the **Parks, Recreation & Historic Sites** division (✉ 205 Butler St. SE, Suite 1352, Atlanta 30334, ☎ 404/656–3530, 800/864–7275 reservations, 770/389–7275 local reservations) has information on Georgia's parks.

Visitor Information

The **Georgia Department of Industry, Trade, and Tourism** (✉ Box 1776, Atlanta 30301, ☎ 404/656–3590 or 800/847–4842, FAX 404/651–9063) is the best source for visitor information around the state.

3 NORTH CAROLINA

Historical sites and natural wonders are plentiful in North Carolina, from Old Salem in Winston-Salem, where the 1700s spring to life today, to the Great Smoky and Blue Ridge mountains. On the Cape Hatteras and Cape Lookout national seashores, lighthouses stand as they have for 200 years, and unspoiled beaches stretch for miles. You'll find sophisticated shopping and dining in Charlotte; first-class golf in the Sandhills; and high technology, health care, and culture within the Triangle, a shape traced by Raleigh, Durham, and Chapel Hill.

By Lisa H. Towle

THE FIRST STANZA OF NORTH CAROLINA'S OFFICIAL toast reads: "Here's to the land of the longleaf pine/ The summer land where the sun doth shine/ Where the weak grow strong and the strong grow great/ Here's to 'Down Home,' the Old North State!" Sure, it's a bit hyperbolic, but it's catchy and rhythmic. It also speaks to a deeper truth: as much as geography, people have shaped the state's landscape over the years. In a moving 1991 tribute that was both videotaped and printed, the late Charles Kuralt, television journalist, author, and inveterate traveler, noted that North Carolina—his "state of grace"—has been home to Whistler's mother, Billy Graham, Michael Jordan, Chief Manteo, and three U.S. presidents.

In 1524 explorer Giovanni da Verrazano landed on what is now North Carolina's shore and wrote in his log, ". . . as pleasant and delectable [a land] to behold as is possible to imagine." Sixty years later the New World's first English-speaking settlers found their way to the state's eastern edge, which is bordered by 300 mi of beaches, islands, and inlets. Hernando de Soto searched for gold in the western part of the state, an area bounded by two ranges of the southern Appalachians, the Blue Ridge Mountains and the Great Smoky Mountains. In 1540, he and his band of Spanish explorers met the centuries-long residents of the area, the Cherokee, at the ancient village of Guasili close by what is today the town of Murphy. Several centuries later, in 1799, the first gold rush in the United States got its start in the heartland, the Piedmont—near Concord, to be exact—when young Conrad Reed discovered a 17-pound nugget that would eventually be identified as gold. And although North Carolina was the last state to secede during the Civil War, the state provided more troops and supplies to the Confederacy than any other Southern state and suffered the most casualties.

Thanks to efforts of the state and many determined citizens, this history and more has been carefully preserved. A lot of it can be found along 1,500 mi of roadway designated by the state's Department of Transportation as Scenic Byways. Thirty-one such byways (all of them marked with signs) crisscross the state. The soul of North Carolina can be glimpsed on these meandering routes. Here the views can quickly shift from panoramic to intimate, and the jessamine and galax, azaleas and rhododendrons, magnolias and dogwoods, and soft Spanish moss grow undisturbed.

Unlike many other states, North Carolina does not have one city that stands head and shoulders above all others. Rather, due to a confluence of circumstance, custom, and capitalistic acuity, a number of centers of business, art, and education have grown up throughout the state. Citizens, from African-American to Quaker, are proud of their contributions to North Carolina's development and protective of the areas and unique cultures from which they sprang. Indeed, some have described the Old North State as a collection of fiercely independent city-states reminiscent of those in ancient Greece or 19th-century Italy. Taken as a whole, North Carolina is now more urban and suburban than rural. You won't find gritty, noisy, oversize cities here, though. Instead, the pace is a bit slower. Manners and smiles still count, and canopies of hardwoods and pine trees characterize cities and countryside alike.

Because it has a temperate climate, world-class schools, and one of the most dynamic economies in the nation, North Carolina is attracting new residents in record numbers. They come not just from around the country but from around the world, and their influence—through their arts, foods, faiths, and intellects—is unmistakable. Ultimately, how-

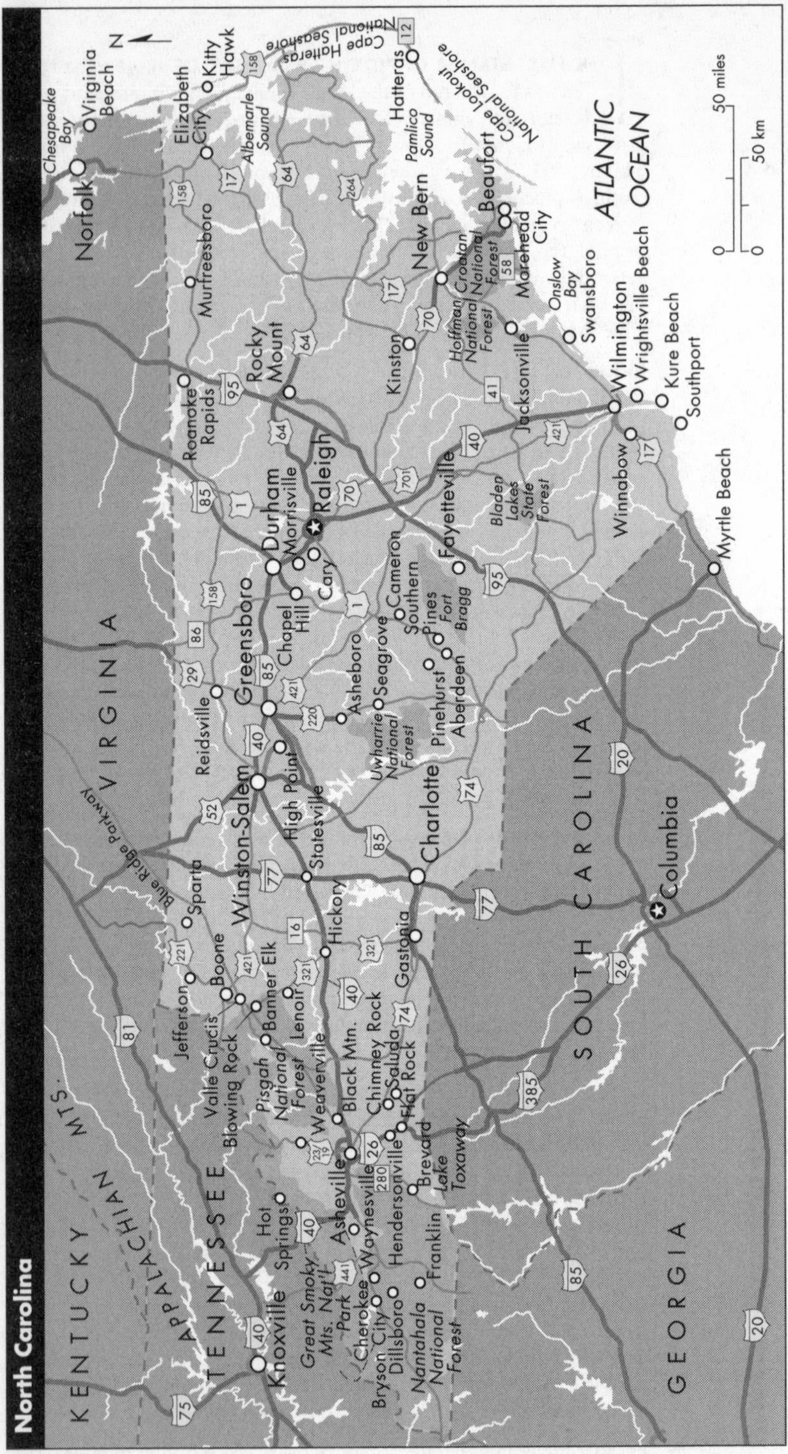
North Carolina
KENTUCKY
VIRGINIA
TENNESSEE
SOUTH CAROLINA
GEORGIA
APPALACHIAN MTS.
ATLANTIC OCEAN
Chesapeake Bay
Norfolk
Virginia Beach
Elizabeth City
Kitty Hawk
Albemarle Sound
Pamlico Sound
Cape Hatteras National Seashore
Hatteras
Cape Lookout National Seashore
Murfreesboro
Roanoke Rapids
Rocky Mount
New Bern
Beaufort
Morehead City
Croatan National Forest
Hoffman National Forest
Kinston
Jacksonville
Onslow Bay
Swansboro
Wilmington
Wrightsville Beach
Kure Beach
Southport
Winnabow
Myrtle Beach
Bladen Lakes State Forest
Fayetteville
Fort Bragg
Raleigh
Durham
Morrisville
Cary
Chapel Hill
Cameron
Southern Pines
Pinehurst
Aberdeen
Seagrove
Asheboro
Uwharrie National Forest
Greensboro
Reidsville
High Point
Winston-Salem
Statesville
Charlotte
Gastonia
Hickory
Lenoir
Sparta
Jefferson
Boone
Valle Crucis
Blowing Rock
Banner Elk
Blue Ridge Parkway
Pisgah National Forest
Weaverville
Black Mtn.
Chimney Rock
Saluda
Flat Rock
Hendersonville
Brevard
Lake Toxaway
Asheville
Hot Springs
Waynesville
Great Smoky Mts. Nat'l. Park
Cherokee
Bryson City
Dillsboro
Franklin
Nantahala National Forest
Knoxville
Columbia
0 50 miles
0 50 km
N

ever, what newcomers, both permanent and transitory, find is that one of the great appeals of North Carolina lies in its timelessness. In 1749, Peter Jefferson, the father of Thomas Jefferson, and his group of surveyors discovered a river in western North Carolina. Because they thought it was a large branch of the Mississippi River no one had seen before, they named it the New River. Later, archaeologists determined that it is actually the oldest river in the United States and the second oldest in the world, after the Nile. Today, amid majestic scenery, its two forks continue to flow.

Pleasures and Pastimes

Beaches

From the thin band of barrier islands known as the Outer Banks, along the northern coastline, to the area around Wilmington and the Cape Fear Coast, to the South Brunswick Islands near the South Carolina border, North Carolina's beaches are a year-round destination. You can visit national seashores or wildlife refuges, go surfing, diving, fishing, hiking, bird-watching, hang gliding—or just watch the waves. North Carolinians are proud that the nation's first national seashore, Cape Hatteras, is in their state, as is Roanoke Island, where the country's first European settlers landed more than 400 years ago.

Dining

In North Carolina's cities, risotto and dim sum are becoming as common as grits and corn bread. Ethnic specialties of all kinds are available, as well as contemporary American cuisine. The Sandhills, too, have a number of sophisticated restaurants. But you can find plenty of good old-fashioned Southern cooking, including Southern-fried chicken, Brunswick stew, ham, vegetables, biscuits, and fruit cobblers. Chopped or sliced pork barbecue is still a big item.

By far the best fare around the Outer Banks is fresh seafood. Raw bars serve oysters and clams on the half shell, and seafood houses offer fresh crabs (soft-shells in season, early in the summer) and whatever local fish—tuna, wahoo, mahimahi—have been hauled in that day. Cuisine in the Wilmington and Morehead City areas is strong on seafood, whether it's shrimp, Atlantic blue crab, or king mackerel, but pork barbecue and international cuisines are also options.

From Cherokee County to Asheville, the dining choices are many: upscale restaurants, middle-of-the-road country fare, and fast-food eateries. Fresh mountain trout, as well as such game meats as pheasant and venison, are regional specialties. Beer, wine, and liquor by the drink are permitted in Blowing Rock, Banner, Elk, and Beech Mountain; beer and wine only in Boone.

Unless otherwise noted, neat, casual wear (including golf wear in the Sandhills) is acceptable throughout North Carolina.

CATEGORY	COST*
$$$$	over $35
$$$	$25–$35
$$	$15–$25
$	under $15

**per person for a three-course meal, excluding drinks, service, and 6%–7% sales tax (depending on county)*

Historic Places

Opportunities abound to get out of the fast lane and onto the back roads that lead to places where history is kept alive. Whether it's the site of a key battle in the Revolutionary War or the largest troop surrender of the Civil War, a Quaker settlement, or studios where artisans carry on a 200-year-old tradition in pottery, North Carolina cherishes its past. Places to visit are as varied as the site of man's first flight and the architectural legacies of America's industrial barons.

Lodging

In North Carolina's cities, you'll find everything from economy motels to convention hotels to bed-and-breakfasts in lovely historic districts. Most major chains are represented, and some hotels offer great weekend packages. A few warnings, though: During the twice-a-year furniture market in High Point, when 75,000 people descend on the city, empty hotel rooms and rental cars are almost impossible to find. May is graduation time for all of the Triangle's colleges and universities. Hotel rooms and restaurant seats are booked, in some cases, years in advance.

Most lodging options in the Sandhills are in the luxury resort category, with full amenities and services. Many of the prices quoted are for golf packages. However, there are some chain motels in Southern Pines and Aberdeen, as well as a variety of bed-and-breakfasts in the area.

Motels and hotels are clustered up and down the Outer Banks, with rental properties in all the towns that dot the Cape Hatteras National Seashore. Visitors to Wilmington and the Cape Fear Coast, and New Bern and the Central ("Crystal") Coast can choose from among a variety of chains, condos, and resorts overlooking water, whether it be rivers or the ocean. There are also in-town guest houses. Lodging options in the western mountains range from posh resorts to mountain cabins, country inns, and economy chain motels. There's a bed for virtually every pocketbook. When you're planning your trip, always ask about special packages and possible off-season rates.

CATEGORY	COST*
$$$$	over $170
$$$	$120–$170
$$	$75–$120
$	under $75

**All prices are for a standard double room, excluding 6%–12% tax (depending on county).*

following the text of a review is your signal that the property has a Web site, where you will find details and, usually, images; for a link, visit www.fodors.com/urls.

Outdoor Activities

North Carolina's unique geological and biological resources give outdoor enthusiasts a full spectrum of activities. There are hundreds of camping options, from primitive camping to family camping. Hikers and backpackers come here for the trails—one-day hikes to weeklong trips. Quite a few stables offer rental horses, and some have llama treks. Hard-core mountain bikers can ride a 27-mi loop through the Great Smoky Mountains National Park. Local outfitters regularly conduct white-water rafting trips. The state has eight ski resorts, and if you like height but not snow, there's hang gliding across the dunes at Nags Head.

Exploring North Carolina

Charlotte, the state's largest city, is known as a center of high finance in the South and prides itself on its cosmopolitan flair. The cities of the Triad (Greensboro, Winston-Salem, and High Point), in the upper Piedmont, showcase the legacies of some of the state's founding families. The Triangle (Raleigh, Durham, and Chapel Hill), in the central

Piedmont, is the hub of higher education, scientific research, and state-sponsored cultural resources. The Sandhills, on the Coastal Plain, is a favorite with antiques lovers and is recognized worldwide as a golf mecca. On the Outer Banks comes solitude in the form of miles of pristine shore and sea oats. Boating, scuba diving, and fishing are the main pastimes in Morehead City and the Central Coast, while history is alive in genteel New Bern. Wilmington and the Cape Fear Coast aren't just resort vacation spots—they're a thriving business and cultural center for the southeastern portion of North Carolina. In the western mountains, which are anchored by the city of Asheville, you'll find everything from hiking trails and Southern crafts to boot-scoot music and Brahms.

Great Itineraries

North Carolina is a large state and touring it comfortably from end to end could easily take two weeks, although you could whiz through in a week. Many people concentrate each trip on one region: mountains, Piedmont, or Coastal Plain. A week could be spent in each of these, but there are many worthwhile trips of shorter duration.

IF YOU HAVE 3 DAYS

Start your tour of the Outer Banks from its north end, coming in on U.S. 158. Drive north on NC 12 your first morning there to spend time in **Corolla,** visiting the Currituck Beach Lighthouse. After lunch head south through **Kitty Hawk, Kill Devil Hills,** and **Nags Head,** with a stop at the Wright Brothers National Memorial. Spend the first night (and the next) on **Roanoke Island,** where you'll take the second day to visit historical locations and the North Carolina Aquarium. On Day 3, leave Roanoke and spend the day along the **Cape Hatteras National Seashore,** visiting sights on **Hatteras Island** in the morning and **Ocracoke Island** in the afternoon.

IF YOU HAVE 5 DAYS

Asheville is the logical starting point for a tour of the North Carolina mountains. It will take a full first day to cover the Biltmore Estate and neighboring village. Day 2 should be devoted to the attractions south of Asheville, including **Chimney Rock** and the Carl Sandburg Home National Historical Site in **Flat Rock.** Another day back in Asheville will allow you to visit the remaining area attractions, including Pack Place. On the fourth morning begin your journey up the **Blue Ridge Parkway,** lingering at the many scenic stopping points along the way, and arrive in the **Boone** area for the night. Day 5 will be occupied with High Country activities, including visiting the Tweetsie Railroad in **Blowing Rock.**

IF YOU HAVE 7 DAYS

With a full week at your disposal, you can do a whirlwind tour from one end of North Carolina to the other. Start your journey in **Asheville,** touring the Biltmore Estate. Next head for **Charlotte**; be sure to visit Discovery Place and the Mint Museum of Craft + Design during your day here. The Triad and the historical attractions of Old Salem are the focus of the third day; overnight in **Winston-Salem.** The next two days will allow time for a taste of the Triangle, including the Duke University campus and Sarah Duke Gardens in **Durham,** the Morehead Planetarium and Franklin Street shopping in **Chapel Hill,** and the museums and capitol area of **Raleigh.** Your sixth day should be spent in the Sandhills area enjoying antiques shops and the world-class golf in **Pinehurst.** Wind up your visit in **Wilmington,** where you can visit the historic downtown and USS *North Carolina* Battleship Memorial or just head for the nearby beaches.

When to Tour North Carolina

North Carolina particularly shines in the spring (April and May) and fall (September and October), when the weather is especially temperate and the trees and flowers burst with color. At these times, you'll avoid the peak tourist season. Summer trips are best spent in the mountains or at the coastal beaches, where temperatures are significantly cooler. In winter many mountain attractions close just as the ski resorts open for the season.

CHARLOTTE

Though Charlotte dates from Revolutionary War times (it is named for King George III's wife, Queen Charlotte), its Uptown is distinctively New South, with gleaming skyscrapers. Uptown encompasses all of downtown Charlotte, its business and cultural heart and soul. It's also home to the government center and some residential neighborhoods. More and more, public art is displayed in the city. Examples of this are the sculptures at the four corners of Trade and Tryon streets. Erected at Independence Square, they symbolize Charlotte's beginnings: a gold miner (commerce), a mill worker (the city's textile heritage), an African-American railroad builder (transportation), and a mother holding her baby aloft (the future). Residents of the Queen City won't hesitate to tell you that theirs is the largest city in the Carolinas and the second-largest banking center in the nation.

Heavy development has created some typical urban problems. Outdated road systems make traffic a nightmare during rush hour, and virtually all the city's restaurants are packed on weekends. But the locals' Southern courtesy is contagious, and people still love the traditional pleasure of picnicking in Freedom Park.

You'll be able to walk around Uptown and the Fourth Ward, and buses are adequate for getting around within the city limits; otherwise, you will need a car to tour.

Numbers in the text correspond to numbers in the margin and on the Charlotte map.

Uptown Charlotte

Uptown Charlotte is ideal for walking. The city was laid out in four wards around Independence Square, at Trade and Tryon streets. The Square, as it is known, is the center of the Uptown area.

A Good Walk

Stop first at **INFO! Charlotte** (✉ 330 S. Tryon St., ☎ 704/331–2700) for information on a self-guided walking tour of the Fourth Ward (☞ *below*) and a historic tour of Uptown, as well as maps and brochures. You can park your car in an open lot a few blocks east of the Square. Take a stroll north on Tryon Street and enjoy the ambience of this revitalized area, noting the outdoor sculptures on the plazas and the creative architecture of some of the newer buildings, including the **Bank of America Corporate Center** ①.

Walk two blocks west on Trade Street from the Square to the **First Presbyterian Church** (✉ 200 W. Trade St.) and begin exploring the **Fourth Ward** ②, Charlotte's new "old" city. It's a refreshing change from the newly developed parts of town. The brochure available at INFO! Charlotte (☞ Visitor Information *in* Charlotte A to Z, *below*) leads you to 18 historic sites.

Charlotte

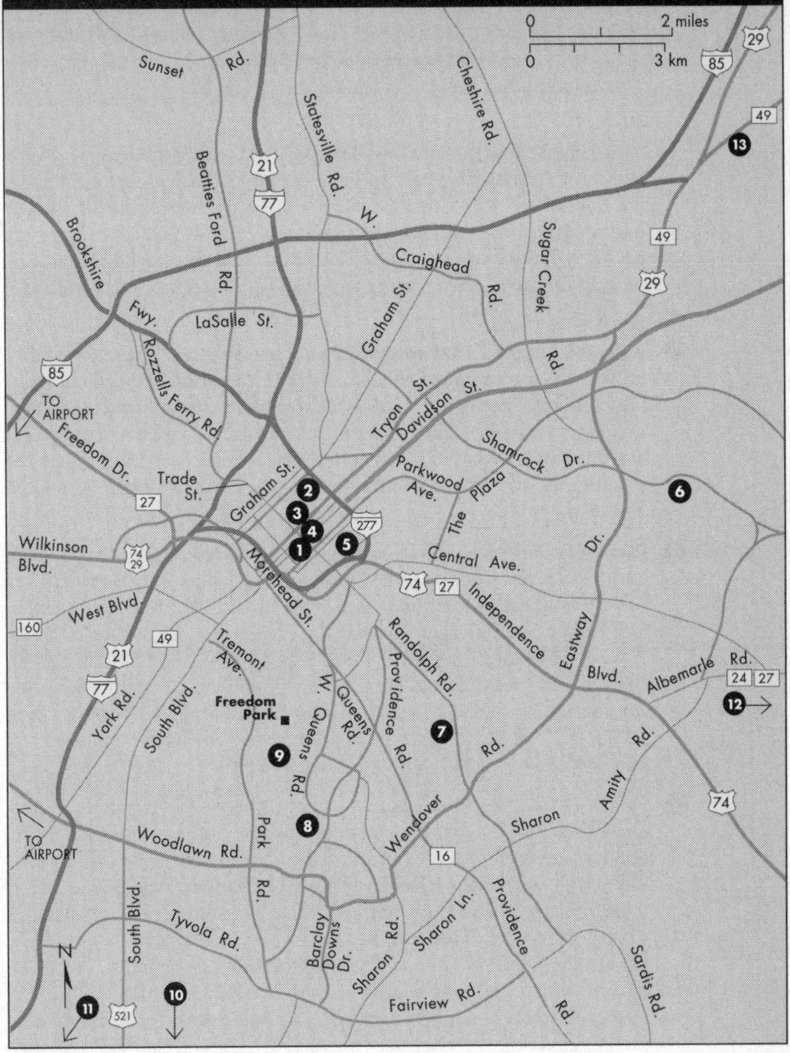

Afro-American Cultural Center **5**

Bank of America, Corporate Center **1**

Charlotte Nature Museum **9**

Discovery Place **3**

Fourth Ward **2**

Hezekiah Alexander Homesite and Charlotte Museum of History . . . **6**

James K. Polk Memorial. **10**

Lowe's Motor Speedway. **13**

Mint Museum of Art . . **7**

Mint Museum of Craft + Design **4**

Paramount's Carowinds. **11**

Reed Gold Mine State Historic Site **12**

Wing Haven Gardens and Bird Sanctuary. . . **8**

When you're done exploring the Fourth Ward, head south to North Tryon Street just above 6th Street, where you will find the science and technology museum **Discovery Place** ③, a leading attraction. Finish your walk at the new **Mint Museum of Craft + Design** ④, which showcases North Carolina's rich crafts tradition.

TIMING

You can spend a pleasant half day to a day touring these areas. Allow an hour to browse through the Bank of America Corporate Center and Founders Hall. You can tour the Fourth Ward in an hour or so. The bulk of your time will be spent in Discovery Place, which can occupy as much of the day as you wish. You can avoid the workday bustle by visiting on the weekend, but note Discovery Place's Sunday hours.

Sights to See

❶ **Bank of America Corporate Center.** This 60-story structure with a crown-like top designed by Cesar Pelli is one of the city's most striking buildings. Its main attraction is three philosophical frescoes by Ben Long that symbolize the city's past, present, and future. Also in the tower are the **North Carolina Blumenthal Performing Arts Center** and the restaurants, shops, and exhibition space of **Founders Hall.** ✉ *100 N. Tryon St.*

★ ❸ **Discovery Place.** At Charlotte's premier attraction, the wonderful hands-on **Science Museum** is a priority; also allow at least two hours for the **aquariums,** the three-story **rain forest,** the **Omnimax theater,** and **Kelly Space Voyager Planetarium,** the largest in the United States. A ham radio room, a puppet theater, and a 10-ft model of an eyeball that you can walk through are other highlights. Check the schedule for special exhibits. ✉ *301 N. Tryon St.,* ☎ *704/372–6261 or 800/935–0553.* *$6.50 for 1 area, plus $3 for any additional area visited.* *Weekdays 9–5, Sat. 9–6, Sun. 1–6.*

❷ **Fourth Ward.** Charlotte's popular old neighborhood began as a political subsection created for electoral purposes in the mid-1800s. The architecture and atmosphere of this quiet, homespun neighborhood provide a feeling for life in a less hectic time. A brochure available at INFO! Charlotte (☞ Visitor Information *in* Charlotte A to Z, *below*) includes 18 historic places of interest. Be sure to stop by **Old Settlers Cemetery,** behind the **First Presbyterian Church** (✉ 200 W. Trade St., ☎ 704/332–5123), which contains tombstones that date from the 1700s. The Gothic Revival church, which takes up a city block and faces West Trade Street, reflects the prosperity of the early settlers and their descendants. **Fourth Ward Park** is an oasis in the middle of the city. **Alexander Michael's** (✉ 401 W. 9th St., ☎ 704/332–6789) is a favorite eatery. **Poplar Street Books** is housed in the Victorian Young-Morrison House (✉ 226 W. 10th St.). U.S. president Taft spent the night in the **McNinch House** (✉ 511 N. Church St.), now a restaurant, when he visited Charlotte in 1909. **Spirit Square** (✉ 345 N. College St.), in a former church, includes galleries, a performing arts center, and classrooms that used to be the sanctuary for the First Baptist Church. The **public library** (✉ 310 N. Tryon St.), which contains a mural reproducing a Romare Bearden painting, is open weekdays 9–9, Saturday 9–6, and Sunday 2–6.

❹ **Mint Museum of Craft + Design**. A sister to the Mint Museum of Art (☞ Greater Charlotte, *below*), the museum is in what used to be an upscale women's clothing store. The gallery alone is 16,000 square ft. Add on the permanent collections of ceramics, glass, fiber, metal, and wood, and you have one of the country's major crafts museums. You can use your receipt from the crafts museum to enter the Mint Museum of Art free on the same day. ✉ *220 N. Tryon St.,* ☎ *704/337–2000.* 🎟 *$6.* ⏲ *Tues.–Thurs. and Sat. 10–7, Fri. 10–9, Sun. noon–5.*

Greater Charlotte

Beyond Uptown and farther afield lie many of Charlotte's most interesting sights, from gardens to museums. You can reach the ones listed below by car or by city bus; for visits elsewhere, a car is essential.

A Good Tour

From Uptown, follow 7th Street east and turn north on North Myers Street to visit the galleries of the **Afro-American Cultural Center** ⑤. Continue east on 7th Street past I–277 to Central Avenue; go east on Central Avenue 3 mi to Eastway Drive, north on Eastway Drive 1½ mi to Shamrock Drive, and east on Shamrock Drive to the **Hezekiah Alexander Homesite and Charlotte Museum of History** ⑥, where you can see the county's oldest building. Return west on Shamrock Drive to Eastway Drive and travel south on Eastway Drive past Central Avenue until it becomes Wendover Road. Continue on Wendover Road 1⅔ mi to Randolph Road and then turn right on Randolph Road to visit the **Mint Museum of Art** ⑦, a wide-ranging collection in a former mint. The next stop, **Wing Haven Gardens and Bird Sanctuary** ⑧, is in Myers Park, a handsome neighborhood. One approach to this area is to drive north on Randolph Road to South Laurel Avenue, which leads south to Providence Road (NC 16). Follow Providence Road south to Queens Road to Selwyn Avenue and then turn west on Ridgewood Avenue. More experience with nature can be found at the **Charlotte Nature Museum** ⑨, next to Freedom Park. To get here, continue west on Ridgewood Avenue to Westfield Road, take Westfield Road north to Sterling Avenue, and then follow Sterling Avenue north to the museum.

TIMING

You can spend a leisurely day touring these sights, which are within a few miles of each other.

Sights to See

❺ **Afro-American Cultural Center.** In a historic former church, this center, with its galleries and theater, serves as a showcase for art, music, drama, and dance. ✉ *401 N. Myers St.,* ☎ *704/374–1565.* 🎟 *Free.* ⏲ *Tues.–Sat. 10–6, Sun. 1–5.*

❾ **Charlotte Nature Museum.** Though affiliated with Discovery Place, the museum is in the southeast section of the city. You'll find a butterfly exhibit, live animals, nature trails, nature films, and hands-on exhibits just for children. ✉ *1658 Sterling Ave. (next to Freedom Park),* ☎ *704/372–0471.* 🎟 *$3.* ⏲ *Weekdays 9–5, Sat. 10–5, Sun. 1–5.*

❻ **Hezekiah Alexander Homesite and Charlotte Museum of History.** The stone house, built in 1774, is the oldest dwelling in the county. Alexander and his wife, Mary, reared 10 children in this house and farmed the land. Costumed docents give guided tours weekdays at 1:15 and 3:15. Seasonal events commemorate the early days. Permanent and rotating exhibits in the museum span 300 years of southern Piedmont history. ✉ *3500 Shamrock Dr.,* ☎ *704/568–1774.* 🎟 *Museum $3, homesite $4, combination ticket $6.* ⏲ *Tues. 10–9, Wed.–Sat. 10–5, Sun. 1–5.*

★ ❼ **Mint Museum of Art.** Built in 1836 as a U.S. Mint, this building has served as a home for art since 1936. Among the holdings in its impressive permanent collections are American and European paintings, furniture, and decorative arts; African, pre-Columbian, and Spanish colonial art; porcelain and pottery; and regional crafts and historic costumes.

You can use your receipt from this museum to enter the Mint Museum of Craft+Design (☞ Uptown Charlotte, *above*) free on the same day. ✉ *2730 Randolph Rd.*, ☎ *704/337–2000.* *$6.* ⏲ *Tues. 10–10, Wed.–Sat. 10–5, Sun. noon–5.*

❽ **Wing Haven Gardens and Bird Sanctuary.** In Myers Park, one of Charlotte's loveliest neighborhoods, 4 acres of gardens developed by the Clarkson family are home to more than 135 species of birds. ✉ *248 Ridgewood Ave.*, ☎ *704/331–0664.* *Free.* ⏲ *Sun. 2–5, Tues. 3–5, Wed. 10–noon, or by appointment.*

Other Area Attractions

Historic sites, a speedway, and a theme park provide plenty to explore beyond the city.

❿ **James K. Polk Memorial.** A state historic site south of Charlotte marks the humble 1795 birthplace and childhood home of the 11th president. Guided tours of the log cabins (replicas of the originals) are available. ✉ *308 S. Polk St., Pineville*, ☎ *704/889–7145.* *Free.* ⏲ *Apr.–Oct., Mon.–Sat. 9–5, Sun. 1–5; Nov.–Mar., Tues.–Sat. 10–4, Sun. 1–4.*

⓭ **Lowe's Motor Speedway.** Learn all about NASCAR racing, one of the nation's fastest-growing sports, at this state-of-the-art, 167,000-seat facility; browse through the gift shop; or even take a "hot laps" (160 mph) lesson at the track through the **Richard Petty Driving Experience** (☎ 704/455–9443) or **Fast Track Driving School** (☎ 704/455–1700). Classes are given year-round except during event weeks in May and October. ✉ *5555 U.S. 29, Harrisburg, northeast of Charlotte*, ☎ *704/455–3200.* *$6.* ⏲ *Mon.–Sat. 9–5, Sun. 1–5.*

⓫ **Paramount's Carowinds.** A 100-acre amusement park on the South Carolina state line has rides and attractions based on films. Costumed movie characters and actors greet visitors, and the Palladium offers musical concerts with star entertainers. Rides include the heart-stopping Drop Zone. ✉ *14523 Carowinds Blvd.*, ☎ *704/588–2600 or 800/888–4386.* *$35.* ⏲ *Apr.–May weekends; June–mid-Aug. daily; mid-Aug.–early Oct., weekends. Park usually opens around 10; closing hrs vary.*

⓬ **Reed Gold Mine State Historic Site.** This area, east of Charlotte in Cabarrus County, is where America's first documented gold rush began, following Conrad Reed's discovery of a 17-pound nugget in 1799. Forty-minute guided underground tours of the gold mine are available, as well as seasonal gold panning, walking trails, and a stamp mill. ✉ *9621 Reed Mine Rd., north of NC 24/27, Locust, follow signs beyond town*, ☎ *704/786–8337.* *Free, gold panning $2 per pan.* ⏲ *Apr.–Oct., Mon.–Sat. 9–5, Sun. 1–5; Nov.–Mar., Tues.–Sat. 10–4, Sun. 1–4; call for tour schedules.*

Dining

$$$–$$$$ ✕ **Campania.** Warmth is the byword for this restaurant in a country club community. The walls are golden and textured, there is richly toned wood and lots of candlelight, and the music is genuine Italian, from opera to contemporary. The food, too, is about as authentic as it gets outside southern Italy. The *gamberoni Mergellina,* shrimp sautéed in garlic butter and herbs, is sublime. Linguine Posillipo pairs clams with red or white sauce. Veal chops are another main category on the menu. ✉ *6414 Rea Rd.*, ☎ *704/541–8505. AE, D, MC, V.*

$$$–$$$$ ★ ✕ **Lamplighter.** For years one of Charlotte's destination restaurants, the romantic, sophisticated Lamplighter is in a stucco-and-tile house built in 1926. The wine list includes 550 vintages, and the menu is far-ranging, with everything from sushi-grade blackened tuna to roast duck and marinated ostrich fillet. The quiet, intimate lounge is good for cocktails. ✉ *1065 E. Morehead St.,* ☎ *704/372–5343. Reservations essential. AE, DC, MC, V.*

$$$–$$$$ ✕ **Townhouse.** Chef-owner Étienne Jaulin and his wife, Amanda, serve exquisitely prepared American cuisine with a French twist. The atmosphere is unassuming; walls are pale rose, and tables are covered with white linens. The menu shifts frequently as Jaulin encourages sous-chefs to go to the market and "come back with something fun." The end result may be thousand-layer salmon terrine or roasted Dover sole with a sweet pea vanilla sauce. ✉ *1011 Providence Rd.,* ☎ *704/335–1546. AE, D, DC, MC, V.*

$$–$$$ ✕ **Atlantic Beer & Ice Co.** This Uptown eatery in a sprawling three-story building has something for everyone: live entertainment, a cigar and Scotch bar, and billiards tables. The building, with its exposed brick, dark wood, and big windows, envelopes you. The seasonal menu is broad: from knockwurst and pastrami sandwiches to beef Stroganoff. Beef is the best bet. ✉ *330 N. Tryon St.,* ☎ *704/339–0566. AE, DC, MC, V.*

$$–$$$ ✕ **Providence Café.** The signature purple awnings and trendy furnishings lend atmosphere. The menu may be comfortably predictable, with chicken, beef, seafood, and pasta, but the focaccia baked daily on the premises is a standout. It's a great place for Sunday brunch and live jazz on Wednesday evenings. Two more Providence restaurants have opened in the city. ✉ *110 Perrin Pl.,* ☎ *704/376–2008; 15205 John Jay Delaney Dr.,* ☎ *704/540–2244; 8708 J. W. Clay Blvd.,* ☎ *704/549–0050. AE, D, DC, MC, V.*

$$–$$$ ✕ **Thai House.** Fiery pleasure awaits the adventurous diner who samples from a selection of vegetarian, seafood, and classic Thai dishes. The food has proved so popular that two more branches have opened. The *satays* (skewers of meat, fish, or poultry with peanut sauce) are mild enough for any taste buds, and you can order many dishes as spicy or mild as you wish. ✉ *3210 N. Sharon Amity Rd.,* ☎ *704/532–6868; Tower Plaza Shopping Center, 8652 Pineville-Matthews Rd., No. 1000,* ☎ *704/542–6300; 4918 Central Ave.,* ☎ *704/535–6716. AE, D, DC, MC, V.*

$–$$$ ✕ **Landmark Diner.** This spacious and informal place in the Eastland Mall neighborhood is a cut above most other inexpensive restaurants, and it's open until 3 AM on weeknights and 24 hours on weekends. The chocolate cream pie is a must-try. ✉ *4429 Central Ave.,* ☎ *704/532–1153. Reservations not accepted. AE, DC, MC, V.*

$ ✕ **College Place Restaurant.** Simple down-home cookin' and plenty of it is served for breakfast and lunch (7 AM–3 PM). You have to work to spend more than $5. Breakfasts in particular are big and offer any combination of eggs, pancakes, grits, bacon, and sausage, to name just a few items. Lunch has lots of vegetable choices (12), meats, homemade corn bread, and cobblers. This cafeteria and grill is close to the convention center. ✉ *300 S. College St.,* ☎ *704/343–9268. No credit cards. Closed weekends. No dinner.*

Lodging

Hotels and Motels

$$$$ ★ 🏨 **The Park.** Executives, entertainers, sports stars, and heads of state appreciate the privacy and pampering as well as the parklike setting of this hotel on a former estate in the southeast corner of the city. Antique furnishings, polished marble, and art grace the public areas, and the hotel owns more than 20 paintings by French artist Yolanda Ardisonne. Guest rooms have a residential feel; fabrics are lush and used generously. ✉ *2200 Rexford Rd., 28211,* ☎ *704/364–8220 or 800/334–0331,* FAX *704/365–4712. 187 rooms, 7 suites. Restaurant, piano bar, in-room data ports, minibars, pool, spa, 18-hole golf course, health club, business services, meeting rooms, airport shuttle. AE, D, DC, MC, V.*

$$$–$$$$ **Adam's Mark.** This is the city's largest convention hotel, within walking distance of the convention center. The expansive main lobby, with its woodwork and shades of green and gray, has a clubby feel. Guest rooms are done in blues and plums. Bravo!, its popular signature restaurant, serving northern Italian cuisine, is known for its singing waiters. ✉ *555 S. McDowell St., 28204,* ☎ *704/372–4100 or 800/444–2326,* FAX *704/348–4646. 631 rooms, 21 suites. Restaurant, bar, in-room data ports, indoor-outdoor pool, sauna, health club, racquetball, dry cleaning, laundry service, concierge, business services, meeting rooms, airport shuttle, free parking. AE, D, DC, MC, V.*

$$–$$$$ **Hyatt Charlotte at SouthPark.** The focal point of the four-story atrium is a Mexican water fountain surrounded by 25-ft olive trees. Scalini, the restaurant, serves northern Italian cuisine; the Club piano bar is a favorite. The hotel is within walking distance of the upscale SouthPark Mall (☞ Shopping, *below*). ✉ *5501 Carnegie Blvd., 28209-3462,* ☎ *704/554–1234 or 800/233–1234,* FAX *704/554–8319. 258 rooms, 4 suites. Restaurant, piano bar, in-room data ports, indoor pool, hot tub, sauna, health club, business services, airport shuttle. AE, D, DC, MC, V.*

$$ **Comfort Inn–Lake Norman.** This economy motel, north of Charlotte on I–77 near Lake Norman and Davidson College, offers basic guest rooms with coffeemakers. Some rooms have VCRs, microwaves, and whirlpool baths. Jogging trails are nearby. ✉ *20740 Torrence Chapel Rd., Cornelius 28031,* ☎ *704/892–3500 or 800/848–9751,* FAX *704/892–6473. 84 rooms, 6 suites. Pool, business services, meeting room. AE, D, DC, MC, V. CP.*

$ **Bradley Motel.** Clean and functional is what you get with this motel, which has been family-owned and -operated since 1959. Popular with families and NASCAR fans, the Bradley, near the airport and the coliseum, fills up on race weekends. The rooms are large, with full ceramic baths. Impromptu games of volleyball or horseshoes take place on the lawn outside. ✉ *4200 S. I–85 Service Rd., 28214,* ☎ *704/392–3206,* FAX *704/392–5040. 21 rooms. AE, D, MC, V.*

Bed-and-Breakfasts

$$$–$$$$ **Morehead Inn.** Though it's now a commercial venture catering to corporate clients, this B&B in the Dilworth neighborhood was once a private estate and still has all the comforts of a beautiful home. ✉ *1122 E. Morehead St., 28204,* ☎ *704/376–3357 or 888/667–3432,* FAX *704/335–1110. 8 rooms, 2 suites, 1 2-bedroom apartment. In-room data ports, meeting rooms. AE, DC, MC, V. CP.*

$$$ **Inn Uptown.** The inn, an 1891 brick château on the edge of the historic Fourth Ward neighborhood, is popular because of its proximity to Uptown businesses and attractions. Many rooms have fireplaces. Most fun is the Tower Room, with its spiral staircase leading to a tower with a whirlpool bath and skyline view. ✉ *129 N. Poplar St., 28202,* ☎ *704/342–2800 or 800/959–1990,* FAX *704/342–2222. 6 rooms. In-room data ports, business services. AE, D, DC, MC, V. BP.*

$$ ★ **Homeplace.** This spotless early 20th-century Victorian gem in a residential neighborhood has a wraparound porch, fireplaces, and 10-ft ceilings and is full of antiques and memorabilia. Rooms, with four-poster beds, are country Victorian in style. The no-smoking inn is best for adults and older children. ✉ *5901 Sardis Rd., 28270,* ☎ *704/365–1936,* FAX *704/366–2729. 2 rooms, 1 suite. AE, MC, V. BP.*

Nightlife and the Arts

The Arts

The key venue for performing arts is the **North Carolina Blumenthal Performing Arts Center,** or PAC (✉ 130 N. Tryon St., ☎ 704/372–1000). It's home to several resident companies, including the Charlotte Symphony Orchestra, North Carolina Dance Theatre, Charlotte Repertory Theatre, and Opera Carolina. PAC also presents national tours of Broadway musicals. The **Spirit Square Center for the Arts & Education** (✉ 345 N. College St., ☎ 704/372–7469) is an interdisciplinary arts center with classes, exhibits, and national acts such as Wynton Marsalis and Jerry Jeff Walker.

Blockbuster Pavilion (✉ 707 Pavilion Blvd., ☎ 704/549–1292) spotlights a variety of big-name concerts (Tom Petty, Reba McEntire, N'Sync) from spring through fall. The **Paladium Amphitheater** at Paramount's Carowinds (✉ 14523 Carowinds Blvd., ☎ 704/588–2600 or 800/888–4386) presents stars in concert from mid-spring through mid-fall.

Nightlife

Comedy Zone (✉ 5317-A E. Independence Blvd., ☎ 704/568–4242) showcases live comedy nightly except Monday, with two shows Friday and two or three shows Saturday. The **Moon Room** (✉ 433 S. Tryon St., ☎ 704/342–2003), a dimly lighted, funky bar with a coffeehouse atmosphere, presents a variety of entertainment. Friday and Saturday are reserved for live music. **Ri Ra** (✉ 208 N. Tryon St., ☎ 704/333–5554), Gaelic for "uproar" or "a lot of fun," is filled with Irish food, ale, and, on Sunday night, live traditional Irish music.

Outdoor Activities and Sports

Participant Sports

CAMPING

Near Charlotte, camping can be found at **McDowell Park and Nature Reserve** (✉ 15222 York Rd., ☎ 704/588–5224), **Paramount's Carowinds** (✉ 14523 Carowinds Blvd., off I–77, ☎ 704/588–2600 or 800/888–4386), and **Duke Power State Park** (✉ Rte. 2, Troutman, ☎ 704/528–6350).

CANOEING

Inlets on Lake Norman and Lake Wylie are ideal for canoeing, as are some spots of the Catawba River. The Pee Dee River east of Charlotte and the New River in the mountains offer other options.

FISHING

You'll find good fishing in Charlotte's neighboring lakes and streams. A mandatory state license can be bought at local bait and tackle shops or over the phone (with a credit card) from the **North Carolina Wildlife Commission** (☎ 919/715–4091).

GOLF

There are more than 50 golf courses within a 40-mi drive of Uptown Charlotte. The *Metrolina Golf Guide,* a free publication available at INFO! Charlotte (☞ Visitor Information *in* Charlotte A to Z, *below*), has a complete list. **Highland Creek Golf Club** (✉ 7001 Highland Creek Pkwy., ☎ 704/875–9000), an 18-hole, par-72 course with a driving range, is considered by some to be the best public course in Charlotte.

Larkhaven Golf Club (✉ 4801 Camp Stewart Rd., ☎ 704/545–4653) is a championship 18-hole, par-72 course with clubhouse and pro shop. **Paradise Valley Golf Center** (✉ 9309 N. Tryon St., ☎ 704/548–1808), in the university area, has an 18-hole, all par-3 course. The driving range is ½ mi down the street (✉ 9615 N. Tryon St., ☎ 704/548–8114). **Woodbridge Golf Links** (✉ 922 New Camp Creek Church Rd., Kings Mountain, ☎ 704/482–0353), an attractive par-72 course, has 18 holes and a driving range.

SWIMMING

The **Mecklenburg County Aquatic Center** (✉ 800 E. 2nd St., ☎ 704/336–3483) has a 50-meter lap pool, hydrotherapy pool, fitness room, and whirlpool. Open swim times for visitors are 5:30–11 AM, 2–5 PM, and 7–10 PM. The fee is $4.

TENNIS

Tennis courts are available in several Charlotte city parks, including Freedom, Hornet's Nest, Park Road, and Veterans. For details, call the **Charlotte Park and Recreation Department** (☎ 704/336–3854).

Spectator Sports

AUTO RACING

NASCAR races, such as the Coca-Cola 600 and UAW/GM 500, draw huge crowds at the **Lowe's Motor Speedway** (✉ 5555 U.S. 29, Harrisburg, northeast of Charlotte, ☎ 704/455–3200).

BASEBALL

The AAA minor league **Charlotte Knights,** an affiliate of the Chicago White Sox, play from April through August at Knights Castle (✉ 2280 Deerfield Dr., at I–77 and Gold Hill Rd., Fort Mill, SC, ☎ 704/357–8071 or 803/548–8050).

BASKETBALL

The **Charlotte Hornets** NBA team plays from October through April at the Charlotte Coliseum (✉ 100 Hive Dr., ☎ 704/357–0252).

FOOTBALL

The NFL's **Carolina Panthers** play from September to mid-January in the 73,000-seat Ericsson Stadium (✉ 800 S. Mint St., ☎ 704/358–7800).

HOCKEY

The **Charlotte Checkers,** an East Coast Hockey League team, play from mid-October to mid-March at Independence Arena (✉ 2700 E. Independence Blvd., ☎ 704/342–4423).

Shopping

Charlotte is the largest retail center in the Carolinas. The majority of stores are in suburban malls, and villages and towns in outlying areas have regional specialties. Many of the Uptown shops, which can be found in the Overstreet Mall connected by a set of skywalks, are open Monday through Saturday 10–5:30. Most malls are open Monday through Saturday 10–9 and Sunday 1–6. Sales tax is 6%.

Shopping Malls

Carolina Place Mall (✉ 11025 Carolina Place Pkwy., off I–277 at Pineville, ☎ 704/543–9300) is the only Charlotte shopping center with five anchors and interstate access. Ask for a visitor discount card at the customer service center. **Eastland Mall** (✉ 5471 Central Ave., ☎ 704/537–2626), on the east side of town, has an ice-skating rink as well as Belk, Dillard's, JCPenney, Sears, and 112 other retail stores. **SouthPark Mall** (✉ 4400 Sharon Rd., ☎ 704/364–4411), in the most affluent section of the city, offers high-end stores such as Tiffany's, Pottery Barn, Coach, Eddie Bauer, and Godiva Chocolatier.

Concord Mills (✉ 15 mi north of Charlotte, intersection of I–85 and Concord Mills Blvd., Concord, ☎ 704/979–3000 or 877/626–4557) has more than 200 stores and theme restaurants, a 24-screen movie theater, arcades, and even a waterfall and trout pond, arranged around a 1-mi oval walking lane.

The **Outlet Marketplace** (✉ off I–77, Fort Mill, SC, 1 mi south of Charlotte, ☎ 704/377–8630) carries well-known brands at a discount.

Specialty Stores

ANTIQUES

The towns of Waxhaw, Pineville, and Matthews are the best places to find antiques. Waxhaw sponsors an annual antiques fair each February. Shops are usually open from Monday through Saturday in Pineville and Matthews. In Waxhaw, some shops are open on Sunday but closed on Monday. You can find a good selection of antiques and collectibles at the sprawling **Metrolina Expo** (✉ off I–77N at 7100 N. Statesville Rd., ☎ 704/596–4643 or 800/824–3770) on the first and third weekends of the month.

BOOKS AND MAGAZINES

The locally owned and operated **Little Professor Book Center** (✉ Park Road Shopping Center, 4139 Park Rd., ☎ 704/525–9239; South Lake Shopping Center, Lake Norman, ☎ 704/896–7323) has a good selection of contemporary fiction and classics. **Newsstand International** (✉ 5622–128 E. Independence Blvd., ☎ 704/531–0199) carries hardbacks, newspapers, maps, and magazines from around the world.

CRAFTS

The best Charlotte crafts buys are in the **Metrolina Expo** (☞ Antiques, *above*). A number of shows, including the Carolina Craft Shows, held in the fall and spring at the convention center, as well as the Southern Christmas Show and the Southern Spring Show at the Merchandise Mart, showcase a wide variety of items.

FOOD AND PLANTS

The **Charlotte Regional Farmers Market** (✉ 1801 Yorkmount Rd., ☎ 704/357–1269) sells produce, fish, plants, and crafts.

Charlotte A to Z

Arriving and Departing

BY BUS

Greyhound/Carolina Trailways (✉ 601 W. Trade St., ☎ 704/372–0456 or 800/231–2222) serves the Charlotte area.

BY CAR

Charlotte is a transportation hub; I–77 comes in from Columbia, South Carolina, to the south and then continues north to Virginia, intersecting I–40 on the way. I–85 arrives from Greenville, South Carolina, to the southwest and then goes northeast to meet I–40 between Winston-Salem and the Triangle. From the Triangle, I–85 continues northeast to Petersburg, Virginia.

BY PLANE

Charlotte-Douglas International Airport (✉ 5501 Josh Birmingham Blvd., ☎ 704/359–4013) is west of the city off I–85. American, British Airways, Delta, Northwest, TWA, United, US Airways, and their local affiliates serve the facility. For airline telephone numbers, *see* Air Travel *in* Smart Travel Tips A to Z.

Taxis from the airport cost about $15 ($2 each additional person), and airport vans are approximately $8 per person to Uptown. Most major hotels provide complimentary transportation. By car, take the Billy Graham Parkway, then Wilkinson Boulevard (U.S. 74) east to I–277, which leads to the heart of Uptown.

BY TRAIN

Amtrak (✉ 1914 N. Tryon St., ☎ 704/376–4416 or 800/872–7245) offers daily service from Charlotte to Washington, D.C., Atlanta, and points beyond, and there's daily service to cities in the Triangle.

Getting Around

BY BUS

Center City Circuit (☎ 704/332–2227) operates free shuttle service throughout Uptown on weekdays beginning at 7 and 7:30 AM. Look for the Uptown Circuit street signs. **Charlotte Transit** (☎ 704/336–3366) provides public transportation throughout the city. Fares are $1 for local rides and $1.40 for express service within Charlotte.

BY TAXI

Crown Cab (☎ 704/334–6666) and **Yellow Cab** (☎ 704/332–6161) have taxis and airport vans. **University Towncar** (☎ 704/553–2424 or 888/553–2424) caters to business travelers. You won't pay more for the company's flat rate than you would for a cab ride.

Contacts and Resources

EMERGENCIES

Ambulance, police (☎ 911).

GUIDED TOURS

The ***Catawba Queen*** paddle wheeler (✉ U.S. 150, Exit 36, Mooresville, ☎ 704/663–2628) gives dinner cruises and tours on Lake Norman. Reservations are essential.

HOSPITALS

Carolinas Medical Center (✉ 1001 Blythe Blvd., ☎ 704/355–2000). **Presbyterian Hospital** (✉ 200 Hawthorne La., ☎ 704/384–4000).

LATE-NIGHT PHARMACY

Eckerd Drugs (✉ Park Road Shopping Center, ☎ 704/523–3031; 3740 E. Independence Blvd., ☎ 704/536–3600).

RADIO STATIONS

AM: WBT 1110, news, talk, sports; WFNZ 610, all sports. **FM:** WSOC 103.7, country; WFAE 90.7, National Public Radio; WXRC 95.7, rock.

VISITOR INFORMATION

INFO! Charlotte (✉ 330 S. Tryon St., ☎ 704/331–2700 or 800/231–4636) is open weekdays 8:30–5, Saturday 10–4, and Sunday 1–4.

THE TRIAD

Greensboro, Winston-Salem, High Point

North Carolinians group six urban centers in the Piedmont into two threesomes: the Triad and the Triangle (☞ *below*). Although this shorthand is a verbal convenience, it's also testament that the whole can be greater than the sum of the parts. Make no mistake, though: Although they share geography and are scattered along the major arteries of the region, the Triad's major cities have very distinct personalities. Greensboro, to the east, bustles as a business center. Smaller Winston-Salem, to the west, will catch you by surprise with its eclectic arts scene. High

Point, to the south, has managed to fuse the simplicity of Quaker forebears with its role as a world-class furniture market.

Greensboro

96 mi northeast of Charlotte, 26 mi east of Winston-Salem, 58 mi west of Durham.

With 200,000 citizens, Greensboro is the largest population center in the Triad, and thanks to spacious convention facilities it's an increasingly popular destination for business travelers. Yet this city, named in honor of General Nathanael Greene, a Revolutionary War hero, takes pride in its role in American history and has taken great pains to preserve and showcase the sights of past eras.

With the exception of Old Greensborough and the downtown historic district, however, walking is not a comfortable sightseeing option. To tour the grand historic homes, glimpse monuments to famous native sons and daughters—Dolley Madison, Edward R. Murrow, O. Henry—or visit one of the many recreation areas, you'll need a car.

Guilford Courthouse National Military Park, the nation's first Revolutionary War park, has monuments, military memorabilia, and more than 200 acres with wooded hiking trails. It memorializes one of the earliest events in the city's history. On March 15, 1781, the Battle of Guilford Courthouse so weakened British troops that they surrendered seven months later at Yorktown. Today many families use the 3 mi of foot trails. ⊠ *2332 New Garden Rd.,* ☎ *336/288–1776.* 🎟 *Free.* ⏲ *Daily 8:30–5.*

Tannenbaum Park, a hands-on history experience near Guilford Courthouse National Military Park, draws you into the life of early settlers. With advance notice costumed re-enactors will escort you through exhibits at the **Colonial Heritage Center** in the visitor center. The restored **1778 Hoskins House** (tours by appointment) and a blacksmith shop and barn are on the property. The park has one of the most outstanding collections of original colonial settlement maps in the country. ⊠ *Visitor center, New Garden Rd. and Battleground Ave.,* ☎ *336/545–5315.* 🎟 *Free.* ⏲ *Tues.–Fri. 9–5, Sat. 10–5, Sun. 1–5.*

Roam through a dinosaur gallery, learn about gems and minerals, and see the lemurs, snakes, and amphibians at the **Natural Science Center of Greensboro.** There's also a planetarium and a petting zoo. ⊠ *4301 Lawndale Dr., adjacent to Country Park,* ☎ *336/288–3769.* 🎟 *$3.50, planetarium $1, prices subject to change for special exhibits and events.* ⏲ *Science center Mon.–Sat. 9–5, Sun. 12:30–5; zoo Mon.–Sat. 10–4:30, Sun. 12:30–4:30.*

The **Greensboro Historical Museum,** in a Romanesque church built in 1892, has exhibits about native son and daughter O. Henry and Dolley Madison, as well as one about the Woolworth sit-in that helped launch the national civil rights movement in the 1960s. ⊠ *130 Summit Ave.,* ☎ *336/373–2043.* 🎟 *Free.* ⏲ *Tues.–Sat. 10–5, Sun. 2–5.*

Greensboro Cultural Center at Festival Park, an architectural showplace, houses 25 visual and performing arts organizations, five art galleries, rehearsal halls, a sculpture garden, a restaurant with outdoor café-style seating, and an outdoor amphitheater. **ArtQuest,** developed by educators and artists, is North Carolina's only permanent interactive children's art gallery. ⊠ *200 N. Davie St.,* ☎ *336/373–2712.* 🎟 *Free.* ⏲ *Weekdays 8 AM–10 PM, Sat. 9–6, Sun. 1–6:30.*

Exhibits and activities at the **Greensboro Children's Museum** are designed for children under 12. They can tour an airplane cockpit with an interactive screen, dig for buried treasure, or wrap themselves in a gigantic bubble. ✉ *220 N. Church St.,* ☎ *336/574–2898.* *$5.50.* *Labor Day–Memorial Day, Tues.–Sat. 9–5, Sun. 1–5; Memorial Day–Labor Day, Mon. 9–5.*

Elm Street, with its turn-of-the-20th-century architecture, is the heart of **Old Greensborough** (✉ 100 block of N. Elm St. to 600 block of S. Elm St., with portions of several other streets), which is listed on the National Register of Historic Places. Stop by the William Fields House, headquarters for the Old Greensborough Preservation Society (✉ 447 Arlington St., ☎ 336/272–6617), to collect your self-guided tour map. The entire tour may be walked in two hours.

In Old Greensborough, the elegant **Blandwood Mansion,** home of former governor John Motley Morehead, is considered the prototype of the Italian villa architecture that swept the country during the mid-19th century. Designed by noted architect Alexander Jackson Davis, the house still contains many of its original furnishings. ✉ *447 W. Washington St.,* ☎ *336/272–5003.* *$5.* *Tues.–Sat. 11–2, Sun. 2–5.*

The **Weatherspoon Art Gallery,** on the campus of the University of North Carolina–Greensboro, consists of six galleries and a sculpture courtyard. It is nationally recognized for its collection and changing exhibitions of 20th-century American art. The permanent collection includes lithographs and bronzes by Henri Matisse. ✉ *Corner of Tate and Spring Garden Sts.,* ☎ *336/334–5770.* *Free.* *Tues. and Thurs.–Fri. 10–5, Wed. 10–8, weekends 1–5.*

Dining and Lodging

$$$–$$$$ ✕ **Paisley Pineapple.** The dining is formal in this romantic Old Greensborough restaurant in a restored 1920s building. The fare on the extensive menu—rack of lamb, grilled veal tenderloin, and sautéed beef tenderloin—tends toward the hearty. On the lighter side are the soups (try the berry bisque if it's available) and seafood. Don't miss the cinnamon-seared salmon. Upstairs, there's a bar with sofas and background music. ✉ *345 S. Elm St.,* ☎ *336/279–8488. AE, MC, V.*

$$–$$$$ ✕ **Gate City Chop House.** This place has a lock on the upscale, everything-is-bigger-here steak house concept in the Triad. The look is masculine and clubby and the portions are geared toward large appetites. Beef is the star to be sure, but there's good to say about other menu items, such as seafood—try the shrimp bisque—and salads. The wine list is respectable. ✉ *106 S. Holden Rd.,* ☎ *336/294–9977. AE, D, DC, MC, V. Closed Sun.*

$$–$$$$ ✕ **Lo Spiedo di Noble.** Murals adorn some walls, and from the upstairs seating area you can see the wood-burning tile oven and the slowly turning spit that turn out Tuscan cuisine such as rack of pork with fresh peach-walnut-thyme compote on a bed of white beans and red chard. The piano bar on the lower level is a nice way to end the evening. A jazz trio plays Wednesday through Saturday evenings. ✉ *172 Battleground Ave.,* ☎ *336/333–9833. AE, D, MC, V.*

$$–$$$ ✕ **Casaldi's Cafe.** Light gray-green is the predominant color in this sleek little trattoria, appearing in the tile floors as well as marble countertops. Wildflowers decorate the tables, and display cases provide a powerful lure to sample the myriad pasta dishes. Particularly popular are the spinach and walnut ravioli and the bow-tie pasta with chicken and mushrooms. ✉ *1310 Westover Terr.,* ☎ *336/379–8191. Reservations not accepted. D, MC, V. Closed Sun.*

$$$$ **O. Henry Hotel.** Named for a famous native son, this is one of the newest and grandest establishments on the city's lodging scene. The decor is somewhat evocative of the Arts and Crafts style, with wood, tapestries, and upholstery in warm tones. Particularly nice touches are the oversize rooms, tiled bathrooms with standing shower stalls and separate tubs, and bed coverlets that are laundered daily. A complimentary breakfast buffet is offered in a sunny pavilion overlooking a small garden. ✉ *624 Green Valley Rd., 27408,* ☎ *336/854–2000,* FAX *336/854–2223. 121 rooms, 10 suites. Restaurant, breakfast room, in-room data ports, in-room safes, refrigerators, room service, pool, exercise room, laundry service, business services, meeting rooms, airport shuttle. AE, D, DC, MC, V. BP.*

$$$ **Sheraton Greensboro Hotel at Four Seasons/Joseph S. Koury Convention Center.** Business travelers are the mainstay here, at the state's largest hotel. Accommodations are standard fare, but the hotel and its nearby sister property, the Park Lane Hotel (☎ 336/294–4565), are convenient to major thoroughfares and the Four Seasons Town Centre (☞ Shopping, *below*), a three-story regional mall. ✉ *3121 High Point Rd., 27407,* ☎ *336/292–9161 or 800/242–6556,* FAX *336/292–1407. 1,014 rooms, 78 suites. 4 restaurants, 4 bars, in-room data ports, pool, wading pool, exercise room, racquetball, nightclub, video games, business services, convention center, meeting rooms, airport shuttle, kennel. AE, D, DC, MC, V.*

$$ ★ **Biltmore Greensboro Hotel.** In the heart of the central business district, the Biltmore has an old-world feel, with 16-ft ceilings, a cage elevator, and a lobby area with walnut-paneled walls and a fireplace. Some guest rooms have Victorian or Victorian-style furniture and electric candle sconces. Rates include evening wine and cheese. ✉ *111 W. Washington St., 27401,* ☎ *336/272–3474 or 800/332–0303,* FAX *336/275–2523. 21 rooms, 4 suites. In-room data ports, minibars, refrigerators, business services, meeting room, airport shuttle. AE, D, DC, MC, V. CP.*

$$ **Greenwood Bed and Breakfast.** Eclectic antiques, art, and various other collections fill this 1905 Craftsman-style home in historic Fisher Park. Owners Bob (a former New Orleans chef) and Dolly (a decorator) Guertin serve a full breakfast at the time of your choosing. Café au lait, French bread, eggs Benedict, and crepes suzette come with freshly squeezed orange juice and fruit. Desserts are set out in the evening. This no-smoking B&B is best for older children. ✉ *205 N. Park Dr., 27401,* ☎ *336/274–6350 or 800/535–9363,* FAX *336/274–9943. 5 rooms. Pool, meeting rooms. AE, D, DC, MC, V. BP.*

Nightlife and the Arts

The **Broach Theatre** (✉ 520 S. Elm St., ☎ 336/378–9300) has professional adult (March–June and September–December) and children's (September–June) theater in the Old Greensborough historic district. The **Carolina Theatre** (✉ 310 S. Greene St., ☎ 336/333–2600), a restored vaudeville venue, serves as one of the city's principal performing arts centers, showcasing dance, concerts, films, and plays. The **Greensboro Symphony** (☎ 336/333–7490) and the **Greensboro Opera Company** (☎ 336/273–9472) perform at the Greensboro Coliseum Complex (☞ *below*).

The vast **Greensboro Coliseum Complex** (✉ 1921 W. Lee St., ☎ 336/373–7474) hosts arts and entertainment events throughout the year as well as professional, college, and amateur sports.

The **Eastern Music Festival** (✉ 200 N. Davie St., ☎ 336/333–7450), whose alumni include Wynton Marsalis, brings six weeks of classical music concerts to Greensboro in summer.

Outdoor Activities and Sports

BASEBALL

The **Greensboro Bats,** the Class A farm club for the New York Yankees, play April through September at War Memorial Stadium (✉ corner of Lindsay and Yanceyville Sts., ☎ 336/333–2287).

CAMPING

Some good choices are **Greensboro KOA** (✉ 2300 Montreal Ave., ☎ 336/274–4143 or 800/562–4143), **Hagan-Stone Park** (✉ 5920 Hagan-Stone Rd., ☎ 336/674–0472), and **Outdoor Center YMCA** (✉ 4924 Tapawingo Trail, ☎ 336/697–0525).

GOLF

Golfers can choose from among 27 public courses and four driving ranges. **Bryan Park and Golf Club** (✉ 6275 Bryan Park Rd., Browns Summit, ☎ 336/375–2200) is a highly regarded non-metal-spike, par-72 course north of Greensboro. The **Grandover Resort/Grandover Golf Club** (✉ One Thousand Club Dr., ☎ 336/294–1800 or 800/472–6301) has two par-72 courses. The **Greensboro National Golf Club** (✉ 330 Niblick Dr., Summerfield, ☎ 336/342–1113), 15 minutes north of Greensboro, is a par-72 course.

The PGA's **Greater Greensboro Chrysler Classic** is held each April at the Forest Oaks Country Club (✉ U.S. 421S, ☎ 336/379–1570).

HIKING

The **Bog Garden** (✉ on Hobbs Rd. north of Friendly Ave., ☎ 336/373–2199) has an elevated wooden walkway through a swampy area with more than 8,000 individually labeled trees, shrubs, ferns, and wildflowers. There are walking trails and an exercise course at the 120-acre **Oka T. Hester Park** (✉ 910 Ailanthus St., ☎ 336/373–2937).

TENNIS

Greensboro Jaycee Park (✉ Forest Lawn Dr. off Pisgah Church Rd., adjacent to Country Park, ☎ 336/545–5342) has sports facilities including a tennis center with 12 soft championship courts.

Shopping

OUTLET CENTERS

The 50 stores at the **Burlington Manufacturers Outlet Center** (✉ off Exit 145 at I–85, ☎ 336/227–2872) make the area off I–85 near Burlington (about 20 mi east of Greensboro) a mecca for bargain hunters.

SHOPPING DISTRICTS AND MALLS

Four Seasons Town Centre (✉ I–40 at High Point Rd., ☎ 336/292–0171) holds more than 200 major stores, specialty shops, restaurants, a first-run movie theater, a US Airways ticket office, and a post office. Head to **Old Greensborough** (☞ Greensboro, *above*) for antiques shops and bookstores.

SPECIALTY STORES

Replacements, Ltd. (✉ I–85/40 at Mt. Hope Church Rd., Exit 132, ☎ 800/737–5223), the world's largest retailer of discontinued and active china, crystal, flatware, and collectibles, stocks nearly 6 million pieces of inventory and 125,000 patterns. The cavernous showroom is open 8–9 daily and free tours are given.

Side Trips from Greensboro

CHARLOTTE HAWKINS BROWN MEMORIAL STATE HISTORIC SITE

10 mi east of Greensboro.

On the site of the Palmer Institute, the memorial honors the African-American woman who founded the school in 1902. Before closing in 1971, this accredited preparatory school for African-Americans was recognized as one of the country's best and had expanded to more than 350 acres of land. There is a visitor center and a gift shop. ✉ *6136 Burlington Rd., Sedalia, off I–85, Exit 135,* ☎ *336/449–4846.* 🎫 *Free.* ⏲ *Oct.–Apr., Tues.–Fri. 10–4, Sun. 1–4; May–Sept., Mon.–Sat. 9–5, Sun. 1–5.*

CHINQUA-PENN PLANTATION

★ *25 mi north of Greensboro.*

The **Chinqua-Penn Plantation**, a National Historic Register English-country mansion, was built by tobacco and utility magnates Jeff and Betsy Penn in 1925. The Penns, world travelers, filled the 27-room house with an eclectic collection of artifacts representing 30 countries. The estate also has a Chinese pagoda, a three-story clock tower, greenhouses, and formal gardens—even a cemetery for all the Penns' beloved dogs. ✉ *2138 Wentworth St., Reidsville,* ☎ *336/349–4576 or 800/948–0947.* 🎫 *$13.* ⏲ *Mar.–Dec., Tues.–Sat. 9–5, Sun. noon–5.*

Winston-Salem

81 mi north of Charlotte, 26 mi west of Greensboro.

Winston-Salem residents' donations to the arts are among the highest per capita in the nation: The city bills itself as the City of the Arts, and its museums show the benefits of this support. The North Carolina School of the Arts commands international attention. Salem College, the oldest women's college in the country, is here, as is Wake Forest University, where writer Maya Angelou teaches. Old Salem, a restored 18th-century Moravian town within the city, has been a popular attraction since the early 1950s.

Staff at the **Winston-Salem Visitor Center** (✉ 601 N. Cherry St., ☎ 336/777–3796 or 800/331–7018) will assist with directions and help you make dining and lodging reservations.

★ Founded in 1766 as a Moravian Congregation town and backcountry trading center, **Old Salem** has become one of the nation's most authentic and well-documented colonial sites. At this living history museum with more than 80 restored and original buildings, costumed interpreters re-create household activities and trades common in Salem in the late 18th and early 19th centuries. You can participate in African-American programs that include a stop by St. Philip's Church, the state's oldest-standing African-American church. Old Salem is home to museum shops, the Old Salem Furniture & Accessories Shop, the 1816 Salem Tavern restaurant, and the Winkler Bakery (don't pass up the Moravian sugar cake). The village is a few blocks from downtown Winston-Salem and near Business I–40 (take the Old Salem/Salem College exit). ✉ *600 S. Main St.,* ☎ *336/721–7300 or 888/653–7253.* 🎫 *$15; combination ticket with Museum of Early Southern Decorative Arts (☞ below) $20.* ⏲ *Mon.–Sat. 9–5, Sun. 12:30–5.*

★ The **Museum of Early Southern Decorative Arts (MESDA),** on the southern edge of Old Salem, is the only museum dedicated to exhibiting and researching the regional decorative arts of the early South. Twenty-four intricately detailed period rooms and six galleries showcase the furniture, painting, ceramics, and metalware made and used regionally through 1820. The bookstore carries current and hard-to-find books on Southern decorative arts, culture, and history. ✉ *924 S. Main St.,* ☎ *336/721–7360 or 888/653–7253.* 🎫 *$10; combination ticket with Old Salem (☞ above) $20.* ⏲ *Mon.–Sat. 10:30–4:30, Sun. 1:30–4:30.*

The **SciWorks** complex includes a 120-seat planetarium, 15-acre Environmental Park, and 45,000 square ft of exhibits that are interactive or hands-on, including the Coastal Encounters wet lab. ✉ *400 W. Hanes Mill Rd.,* ☎ *336/767–6730.* *Museum $7, the Works (planetarium, park, and museum) $8.* ⊙ *Mon.–Sat. 10–5.*

You can take a guided tour through the exhibits on tobacco growing and auctioning at **R. J. Reynolds Whitaker Park,** view historical memorabilia related to the tobacco industry, and visit the gift shop. Tours of the factory floor are no longer offered, however. ✉ *1100 Reynolds Blvd.,* ☎ *336/741–5718.* *Free.* ⊙ *Weekdays 8–6.*

Historic Bethabara Park, set in a wooded 195 acres, is the site of the first Moravian settlement (1753) in North Carolina. Bethabara—meaning "house of passage"—was to be temporary until the town of Salem was established. You can tour restored buildings such as the 1788 congregation house and explore the foundations of the town. Children love the reconstructed fort from the French and Indian War and the wildlife preserve. ✉ *2147 Bethabara Rd.,* ☎ *336/924–8191.* *$1.* ⊙ *Exhibit buildings Apr.–Nov., weekdays 9:30–4:30, weekends 1:30–4:30; guided tours Apr.–Nov. or by appointment. Brochures for self-guided walking tour available year-round at visitor center.*

The **Museum of Anthropology** has exhibits of peoples and cultures of the Americas, Asia, Africa, and Oceania. The Museum Shop holds special sales in May and December. ✉ *Wake Forest University, Reynolda campus, Wingate Rd.,* ☎ *336/758–5282.* *Free.* ⊙ *Tues.–Sat. 10–4:30.*

Reynolda House Museum of American Art, formerly the home of tobacco magnate Richard Joshua Reynolds and his wife, Katherine, is filled with American paintings, prints, and sculptures by such artists as Thomas Eakins, Frederick Church, and Georgia O'Keeffe. There's also a costume collection, as well as vintage clothing and toys used by the Reynolds children. The museum is next to **Reynolda Village,** a collection of shops, restaurants, and gardens that fill the estate's original outer buildings. ✉ *2250 Reynolda Rd.,* ☎ *336/725–5325.* *$6.* ⊙ *Tues.–Sat. 9:30–4:30, Sun. 1:30–4:30.*

Exhibits at the **Southeastern Center for Contemporary Art (SECCA),** near Reynolda House, showcase regional arts and crafts as well as works by nationally known artists. The Centershop sells many one-of-a-kind pieces. ✉ *750 Marguerite Dr.,* ☎ *336/725–1904.* *$3.* ⊙ *Tues.–Sat. 10–5, Sun. 2–5.*

Just south of the city, **Tanglewood Park,** the home of the late William and Kate Reynolds, is now open to the public; in addition to golfing, boating, hiking, fishing, horseback riding, and swimming, it puts on a holiday lights festival, the largest such display in the Southeast. The **Tanglewood Festival of Lights** runs from mid-November to mid-January annually. ✉ *U.S. 158 off I–40, Clemmons,* ☎ *336/778–6300.* *$2 per car, separate fees for each activity.* ⊙ *Daily dawn–dusk.*

Dining and Lodging

$$$–$$$$ ✕ **Southbound Bistro and Grille.** Housed in a building erected in 1913 as the headquarters for Southbound Railway, this restaurant is anything but old-fashioned. It has a weekly-changing menu, with everything from grilled steak with fried sweet potatoes to grilled ostrich topped with honeyed onions and spicy cantaloupe chutney. ✉ *300 S. Liberty St.,* ☎ *336/723–0322. AE, MC, V. Closed Sun. No lunch Sat.*

$$–$$$$ ✕ **Noble's Grille.** French and Mediterranean flavors influence the menu, which changes nightly. Entrées are grilled or roasted over an oak-and-hickory fire, from braised rabbit with black-pepper fettuccine to Carolina *poussin* (young chicken) with polenta. The dining room, with tall windows and track lighting, has a view of the kitchen grill. ✉ *380 Knollwood St.,* ☎ *336/777–8477. AE, DC, MC, V.*

$$$ ✕ **Leon's Café.** This eatery in a renovated building near Old Salem serves some of the best food in town—fresh seafood, chicken breasts with raspberry sauce, lamb, and other specialties. The restaurant's dark colors are set off by artwork and lacy window treatments. ✉ *924 S. Marshall St.,* ☎ *336/725–9593. AE, D, MC, V.*

$$–$$$ ✕ **Old Salem Tavern Dining Room.** Although Moravian dishes such as chicken potpie and sauerbraten are the highlight of the lunch menu, dinner is more varied. In the warm months drinks are served under the arbor, and open-air seating draws diners to the covered back porch. ✉ *736 S. Main St.,* ☎ *336/748–8585. AE, MC, V.*

$$–$$$ ✕ **The Vineyards.** The innovative seasonal menu, with such dishes as grilled swordfish on a bed of black-eyed-pea salsa, and stuffed eggplant, attracts diners to this Reynolda Village restaurant. Locals have voted the homemade bread pudding the best in town. ✉ *120 Reynolda Village Rd.,* ☎ *336/748–0269. AE, MC, V.*

$$–$$$$ **Adam's Mark Winston Plaza Hotel.** Centrally located off I–40, the hotel is housed in two towers connected by a climate-controlled skywalk. The East Tower has a traditional look while the West Tower is a bit sleeker and more contemporary. The Cherry Street Bar, with its smoothly tailored living-room atmosphere, is a great place to relax. ✉ *425 N. Cherry St., 27101,* ☎ *336/725–3500 or 800/444–2326,* FAX *336/721–2240. 605 rooms, 26 suites. Restaurant, 2 bars, in-room data ports, room service, indoor pool, sauna, steam room, exercise room, dry cleaning, laundry service, business services, meeting rooms, parking (fee). AE, D, DC, MC, V.*

$$–$$$$ **Henry F. Shaffner House.** Accessible to downtown and Old Salem, this B&B is a favorite with business travelers and honeymooning couples. The rooms in the restored English Tudor house are furnished in 19th-century Victorian elegance. Rates include breakfast as well as afternoon tea and evening wine and cheese. ✉ *150 S. Marshall St., 27101,* ☎ *336/777–0052 or 800/952–2256,* FAX *336/777–1188. 9 rooms. Restaurant, in-room data ports, business services, meeting room. AE, MC, V. BP, CP.*

$$$ **Brookstown Inn.** Handmade quilts, two-person tubs, and wine and cheese or freshly baked cookies in the lobby are amenities at this inn, built in 1837 as a textile mill. ✉ *200 Brookstown Ave., 27101,* ☎ *336/725–1120 or 800/845–4262,* FAX *336/773–0147. 40 rooms, 31 suites. In-room data ports, business services, meeting rooms. AE, DC, MC, V. CP.*

$–$$ **Tanglewood Manor House Bed & Breakfast.** The former home of a branch of the Reynolds family includes 10 rooms in the antiques-filled manor house, 18 rooms in a more contemporary motel behind the house, and four cottages on Mallard Lake in Tanglewood Park. Those staying in the motel can purchase the Continental breakfast served in the manor house. Admissions to the park and swimming pool are included; a fishing license is extra. Greens fees at park courses are discounted. ✉ *U.S. 158 off I–40, Clemmons 27012,* ☎ *336/778–6300,* FAX *336/778–6379. 28 rooms, 4 cottages, guest house. Picnic area, pool, wading pool, driving range, 2 18-hole golf courses, horseback riding, fishing, playground, meeting rooms. AE, DC, MC, V. CP.*

$–$$ **Comfort Inn–Cloverdale.** Off I–40 Business near downtown and Old Salem, this immaculately kept property has rooms with microwaves and refrigerators. ✉ *110 Miller St., 27103,* ☎ *336/721–0220 or 800/228–5150,* FAX *336/723–2117. 122 rooms. In-room data ports, pool, sauna, exercise room, meeting room. AE, D, DC, MC, V. CP.*

Nightlife and the Arts

THE ARTS

Many North Carolina School of the Arts musical and dramatic performances are held at the **Stevens Center** (☒ 405 W. 4th St., ☎ 336/721–1945), a restored 1929 movie palace downtown that is part of the NCSA campus. The Broadway Preview Series shows first-run productions before they move on to Broadway engagements.

NIGHTLIFE

Burke Street Pub (☒ 1110 Burke St., ☎ 336/750–0097) is an Irish-style pub with music, dancing, games, and sports TV. In the Adam's Mark Winston Plaza, the **Cherry Street Bar** (☒ 425 N. Cherry St., ☎ 336/725–3500) has cozy chairs and smart decor. **Lucky 32** (☒ 109 S. Stratford Rd., ☎ 336/777–0032), a fine bar adjoining a restaurant, caters to a professional crowd.

Outdoor Activities and Sports

BASEBALL

The **Winston-Salem Warthogs,** a Class A affiliate of the Chicago White Sox, play from April through August at Ernie Shore Field (☒ 401 Deacon Blvd., ☎ 336/759–2233).

BASKETBALL

Winston-Salem's Atlantic Coast Conference entry is the Wake Forest University **Demon Deacons** (☎ 336/758–3322 or 888/758–3322).

GOLF

Tanglewood Park Golf Club (☒ NC 158, Clemmons, ☎ 336/778–6320) has two fine 18-hole, par-72 courses, the Reynolds Course and the Championship Course, where the Vantage Championship is played each year. **Reynolds Park Golf Course** (☒ 2931 Reynolds Park Rd., ☎ 336/650–7660) has 18 holes with a view of the city skyline and a par 71.

Shopping

SHOPPING DISTRICTS AND MALLS

The **Art District** at 6th and Trade streets (just behind the Winston-Salem Visitor Center) has several galleries and arts-and-crafts shops. **Reynolda Village** is near the Reynolda House Museum of American Art (☞ Winston-Salem, *above*). **Stratford Place,** a collection of upscale shops, restaurants, and cafés, is off I–40 Business in the Five Points area, where Country Club, Miller Road, and 1st Street converge.

At 1.8 million square ft, and with more than 200 stores, **Hanes Mall** (☒ Silas Creek Pkwy. and Hanes Mall Blvd.) is one of the largest indoor malls in the Carolinas.

CRAFTS

All items at the **Piedmont Craftsmen's Shop and Gallery** (☒ 1204 Reynolda Rd., ☎ 336/725–1516) are juried. An annual fair is held in November. **erl Originals** (☒ 3069 Trenwest Dr., ☎ 336/760–4363), near I–40 and Hanes Mall, has 8,000 square ft of gallery space and represents more than 300 artists.

High Point

76 mi northeast of Charlotte, 20 mi southwest of Greensboro.

Originally settled by Quakers in the 1700s, High Point was incorporated in 1859. Its name is derived from its former position as the highest point on the railroad between Goldsboro and Charlotte. Today when people think of High Point, they think of furniture, for it is home to the twice-a-year (April and October) International Home Furnishings Market, the largest wholesale furniture market in the world (not open to the public). Tens of thousands of buyers and others associated with the trade "go to market" and in the process lend a sophistication to this warm and hospitable city. Retail outlets here offer furniture and home accessories at bargain prices.

The **High Point Museum/Historical Park,** focusing on Piedmont history and Quaker heritage, includes the 1786 Haley House and a mid-1700s blacksmith shop and weaving house. Exhibits highlight furniture, pottery, communication, transportation, and military artifacts. Tours of the buildings are available weekends and are conducted by costumed staff. ✉ *1859 E. Lexington Ave.,* ☎ *336/885–6859.* 🎫 *Free.* ⏲ *Museum Tues.–Sat. 10–4, Sun. 1–4; park buildings weekends 1–4.*

The **Furniture Discovery Center,** in a renovated fabric warehouse downtown, simulates the furniture design and manufacturing process. It has a Furniture Hall of Fame and an extensive miniature collection exhibited in room displays. ✉ *101 W. Green Dr.,* ☎ *336/887–3876.* 🎫 *$5; combination ticket with Angela Peterson Doll and Miniature Museum (☞ below) $8.50.* ⏲ *Apr.–Oct., weekdays 10–5, Sat. 9–5; Sun. 1–5; Nov.–Mar., Tues.–Fri. 10–5, Sat. 9–5, Sun. 1–5.*

The **Angela Peterson Doll and Miniature Museum** houses the collection of one woman: more than 1,700 dolls, costumes, miniatures, and dollhouses. ✉ *101 W. Green Dr.,* ☎ *336/885–3655.* 🎫 *$4; combination ticket with Furniture Discovery Center (☞ above) $8.50.* ⏲ *Apr.–Oct., weekdays 10–4:30, Sat. 9–4:30, Sun. 1–4:30; Nov.–Mar., Tues.–Sat. 10–4:30, Sun. 1–4:30.*

OFF THE BEATEN PATH

MENDENHALL PLANTATION – A few miles northwest of High Point is this well-preserved example of 19th-century Quaker domestic architecture. The Mendenhalls opposed slavery, and here you'll find one of the few surviving false-bottom wagons, used to help slaves escape to freedom on the Underground Railroad. ✉ *603 W. Main St., Jamestown,* ☎ *336/454–3819.* 🎫 *$2.* ⏲ *Mid-Apr.–Nov., weekdays 11–2, Sat. 1–4, Sun. 2–4.*

Dining and Lodging

$$$–$$$$ ✕ **J. Basul Noble's.** Locals hold Noble's in very high esteem, and it's not hard to see why. It's architecturally dramatic, with 10-ft pillars, a glass ceiling, and a river-rock wall. Veal dishes are recommended, and you could make a meal out of the fine breads (baked daily on the premises) and desserts served here. There's live jazz Thursday through Saturday. ✉ *101 S. Main St.,* ☎ *336/889–3354. AE, DC, MC, V.*

$$–$$$ ✕ **Atrium Cafe.** Wall murals and a teal-and-peach color scheme create a casual and elegant atmosphere. Veal, duck, and fish dishes are standouts, but the pasta and mushrooms with marinara sauce proves the Atrium can appeal to vegetarians, too. It's near the top of the Atrium Furniture Mall (☞ Shopping, *below*). ✉ *430 S. Main St.,* ☎ *336/889–9934. AE, D, DC, MC, V.*

$$–$$$ 🏨 **Radisson Hotel High Point.** The central location makes the Radisson a favorite with people coming to town for weekend shopping trips. Guest rooms are standard, but each suite is outfitted with furniture from the different manufacturers represented in the area. ✉ *135 S. Main St., 27260,* ☎ *336/889–8888,* FAX *336/885–2737. 239 rooms, 13 suites. Restaurant, bar, in-room data ports, indoor pool, exercise room, business services, meeting rooms, airport shuttle, parking (fee). AE, D, DC, MC, V.* 🏆

$$ 🏨 **Premier Bed & Breakfast.** A local furniture designer owns this three-story B&B, a 1930s-era home in a historic neighborhood. It's just a mile north of downtown, near the furniture outlets and shopping. You can relax while sipping wine by the fireplace or on the front porch swing. ✉ *1001 Johnson St., 27262,* ☎ *336/889–8349. 6 rooms. Meeting room. MC, V. BP.*

Nightlife and the Arts

Headquartered in High Point is the **North Carolina Shakespeare Festival.** The professional troupe performs from August through October and in December at the High Point Theatre (✉ 305 N. Main St., Suite 200, ☎ 336/841–2273).

Outdoor Activities and Sports

GOLF

There are four public golf courses in High Point: three have 18 holes and one has 9. Contact the High Point Convention and Visitors Bureau (☞ Visitor Information *in* The Triad A to Z, *below*) for information. Pete Dye designed the par-72 course at **Oak Hollow** (✉ 3400 N. Centennial St., ☎ 336/883–3260).

HIKING

The 376-acre **Piedmont Environmental Center** (✉ 1220 Penny Rd., ☎ 336/883–8531) has 11 mi of hiking trails adjacent to City Lake Park, with recreation opportunities and a nature preserve. There's also access to a 6-mi greenway trail.

SOCCER

The **Carolina Dynamo,** a United Soccer League team, play at A. J. Simeon Stadium (✉ 2920 School Park Rd., ☎ 336/884–5255) from April to August.

TENNIS

In Oak Hollow Lake Park, the **Reitzel Tennis Center** (✉ 3431 N. Centennial St., ☎ 336/883–3493) has four indoor courts, eight clay courts, and two hard courts. Reservations are a must.

Shopping

There are more than 60 retail **furniture stores** in and around High Point. The 36 stores in the **Atrium Furniture Mall** (✉ 430 S. Main St., ☎ 336/882–5599) carry items by more than 700 manufacturers of furniture and home accessories.

Oak Hollow Mall (✉ 921 Eastchester Dr., ☎ 336/886–6255) has 105 specialty stores, restaurants, and department stores.

Art shows rotate through the **Theatre Art Galleries** (✉ 220 E. Commerce Ave., ☎ 336/887–3415), open weekdays noon–5 and weekends by appointment but closed during market weeks in April and October.

The Triad A to Z

Arriving, Departing, and Getting Around

BY BUS

Greyhound/Carolina Trailways (☎ 800/231–2222) has service in the area.

BY CAR

Greensboro and Winston-Salem are on I–40, which runs from Asheville in the west to Wilmington in southeastern North Carolina. I–40 and I–85 are combined coming into the Triad from the east, but in Greensboro, I–85 splits off to head southwest to Charlotte. High Point is off a business bypass of I–85 southwest of Greensboro.

BY PLANE

Just west of Greensboro, the **Piedmont Triad International Airport** (✉ 6451 Bryan Blvd., Greensboro, ☎ 336/665–5666) is off NC 68 N from

I–40W; it's served by American, Continental, Atlantic Southeast Airlines, Eastwind, Northwest, United, and US Airways. For airline telephone numbers, *see* Air Travel *in* Smart Travel Tips A to Z.

Taxi service to and from the airport is provided by **Airport Express** (☎ 800/934–8779) and other tour, charter, limousine, and cab services, including the **Golden Eagle Cab Company** (☎ 336/724–6481) and **Piedmont Executive Transportation** (☎ 336/723–2179).

BY TRAIN

There are **Amtrak** stations in Greensboro (✉ 2603 Oakland Ave., ☎ 336/855–3382 or 800/872–7245) and High Point (✉ 100 W. High St., ☎ 336/841–7245 or 800/872–7245).

Contacts and Resources

EMERGENCIES

Ambulance, police (☎ 911).

GUIDED TOURS

Carolina Treasures and Tours (✉ 1031 Burke St., ☎ 336/631–9144) offers a look at historic Winston-Salem.

RADIO STATIONS

AM: WSJS 600, news, talk; WAAA 980, urban contemporary. **FM:** WFDD 88.5, National Public Radio; WKRR 92.3, rock; WJMH 102.1, urban contemporary; WTQR 104.1, country.

VISITOR INFORMATION

The following provide maps, brochures, and flyers on attractions, accommodations, and services. **Greensboro Area Convention & Visitors Bureau** (✉ 317 S. Greene St., 27401, ☎ 336/274–2282 or 800/344–2282). **High Point Convention & Visitors Bureau** (✉ 300 S. Main St., 27260, ☎ 336/884–5255 or 800/720–5255). **Winston-Salem Convention & Visitors Bureau** (✉ Box 1409, 27102, ☎ 336/728–4200 or 800/331–7018). In Winston-Salem, a visitor's **reception center** in the City Market building (✉ 601 N. Cherry St., ☎ 336/777–3796) is open daily.

THE TRIANGLE

Raleigh, Durham, Chapel Hill

The cities of Raleigh, Durham, and Chapel Hill make up the Triangle, with Raleigh to the east, Durham to the north, Chapel Hill to the west, and, in the center, Research Triangle Park—a renowned complex of corporations and public and private research facilities set in 6,800 acres of lake-dotted pineland that attracts scientists, academicians, and businesspeople from all over the world. Throughout the Triangle, an area that's been characterized as "trees, tees, and Ph.D.s," politics and basketball are always hot topics. The NCAA basketball championship has traded hands among the area's three schools.

Raleigh

143 mi northeast of Charlotte, 104 mi east of Winston-Salem.

Raleigh is Old South and New South, down-home and upscale, all in one. Named for Sir Walter Raleigh (who established the first English colony on the coast in 1585), it's the state capital and the biggest of the three cities. Many of the state's largest and best museums are here, as are North Carolina State University and six other universities and colleges.

Artspace **24**
Capital Area Visitor Center **14**
City Market . . **23**
Executive Mansion **16**
Exploris **22**
Fayetteville Street Mall . . . **21**
North Carolina Museum of History. **19**
North Carolina Museum of Natural Sciences **18**
Oakwood Historic District. **15**
State Capitol **20**
State Legislative Building **17**

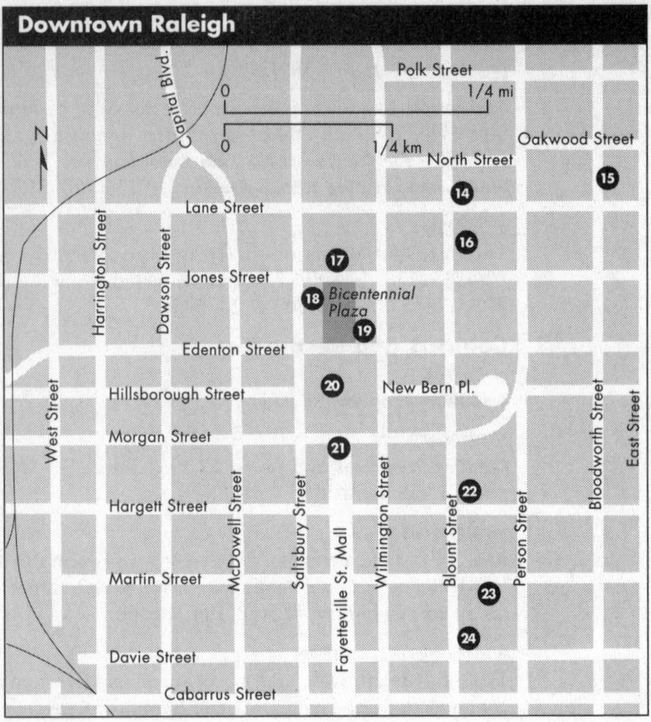

Numbers in the text correspond to numbers in the margin and on the Downtown Raleigh map.

A Good Walk

Downtown, the streets are laid out in an orderly grid with the State Capitol as the hub. Most downtown Raleigh attractions are state government buildings, historic buildings, and museums and are free to the public. Begin at the **Capital Area Visitor Center** ⑭, where you can pick up maps and brochures, including a self-guided walking tour of the **Oakwood Historic District** ⑮. To get to Oakwood, travel east from the visitor center on Lane Street. After finishing your walk through Oakwood, stroll by the **Executive Mansion** ⑯, home to governors since 1891. It's on Blount Street between Lane and Jones streets.

Follow Jones Street west past Wilmington Street to visit the **State Legislative Building** ⑰. Cross Jones to the Bicentennial Plaza, flanked by the **North Carolina Museum of Natural Sciences** ⑱ to the west and the **North Carolina Museum of History** ⑲ to the east. Continue south across Edenton Street to Capitol Square and the **State Capitol** ⑳.

Starting just south of the capitol across Morgan Street and continuing for four blocks is the **Fayetteville Street Mall** ㉑, a pedestrian-only walkway. From the mall, walk two blocks east on Hargett Street to **Exploris** ㉒, a children's museum. One block south is the **City Market** ㉓, a revitalized area between Blount and Person streets. Just south of the market are the studios and galleries of **Artspace** ㉔, at the corner of Blount and Davie streets.

TIMING

You'll need several hours just to hit the sights of this walk and even more time if you tend to get hooked on museums.

Sights to See

24 **Artspace.** Adjacent to the Moore Square art district, Artspace is a refurbished auto dealership where the public can watch 40 artists working in open studios and talk with them about their work. It has exhibition galleries and arts education programs. Most of the art is for sale. ✉ *201 E. Davie St.,* ☎ *919/821–2787.* *Free.* ⏲ *Tues.–Sat. 10–6.*

14 **Capital Area Visitor Center.** Here, you can pick up maps and brochures and schedule tours of limited-access facilities such as the Executive Mansion (☞ *below*). ✉ *301 N. Blount St.,* ☎ *919/733–3456.* ⏲ *Weekdays 8–5, Sat. 9–5, Sun. 1–5.*

23 **City Market.** This revitalized area with cobblestone streets is home to specialty shops, art galleries, restaurants, a comedy club, and a small farmers' market. The free Entertainment Trolley shuttles between the market and other downtown restaurant and nightlife locations from 6:40 PM to 1:40 AM Thursday through Saturday. ✉ *Martin St. and Moore Sq.,* ☎ *919/828–4555.* ⏲ *Stores Mon.–Sat. 10–5:30, restaurants Mon.–Sat. 7 AM–1 AM and Sun. 11:30–10.*

16 **Executive Mansion.** The mansion is a brick early 20th-century Queen Anne cottage–style structure with gingerbread trim and manicured lawns. Tour hours vary; check with the **Capital Area Visitor Center** (☞ *above*). ✉ *200 N. Blount St.,* ☎ *919/733–3456.* *Free.*

22 **Exploris.** This 84,000-square-ft architectural showplace is a learning center that stands apart from most other children's museums. It emphasizes a global perspective, as opposed to specific health and natural science topics. Exhibits explore language, culture, geography, global trade, and communications. ✉ *201 E. Hargett St.,* ☎ *919/834–4040.* *$7.* ⏲ *Tues.–Sat. 9–5, Sun. noon–5.*

21 **Fayetteville Street Mall.** Extending from the State Capitol to the Raleigh Civic and Convention Center, this pedestrian walkway provides entrance to a number of high-rise office buildings. The shops and restaurants in the area cater to the weekday business crowd.

19 **North Carolina Museum of History.** Founded in 1898, the museum is now in a state-of-the-art facility on Bicentennial Plaza. It uses artifacts, audiovisual programs, and interactive exhibits to bring the state's history to life. Exhibits include the *N.C. Sports Hall of Fame*; *N.C. Folklife*; and *Militaria, Politics, and Society.* ✉ *5 E. Edenton St.,* ☎ *919/715–0200.* *Free.* ⏲ *Tues.–Sat. 9–5, Sun. noon–5.*

★ 18 **North Carolina Museum of Natural Sciences.** At 200,000 square ft, the new museum is the largest of its kind in the Southeast. It has permanent exhibits and dioramas that celebrate the incredible diversity of species in the state. There are enough animals and insects—including butterflies, hummingbirds, snakes, and a two-toed sloth—to qualify for a small zoo. One signature exhibit contains rare whale skeletons. The pièce de résistance, however, is the *Terror of the South* exhibit, featuring the dinosaur skeleton of "Acro," a giant carnivore that lived in the South 110 million years ago. ✉ *11 W. Jones St.,* ☎ *919/733–7450 or 877/462–8724.* *Free.* ⏲ *Mon.–Sat. 9–5, Sun. 1–5.*

15 **Oakwood Historic District.** Many fine examples of Victorian architecture can be seen in this tree-shaded neighborhood. Self-guided walking tours of the area, which encompasses 20 blocks bordered by Person, Edenton, Franklin, and Watauga/Linden streets, are available at the **Capital Area Visitor Center** (☞ *above*). Adjacent to historic Oakwood is **Oakwood Cemetery** (✉ 701 Oakwood Ave., ☎ 919/832–6077). Established in 1869, it is the resting place of 2,800 Confederate soldiers,

Civil War generals, governors, and numerous U.S. senators. Free maps are available at the cemetery office.

20 **State Capitol.** A beautifully preserved example of Greek Revival architecture from 1840, the capitol once housed all the functions of state government. Today it's part museum, part executive offices. The capitol contains, under the domed rotunda, a copy of Antonio Canova's statue of George Washington depicted as a Roman general with tunic, tight-fitting body armor, and a short cape. ✉ *Capitol Sq. (1 E. Edenton St.),* ☎ *919/733–4994.* ⏲ *Mon.–Sat. 9–5, Sun. 1–5.*

17 **State Legislative Building.** One block north of the State Capitol, this complex hums with lawmakers and lobbyists when the legislature is in session. It's fun to watch from the gallery. A free guided tour is also available through the **Capital Area Visitor Center** (☞ *above*). ✉ *Salisbury and Jones Sts.,* ☎ *919/733–7928.* ⏲ *Weekdays 8–5, Sat. 9–5, Sun. 1–5.*

Other Area Attractions

The city is spread out, so a car is almost a necessity for museums and parks beyond downtown.

OFF THE BEATEN PATH

AVA GARDNER MUSEUM – This museum in the hometown of the legendary beauty and movie star has memorabilia that trace her life from childhood on the farm to Hollywood glory days. It's about 30 mi east of Raleigh in downtown Smithfield. ✉ *205 S. 3rd St., Smithfield,* ☎ *919/934–5830 or 919/934–0887.* 🎫 *$3.* ⏲ *Daily 1–5.*

Joel Lane House. The oldest dwelling in Raleigh was the home of the "father of Raleigh" and dates from the 1760s. Joel Lane sold the state the property on which the capital city grew. Costumed docents tell the story and show the restored house and beautiful period gardens. ✉ *720 W. Hargett St., at St. Mary's St.,* ☎ *919/833–3431.* 🎫 *$3.* ⏲ *Mar.–mid-Dec., Tues.–Fri. 10–2, 1st and 3rd Sat. of the month 1–4.*

Mordecai Historic Park. You can see the Mordecai family's plantation home and other structures, including the house where President Andrew Johnson was born in 1808. One-hour guided tours are given on the half hour. You can also board a trolley for a narrated 45-minute tour of historic Raleigh ($5). ✉ *1 Mimosa St., at Wake Forest Rd.,* ☎ *919/834–4844.* 🎫 *$4.* ⏲ *Mon. and Wed.–Sat. 10–3, Sun. 1–3.*

★ **North Carolina Museum of Art.** On the west side of Raleigh, the NCMA houses 5,000 years of artistic heritage, including one of the nation's largest collections of Jewish ceremonial art. Other exhibits range from ancient Egyptian times to the present, from the Old World to the New. The museum hosts touring exhibitions of works by such artists as Caravaggio and Rodin. The glass-wall **Museum Café** looks out on an outdoor performance center–cum–sculpture that when viewed from above spells the words PICTURE THIS. ✉ *2110 Blue Ridge Rd.,* ☎ *919/839–6262, 919/833–3548 restaurant.* 🎫 *Free.* ⏲ *Tues.–Thurs. and Sat. 9–5, Fri. 9–9, Sun. 11–6; Tues.–Sun. tours 1:30.*

Pullen Park. In summer crowds come to picnic and ride the 1911 Dentzel carousel, the train, and pedal boats. You can swim here in a large public aquatic center, explore an arts-and-crafts center, or, if the timing is right, see a play at the Theater in the Park. ✉ *520 Ashe Ave., near North Carolina State University,* ☎ *919/831–6468 or 919/831–6640.* 🎫 *Fees vary.* ⏲ *Park daily dawn–dusk; rides Memorial Day–Labor Day, Mon.–Thurs. 10:30–6:30, Fri.–Sat. 10:30–8, Sun. 1–8.*

Dining and Lodging

$$$$ ★ ✕ **Second Empire.** Wood paneling, crown molding and high ceilings, floral arrangements, muted lighting, and well-spaced tables make for a calming and elegant dining experience. The regularly changing menu has a regional flavor; the food is best described as art on a plate, intricately styled so that colors, textures, and tastes fuse. For an entrée you might get roasted mahimahi, paired with collard greens, butternut squash, and garlic cream. A wood-and-brass tavern in the lower level has a simpler and less expensive menu. ✉ *300 Hillsborough St.,* ☎ *919/829–3663. AE, MC, V. Closed Sun.*

$$$–$$$$ ✕ **Angus Barn.** A huge rustic barn houses a Raleigh tradition that has won virtually every major dining award. The astonishing wine and beer list is 35 pages. The restaurant is known for its steaks, baby-back ribs, prime rib, and fresh seafood and for its clubby Wild Turkey lounge. Desserts are heavenly. Reservations aren't accepted for Saturday dinner. ✉ *U.S. 70W (Glenwood Ave.) near Aviation Pkwy.,* ☎ *919/781–2444. AE, D, DC, MC, V.*

$$$–$$$$ ✕ **Margaux's.** Eclectic is the key word for the cuisine at this north Raleigh fixture, where a massive stone fireplace warms the intimate setting. A blackboard lists the diverse specials, such as red chili fettuccine with goat cheese, lamb with coconut curry sauce, or grilled shrimp and crawfish tostada with roasted corn, black beans, and salsa *verde.* ✉ *8111 Creedmoor Rd.,* ☎ *919/846–9846. AE, DC, MC, V.*

$$–$$$ ✕ **Tony's Bourbon Street Oyster Bar.** The atmosphere—already festive with red walls, feather masks, and street lamps from New Orleans—jumps up a notch with live music Thursday, Friday, and Saturday evenings. Cajun and Creole dishes such as gumbo, jambalaya, and crawfish étouffée are served in the large, open dining room, or the oyster bar. Cary, near the entrance to Research Triangle Park, is 25 minutes from downtown Raleigh. ✉ *107 Edinburgh Dr., MacGregor Village Shopping Center, Cary,* ☎ *919/462–6226. AE, MC, V.*

$–$$$ ✕ **Greenshields Brewery & Pub.** You can sip beer and ale brewed on the premises with your soup, salad, sandwich, or such entrées as fish-and-chips, shepherd's pie, and steak in this English-style pub. Oak paneling and working fireplaces enhance the mood. ✉ *214 E. Martin St., City Market,* ☎ *919/829–0214. AE, D, MC, V.*

$ ✕ **Big Ed's City Market Restaurant.** A must for breakfast or lunch, Big Ed's is filled with antique farm implements and the owner's political memorabilia, including pictures of presidential candidates who have stopped at this landmark. Every Saturday morning a Dixieland band plays in front of the restaurant. Come here for down-home cookin' and don't miss the biscuits. ✉ *220 Wolfe St., City Market,* ☎ *919/836–9909. Reservations not accepted. No credit cards. Closed Sun. No dinner.*

$$$ 🏨 **Courtyard by Marriott–Airport.** Convenient to the airport and Research Triangle Park, this chain property offers many amenities without hefty rates. Rooms are predictably modern. The dining room is for guests only. ✉ *2001 Hospitality Ct., Morrisville, 27560,* ☎ *919/467–9444 or 800/321–2211,* FAX *919/467–9332. 140 rooms, 12 suites. Dining room, in-room data ports, pool, hot tub, exercise room, airport shuttle. AE, D, DC, MC, V. CP.*

$$$ 🏨 **North Raleigh Hilton.** This is a favorite spot for corporate meetings. The standard rooms are done in mauve and green. You can dine in Lofton's restaurant and listen to the piano afterward in the lobby bar. Bowties (☞ Nightlife and the Arts, *below*) is a popular nightspot for dancing. ✉ *3415 Wake Forest Rd., 27609,* ☎ *919/872–2323 or 800/445–8667,* FAX *919/876–0890. 331 rooms, 7 suites. Restaurant, 2 bars, in-room data ports, indoor pool, exercise room, nightclub, business services, meeting rooms, airport shuttle. AE, D, DC, MC, V.*

$$$ **Quality Suites Hotel.** Minutes from downtown, Quality Suites has luxurious two-room suites equipped with cassette stereos, microwaves, and wet bars. The manager's evening reception and the cooked-to-order breakfast are included in the rate. ✉ *4400 Capital Blvd., 27604,* ☎ *919/876–2211 or 800/543–5497,* FAX *919/790–1352. 114 suites. Breakfast room, in-room data ports, in-room VCRs, minibars, refrigerators, pool, exercise room, business services, meeting rooms. AE, D, DC, MC, V. BP.*

$$–$$$ **Raleigh Marriott Crabtree Valley.** In one of the city's most luxurious hotels, fresh floral arrangements adorn the elegantly decorated public rooms. Standard rooms have soft colors such as cream, Asian floral prints, and dark cherry-wood furnishings. Guests can dine at J. W.'s Steakhouse and at Quinn's, a lounge where light fare and drinks are served daily. ✉ *4500 Marriott Dr. (U.S. 70W near Crabtree Valley Mall), 27612,* ☎ *919/781–7000 or 800/228–9290,* FAX *919/781–3059. 375 rooms, 4 suites. Restaurant, bar, in-room data ports, indoor-outdoor pool, hot tub, exercise room, business services, meeting rooms, airport shuttle. AE, D, DC, MC, V.*

$$–$$$ **William Thomas House.** A stately but not stuffy Victorian home is a B&B on the edge of downtown Raleigh a few blocks from the governor's mansion. Rooms, named for family members, are traditionally and elegantly decorated and have oversize windows and 12-ft ceilings. The richly hued common rooms are filled with heirlooms such as a grand piano from 1863 and antique china. ✉ *530 N. Blount St., 27604,* ☎ *919/755–9400 or 800/653–3466,* FAX *919/755–3966. 4 rooms. Fans, in-room data ports, refrigerators. AE, D, DC, MC, V. BP.*

$ **Hampton Inn & Suites.** In the southwest corner of Cary, right over the Raleigh line, this recently built hotel is just minutes from Raleigh's Entertainment & Sports Arena, the State Fairgrounds, and North Carolina State University. Rooms are typical of the chain; you'll need a car to get to restaurants. ✉ *111 Hampton Woods La., Cary 27607,* ☎ *919/233–1798 or 800/426–7866,* FAX *919/854–1166. 126 rooms. In-room data ports, no-smoking floor, refrigerators, pool, exercise room, baby-sitting, laundry service, business services, meeting rooms. AE, D, DC, MC, V.*

$ **Ramada Inn Crabtree.** Rooms are comfortable in familiar chain style at what may be the friendliest motel in town. It's also where football and basketball teams like to stay when they're here for a game, as evidenced by the sports memorabilia in the Brass Bell Lounge. ✉ *3920 Arrow Dr. (U.S. 70 and Beltline/I–440), 27612,* ☎ *919/782–7525 or 800/441–4712,* FAX *919/781–0435. 157 rooms, 17 suites. Restaurant, bar, in-room data ports, pool, exercise room, business services, meeting rooms, airport shuttle. AE, D, DC, MC, V.*

Nightlife and the Arts

THE ARTS

The **North Carolina Theatre** (✉ 1 E. South St., ☎ 919/831–6060), a professional nonprofit theater, produces five Broadway musicals a year. The **North Carolina Symphony** (✉ 2 E. South St., ☎ 919/733–2750) gives more than 200 concerts throughout the state annually, but its home venue is the elegant Memorial Auditorium. The **Carolina Ballet** (✉ 2914 Kildaire Farm Rd., Cary, ☎ 919/831–6060) performs from mid-October to mid-June in Memorial Auditorium and other venues. The **North Carolina State University Arts Programs** (☎ 919/515–1100) include the Center Stage series, host to professional touring productions and world-class artists. All arts program performances are open to the public.

Alltel Pavilion at Walnut Creek (✉ 3801 Rock Quarry Rd., ☎ 919/831–6666), known as "The Creek," accommodates 20,000. Headliners appear from spring through mid-fall and cover the musical spectrum. This is the most attended amphitheater on the East Coast.

NIGHTLIFE

The **Berkeley Café** (✉ 217 W. Martin St., ☎ 919/821–0777) is one of the hottest gathering places in the Triangle for live music: rock and roll, R&B, and blues. **Bowties** (✉ North Raleigh Hilton, 3415 Wake Forest Rd., ☎ 919/878–4917) is a popular after-hours spot for dancing. **Charlie Goodnight's Comedy Club** (✉ 861 W. Morgan St., ☎ 919/828–5233) combines dinner with a night of laughs. Alumni include Jay Leno, Jerry Seinfeld, and Brett Butler. **Tir na nog** (✉ 218 S. Blount St., ☎ 919/833–7795) has Irish entertainers, Murphy's Irish Amber, Guinness, and even whiskey on tap. You can munch on simple Irish pub grub or contemporary fare. The owners and a good portion of the staff are Irish, so authenticity is what distinguishes this bar, whose name means "land of eternal youth." In the warehouse district is the **Warehouse Restaurant and Entertainment Center** (✉ 427 S. Dawson St., ☎ 919/836–9966), with a huge dance floor and game room.

Outdoor Activities and Sports

BASEBALL

The **Carolina Mudcats** (☎ 919/269–2287), the AA affiliate of the Colorado Rockies, play April through August at Five County Stadium in Zebulon, about 20 mi east of Raleigh.

BASKETBALL

Raleigh's Atlantic Coast Conference entry is the North Carolina State University **Wolfpack** (☎ 919/515–2106 or 800/310–7225).

BIKING

Raleigh has 40 mi of greenways for biking or walking, and maps are available through the **Raleigh Division of Transportation** (☎ 919/890–3430).

CAMPING

Try the North Carolina State Fairgrounds, William B. Umstead State Park, Clemmons State Forest near Clayton, or Jordan Lake between Apex and Pittsboro. For details, call the Greater Raleigh Convention and Visitors Bureau (☞ Visitor Information *in* The Triangle A to Z, *below*) or the North Carolina Division of Tourism, Film and Sports Development (☞ Visitor Information *in* North Carolina A to Z, *below*).

FISHING

Jordan Lake, a 13,900-acre reservoir in Apex, is a favorite fishing spot. Others are Lake Wheeler in Raleigh and the Falls Lake State Recreation Area in Wake Forest.

FITNESS

The **Central YMCA** (✉ 1601 Hillsborough St., ☎ 919/832–6601) will permit visitors to use its facilities for a few dollars provided they have a YMCA membership elsewhere. The **Cary Family YMCA** (✉ 101 YMCA Dr., at Cary Pkwy., Cary, ☎ 919/469–9622) doesn't charge if you are already a member of a Y elsewhere. It has an indoor lap track, two pools, high-tech exercise machines, and a weight room.

GOLF

There are 20 golf courses, either public or semiprivate, within a half-hour drive of downtown Raleigh. **Cheviot Hills Golf Course** (✉ 7301 Capitol Blvd., ☎ 919/876–9920) is a par-71 championship course. **Devil's Ridge Golf Club** (✉ Holly Springs Rd., Cary, ☎ 919/557–6100), about 15 mi from Raleigh, is a challenging par-72 course with large, rolling greens. **Lochmere Golf Club** (✉ Kildaire Farm Rd., Cary, ☎ 919/851–0611) provides a friendly atmosphere, good value, and a challenge at par-71. A 30-minute drive from Raleigh is the **Neuse Golf Club** (✉ NC 42 E, Clayton, ☎ 919/550–0550), an attractive par-72 course on the banks of the Neuse River.

HOCKEY

The NHL's **Carolina Hurricanes** play in the 21,000-seat Raleigh Entertainment & Sports Arena (☎ 919/467–7825 or 888/645–8491).

JOGGING

Runners frequent Shelley Lake, the track at North Carolina State University, and the **Capital Area Greenway** system (☎ 919/831–6833 for a map).

SOCCER

The **Raleigh Capital Express** competes in the A League's Atlantic Conference April through September. Home games are played in the WRAL Soccer Center (✉ 7700 Perry Creek Rd., ☎ 919/786–1313).

TENNIS

More than 80 courts in Raleigh city parks are available for use; call 919/872–4128 for details.

Shopping

SHOPPING MALLS AND OUTLET CENTERS

Cameron Village Shopping Center (✉ 1900 Cameron St.), Raleigh's first shopping center, contains specialty shops and boutiques and restaurants. **Crabtree Valley Mall** (✉ Glenwood Ave., U.S. 70) is one of the South's largest enclosed malls and has more than 240 specialty stores, including Pottery Barn, Abercrombie & Fitch, and Williams-Sonoma. Department stores include Lord & Taylor, Hudson-Belk, Hecht's, and Sears. **Prime Outlets** (✉ Exit 284 off I–40, Airport Blvd., Morrisville, between Raleigh and Durham, ☎ 919/380–8700) is decidedly un-mall-like with its wooden floors and greenery. The area's only factory outlet center has more than 40 stores, including Off Fifth (Saks Fifth Avenue) and Geoffrey Beene.

ART AND ANTIQUES

City Market (☞ Sights to See, *above*) is a revitalized shopping area with an array of shops and art galleries. At **Artspace** (☞ Sights to See, *above*), you can visit artists' studios and purchase their works. The merchandise changes daily at **Carolina Antique Mall** in Cameron Village (☞ *above*), where 75 dealers stock the floor.

FOOD

Open year-round, the 60-acre **State Farmers' Market** (✉ Lake Wheeler Rd. and I–40, ☎ 919/733–7417 market; 919/833–7973 restaurants) includes a garden center, seafood restaurant, and a down-home restaurant. **Wellspring Grocery** (✉ 3540 Wade Ave., ☎ 919/828–5805) has outstanding produce, fresh-baked breads, health foods, and specialty items, as well as a place to sit and eat your purchases.

Durham

23 mi northwest of Raleigh on I–40 and NC 147 (Durham Freeway).

Durham has three of North Carolina's 22 National Historic Landmarks and long ago shed its tobacco-town image. It is now known as the City of Medicine for the medical and research centers at Duke University, one of the top schools in the nation. With more than 20,000 employees, Duke is not only the largest employer in Durham but also one of the largest in the state. Warehouses and mills around the city have been converted to chic shops, offices, and condos.

Duke Chapel 27
Duke Homestead . . 30
Hayti Heritage Center 26
North Carolina Central University Art Museum 25
North Carolina Museum of Life and Science 29
Sarah P. Duke Gardens 28
West Point on the Eno . . . 31

Durham

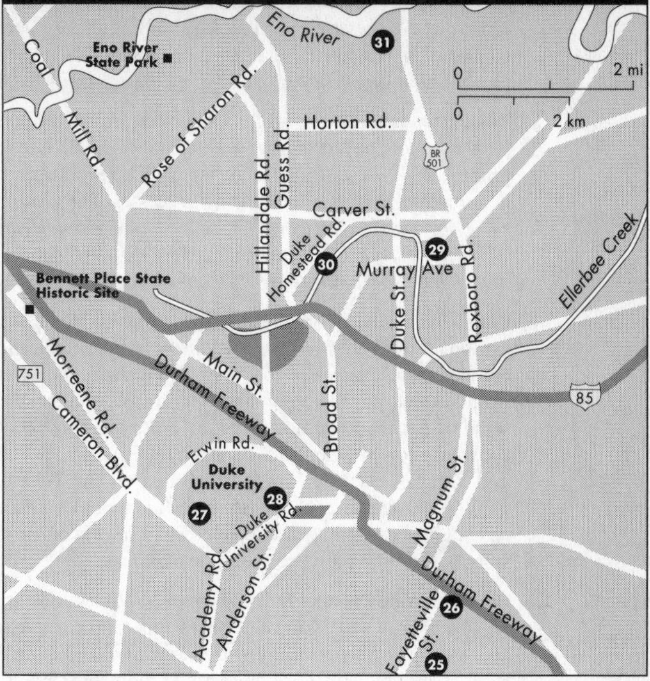

Numbers in the text correspond to numbers in the margin and on the Durham map.

A Good Drive

Durham has some areas appropriate for a good walk, such as Duke University's campus. However, to save time and ensure that you get the real flavor of this relatively compact, single-city county, it's best to drive. Start your tour 1½ mi south of downtown, exiting the Durham Freeway (NC 147) at Fayetteville Street, along which you will find the **North Carolina Central University Art Museum** ㉕ and the **Hayti Heritage Center** ㉖.

The next stop is about 3 mi away. Return to the Durham Freeway and continue northwest to the exit at Chapel Hill Street. Follow Chapel Hill west into the West Campus of **Duke University,** which includes the **Duke Chapel** ㉗ and the **Sarah P. Duke Gardens** ㉘. Return to Chapel Hill Street and take it past the Durham Freeway to Duke Street and turn left toward the northern sections of the city, about 3½ mi. Continue past I–85 and make a right at Murray Avenue, which will quickly bring you to the **North Carolina Museum of Life and Science** ㉙. Return to Duke Street, heading north a short distance, and turn left onto Carver Street, which leads to Duke Homestead Road, along which lies **Duke Homestead** ㉚. Retrace your path back to Duke Street, following it north until it merges with U.S. 501. Take U.S. 501 about 3½ mi to the conclusion of your tour at **West Point on the Eno** ㉛.

TIMING

You should allow 1 to 1½ days to explore these Durham highlights; select a number of sights that interest you if you have only a day.

Sights to See

★ 27 **Duke Chapel.** A Gothic-style gem built in the early 1930s, the chapel is the centerpiece of the campus. Modeled after Canterbury Cathedral, it has 77 stained-glass windows and a 210-ft bell tower. ✉ *Chapel Dr., West Campus of Duke University,* ☎ *919/681–1704.* ⏲ *Daily 8 AM–9 PM.*

30 **Duke Homestead.** The Duke family empire began here in the 1860s with tobacco, and it is now a National Historic Landmark. You can tour the small wood-frame factories, pack house, and curing barn; guides demonstrate early manufacturing processes. The visitor center exhibits early tobacco advertising. ✉ *2828 Duke Homestead Rd.,* ☎ *919/477–5498.* *Free.* ⏲ *Apr.–Oct., Mon.–Sat. 9–5, Sun. 1–5; Nov.–Mar., Tues.–Sat. 10–4, Sun. 1–4.*

Duke University. A stroll along the beautiful tree-lined streets of this campus is a lovely way to spend a few hours. In all, the university encompasses 525 acres in the heart of Durham. The East Campus, off Broad Street, has Georgian architecture and the **Duke University Museum of Art** (✉ Buchanan Blvd. at Trinity Ave., ☎ 919/684–5135), a showcase for pre-Columbian, African, Russian, European medieval, and Renaissance art. A mile or so away is the West Campus, dominated by **Duke Chapel** (☞ *above*) on Chapel Drive and late-Gothic-style buildings. The sprawling medical school is on Erwin Road. A bus system and bike paths connect the campuses.

26 **Hayti Heritage Center.** One of Durham's oldest ecclesiastical structures, St. Joseph's A.M.E. Church houses this center for African-American art. In addition to exhibitions of traditional and contemporary art by local, regional, and national artists, the center hosts special events such as the Black Diaspora Film Festival. ✉ *804 Old Fayetteville St.,* ☎ *919/683–1709 or 800/845–9835.* *Free; fees for special events vary.* ⏲ *Weekdays 9–5, Sat. 10–2:30.*

25 **North Carolina Central University Art Museum.** African-American art is showcased at the nation's first liberal arts college for African-Americans. Besides the permanent collection you can see works by students and local artists. ✉ *1801 Fayetteville St.,* ☎ *919/560–6211.* *Free.* ⏲ *Tues.–Fri. 9–5, Sun. 2–5.*

29 **North Carolina Museum of Life and Science.** Here you can create a tornado, encounter dinosaurs on the prehistoric trail, view NASA artifacts, and ride a train through a wildlife sanctuary. The nature center has such native North Carolina animals as flying squirrels. The three-story **Magic Wings Butterfly House** has a tropical butterfly conservatory and includes the Insectarium, where you can see and hear live insects under high magnification and amplification. ✉ *433 Murray Ave., off I–85,* ☎ *919/220–5429.* *Museum $8, train ride $1.50.* ⏲ *Mon.–Sat. 10–5, Sun. noon–5.*

★ 28 **Sarah P. Duke Gardens.** These 55 acres, complete with a wisteria-draped gazebo and a Japanese garden with a lily pond teeming with fat goldfish, have more than 5 mi of pathways through formal plantings and woodlands. ✉ *Main entrance on Anderson St., West Campus of Duke University,* ☎ *919/684–3698.* *Free.* ⏲ *Daily 8–dusk.*

31 **West Point on the Eno.** Included in a city park on the banks of the Eno River are a 19th-century blacksmith shop, an 1880s home, and a restored mill dating from 1778. It's the site of an annual three-day folklife festival surrounding the Fourth of July; musicians, artists, and craftspeople come from around the region. ✉ *5101 N. Roxboro Rd. (U.S. 501N),* ☎ *919/471–1623.* *Free.* ⏲ *Daily 8–sunset, historic buildings weekends only 1–5.*

Other Area Attractions

Bennett Place State Historic Site. In this farmhouse in April 1865, Confederate general Joseph E. Johnston surrendered to U.S. general William T. Sherman, 17 days after Lee's surrender to Grant at Appomattox. The two generals then set forth the terms for a "permanent peace" between the South and the North. Historical reenactments are held annually. ✉ *4409 Bennett Memorial Rd., 10 mi from downtown,* ☎ *919/383–4345.* *Free.* *Apr.–Oct., Mon.–Sat. 9–5, Sun. 1–5; Nov.–Mar., Tues.–Sat. 9–5, Sun. 1–5.*

Eno River State Park. The park's 2,733 acres include hiking trails, a picnic area, rough camping, and Class II rapids (after a heavy rain). ✉ *6101 Cole Mill Rd.,* ☎ *919/383–1686.* *Free.* *Daily 8–sunset.*

Dining and Lodging

$$$–$$$$ ★ ✕ **Magnolia Grill.** This bistro is consistently one of the area's finest, most innovative places to dine. The food is as eye-catching as the art on the walls. On the daily menu you may find grilled jumbo sea scallops on spicy black beans with blood-orange-and-onion marmalade or grilled hickory-smoked pork tenderloin in a sun-dried cherry sauce. ✉ *1002 9th St.,* ☎ *919/286–3609. MC, V. Closed Sun. No lunch.*

$$–$$$$ ✕ **Café Parizäde.** This Erwin Square Mediterranean restaurant gets high marks for its food and service. Soft lighting, white tablecloths, and ceiling murals give the place an elegant feel. One appetizer is fried calamari with jalapeño-tomato salsa; some entrées are fettuccine with fresh salmon and black-pepper dill cream, sesame pasta with scallops, and roast duck with fresh vegetables. ✉ *2200 W. Main St.,* ☎ *919/286–9712. AE, D, DC, MC, V. No lunch weekends.*

$$–$$$ ✕ **Pop's.** The roof is rough tin and the sculptures rusty industrial, while the lattice walls are covered in silk flowers and vines. Like the decor, the menu is eclectic, with Italian and contemporary cuisine. You can get a grilled pork chop with polenta or *fritto misto* calamari (batter-fried squid). Arrive early; it fills up quickly. ✉ *810 W. Peabody St.,* ☎ *919/956–7677. MC, V. Closed Mon.*

$$$–$$$$ ★ ✕ **Washington Duke Inn & Golf Club.** On the campus of Duke University, this luxurious hotel overlooks a Robert Trent Jones golf course. Rooms evoke the feeling of an English country inn, with floral bedspreads and creamy striped wall coverings. On display in the public rooms are memorabilia belonging to the Duke family, for whom the hotel and university are named. At the truly elegant Fairview restaurant, you can start with Moroccan spiced lamb sausage or chestnut soup with rosemary cream and then move on to entrées such as breast of Muscovy duck with mashed white beans, roasted garlic, and sweet-and-sour cranberry sauce. ✉ *3001 Cameron Blvd., 27706,* ☎ *919/490–0999 or 800/443–3853,* FAX *919/688–0105. 164 rooms, 7 suites. Restaurant, bar, in-room data ports, pool, driving range, 18-hole golf course, putting green, 12 tennis courts, exercise room, jogging, business services, meeting rooms, airport shuttle. AE, D, DC, MC, V.*

$$–$$$$ **Arrowhead Inn.** Brick chimneys and tall Doric columns distinguish this bed-and-breakfast inn in an 18th-century white-clapboard farmhouse. It's a few miles outside Durham and has a homelike setting, with antiques, old plantings, fireplaces, and a log cabin in the garden. ✉ *106 Mason Rd., 27712,* ☎ *919/477–8430 or 800/528–2207,* FAX *919/471–9538. 9 rooms, 2 suites. Picnic area, business services. AE, D, DC, MC, V. BP.*

$$–$$$$ **Blooming Garden Inn.** Truly a bright spot in the Holloway Historic District, this B&B is painted yellow outside. Inside, the inn explodes with color and warmth, thanks to exuberant hosts Dolly and Frank Pokrass. Breakfast might be walnut crepes with ricotta cheese and warm raspberry sauce. A sister B&B, the Victorian Holly House across the street, accommodates people on extended stays. ✉ *513 Holloway St., 27701,* ☎ *919/687–0801 or 888/687–0801,* FAX *919/688–1401. 4 rooms, 2 suites. AE, D, DC, MC, V. BP.*

Nightlife and the Arts

The 1926 Beaux Arts **Carolina Theatre** (✉ 309 W. Morgan St., ☎ 919/560–3040) hosts film festivals, orchestras, and operas, as well as the International Jazz Festival (March) and the American Dance Festival (June).

Outdoor Activities and Sports

BASEBALL

The **Durham Bulls,** a tradition since 1902, were immortalized in the hit movie *Bull Durham.* The AAA team, an affiliate of the Tampa Bay Devil Rays, plays at their stadium near downtown (✉ 409 Blackwell St., ☎ 919/687–6500).

BASKETBALL

Durham's Atlantic Coast Conference team is Duke's **Blue Devils** (☎ 919/681–2583 or 800/672–2583).

CAMPING

Try the **Eno River State Park** (✉ 6101 Cole Mill Rd., ☎ 919/383–1686). For information, call the North Carolina Division of Tourism, Film and Sports Development (☞ Visitor Information *in* North Carolina A to Z, *below*).

GOLF

Durham has four 18-hole public golf courses. **Duke University** (✉ Cameron Blvd. and Science Dr., ☎ 919/681–2288) has a Robert Trent Jones course, with a par 72. **Hillandale Golf Course** (✉ Hillandale Rd., ☎ 919/286–4211) has a par-71 George Cobb course.

TENNIS

The city's **Parks and Recreation Department** (☎ 919/560–4355) has information on the city's 72 public tennis courts.

Shopping

SHOPPING DISTRICTS AND MALLS

Durham's **9th Street** has funky shops and restaurants. **Brightleaf Square** (✉ 905 W. Main St., ☎ 919/682–9229) is an upscale shopping-entertainment complex housed in old tobacco warehouses in the heart of downtown. **Northgate Mall** (✉ 1058 W. Club Blvd., ☎ 919/286–4400) draws shoppers from all parts of the Triangle. Kids enjoy riding the old-fashioned carousel while adults can choose from among three department stores and nearly 200 specialty stores.

CRAFTS

One World Market (✉ 1918 Perry St., ☎ 919/286–2457) carries unique, affordable gifts. One goal of the store is to provide increased self-employment for low-income crafters from around the world.

FOOD

Fowler's Gourmet (✉ 112 S. Duke St., ☎ 919/683–2555) stocks everything from exotic spices to wines, fresh seafood, and European chocolates. Customized gift baskets are shipped all over the country. **Wellspring Grocery** (✉ 621 Broad St., ☎ 919/286–2290) has outstanding fresh produce, soups, salads, and sandwiches prepared daily.

Chapel Hill

12 mi southwest of Durham on U.S. 15–501, 28 mi northwest of Raleigh.

Chapel Hill may be the smallest city in the Triangle, but its reputation as a seat of learning—and of liberalism—looms large. The home of the nation's first state university, the 208-year-old University of North Carolina (UNC), Chapel Hill retains the feel of a quiet, tree-shaded village while crowded with students and retirees.

Morehead Planetarium, where the original *Apollo* astronauts and many since have trained, is one of the largest in the country. You can learn about the constellations and take in laser-light shows. ✉ *250 E. Franklin St.,* ☎ *919/962–1236, 919/549–6863 show information.* 🎫 *$4.* 🕓 *Mon. 12:30–5, Tues.–Fri. and Sun. 12:30–5 and 7–9:45, Sat. 10–5 and 7–9:45; call ahead for show times.*

★ **Franklin Street,** in the heart of downtown Chapel Hill, is lined with bicycle shops, bookstores, clothing stores, restaurants and coffee shops, and a movie theater.

Franklin Street runs along the northern edge of the **University of North Carolina** campus, which is filled with oak-shaded courtyards and stately old buildings. The **Louis Round Wilson Library** (✉ South St., ☎ 919/962–0114) is home to the largest single collection of state literature in the nation. Its North Carolina Collection Gallery (919/962–1172) has exhibits of rare books, photos, and oil portraits. Several historic rooms highlight topics in the state's history, such as the Walter Raleigh Room. The university's **Ackland Art Museum** (✉ Columbia and Franklin Sts., ☎ 919/406–9837) showcases some of the Southeast's strongest collections of art from India and of Western art, as well as old-master paintings and sculptures. Of special interest is North Carolina folk art.

The **ArtsCenter** (✉ 300G E. Main St., Carrboro, ☎ 919/929–2787) has exhibits, offers classes of all kinds for children, and hosts dance, theater, and music events.

The **North Carolina Botanical Garden,** south of downtown via U.S. 15–501 Bypass, has the largest collection of native plants in the Southeast. Nature trails wind through a 300-acre Piedmont forest; the herb garden and carnivorous plant collection are impressive. ✉ *Old Mason Farm Rd.,* ☎ *919/962–0522.* 🎫 *Free.* 🕓 *Apr.–Oct., weekdays 8–5, Sat. 10–5, Sun. 1–5; Nov.–Mar., weekdays 8–5, Sat. 9–6, Sun. 1–6.*

Dining and Lodging

$$$ ✕ **Il Palio Ristorante.** Tuscan cuisine and attentive service are the hallmarks of this restaurant in the sumptuous Siena Hotel (☞ *below*). You won't be hurried here, which is a good thing, since it takes a while just to get through the antipasto while you anticipate entrées such as *filetto di branzino*—black grouper filled with greens and wrapped with prosciutto, in a saffron broth. ✉ *1505 E. Franklin St.,* ☎ *919/929–4000. AE, D, DC, MC, V.*

$$–$$$ ✕ **Aurora.** Northern Italian cuisine is the specialty. The changing menu may include succulent sea scallops and shiitake mushrooms in rosemary and white wine, fresh chive pasta stuffed with four cheeses and tossed with walnut sauce, or veal with apples. ✉ *1350 Raleigh Rd. (NC 54 Bypass),* ☎ *919/942–2400. AE, MC, V.*

$$–$$$ ✕ **Crook's Corner.** This small, often noisy restaurant is an exemplar of Southern chic. It turns out such regional specialties as snapper with mint, pecans, and oranges, as well as hot pepper jelly, crab gumbo, and buttermilk pie. A wall of bamboo and a waterfall fountain make the patio a delightful alfresco experience. Look for the pink pig atop the building. ✉ *610 W. Franklin St.,* ☎ *919/929–7643. AE, MC, V.*

$$–$$$ ✕ **Pyewacket Restaurant.** What began as a hole-in-the-wall vegetarian restaurant in 1977 has become one of Chapel Hill's most popular eateries. Now with bigger digs and courtyard dining, Pyewacket has added seafood and pasta specialties to its repertoire. Entrées range from southwestern grilled seafood to spinach lasagna. ✉ *431 W. Franklin St.,* ☎ *919/929–0297. AE, D, DC, MC, V.*

$$$$ ★ ✕ **Fearrington House.** A member of the prestigious Relais & Châteaux group, this country inn is on a 200-year-old farm that has been remade into a residential community resembling a country village. The village mascots, the "Oreo cows" (black on the ends, snow white in the middle), roam the pasture at the entrance. The inn's modern guest rooms, overlooking a courtyard, gardens, and pasture, are furnished with antiques, original art, English pine, and floral print fabrics. The restaurant serves regional food, such as collard-pecan-pesto-stuffed chicken breast with Hoop cheddar grits over a chicory morel gravy. Dinner is prix-fixe. Guests can use the Fearrington Swim & Croquet Club. ✉ *2000 Fearrington Village Center, 8 mi south of Chapel Hill on U.S. 15–501, Pittsboro 27312,* ☎ *919/542–2121,* FAX *919/542–4202. 30 rooms, 2 suites. 2 restaurants, pool, 2 tennis courts, croquet, business services, meeting rooms. AE, MC, V. BP.*

$$$ **Siena Hotel.** The love affair Sam and Susan Longiotti have with Siena, Italy, has carried over to their posh, European-style hotel, arguably the nicest in Chapel Hill. The lobby and rooms have imported furniture, and fabrics and artwork that conjure the Italian Renaissance. The friendly staff and the pleasant atmosphere more than make up for the location—off a main road, surrounded by the parking lot (and some trees). Rates include a breakfast buffet served by Il Palio, the in-house restaurant (☞ *above*). ✉ *1505 E. Franklin St., 27514,* ☎ *919/929–4000 or 800/223–7379,* FAX *919/968–8527. 68 rooms, 12 suites. Restaurant, bar, picnic area, in-room data ports, business services, meeting rooms, airport shuttle. AE, DC, MC, V. BP.*

Nightlife and the Arts

THE ARTS

The **Dean E. Smith Center** (✉ Skipper Bowles Dr., on the UNC campus, ☎ 919/962–7777) is the place to see the university's men's basketball games, special events, and concerts. **Playmakers Repertory Company** (✉ Country Club Dr., on the UNC campus, ☎ 919/962–7529), a non-profit professional theater, performs six plays annually (September–May) at the Paul Green Theatre.

NIGHTLIFE

The Chapel Hill area is the place to hear live rock and alternative bands. **Cat's Cradle** (✉ 300 E. Main St., Carrboro, ☎ 919/967–9053) is smoky and dark and presents entertainment nightly.

Outdoor Activities and Sports

BASKETBALL

The University of North Carolina's **Tarheels** (☎ 919/962–2296 or 800/722–4335) are Chapel Hill's Atlantic Coast Conference team.

BIKING

Chapel Hill is a great town for biking; for a bicycling map, contact the **Chapel Hill/Orange County Visitors Bureau** (☞ Visitor Information *in* the Triangle A to Z, *below*).

GOLF

There are three public golf courses in Orange County; Chapel Hill has one of them: **Finley Golf Course** (✉ Finley Golf Course Rd., off NC 54 on the UNC campus, ☎ 919/962–2349) is a championship par-72 course with a driving range and putting green.

TENNIS

There are 21 public courts in Chapel Hill. For information call the **Chapel Hill Parks and Recreation Department** (☎ 919/968–2784).

Shopping

SHOPPING DISTRICTS AND MALLS

Minutes from downtown, the lively **Eastgate Shopping Center** (✉ between E. Franklin St. and U.S. 15–501) sells everything from antiques to wine. **Fearrington Village,** a planned community 8 mi south of Chapel Hill on U.S. 15–501 in Pittsboro, has upscale shops selling art, garden items, handmade jewelry, and more. **Franklin Street** in Chapel Hill has a wonderful collection of shops, including bookstores, art galleries, crafts shops, and clothing stores.

BOOKS

At **McIntyre's Fine Books and Bookends** (✉ Fearrington Village, U.S. 15–501, Pittsboro, ☎ 919/542–3030), an independent operation, you can read by the fire in one of the cozy rooms. It has extensive collections of travel and gardening books.

FOOD

A Southern Season (✉ Eastgate Mall, ☎ 919/929–9466 or 800/253–3663) stocks everything from wine to such Tarheel treats as barbecue sauces, peanuts, and hams. The Weathervane Café has indoor and alfresco dining. **Wellspring Grocery** (✉ 81 S. Elliott Rd., ☎ 919/968–1983) has fresh produce and health foods.

The Triangle A to Z

Arriving and Departing

BY BUS

Greyhound/Carolina Trailways (☎ 800/231–2222) serves Raleigh, Durham, and Chapel Hill.

BY CAR

U.S. 1, which runs north–south through the Triangle and the Sandhills, also links to I–85 going northeast. U.S. 64, which makes an east–west traverse across the Triangle, continues eastward all the way to the Outer Banks. I–95 runs northeast–southwest to the east of the Triangle and the Sandhills, crossing U.S. 64 and I–40 on its way from Virginia to South Carolina.

BY PLANE

The **Raleigh-Durham International Airport** (✉ 1600 Terminal Blvd., Morrisville, ☎ 919/840–2123), off I–40 between the two cities, is served by 19 airlines, including American, Continental, Delta, Northwest, TWA, United, US Airways, Midway, and Southwest. For airline telephone numbers, *see* Air Travel *in* Smart Travel Tips A to Z. If you're driving from the airport to Raleigh, take I–40 east to Exit 285; for Chapel Hill, take I–40 west to Exits 273, 270, and 266; for Durham, also take I–40 west to NC 147. It takes about 20 minutes to get to any of the three cities.

BY TRAIN

The **Amtrak** (✉ 320 W. Cabarrus St., Raleigh, ☎ 919/833–7594 or 800/872–7245; 400 W. Chapel Hill St., Durham, ☎ 919/956–7932 or 800/872–7245; 211 N. Academy St., Cary, ☎ 800/872–7245) *Carolinian* has one daily train northbound and one southbound, with stops in

Raleigh, Cary, Durham, and 10 other Piedmont cities. The in-state *Piedmont* connects nine cities between Raleigh and Charlotte each day.

Getting Around

BY BUS

Capital Area Transit (☎ 919/833–5701) is Raleigh's public transport system. Fares are 75¢. **Chapel Hill Transit** (☎ 919/968–2769), at 75¢ a ride, takes you around the city. **Durham Area Transit Authority** (☎ 919/688–4587) is Durham's intracity bus system. Fares are 75¢, transfers 10¢. **Triangle Transit Authority** (☎ 919/549–9999), which links downtown Raleigh with Cary, Research Triangle Park, Durham, and Chapel Hill, runs weekdays except major holidays. Rates start at $1.

BY TAXI

More than 25 taxi companies serve the Triangle; fares are calculated by the mile. **City Taxi** (✉ Raleigh, ☎ 919/832–1489). **National Cab** (✉ Raleigh-Durham Airport, ☎ 919/469–1333). **Orange Cab** (✉ Durham, ☎ 919/682–6111).

Contacts and Resources

EMERGENCIES

Ambulance, police (☎ 911). For minor emergencies, go to one of the many urgent-care centers in Raleigh, Cary, Durham, and Chapel Hill.

GUIDED TOURS

The **Capital Area Visitor Center** (✉ 301 N. Blount St., 27611, ☎ 919/733–3456) in Raleigh offers maps, brochures, and free tours of government buildings; it's open weekdays 8–5, Saturday 9–5, Sunday 1–5.

The **Historic Chapel Hill/UNC Trolley Tour** (☎ 919/942–7818) operates April to November 15, Wednesday at 2. Fare is $5; call on weekdays for reservations.

LATE-NIGHT PHARMACIES

Eckerd Drug Store (✉ Lake Boone Shopping Center, Wycliff Rd., Raleigh, ☎ 919/781–4070) is open 24 hours. The **Wal-Mart** pharmacy (✉ 6600 Glenwood Ave., Raleigh, ☎ 919/783–9693) is open 24 hours. **Eckerd Drugs** (✉ 3527 Hillsborough Rd., Durham, ☎ 919/383–5591) is open 8 AM–midnight weekdays and 9 AM–11 PM weekends.

RADIO STATIONS

AM: WPTF 680, news, talk; WRBZ 850, talk. **FM:** WCPE 89.7, classical; WUNC 91.5, National Public Radio; WRAL 101.5, adult contemporary; WQDR 94.7, country; WRDU 106.1, rock.

VISITOR INFORMATION

Chapel Hill/Orange County Visitors Bureau (✉ 501 W. Franklin St., Suite 104, Chapel Hill 27516, ☎ 919/968–2060 or 888/968–2060). The **Downtown Chapel Hill Welcome Center** has maps, brochures, and flyers on attractions, accommodations, and services. ✉ *Bank of America Center, 137 E. Franklin St.,* ☎ *919/929–9700.* ⏲ *Tues.–Sat. 10–4.*

Durham Convention & Visitors Bureau (✉ 101 E. Morgan St., 27701, ☎ 919/687–0288 or 800/446–8604). The **Durham Bullhorn** provides 24-hour recorded information on events and activities (☎ 919/688–2855 or 800/772–2855).

Greater Raleigh Convention and Visitors Bureau (✉ Bank of America Bldg., 421 Fayetteville Street Mall, Suite 1505, 27601, ☎ 919/834–5900 or 800/849–8499).

THE SANDHILLS

Southern Pines, Pinehurst

Because of their sandy soil—they were once Atlantic beaches—the Sandhills weren't of much use to early farmers, most of whom switched to lumbering and making turpentine for a livelihood. Since the turn of the 20th century, however, this area with its gently undulating hills has proved ideal for golf and tennis. Promoters call it the Golf Capital of the World; the Tufts Archives honors the sport and the founding of Pinehurst. First-class resorts are centered on the 40 championship golf courses, including the famed Pinehurst Number 2. Public tennis courts can be found in many communities, and the area has also long been popular with horse owners.

The Highland Scots who settled the area left a rich heritage perpetuated through festivals and gatherings. In Colonial times, English potters were attracted to the rich clay deposits in the soil, and today their descendants and others turn out beautiful wares that are sold in more than 40 local shops.

Southern Pines

104 mi east of Charlotte, 71 mi southwest of Raleigh.

Southern Pines, the center of the Sandhills, is a good place to start your visit to the area.

Sandhills Horticultural Gardens has a wetland area that can be observed from elevated boardwalks. It's part of a 15-acre series of gardens showcasing roses, fruits and vegetables, herbs, conifers, hollies, a formal English garden, pools, and a waterfall. ✉ *2200 Airport Rd., Sandhills Community College campus,* ☎ *910/695–3882 or 800/338–3944.* 🎫 *Free.* ⏲ *Daily sunrise–sunset.*

The **Shaw House,** the oldest structure in town (circa 1820), serves as headquarters for the Moore County Historical Association. There are three historic houses on the property and one about 15 mi away. ✉ *S.W. Broad St. and Morganton Rd.,* ☎ *910/692–2051.* 🎫 *Free.* ⏲ *Apr.–Dec., Wed.–Sun. 1–4.*

Weymouth Center, former home of author and publisher James Boyd, hosts numerous concerts and lectures. Boyd, who died in 1944, was visited by many well-known writers; his home served as a cultural center for the area. The North Carolina Literary Hall of Fame is here, and a writer-in-residence program has hosted more than 600 writers. ✉ *555 E. Connecticut Ave.,* ☎ *910/692–6261.* 🎫 *Free.* ⏲ *Weekdays 10–noon and 2–4; call ahead to arrange tours.*

Weymouth Woods Sandhills Nature Preserve, on the eastern outskirts of town, is a 571-acre wildlife preserve with 4 mi of hiking trails, a beaver pond, and a naturalist on staff. ✉ *1024 N. Fort Bragg Rd. (off U.S. 1),* ☎ *910/692–2167.* 🎫 *Free.* ⏲ *Apr.–Oct., daily 9–7; Nov.–Mar., daily 9–6.*

OFF THE BEATEN PATH

CAMERON – Cameron, which hasn't changed much since the 19th century, is the place to shop for antiques. Approximately 60 antiques dealers operate out of several stores. The town itself, off U.S. 1, has been declared a historic district. Most shops are open Tuesday through Saturday 10–5, Sunday 1–5; call the historic district office (☎ 910/245–7001) for information. The town is 12 mi north of Southern Pines.

Dining and Lodging

$–$$$$ ✕ **Lob Steer Inn.** Salad and dessert bars complement generous broiled seafood and prime rib dinners at this casual, dimly lit steak house. ✉ *U.S. 1, ☎ 910/692–3503. Reservations essential. AE, DC, MC, V. No lunch.*

$$$$ **Pine Needles Lodge and Golf Club.** One of the bonuses of staying at this informal lodge is the chance to meet Peggy Kirk Bell, a champion golfer and golf instructor. She built the resort with her late husband and continues to help run it. It was host to the 1996 U.S. Women's Open and has been awarded the championship again for 2001. The rooms are done in a rustic style; many have exposed beams. ✉ *1005 Midland Rd., Box 88, 28387, ☎ 910/692–7111 or 800/747–7272, FAX 910/692–5349. 71 rooms. Bar, dining room, snack bar, in-room data ports, pool, driving range, 18-hole golf course, putting green, 2 tennis courts, bicycles, business services, meeting rooms, airport shuttle. AE, MC, V. FAP.*

$$$ **Mid Pines Inn and Golf Club.** This resort community includes a Georgian-style clubhouse and a golf course designed by Donald Ross that has been the site of numerous tournaments. The spacious rooms in the 1921 inn are Wedgwood blue, with American antiques or good copies. Jackets are required in the dining room. ✉ *1010 Midland Rd., 28387, ☎ 910/692–2114 or 800/323–2114, FAX 910/692–4615. 112 rooms, 5 houses, 7 villas. Bar, dining room, snack bar, pool, 18-hole golf course, putting green, 4 tennis courts, business services, meeting rooms, airport shuttle. AE, D, DC, MC, V.*

Outdoor Activities and Sports

There are many excellent 18-hole golf courses here. **Club at Longleaf** (✉ 2001 Midland Rd., ☎ 910/692–6100 or 800/889–5323) was built on a former horse farm. The front nine of the par-71 course plays through posts, rails, and turns of the old racetrack. **Mid Pines Golf Club** (✉ 1010 Midland Rd., ☎ 910/692–2114 or 800/323–2114) is a golf getaway with a Donald Ross–designed par-72 course. **Pine Needles Resort** (✉ 1005 Midland Rd., ☎ 910/692–7111 or 800/747–7272) has a Donald Ross–designed par-71 course complemented by practice facilities, grass tennis courts, and an outdoor swimming pool. **Talamore at Pinehurst** (✉ 1595 Midland Rd., ☎ 910/692–5884 or 800/552–6292), with its unusual llama caddies, is a par-71 course designed by Rees Jones.

Shopping

Country Bookshop (✉ 140 N.W. Broad St., ☎ 910/692–3211), in the historic downtown district, often has regional authors do readings and signings; the store stocks lots of children's books.

Pinehurst

6 mi west of Southern Pines.

Pinehurst, a New England–style village with quiet, shaded streets and immaculately kept cottages, was laid out in the late 1800s in a wagon-wheel design by landscape genius Frederick Law Olmsted. Annie Oakley lived here for a number of years and headed the gun club. Today, it is a mecca for sports enthusiasts, retirees, and tourists.

Tufts Archives recounts the founding of Pinehurst in the letters, pictures, and news clippings, dating from 1895, of James Walker Tufts, who served as president of the United States Golf Association. Golf memorabilia are on display. ✉ *Given Memorial Library, 150 Cherokee Rd., ☎ 910/295–6022 or 910/295–3642.* ⏲ *Weekdays 9:30–5, Sat. 9:30–12:30.*

Dining and Lodging

$ ✕ **Pinehurst Playhouse Restaurant.** This casual eatery in the shop-filled Theater Building is in the heart of the village. It's *the* place to meet for soups and sandwiches. ✉ *W. Village Green,* ☎ *910/295–8873. Reservations not accepted. No credit cards. Closed Sun. No dinner.*

$$$$ ✕🏨 **Holly Inn.** Listed on the National Register of Historic Places, this hotel, affiliated with the Pinehurst Resort (☞ *below*), was the first in the village. Molding, lighting, and plumbing fixtures, based on research from local archives, recall the 1890s, the decade of its opening. Luxuries include silk hangers; embroidered robes; and afternoon sandwiches, cookies, and ice tea. A two-night stay is required. The menu at 1895, the bistro-style restaurant, changes with the seasons. Signature dinner entrées include pinecone-smoked free-range chicken with truffles, tarragon-scented roast tenderloin of veal, and Carolina blue-crab hash served with Madeira and orange basil hollandaise sauce. Jackets are required at the restaurant. ✉ *Cherokee Rd., 28374,* ☎ *910/295–2300 or 800/682–6901,* FAX *910/295–0988. 78 rooms, 7 suites. Restaurant, bar, in-room data ports, pool, golf and tennis privileges, croquet, business services, meeting rooms. AE, DC, MC, V. MAP.*

$$$–$$$$ ★ ✕🏨 **Pinehurst Resort and Country Club.** The Pinehurst, a venerable resort hotel in operation for nearly a century, has never lost the charm that founder James Tufts intended it to have. Civilized decorum rules in the spacious public rooms, on the rocker-lined wide verandas, and amid the gardens. Guest rooms are elegantly traditional. You can tee off on one of eight signature golf courses. Two blocks away the Manor Inn, a Pinehurst property with 45 rooms, has the feel of a cozy bed-and-breakfast. Manor Inn guests have access to all the resort and country club facilities, including the Carolina Dining Room. Known for its fine five-course meals, the restaurant is formal and requires a jacket. Try the veal medallions with applejack cream sauce, grilled apples, and caramelized Vidalia onions. ✉ *1 Carolina Vista Dr., Box 4000, 28374,* ☎ *910/295–6811 or 800/487–4653,* FAX *910/295–8503. 338 rooms, 130 condominiums. 2 restaurants, bar, in-room data ports, 5 pools, massage, 8 18-hole golf courses, 24 tennis courts, croquet, health club, windsurfing, boating, fishing, bicycles, children's programs, business services, meeting rooms. AE, D, DC, MC, V.*

$$$ ✕🏨 **Magnolia Inn.** This 102-year-old inn, once just a hangout for golfing buddies, is tastefully decorated with unusual antiques. Most guest rooms are in the Victorian style with wicker and brass beds; bathrooms have original fixtures such as claw-foot tubs. The inn's dining rooms ($$$–$$$$), with their dusty-rose wallpaper and fireplaces, have a cozy feel. Superb dinner choices are the grilled Norwegian salmon or roasted herb-crusted rack of lamb. There's also an English-style pub. ✉ *Magnolia and Chinquapin Rds., Box 818, 28370,* ☎ *910/295–6900 or 800/526–5562,* FAX *910/215–0858. 11 rooms. Dining room, pool, business services. AE, MC, V. BP.*

$$ 🏨 **Pine Crest Inn.** Chintz and mahogany fill the rooms of this slightly faded gem once owned by golfing great Donald Ross. The chefs whip up meals reminiscent of Sunday supper: homemade soups, fresh seafood dishes, and the house special, stuffed pork chops. Mr. B's Bar is the liveliest nightspot in town. Guests have golf and tennis privileges at local clubs. ✉ *Dogwood Rd., Box 879, 28370,* ☎ *910/295–6121 or 800/371–2545,* FAX *910/295–4880. 40 rooms. Dining room, bar. AE, D, DC, MC, V. MAP.*

Outdoor Activities and Sports

GOLF

Pinehurst Resort and Country Club (✉ 1 Carolina Vista Dr., ☎ 910/295–6811 or 800/487–4653) has eight courses designed by masters such as Donald Ross, including the famed and challenging par-72 Number 2.

The par-71 **Pit Golf Links** (✉ NC 5, ☎ 910/944–1600 or 800/574–4653) was designed by Dan Maples and sculpted from a 230-acre sand quarry.

HORSEBACK AND CARRIAGE RIDING

Riding instruction and carriage rides are available by appointment at **Pinehurst Stables** (✉ NC 5, ☎ 910/295–8456).

TENNIS

The **Lawn and Tennis Club of North Carolina** (✉ 1 Merrywood, ☎ 910/692–7270) and **Pinehurst Resort and Country Club** (✉ Carolina Vista Dr., ☎ 910/295–8556) are known for their daily clinics.

Aberdeen

5 mi southeast of Pinehurst, 5 mi southwest of Southern Pines.

Aberdeen, a small town of Scottish ancestry, has a beautifully restored early 20th-century train station and plenty of shops with antiques and collectibles. The **Bethesda Presbyterian Church,** on Bethesda Road east of town, was founded in 1790. The present wooden structure, which is used for weddings, funerals, and reunions, was built in the 1860s and has bullet holes from a Civil War battle. The cemetery, where many early settlers are buried, is always open.

Malcolm Blue Farm, one of the few remaining examples of the 19th-century Scottish homes that dotted the area, has farm buildings and an old gristmill. A September festival recalls life here in the 1800s. The farm and museum are part of the North Carolina Civil War Theme Trail. ✉ *Bethesda Rd.,* ☎ *910/944–7558, 910/944–9483 museum.* *Free.* *Thurs.–Sat. 1–4.*

OFF THE BEATEN PATH

FORT BRAGG/POPE AIR FORCE BASE – This army–air force duo outside Fayetteville, 45 mi east of Aberdeen via NC 211 and U.S. 401, is one of the world's largest military complexes. Pope hosts an open house and air show annually (☎ 910/394–4183). Bragg, the biggest army post east of the Mississippi, is open year-round, and self-guided tours are available. The welcome center (☎ 910/907–2026) at the corner of Randolph and Knox streets on Fort Bragg has maps indicating public access areas. Free sites include the 82nd Airborne Division War Memorial Museum (☎ 910/432–3443), which tells the story of this unit famous from World War I through Desert Storm. ✉ *Off NC 24 or the All American Fwy. Some sites closed Mon.*

Lodging

$–$$ **Inn at Bryant House.** One block east of U.S. 1, this charming downtown B&B, built in 1913, is a home away from home. All rooms are individually decorated; some have canopy beds. The inn has golf packages and arranges tennis and horseback riding. ✉ *214 N. Poplar St., 28315,* ☎ *910/944–3300 or 800/453–4019,* FAX *910/944–8898. 9 rooms, 7 with bath. AE, D, MC, V. CP.*

Outdoor Activities and Sports

Legacy Golf Links (✉ U.S. 15–501S, ☎ 910/944–8825 or 800/344–8825) has the first American course designed by Jack Nicklaus II (par 72).

Seagrove

35 mi northwest of Pinehurst via NC 211 and U.S. 220.

Potters, some of whom are carrying on traditions that have been in their families for generations and others who are newer to the art, handcraft mugs, bowls, pitchers, platters, vases, and clay "face jugs" in the ★ **Seagrove** area. More than 90 potteries are scattered along and off Route 705 and U.S. 220. Some of the work of local artisans is exhibited in national museums, including the Smithsonian. Most shops are open Tuesday through Saturday 10–5.

★ The **North Carolina Pottery Center,** a museum and educational facility, has exhibitions of pottery from around the state and maps locating the various studios around the area. ✉ *250 East Ave.,* ☎ *336/873–8430.* ⏲ *Tues.–Sat. 10–4.*

Asheboro

13 mi north of Seagrove, 23 mi south of Greensboro on U.S. 64.

Asheboro, the seat of Randolph County, sits in the Uwharrie National Forest, a haven for hikers, bikers, horseback riders, and fisherfolk. This part of the southern Piedmont is a lovely place to view scenery and visit crafts shops. You can also visit the **American Classic Motorcycle Museum** (✉ 11740 U.S. 64W, ☎ 336/629–9564) or the **Foundation for Aircraft Conservation Flying Museum** (✉ 2222 Pilot View Rd., ☎ 336/625–0170).

★ The **North Carolina Zoological Park,** a 1,500-acre home for more than 1,100 animals and 60,000 exotic and tropical plants, was the first zoo in the country designed from the get-go as a natural habitat facility. The park includes the 300-acre African Pavilion, an aviary, a gorilla habitat, a Sonoran Desert habitat, and a 200-acre North American habitat with polar bears and sea lions. You can take a tram between areas. ✉ *4401 Zoo Pkwy.,* ☎ *336/879–7000 or 800/488–0444.* *$8, including tram ride.* ⏲ *Apr.–Oct., daily 9–5; Nov.–Mar., daily 9–4.*

Sandhills A to Z

Arriving, Departing, and Getting Around

BY CAR

U.S. 1 runs north–south through the Sandhills and is the recommended route from the Raleigh-Durham area, a distance of about 70 mi.

BY PLANE

US Airways Express (☎ 800/428–4322) serves the **Moore County Airport** (✉ NC 22, Southern Pines, ☎ 910/692–3212), with connections from **Charlotte-Douglas International Airport** (☎ 704/359–4013), **Raleigh-Durham International Airport** (☎ 919/840–2123), and the **Piedmont Triad International Airport** (☎ 336/665–5666). Many lodging establishments run shuttle services.

BY TRAIN

Amtrak (☎ 910/692–6305 or 800/872–7245) southbound and northbound trains, one daily in each direction, stop in Southern Pines.

Contacts and Resources

EMERGENCIES

Ambulance, police (☎ 911). **Moore Regional Hospital** (✉ 155 Memorial Dr., Pinehurst, ☎ 910/215–1111) has an emergency room.

RADIO STATIONS

AM: WKHO 550, easy listening; WEEB 990, news, talk; WQNX 1350, talk. **FM:** WIOZ 107, easy listening.

VISITOR INFORMATION

Pinehurst Area Convention and Visitors Bureau (✉ 1480 U.S. 15–501N, Box 2270, Southern Pines 28388, ☎ 910/692–3330 or 800/346–5362) serves the Pinehurst, Southern Pines, and Aberdeen area. For details on local events, call the **events hot line** (☎ 910/692–1600). **Moore County Parks and Recreation Department** (☎ 910/947–2504) can provide recreation information.

THE OUTER BANKS

Cape Hatteras, Cape Lookout

North Carolina's Outer Banks, a series of barrier islands on the Atlantic Ocean, stretch from the Virginia state line south to Cape Lookout. Throughout history these waters have been the nemesis of shipping, gaining the nickname the Graveyard of the Atlantic; the network of lighthouses and lifesaving stations draws visitors today, and the many submerged wrecks attract scuba divers. The islands' coves and inlets offered privacy to pirates—the notorious Blackbeard lived and died here. For many years the Outer Banks remained isolated, home only to a few families who made their living by fishing. Today the islands, linked by bridges and ferries, have become popular destinations. Much of the area is included in the Cape Hatteras and Cape Lookout national seashores. The largest towns are Kitty Hawk, Kill Devil Hills, Nags Head, and Manteo.

On the inland side of the Outer Banks is the historic Albemarle region, a remote area of small villages and towns surrounding Albemarle Sound. Edenton was the colonial capital for a while, and many of its early structures are preserved.

You can tour the Outer Banks from the south end, by taking a car ferry to Ocracoke Island or, as in the following route, from the north end. You can drive the 120-mi stretch of NC 12 from Corolla to Ocracoke in a day, but be sure to allow plenty of time in summer to wait for the ferry connecting the islands and for exploring the undeveloped beaches, historic lifesaving stations, and charming beach communities stretched along the national seashores. Rentals are available throughout the area, with the highest concentration of accommodations between Kill Devil Hills and Nags Head. Mile markers (MM) indicate addresses for sites where there aren't many buildings. Be aware that during major storms and hurricanes the roads and bridges become clogged with traffic following the blue-and-white evacuation signs.

Numbers in the margin correspond to points of interest on the Outer Banks map.

Corolla, Duck, and Kitty Hawk

Kitty Hawk: 87 mi south of Norfolk, Va., via U.S. 17 and U.S. 158; 215 mi east of Raleigh via U.S. 64 and NC 12. Duck: 7 mi north of Kitty Hawk. Corolla: 19 mi north of Duck.

The small settlements of Corolla and Duck are largely seasonal residential enclaves full of summer rental condominiums. **Duck** has a growing number of restaurants and shopping outlets. The Currituck Beach Lighthouse in **Corolla** is the northernmost lighthouse on the Outer Banks. Drive slowly in Corolla; wild ponies wander free here and al-

The Outer Banks

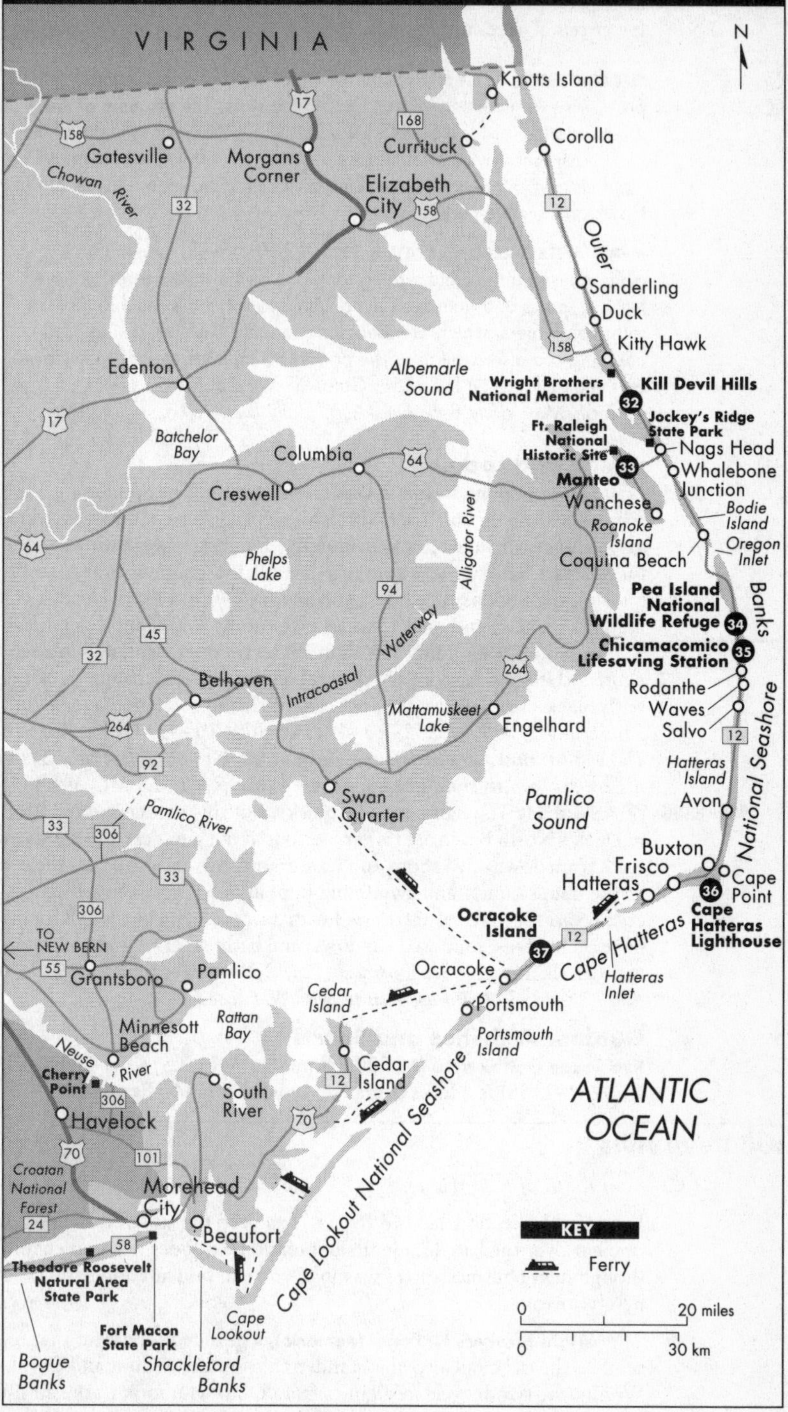

ways have the right of way. **Kitty Hawk,** with a few thousand permanent residents, is among the quieter of the beach communities, with fewer rental accommodations.

OFF THE BEATEN PATH

ELIZABETH CITY – This city's historic district has the largest number of pre–Civil War commercial buildings in the state. The **Museum of the Albemarle** (✉ 1116 U.S. 17S, ☎ 252/335–1453), an affiliate of the North Carolina Museum of History (☞ Raleigh, *above*), has displays on local history; admission is free. Elizabeth City is 50 mi northwest of Kitty Hawk on the Albemarle Sound.

MERCHANTS MILLPOND STATE PARK – A 200-year-old man-made millpond and an ancient swamp form one of the state's rarest ecosystems. Cypress and gum trees hung with Spanish moss reach out of the still, dark waters, which are ideal for canoeing. Fishing, hiking, and camping are also available. The park is 80 mi northwest of Kitty Hawk, on the mainland. ✉ *U.S. 158, Gatesville,* ☎ *252/357–1191.* *Free.* ⏲ *Sept.–May, daily 8–8; June–Aug., daily 8 AM–9 PM.*

Dining and Lodging

$$$$ **Sanderling Inn Resort & Conference Center.** The Sanderling, on a remote beach 5 mi north of Duck, is a fine place to be pampered. Recreation choices include tennis, swimming, and nature walks through the Pine Island Sanctuary. Though it has all the contemporary conveniences, the inn has the stately, mellow look of old Nags Head. Ceiling fans, wicker, and neutral tones give rooms a cool and casual feel. The ambitious restaurant ($$$; dinner reservations essential) is in a renovated lifesaving station; try the crab cakes, roast Carolina duckling with black cherry sauce, or fricassee of shrimp. ✉ *1461 Duck Rd., Sanderling 27949,* ☎ *252/261–4111 or 800/701–4111,* FAX *252/261–1638. 88 rooms, 29 efficiencies. Restaurant, bar, pool, hot tub, 2 tennis courts, health club, library, meeting rooms. AE, D, MC, V.*

$$$–$$$$ **Advice 5¢.** The name may be quirky, but this contemporary B&B in Duck's North Beach area is very serious about guest care. Just a short walk from downtown shops and restaurants, Advice also offers the use of the tennis courts and swimming pool at Sea Pines, a nearby property. Beds in each room are dressed with crisp, colorful linens. All rooms have ceiling fans, shuttered windows, and baths stocked with thick cotton towels. ✉ *111 Scarborough La., 27949,* ☎ *252/255–1050 or 800/238–4235. 4 rooms, 1 suite. MC, V. Closed Dec.–Jan. CP.*

Outdoor Activities and Sports

Sea Scape Golf Course (✉ 300 Eckner St., MM 2.5, Kitty Hawk, ☎ 252/261–2158) is a links course set amid the dunes. Par is 72.

Kill Devil Hills

32 *4 mi south of Kitty Hawk.*

Kill Devil Hills, on U.S. 158 Bypass, has been the site of rapid development over the last decade. Its population explodes in summer, and though many businesses are seasonal, you can find anything you need here year-round.

★ The **Wright Brothers National Memorial,** a granite monument that resembles the tail of an airplane, stands as a tribute to Wilbur and Orville Wright, the two bicycle mechanics from Ohio who took to the air on December 17, 1903. You can see a replica of the *Flyer* and stand on the spot where it made four takeoffs and landings, the longest flight a distance of 852 ft. Exhibits and an informative talk by a National Park Service ranger bring the event to life. The Wrights had to bring in the unassembled airplane by boat, along with all their food and supplies for building a camp. They made four trips to the site, beginning in 1900. The First Flight is commemorated annually. ✉ *Off U.S. 158, between MM 7 and MM 8,* ☎ *252/441–7430.* *$4 per car or $2 per person.* ⏲ *Daily 9–5; extended hrs in summer.*

Kill Devil Hills has 5 mi of **beach** with 27 public access areas with limited parking off NC 12. Some have off-road vehicle access. Because of the number of rental cottages and hotels, this beach tends to have more people, but it is seldom uncomfortably crowded.

Dining and Lodging

$$–$$$ ✕ **Flying Fish Cafe.** While the interior of this downtown café is brightly colored and casual, the food and wine are taken very seriously. A perennial favorite entrée is shrimp on spinach fettuccine with feta cheese. ✉ *2003 Croatan Hwy., off U.S. 158,* ☎ *252/441–6894. AE, D, MC, V. No lunch weekends.*

$$$–$$$$ **Ramada Inn.** Guest rooms in this convention-style hotel have private balconies, some with ocean views. Peppercorns restaurant, overlooking the ocean, serves breakfast and dinner, and lunch is available on the sundeck next to the pool. ✉ *1701 S. Virginia Dare Trail, off U.S. 158, MM 9.5, Box 2716, 27948,* ☎ *252/441–2151 or 800/635–1824,* FAX *252/441–1830. 172 rooms. Restaurant, bar, in-room data ports, indoor pool, hot tub, shuffleboard, volleyball, business services, meeting rooms. AE, D, DC, MC, V.*

Nags Head

4 mi south of Kill Devil Hills.

Nags Head got its name because Outer Bankers hoping for shipwrecks would tie lanterns around the heads of their horses to lure merchant ships onto the shoals, thus profiting from the cargo that washed ashore. This is a very commercialized and congested area. On the upside, there are many restaurants, motels, hotels, and shops from which to choose.

Nags Head has 11 mi of **beach** with 33 public access areas, all with parking and some with rest rooms and showers. One point of interest is mile marker 11.5, the first North Carolina Historic Shipwreck Site. The USS *Huron* lies in 20 ft of water off the Nags Head Pier.

Coquina Beach (✉ off NC 12, 8 mi south of U.S. 158) in the **Cape Hatteras National Seashore** (☞ *below*) is considered by some to be the best swimming hole on the Outer Banks. The wide-beamed ribs of the shipwreck *Laura Barnes* rest in the dunes here. Picnic shelters are available.

Jockey's Ridge State Park still has the tallest sand dune in the East (about 88 ft), though it has lost some 22 ft since the 1930s thanks to the million visitors a year who carry sand away. It's a popular spot for hang gliding, kite flying, and sandboarding. ✉ *U.S. 158 Bypass, MM 12,* ☎ *252/441–7132.* *Free.* ⏲ *Daily 8–sunset.*

Dining and Lodging

$$$–$$$$ ✕ **Owens' Restaurant.** In an old Nags Head–style clapboard cottage, Owens' has been in the same family since 1946. Though the menu features pasta and beef, the seafood is the star—especially the coconut shrimp and lobster bisque. The brass-and-glass Station Keeper's Lounge has entertainment. ✉ *U.S. 158, MM 17,* ☎ *252/441–7309. Reservations not accepted. AE, D, DC, MC, V. Closed Jan.–Feb. No lunch.*

$$–$$$ ✕ **Windmill Point.** The menu changes but you can always count on the signature seafood trio: diners may choose any combination of three fish. The preparation is at the whim of the chef: lightly poached or grilled, and topped with roasted red pepper and capers, or shredded cucumber and dill, or a pineapple salsa. The restaurant has stunning views of the sound at sunset, eye-catching memorabilia from the luxury liner SS *United States,* and yes, a real windmill. ✉ *U.S. 158 Bypass, MM 16½,* ☎ *252/441–1535. AE, D, DC, MC, V.*

$$$–$$$$ ★ **First Colony Inn.** This historic three-story B&B has encircling verandas for great ocean views. Two rooms have wet bars, kitchenettes, and whirlpool baths; others have four-poster or canopy beds, handcrafted armoires, and English antiques. The entire property is no-smoking. ✉ *6720 S. Virginia Dare Trail, 27959,* ☎ *252/441–2343 or 800/368–9390,* FAX *252/441–9234. 26 rooms. Picnic area, in-room data ports, pool, beach, business services. AE, D, MC, V. CP.*

Outdoor Activities and Sports

GOLF

Nags Head Golf Links (✉ 5615 S. Seachase Dr., MM 15, ☎ 252/441–8074 or 800/851–9404) has a par-71 course with ocean views.

HANG GLIDING

Lessons and gear are provided by **Kitty Hawk Kites** (✉ U.S. 158, MM 13, ☎ 252/441–4124 or 800/334–4777), the oldest hang-gliding school on the East Coast.

Roanoke Island

10 mi southwest of Nags Head.

On a hot July day in 1587, 117 men, women, and children left their boat and set foot on Roanoke Island to make the first permanent English settlement in the New World. Three years later they disappeared without a trace, leaving a mystery that continues to intrigue historians. Today Roanoke Island is a sleepy, well-kept place that hasn't succumbed to full-scale commercialism. Much of the 12-mi-long island remains wild. In summer, Roanoke and its two villages—picturesque Manteo, whose waterfront provides a pleasant combination of residential and commercial development, and Wanchese, a commercial fishing community—come alive. The island is reached by U.S. 64/264
33 from U.S. 158 Bypass. **Manteo** has some sights related to the island's history as well as an aquarium.

A history, education, and cultural arts complex opposite the waterfront in Manteo, **Roanoke Island Festival Park** includes the *Elizabeth II* State Historic Site. Costumed interpreters conduct tours of the 69-ft ship, a re-creation of a 16th-century vessel, except when it is on educational voyages in the off-season (call ahead). The complex also has plays, concerts, arts and crafts exhibitions, and special programs. ✉ *Downtown Manteo,* ☎ *252/473–1144.* *$8.* ⏲ *Mar., daily 10–5; Apr.–Oct., daily 9–6; Nov.–Dec., daily 10–5.*

Clustered together on the outskirts of Manteo are the lush **Elizabethan Gardens,** a re-creation of a 16th-century English garden, established as a memorial to the first English colonists. They are impeccably maintained by the Garden Club of North Carolina. ✉ *1411 U.S. 64/264, 3 mi north of downtown Manteo,* ☎ *252/473–3234.* *$5.* ⏲ *Apr.–May and Sept.–Oct., daily 9–6; June–Aug., daily 9–7; Dec.–Feb., weekdays 10–4.*

Fort Raleigh National Historic Site is a restoration of the original 1585 earthworks that marks the beginning of English colonial history in America. Be sure to see the orientation film and then take a guided tour of the fort. A nature trail leads to an outlook over Roanoke Sound. ✉ *Off U.S. 64/264, 3 mi north of Manteo,* ☎ *252/473–5772.* *Free.* ⏲ *Daily 9–5; extended hrs in summer.*

The ***Lost Colony,*** begun in 1937, is the country's first and longest-running outdoor drama. It reenacts the story of the first colonists who settled here in 1587 and then disappeared, and it is staged at the Waterside Amphitheatre. ✉ *1409 U.S. 64/264,* ☎ *252/473–3414 or 800/488–5012.* *$16 (reservations essential).* ⏲ *Performances June–Aug., Sun.–Fri. at 8:30 PM.*

The **North Carolina Aquarium at Roanoke Island,** overlooking Croatan Sound, has been expanded to twice its former size. *The Graveyard of the Atlantic* is the centerpiece exhibit. It is a 285,000-gallon ocean tank containing the re-created remains of the USS *Monitor,* sunken off Hatteras Island (☞ *below*). ✉ *Airport Rd., off U.S. 64,* ☎ *252/473–3493.* *$3.* ⏲ *Daily 9–5.*

OFF THE BEATEN PATH

EDENTON – Rich with history, North Carolina's first permanent settlement and the colony's first capital is a placid, immensely scenic place on the north side of the Albemarle Sound (65 mi west of Manteo). Originally incorporated in 1715 with the name the Towne on Queen Anne's Creek, the spot was renamed Edenton seven years later in honor of Governor Charles Eden. A fine collection of 18th-century buildings has been well maintained. Stop by the visitor center (✉ 108 N. Broad St., ☎ 252/482–2637) to hear tales about the colonists, such as the women of the Edenton Tea Party, who fought for liberty. An inexpensive pamphlet serves as a guide on a 1½-mi walking tour. Guided tours of the historic district are available and are recommended. Some highlights are the Jacobean-style Cupola House and Gardens, the Chowan County Courthouse (1767), and St. Paul's Episcopal Church.

Dining and Lodging

$$ ✕ **Weeping Radish Brewery and Restaurant.** This Bavarian-style restaurant and microbrewery is known for its German cuisine and the annual Octoberfest weekend held after Labor Day, which showcases German and blues bands. Brewery tours are offered free of charge upon request. The beer is superb. ✉ *U.S. 64, Manteo,* ☎ *252/473–1157. D, MC, V.*

$$$ ✕ **Tranquil House Inn.** This 19th-century-style waterfront inn is only a few steps from shops, restaurants, and the Roanoke Island Festival Park (☞ *above*), and bikes are provided for more distant adventures. Handmade comforters give rooms a cozy feel. Wine and cheese each evening are part of the rate. The restaurant, 1587 ($$$–$$$$), serves inventive entrées such as sesame-crusted tuna with wasabi vinaigrette and shiitake mushrooms. ✉ *405 Queen Elizabeth Ave., Box 2045, Manteo 27954,* ☎ *252/473–1404 or 800/458–7069,* FAX *252/473–1526. 25 rooms. Restaurant, business services, meeting rooms. AE, D, MC, V. Closed Dec.–Jan. CP.*

Cape Hatteras National Seashore

Extends 70 mi south of Nags Head.

★ **Cape Hatteras National Seashore** has more than 70 mi of unspoiled beaches stretching from south Nags Head to Ocracoke Inlet across three narrow islands: Bodie, Hatteras, and Ocracoke. The islands are linked by NC 12 and the Hatteras Inlet ferry. This coastal area is ideal for swimming, surfing, windsurfing, diving, boating, and other water activities. It's easy to find your own slice of beach as you drive south down NC 12, but park only in designated areas. If you want to swim, beware of strong tides and currents—there are no lifeguard stations. Fishing piers can be found in Rodanthe, Avon, and Frisco. For information, *see* Visitor Information *in* the Outer Banks A to Z, *below.*

Hatteras Island

15 mi south of Nags Head.

The Herbert C. Bonner Bridge arches for 3 mi over Oregon Inlet and carries traffic to Hatteras Island, known as the "blue marlin capital of the world." The island, a 33-mi-long ribbon of sand, juts out into the Atlantic Ocean; at its most distant point (Cape Hatteras), Hatteras is 25 mi from the mainland. About 85% of the island belongs to Cape Hatteras National Seashore, and the remainder is privately owned in seven small, quaint villages strung along NC 12, the island's fragile lifeline to points north.

34 **Pea Island National Wildlife Refuge,** between Oregon Inlet and Rodanthe, is made up of more than 5,000 acres of marsh. This birder's paradise, with observation platforms and spotting scopes, is on the Atlantic Flyway: More than 265 species are sighted regularly, including endangered peregrine falcons and piping plovers. NC 12 travels through marsh areas, and you can hike or drive, depending on the terrain. A visitor center, 5 mi south of Oregon Inlet on NC 12, has an informational display. ✉ *Pea Island Refuge Headquarters, NC 12,* ☎ *252/473–1131.* *Free.* *May–Sept., daily 9–4; Oct.–Apr., weekdays 9–4.*

35 In Rodanthe, the restored 1911 **Chicamacomico Lifesaving Station** has a museum that tells the story of the 24 stations that once lined the Outer Banks. Living-history reenactments are performed June–August. ✉ *Off NC 12,* ☎ *252/987–1552.* *Free.* *May–Oct., Tues., Thurs., and Sat. 11–5.*

36 **Cape Hatteras Lighthouse,** about 30 mi south of Rodanthe, is a beacon to ships offshore. At 208 ft this is the tallest brick lighthouse in the world, and it's painted with distinctive black and white spirals. During the summer the Principal Keeper's quarters are open for viewing. Offshore lie the remains of the USS *Monitor,* a Confederate ironclad ship that sank in 1862. The visitor center here provides information on the National Seashore. ✉ *Hatteras Island Visitor Center, off NC 12 near Buxton,* ☎ *252/995–4474.* *Free.* *Daily 9–5.*

Dining

$–$$$ ✕ **Tides.** Just south of the entrance for the Cape Hatteras Lighthouse, this place is popular for its good service, well-prepared food, and homey atmosphere. In addition to offering the usual seafood, the menu has chicken and ham. It's also a favorite breakfast spot. ✉ *NC 12, Buxton,* ☎ *252/995–5988. MC, V. Closed Dec.–early Apr.*

Ocracoke Island

37 *Southwest of Hatteras Island.*

Much of Ocracoke Island is part of Cape Hatteras National Seashore. A free ferry that leaves every hour during the day will take you from Hatteras to the island in 40 minutes; other ferries leave from the mainland. Ocracoke was cut off from the world for so long that locals still speak in quasi-Elizabethan accents. Today, however, the island is a refuge for visitors. A village of shops, motels, and restaurants is around Silver Lake Harbor, where the pirate Blackbeard met his death in 1718. The Ocracoke Lighthouse is a photographer's dream. The **Ocracoke Island Visitor Center** (✉ Ocracoke Village, south end of NC 12 on Silver Lake, ☎ 252/928–4531), run by the National Park Service, provides information.

Ocracoke Island **beaches** are among the least populated and most beautiful on the Cape Hatteras National Seashore. Four public access

Close-Up

NORTH CAROLINA'S PIRATES

NORTH CAROLINA'S COAST was a magnet for marauding sea dogs during the Golden Age of Piracy, a period that spanned the 17th and 18th centuries. Among its visitors was Stede Bonnet, captured in the Cape Fear region in 1718 but escaped; Anne Bonny, daughter of a plantation owner, wife of one pirate and lover of another; Charles Vane, whose crew mutinied; and Paul Williams, who accepted King George I's pardon, only to return to piracy.

The most notorious buccaneer of them all was Blackbeard, whose two-year reign of terror began in 1716: cultivating fear by strapping on six pistols and six knives, tying his luxuriant beard into pigtails and, legend has it, lighting matches under his hat to give the illusion that his head was smoking, Blackbeard attacked ships in the Caribbean and settlements along the coasts of Virginia and the Carolinas.

At least three of his ships sank in North Carolina's waters; archaeologists are retrieving artifacts from what is likely the flagship, *Queen Anne's Revenge,* which ran aground on a sandbar near Beaufort Inlet in May of 1718. The following November a seafaring posse caught Blackbeard in one his favorite playgrounds, Ocracoke Inlet. The pirate was decapitated and his head hung from a conquering ship. Still sought are the hulks of Blackbeard's lost ships and his treasure.

–By Lisa H. Towle

areas have parking, as well as off-road vehicle access. At the **Ocracoke Pony Pen** (✉ NC 12, 6 mi southwest of the Hatteras–Ocracoke ferry landing), you can observe from a platform what some believe are the direct descendants of Spanish mustangs that once roamed wild on the island.

Dining and Lodging

$–$$ ✕🏨 **Island Inn and Dining Room.** The inn, built as a private lodge back in 1901, shows its age a bit but is full of Outer Banks character and is being upgraded gradually. Some rooms are in a modern wing, and these are good for families. The large rooms in the Crow's Nest on the third floor are the best; they have cathedral ceilings and look out over the island. The restaurant ($–$$) is known for its oyster omelet, crab cakes, and hush puppies. This is a no-smoking property. ✉ *Corner of Lighthouse Rd. and NC 12, Box 9, 27960,* ☎ *252/928–4351, 877/456–3466 inn, 252/928–7821 dining room;* FAX *252/928–4352. 35 rooms, 4 villas. Restaurant, in-room data ports, pool, airport shuttle. D, MC, V.*

Cape Lookout National Seashore

Southwest of Ocracoke Island via Cedar Island.

★ **Cape Lookout National Seashore** extends for 55 mi from Portsmouth Island to Shackleford Banks and includes 28,400 acres of uninhabited land and marsh. The remote, sandy islands are linked to the mainland by private ferries. Ferry service is available from Harkers Island to the Cape Lookout Light area, from Davis to Shingle Point, from Atlantic to an area north of Drum Inlet, and from Ocracoke to Portsmouth Village. Portsmouth, a deserted village that was inhabited from 1753 until the early 1970s, is being restored and is open to the public from April to early November. To the south, wild ponies roam Shackleford Banks. Four-wheel-drive vehicles are allowed on the beach, and primitive camping is available. For information, *see* Visitor Information *in* the Outer Banks A to Z, *below.*

The Outer Banks A to Z

Arriving, Departing, and Getting Around

BY BOAT

Seagoing visitors travel the Intracoastal Waterway through the Outer Banks and Albemarle region. Boats may dock at nearly 150 marinas, including **Elizabeth City** (☎ 252/338–2886), **Manteo Waterfront Docks** (☎ 252/473–3320), and **National Park Service Silver Lake Marina** (☎ 252/928–5111) in Ocracoke. For a complete list of facilities, see the *North Carolina Coastal Boating Guide,* compiled by the **North Carolina Department of Transportation** (☎ 919/733–2520).

BY CAR

U.S. 158 links the Outer Banks with U.S. 17 leading to Norfolk, Virginia, and other places north. NC 12 goes north toward Corolla and south toward Ocracoke. From Ocracoke there are **car ferries** to Cedar Island and Swan Quarter on the mainland. You need a reservation for the ferry (☎ 800/293–3779).

BY FERRY

For information about the state-run ferry system and its schedules and costs, call the North Carolina Department of Transportation's **Ferry Information Line** (☎ 800/293–3779).

BY PLANE

The closest commercial airports are the **Raleigh-Durham International Airport** (✉ 1600 Terminal Blvd., Morrisville, ☎ 919/840–2123), a five-hour drive, and, in Virginia, **Norfolk International** (✉ 2200 Norview Ave., ☎ 757/857–3351), a 1½-hour drive, both of which are served by major carriers, including American, Continental, Delta, and US Airways. For airline telephone numbers, *see* Air Travel *in* Smart Travel Tips A to Z. **Southeast Air** (☎ 252/473–3222 or 800/289–8202) and **Outer Banks Airways** (☎ 252/473–2227) provide charter service between the **Dare County Regional Airport** (✉ 410 Airport Rd., Manteo, ☎ 252/473–2600) and major cities along the East Coast.

BY TAXI

Beach Cabs (☎ 252/441–2500 or 800/441–2503), based in Nags Head, offers 24-hour service from Norfolk to Ocracoke and towns in between. **Outer Banks Limousine Service** (☎ 252/261–3133 or 800/828–5466), headquartered in Kill Devil Hills, serves the entire area and Norfolk International.

BY TRAIN

Amtrak service (☎ 800/872–7245) is available to Norfolk, Virginia, about 75 mi to the north.

Contacts and Resources

EMERGENCIES

Dial 911 for emergencies on Oregon Inlet, Roanoke Island, Hatteras Island, and Ocracoke Island. The **Healtheast/Outer Banks Medical Center** (✉ 2808 S. Croatan Hwy., Nags Head, ☎ 252/441–7111) is open 24 hours a day. **Beach Medical Care** (✉ 5200 N. Croatan Hwy., MM 1.5, Kitty Hawk, ☎ 252/261–4187) provides help around the clock. For **Coast Guard** assistance, dial ☎ 252/995–6411.

GUIDED TOURS

Historic Albemarle Tour, Inc. (✉ 1 Harding Sq., Washington, ☎ 252/974–2950 or 800/734–1117) runs guided tours of Edenton and publishes a brochure on a self-guided tour of the Albemarle Region.

Kitty Hawk AeroTours leaves from the First Flight Airstrip or from Manteo for Kitty Hawk, Corolla, Cape Hatteras, Ocracoke, Portsmouth Island, and other areas along the Outer Banks. ✉ *Behind Wright Brothers Monument, U.S. 158, MM 8, Kill Devil Hills,* ☎ *252/441–4460.* ⊙ *Tours Mar.–Labor Day.*

The **North Carolina Aquarium at Roanoke Island** (✉ Airport Rd., Manteo, ☎ 252/473–3493) sponsors summer boat tours of the estuary and the sound.

OUTDOOR ACTIVITIES AND SPORTS

Camping is permitted in four designated areas along the **Cape Hatteras National Seashore** (✉ Rte. 1, Box 675, Manteo 27954, ☎ 252/473–2111). These campgrounds can serve tents, trailers, and motor homes. All camping at **Cape Lookout National Seashore** (✉ 131 Charles St., Harkers Island 28531, ☎ 252/728–2250) is in the primitive style and is allowed from mid-April through mid-October. Be sure to take extralong tent stakes for sand, and don't forget insect repellent. All sites are available on a first-come, first-served basis, except Ocracoke, where reservations are accepted. For information about private campgrounds, contact the **Dare County Tourist Bureau** (☎ 252/473–2138 or 800/446–6262).

Fishing, whether surf casting or deep-sea, is wonderful here. You don't need a license for saltwater fishing. You can board a charter boat or head your own craft out of **Oregon Inlet Fishing Center** (☎ 252/441–6301 or 800/272–5199) or **Pirates Cove Yacht Club and Marina** (☎ 252/473–3906 or 800/367–4728) in Manteo. For fishing regulations, call the North Carolina Division of Marine Fisheries (☎ 252/726–7021).

With more than 1,500 known shipwrecks off the coast of the Outer Banks, **scuba-diving** opportunities are virtually unlimited. The USS *Monitor* is off-limits, however. The USS *Huron* Historic Shipwreck Preserve, which lies offshore between mile markers 11 and 12, is a popular diving site. Full-service dive shops include **Outer Banks Dive Center** (✉ 3917 S. Croatan Hwy., Nags Head, ☎ 252/449–8349).

Surfing and **windsurfing** are excellent on the Outer Banks. For lessons and rentals, including windsurfing and kayaking, contact **Kitty Hawk Water Sports** (✉ U.S. 158, MM 16.5, Nags Head, ☎ 252/441–6800 or 800/334–4777) or **Bert's Surf Shop** (✉ U.S. 158, MM 10, Nags Head, ☎ 252/441–1939; U.S. 158, MM 4, Kitty Hawk, ☎ 252/261–7584).

RADIO STATIONS

AM: WGAI 560, adult contemporary; WOBR 1530, vacation information, news. **FM:** WNHW 92, country; WOBR 95.3, adult contemporary; WVOD 99.1, beach, Top 40; WRSF 105.7, country.

VISITOR INFORMATION

Dare County Tourist Bureau (✉ 704 S. U.S. 64/264, Box 399, Manteo 27954, ☎ 252/473–2138 or 800/446–6262) operates two additional information centers. The **Aycock Brown Welcome Center** (✉ U.S. 158, MM 1.25, Kitty Hawk, ☎ 252/261–4644) is open daily 8:30–6:30 and offers extensive resources including maps and ferry schedules. The smaller **Hatteras Island Welcome Center** (☎ no phone) is right before Bodie Island, just south of the Whalebone Junction intersection of NC 12 near Cape Hatteras National Seashore's northern entrance. This center is open from Memorial Day to October 1, daily 9–5, and on weekends in April, May, and November. The bureau can also direct you to agencies that arrange housing rentals.

The **National Park Service's Group Headquarters,** at Fort Raleigh National Historic Site in Manteo (✉ Off U.S. 64/264), has a 24-hour general information line (☎ 252/473–2111) about Cape Hatteras National Seashore, or you can write the Superintendent (✉ Rte. 1, Box 675, Manteo, 27954).

The **National Park Service, Cape Lookout National Seashore** (✉ 131 Charles St., Harkers Island, 28531, ☎ 252/728–2250) has information about visiting Cape Lookout.

NEW BERN AND THE CENTRAL COAST

Craven County—home to New Bern; a good chunk of the 157,000-acre Croatan National Forest; and Cherry Point, the world's largest Marine Corps Air Station—is by turns genteel and historic, modern and commercialized, rural and wild. Golfers, boaters, and a growing number of retirees find the area a haven.

Neighboring Carteret County, with nearly 80 mi of ocean coastline, is known as the Central or "Crystal" Coast. It is composed of the south-facing beaches along the barrier island Bogue Banks (Atlantic Beach, Pine Knoll Shores, Indian Beach, Salter Path, and Emerald Isle), three mainland townships (Morehead City, Beaufort, and Newport), and a series of small, unincorporated "Down East" communities traversed by a portion of U.S. 70 that's a Scenic Byway.

New Bern

112 mi southeast of Raleigh.

The pace is quiet and slow in New Bern, the second oldest town in North Carolina. Settled in 1710 by Swiss and German colonists and named for Bern, Switzerland, the city has a heraldic Swiss black bear symbol that is everywhere. New Bern, the state capital from the period of English rule until immediately after the Revolution, is where North Carolina's first newspaper was printed and Pepsi Cola was invented. History is taken seriously here; there are more than 150 sites included in the National Register of Historic Places.

Sailors and sun seekers will enjoy the area, as the Neuse and Trent rivers are perfect for activities such as water-skiing and crabbing. The historic downtown area is filled with shops, many of them selling antiques. As in much of North Carolina, golf is a favorite New Bern pastime.

The reconstructed **Tryon Palace,** an elegant Georgian building, was the colonial capitol and the home of Royal Governor William Tryon during the 1770s. It was rebuilt according to architectural drawings of the original palace and furnished with English and American antiques according to Governor Tryon's inventory. An audiovisual orientation will prep you for a tour of the house led by costumed guides. In summer actors deliver monologues detailing a day in the life of the governor. Tours of the 18th-century formal gardens are self-guided. The stately **John Wright Stanly House** (circa 1783), the **Dixon-Stevenson House** (circa 1826), and **New Bern Academy** (circa 1809) are within or near the 13-acre Tryon Palace complex. ✉ *610 Pollock St.,* ☎ *252/514–4900.* *Palace and gardens $7, tour of all buildings and gardens $12.* ⊙ *Mon.–Sat. 9–5, Sun. 1–5.*

Dining and Lodging

$$–$$$$ ✕ **The Flame.** The considerate staff at this dark, woodsy steak house, with decor that's vaguely reminiscent of the Victorian era, helps make dinners special. Steak, lobster, grilled shrimp, and teriyaki chicken are all good bets. ✉ *2303 Neuse Blvd.,* ☎ *252/633–0262. AE, D, DC, MC, V. Closed Sun. No lunch.*

$ ✕ **Pollock Street Deli.** Good-size crowds gather in the tiny rooms of an authentic colonial house in the historic district and its sidewalk tables for a wide variety of classic deli treats or Sunday brunch. Service can be leisurely. ✉ *208 Pollock St.,* ☎ *252/637–2480. AE, MC, V. No dinner Sun.*

$$–$$$ ★ ✕ **Harvey Mansion Historic Inn.** The upstairs dining area at Beat and Carolyn Zuttel's inn consists of six small dining rooms with 11½-ft ceilings and decorative fireplaces. Guest rooms have four-poster beds, plush carpeting, and extraplush mattresses. The mansion, a striking 1797 house, also serves as an art gallery, and the cellar, with its exposed beams, is a low-key pub. ✉ *221 S. Front St., 28563,* ☎ *252/638–3205 or 800/638–3205,* FAX *252/638–3206. 3 rooms. Restaurant, pub, meeting rooms. AE, D, DC, MC, V.*

$$$ **Sheraton Grand.** At the confluence of the Neuse and Trent rivers, this Sheraton—with marina facilities—is actually two properties in one. A hotel has guest rooms overlooking the Trent River, and rooms at the inn have either waterfront or city views. An executive level contains suites. ✉ *100 Middle St., 28560,* ☎ *252/638–3585,* FAX *252/638–8112. 172 rooms. Restaurant, bar, in-room data ports, pool, business services, meeting rooms, airport shuttle. AE, D, DC, MC, V.*

$$ ★ **Harmony House Inn.** At this historic B&B convenient to all the attractions, guests sleep in spacious rooms that once lodged Yankee soldiers during the Civil War. Today, rooms are furnished with a mix of antiques and reproductions. The inn serves complimentary white and dessert wines in the evening. ✉ *215 Pollock St., 28560,* ☎ *252/636–3810 or 800/636–3113,* FAX *252/636–3810. 10 rooms. In-room data ports, business services, airport shuttle. AE, D, MC, V. BP.*

Morehead City

35 mi southeast of New Bern.

Morehead City is a fishing and boating center across Bogue Sound from the barrier island Bogue Banks. Popular family beaches on the island are **Atlantic Beach** and **Emerald Isle.** Among the more developed areas are these beach towns, as well as Pine Knoll Shores; all appeal to families.

The **North Carolina Aquarium at Pine Knoll Shores,** in a maritime forest on Bogue Banks, has a 2,000-gallon salt-marsh tank with live alligators, a loggerhead turtle nursery, and a shipwreck exhibit. ✉ *Salter Path Rd., MM 7, Atlantic Beach,* ☎ *252/247–4004.* *$3.* *Daily 9–5.*

Dining and Lodging

$$–$$$ ✕ **West Side Cafe.** A favorite among locals, this small café takes pride in serving fresh seafood any way you can eat it. Dinner is a delight here; sometimes there's live entertainment. ✉ *4370-A Arendell St.,* ☎ *252/240–0588. MC, V.*

$–$$$ ✕ **Sanitary Fish Market & Restaurant.** Sixty-one years ago, when the Sanitary was founded, many fish houses were ill-kept. The owners wanted to signal their difference. Clean, simple, and generous are bywords at this waterfront place where diners sit on wooden benches. It can get noisy (the restaurant seats 600), but guests from around the world gush about the food. ✉ *501 Evans St.,* ☎ *252/247–3111. D, MC, V.*

$$ **Windjammer Inn.** This is the place for people focused on one thing: easy access to the ocean. What you get here is straightforward—a comfortable oversize room with a private balcony and ocean view. The five-story, glass-enclosed elevator sets the inn apart from typical beach lodging. A two-night minimum stay is required on summer weekends. ✉ *Salter Path Rd. in Pine Knoll Shores, Atlantic Beach 28512,* ☎ *252/247–7123 or 800/233–6466,* FAX *252/247–0133. 46 rooms. In-room data ports, refrigerators, pool. AE, D, MC, V.*

$–$$ **Best Western Buccaneer.** The inn sits beside the Morehead Plaza shopping center, a 10-minute drive from Atlantic Beach. Rooms are attractive and comfortable. ✉ *2806 Arendell St., 28557,* ☎ *252/726–3115 or 800/682–4982,* FAX *252/726–3864. 91 rooms. Restaurant, pool, business services, meeting room. AE, D, DC, MC, V. BP.*

Beaufort

3 mi east of Morehead City.

Beaufort, a small seaport with a bustling boardwalk, brims with charm. The third-oldest town in North Carolina, it was named for Henry Somerset, Duke of Beaufort.

The **Beaufort Historic Site,** in the center of town, consists of restored buildings dating from 1767 to 1859, including the **Carteret County Courthouse** and the **Apothecary Shop and Doctor's Office.** Don't miss the **Old Burying Grounds** (1731). Here Otway Burns, a privateer in the War of 1812, is buried under his ship's cannon; a nine-year-old girl who died at sea is buried in a rum keg; and an English soldier saluting the king is buried upright in his grave. Tours on an English-style double-decker bus and guided walking tours depart from the visitor center. ✉ *130 Turner St.,* ☎ *252/728–5225.* *Bus tour $6, bus and walking tour $10.* *Visitor center Easter–Oct., Mon.–Sat. 9:30–5, Sun. 1:30–4; Nov.–Easter, Mon.–Sat. 10–4, Sun. 1:30–4.*

Beaufort's **North Carolina Maritime Museum** documents the state's seafaring and coastal history and includes an exhibit about the infamous pirate Blackbeard and the discovery of his flagship near Beaufort Inlet (☞ Close-Up: North Carolina's Pirates, *above*). The museum includes the **Watercrafts Center,** across the street, which gives boat-building classes. Its education staff also provides year-round programs, including trips to the marsh and barrier islands. ✉ *315 Front St.,* ☎ *252/728–7317.* *Museum Mon.–Sat. 8–5, Sun. 1–5; watercrafts center Tues.–Fri. 9–5, Sat. 10–5, Sun. 1–5.* *Free.*

Dining and Lodging

$–$$$ ✕ **Clawson's 1905 Restaurant and Pub.** Housed in what was a general store in the early 1900s, Clawson's serves hearty food such as ribs, steaks, pasta, and local seafood. It gets very crowded in summer, so arrive early for both lunch and dinner. The coffee bar opens at 7 AM. ✉ *425 Front St.,* ☎ *252/728–2133. D, MC, V.*

$$–$$$ ★ **Langdon House.** You'll sleep surrounded by antiques at this B&B built in 1733. The host provides everything from sightseeing suggestions to sumptuous Southern breakfasts and full beach baskets for picnics. ✉ *135 Craven St., 28516,* ☎ *252/728–5499,* FAX *252/728–1717. 4 rooms. No credit cards. BP.*

New Bern and the Central Coast A to Z

Arriving, Departing, and Getting Around

BY BOAT

The Intracoastal Waterway provides access to many Central Coast destinations, including Beaufort, Morehead City, and Emerald Isle. Beaufort has plentiful anchorage and more than 35 marinas, including the **Beaufort Town Docks** (☎ 252/728–2053) and the **Morehead City Yacht Basin** (☎ 252/726–6862).

New Bern can be reached via the Neuse River from Pamlico Sound. Several marinas are available here, including the **Sheraton Grand Marina** (☎ 252/638–3585). You can dock for the day (but not overnight) at the public docks of **Union Point Park** (☎ 252/636–4060).

The *North Carolina Coastal Boating Guide,* compiled by the **North Carolina Department of Transportation** (☎ 919/733–2522), has a comprehensive list of facilities for boaters.

BY BUS

Greyhound/Carolina Trailways serves Morehead City (✉ 105 N. 13th St., ☎ 252/726–3029 or 800/231–2222) and New Bern (✉ 504 Guion St., ☎ 252/633–3100 or 800/231–2222).

BY CAR

U.S. 70 connects New Bern, Morehead City, and Beaufort with points to the west, including Raleigh and I–95. East of Beaufort, U.S. 70 connects to NC 12, which continues on the Outer Banks via ferry. U.S. 17 leads north from New Bern toward the Albemarle region and south to Wilmington. NC 58 runs the length of the Bogue Banks, while NC 24 follows the mainland shore from Morehead City south to Swansboro.

BY FERRY

For information about the state-run ferry system, call the North Carolina Department of Transportation's **ferry information line** (☎ 800/293–3779).

BY PLANE

US Airways Express (☎ 800/428–4322) flies into **Craven County Regional Airport** (✉ U.S. 70, New Bern, ☎ 252/638–8591), where charter service and car rentals are available.

BY TAXI

A-1 Yellow Cab Co. (☎ 252/728–3483) serves Atlantic Beach, Beaufort, Morehead City, and the airport. **Safeway Taxi Co.** (☎ 252/633–2828) operates in the New Bern area.

Contacts and Resources

BEACHES

NC 58 passes through all of the beach communities on the Bogue Banks, and locations are noted by mile markers (MM). Points of public access along the shoreline are marked by orange-and-blue signs. Lifeguards monitor some of the beaches. Contact the Carteret County Tourism Development Bureau (☞ Visitor Information, *below*) for information. You can fish, swim, picnic, and hike at **Fort Macon State Park** (☎ 252/726–3775), outside Morehead City.

EMERGENCIES

Ambulance, police (☎ 911). **Coast Guard assistance** (☎ 252/247–4598). For emergencies, contact **Carteret General Hospital** (✉ 3500 Arendell St., ☎ 252/247–1540) in Morehead City or **Craven Regional Medical Center** in New Bern (✉ 2300 Neuse Blvd., ☎ 252/633–8111).

OUTDOOR ACTIVITIES AND SPORTS

The Atlantic Beach King Mackerel Tournament is held on the Crystal Coast in September, and one of the largest and oldest **sportfishing** contests, the Big Rock Blue Marlin Tournament, is held in various locations each June. Fishing piers are found mostly on Bogue Banks and are closed during the winter. Dozens of charter boats operate year-round. In New Bern, bass fishing tournaments are popular, as is **crabbing** in the Neuse River. For information on sportfishing and crabbing, contact the Craven County Convention and Visitors Bureau (☞ Visitor Information, *below*).

Golf courses are abundant, and locals prefer to play in the spring and fall months, when it's cooler. For a list of courses and help with reservations, contact **Crystal Coast Regional Golf Association** (✉ 801 Arendell St., Box 1193, Morehead City 28557, ☎ 888/991–7529). Two notable courses are the par-72, 18-hole course at **Carolina Pines Gold and Country Club** (✉ 390 Carolina Pines Blvd., off NC 70, between New Bern and Havelock, ☎ 252/444–1000) and the par-72, 18-hole course designed by Rees Jones at the **Emerald Golf Club** (✉ 5000 Clubhouse Dr., on NC 70 Bypass, ☎ 252/633–4440).

Morehead City is consistently rated as a top **scuba diving** destination in North America. Two popular wreck sites are the *Schurz,* sunk in World War I, and the *Papoose,* a World War II tanker inhabited by docile sand sharks. **Olympus Dive Center** (✉ 713 Shephard St., Morehead City, ☎ 252/726–9432) has five dive boats and offers full- and half-day charters, equipment rental, and lessons.

RADIO STATIONS

AM: WMBL 740, easy listening. **FM:** WRHT 96.3, Top 40; WMGV 103.3, adult contemporary; WTEB 89.3, National Public Radio.

VISITOR INFORMATION

The **Carteret County Tourism Development Bureau** operates two visitors centers, one in Morehead City (✉ 3409 Arendell St., 28557, ☎ 800/786–6962) and one on NC 58 just north of the Cameron Langston Bridge to Emerald Isle (✉ 263 NC 58, Swansboro 28584, ☎ 252/393–3100). **Craven County Convention and Visitors Bureau** (✉ 314 S. Front St., New Bern 28560, ☎ 252/637–9400 or 800/437–5767) is open weekdays 8:30–5, Saturday 9–5, and Sunday 10–4.

WILMINGTON AND THE CAPE FEAR COAST

Wilmington and the Cape Fear Coast area, between the Cape Fear River and the Atlantic Ocean near the south end of the North Carolina coast, are simultaneously a beach resort and a shipping and trading center. Artists, golfers, history buffs, naturalists, and shoppers will all find something of interest here. The old seaport town of Wilmington has much to celebrate these days, including a once-decayed downtown that has been transformed with new places to shop and dine. On the surrounding Cape Fear Coast, you can tour old plantation houses and azalea gardens, study sea life at the state aquarium, or bask in the sun at nearby beaches.

Wilmington

130 mi south of Raleigh.

The city's long history, including its part in the American Revolution and its role as the main port of the Confederacy, is revealed in sights downtown and in the surrounding area. Chandler's Wharf, the Cotton Exchange, and Water Street Market are old buildings now used as shopping and entertainment centers. *Henrietta II,* a paddle wheeler similar to those that plied the waters of the Cape Fear River, has been put into service as a tourist vessel. Wilmington, also a college town, has special annual events such as the Azalea Festival, North Carolina Jazz Festival, Christmas candlelight tours, and fishing tournaments.

At the **USS *North Carolina* Battleship Memorial** you can tour a ship that participated in every major naval offensive in the Pacific during World War II. The self-guided tour takes about two hours, and a 10-minute film is shown throughout the day. Narrated tours on cassette can be rented. Warning: a climb down into the ship's interior is not for the claustrophobic. The ship can be reached by car or by taking the river taxi from Riverfront Park, Memorial Day through Labor Day, for a cost of $2. ✉ *Junction of U.S. 74/76 and U.S. 17 and 421, west bank of Cape Fear River,* ☎ *910/251–5797.* 🎫 *$8.* ⏲ *Mid-May–mid-Sept., daily 8–8; mid-Sept.–mid-May, daily 8–5.*

The **Cotton Exchange,** a shopping-dining complex, is in eight restored buildings on the Cape Fear River that have flourished as a trading center since pre–Civil War days. ✉ *321 N. Front St.,* ☎ *910/343–9896.* ⏲ *Mon.–Sat. 10–5:30; some stores also evenings and Sun. 1–5.*

The **Cape Fear Museum** traces the natural, cultural, and social history of the lower Cape Fear region from its beginnings to the present. One exhibit follows the youth of one of Wilmington's most famous native sons, basketball superstar Michael Jordan. ✉ *814 Market St.,* ☎ *910/341–7413.* 🎫 *$4.* ⏲ *Labor Day–Memorial Day, Tues.–Sat. 9–5, Sun. 2–5; Memorial Day–Labor Day, daily 9–5.*

Built in 1770 on the foundations of a jail, the **Burgwin-Wright Museum House** is a fine restoration of a colonial gentleman's town house and includes seven distinct period gardens. In April 1781 General Cornwallis used the house as his headquarters. ✉ *224 Market St.,* ☎ *910/762–0570.* 🎫 *$5.* ⏲ *Tues.–Sat. 10–3:30.*

St. John's Museum of Art is known for its 13 prints by Mary Cassatt, as well as for its works by North Carolina artists. The museum is housed in three buildings, including the 1804 Masonic Lodge Building, the oldest such lodge in the state. There is also a sculpture garden. ✉ *114 Orange St.,* ☎ *910/763–0281.* 🎫 *$3.* ⏲ *Tues.–Sat. 10–5, Sun. noon–4.*

The **Zebulon Latimer House,** built in 1852 in the Italianate style, is a reminder of opulent antebellum living. The Lower Cape Fear Historical Society is based here; it offers guided walking tours of the downtown historic district that depart from the house on Wednesday and Saturday mornings at 10. ✉ *126 S. 3rd St.,* ☎ *910/762–0492.* 🎫 *$5.* ⏲ *Weekdays 10–3:30, weekends noon–5.*

Chandler's Wharf (✉ 225 S. Water St.) contains shops and some seafood restaurants such as Elijah's. It's a great place to conclude a tour of downtown Wilmington.

Greenfield Lake and Gardens offers picnic spots and canoe and paddleboat rentals on a 180-acre lake bordered by cypress trees laden with Spanish moss. In April, the area is ablaze with azaleas. ✉ *S. 3rd St. (U.S. 421), 2½ mi south of downtown,* ☎ *910/763–9371.* 🎫 *Free.* ⏲ *Daily.*

At **Poplar Grove Historic Plantation,** an 1850 Greek Revival manor house 9 mi northeast of downtown, you can tour the manor house and outbuildings, see crafts demonstrations, shop in the country store, and pet the farm animals. ✉ *10200 U.S. 17, Scotts Hill,* ☎ *910/686–9989.* 🎫 *Guided tours $7.* ⏲ *Feb.–Dec., Mon.–Sat. 9–5, Sun. noon–5.*

The **New Hanover County Arboretum** has 33 exhibits, including magnolia and patio gardens, 100 varieties of shade-loving camellias, a salt-spray garden, and a children's garden with a maze. ✉ *6206 Oleander Dr.,* ☎ *910/452–6393.* 🎫 *Free.* ⏲ *Daily sunrise–sunset.*

OFF THE BEATEN PATH

MOORE'S CREEK NATIONAL BATTLEFIELD – Military history buffs will appreciate this site, where American patriots defeated the Loyalists in 1776. ✉ *200 Moores Creek Rd., Currie, 20 mi northwest of Wilmington on Rte. 210,* ☎ *910/283–5591.* *Free.* *Daily 8–5.*

Dining and Lodging

$$–$$$$ ✕ **Pilot House.** This Chandler's Wharf restaurant is known for its seafood, pastas, fresh vegetables, and Carolina seafood bisque. You can dine indoors at tables with linen tablecloths secured by vases of fresh flowers or outdoors overlooking the Cape Fear River. Sunday brunch, which starts at 11:30, is popular. ✉ *2 Ann St.,* ☎ *910/343–0200. AE, D, DC, MC, V.*

$$–$$$ ✕ **Water Street Restaurant and Sidewalk Café.** A restored, two-story brick waterfront warehouse dating from 1835 holds an outdoor café and restaurant that serves up Greek, Mexican, Middle Eastern, and other ethnic cooking. Seafood chowder is made daily on the premises. ✉ *5 Water St.,* ☎ *910/343–0042. AE, MC, V.*

$ ✕ **Mollye's.** Some people may recognize this little downtown restaurant from the *Dawson's Creek* television show. It specializes in salads, soups, roll-ups, and fruit dishes. The wine bar is open nightly and there's live music on weekends. ✉ *118 Princess St.,* ☎ *910/772–9989. D, MC, V.*

$$$–$$$$ **Inn at St. Thomas Court.** Many of the clients here are businesspeople and members of the entertainment community in the area to make movies or TV shows. In the heart of the historic district, former commercial buildings, an antebellum home, and a convent have been meticulously transformed into luxurious suites, each decorated in a different theme—classic movies, nautical heritage, and country French, for example. It's best for older children. ✉ *101 S. 2nd St., 28401,* ☎ *910/343–1800 or 800/525–0909,* FAX *910/251–1149. 40 suites. In-room data ports, in-room VCRs, business services, meeting rooms. AE, D, DC, MC, V. CP.*

$$$ **Hilton-Riverside.** Overlooking the Cape Fear River on one side and the city on the other, the spacious Hilton is one of the most convenient places to stay in town. The lobby is plush; guest rooms are traditional, with dark woods and autumn colors. ✉ *301 N. Water St., 28401,* ☎ *910/763–5900 or 800/445–8667,* FAX *910/763–0038. 262 rooms, 11 suites. Restaurant, bar, in-room data ports, pool, dock, business services, meeting rooms, airport shuttle. AE, D, DC, MC, V.*

$$ **Catherine's Inn.** This two-story Italianate home, built in 1883 in what is now a historic district overlooking the Cape Fear River, is a B&B with hardwood floors, a sunken garden, four-poster and canopy beds, and private phones in each room. Many items were collected by the innkeepers over the years. This is the only inn in the area with a direct view of the river. ✉ *410 S. Front St., 28401,* ☎ *910/251–0863 or 800/476–0723,* FAX *910/772–9550. 5 rooms. MC, V. BP.*

$$ **Hampton Inn.** It's not luxurious, but this moderately priced chain motel is only 3 mi from downtown and 6 mi from Wrightsville Beach. It offers such extras as in-room movies and free local calls. ✉ *5107 Market St., 28403,* ☎ *910/395–5045 or 800/426–7866,* FAX *910/799–1974. 118 rooms. In-room data ports, pool, exercise room, business services, meeting room. AE, D, DC, MC, V. CP.*

Nightlife and the Arts

THE ARTS

The city has its own symphony orchestra, oratorio society, civic ballet, and concert association; and the North Carolina Symphony makes four appearances here each year. For information, contact the Cape Fear Coast Convention and Visitors Bureau (☞ Visitor Information *in* Wilmington and the Cape Fear Coast A to Z, *below*). **Thalian Hall Center for the Performing Arts** (✉ 310 Chestnut St., ☎ 910/343–3664 or 800/523–2820), an opera house built between 1855 and 1858 and restored to its former grandeur, hosts more than 250 theater, dance, and musical performances each year. Theatrical productions are staged by the Thalian Association, Opera House Productions, and Tapestry Players. The annual **Wilmington Jazz Festival,** held in February, and the **Blues Festival,** in August, draw crowds.

NIGHTLIFE

A favorite waterfront haunt is the **Ice House Beer Garden** (✉ 115 S. Water St., ☎ 910/251–1158 or 910/763–2084), an indoor and outdoor bar with live rhythm and blues. **Rockit's Rhythm & Sports Grille** (✉ 5025 Market St., ☎ 910/791–2001) is known for its music (rock, blues, beach). It's also a great place to play pool or watch a game.

Outdoor Activities and Sports

There are approximately 40 public-access golf courses in the Greater Wilmington area. **Beau Rivage Plantation Golf Club** (✉ 6230 Carolina Beach Rd., ☎ 910/395–1300) is a par-72 course in a natural links setting. The **Cape Golf & Racquet Club** (✉ 535 The Cape Blvd., ☎ 910/799–3110) is a par-72 resort course with a driving range.

South Brunswick County, about 30–40 mi from Wilmington on the coast, is golf heaven, especially the areas around Calabash, Sunset Beach, and Ocean Isle. **Lockwood Folly Golf Links** (✉ 100 Club House Dr., Holden Beach, ☎ 910/842–5666 or 800/443–7891) is a highly rated par-72 resort course. **Marsh Harbour Golf Links** (✉ NC 179, Calabash, ☎ 910/579–3161 or 800/552–2660) has a highly-rated par-71 course, offering views of marsh and marina activity. **Oyster Bay Golf Links** (✉ NC 179, Sunset Beach, ☎ 910/579–3528 or 800/552–2660) is known for its oyster-shell hazards, gator sightings, and par 70. **Sea Trail Plantation** (✉ 211 Clubhouse Rd., Sunset Beach, ☎ 910/579–4350 or 800/624–6601) has three courses designed by Dan Maples, Rees Jones, and Willard Byrd, respectively, with pars from 54 to 72.

Shopping

The city has fun shopping at Chandler's Wharf, the Cotton Exchange, and the Water Street Market; it also has shops in the downtown historic district, as well as shopping malls and outlets.

Wrightsville Beach

12 mi east of Wilmington.

Wrightsville Beach is a small, quiet island community that's very family oriented. It has a number of fine restaurants, and beaches good for swimming, boating, and surfing.

Dining and Lodging

$$$–$$$$ ✕ **Ocean Terrace Restaurant.** Part of the Blockade Runner Resort (☞ *below*), this restaurant attracts crowds with its weekend buffets and jazz brunch on Sunday. Regular dishes include grilled New York strip steak with bourbon-shallot butter; almond-breaded flounder with shrimp; and chicken breast with toasted pecans, pears, and apples. ✉ *Blockade Runner Resort Hotel and Conference Center, 275 Waynick Blvd.,* ☎ *910/256–2251 or 800/541–1161. Reservations essential. AE, D, DC, MC, V.*

$$–$$$ ✕ **Oceanic Restaurant and Grill.** You'll have a panoramic view of the Atlantic for miles around—a great backdrop for the fresh seafood, steaks, and chicken. Dinner on the pier at sunset is a real treat. ✉ *703 S. Lumina St.,* ☎ *910/256–5551. AE, MC, V.*

$$$$ **Blockade Runner Resort Hotel and Conference Center.** This oceanside complex is widely known for its Ocean Terrace Restaurant (☞ *above*) and supervised summer children's programs. Guest rooms, done in bright colors, overlook either the Intracoastal Waterway or, for a higher price, the ocean. Service can be uneven, especially at the height of the season, but the hotel's beachfront location and guaranteed parking keep them coming back. ✉ *275 Waynick Blvd., 28480,* ☎ *910/256–2251 or 800/541–1161,* FAX *910/256–5502. 147 rooms, 3 suites. Restaurant, bar, indoor-outdoor pool, exercise room, beach, boating, bicycles, business services, meeting rooms, airport shuttle. AE, D, DC, MC, V.*

Kure Beach

17 mi south of Wilmington.

Kure Beach is a resort community that's a bit livelier than Wrightsville Beach (☞ *above*) as it's next to Carolina Beach, which has amusement parks and a boardwalk with bars. Historic site Fort Fisher and the North Carolina Aquarium provide further interest. In some places, twisted live oaks still grow behind the dunes. The community has miles of beaches; public access points are marked by orange-and-blue signs.

Fort Fisher State Historic Site marks the largest and one of the most important earthworks fortifications in the South during the Civil War. A reconstructed battery and Civil War relics and artifacts from sunken blockade-runners are on site. The fort is part of **Fort Fisher Recreation Area,** with 4 mi of undeveloped beach. ✉ *U.S. 421,* ☎ *910/458–5538.* *Free.* *Apr.–Oct., Mon.–Sat. 9–5, Sun. 1–5; Nov.–Mar., Tues.–Sat. 10–4, Sun. 1–4.*

Lodging

$$$–$$$$ **Docksider Inn.** The nautical theme is no surprise given that this is a waterfront hotel. The inn is furnished in light-color beach-type furniture. Owners Kip and Maureen Darling have another property a block away on Atlantic Avenue. The five contemporary luxury suites of Darlings by the Sea are for adults only. Each has an expansive ocean view, custom-made drapes, bed skirting, and cabinetry. There are whirlpools for two and wet bars. ✉ *202 Fort Fisher Blvd. (U.S. 421), 28449,* ☎ *910/458–4200 or 800/383–8111,* FAX *910/458–6468. 34 rooms. Pool, beach. AE, D, MC, V.*

Southport

30 mi south of Wilmington.

This small town, which sits quietly at the mouth of the Cape Fear River, is listed on the National Register of Historic Places. An increasingly desirable retirement spot, Southport retains its village charm and character. Stately and distinctive homes, antiques stores, gift shops, and restaurants line streets that veer to accommodate ancient oak trees. The town, portrayed in Robert Ruark's novel *The Old Man and the Boy,* is ideal for walking; it's also popular with moviemakers—*Crimes of the Heart* was filmed here.

If you're approaching the town from Fort Fisher and NC 421, the **Southport–Fort Fisher Ferry,** a state-operated car ferry, provides a river ride between Old Federal Point at the tip of the spit and the mainland. The Old Baldy lighthouse on Bald Head Island is seen en route. It's best to arrive 30 minutes prior to ferry departure, as it's first-come, first-served. ☎ *910/458–3329.* *$3 per car.* *Ferries run mid-Mar.–mid-*

Nov., daily every 45 mins 6:15 AM–9:15 PM; mid-Nov.–mid-Mar., daily every 1½ hrs 6:15 AM–4:45 PM.

Lodging

$$–$$$ **Bald Head Island Resort.** Reached by ferry from Southport, this private, self-contained, car-less community complete with grocery store and restaurants has bleached-wood villas and shingle cottages. You can explore the semitropical island on foot, by bicycle, or in a golf cart. Pastimes are watching the loggerhead turtles and taking a guided tour through the maritime forest. Accommodations include rental condos, villas, cottages, and a privately owned bed-and-breakfast; a two-night minimum stay is required. The ferry (☎ 910/457–5003) costs $15 per person round-trip and runs on the hour, 8–6 (except noon on weekdays), from Southport. Advance reservations are necessary for both the ferry and resort. ✉ *Bald Head Island, 28461,* ☎ *910/457–5000 or 800/234–1666,* FAX *910/457–9232. 195 condos, villas, and cottages; 15 rooms in B&B. 3 restaurants, pool, 18-hole golf course, 4 tennis courts, croquet, boating, fishing. AE, DC, MC, V.*

Outdoor Activities and Sports

For golf, the par-72 **Gauntlet at St. James Plantation** (✉ NC 211, ☎ 910/253–3008 or 800/247–4806) lives up to its reputation as a challenging course.

Winnabow

12 mi north of Southport, 18 mi south of Wilmington.

Winnabow is more of a crossroads than a town to visit; the draws here are gardens and a historic site, both off NC 133 near the Cape Fear ★ River. The house at **Orton Plantation Gardens** is not open to the public, but the 20 acres of beautiful, comprehensive gardens are great for strolling. The former rice plantation holds magnolias, ancient oaks, and all kinds of ornamental plants; the grounds are a refuge for waterfowl. ✉ *9149 Orton Rd. SE, off NC 133,* ☎ *910/371–6851.* *$8.* ⏲ *Mar.–Aug., daily 8–6; Sept.–Nov., daily 10–5.*

At **Brunswick Town State Historic Site** you can explore the excavations of a colonial town; see Fort Anderson, a Civil War earthworks fort; and have a picnic. Special events include reenactments of Civil War encampments. ✉ *8884 St. Phillips Rd., off NC 133,* ☎ *910/371–6613.* *Free.* ⏲ *Apr.–Oct., Mon.–Sat. 9–5, Sun. 1–5; Nov.–Mar., Tues.–Sat. 10–4, Sun. 1–4.*

Wilmington and the Cape Fear Coast A to Z

Arriving, Departing, and Getting Around

BY BOAT

A number of hotels provide docking facilities for guests. The Wilmington area has **public marinas** at **Carolina Beach State Park** (☎ 910/458–7770) and **Wrightsville Beach** (☎ 910/256–6666). Public boat access is also offered at Atlantic Marina, Masonboro Boat Yard and Marina, Seapath Transient Dock, and Wrightsville Gulf Terminal. The *North Carolina Coastal Boating Guide,* compiled by the **North Carolina Department of Transportation** (☎ 919/733–2522), has a comprehensive list of marinas and facilities for boaters. A state-run car ferry connects Fort Fisher with Southport on the coast.

BY BUS

Greyhound/Carolina Trailways serves the Union Bus terminal (✉ 201 Harnett St., ☎ 910/762–6625 or 800/231–2222). The **Wilmington**

Transit Authority (☏ 910/343–0106) provides service Monday–Saturday for 75¢ a ride.

BY CAR

Wilmington is linked to Raleigh by I–40 and to New Bern by U.S. 17.

BY PLANE

US Airways and Atlantic Southeast Airlines serve the **Wilmington International Airport** (✉ 1740 Airport Blvd., ☏ 910/341–4125). For airline telephone numbers, *see* Air Travel *in* Smart Travel Tips A to Z.

Contacts and Resources

BEACHES

Three beaches—Wrightsville, Carolina, and Kure—are within a short drive from Wilmington, and miles and miles of sand stretch northward to the Outer Banks and southward to South Carolina. The beaches offer activities from fishing to sunbathing to scuba diving, and the towns here have a choice of accommodations. Approximately 100 points of public access along the shoreline are marked by orange-and-blue signs. Some of the smaller beaches have lifeguards on duty, and many are accessible to people with disabilities. Some fishing piers are open to the public. Contact the Cape Fear Coast Convention and Visitors Bureau (☞ Visitor Information, *below*) for more information. Camping, fishing, swimming, and picnicking are permitted at **Carolina Beach State Park** (☏ 910/458–8206, 910/458–7770 marina).

EMERGENCIES

Ambulance, police (☏ 911). **Coast Guard assistance** (☏ 910/343–4881). For emergency medical attention, contact the **Cape Fear Memorial Hospital** (✉ 5301 Wrightsville Ave., ☏ 910/452–8100) or the **New Hanover Regional Medical Center** (✉ 2131 S. 17th St., ☏ 910/343–7000), a regional trauma center.

GUIDED TOURS

From April through December, **Cape Fear Riverboats, Inc.** (✉ docked at the Hilton in downtown Wilmington, ☏ 910/343–1611 or 800/676–0162) runs a variety of cruises aboard a stern-wheel riverboat, the *Henrietta II,* that departs from Riverfront Park. Cost is $9–$32. **Cape Fear Tours** (✉ 8112 Sidbury Rd., Wilmington, ☏ 910/686–7744) gives walking and driving tours of the Wilmington Historic District, mansions, and the beaches. Individual tours are $20 per hour.

OUTDOOR ACTIVITIES AND SPORTS

There's surf **fishing** on the piers that dot the coast, and charter boats are available for off-shore fishing. Four major tournaments, for substantial prize money, are held each year—the Cape Fear Marlin Tournament, the Wrightsville Beach King Mackerel Tournament, the East Coast Open King Mackerel Tournament, and the U.S. Open King Mackerel Tournament. For information, contact the Cape Fear Coast Convention and Visitors Bureau (☞ Visitor Information, *below*).

Some top **golf** choices are listed in this section, but for more information contact the Cape Fear Coast Convention and Visitors Bureau (☞ Visitor Information, *below*) or the **South Brunswick Islands Chamber of Commerce** (✉ 4948 Main St., Box 1380, Shalotte 28459, ☏ 910/754–6644).

Wrecks such as the World War II tanker *John D. Gill* make for exciting **scuba diving** off the coast. **Aquatic Safaris** (✉ 5751–4 Oleander Dr., Wilmington, ☏ 910/392–4386) rents equipment and leads trips.

Surfing and **board sailing** are popular at area beaches, and rentals are available at shops in Wilmington, Wrightsville Beach, and Carolina Beach.

RADIO STATIONS

AM: WAAV 980, news, talk; WBMS 1340, news, talk, sports. **FM:** WHQR 91.3, National Public Radio; WGNI 102.7, adult contemporary and Top 40; WWQQ 101.3, country; WSFM 107.5, classic rock.

VISITOR INFORMATION

Cape Fear Coast Convention and Visitors Bureau (✉ 24 N. 3rd St., Wilmington 28401, ☎ 910/341–4030 or 800/222–4757) is in the Old Courthouse downtown and has an information center on the boardwalk along the Cape Fear River open weekdays 8:30–5, Saturday 9–4, Sunday 1–4.

THE MOUNTAINS

Cherokee, Asheville, and the High Country

The majestic peaks, meadows, and valleys of the Appalachian, Blue Ridge, and Smoky mountains characterize the western corner of the state, which is divided into three distinct regions: the southern mountains, home to the Cherokee reservation; the northern mountains, known as the High Country (Blowing Rock, Boone, Banner Elk); and the central mountains, anchored by Asheville, for decades a retreat for the wealthy and famous. National parks, national forests, handmade-crafts centers, and the Blue Ridge Parkway are the area's main draws, providing prime opportunities for shopping, skiing, hiking, bicycling, camping, fishing, canoeing, or just taking in the views.

At the southern terminus of the Blue Ridge Parkway and the North Carolina entrance to the Great Smoky Mountains lies the homeland of the Eastern Band of the Cherokee Indians. Through a blending of museums, dramas, assorted outdoor attractions, and everyday living, the Cherokee attempt to explain what's precious in their Land of the Blue Mist.

The biggest city in the mountains, Asheville has a lovely setting, a choice of hotels and restaurants, and a thriving arts community. The city's revitalized downtown has good shopping, galleries, museums, restaurants, and nightlife.

Picture-book towns such as Boone, Blowing Rock, and Banner Elk have boomed in the 30 years since the introduction of snowmaking equipment. Luxury resorts now dot the valleys and mountaintops, and you can take advantage of the many crafts shops, music festivals, and theater offerings. The passing of each season is a visual event here, and autumn is the star.

Cherokee

165 mi west of Charlotte, 50 mi west of Asheville.

The 56,000-acre Cherokee Indian Reservation is known as the Qualla Boundary, and the town of Cherokee is its capital. Truth be told, there are two Cherokees. There's the side with sometimes tacky pop culture, designed to appeal to mass numbers of tourists, many of whom are visiting nearby Great Smoky Mountains National Park. Another Cherokee explores the rich heritage of the tribe's Eastern Band. Though now relatively small in number—tribal enrollment is 11,000—these people and their ancestors have been responsible for keeping alive the Cherokee culture. They are the descendants of those who hid in the Great

Smoky Mountains to avoid the forced removal of the Cherokee Nation to Oklahoma in the 19th century, known as the Trail of Tears. They are survivors, extremely attached to the hiking, swimming, trout fishing, and natural beauty of their ancestral homeland.

The **Museum of the Cherokee Indian,** with displays and artifacts that cover 10,000 years, is one of the best Native American museums in the United States. Computer-generated images, lasers, specialty lighting, and sound effects help re-create events in the history of the Cherokee: children stop to play a butter bean game while adults shiver along the snowy Trail of Tears. The museum has an art gallery and an outdoor living exhibit of Cherokee life in the 15th century. ✉ *U.S. 441 at Drama Rd.,* ☎ *828/497–3481.* 🎫 *$6.* ⏲ *June–Aug., Mon.–Sat. 9–8, Sun. 9–5; Sept.–May, daily 9–5.*

The **Qualla Arts and Crafts Mutual,** across the street from the Museum of the Cherokee Indian, is a cooperative that displays and sells items created by 300 Cherokee craftspeople. The store also has a large section of baskets, masks, and wood carvings. ✉ *U.S. 441 at Drama Rd.,* ☎ *828/497–3103.* ⏲ *June–Aug., daily 8–8; Sept.–Oct., daily 8–6; Nov.–May, daily 8–4:30.*

At the historically accurate, re-created **Oconaluftee Indian Village,** guides in native costumes will lead you through a village of 225 years ago while others demonstrate traditional skills such as weaving, pottery, canoe construction, and hunting techniques. ✉ *U.S. 441 at Drama Rd.,* ☎ *828/497–2315.* 🎫 *$10.* ⏲ *May 15–Oct. 25, daily 9–5:30.*

Every mountain county has significant deposits of gems and minerals, and at the **Smoky Mountain Gold and Ruby Mine,** on the Qualla Boundary, you can search for gems such as aquamarines. Children love panning precisely because it can be wet and messy. Here they're guaranteed a find. Gem ore can be purchased, too: gold ore costs $5 per bag. ✉ *U.S. 441N,* ☎ *828/497–6574.* 🎫 *$4–$10, depending on the gems.* ⏲ *Mar., weekends 9–6; Apr.–Nov., daily 10–9.*

Dining and Lodging

$–$$ ✕ **Nantahala Village Restaurant.** This roomy rock-and-cedar restaurant with front-porch rocking chairs is about 10 mi southwest of Cherokee and is a local favorite. The food isn't fancy, but choices such as trout, chicken, and country ham are good and filling. Sunday brunch has some surprises: *huevos rancheros* (tortilla with fried eggs and salsa) and eggs Benedict, to name a couple. ✉ *9400 U.S. 19W, Bryson City,* ☎ *828/488–9616 or 800/438–1507. D, MC, V. Closed Dec.–Mar.*

$$$–$$$$ ✕🏨 **Hemlock Inn.** Even if you're not a guest at the inn, which is built on a small mountain that overlooks three valleys, you can make a reservation for dinner ($$) Monday through Saturday, and lunch on Sunday. The one-price, all-you-can-eat meals are prepared with regional foods, including locally grown fruits and vegetables and mountain honey. Each cozy room is decorated with antiques and area crafts. ✉ *Galbraith Creek Rd., 1 mi north of U.S. 19W, Bryson City 28713,* ☎ *828/488–2885,* FAX *828/488–8985. 29 rooms. Restaurant, recreation room. D, MC, V. Closed Nov.–mid-Apr. MAP.*

$–$$ 🏨 **Holiday Inn Cherokee.** Guest rooms are standard chain fare, but the staff at this well-equipped, full-service facility is very friendly. The Chestnut Tree restaurant has dinner buffets that are veritable groaning boards, and the native crafts shop, the Hunting Ground, with works by local artists, is a nice touch. ✉ *U.S. 19S, 28719,* ☎ *828/497–9181 or 800/465–4329,* FAX *828/497–5973. 150 rooms, 4 suites. Restaurant, indoor pool, outdoor pool, wading pool, sauna, recreation room, playground, meeting room. AE, D, DC, MC, V.*

Nightlife and the Arts

THE ARTS

Unto These Hills Outdoor Drama (✉ Mountainside Theater on Drama Rd., off U.S. 441N, ☎ 828/497–2111) is a colorful and well-staged history of the Cherokee from the time of Spanish explorer Hernando de Soto's visit in 1540 to the infamous Trail of Tears. It runs from mid-June to mid-August, and tickets are $11–$14.

NIGHTLIFE

The 175,000-square-ft **Harrah's Cherokee Casino** (✉ U.S. 19 off U.S. 441 N, ☎ 828/497–7777) has action 24 hours a day. Its 2,400 gaming machines, video poker, video blackjack, and video craps make it the largest casino in a 500-mi radius. The complex also has a 1,500-seat concert hall, three restaurants, and a child-care area.

Outdoor Activities and Sports

FISHING

There are 30 mi of regularly stocked trout streams on the **Cherokee Indian Reservation.** To fish in tribal water, you need a tribal fishing permit, available at nearly two dozen reservation businesses. The $7 permit is valid for one day. For information, call ☎ 828/497–5201 or 800/438–1601.

HIKING

In the downtown area you can cross the Oconaluftee River on a footbridge to **Oconaluftee Islands Park & Trail** (✉ across from Cherokee Elementary School on U.S. 441) and walk a trail around the perimeter of the Island Park, which also has picnic facilities. The flat 1½-mi **Oconaluftee River Trail** begins at the Great Smoky Mountains National Park entrance sign on U.S. 441 (near the entrance to the Blue Ridge Parkway) and ends at the Mountain Farm Museum/Park Visitor Center. A five-minute hike from the Mingo Falls Campground area (✉ Big Cove Rd. about 4 mi north of Acquoni Rd.) will reward you with a view of the 200-ft-high **Mingo Falls.**

Great Smoky Mountains National Park

3 mi north of Cherokee.

★ Natural assets help make the **Great Smoky Mountains National Park** the most visited national park in the United States. No mountains in the world are older, and no place on earth can claim such biological diversity: more than 1,600 types of wildflowers and more than 140 species of trees flourish in this wildlife sanctuary. The Appalachian Trail runs along the crest of the mountains through the park, the largest protected land area east of the Rocky Mountains. Within its 800 square mi (276,000 acres lie in North Carolina, 244,000 in Tennessee) are 800 mi of trails, more than 600 mi of trout streams, and some 200,000 acres of virgin forest.

The Smokies are so named because of the frequently occurring smoke-like blue mist that hovers in the air and can get so dense as to obscure mountaintops. In actuality, the "smoke" occurs when vegetation releases water vapor and natural oils produced by plants into the air. Along the twists and turns of the Blue Ridge Parkway are scores of scenic overlooks, and many byways lead to areas that grip the imagination.

U.S. Highway 441 is the only road that passes all the way through the park. Fishing permits and visitor information are available at ranger stations at the north and south entrances. Depending on your location, the Oconoluftee Visitors Center (☎ 828/497–1900) is the terminus of the Blue Ridge Parkway or its starting point. Adjacent to the visitor center, at mile marker 469.1, is **Mountain Farm Museum,** a re-created pioneer homestead. ✉ *107 Park Headquarters Rd., Gatlinburg, TN 37738,* ☎ *423/436–5615.* *Free.*

Dillsboro

13 mi southeast of Cherokee on U.S. 441.

The tiny town of Dillsboro in Jackson County has a big reputation for good shopping, particularly if you favor folk art and crafts. The popular train rides of the **Great Smoky Mountains Railway** include six regular excursions and six special trips on diesel-electric or steam locomotives. Open-sided cars or cabooses are ideal for picture taking as the mountain scenery glides by. There's a train museum, too. ✉ *119 Front St.,* ☎ *828/586–8811 or 800/872–4681.* *$21–$64; some rides include a meal.* *Mar.–Dec.; call for schedule.*

Franklin

32 mi south of Cherokee on U.S. 441.

Franklin, the Macon County seat, lies at the convergence of U.S. 441, U.S. 64, and NC 28. In the 1500s, Hernando de Soto came in search of gold and overlooked the wealth of gemstones for which this area is so famous. A dozen gem mines and nearly as many gem stores are nearby.

The **Scottish Tartans Museum** has the official registry of all publicly known tartans and is the American extension of the Scottish Tartans Society. Scottish heritage can be traced in the research library. ✉ *86 E. Main St.,* ☎ *828/524–7472.* *$1.* *Mon.–Sat. 10–5, Sun. 1–5.*

Waynesville

17 mi east of Cherokee on U.S. 19.

This is where the Blue Ridge Parkway meets the Great Smokies. Pretty, arty Waynesville is the seat of Haywood County. About 40% of the county is occupied by the Great Smoky Mountains National Park, Pisgah National Forest, and the Harmon Den Wildlife Refuge.

The **Museum of North Carolina Handicrafts,** in the Shelton House (circa 1875), has a comprehensive exhibit of 19th-century heritage crafts as well as a working pioneer village and railroad memorabilia. ✉ *307 Shelton St.,* ☎ *828/452–1551.* *$4.* *May–Oct., Tues.–Fri. 10–4.*

Cold Mountain, the vivid best-seller by Charles Frazier, has made a destination out of the real **Cold Mountain.** Located about 15 mi from Waynesville in the Shining Rock Wilderness Area of Pisgah National Forest, the 6,030-ft rise has until recently stood in relative isolation. But now, people want to see the region that Inman and Ada, the book's Civil War–era protagonists, called home.

There are different ways to experience Cold Mountain. For a view of the splendid mass—or at least of the surrounding area—stop at any of a number of overlooks off the Blue Ridge Parkway. Try the Cold Mountain Parking Overlook just past mile marker 411.9; the Wagon Road Gap parking area at mile marker 412.2; or the Waterrock Knob Interpretative Station at mile marker 451.2. You can climb the mountain, but beware, as the hike to the summit is rather strenuous. No campfires are allowed in Shining Rock, so you'll need a stove if you wish to cook. Inform the ranger station (☎ 828/877–3350) if you plan to hike or camp.

Those who want a more interpretive experience might consider Cold Mountain tours by **Southern Safari** (✉ Box 8237, Asheville 28814, ☎ 800/454–7374). In addition to the popular 11-mi guided hiking tours for small groups, which culminate in a "French country picnic" atop the mountain, this company has a historical driving tour. About six hours long, the tour includes visits to Waynesville and various points of interest along the Blue Ridge Parkway brought to life in the novel.

Lodging

$$$$ **The Swag.** This exquisite, rustic inn sits high atop the Cataloochee Divide overlooking a swag—a deep depression in otherwise high ground. Its 250 wooded acres share a border with Great Smoky Mountains National Park and have access to the park's hiking trails. Guest rooms and cabins were assembled from six authentic log structures transported here. All have rough wooden walls, exposed beams, and wooden floors and are furnished with Early American crafts. A two-night minimum stay is required. ✉ *2300 Swag Rd., 28786,* ☎ *828/926–0430 or 800/789–7672,* FAX *828/926–2036. 16 rooms, 3 cabins. Dining room, pond, massage, sauna, badminton, croquet, racquetball, library, business services. AE, D, MC, V. Closed Dec.–Apr. FAP.*

Asheville

50 mi east of Cherokee, 115 mi west of Charlotte.

The largest and most cosmopolitan city in the mountains, Asheville has been rated America's favorite place to live among cities of its size. It has scenic beauty, a good airport and road system, a moderate four-season climate, and a thriving arts community. Banjo pickers are as revered as violinists, and mountain folks mix with city slickers. Experience the renaissance of the city's downtown, a pedestrian-friendly place with upscale shopping, art galleries, museums, restaurants, and nightlife.

Downtown Asheville is noted for its eclectic architecture. The **Battery Park Hotel** (1924) is neo-Georgian; the **Flatiron Building** (1924) is neoclassical; the **Basilica of St. Lawrence** (1912) is Spanish Baroque; **Pack Place,** formerly known as Old Pack Library (1925), is in Italian Renaissance style; the **S&W Cafeteria** (1929) is Art Deco. In fact, the city has the largest collection of Art Deco buildings in the Southeast except for Miami.

The 92,000-square-ft **Pack Place Education, Arts & Science Center,** in downtown Asheville, houses the **Asheville Art Museum, Colburn Gem & Mineral Museum, Health Adventure,** and **Diana Wortham Theatre.** The **YMI Cultural Center,** also maintained by Pack Place, is across the street. ✉ *2 S. Pack Sq.,* ☎ *828/257–4500.* *$4 per museum, $12 combination ticket.* ⏲ *June–Oct., Tues.–Sat. 10–5, Sun. 1–5; Nov.–May, Tues.–Sat. 10–5.*

Asheville's most famous son, Thomas Wolfe, grew up in a Queen Anne–style home that his mother ran as a boarding house. The home, a state historic site, burned as a result of arson. It is closed while undergoing restoration. However, the visitor center at the **Thomas Wolfe Memorial** remains open, showing a video about Wolfe and displaying photographs and other memorabilia related to the author and his career. Some items salvaged from the house are also here. ✉ *52 Market St.,* ☎ *828/253–8304.* *$1.* ⏲ *Apr.–Oct., Mon.–Sat. 9–5, Sun. 1–5; Nov.–Mar., Tues.–Sat. 10–4, Sun. 1–4.*

★ The astonishing **Biltmore Estate,** which faces Biltmore Village, was built in the 1890s as the private home of George Vanderbilt. This 250-room French Renaissance château is America's largest private residence (some of Vanderbilt's descendants still live on the grounds but open the bulk of the home and grounds to visitors). Richard Morris Hunt designed it, and Frederick Law Olmsted landscaped the original 125,000-acre estate (now 8,000 acres). It took 1,000 men five years to complete the gargantuan project. On view are the priceless antiques and art collected by the Vanderbilts, and 75 acres of gardens and formally landscaped grounds. You can also see the state-of-the-art winery and take Christmas candlelight tours of the house. Allow a full day to tour the house and grounds. ✉ *Exit 50 off I–40E,* ☎ *828/255–1700 or 800/624–1575.* *$32; prices for special events vary.* ⏲ *Jan.–Mar., daily 9–5; Apr.–Dec., daily 8:30–5.*

The **North Carolina Arboretum,** 426 acres that were part of the original Biltmore Estate, completes Frederick Law Olmsted's dream of creating a world-class arboretum in the western part of the state. It features southern Appalachian flora in a stunning number of settings, including the Blue Ridge Quilt Garden, with bedding plants that are arranged in patterns reminiscent of Appalachian quilts. There is also the formal Stream Garden, which capitalizes on the Bent Creek trout stream that runs through the grounds. An extensive network of trails is available for walking or mountain biking. ✉ *100 Frederick Law Olmsted Way, 10 mi southwest of downtown Asheville, adjacent to Blue Ridge Pkwy. (near I–26 and I–40),* ☎ *828/665–2492.* *Free; call for group tour fees.* ⏲ *Visitor education center Mon.–Sat. 9–5, Sun. noon–5; gardens and grounds daily 8 AM–9 PM.*

OFF THE BEATEN PATH

PENLAND SCHOOL OF CRAFTS – This world-famous institution about 45 mi northeast of Asheville on a remote mountaintop is the oldest and largest school for high-quality mixed-media arts and crafts in North America. It has classes in books and paper, glassblowing, ceramics, textile arts, and other media. A gallery displays works (some are for sale; call to check hours and winter closing). Classes aren't open to the public, but you can call about a free campus tour. ✉ *Penland Rd. off NC 19/23, Penland,* ☎ *828/765–2359 school, 828/765–6211 gallery and campus tours.*

Dining and Lodging

$$$–$$$$ ✕ **Windmill European Grill.** The menu at this cool, dark, and cozy cellar restaurant is a mix of German, Italian, Middle Eastern, and Indian cuisines. ✉ *85 Tunnel Rd.,* ☎ *828/253–5285. AE, D, MC, V. Closed Sun.–Mon. No lunch.*

$$–$$$$ ✕ **The Market Place.** Clean lines, neutral colors, and brushed steel mobiles create a sophisticated setting. The food offers refreshing twists on ingredients indigenous to the mountains (game and trout) and the South in general. Possible entrées are smoked trout and green apple salad, or tenderloin of pork with a sweet potato timbale. Iron gates open onto an exterior courtyard and dining patio. ✉ *20 Wall St.,* ☎ *828/252–4162. AE, MC, V. Closed Sun. No lunch.*

$$ ✕ **Café on the Square.** When owners Bill and Shelagh Byrne moved to Asheville from San Francisco, they brought California-Continental cuisine with them. The local business crowd frequents this elegant and airy restaurant during lunch, but theatergoers favor it for dinner. The menu, which lists from four to eight specials at each meal, is heavy on fresh seafood and pastas cooked with salsas, chutneys, and simple marinades. The signature dishes are hickory-smoked chicken in a marsala-and-shiitake-mushroom sauce and a rich peanut-butter pie. ✉ *1 Biltmore Ave.,* ☎ *828/251–5565. AE, D, MC, V. Closed Sun.*

$–$$ ✕ **The Laughing Seed Café.** You'll get more than brown rice and beans at this vegetarian eatery. The extensive menu ranges from fruit drinks to sandwiches and pizzas to dinner specialties influenced by the flavors of India, China, and Morocco. ✉ *40 Wall St.,* ☎ *828/252–3445. AE, D, MC, V. Closed Tues.*

$–$$ ✕ **West Side Grill.** A '50s-style diner, the West Side has a little bit of everything, including daily blue-plate specials, from Mile-High Meat Loaf to Southern-fried catfish. Vegetarians have a number of choices, including the focaccia veggie melt and the blackened garden burger. ✉ *1190 Patton Ave.,* ☎ *828/252–9605. Reservations not accepted. AE, D, MC, V.*

$$$$ ★ ✕ **Grove Park Inn Resort.** With its supervised children's activities, racquetball and tennis courts, special weekend packages, and views of the Blue Ridge Mountains, this is Asheville's premier resort. Since the resort's opening in 1913, the guest list has included Henry Ford, Thomas Edison, F. Scott Fitzgerald, and, more recently, Justice Sandra Day O'Conner and Michael Jordan. The inn is furnished with oak antiques in the Arts and Crafts style. The restaurants offer plenty of choices: Horizons specializes in game dishes from ostrich to boar; you can also order free-range chicken. ✉ *290 Macon Ave., 28804,* ☎ *828/252–2711 or 800/438–5800;* FAX *828/253–7053 guests, 828/252–6102 reservations. 498 rooms, 12 suites. 4 restaurants, 3 bars, indoor pool, outdoor pool, hot tub, spa, 18-hole golf course, putting green, 9 tennis courts, health club, nightclub, playground, business services, meeting rooms. AE, D, DC, MC, V.*

$$$$ ★ ✕ **Richmond Hill Inn.** Once a private residence, this elegant Victorian mansion is on the National Register of Historic Places. Many rooms in the mansion are furnished with canopy beds, Victorian sofas, and other antiques, while the more modern cottages have contemporary pine poster beds. Gabrielle's is known for its innovative cuisine, cherrywood paneling, and three-tier chandelier. Reservations are necessary here but not at the Arbor Grille, a glass-enclosed sun porch. Gabrielle's is only open to the public for dinner and Sunday brunch; jacket and tie are required. ✉ *87 Richmond Hill Dr., 28806,* ☎ *828/252–7313 or 888/742–4536,* FAX *828/252–8726. 24 rooms, 3 suites, 9 cottages. 2 restaurants, croquet, library, business services, meeting rooms. AE, MC, V. BP.*

$$$–$$$$ **Cedar Crest Victorian Inn.** Biltmore craftspeople constructed this beautiful cottage, with its leaded-glass front door and corbeled brick fireplaces, as a private residence in 1891. The lovingly restored guest rooms are furnished with period antiques. You are treated to afternoon tea, evening coffee or chocolate, and a breakfast of fruit, pastry, and coffee. It's best for older children. ✉ *674 Biltmore Ave., 28803,* ☎ *828/252–1389 or 800/252–0310,* FAX *828/252–7667. 9 rooms, 2 cottage suites. Croquet, business services. AE, D, DC, MC, V.*

$$$–$$$$ ✕ **Haywood Park Hotel.** The lobby of this Art Deco downtown hotel, once a department store, has golden oak woodwork accented with gleaming brass. The suites are spacious, with baths done in Spanish marble. The hotel's elegant restaurant, 23 Page, serves seafood and game. A favorite entrée is grilled lamb chop with radicchio and artichoke mousse. Adjoining the property is a shopping galleria. ✉ *1 Battery Park Ave., 28801,* ☎ *828/252–2522 or 800/228–2522,* FAX *828/253–0481. 33 suites. Restaurant, bar, in-room data ports, sauna, exercise room, laundry service, business services, meeting rooms. AE, D, DC, MC, V. CP.*

$$ **Comfort Inn.** This chain hotel, off I–240 near the River Ridge Outlet Mall, has a fireplace in a large sitting area. Most guest rooms are standard fare, but suites have private balconies and dinette areas. ✉ *800 Fairview Rd., 28803,* ☎ *828/298–9141,* FAX *828/298–6629. 149*

rooms, 28 suites. Pool, business services, meeting rooms. AE, D, DC, MC, V. CP.

$$ **Hampton Inn.** You can relax beside the fire in the lobby at this motel off I–26 that's convenient to downtown. Some guest rooms have whirlpool baths. ✉ *1 Rocky Ridge Rd., 28806,* ☎ *828/667–2022 or 800/426–7866,* FAX *828/665–9680. 121 rooms. In-room data ports, indoor pool, sauna, exercise room, business services, meeting rooms, airport shuttle. AE, D, DC, MC, V. CP.*

$–$$ **Mountaineer Inn.** A fixture along Tunnel Road for nearly 40 years, the Mountaineer is ever popular with families and others who care less about fancy than they do about affordable, comfortable surroundings. ✉ *155 Tunnel Rd., 28805,* ☎ *828/254–5331 or 800/255–4080,* FAX *828/254–5331. 79 rooms. In-room data ports, pool, business services, meeting rooms. AE, D, MC, V. CP.*

Nightlife and the Arts

An intimate, smoke-free listening room, **Be Here Now** (✉ 5 Biltmore Ave., ☎ 828/258–2071) has dancing and concerts. It's one of the region's premier music clubs, drawing a varied clientele and artists ranging from Doc Watson to the Second City comedy troupe. One of the best nightspots in town is **Gatsby's** (✉ 13 W. Walnut St., ☎ 828/254–4248), a cornerstone of the revitalized downtown. World-class acts range from blues to alternative rock.

Outdoor Activities and Sports

For other activities, *see* The Mountains A to Z, *below.*

GOLF

Colony Lake Lure Golf Resort (✉ 201 Blvd. of the Mountains, Lake Lure, ☎ 828/625–2888 or 800/260–1040), 5 mi from Asheville, has two 18-hole, par-72 courses known for their beauty. **Etowah Valley Country Club and Golf Lodge** (✉ U.S. 64, Etowah, ☎ 828/891–7141 or 800/451–8174), about 20 mi from Asheville, has three very different (one par-72, two par-73) 18-hole courses with good package deals. **Grove Park Inn Resort** (✉ 290 Macon Ave., ☎ 828/252–2711 or 800/438–5800) has a beautiful par-71 course.

HORSEBACK RIDING

Trail rides are offered by stables throughout the region between April and November, including **Pisgah View Ranch** (✉ Rte. 1, Candler, ☎ 828/667–9100) in the central mountains and **Cataloochee Ranch** (✉ Rte. 1, Maggie Valley, ☎ 828/926–1401 or 800/868–1401) in the southern mountains.

LLAMA TREKS

One-day and overnight hikes with llamas carrying your pack through local forests are arranged by **Windsong Llama Treks, Ltd.** (✉ 120 Ferguson Ridge Rd., Clyde, ☎ 828/627–6111). **Avalon Llama Trek** (✉ 310 Wilson Cove Rd., Swannanoa, ☎ 828/298–5637) leads trips on the lush trails of the Pisgah National Forest.

SKIING

Ski resorts in the Asheville area include **Cataloochee** (✉ Rte. 1, Maggie Valley, ☎ 828/926–0285 or 800/768–0285), **Fairfield-Sapphire Valley** (✉ 4000 U.S. 64W, Sapphire Valley, ☎ 828/743–3441 or 800/533–8268), and **Wolf Laurel** (✉ Rte. 3, Mars Hill, ☎ 828/689–4111).

Shopping

Biltmore Village (✉ Hendersonville Rd., ☎ 828/274–5570) on the Biltmore Estate is a cluster of specialty shops, restaurants, galleries, and hotels in a setting with a decided early 20th-century English-hamlet feel. Everything from children's books to music, antiques, and wearable art can be found.

Grovewood Gallery at the Homespun Shops (✉ 111 Grovewood Rd., ☎ 828/253–7651), adjacent to the Grove Park Inn and established by Mrs. George Vanderbilt, sells furniture and contemporary and traditionally crafted woven goods made on the premises.

Side Trips from Asheville

Within 40 mi of Asheville are towns with parks and historic sites. Some are resort destinations in themselves.

BREVARD

40 mi southwest of Asheville on NC 280.

Plenty of nearby waterfalls and the **Brevard Music Center** (☎ 828/884–2011), which has a seven-week music festival each summer, are draws in this resort town. Nearby Pisgah National Forest has the **Cradle of Forestry in America National Historic Site** (✉ 1001 Pisgah Hwy., ☎ 828/884–5823).

At **Sliding Rock** in summer, you can skid 150 ft on a natural water slide. Wear old jeans and tennis shoes and bring a towel. ✉ *Pisgah National Forest, north of Brevard, off U.S. 276,* ☎ *828/877–3265.* *Free.* *Memorial Day–Labor Day, daily 10–5:30.*

CHIMNEY ROCK

25 mi southeast of Asheville on U.S. 64/74A.

This town is deep in the Blue Ridge Mountains. At **Chimney Rock Park** an elevator travels through a 26-story shaft of rock for a staggering view of Hickory Nut Gorge and the surrounding mountains. Trails, open year-round, lead to 400-ft Hickory Nut Falls, where *The Last of the Mohicans* was filmed. ✉ *U.S. 64/74A,* ☎ *828/625–9611 or 800/277–9611.* *$11.* *Daily 8:30–4:30.*

FLAT ROCK

21 mi southwest of Chimney Rock, 25 mi south of Asheville via I–26.

Flat Rock has been a summer resort since the mid-19th century. The ★ **Carl Sandburg Home National Historic Site** is the spot to which the poet and Lincoln biographer Carl Sandburg moved with his wife, Lilian, in 1945. Guided tours of their house, Connemara, where Sandburg's papers still lie scattered on his desk, are given by the National Park Service. In summer, *The World of Carl Sandburg* and *Rootabaga Stories* are presented at the amphitheater. ✉ *1928 Little River Rd.,* ☎ *828/693–4178.* *$3.* *Daily 9–5.*

The **Flat Rock Playhouse** (✉ Greenville Hwy., ☎ 828/693–0731) has a high reputation for summer stock theater. The season runs from May to mid-December.

SALUDA

30 mi southeast of Asheville.

At the top of the steepest railroad grade east of the Rockies, this salubrious town along the tracks is strung with antiques and crafts shops in 19th-century brick buildings. The surrounding area has apple orchards, woods, and waterfalls.

WEAVERVILLE

18 mi north of Asheville via U.S. 23/19.

This town's state historic site, the **Zebulon B. Vance Birthplace,** has a reconstructed two-story log cabin and several outbuildings. This is where Vance, governor of North Carolina during the Civil War and later a

Close-Up

ARTS AND CRAFTS IN THE MOUNTAINS

A CENTURY AGO, AS YOUNG **GEORGE VANDERBILT** prepared to build a retreat in then-bucolic Asheville, he and an architect traveled the French countryside looking for elements of designs that could be incorporated into the home he had modeled after a 16th-century Loire Valley château. A legion of craftspeople labored long to create the Biltmore Mansion, including its unlikely gargoyles and grotesques. Decades later, in the 1970s, two tiny Episcopal churches in Glendale Springs and West Jefferson became home to Ben Long frescoes stunning enough to be in a great cathedral.

The message is this: when it comes to arts and crafts in western North Carolina, expect the unexpected. (Note: if a place mentioned here isn't described elsewhere in the chapter, an address or telephone number is given.) There's so much more going on than first meets the eye. And that's the fun of it: the hunt. Sometimes handmade treasures are found out in the open: more than 85 crafts fairs are held annually throughout the rural 21-county region. At the Balsam Mountain Inn (✉ Off NC 23/74, Balsam, ☎ 828/456–9498) just off the Blue Ridge Parkway near Waynesville, the work of a range of artisans is tastefully showcased year-round.

More than 4,000 people here earn part or all of their living from crafts, and many of them can be found "around the bend" and in homes tucked back in forested hollows. They patiently coax form from clay and wood and metal, and because art is close to the heart, they are usually happy to talk about what they do. So go ahead—explore. Interesting roads that are off the map can lead to workshops. If hours are posted, however, it's best to respect them; time is precious.

In the beginning, it was practical function, not notions of folk art, behind all the quilting, weaving, woodworking, and pottery making. By the latter part of the 19th century, though, missionaries, social workers, and women of means—Frances Goodrich and Edith Vanderbilt among them—began to recognize that the things of day-to-day life contained artistry and thus economic salvation for a beautiful but isolated and impoverished area.

Today, utility and aesthetics have melded. From furnaces in the northwest counties of Mitchell and Yancey come gobs of hot liquid that are shaped by hand into art glass prized by collectors and dealers worldwide. Many glassblowers have perfected their métier at the prestigious Penland School of Crafts, whose courses include printmaking, wood, surface design, metals, drawing, clay, and fibers. The work of students and graduates, much of it contemporary, is on display in area galleries including Penland's own extensive gallery shop.

In the tiny village of Crossnore in southern Avery County, a rock cottage houses the Crossnore School's Weaving Room (✉ U.S. 221, ☎ 828/733–4660). Favored here are patterns used by the early settlers of the Appalachians; however, in a nod to modernity the ladies spin with easy-care rayon and synthetics as well as with cotton, wool, and linen.

On the Cherokee Reservation, in the shadow of the Smoky Mountains, elders pass on to children the secrets of finger weaving, wood carving, mask and beaded jewelry making. Their work, intricate and colorful and found in shops such as Medicine Man Crafts (✉ U.S. 441, ☎ 828/497–2202) in downtown Cherokee, is ageless, a connective thread to a time that predates the United States by thousands of years.

U.S. senator, grew up. Crafts and chores typical of his period are often demonstrated. Picnic facilities are available. An entrance to the Blue Ridge Parkway is nearby. ✉ *911 Reems Creek Rd. (Rte. 1103),* ☎ *828/645–6706.* *Free.* *Apr.–Oct., Mon.–Sat. 9–5, Sun. 1–5; Nov.–Mar., Tues.–Sat. 10–4, Sun. 1–4.*

Lake Toxaway

40 mi southwest of Asheville.

A century ago, a group called the Lake Toxaway Company created a 640-acre lake in the high mountains between Brevard and Cashiers. Nearby, a grand 500-room hotel built with the finest materials, providing the most modern conveniences, and serving European cuisine, attracted many of the country's elite. That hotel is long gone, but the scenic area, which some still call "America's Switzerland," has a number of fine resorts and some of the priciest real estate in the North Carolina mountains.

Those who love nature, even if it's just looking at it, will enjoy being in this mountain wilderness. And for those to whom shopping is a sport, a number of upscale stores—many specializing in antiques and regional arts and crafts—can be found.

Lodging

$$$$ **Earthshine Mountain Lodge.** You can have as much solitude or adventure as you want at this spacious cedar log cabin with stone fireplaces. The lodge, which sits on 70 acres midway between Brevard and Cashiers on a ridge that adjoins the Pisgah National Forest, offers horseback riding, hiking, fishing, and even an opportunity to gather berries, feed the goats, or master some Cherokee skills. In the evening guests may gather around an open fire to sing songs, square dance, or exchange stories. A minimum stay of two nights is required. ✉ *Golden Rd., off Silversteen Rd. off U.S. 64, Box 216C, 28747,* ☎ *828/862–4207. 10 rooms. Hiking, horseback riding, fishing, baby-sitting, children's programs (ages 6 and up), meeting rooms. D, MC, V. FAP.*

$$$$ **Greystone Inn.** In 1915, Savannah resident Lucy Molz built a second home in Lake Toxaway. Today, the six-level Swiss-style mansion is an inn listed on the National Register of Historic Places. Guest rooms have antiques or period reproductions, while suites that border the lake of this mountain resort are modern. Rates include breakfast and dinner, afternoon tea and cake, and cocktails. The inn is open January through March, weekends only. ✉ *Greystone La., 28747,* ☎ *828/966–4700; 800/824–5766 outside NC,* FAX *828/862–5689. 33 rooms. Dining room, in-room VCRs, pool, lake, massage, driving range, 18-hole golf course, putting green, 5 tennis courts, children's programs, business services. AE, MC, V. MAP.*

Hot Springs

30 mi northwest of Asheville via U.S. 23/19 and 25/70 past Marshall.

This picturesque village is a way station for hikers on the Appalachian Trail. The **Hot Springs Spa**'s mineral springs maintain a natural 100°F temperature year-round and have, since the turn of the 20th century, provided relief for visitors suffering a variety of ailments, including rheumatism and pelvic troubles. Massage therapy is also available. ✉ *315 Bridge St.,* ☎ *828/622–7676 or 800/462–0933.* *$12–$30 per hr, depending on time of day and number of people in tub.* *Daily 9 AM–11 PM; hrs variable Dec.–Jan. (call in advance).*

Dining and Lodging

$ ✕🏨 **Bridge Street Café & Inn.** This renovated storefront, circa 1922, is right on the Appalachian Trail and overlooks Spring Creek. Upstairs are brightly decorated rooms and two baths filled with antiques. One bathroom has a claw-foot tub. The café ($$–$$$) downstairs has a wood-fired oven and grill from which emerge delicious pizzas. ✉ *Bridge St., Box 502, 28743,* ☎ *828/622–0002,* FAX *828/622–7282. 4 rooms share 2 baths. Restaurant. AE, D, MC, V. Closed Nov.–mid-Mar.*

Blue Ridge Parkway

Entrance 2 mi east of Asheville, off I–40.

★ The beautiful **Blue Ridge Parkway** (✉ Superintendent, Blue Ridge Pkwy., 199 Hemphill Knob Rd., Asheville 28803, ☎ 828/298–0398,) gently winds through mountains and meadows and crosses mountain streams for more than 469 mi on its way from Cherokee, North Carolina, to Waynesboro, Virginia. This is the most scenic route from Asheville to Boone and Blowing Rock. The parkway is generally open year-round but often closes during inclement weather. Maps and information are available at visitor centers along the highway. Mile markers (MM) identify points of interest and indicate the distance from the parkway's starting point in Virginia.

The **Folk Art Center** sells authentic mountain crafts made by members of the Southern Highland Craft Guild. ✉ *Blue Ridge Pkwy., MM 382,* ☎ *828/298–7928.* ⏲ *Daily 9–6.*

You can tour an underground mine or dig for gems of your own at **Emerald Village.** ✉ *McKinney Mine Rd. at Blue Ridge Pkwy., MM 334, Little Switzerland,* ☎ *828/765–6463 or 877/389–4653.* 🎫 *Mine $4, plus cost of gem bucket chosen ($3–$100). A $50 bucket guarantees you a stone, which will be cut free of charge; $100 guarantees 2.* ⏲ *June–Labor Day, daily 9–6, May and Sept.–Oct., daily 9–5.*

Linville Caverns are the only caverns in the Carolinas. The caverns go 2,000 ft beneath Humpback Mountain and have a year-round temperature of 51°F. North of Asheville, exit the parkway at mile marker 317.4 and turn left onto U.S. 221. ✉ *U.S. 221 between Linville and Marion,* ☎ *828/756–4171.* 🎫 *$5.* ⏲ *June–Labor Day, daily 9–6; Apr.–May and Sept.–Oct., daily 9–5; Nov. and Mar., daily 9–4:30; Dec.–Feb., weekends 9–4:30.*

From the **Linville Falls Visitor Center** (✉ Rte. 1, Spruce Pine, ☎ 828/765–1045), at mile marker 316.3, a ½-mi hike leads to one of North Carolina's most photographed waterfalls. The easy trail winds through evergreens and rhododendrons to overlooks with views of the series of cascades tumbling into Linville Gorge. There's also a campground and a picnic area.

Just off the parkway at mile marker 305, **Grandfather Mountain** soars to 6,000 ft and is famous for its Mile-High Swinging Bridge, a 228-ft-long bridge that sways over a 1,000-ft drop into the Linville Valley. There are also hiking and picnicking. The **Natural History Museum** has exhibits on native minerals, flora and fauna, and pioneer life. The annual **Singing on the Mountain** in June is an opportunity to hear old-time gospel music and preaching, and the **Highland Games in July** bring together Scottish clans from all over North America for athletic events and Highland dancing. ✉ *Blue Ridge Pkwy. and U.S. 221, Linville,* ☎ *828/733–4337 or 800/468–7325.* 🎫 *$10.* ⏲ *Apr.–mid-Nov., daily 8–dusk; mid-Nov.–Mar., daily 8–5, weather permitting.*

Parks along the parkway include **Julian Price Park** (MM 295–298.1), which has hiking, canoeing on a mountain lake, trout fishing, and camping. The **Moses H. Cone Park** (MM 292.7–295) has a turn-of-the-20th-century manor house (home of a textile magnate) that's now the Parkway Craft Center. The center sells fine work by area craftspeople.

Dining and Lodging

$$$$ ★ ✕🏨 **Eseeola Lodge and Restaurant.** Rebuilt in 1936 after a fire, this lakeside lodge, best described as dressed-up rustic, sits 3,800 ft above sea level and is one sure way to beat summer's heat. Golf is a passion here, but the diversions are many. The lovely grounds are manicured, and rich chestnut paneling and stonework grace the public areas. Entrées at the restaurant may include free-range chicken and rainbow trout; jacket and tie are required at dinner. ✉ *U.S. 221, Linville 28646,* ☎ *828/733–4311 or 800/742–6717,* FAX *828/733–3227. 19 rooms, 5 suites, 1 cottage. Restaurant, bar, pool, 18-hole golf course, putting green, 8 tennis courts, croquet, exercise room, boating, fishing, business services. MC, V. Closed late Oct.–mid-May. MAP.*

Outdoor Activities and Sports

HIKING

More than 100 trails lead off the Blue Ridge Parkway, from easy strolls to strenuous hikes. For more information on parkway trails, contact the Blue Ridge Parkway (☞ *above*). Another good source is *Walking the Blue Ridge: A Guide to the Trails of the Blue Ridge Parkway,* by Leonard Adkins, available at most parkway visitor center gift shops. The **Bluff Mountain Trail** at Doughton Park (MM 238.5) is a moderately strenuous 7½-mi trail winding through forests, pastures, and valleys, and along the mountainside. Moses H. Cone Park's (MM 292.7) **Figure 8 Trail** is an easy and beautiful trail that the Cone family designed for their morning walks. The ½-mi loop winds through a tunnel of rhododendrons and a hardwood forest. Those who tackle the ½-mi, strenuous **Waterrock Knob Trail** (MM 451.2), near the south end of the parkway, will be rewarded with spectacular views from the 6,400-ft-high Waterrock Knob summit.

ROCK CLIMBING

One of the most challenging climbs in the country is the **Linville Gorge** (MM 317), often called "the Grand Canyon of North Carolina." Permits are available from the district forest ranger's office in Marion (☎ 828/652–2144) or from the Linville Falls Texaco station on U.S. 221.

SKIING

Cross-country skiing is offered at **Moses H. Cone Park** (☎ 828/295–7591) and at **Linville Falls** on the **Blue Ridge Parkway** and at **Roan Mountain** (☎ 615/772–3303). Tours and equipment are available from **High Country Ski Shop** (☎ 828/733–2008) in Pineola on U.S. 221.

Blowing Rock

86 mi northeast of Asheville, 93 mi west of Winston-Salem.

Blowing Rock, a mecca for mountain visitors since the 1880s, has retained the flavor of a quiet village. About a thousand people are permanent residents, but the population swells each summer. To retain the rural atmosphere, the community banded together to prohibit large hotels and motels. Blowing Rock is the inspiration for the small town in resident Jan Karon's novels about country life in the fictional town of Mitford. To get here from the Blue Ridge Parkway, take U.S. 221/321 to just north of the entrance to Moses H. Cone Park.

The **Blowing Rock** looms 4,000 ft over the Johns River Gorge. If you throw your hat over the sheer precipice, it may come back to you, should the wind gods be playful. The story goes that a Cherokee man and a Chickasaw maiden fell in love. Torn between his tribe and his love, he jumped from the cliff, but she prayed to the Great Spirit, and he was blown safely back to her. ✉ *Off U.S. 321,* ☎ *828/295–7111.* 🎫 *$4.* ⊙ *June–Oct., Sun.–Thurs. 8:30–7, Fri.–Sat. 8:30–8; Nov.–Dec. daily 9–5; Jan.–Feb. weekends 8–8; Mar.–May daily 9–5.*

The **Tweetsie Railroad** is a popular Wild West theme park centered on a steam locomotive beset by robbers. A petting zoo, a country fair, rides, gold panning, a saloon show, and concessions are also here. ✉ *U.S. 321/221, off Blue Ridge Pkwy., MM 291,* ☎ *828/264–9061 or 800/526–5740.* 🎫 *$20.* ⊙ *Mid-May–mid-Aug., daily 9–6; mid-Aug.–Oct., Fri.–Sun. 9–6.*

Lodging

$$$–$$$$ **The Inn at Ragged Gardens.** With a grand stone staircase in the entry hall, colorful gardens, richly toned chestnut paneling, and the chestnut bark siding found on many older homes in the High Country, it's no wonder that this manor-style house in the heart of Blowing Rock gets rave reviews. Guests appreciate the attention to detail: the European and American antiques blended with contemporary art and the all-hours butler's pantry. All rooms have fireplaces and some have whirlpools and private balconies. It's best for older children. A two-night minimum is required on weekends. ✉ *203 Sunset Dr., 28605,* ☎ *828/295–9703. 6 rooms, 2 suites. Meeting room. MC, V. BP.*

$$$ **Chetola Resort.** This small resort, named for the Cherokee word meaning "haven of rest," grew out of an early 20th-century stone-and-wood lodge. The original building now houses the resort's restaurant and meeting rooms and is adjacent to the 1988 lodge. Guest rooms in the lodge have private balconies facing either the mountains, the lake, or both. Condominiums are spread among the hills. The property adjoins Moses H. Cone Park, with its hiking trails and riding facilities. ✉ *N. Main St., Box 17, 28605,* ☎ *828/295–5500 or 800/243–8652,* FAX *828/295–5529. 37 rooms, 5 suites, 62 condominiums. 2 restaurants, piano bar, indoor pool, hot tub, massage, 5 tennis courts, exercise room, racquetball, boating, fishing, bicycles, playground, business services, meeting rooms. AE, D, MC, V.*

$$–$$$ **Maple Lodge Bed & Breakfast.** Blowing Rock's oldest continuously operating bed-and-breakfast is just off Main Street, with its shops and restaurants. Built in 1946, the inn has a wonderful garden, pine paneling in the foyer and twin parlors, and pine ceilings and woodwork throughout. Some rooms are small, but most can hold a queen-size bed, antique dresser, table, and chair comfortably. The full breakfast, served in an enclosed porch, includes delicious homemade breads and muffins. ✉ *152 Sunset Dr., 28605,* ☎ *828/295–3331,* FAX *828/295–9986. 10 rooms, 1 suite. Fans. AE, D, MC, V. Closed Jan.–Feb. BP.*

$–$$ **Alpine Village Inn.** This motel in the heart of Blowing Rock harks back to a simpler time. Its rooms are neat as a pin and attractive in a homey way. Owners Rudy and Lynn Cutrera have decorated them with antiques, quilts, even flowers on holidays. Room refrigerators are available and morning coffee is served. ✉ *297 Sunset Dr., 28605,* ☎ *828/295–7206. 15 rooms. AE, D, MC, V.*

Outdoor Activities and Sports

HORSEBACK RIDING

Blowing Rock Stables (✉ U.S. 221, ☎ 828/295–7847) runs trail rides.

SKIING

There's downhill skiing at **Appalachian Ski Mountain** (✉ 940 Ski Mountain Rd., ☎ 828/295–7828 or 800/322–2373).

Shopping

Bolick Pottery (✉ NC 8 off U.S. 321, Lenoir, ☎ 828/295–3862), 3 mi southeast of Blowing Rock, sells mountain crafts and pottery handcrafted by Glenn and Lula Bolick, fifth-generation potters. **Goodwin Weavers** (✉ off U.S. 321 Bypass, ☎ 828/295–3394) sells bedspreads, afghans, and other goods woven in the traditional mountain style, plus home furnishings designed by North Carolina artist Bob Timberlake.

Boone

8 mi north of Blowing Rock.

Boone, named for frontiersman Daniel Boone, is a city of several thousand residents at the convergence of three major highways—U.S. 321, U.S. 421, and NC 105. You'll find mountain crafts in stores and at crafts fairs here. **Mast General Store** at the Old Boone Mercantile (✉ 630 W. King St., ☎ 828/262–0000) is a classic general store.

Horn in the West, a project of the Southern Appalachian Historical Association, is an outdoor drama that traces the story of Daniel Boone's life. ✉ *Amphitheater off U.S. 321,* ☎ *828/264–2120.* 🎫 *$12.* ⏲ *Performances nightly at 8, except Mon. mid-June–mid-Aug.*

The **Appalachian Cultural Museum** examines the lives of Native Americans and African-Americans in the High Country; showcases the successes of such mountain residents as stock-car racer Junior Johnson and country singers Lula Belle and Scotty Wiseman; and exhibits a vast collection of antique quilts, fiddles, and handcrafted furniture. ✉ *University Hall near Greene's Motel, U.S. 321,* ☎ *828/262–3117.* 🎫 *$4.* ⏲ *Tues.–Sat. 10–5, Sun. 1–5.*

Dining and Lodging

$–$$$ ✕ **Mike's Inland Seafood.** Calabash-style (lightly battered and fried) or broiled, the seafood here couldn't taste better if it were served at the ocean. There's a branch in Banner Elk. ✉ *U.S. 321,* ☎ *828/262–5605. AE, DC, MC, V. Closed Mon.*

$$$$ 🏨 **Hound Ears Lodge and Club.** This alpine inn, overlooking Grandfather Mountain and a lush golf course, offers amenities such as a pool secluded in a natural grotto and comfortable, well-kept rooms dressed in Waverly print fabrics. From April through October, the room rate for special packages includes breakfast and dinner. The dining area is open only to guests and members; reservations are required, as are a jacket and tie for dinner. ✉ *328 Shulls Mill Rd., off NC 105, 6 mi from Boone, Box 188, 28605,* ☎ *828/963–4321,* FAX *828/963–8030. 29 rooms. Dining room, pool, 18-hole golf course, 6 tennis courts, business services, meeting rooms. AE, MC, V.*

$–$$ 🏨 **High Country Inn.** A honeymoon destination that draws skiers, golfers, and other groups interested in the discount packages, the inn, made of native stone and surrounded by ponds, has accommodations that range from luxurious to comfortable. Geno's, a popular sports bar and restaurant, is here. ✉ *1785 NC 105 S, Box 1339, 28607,* ☎ *828/264–1000 or 800/334–5605,* FAX *828/262–0073. 118 rooms, 2 suites, 2 log cabins. Restaurant, bar, indoor-outdoor pool, hot tub, sauna, exercise room, meeting rooms. AE, D, MC, V.*

$–$$ 🏨 **Smoketree Lodge.** Views of Grandfather Mountain and an in-house art gallery showing the work of local artists are highlights of this mountain inn near the ski slopes. All rooms are fully equipped and have a kitchenette; use of laundry facilities is free. ✉ *11914 NC 105 S, Box*

3407, 28607, ☎ 828/963–6505 or 800/422–1880, FAX 828/963–7815. 46 rooms. Indoor pool, hot tub, exercise room. AE, D, MC, V.

OFF THE BEATEN PATH **BLUE RIDGE MOUNTAIN FRESCOES** – In the 1970s, North Carolina artist Ben Long and his students painted four luminous big-as-life frescoes in two churches about 45 mi northeast of Boone in Ashe County, past Blue Ridge Parkway mile marker 258.6. *The Last Supper* is in the Glendale Springs Holy Trinity Church; the others, including *Mary, Great with Child,* are in St. Mary's Episcopal Church at Beaver Creek near West Jefferson. Signs from the parkway lead to the churches. ☎ *336/982–3076.* *Free.* *Freely accessible. Guide service available by prior arrangement.*

Outdoor Activities and Sports

CANOEING AND WHITE-WATER RAFTING

Near Boone and Blowing Rock, the New River, a federally designated Wild and Scenic River (Classes I and II rapids) provides excitement for canoeists and rafters, as do the Watauga River, Wilson Creek, and the Toe River. One outfitter is **Wahoo's Adventures** (☎ 828/262–5774 or 800/444–7238).

GOLF

Western North Carolina has many challenging courses. North Carolina High Country Host (☞ Visitor Information *in* The Mountains A to Z, *below*) has information on public courses in Boone, Seven Devils, Newland, and West Jefferson. **Boone Golf Club** (✉ Fairway Dr., ☎ 828/264–8760) is a good par-71 course for the whole family. **Hound Ears Club** (✉ NC 105, ☎ 828/963–4312) has an 18-hole course with great mountain views (par 72). **Linville Golf Club** (✉ Linville, ☎ 828/733–4363), 17 mi from Boone, has a par-72 Donald Ross course.

Valle Crucis

5 mi south of Boone.

This tiny mountain town has the state's first rural historic district; vintage stores line the downtown streets. Everything from ribbons and calico to brogans and overalls is sold in the **Mast General Store** (✉ NC 194, ☎ 828/963–6511). Built in 1882, the store has plank floors worn to a soft sheen and a potbellied stove.

Dining and Lodging

$$$–$$$$ ✕ **Mast Farm Inn.** You can turn back the clock and still enjoy modern amenities at this charming pastoral inn, built in the 1800s and now on the National Register of Historic Places. Rooms are in the farmhouse or in log outbuildings. The restaurant uses locally and organically grown vegetables and local trout. Organic gardening demonstrations are held in the Inn's gardens. ✉ *2543 Broadstone Rd., Box 704, 28691,* ☎ *828/963–5857,* FAX *828/963–6404 or 888/963–5857. 9 rooms, 6 cottages. Restaurant. MC, V. BP.*

Banner Elk

6 mi southwest of Valle Crucis, 11 mi southwest of Boone.

Banner Elk is a popular ski resort town surrounded by the lofty peaks of Grandfather, Hanging Rock, Beech, and Sugar mountains.

Dining and Lodging

$$–$$$$ ✕ **Stonewalls.** This contemporary rustic restaurant affords one of the best views of Beech Mountain. Fare includes steak, prime rib, fresh seafood, chicken, and homemade desserts. The salad bar is superb. ✉ *NC 184,* ☎ *828/898–5550. AE, MC, V. No lunch.*

$–$$$ **The Inns of Beech Mountain.** As these two Appalachian Mountain resorts—the Beech Alpen Inn and the Top of Beech Inn—are in eastern America's highest town, they overlook the slopes of the Blue Ridge Mountains. The staff is friendly at these country inns, and some rooms have fireplaces and balconies. The restaurant at Beech Alpen is open for dinner only. ✉ *700 Beech Mountain Pkwy., 28604,* ☎ *828/387–2252. 50 rooms. Restaurant. AE, D, MC, V. CP.*

Outdoor Activities and Sports

CANOEING AND WHITE-WATER RAFTING

The many rivers in the Banner Elk area provide a variety of possibilities. Outfitters include **Edge of the World Outfitters** (✉ NC 184, ☎ 828/898–9550 or 800/789–3343).

HORSEBACK RIDING

Banner Elk Riding Stables (✉ NC 184, ☎ 828/898–5424) runs trail rides.

SKIING

There's downhill skiing at **Ski Beech** (✉ NC 184, Beech Mountain, ☎ 828/387–2011 or 800/438–2093), **Sugar Mountain** (✉ off NC 184, Banner Elk, ☎ 828/898–4521 or 800/784–2768), and **Hawksnest Golf and Ski Resort** (✉ 1800 Skyland Dr., Seven Devils, ☎ 828/963–6561 or 800/822–4295). For **ski conditions,** call ☎ 800/962–2322.

The Mountains A to Z

Arriving, Departing, and Getting Around

BY BUS

Greyhound/Carolina Trailways (✉ 2 Tunnel Rd., ☎ 828/253–5353 or 800/231–2222) serves Asheville.

BY CAR

I–40 runs east and west through Asheville. I–26 runs from Charleston, South Carolina, to Asheville. I–240 forms a perimeter around the city. U.S. 23–19A is a major north and west route. The Blue Ridge Parkway runs northeast from Great Smoky Mountains National Park to Shenandoah National Park in Virginia, passing Cherokee, Asheville, and the High Country. U.S. 221 runs north to the Virginia border through Blowing Rock and Boone and intersects I–40 at Marion. U.S. 321 intersects I–40 at Hickory and heads to Blowing Rock/Boone.

BY PLANE

Asheville Regional Airport (✉ 708 Airport Rd., Fletcher, ☎ 828/684–2226) is served by Midway Connections, Atlantic Southeast Airlines, ComAir, and US Airways. For airline telephone numbers, *see* Air Travel *in* Smart Travel Tips A to Z. US Airways Express (☎ 800/428–4322) serves the **Hickory Airport** (✉ U.S. 321, ☎ 828/323–7408), about 40 mi from Blowing Rock.

Contacts and Resources

EMERGENCIES

Dial 911 for **police** and **ambulance** everywhere but the Cherokee Reservation, where the police can be reached at 828/497–4131 and the EMS service at 828/497–6402. **Memorial Mission** (✉ 509 Biltmore Ave., Asheville, ☎ 828/255–4000). **Watauga Medical Center** (✉ 336 Deerfield Rd., Boone, ☎ 828/262–4100). **Cannon Memorial Hospital** (✉ 805 Shawneehaw Ave., Banner Elk, ☎ 828/898–5111). **Blowing Rock Hospital** (✉ 416 Chestnut Dr., Blowing Rock, ☎ 828/295–3136).

GUIDED TOURS

A brochure entitled **"The Asheville Urban Trail,"** available at the Asheville Area Chamber of Commerce (✉ 151 Haywood St., ☎ 828/258–6100), provides a self-guided 1½-mi walking tour of downtown.

OUTDOOR ACTIVITIES AND SPORTS

There are **camping** opportunities at the five developed, or "frontcountry," campgrounds in the North Carolina part of Great Smoky Mountains National Park; one of these, Smokemont, accepts reservations through the **National Park Service Reservation Service** (☎ 800/365–2267). The remaining four campgrounds—Balsam Mountain, Big Creek, Cataloochee, and Deep Creek—are first-come, first-served only. All frontcountry camping in the park is primitive by design. For more information on campgrounds, including those in Tennessee, as well as regulations and restrictions, contact the **Great Smoky Mountains National Park Headquarters** (✉ 107 Park Headquarters Rd., Gatlinburg, TN 37738, ☎ 865/436–1230 or 865/436–1231 for inquiries about backcountry camping).

For **canoeing** and **whitewater rafting** in the Asheville area, the Chattooga, Nolichucky, French Broad, Nantahala, Ocoee, and Green rivers offer Class I–V rapids. One of the largest area outfitters is **Nantahala Outdoor Center** (✉ 13077 U.S. 19W, Bryson City, ☎ 828/488–2175 or 800/232–7238).

Western North Carolina offers many challenging **golf** courses. For a complete listing of public courses in Asheville, Black Mountain, Brevard, Hendersonville, Lake Lure, Old Fort, and Waynesville, contact the Asheville Convention and Visitors Bureau (☞ Visitor Information, *below*).

Anyone into serious **hiking** can explore the Appalachian Trail, which runs along the crest of the Appalachian Mountains at the North Carolina–Tennessee border. It can be picked up at several points, including the Newfound Gap parking area in **Great Smoky Mountains National Park** (☎ 615/436–5615) and **Grandfather Mountain** (☎ 828/733–4337), where you can get trail maps.

RADIO STATIONS

AM: WSKY 1230, talk; WZQR 1350, country. **FM:** WCQS 88.1, National Public Radio; WSPA 98.9, easy listening; WKSF 99.9, country.

VISITOR INFORMATION

In Asheville, the **Asheville Convention and Visitors Bureau** (✉ 151 Haywood St., Box 1010, 28802, ☎ 828/258–6102 or 800/257–1300) will answer questions and provide maps. The **Cherokee Visitors Center** (✉ U.S. 441 Business, ☎ 828/497–9195 or 800/438–1601) provides information on the reservation. **North Carolina High Country Host** (✉ 1701 Blowing Rock Rd., Boone 28607, ☎ 828/264–1299 or 800/438–7500) is a complete information center for the High Country counties of Watauga, Ashe, and Avery. **Smoky Mountain Host of NC** (✉ 4437 Georgia Rd., Franklin 28734, ☎ 828/369–9606 or 800/432–4678) has information about the state's seven westernmost counties.

NORTH CAROLINA A TO Z

Arriving and Departing

By Bus

Greyhound/Carolina Trailways (☎ 800/231–2222) links the cities of North Carolina with major cities in the southeastern United States.

By Car

I–40 traverses the state from Asheville in the west to Wilmington in the east. I–85 passes through the Triangle, the Triad, and Charlotte as it crosses from northeast to southwest. I–77 passes through the western part of the state from Virginia through Charlotte to South Carolina, and I–95 carries north–south traffic in the eastern part of the state.

By Plane

Among the major airports in the state are **Charlotte-Douglas International Airport** (✉ 5501 Josh Birmingham Blvd., ☎ 704/359–4013), the **Piedmont Triad International Airport** (✉ 6451 Bryan Blvd., Greensboro, ☎ 336/665–5666), and the **Raleigh-Durham International Airport** (✉ 1600 Terminal Blvd., Morrisville, ☎ 919/840–2123).

By Train

Amtrak (☎ 800/872–7245) offers daily service from major cities on the eastern seaboard to the state's main population centers, including Charlotte, Greensboro, Raleigh, Durham, and Southern Pines.

Getting Around

By Bicycle

North Carolina has more than 5,000 mi of mapped and signed bicycle routes, many on scenic country roads. For maps and information, contact the **Division of Bicycle and Pedestrian Transportation** (✉ Box 25201, Raleigh 27611, ☎ 919/733–2804).

By Bus

Greyhound/Carolina Trailways (☎ 800/231–2222) links cities and towns throughout the state.

By Car

The speed limit on interstates varies; it's generally 65 or 70 mph. Right turns on red are permitted unless otherwise indicated. The official *State Transportation Map* may be ordered from the **North Carolina Department of Transportation** (✉ Public Affairs Division, Box 25201, Raleigh 27611, ☎ 919/733–7600, 800/847–4862 outside NC). Copies of the state's booklet about **Scenic Byways** are available at North Carolina welcome and visitor centers. To order a single copy, call ☎ 919/733–2920 or write to the Department of Transportation's (☞ *above*) Roadside Environmental Unit.

By Ferry

Ferries connect coastal communities. Routes and schedules are printed on the official North Carolina *State Transportation Map* (☞ By Car, *above*) and are available by phone from the Department of Transportation (☎ 800/293–3779).

By Train

Amtrak (☎ 800/872–7245) offers daily service between a number of cities and towns.

Contacts and Resources

Emergencies

In almost all cities and towns dial 911 for police or ambulance in an emergency. Most hospital emergency rooms are open 24 hours a day. Smaller ones are often connected by air evacuation systems to major trauma centers.

Fishing

A mandatory state license can be bought at local bait and tackle shops or over the phone (with a credit card) from the **North Carolina Wildlife**

Commission (☎ 919/715–4091). Cost for nonresidents is as follows: one day $10, three days $15, and year pass $30.

Visitor Information

The **North Carolina Division of Tourism, Film and Sports Development** (✉ 301 N. Wilmington St., Raleigh 27601, ☎ 919/733–4171 or 800/847–4862, FAX 919/733–8582) has information packets and an information line. Operators will answer questions about everything from beaches to snow conditions.

4 SOUTH CAROLINA

South Carolina's scenic Lowcountry shoreline is punctuated by the historic yet vibrant port city of Charleston, with its elegant homes and fine museums. The recreational resorts of Myrtle Beach and Hilton Head anchor each end of the coast. Columbia, the state capital, is set in the fertile interior of the state, which stretches toward the Blue Ridge Mountains. Also to the west are the rolling fields of Thoroughbred Country. Upcountry South Carolina, at the northwestern tip of the state, is noted for incredible mountain scenery and white-water rafting.

Updated by Mary Sue Lawrence

FROM ITS LOWCOUNTRY SHORELINE, with wide sand beaches, spacious bays, and forests of palmettos and moss-draped live oaks, South Carolina extends into an undulating interior region rich with fertile farmlands, then reaches toward the Blue Ridge Mountains, whose foothills are studded with scenic lakes, forests, and wilderness hideaways. What this smallest of Southern states lacks in land area it makes up for in diversity and enthusiasm. People here like to celebrate. Every month of the year there's a local festival that turns on regional pride, feting critters such as jumping frogs, edibles such as peaches and watermelons, or rarefied delicacies such as okra and chitterlings. South Carolina owes much of its growth to the tourism industry, which brings more than $14 billion and 29 million people to the state each year.

The historic port city of Charleston, although lovingly preserved, is not a museum city. Many of its treasured double-galleried antebellum homes are authentically furnished house museums, just as many are home to Charlestonians and newcomers. Residents air their quilts over piazzas, walk their dogs down cobblestone streets, and tend their famous gardens in much the same way their ancestors did 300 years ago. Locals bravely rebounded from Hurricane Hugo, which hit in 1989, to painstakingly rebuild and renovate, making the city perhaps as gleaming and fresh as it was during the 18th century. Renovation continues to expand to the far reaches of the downtown historic district, extending across the Cooper River Bridge and out of the town of Mount Pleasant into Awendaw and McClellanville. Culturally vibrant, Charleston nurtures theater, dance, music, and visual arts, showcased each spring during the internationally acclaimed Spoleto Festival USA.

Myrtle Beach is the glitzy jewel of the Grand Strand, a 60-mi stretch of wide white-sand beaches and recreational activities, especially golf, a top attraction throughout the state. South from Myrtle Beach to Georgetown, it's almost one continuous community. Georgetown itself is enjoying a healthy tourism trade, offering a small-town respite smack-dab between the big-city sophistication of Charleston and amusement-park excitement of Myrtle Beach.

To the south, tasteful, low-key Hilton Head—divided into several self-contained resorts—also offers beautiful beaches and wonderful golf and tennis. A toll expressway was completed in 1997 to help handle traffic to the resort areas. Sun City, a large, newly developed retirement community, is attracting scores of fifty-somethings to the area.

Nearby is the port city of Beaufort, with lovely streets dotted with preserved 18th-century homes. A stopover popular with New York-to-Florida commuters, it's also the favorite of early retirees in search of small-town life and great deals on real estate; many have converted its historic houses into B&Bs.

Columbia, the state capital, is a busy and historic city blessed by three rushing rivers. Besides museums and a good minor-league baseball team, the city has one of the country's top zoos and a riverside botanical garden. The University of South Carolina, with a student body of 40,000, means that nightlife and cheap and cheerful restaurants are plentiful. Nearby lakes and state parks provide abundant outdoor recreation and first-rate fishing, and the Congaree Swamp National Monument has the oldest and largest trees east of the Mississippi.

Thoroughbred Country, centered on the town of Aiken, is a peaceful area of rolling pastures where top racehorses are trained. In this part of the state, charming, old-fashioned towns such as Abbeville and Cheraw draw more and more visitors with their history, abundant outdoor activities, sleepy main streets, and friendly residents.

Upcountry South Carolina, at the northwestern tip, is less visited than the rest of the state but repays time spent here with dramatic mountain scenery, excellent hiking, and challenging white-water rafting. Greenville has seen a dramatic growth spurt in the last few years. Downtown Greenville is changing rapidly; new cafés, shops, and boutiques, plus a newfound cultural diversity, are breathing fresh life into the old city.

Pleasures and Pastimes

Beaches

South Carolina's mild climate makes the surf enjoyable from April through October. The beaches are expanses of white sand—some serene and secluded, others bustling and lined with high-rises. You can choose the high-voltage action at busy Myrtle Beach or the more low-key scene on the resort island of Hilton Head, or just stroll the sands at Huntington Beach State Park.

Dining

South Carolinians love to cook and share good food, from dishes marinated in tradition to the creatively contemporary. Lowcountry specialties include she-crab soup, stuffed oysters, and infinite variations on pecan pie. Seafood—often the fresh catch of the day—is likely to be traditionally prepared on the Grand Strand and gussied up on Hilton Head. Elsewhere in the state, try barbecue and look for a variety of cuisine, from cosmopolitan to country cookery. And don't write off grits until you've tasted them laced with cheese, topped with *tasso* (spiced ham) gravy, or folded into a veal or quail entrée.

CATEGORY	COST*
$$$$	over $40
$$$	$30–$40
$$	$20–$30
$	under $20

**per person for a three-course meal, excluding drinks, service, and 5% tax*

Gardens

Gardening devotees can and do build vacations around South Carolina gardens, where camellias, azaleas, other flowering shrubs, and blooming trees abound. Along the coast are some of the nation's most famous, including Middleton Place, with the oldest landscaped garden in America; Cypress Gardens, where cypress trees tower in dark waters with azaleas on the banks; and Brookgreen Gardens, with a superb outdoor sculpture collection set amid giant oaks and colorful flowers. Inland, remarkable gardens planted with roses, irises, or mountain laurel make some small towns a worthwhile side trip. Along the way, you can see peach orchards in bloom in spring.

Lodging

From predictable but dependable chains to luxurious resort hotels and quaint B&Bs, accommodations are available for every budget. Reservations are a must, especially on the coast, and prices do vary with the seasons—in fact, winter rates in Charleston and along the coast can be a pleasant surprise. The charms of historic Charleston in particular can be enhanced by a stay at one of its many inns, most in restored structures. Some are reminiscent of European inns; others are tastefully contemporary.

South Carolina

Charlotte
NORTH CAROLINA
Fayetteville
Monroe
Rockingham
Pageland
Cheraw
Bennettsville
Lumberton
Sandhills State Forest
Whiteville
Camden
Darlington
Florence
Great Pee Dee R.
Marion
Sumter
Woods Bay State Park
Lake City
Calabash
Conway
Atlantic Beach
North Myrtle Beach
Windy Hill Beach
Surfside Beach
Myrtle Beach
Manchester State Forest
Murrells Inlet
Litchfield Beach
Black R.
Orangeburg
Lake Marion
St. Stephen
Andrews
Pawleys Island
Georgetown
Santee R.
Lake Moultrie
Hampton Plantation State Park
Francis Marion National Forest
McClellanville
Edisto R.
Cypress Gardens
Summerville
Mount Pleasant
Middleton Place
Charleston
Isle of Palms
Sullivans Is.
ATLANTIC OCEAN
Osborn
James Is.
Folly Is.
Johns Is.
Kiawah Is.
Seabrook Is.
Edisto Island
St. Helena Island
Hunting Island State Park
Hunting Island
Fripp Is.
Parris Island
Bluffton
Daufuskie Is.
N
0
100 miles
0
150 km

CATEGORY	CHARLESTON AND THE COAST*	OTHER AREAS*
$$$$	over $200	over $150
$$$	$150–$200	$110–$150
$$	$100–$150	$75–$110
$	under $100	under $75

**All prices are for a standard double room, excluding 7% tax.*

following the text of a review is your signal that the property has a Web site, where you will find details and, usually, images; for a link, visit www.fodors.com/urls.

Outdoor Activities

South Carolina's many rivers and lakes afford a range of activities, including boating, fly- and deep-water fishing, kayaking, sailboarding, sailing, tubing, and, in the Upcountry, whitewater rafting. Canoeing is popular on waters near Columbia. Anglers frequently break records with hauls of largemouth bass, stripers, crappie, and catfish caught in Lakes Marion and Moultrie. The first passages of the Palmetto Trail—a hiking, mountain biking, and horseback riding trail that will eventually wind 400 mi across the state—are open: the High Hills of Santee Passage, the Lake Moultrie Passage, and the Swamp Fox Passage in Francis Marion National Forest. Golfing, of course, reigns supreme practically year-round; the state has more than 380 courses.

Exploring South Carolina

South Carolina has three regions—its 200-mi coastline, its interior heart, and its hilly north country. Charleston and points south are the Lowcountry, distinguished by aristocratic elegance and an accent unlike any other in the South. Because Hilton Head Island, in the southern part of the state, has become world renowned as a posh resort, it is treated separately here, along with the coastal towns near it. Natives consider the upper coasts part of what they call the Pee Dee (after the Pee Dee River), but the world knows Myrtle Beach and its environs by their more famous other name—the Grand Strand. It refers to the sandy strip of beaches more than 60 mi long.

The Heartland, including the Midlands core of the state, is an eclectic collection of towns and the capital city, Columbia. It also includes Thoroughbred Country, lush pasture for Triple Crown contenders. The Upcountry, noted for mountain scenery, is in the northwest.

Great Itineraries

To enjoy South Carolina to the fullest, you need a week or more to savor the coast and visit briefly inland. But you can have a memorable experience, however fleeting, by choosing sights that strike your fancy and promising yourself to return another time for more. The Lowcountry and Charleston are priorities; every traveler to South Carolina should visit that historic city—and most want to. With a bit more time, you can travel north from there to the Grand Strand or south to Hilton Head or west into the Heartland. If you have 10 days or so, you can add Thoroughbred Country and the Upcountry to your itinerary.

IF YOU HAVE 1 DAY

Spend the day in the historic district in **Charleston.** Take a carriage ride through it for a look at some of the city's most elegant homes. Then browse through the shops in the Old City Market area, where most of the carriage tours begin and end. After that, walk south along East Bay Street or any side streets on your way to a couple of the area's museums. Here, wander the tree-shaded streets, discovering courtyard gardens and all the little surprises that reveal themselves to those who seek them out.

IF YOU HAVE 2–3 DAYS

Charleston has so many charms—a rich antebellum and Civil War history, plantations and historic homes, beaches, golf, and superb restaurants—that you could spend a week here. Expand your itinerary on Day 2 by adding more sights within the historic district (it takes time to tour the house museums), by browsing in the Shops at Charleston Place or along King Street, and by including the Charleston Museum and other nearby museums. On the afternoon of Day 2 or Day 3, you could visit Mount Pleasant, with access to Fort Sumter National Monument, nice beaches, and Boone Hall Plantation to the north. Or you could head west of the Ashley River to visit Charles Towne Landing State Park and Magnolia Plantation and Gardens.

IF YOU HAVE 5–6 DAYS

On Day 4, take a leisurely exit from Charleston along SC 61 and see **Drayton Hall** and **Middleton Place** as you make your way inland for a quick visit to **Columbia,** with its State House, historic university campus, and zoo and botanical garden. Another choice is to take U.S. 17 north toward the beaches of the **Grand Strand,** where you can stay in busy **Myrtle Beach** or more quiet **Pawleys Island,** or south toward **Beaufort** or **Hilton Head Island.** There are beautiful gardens, stately plantations, and fine museums in both directions, or you may choose to go by boat on the ocean or Intracoastal Waterway.

IF YOU HAVE 10 DAYS

Follow the itineraries above and then extend your time in **Columbia.** Take a canoe ride on the scenic Saluda River or down the Congaree River, and visit Congaree Swamp National Monument. Browse in the South Carolina State Museum and enjoy shopping and dining in the Congaree Vista, a district stretching six blocks from the Congaree River. Take a day trip to historic, horsey **Camden** or **Aiken** to get the flavor of other Heartland towns. On Day 8, head to the Upcountry for magnificent scenery. You can explore **Greenville,** perhaps driving north to the Cherokee Foothills Scenic Highway or to Kings Mountain National Military Park, a Revolutionary War site. You might head west and raft on the Chattooga River and spend your last night and day in **Pendleton,** with its historic district and proximity to Clemson and the South Carolina State Botanical Garden.

When to Tour South Carolina

South Carolina is loveliest in spring, when azaleas, dogwood, and other flowering bushes and trees are in bloom, but flowers brighten every season—even winter, when pansies and camellias thrive. Between mid-March and mid-April, you can catch tours of private mansions in Charleston, and the city is alive with Spoleto events in May and June. Beaufort holds its Water Festival in mid-July. For price breaks on the coast, consider visiting in the off-season, October through February, but remember that some restaurants and a few attractions close around that time, and the water may be cool.

CHARLESTON

At first glimpse, Charleston resembles an 18th-century etching come to life. Its low-profile skyline is punctuated with the spires and steeples of 181 churches, representing 25 denominations—the reason that Charleston, known for religious freedom during its formation, is called the "Holy City." Parts of the city appear frozen in time; block after block of old downtown structures have been preserved and restored for residential and commercial use, and some brick and cobblestone streets remain. Charleston has survived three centuries of epidemics, earthquakes, fires, and hurricanes, and it is today one of the South's loveliest and best-preserved cities. It is not a museum, however: Throughout the year festivals (☞ Festivals *in* Nightlife and the Arts, *below*) add excitement and sophistication.

Besides the historic district (which we've divided, for ease of exploration, into two parts: the area north of Broad Street, and the Battery and area south of Broad Street), a visit to the city can easily include nearby towns, plantations and outstanding gardens, and historic sites, whether in Mount Pleasant or the area west of the Ashley River.

North of Broad

To really appreciate Charleston, you must walk its streets. The downtown historic district, roughly bounded by Calhoun Street to the north, the Cooper River to the east, the Battery to the south, and Legare Street to the west, is large, with 2,000 historic homes and buildings on the southeastern tip of the Charleston peninsula. In a fairly compact area you'll find churches, museums, and lovely views at every turn.

The area north of Broad Street has some of the finest historic homes and neighborhoods in the city, including Mazyck/Wraggborough neighborhood, where you'll find the Aiken-Rhett House. Large tracts of land made this area ideal for urban plantations during the early 1800s. While there are a number of pre-Revolutionary buildings here (including the Old Powder Magazine, the oldest public building in Charleston), in general, the farther north you travel on the peninsula, the newer the development. Still, because the peninsula was built-out by the early 1900s, North of Broad is rich with historic buildings from the 19th century and is often a treasure trove, as most tourists are busy conquering the waterfront area.

Numbers in the text correspond to numbers in the margin and on the Charleston map.

A Good Walk

Before you begin touring, drop by the **Visitor Information Center** ① on Meeting Street for an overview of the city, a map, and tickets for shuttle services if you want to give your feet a break. Start across the street at the **Charleston Museum** ②, with its large decorative arts collection; then turn right on Ann Street and follow it to Elizabeth Street to the palatial **Aiken-Rhett House** ③. After touring the house, head south down Elizabeth Street and turn right on John Street for the **Joseph Manigault Mansion** ④, another impressive house museum dating to the early 1800s. From here, return to Meeting Street and walk south toward Calhoun Street, passing the **Old Citadel Building** ⑤, converted into an Embassy Suites (☞ Lodging, *below*). Take a left on Calhoun Street; a half block down on your left is the **Emanuel African Methodist Episcopal Church** ⑥, where Denmark Vesey was a member. From here, you may want to use the shuttle bus DASH to give your feet a rest, or cross the street to Marion Square Mall for a drink and a break.

Retrace your steps on Calhoun Street (passing the Francis Marion Hotel, in the 1920s the highest building in the Carolinas) and continue two blocks west to St. Phillips Street, where you turn left to end up in the midst of the romantic campus of the **College of Charleston** ⑦, the oldest municipal college in the country. Enter through one of the gated openings on St. Phillips Street for a stroll under the many moss-draped trees. Then head east to King Street, Charleston's main shopping thoroughfare, and turn right; turn left on Hasell Street to see **Congregation Beth Elohim** ⑧, a Greek Revival building. Keep walking down Hasell Street, turn right on Meeting Street, and then turn left down Pinckney

Aiken-Rhett House 3
American Military Museum 9
The Battery 29
Calhoun Mansion . . . 27
Charleston Museum . . . 2
Charleston Place 12
Circular Congregational Church 16
City Hall 23
College of Charleston 7
Congregation Beth Elohim 8
Dock Street Theatre 20
Edmondston-Alston House. 28
Emanuel African Methodist Episcopal Church 6
French Protestant (Huguenot) Church 19
Gibbes Museum of Art 15
Heyward-Washington House. 25
Joseph Manigault Mansion 4
Market Hall 10
Nathaniel Russell House. 26
Old Citadel Building 5
Old City Market. 11
Old Exchange Building/Provost Dungeon. 22
Old Powder Magazine. 17
St. John's Lutheran Church. 13
St. Michael's Episcopal Church 24
St. Philip's Episcopal Church 18
South Carolina Aquarium 31
Unitarian Church 14
Visitor Information Center 1
Waterfront Park 21
White Point Gardens 30

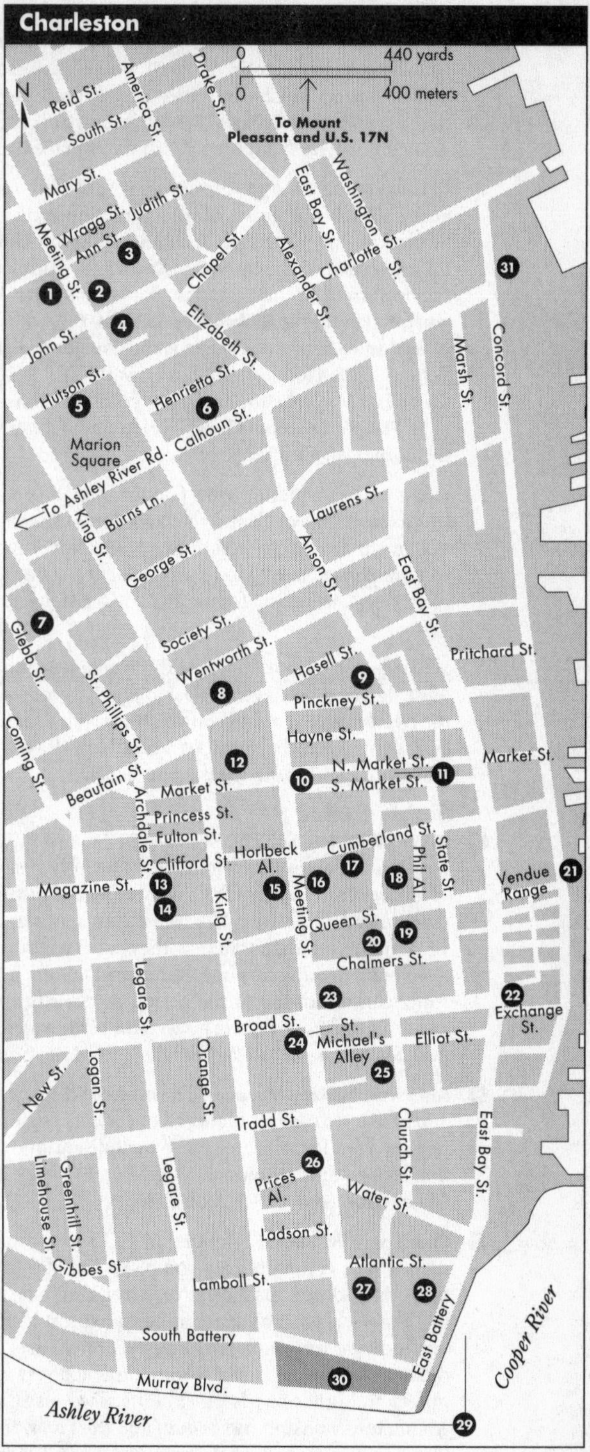

Street to the **American Military Museum** ⑨. Two blocks to the south are **Market Hall** ⑩ and the bustling **Old City Market** ⑪. Now is a good time for a carriage tour, many of which leave from here (☞ Contacts and Resources *in* Charleston A to Z, *below*). Across Meeting Street is the classy **Charleston Place** ⑫, with its graceful hotel and cluster of shops. You can browse from one end to the other, exiting on King Street.

Facing you on the opposite corner is Saks Fifth Avenue; cross the street and walk a block down Market Street, turning left on quiet Archdale Street to wander through **St. John's Lutheran Church** ⑬ and the peaceful graveyard of the **Unitarian Church** ⑭. Turn left on Queen Street at the bottom of Archdale and walk two blocks to Meeting Street, where you turn left for the **Gibbes Museum of Art** ⑮, with its spectacular stained-glass dome. Across the street is the **Circular Congregational Church** ⑯. Behind it, on Cumberland Street, is the **Old Powder Magazine** ⑰. To the left as you face the building, you'll catch a glimpse of the steeple of **St. Philip's Episcopal Church** ⑱, famous in the city's skyline; it's around the corner on Church Street.

Cross over to picturesque Church Street to the **French Protestant (Huguenot) Church** ⑲ and the **Dock Street Theatre** ⑳ across the street. You might detour east here, down Queen Street and along Vendue Range to **Waterfront Park** ㉑ to relax in a bench swing overlooking beautiful river views, dramatic fountains, and a fishing pier.

TIMING

Set aside two to four hours for this walk, depending on your pace. Most of the house museum tours last about 40 minutes, so you might choose the two or three that interest you most. If it's high summer, you'll likely be moving with the speed of a Southern drawl, so pace yourself and make use of all those Charleston benches.

Sights to See

❸ **Aiken-Rhett House.** This stately 1819 mansion, with its original wallpaper, paint colors, and some of its furnishings, was the headquarters of Confederate general P. G. T. Beauregard during his 1864 Civil War defense of Charleston. The house, kitchen, slave quarters, and work yard are maintained much as they were when the original occupants lived here, making this one of the most complete examples of African-American urban life of the period. ✉ *48 Elizabeth St.,* ☎ *843/723–1159.* 🎫 *$7; combination ticket with Nathaniel Russell House and Old Powder Magazine (☞ below) $14.* ⏲ *Mon.–Sat. 10–5, Sun. 2–5.*

❾ **American Military Museum.** The museum displays hundreds of uniforms and artifacts from all branches of service, beginning with the Revolutionary War. Its collections also include antique toy soldiers, war toys, miniatures, and weaponry. ✉ *40 Pinckney St.,* ☎ *843/723–9620.* 🎫 *$5.* ⏲ *Mon.–Sat. 10–6, Sun. 1–6.*

★ ❷ **Charleston Museum.** Founded in 1773, the country's oldest city museum is in a contemporary complex. The 500,000 items in the collection—in addition to Charleston silver, fashions, toys, snuff boxes, and the like—include objects relating to natural history, archaeology, and ornithology. Its South Carolina decorative arts holdings are extraordinary. The Discover Me Room, designed just for children, has computers and other hands-on exhibits. Two historic homes—the **Joseph Manigault Mansion** (☞ *below*) and the **Heyward-Washington House** (☞ *below*)—are part of the museum. ✉ *360 Meeting St.,* ☎ *843/722–2996.* 🎫 *$8, museum and houses $18, 2 of the 3 sights $12.* ⏲ *Mon.–Sat. 9–5, Sun. 1–5.*

12 **Charleston Place.** The city's only world-class hotel, this Orient Express property is flanked by a four-story complex of upscale boutiques and specialty shops (☞ Shopping, *below*). Peek into the lobby or have cocktails or tea in the intimate Lobby Lounge. Entrances for the garage and reception area are on Hasell Street between Meeting and King streets. ✉ *130 Market St.,* ☎ *843/722–4900.*

16 **Circular Congregational Church.** The corners of this unusual Romanesque church were rounded off, they say, so the devil would have no place to hide. Simple but pretty, it has a beamed, vaulted ceiling. ✉ *150 Meeting St.,* ☎ *843/577–6400.* ⏲ *Call for tour schedule.*

7 **College of Charleston.** The lovely, tree-shaded campus of this college, founded in 1770, has a graceful main building, the Randolph House (1828), designed by Philadelphia architect William Strickland. It provides a romantic backdrop for the Cistern, often used as a grassy stage for concerts and other activities. Within the college, centered at the corner of George and St. Phillips streets, is the **Avery Research Center for African-American History and Culture,** which traces the heritage of Lowcountry African-Americans. ✉ *Avery Research Center, 125 Bull St.,* ☎ *843/953–7609.* 🎟 *Free. Mon.–Sat. noon–5, mornings by appointment.*

8 **Congregation Beth Elohim.** Considered one of the nation's finest examples of Greek Revival architecture, this temple was built in 1840 to replace an earlier one—the birthplace of American Reform Judaism in 1824—that was destroyed by fire. ✉ *90 Hasell St.,* ☎ *843/723–1090.* ⏲ *Weekdays 10–noon.*

NEED A BREAK? On your way to the cluster of sights around Meeting Street, pick up a batch of Charleston's famed benne wafers at **Olde Colony Bakery** (✉ 280 King St., between Society and Wentworth Sts., ☎ 843/722–2147). *Benne* is an African word used by slaves to describe the sesame seeds on these delicacies.

20 **Dock Street Theatre.** Built on the site of one of the nation's first playhouses, the building combines the reconstructed early Georgian playhouse and the preserved Old Planter's Hotel (circa 1809). The theater, which offers fascinating backstage views, welcomes visitors except when technical work for a show is under way. ✉ *135 Church St.,* ☎ *843/720–3968.* 🎟 *Free tours; call ahead for ticket prices and performance times.* ⏲ *Weekdays 10–4.*

6 **Emanuel African Methodist Episcopal Church.** Home of the South's oldest A.M.E. congregation, the church had its beginnings in 1818. It was closed in 1822 when authorities learned that Denmark Vesey had used the sanctuary to plan his slave insurrection, but the church reopened in 1865 at the present site. ✉ *110 Calhoun St.,* ☎ *843/722–2561.* ⏲ *Daily 9–4.*

19 **French Protestant (Huguenot) Church.** This church is the only one in the country still using the original Huguenot liturgy, which can be heard in a special service held each spring. ✉ *110 Church St.,* ☎ *843/722–4385.* ⏲ *Weekdays 10–12:30 and 2–4.*

NEED A BREAK? For a great view of the harbor and Waterfront Park, the **Vendue Inn** (☞ Lodging, *below*) on Vendue Range, at the end of Queen Street, serves lunch, drinks, and appetizers alfresco on the city's only Rooftop Lounge.

15 **Gibbes Museum of Art.** The collections of American art include notable 18th- and 19th-century portraits of Carolinians and an outstanding

group of more than 400 miniature portraits. Don't miss the miniature rooms—intricately detailed with fabrics and furnishings and nicely displayed in shadow boxes inset in dark-paneled walls—or the Tiffany-style stained-glass dome in the rotunda. ✉ *135 Meeting St.,* ☎ *843/722–2706.* 🎫 *$5.* ⏲ *Tues.–Sat. 10–5, Sun.–Mon. 1–5.*

❹ **Joseph Manigault Mansion.** A National Historic Landmark and an outstanding example of neoclassical architecture, this home was designed by Charleston architect Gabriel Manigault in 1803 and is noted for its carved-wood mantels and elaborate plasterwork. Some furnishings are British and French but most are Charleston antiques; some rare tricolor Wedgwood pieces are noteworthy. ✉ *350 Meeting St.,* ☎ *843/723–2926.* 🎫 *$7; for combination ticket, see the Charleston Museum (☞ above).* ⏲ *Mon.–Sat. 10–5, Sun. 1–5.*

❿ **Market Hall.** Built in 1841 and modeled after the Temple of Nike in Athens, this imposing landmark building includes the **Confederate Museum,** where the Daughters of the Confederacy preserve and display flags, uniforms, swords, and other Civil War memorabilia. At press time, the museum, heavily damaged by Hurricane Hugo in 1989, was closed for renovation and may remain so into 2001; however, costumed guides sometimes stand outside and describe the facility for visitors. The collection is temporarily housed at 34 Pitt Street; admission is $2, and it's open Saturday noon–4, Sunday 1–4. ✉ *88 Meeting St.,* ☎ *843/723–1541.*

❺ **Old Citadel Building.** Built in 1822 to house state troops and arms, the Old Citadel Building faces Marion Square. This is where the Carolina Military College—the Citadel—had its start. The fortresslike building is now the Embassy Suites Historic Charleston (☞ Lodging, *below*), and the Citadel is now on the Ashley River.

⓫ **Old City Market.** A series of low sheds that once housed produce and fish markets, this area is often called the Slave Market, although Charlestonians dispute that slaves ever were sold there. It now has restaurants, shops, gimcracks and gee-gaws for children, vegetable and fruit vendors, and local "basket ladies" weaving and selling sweet-grass, pine-straw, and palmetto-leaf baskets—a craft passed down through generations from their West African ancestors. ✉ *Market St. between Meeting and E. Bay Sts.* ⏲ *Daily 9–sunset; hrs may vary.*

NEED A BREAK? Just across the street from the Old City Market and Charleston Place, **Café Cafe** (✉ 177 Meeting St., corner of Market, ☎ 843/723–3622) serves hearty sandwiches, inventive wraps, homemade soups, and great coffees and desserts throughout the day; some evenings there's live music, too.

⓱ **Old Powder Magazine.** This structure was built in 1713 and used during the Revolutionary War. It is now a museum with costumes, armor, and other artifacts from 18th-century Charleston, plus a fascinating audiovisual tour. ✉ *79 Cumberland St.,* ☎ *843/805–6730.* 🎫 *$2; combination ticket with Aiken-Rhett House (☞ above) and Nathaniel Russell House (☞ below) $14.* ⏲ *Mon.–Sat. 10–5, Sun. 2–5.*

⓭ **St. John's Lutheran Church.** This Greek Revival church was built in 1817 for a congregation that celebrated its 250th anniversary in 1992. Notice the fine craftsmanship in the delicate wrought-iron gates and fence. Musicians may be interested in the 1823 Thomas Hall organ case. ✉ *5 Clifford St.,* ☎ *843/723–2426.* ⏲ *Weekdays 9–3.*

⓲ **St. Philip's Episcopal Church.** The graceful late-Georgian church is the second on its site; the congregation's first building burned down in 1838.

In the graveyard on the church's side of the street, Charlestonians are buried; in the graveyard on the other side, "foreigners" lie (including John C. Calhoun, who was from Abbeville, South Carolina). ✉ *146 Church St.,* ☎ *843/722–7734.* ⏲ *By appointment.*

14 **Unitarian Church.** Completed in 1787, this church was remodeled in the mid-19th century using plans inspired by the Chapel of Henry VII in Westminster Abbey. The Gothic fan-tracery ceiling was added during that renovation. An entrance to the church grounds is on 161½–163 King Street, amid the antiques shops there. The secluded and romantically overgrown graveyard invites contemplation. ✉ *8 Archdale St.,* ☎ *843/723–4617 weekdays 8:30–2:30.* ⏲ *Call ahead for hrs.*

1 **Visitor Information Center.** The center gives a fine introduction to the city and sells tickets for shuttle services (☞ Getting Around *in* Charleston A to Z, *below*). Parking is 65¢ per hour; the first hour is free if you purchase a shuttle pass. Take time to see *Forever Charleston,* an insightful 20-minute film. ✉ *375 Meeting St.,* ☎ *843/853–8000 or 800/868–8118.* 🎫 *Film $2.50.* ⏲ *Mar.–Oct., daily 8:30–5:30; Nov.–Feb., daily 8:30–5; shows daily 9–5 on the ½ hr.*

21 **Waterfront Park.** A sprinkle from the park's interactive fountain will refresh you on hot summer days. Here, you'll also find swings, a fishing pier, picnic tables, and gardens overlooking Charleston Harbor. It's at the foot of Vendue Range, along the east side of Charleston Harbor. ☎ *843/724–7321.* 🎫 *Free.*

The Battery and South of Broad

Along the Battery, on the point of a narrow peninsula bounded by the Ashley and Cooper rivers, handsome mansions, surrounded by gardens, face the harbor. Their distinctive look is reminiscent of the West Indies: before coming to the Carolinas in the late 17th century, many early British colonists had first settled on Barbados and other Caribbean isles, where they'd built houses with high ceilings and broad piazzas at each level to catch the sea breezes. In Charleston, they adapted these designs. One new type—narrow two- to four-story "single houses" built at right angles to the street—emerged partly because buildings were taxed according to the length of their frontage.

Heavily residential, the area south of Broad Street has many beautiful private homes, almost all of which have a plaque with a short written description of the home's history. You might get a peek at tucked-away, English-style gardens, too. An open gate in Charleston once signified that visitors were welcome to venture inside for a closer look at the owner's garden. Open gates are rare today, but keep an eye out, as you never know when you'll get lucky.

Numbers in the text correspond to numbers in the margin and on the Charleston map.

A Good Walk

Start at the top of Broad Street at the **Old Exchange Building/Provost Dungeon** ㉒, which held prisoners during the American Revolution. Two blocks down Broad Street are the Four Corners of Law, including **City Hall** ㉓, with some historical displays and portraits, and **St. Michael's Episcopal Church** ㉔, the city's oldest surviving church. In the famously affluent South of Broad neighborhood are several of the city's lavish house museums. The **Heyward-Washington House** ㉕ is a block south of Broad on Church Street. Next to it is the picturesque Cabbage Row, the inspiration for Catfish Row in *Porgy and Bess.* The **Nathaniel Russell House** ㉖ and the **Calhoun Mansion** ㉗ are on Meeting Street, about

Close-Up

ANTEBELLUM CHARLESTON: THE GOLDEN YEARS

CHARLESTON, CALLED CHARLES TOWNE until the British left in 1783, boomed with the plantation economy in the years before the Civil War. South Carolina's rice, indigo, and cotton crops produced an extraordinary concentration of wealth, making a few hundred plantation owners, merchants, and shippers rich. Rice was the most profitable export; the labor source used to grow the rice—slaves—was the most profitable import. Cotton, too, was a huge moneymaker; by the outbreak of the Civil War in 1861, cotton accounted for 57% of the nation's exports.

From Charleston's beginnings, the planter aristocracy set out to entertain itself in style, seeking a social and cultural lifestyle to match its financial success. By the mid-17th century, the city had a thriving musical community. The first playhouse, the original Dock Street Theatre, was open for business. There were dances and concerts; the town attracted some of the most important performers in colonial America. During the 1770s there were more than 23 singing and dancing masters teaching in the city, which also had a reputation for turning out the Colonies' best Shakespearean productions.

The city boasted talented goldsmiths, silversmiths, gunsmiths, tobacconists, brewers, and cabinetmakers and was one of the best shopping towns in North America. Immigrants and others seeking religious freedom poured into Charleston. More than 200 private residences were built during this boom. Though Charleston had half the population of New York during the early 1770s, its annual export trade exceeded the tonnage that passed through New York's port.

Until the Civil War, Charleston's fortunes continued to grow. The city's native sons played a huge part in the forming of the new national government; four Charlestonians signed the U.S. Constitution. Writers and artists filled the city. Charlestonian Robert Mills, who designed the Washington Monument, also designed many buildings in Charleston. George Washington toured Charleston in 1791, staying in many of the city's now historic homes.

Charleston thrived as the social and cultural center of planter families. The social season, from late January to March, was defined by balls, dinners, masquerades, concerts, plays, and horse races. The elite and their slaves moved from the plantations to their Charleston residences, embellished with silk curtains, Dutch linens, French china, English silver, and lavish ornamental gardens. They commissioned famous portrait artists and European craftsmen and gave extravagant dinners where guests were served by black slaves. Lowcountry gentlemen joined private clubs and favored fox hunts, races, and gambling. Lowcountry sons traveled to England for their education. By the 1840s, construction pervaded the city: City Hall was under renovation; the Battery was being made into a city park; and such buildings as the four-story Charleston Hotel had become part of the emerging cityscape. By 1850 the city's population had grown to nearly 43,000.

When the Union-held Fort Sumter was bombarded on April 11, 1861, Charlestonians celebrated. But the merriment, along with the years of splendor and luxury, was soon over; the collapse of slavery ended the plantation system, sending much of the state's economy into depression.

two blocks apart. Around the corner is the **Edmondston-Alston House** ㉘, overlooking Charleston's famous **Battery** ㉙ and the Charleston harbor. A park bench in the shade of **White Point Gardens** ㉚, so named because of the bleached whiteness of oyster shells left here by Native Americans, is a splendid spot for a rest. From here, go north along the Cooper River to the **South Carolina Aquarium** ㉛ by shuttle or by car.

TIMING

Plan to spend two to four hours doing this walk, depending on your pace and which buildings you visit. A trip to the aquarium can add two or so hours; you may wish to split the trip into two half-days.

Sights to See

㉙ **The Battery.** This sea wall and promenade has sweeping views of Charleston Harbor. ✉ *Murray Blvd.*

㉗ **Calhoun Mansion.** Opulent by Charleston standards, this is a no-holds barred example of Victorian taste. Built in 1876, it's notable for ornate plasterwork, fine wood moldings, and a 75-ft dome ceiling. ✉ *16 Meeting St.,* ☎ *843/722–8205.* 🎫 *$10.* ⏲ *Feb.–Dec., Wed.–Sun. 10–4.*

㉓ **City Hall.** The intersection of Meeting and Broad streets is known as the Four Corners of Law, representing the laws of nation, state, city, and church. On the northeast corner is graceful City Hall, dating from 1801. The second-floor Council Chamber has a variety of historical displays and portraits, including John Trumbull's 1791 satirical portrait of George Washington and Samuel F. B. Morse's likeness of James Monroe. ✉ *80 Broad St.,* ☎ *843/577–6970 or 843/724–3799.* 🎫 *Free.* ⏲ *Weekdays 10–5.*

OFF THE BEATEN PATH

COLONIAL LAKE – Joggers, walkers, and folks looking for a tranquil city spot flock to this small man-made lake circled by a wide sidewalk, trees, and benches. In the late 19th century, Colonial Common, as it was called at the time, was a popular gathering place for Victorian Charleston. Today it is surrounded by stately Victorian buildings. ✉ *Ashley and Rutledge Aves. to the east and west, Broad and Beaufain Sts. to the north and south,* ☎ *843/724–7327.*

㉘ **Edmondston-Alston House.** With commanding views of Charleston Harbor, this imposing home was built in 1825 in late Federal style and transformed into a Greek Revival structure during the 1840s. It is tastefully furnished with antiques, portraits, Piranesi prints, silver, and fine china. ✉ *21 E. Battery,* ☎ *843/722–7171.* 🎫 *$7; combination ticket with Middleton Place (☞ below) $24.* ⏲ *Tues.–Sat. 10–4:30, Sun.–Mon. 1:30–4:30.*

㉕ **Heyward-Washington House.** Built in 1772 by rice king Daniel Heyward, this home was the backdrop for DuBose Heyward's book *Porgy,* which was the basis for the beloved folk opera *Porgy and Bess.* The neighborhood, known as Cabbage Row, is central to Charleston's African-American history. President George Washington stayed in the house during his 1791 visit. It is full of fine period furnishings by such local craftsmen as Thomas Elfe, and its restored 18th-century kitchen is the only one in Charleston open to visitors. ✉ *87 Church St.,* ☎ *843/722–0354.* 🎫 *$8; for combination ticket, see Charleston Museum (☞ above).* ⏲ *Mon.–Sat. 10–5, Sun. 1–5.*

★ ㉖ **Nathaniel Russell House.** One of the nation's finest examples of Adams-style architecture, the Nathaniel Russell House was built in 1808. The interior is distinguished by its ornate detailing, its lavish period furnishings, and the "flying" circular staircase that spirals three stories with no apparent support. ✉ *51 Meeting St.,* ☎ *843/724–8481.* 🎫 *$7; combination ticket with Aiken-Rhett House and Old Powder Magazine (☞ above) $14.* ⏲ *Mon.–Sat. 10–5, Sun. 2–5.*

22 **Old Exchange Building/Provost Dungeon.** Originally a customs house, the British used it for prisoners during the Revolutionary War. Today a tableau of lifelike mannequins recalls this era. ✉ *122 E. Bay St.,* ☎ *843/727–2165.* 🎫 *$6.* ⏲ *Daily 9–5.*

24 **St. Michael's Episcopal Church.** Modeled after London's St. Martin-in-the-Fields and completed in 1761, this is Charleston's oldest surviving church. Its steeple clock and bells were imported from England in 1764. ✉ *14 St. Michael's Alley,* ☎ *843/723–0603.* ⏲ *Weekdays 9–5, Sat. 9–noon.*

NEED A BREAK? On your way down Broad Street toward Church Street, duck into the dark-paneled, tin-ceiling **Blind Tiger Pub** (✉ 38 Broad St., ☎ 843/577–0088) for a drink or beer in the beer garden out back, or a meal from the Four Corners Cafe next door.

★ 31 **South Carolina Aquarium.** The 322,000-gallon Great Ocean Tank has the tallest aquarium window in North America. Exhibits have more than 10,000 living organisms, representing more than 500 species. Visitors travel through the five major regions of the Southeast Appalachian Watershed as found in South Carolina: the Blue Ridge Mountains, the Piedmont, the Coastal Plain, the Coast, and the Ocean. Bring the little ones for the special toddler displays. ✉ *3250 Concord St.,* ☎ *843/720–1990 or 800/722–6455.* 🎫 *$14.* ⏲ *July–Aug., daily 9–7; Mar.–June and Sept.–Oct., daily 9–5; Nov.–Feb., daily 10–5.*

30 **White Point Gardens.** Pirates once hung from gallows here; now this small garden, with a gazebo, Charleston benches, and views of the harbor and Fort Sumter, is the number one marriage site in the city. Children love to climb on the cannon and cannonball replicas. ✉ *Murray Blvd. and E. Battery,* ☎ *843/724–7327.* ⏲ *Weekdays 9–5, Sat. 9–noon.*

Mount Pleasant and Vicinity

East of Charleston across the Cooper River bridges, via U.S. 17N, is the town of Mount Pleasant, named not for a mountain or a hill but for a plantation in England from which some of the area's settlers hailed. In its Old Village neighborhood are antebellum homes and a sleepy, old-time town center with shops and cafés. Along Shem Creek, where the local fishing fleet brings in the daily catch, are good seafood restaurants. Other attractions in the area are museums, plantations, and, farther north, the Cape Romain National Wildlife Refuge.

A Good Tour

There's enough adventure here to stretch over a number of days, especially if you're a war history buff. On the first day you might drive to **Patriots Point,** veering right off the Cooper River Bridge onto Coleman Boulevard in the direction of Sullivan's Island and the Isle of Palms. Turn right at the signs, and then board the museum ships for tours. From here you can catch the ferry for a harbor ride to **Fort Sumter National Monument.** Later, continue along Coleman Boulevard and, just after crossing the boat-lined docks and restaurants at Shem Creek, turn right at Whilden Street for a drive through the Old Village. Returning to Coleman Boulevard, you'll pass the Common, a cluster of shops on your left. Stop here for the **Museum on the Common,** featuring the *Hurricane Hugo Revisited* exhibit. As you make your way across the Ben Sawyer Bridge to Sullivan's Island and the Isle of Palms, you'll see how the area has recovered from Hugo. Follow the signs to **Fort Moultrie.** Spend the rest of the day relaxing on the beach or bicycling through Sullivan's Island, a residential community scattered with early 20th-century beach houses, or the Isle of Palms, which has a pavilion and more abundant parking.

Another day, drive out U.S. 17N 8 mi to **Boone Hall Plantation** and its famous Avenue of Oaks, stopping at nearby **Charles Pinckney National Historic Site,** with interpretations of African-American life on the plantation. Bring a picnic and rent bikes at **Palmetto Islands County Park,** across Boone Hall Creek from the plantation; you'll need a swimsuit for Splash Island, a mini–water park. Another option is a ferry ride and visit to Bull Island, part of the **Cape Romain National Wildlife Refuge,** one of the nation's most pristine wildlife areas. The Sewee Visitor & Environmental Education Center (on U.S. 17 heading north) has information and exhibits on the refuge as well as live birds of prey, red wolves, and trails.

TIMING

You need three days to see all the attractions here; if you have one day or less, choose a few based on your interests.

Sights to See

★ **Boone Hall Plantation.** This plantation is approached along one of the South's most majestic avenues of oaks, which was the model for the grounds of Tara in *Gone With the Wind.* You can tour the first floor of the classic columned mansion, which was built in 1935 incorporating woodwork and flooring from the original house. The primary attraction is the grounds, with formal azalea and camellia gardens, as well as the original slave quarters—the only "slave street" still intact in the Southeast—and the cotton-gin house used in the made-for-television movies *North and South* and *Queen.* ✉ *1235 Long Point Rd., off U.S. 17N,* ☎ *843/884–4371.* 🎫 *$12.50.* ⏲ *Apr.–Labor Day, Mon.–Sat. 8:30–6:30, Sun. 1–5; Labor Day–Mar., Mon.–Sat. 9–5, Sun. 1–4.*

NEED A BREAK? Driving north of Mount Pleasant along U.S. 17, you'll see **basket ladies** at roadside stands. If you have the heart to bargain, you *may* be able to purchase the baskets at somewhat lower prices than in Charleston. But remember that you are buying a nearly lost art, and sweet grass is no longer plentiful in the wild.

Cape Romain National Wildlife Refuge. A grouping of barrier islands and salt marshes, this 60,000-acre refuge is one of the most outstanding in the country. At the Sewee Visitor & Environmental Education Center you can view exhibits about the refuge and arrange to take a ferry to Bull Island for a day visit. The island is a nearly untouched wilderness; the beach here, strewn with bleached driftwood, is nicknamed Bone Beach. ✉ *5821 U.S. 17N, Awendaw,* ☎ *843/928–3368.* 🎫 *Free.* ⏲ *Daily 9–5.*

Charles Pinckney National Historic Site. Across the street from Boone Hall, this is the only protected remnant of the country estate of Charles Pinckney, drafter and signer of the Constitution. A self-guided tour explores many fascinating interpretations of African-American life, including the plantation owner–slave relationship. You can also tour an 1820s tidewater cottage. ✉ *1254 Long Point Rd., off U.S. 17N,* ☎ *843/881–5516,* FAX *843/881–7070.* 🎫 *Free.* ⏲ *Daily 9–5.*

Fort Moultrie. Here Colonel William Moultrie's South Carolinians repelled a British assault in one of the first Patriot victories of the Revolutionary War. Completed in 1809, this is the third fort on this site at **Sullivan's Island,** which you'll reach on SC 703 off U.S. 17N. A 20-minute film tells the history of the fort. ✉ *W. Middle St., Sullivan's Island,* ☎ *843/883–3123.* 🎟 *$2.* ⏲ *Daily 9–5.*

★ **Fort Sumter National Monument.** It was here, on a man-made island in Charleston Harbor, that the first shot of the Civil War was fired, on April 12, 1861, by Confederate forces. After a 34-hour bombardment, Union forces surrendered and Confederate troops occupied Sumter, which became a symbol of Southern resistance. The Confederacy held the fort, despite almost continual bombardment, for nearly four years, and when it was finally evacuated, it was a heap of rubble. Today National Park Service rangers conduct free guided tours of the restored structure, which includes a free **museum** (☎ 843/883–3123) with historical displays. The fort is reached from either Charleston's Municipal Marina or Patriots Point. ☎ *843/722–1691.* 🎟 *Ferry fare $11.* ⏲ *Tours usually leave from Municipal Marina daily at 9:30, noon, and 2:30, but they vary by season. Tours leave from Patriots Point daily at 10:45 and 1:30; Apr.–Labor Day, additional tour at 4.*

Museum on the Common. This small museum has an outdoor maritime museum and a Hurricane Hugo exhibit prepared by the South Carolina State Museum; it shows the 1989 storm damage through video and photos. ✉ *217 Lucas St., Shem Creek Village,* ☎ *843/849–9000.* 🎟 *Free.* ⏲ *Mon.–Sat. 10–4.*

Palmetto Islands County Park. You'll find a Big Toy playground, 2-acre pond, paved trails, an observation tower, marsh boardwalks, and a "water island" at this park across Boone Hall Creek from Boone Hall Plantation. Bicycles and pedal boats can be rented in season. ✉ *U.S. 17N, ½ mi past Snee Farm, turn left onto Long Point Rd.,* ☎ *843/884–0832.* 🎟 *$1.* ⏲ *Apr. and Sept.–Oct., daily 9–6; May–Aug., daily 9–7; Nov.–Feb., daily 10–5; Mar., daily 10–6.*

★ **Patriots Point.** Tours are available on all vessels here at the world's largest naval and maritime museum, now home to the Medal of Honor Society. Berthed here are the aircraft carrier *Yorktown,* the World War II submarine *Clamagore,* the destroyer *Laffey,* the nuclear merchant ship *Savannah,* and the cutter *Ingham,* responsible for sinking a U-boat during World War II. The film *The Fighting Lady* is shown regularly aboard the *Yorktown,* and there is a Vietnam exhibit. ✉ *Foot of Cooper River Bridges,* ☎ *843/884–2727.* 🎟 *$11.* ⏲ *Labor Day–Mar., daily 9–6:30; Apr.–Labor Day, daily 9–7:30.*

West of the Ashley River

A Good Tour

The sights covered here are each a few miles apart along Ashley River Road, SC 61, about 10 mi northwest of downtown Charleston over the Ashley River Bridge. Still, you'll need time to see them all. One day you could spend a few hours exploring **Charles Towne Landing State Park,** veering off SC 61 onto Old Towne Road (SC 171); then finish your day at **Middleton Gardens.** Another day you might tour the majestic simplicity of **Drayton Hall** before continuing on to **Magnolia Plantation and Gardens** and all their splendor.

TIMING

Nature and garden enthusiasts can easily spend a full day at Magnolia Gardens, Middleton Gardens, or Charles Towne Landing State Park, so budget your time accordingly. Spring is a peak time for the gardens, although they are lovely throughout the year.

Sights to See

★ **Charles Towne Landing State Park.** Commemorating the site of the original 1670 Charleston settlement, this park on SC 171N across the Ashley River Bridge has a reconstructed village and fortifications, English park gardens with bicycle trails and walkways, and a replica 17th-century vessel moored in the creek. In the animal park, native species roam freely—among them alligators, bison, pumas, bears, and wolves. Bicycle and kayak rentals and cassette and tram tours are available. ✉ *1500 Old Towne Rd.,* ☎ *843/852–4200.* *$5.* *Memorial Day–Labor Day, daily 9–6; Labor Day–Memorial Day, daily 9–5.*

★ **Drayton Hall.** Considered the nation's finest example of unspoiled Georgian-Palladian architecture, this mansion is the only plantation house on the Ashley River to have survived the Civil War. A National Historic Landmark, built between 1738 and 1742, it is an invaluable lesson in history as well as in architecture. Drayton Hall has been left unfurnished to highlight the original plaster moldings, opulent hand-carved woodwork, and other ornamental details. ✉ *3380 Ashley River Rd.,* ☎ *843/766–0188.* *$8; Mar.–Apr. and Sept.–Oct. $10.* *Guided tours Mar.–Oct., daily 10–4; Nov.–Feb., daily 10–3.*

Magnolia Plantation and Gardens. The 50-acre informal garden, begun in 1685, has a huge collection of azaleas and camellias. A tram will take you for an overall tour with three stops. You can canoe through the 125-acre Waterfowl Refuge, explore the 30-acre **Audubon Swamp Garden** along boardwalks and bridges, or walk or bicycle more than 500 acres of wildlife trails. Tours of the manor house, built during Reconstruction, depict plantation life. The grounds also hold a petting zoo and a miniature-horse ranch. ✉ *Ashley River Rd.,* ☎ *843/571–1266 or 800/367–3517.* *$10; house tour $6 extra; tram tour $5 extra; swamp tour $5 extra.* *Daily 8–5:30.*

★ **Middleton Place.** The nation's oldest landscaped gardens, dating from 1741, are magnificently ablaze with camellias, magnolias, azaleas, roses, and flowers of all seasons planted in floral *allées* and terraced lawns and around ornamental lakes. Much of the mansion was destroyed during the Civil War, but the south wing has been restored and houses impressive collections of silver, furniture, paintings, and historic documents. In the stable yard craftspeople use authentic tools and equipment to demonstrate spinning, blacksmithing, and other domestic skills from the plantation era. Farm animals, peacocks, and other creatures roam freely. The Middleton Place restaurant serves Lowcountry specialties for lunch daily; a gift shop carries local arts, crafts, and souvenirs. Also on the grounds is a modern, Danish-style inn (access to the gardens is included in the room price) with floor-to-ceiling windows dramatizing views of the Ashley River; here you can sign up for kayaking and biking tours. ✉ *Ashley River Rd.,* ☎ *843/556–6020 or 800/782–3608.* *$14; house tours $7 extra.* *Daily 9–5; house tours Tues.–Sun. 10–4:30, Mon. 1:30–4:30.*

OFF THE BEATEN PATH

AMERICAN CLASSIC TEA PLANTATION – On a small rural island about 20 mi west of Charleston on SC 700 is the country's only commercial tea plantation. Tours run from May through October and cover tea history, harvesting, and production and include a discussion with the plantation's official tea-taster. The tour ends with tea and cookies. ✉ *6617 Maybank Hwy., Wadmalaw Island,* ☎ *800/443–5987.* Free. *May–Oct., 1st Sat. each month 10–1:30.*

ANGEL OAK – This magnificent live oak has a massive canopy which creates 17,000 square ft of shade. Long a favorite with local children because of its bending branches that slope gently, armlike to the ground,

Angel Oak is believed to be more than 1,400 years old. It is about 15 mi west of Charleston off SC 700. ✉ *3688 Angel Oak Rd., Johns Island,* ☎ *843/559–3496.* *Free.* ⏲ *Daily 9–4:45.*

Dining

She-crab soup, sautéed shrimp and grits, variations on pecan pie, and other Lowcountry specialties are served all over the Charleston area—as are creative contemporary dishes crafted by local chefs. Outstanding eateries, from seafood houses to elegant French restaurants, make Charleston a mecca for gastronomes. Trendy Mount Pleasant, across the East Cooper Bridge, has a number of good restaurants.

Contemporary

$$$–$$$$ ✕ **McCrady's.** This revamped restaurant, in a 1778 tavern, has locals raving over its potato gnocchi, tuna tartare, grouper with creamy leek sauce and truffle oil, herb-marinated rack of lamb with mint drizzle, and molten chocolate cake. ✉ *2 Unity Alley,* ☎ *843/577–0025. No lunch. AE, MC, V.*

$$$–$$$$ ★ ✕ **Peninsula Grill.** Surrounded by walls covered in olive-green velvet, black iron chandeliers, and 18th-century-style portraits, diners at this busy spot in the Planters Inn (☞ Lodging, *below*) can feast on such delights as lobster citron, wild mushroom grits with oysters, and New Zealand benne-seed-encrusted rack of lamb. For dessert, try the divine lemon tart with lemon sorbet, lemon crisps, and candied lemon. ✉ *112 N. Market St.,* ☎ *843/723–0700. No lunch. AE, D, DC, MC, V.*

$–$$$ ✕ **Sermet's Corner.** Colorful, bold artwork by chef Sermet Aslan decorates the walls of this lively eatery. The Mediterranean menu has *panini* (grilled Italian sandwiches), seafood, and flavorful pastas; the poached pear salad and lavender pork are favorites. ✉ *276 King St.,* ☎ *843/853–7775. AE, MC, V.*

French

$$$$ ✕ **Robert's of Charleston.** After a 10-year sabbatical, Charleston's classically trained singer and chef reopened his restaurant. The special experience is much the same: four rich, generously portioned courses with lovely wines, impeccable service, and the best of Broadway tunes in a warm, intimate dining room. Signature dishes are scallop mousse with lobster sauce, duckling with grilled vegetables, and roast tenderloin with bordelaise (wine sauce with brown stock and herbs) sauce. ✉ *182 E. Bay St.,* ☎ *843/577–7565. No lunch. MC, V.*

$–$$ ✕ **Gaulart and Maliclet Café Restaurant.** This casual, chic eatery serves Continental dishes—breads and pastries, soups, salads, sandwiches, and specials such as seafood Normandy and chicken sesame. ✉ *98 Broad St.,* ☎ *843/577–9797. AE, D, MC, V. Closed Sun. No dinner Mon.*

Italian

$$$ ✕ **Fulton Five.** There are just 15 tables in this romantic restaurant on a side road off King Street. The chartreuse walls and antique brass accents provide the perfect setting to savor northern Italian specialties like risotto; lemon sherbet with Campari; and antipasto Spoleto, mozzarella and prosciutto wrapped in a romaine lettuce leaf and drizzled with olive oil and diced tomatoes. ✉ *5 Fulton St.,* ☎ *843/853–5555. AE, DC, MC, V. Closed Sun., late Aug.–1st wk Sept. No lunch.*

$–$$ ✕ **Il Cortile del Re.** Great wines, hearty soups and pastas, and lovely cheeses and breads make it feel just like Tuscany. Tucked off King Street behind a women's clothing shop, this hard-to-find spot has a cozy back room and a romantic courtyard with a crumbling brick wall. ✉ *193 King St.,* ☎ *843/853–1888. AE, DC, MC, V. Closed Mon.–Sun. No lunch Thurs.–Sat.*

Dining

Alice's Fine Foods . . . **11**
Anson **22**
Barbadoes Room . . . **36**
Boathouse Restaurant **2, 8**
Carolina's **43**
Charleston Grill **28**
Elliott's on the Square. . . **14**
Fulton Five **29**
Gaulart and Maliclet Café Restaurant **37**
High Cotton **39**
Hominy Grill **9**
Il Cortile del Re. **30**
J. Bistro **5**
Louis's Restaurant . . . **24**
Magnolias **42**
McCrady's. **34**
Peninsula Grill **25**
Robert's of Charleston . . **41**
Sermet's Corner **19**
Slightly North of Broad **40**
Sticky Fingers **26**
The Wreck **3**

Lodging

Ansonborough Inn . . **21**
Best Western King Charles Inn **20**
Cannonboro Inn and Ashley Inn **15**
Charleston Place. . . . **27**
Doubletree Guest Suites Historic Charleston . . **23**
1837 Bed and Breakfast and Tea Room **17**
Elliott House Inn **35**
Embassy Suites Historic Charleston **12**
Francis Marion Hotel. . . **14**
Guilds Inn **7**
Hampton Inn Charleston Airport . . . **1**
Hampton Inn Historic District **10**
Hayne House **44**
Harborview Inn **33**
Holiday Inn Charleston/Mount Pleasant. **4**
Holiday Inn Historic District. **13**
John Rutledge House Inn **38**
Meeting Street Inn. . . **31**
Mills House Hotel . . . **36**
Planters Inn **25**
Phoebe Pember House . . **16**
Red Roof Inn **6**
Two Meeting Street . . **45**
Vendue Inn. **32**
Wentworth Mansion. . . **18**

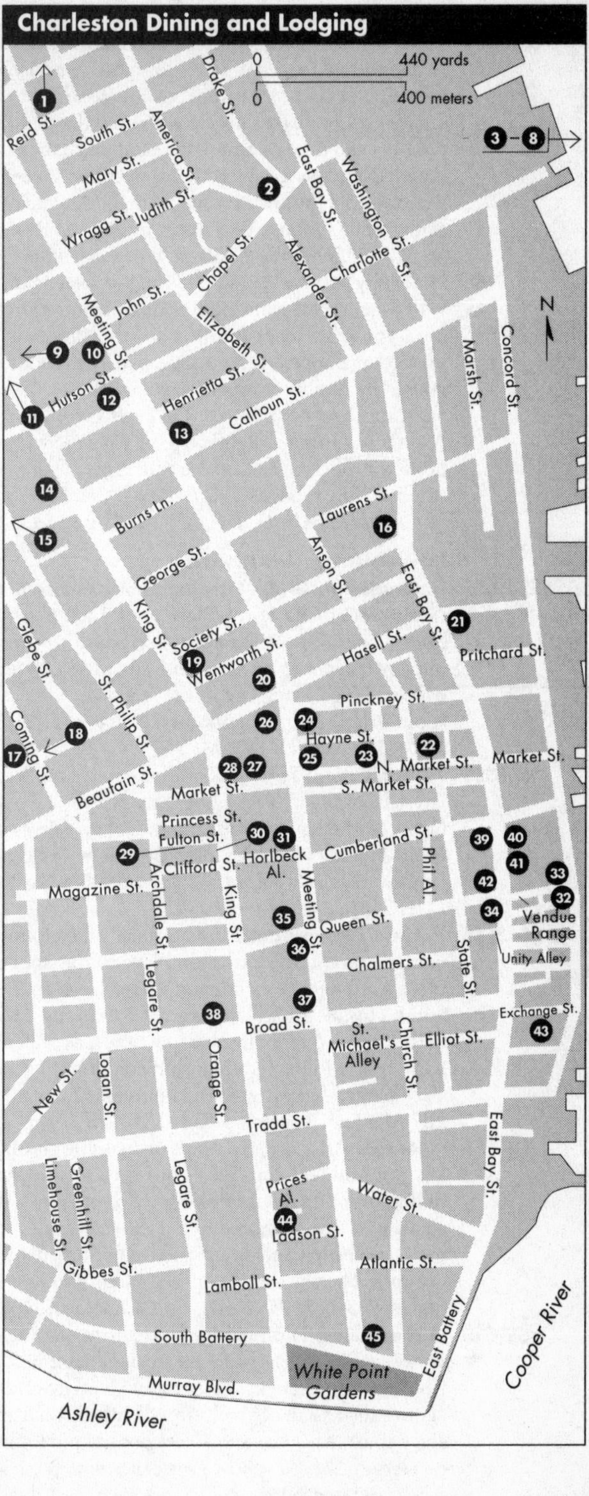

Lowcountry

$$–$$$$ ✕ **Carolina's.** Lively and bustling, Carolina's has long been a favorite. Black-and-white decor, terra-cotta tiles, and 1920s French posters create a casual bistro atmosphere. Fans return for the "appeteasers" such as crowder pea cakes (made with crowder peas, spices, egg, and bread crumbs) and fried calamari, plus smoked baby-back ribs and pasta with crawfish and tasso (spiced ham) in cream sauce. Dinner entrées are selections from the grill: among them, pork tenderloin with Jamaican seasoning and salmon with cilantro, ginger, and lime butter. ✉ *10 Exchange St.,* ☎ *843/724–3800. Reservations essential. D, MC, V. No lunch.*

$$ ★ ✕ **Slightly North of Broad.** This high-ceiling haunt with brick-and-stucco walls has several seats looking directly into the exposed kitchen. From here you'll see chef Frank Lee laboring over his inventive dishes: sautéed quail filled with sausage, pad Thai noodles with shrimp or pork, and an incredible Southern vegetable plate. You can order most items as an appetizer or an entrée. The extensive wine list is moderately priced. A sister restaurant, Slightly Up the Creek (✉ 130 Mill St., ☎ 843/884–5005), at Shem Creek in Mount Pleasant, has waterfront views and similarly fine food. ✉ *192 E. Bay St.,* ☎ *843/723–3424. Reservations not accepted. AE, D, DC, MC, V. Closed Sun. No lunch Sat.*

Lowcountry/Southern

$$$–$$$$ ✕ **Charleston Grill.** With its clubby chairs and dark paneling, the restaurant at Charleston Place (☞ Lodging, *below*) is comfortably elegant. Chef Bob Waggoner's new South cuisine includes lobster tempura over lemon grits; salad with spicy fried oysters; and beef medallions over whipped black-eyed peas in a roasted pecan and shiitake mushroom sauce. Many nights there's live jazz. ✉ *224 King St.,* ☎ *843/577–4522. AE, D, DC, MC, V.*

$$–$$$$ ✕ **High Cotton.** This brick-walled eatery studded with palm trees is the latest from the owners of Slightly North of Broad (☞ *above*) and Elliott's on the Square (☞ *below*). Diners enjoy spit-roasted and grilled meats and fish. The chocolate souffle with blackberry sauce and praline souffle are fabulous. ✉ *199 East Bay St.,* ☎ *843/724–3815. AE, D, DC, MC, V. No lunch.*

$$–$$$$ ✕ **Louis's Restaurant.** Louis Osteen's fans followed him from his former restaurant at Charleston Place to this spot across the street. This place has a light, very contemporary Japanese feel, and serves the new South cuisine for which the chef is famous. Here you'll find his she-crab soup and crab and lobster cakes, as well as roasted Chilean sea bass, roasted duck, and lamb medallions. The inventive menu at the sleek bar, including fresh tuna burgers and pickled eggs, is inviting. ✉ *200 Meeting St.,* ☎ *843/853–2550. AE, D, DC, MC, V. No lunch.*

$$–$$$ ✕ **Anson.** After an afternoon of strolling through the Old City Market, you can walk up Anson Street to this softly lighted, gilt-trimmed dining room. Framed by about a dozen French windows, Anson's has elegant booths anchored by marble-top tables. New South specialties include shrimp and grits, fried corn bread oysters, and barbecued grouper. The she-crab soup is some of the best around. ✉ *12 Anson St.,* ☎ *843/577–0551. AE, D, DC, MC, V. No lunch.*

$$–$$$ ★ ✕ **Magnolias.** This popular place, in an 1823 warehouse, is a local favorite, with a magnolia theme in vivid paintings, etched glass, wrought iron, and candlesticks. The uptown Down South cuisine shines in specialties such as an egg roll stuffed with chicken and collard greens with spicy mustard sauce and sweet pepper puree. Equally innovative appetizers are seared yellow grits cakes with tasso gravy and yellow corn relish, and sautéed greens. There's even fried chicken with mashed potatoes and mushroom gravy. You may also want to try the **Blossom Café** (✉ 171 E. Bay St., ☎ 843/722–9200), owned by the same people but

with a more Continental menu, including pizzas cooked in a wood-burning oven, pastas, and fish. ✉ *185 E. Bay St.,* ☎ *843/577–7771. Reservations essential. AE, DC, MC, V.*

$$ ✕ **Elliott's on the Square.** This bright and cheerful restaurant in the Francis Marion Hotel (☞ Lodging, *below*) serves Southern Sunday-dinner-style entrées for lunch and dinner, including black-eyed pea cakes, fried chicken, BBQ salmon over grits, and butter pound cake. The food may be down-home, but the service is not. ✉ *387 King St.,* ☎ *843/724–8888. AE, D, DC, MC, V.*

$–$$$ ✕ **J. Bistro.** Funky steel cutouts liven up the outside and inside walls of this Mount Pleasant eatery. The lighting is whimsical and hangs low over tables lined up against a banquette. A varied list of appetizers and small plates makes this a great place to graze. Choose from such innovations as steamed lobster wontons, grouper with champagne crabmeat cream sauce, and pecan-crusted catfish over grits. The lamb chop is superb. ✉ *819 Coleman Blvd., Mount Pleasant,* ☎ *843/971–7778. Reservations essential. AE, MC, V.* ⊗ *Closed Mon. No lunch. No dinner Sun.*

$–$$ ✕ **Sticky Fingers.** Specializing in ribs six ways (Memphis-style wet and dry, Texas-style wet and dry, Carolina sweet, and Tennessee whiskey) and barbecue, this family-friendly restaurant has locations downtown and in Mount Pleasant and Summerville. Tuesday night is children's night, with supervised games and cartoons in a playroom. ✉ *235 Meeting St.,* ☎ *843/853–7427 or 800/671–5966; U.S. 17 Bypass, Mount Pleasant,* ☎ *843/856–9840; 1200 N. Main St., Summerville,* ☎ *843/875–7969. AE, DC, MC, V.*

$ ★ ✕ **Alice's Fine Foods.** The food Southerners crave is here in its original, beloved form: baked or fried chicken, ribs, fried fish, and other entrées come with a choice of three home-cooked vegetables and side dishes, including green beans, collard greens, red rice, macaroni-and-cheese pie, okra and tomatoes, lima beans, rice and gravy, yams, and squash. ✉ *468–470 King St.,* ☎ *843/853–9366. MC, V.*

$ ✕ **Hominy Grill.** Locals lunch and brunch at this breezy, café-style restaurant. Though a bit off the beaten path, it's worth a special trip. The young chef's Southern upbringing is evident in everything from the vegetable plate (collards, squash casserole, black-eyed-pea cakes with guacamole, and mushroom hominy) to the pimento cheese sandwich or turkey club with homemade french fries. The avocado and *wehani* rice salad with grilled vegetables is a refreshing don't-miss in the summer. Leave room for the excellent buttermilk pie or bread pudding. ✉ *207 Rutledge Ave.,* ☎ *843/937–0930. AE, MC, V.*

Seafood

$$–$$$ ✕ **Barbadoes Room.** This large, airy plant- and light-filled space has a sophisticated island look and a view out to a cheery courtyard garden. The menu includes she-crab soup, blackened shrimp and scallops, and oyster and crab gratin. The extensive breakfast buffet and Sunday brunch are packed. ✉ *115 Meeting St., in the Mills House Hotel,* ☎ *843/577–2400. Reservations essential. D, DC, MC, V.*

$–$$$ ★ ✕ **Boathouse Restaurant.** Large portions of fresh seafood at reasonable prices make both locations of the Boathouse Restaurant wildly popular. The crab dip, fish specials, and lightly battered fried shrimp and oysters are irresistible. Entrées come with heaping helpings of mashed potatoes, grits, collard greens, or blue-cheese coleslaw. The original Isle of Palms location is right on the water. ✉ *101 Palm Blvd., Isle of Palms,* ☎ *843/886–8000;* ✉ *14 Chapel St.,* ☎ *843/886–8000. Reservations essential. AE, DC, MC, V.*

$–$$ ✕ **The Wreck.** Dockside and full of wacky character, this spot serves up such traditional dishes as boiled peanuts, fried shrimp, shrimp pilaf, deviled crab, and oyster platters in a shabby, candlelit screened-in porch and small dining area. ✉ *106 Haddrell St., Mount Pleasant,* ☎ *843/884–0052. Reservations not accepted. No credit cards.*

Lodging

Rates tend to increase during the Spring Festival of Houses and Spoleto, when reservations are essential. The **Charleston Area Convention and Visitors Bureau** (✉ Box 975, Charleston 29402, ☎ 843/853–8000 or 800/868–8118) distributes a Visitor Value Days Card entitling the bearer to 10%–50% off at many accommodations between December 1 and March 1.

Hotels and Motels

$$$$ ★ **Charleston Place.** This Orient Express property, a graceful low-rise structure in the historic district, is surrounded by upscale boutiques and specialty shops. The lobby has a magnificent handblown Venetian-glass chandelier, an Italian marble floor, and antiques from Sotheby's. Rooms are furnished with period reproductions, linen sheets and robes, and fax machines. The hotel is world class. ✉ *130 Market St., 29401,* ☎ *843/722–4900 or 800/611–5545,* FAX *843/724–7215. 400 rooms, 40 suites. 2 restaurants, 2 lounges, minibars, indoor pool, hot tub, sauna, steam room, exercise room, concierge floors. AE, D, DC, MC, V.*

$$$–$$$$ **Embassy Suites Historic Charleston.** The courtyard of the Old Citadel military school where cadets once marched is now a skylighted atrium with stone flooring, armchairs, palm trees, and a fountain. The restored brick walls of the breakfast room and some guest rooms in this contemporary hotel contain original gun ports, reminders that the 1822 building was originally a fortification. Teak and mahogany furniture, safari motifs, and sisal carpeting recall the British colonial era. Breakfast and evening refreshments are complimentary. ✉ *341 Meeting St., 29403,* ☎ *843/723–6900 or 800/362–2779,* FAX *843/723–6938. 153 suites. Lounge, pool, exercise room. AE, D, DC, MC, V. BP.*

$$$–$$$$ **HarborView Inn.** Overlooking the harbor and Waterfront Park, this new inn is close to most downtown attractions. Calming earth tones and rattan are abundant; high ceilings, four poster beds, and sea-grass rugs complete the Lowcountry look. Some of the rooms are in a former 19th-century shipping warehouse with exposed brick walls; some have fireplaces and whirlpool tubs. Continental breakfast, afternoon wine and cheese, and evening cookies are included. ✉ *2 Vendue Range, 29401,* ☎ *843/853–8439 or 888/853–8439,* FAX *843/853–4034. 51 rooms, 1 suite. Concierge, business services. AE, D, DC, MC, V. CP.*

$$$–$$$$ **Mills House Hotel.** Antique furnishings and period decor give charm to a luxurious Holiday Inn property, a reconstruction of an old hostelry on its original site in the historic district. Though rooms are small and a bit standard, the hotel has a lounge with live entertainment and excellent dining in the Barbadoes Room (☞ Dining, *above*). ✉ *115 Meeting St., 29401,* ☎ *843/577–2400 or 800/874–9600,* FAX *843/722–0623. 199 rooms, 16 suites. Restaurant, 2 lounges. AE, D, DC, MC, V.*

$$–$$$$ **Doubletree Guest Suites Historic Charleston.** Across from the City Market, this hotel has a restored entrance portico from an 1874 bank, a refurbished 1866 firehouse, and three lush gardens. The spacious suites, all decorated with 18th-century reproductions and canopy beds, have full kitchens or wet bars with microwave ovens and refrigerators. ✉ *181 Church St., 29401,* ☎ *843/577–2644 or 800/222–8733,* FAX *843/577–2697. 182 suites. Lounge, hot tub, exercise room, business services, meeting rooms. AE, D, DC, MC, V.*

$$–$$$ **Best Western King Charles Inn.** Renovated in 1997, this inn in the historic district is a cut above the typical chain, with a welcoming lobby and sitting area and spacious rooms furnished with 18th-century period reproductions. ✉ *237 Meeting St., 29401,* ☎ *843/723–7451 or 800/528–1234,* FAX *843/723–2041. 91 rooms. Dining room, lounge, pool. AE, D, DC, MC, V.*

$$–$$$ ★ **Francis Marion Hotel.** Built in 1924 as the largest hotel in the Carolinas, the restored Francis Marion is now a Westin property. It retains big-band and tea-dance glamour with its windowed ballrooms, wrought-iron railings, columns, high ceilings, crown moldings, decorative plasterwork, and views of Marion Square and the harbor. A few rooms have their original pedestal sinks and deep tubs. Excellent Southern cuisine can be had at Elliott's on the Square (☞ Dining, *above*). ✉ *387 King St., 29403,* ☎ *843/722–0600,* FAX *843/723–4633. 160 rooms, 66 suites. Restaurant, lounge, health club, meeting rooms. AE, D, DC, MC, V.*

$$–$$$ **Meeting Street Inn.** Built in 1874, this salmon-color former tavern in the historic district overlooks a lovely courtyard with fountains and gardens. Spacious rooms have hardwood floors, high ceilings, and reproduction furniture including four-poster rice beds. ✉ *173 Meeting St., 29401,* ☎ *843/723–1882 or 800/842–8022,* FAX *843/577–0851. 56 rooms. Meeting room. AE, D, DC, MC, V. CP.*

$$ **Holiday Inn Historic District.** Though this hotel changed hands and went through a major renovation, it still draws loyal repeat visitors because of its free parking and location a block from the Gaillard Municipal Auditorium and within walking distance of many must-see spots. Rooms are motel modern. ✉ *125 Calhoun St., 29401,* ☎ *843/805–7900,* FAX *843/805–7700. 133 rooms. Restaurant, lounge, pool, meeting rooms. AE, D, DC, MC, V.*

$–$$ ★ **Hampton Inn–Historic District.** This downtown chain has hardwood floors and a fireplace in the elegant lobby, guest rooms with period reproductions, and a courtyard garden. It is a front-runner in its price category. ✉ *345 Meeting St., 29403,* ☎ *843/723–4000 or 800/426–7866,* FAX *843/722–3725. 166 rooms, 5 suites. Pool. AE, D, DC, MC, V. CP.*

$–$$ **Holiday Inn Charleston/Mount Pleasant.** Just over the Cooper River Bridge, the Holiday Inn is a 10-minute drive from the downtown historic district. Everything has been gracefully done: brass lamps, crystal chandeliers, Queen Anne–style furniture. The suites designated as high-tech have PC cable hookups, large working areas, glossy ultramodern furniture, and refrigerators. ✉ *250 U.S. 17, Mount Pleasant 29464,* ☎ *843/884–6000 or 800/290–4004,* FAX *843/881–1786. 158 rooms. Restaurant, lounge, pool, sauna, exercise room, concierge floor, meeting rooms. AE, D, DC, MC, V.*

$ **Hampton Inn Charleston Airport.** Near the airport in North Charleston, this chain motel is clean and quiet. Guests have access to a health club nearby. ✉ *4701 Saul White Blvd., North Charleston 29418,* ☎ *843/554–7154,* FAX *843/566–9299. 125 rooms. Pool. AE, D, DC, MC, V.*

$ **Red Roof Inn.** At the foot of the Cooper River Bridge about 10 minutes from historic Charleston, this chain motel is clean and well lighted. Rooms have work areas. ✉ *301 Johnnie Dodds Blvd., 29403,* ☎ *843/884–1411 or 800/843–7663,* FAX *843/884–1411. 126 rooms. Pool. AE, D, DC, MC, V.*

Inns and Guest Houses

$$$$ ★ **John Rutledge House Inn.** This 1763 house, built by John Rutledge, one of the framers of the U.S. Constitution, is one of Charleston's most luxurious inns. The ornate ironwork, original woodwork, plaster

moldings, parquet floors, marble fireplaces, and 14-ft ceilings are impressive. A lovely afternoon tea including wine is served in the ballroom, and Continental breakfast and newspapers are delivered to your room. Two charming period carriage houses also accommodate guests. There are whirlpool tubs and fireplaces in some guest rooms. ✉ *116 Broad St., 29401,* ☎ *843/723–7999 or 800/476–9741,* FAX *843/720–2615. 11 rooms in mansion, 4 in each of 2 carriage houses. In-room data ports, business services. AE, D, DC, MC, V. CP.*

$$$$ **Wentworth Mansion.** This spectacular brick mansion, built around 1886 as a private home, is now a luxury inn. Hand-carved marble fireplaces, rich woodwork, Tiffany stained-glass windows, and Second Empire reproductions create an elegant atmosphere in the spacious guest rooms. Breakfast buffet, afternoon tea, wine tastings, evening cordials, turndown service, and on-site parking are included. Rooms have king-size beds and oversize whirlpools; most have gas fireplaces. Circa 1886, in the former carriage house, serves inventive food and is the perfect spot for a special occasion. ✉ *149 Wentworth St., 29403,* ☎ *843/853–1886 or 888/466–1886,* FAX *843/723–8634. 21 rooms. Restaurant, lounge. AE, D, DC, MC, V. BP.*

$$$–$$$$ ★ **Two Meeting Street.** As pretty as a wedding cake and just as romantic, this early 20th-century inn near the Battery has very private honeymoon suites. There are Tiffany windows, carved English oak paneling, and a chandelier from the former Czechoslovakia. Guests are treated to afternoon high tea and Continental breakfast. ✉ *2 Meeting St., 29401,* ☎ *843/723–7322. 7 rooms, 2 suites. No credit cards. CP.*

$$–$$$$ **Hayne House.** One block from the Battery in Charleston's prestigious South of Broad neighborhood, the Hayne house was built in 1755. It has old furnishings but a fresh, light spirit. Rooms are dominated by Federal antiques and other heirlooms from the proprietors' families. Two of the guest rooms are in the main house; the other four are in the kitchen house, with its narrow stairway, colonial brickwork, and chimney. ✉ *30 King St., 29401,* ☎ *843/577–2633,* FAX *843/577–5906. 4 rooms, 2 suites. MC, V. CP.*

$$$ **Ansonborough Inn.** Formerly a stationer's warehouse dating from the early 1900s, this spacious all-suite inn is furnished in period reproductions. It offers hair dryers, irons, a morning newspaper, message service, wine reception, and Continental breakfast, but it's best known for its friendly staff. ✉ *21 Hasell St., 29401,* ☎ *843/723–1655 or 800/522–2073,* FAX *843/527–6888. 37 suites. Meeting room. AE, MC, V. CP.*

$$$ **Planters Inn.** High-ceiling rooms and suites are beautifully appointed with opulent furnishings, including mahogany four-poster beds and marble baths. Twenty-one rooms have a piazza overlooking the garden courtyard. The inn's Peninsula Grill (☞ Dining, *above*) is wonderful. ✉ *112 N. Market St., 29401,* ☎ *843/722–2345 or 800/845–7082,* FAX *843/577–2125. 56 rooms, 6 suites. Restaurant, room service, concierge, business services. AE, D, DC, MC, V.*

$$$ **Vendue Inn.** Many rooms of this elegant yet friendly inn look out over the harbor and Waterfront Park. Guest rooms have four-poster beds, cozy seating areas, and large bathrooms. A full buffet breakfast plus afternoon wine and cheese are complimentary. Climb up to the inn's rooftop terrace bar for sweeping views of the harbor along with drinks and appetizers from the inn's Library Restaurant. ✉ *19 Vendue Range, 29401,* ☎ *843/577–7970 or 800/845–7900. 22 rooms, 24 suites. Restaurant, lounge, exercise room, business services, meeting rooms. AE, D, DC, MC, V. BP.*

$$–$$$ **Phoebe Pember House.** Built in 1807, the mansion still has its separate kitchen and slaves quarters, both of which now have two guest rooms upstairs and a living room, dining room, kitchenette, and garden downstairs. Colors and fabrics are cheerful yet refined; artwork is by Charleston artists. The inn is off a busy street, but the piazza is cocooned by a walled garden overlooking Charleston's port. A Continental breakfast of croissants and fruit is delivered to your room or the piazza. ✉ *26 Society St.,* ☎ *843/722–4186,* FAX *843/722–0557. 7 rooms, carriage house. AE, MC, V. CP.*

$$ **Cannonboro Inn and Ashley Inn.** Two of the most elegant inns in town, these B&B neighbors on the edge of the historic district near the Medical University have luxurious rooms, tastefully decorated in period furnishings. Guests are treated to a full English breakfast on piazzas overlooking Charleston gardens. Use of the bicycles, afternoon refreshments, and convenient parking in an off-street lot are all included. ✉ *Cannonboro: 184 Ashley Ave., 29403,* ☎ *843/723–8572,* FAX *843/723–8007. 6 rooms. Bicycles, business services. MC, V. BP. Ashley: 201 Ashley Ave., 29403,* ☎ *843/723–1848,* FAX *843/579–9080. 6 rooms, 1 suite. Bicycles, business services. AE, D, MC, V. BP.*

$$ **1837 Bed and Breakfast and Tea Room.** Though not as fancy as some of the B&Bs in town, this inn is long on hospitality; you'll get a sense of what it's really like to live in one of Charleston's beloved homes. Restored and operated by two artists-teachers, the home and carriage house have rooms filled with antiques, including romantic canopied beds. A gourmet breakfast of homemade breads and hot entrées such as sausage pie or ham frittata is included in the rate, as is the afternoon tea (open to the public for a nominal price). ✉ *126 Wentworth St., 29401,* ☎ *843/723–7166. 8 rooms. AE, MC, V. BP.*

$$ **Elliott House Inn.** Listen to the chimes of St. Michael's Episcopal Church as you sip wine in the courtyard of this lovely old inn in the heart of the historic district. You can then retreat to a cozy room with period furniture, including canopied four-posters and Oriental carpets. ✉ *78 Queen St., 29401,* ☎ *843/723–1855 or 800/729–1855,* FAX *843/722–1567. 26 rooms. Hot tub, bicycles. AE, D, MC, V. CP.*

$$ **Guilds Inn.** There's no lack of charm at this place in Mount Pleasant's historic and scenic Old Village, a residential area with a soda fountain, antiques shop, and restaurant. The National Historic Register property has hardwood floors, traditional Lowcountry furnishings, and a mix of antiques and reproductions. Rooms have whirlpool tubs. ✉ *101 Pitt St., Mount Pleasant 29464,* ☎ *843/881–0510 or 800/331–0510,* FAX *843/884–5020. 6 rooms. AE, D, MC, V. CP.*

Resort Islands

The semitropical islands dotting the South Carolina coast near Charleston are home to several sumptuous resorts that offer a wide variety of packages. Peak season rates (during spring and summer vacations) range from $140 to $300 per day, double occupancy. Costs drop considerably off-season.

$$$$ **Wild Dunes.** This serene 1,600-acre resort on the Isle of Palms has 250 one- to six-bedroom villas and homes for rent, each with a kitchen and washer and dryer. The plantation-style Boardwalk Inn at Wild Dunes is just a few yards from the beach; many rooms have balconies and overlook the ocean. There are two acclaimed golf courses, a racquet club, a yacht harbor on the Intracoastal Waterway, and a long list of recreational options. Tradewinds Restaurant has lovely views of the waterway; the Grill at the Boardwalk Inn has a piazza for alfresco dining from its Continental menu. ✉ *Box 20575, Charleston 29413,* ☎ *843/886–6000 or 800/845–8880,* FAX *843/886–2916. 250 units, 93 rooms. 4 restaurants, lounge, 2 18-hole golf courses, 19 tennis courts, health club, boating, fishing, bicycles, rollerblading, children's programs. AE, D, DC, MC, V.*

$$$–$$$$ **Kiawah Island Resort.** Choose from 150 inn rooms and 430 completely equipped one- to five-bedroom villas and private homes in two luxurious resort villages on 10,000 wooded acres. There are 10 mi of fine broad beaches and an array of recreational opportunities. Dining options are many and varied. ✉ *12 Kiawah Beach Dr., Kiawah Island 29455,* ☎ *843/768–2121 or 800/654–2924,* FAX *843/768–6099. 150 rooms, 430 villas and private homes. 8 restaurants, 5 18-hole golf courses, 28 tennis courts, boating, fishing, bicycles, shops, children's programs. AE, D, DC, MC, V.*

$$$–$$$$ **Seabrook Island Resort.** A total of 175 completely equipped one- to three-bedroom villas, cottages, and beach houses dot this property. The Beach Club and Island House, open to all guests, are centers for dining and leisure activities. Bohicket Marina Village, the hub of activity around the island, offers three fine restaurants as well as pizza and sub shops. The marina area includes opportunities for shopping as well as scuba diving, deep-sea and inshore fishing charters, and small-boat rentals. ✉ *1002 Landfall Way, Seabrook Island 29455,* ☎ *843/768–1000 or 800/845–2475,* FAX *843/768–3096. 175 units. 3 restaurants, 2 pools, 2 18-hole golf courses, 13 tennis courts, horseback riding, boating, parasailing, fishing, bicycles, children's programs. AE, D, DC, MC, V.*

Nightlife and the Arts

The Arts

CONCERTS

The **Charleston Concert Association** (☎ 843/722–7667) has information on visiting performing arts groups including symphonies, ballets, and operas. The **Charleston Symphony Orchestra** (843/723–7528) presents MasterWorks Series, Downtown Pops, First Union Family Series, and an annual holiday concert at Gaillard Municipal Auditorium (✉ 77 Calhoun St., ☎ 843/577–4500). The orchestra also performs the Sotille Chamber Series at the Sotille Theater (✉ 44 George St., ☎ 843/953–6340) and the Light and Lively Pops at Charleston Southern University (✉ U.S. 78, ☎ 843/953–6340). The College of Charleston has a free **Monday Night Recital Series** (☎ 843/953–8228).

DANCE

Anonymity Dance Company (☎ 843/886–6104 or 800/215–6523), a modern dance troupe, performs throughout the city. The **Charleston Ballet Theatre** (✉ 477 King St., ☎ 843/723–7334) performs everything from classical to contemporary dance at locations around the city. The **Robert Ivey Ballet Company** (☎ 843/556–1343), a semiprofessional company that includes several College of Charleston students, gives a fall and spring program of jazz, classical, and modern dance at the Sotille Theater.

FESTIVALS

The **Fall Candlelight Tours of Homes and Gardens** (✉ Box 521, 29402, ☎ 843/722–4630), sponsored by the Preservation Society of Charleston in September and October, offers an inside look at Charleston's private buildings and gardens.

During the **Festival of Houses and Gardens** (✉ Box 1120, 29202, ☎ 843/724–8484), held during March and April each year, more than 100 private homes, gardens, and historic churches are open to the public for tours sponsored by the Historic Charleston Foundation. There are also symphony galas in stately drawing rooms, plantation oyster roasts, and candlelight tours.

MOJA Arts Festival (✉ Office of Cultural Affairs, 133 Church St., 29401, ☎ 843/724–7305), which takes place during the last week of September and first week of October, celebrates the rich heritage of the African continent and Caribbean influences on African-American culture. It includes theater, dance, and music performances; art shows; films; lectures; and tours of the historic district.

Piccolo Spoleto Festival (✉ Office of Cultural Affairs, 133 Church St., 29401, ☎ 843/724–7305) is the spirited companion festival of Spoleto Festival USA, showcasing the best in local and regional talent from every artistic discipline. There are about 300 events—from jazz performances to puppet shows—held at 60 sites in 17 days from mid-May through early June, and most performances are free.

The **Southeastern Wildlife Exposition** (✉ 211 Meeting St., 29401, ☎ 843/723–1748 or 800/221–5273) in mid-February is one of Charleston's biggest annual events. It displays art by renowned wildlife artists.

Spoleto Festival USA (✉ Box 704, 29402, ☎ 843/722–2764), founded by the composer Gian Carlo Menotti in 1977, has become a world-famous celebration of the arts. For two weeks, from late May to early June, opera, dance, theater, symphonic and chamber music performances, jazz, and the visual arts are showcased in concert halls, theaters, parks, churches, streets, and gardens throughout the city.

The reasonably priced **Worldfest Charleston** (✉ Box 838, 29402, ☎ 843/723–7600 or 800/501–0111), held in mid-November, premieres new films from around the world, offers workshops and seminars, and provides opportunities to meet the producers, directors, and actors.

FILM

The **American Theater** (✉ 446 King St., ☎ 843/722–3456), a renovated theater from the 1940s, shows current movies in a table-and-chairs setting with pizza, burgers, finger foods, beer, and wine. Upstairs there's a virtual reality game center. The **Roxy** (✉ 245 E. Bay St., ☎ 843/853–7699) has films from around the world plus wine, beer, coffee drinks, pastries, sandwiches, and pasta.

THEATER

Several groups, including the Footlight Players and Charleston Stage Company, perform at the **Dock Street Theatre** (✉ 135 Church St., ☎ 843/723–5648). **Pluff Mud Productions** puts on comedies at the Isle of Palms' Windjammer (✉ 1000 Ocean Blvd., ☎ 843/886–8596). Performances by the College of Charleston's theater department and guest theatrical groups are presented during the school year at the **Simons Center for the Arts** (✉ 54 St. Phillips St., ☎ 843/953–5604).

The **Cavallaro** (✉ 1478 Savannah Hwy., ☎ 843/763–9222) is the home of several successful dinner theater productions.

Nightlife

DANCING AND MUSIC

Cumberland's (✉ 26 Cumberland St., ☎ 843/577–9469) has live blues, rock, reggae, and bluegrass Monday through Saturday; the place is also known for wings and cheap beer. Live bands entertain at the **Indigo Lounge** (✉ 5 Faber St., ☎ 843/577–7383) each weekend. The **Mills House Hotel** (✉ 115 Meeting St., ☎ 843/577–2400), favored by an elegant, older crowd, has a lively bar and either a live big band or swing music on Tuesday night. Most evenings **Momma's Blues Palace** (✉ 46 John St., ☎ 843/853–2221) has live music starting at 10 PM. The **Music Farm** (✉ 32 Ann St., ☎ 843/853–3276) features live national and local alternative bands. There's swing-dancing and funky '70s music at **Trio Club** (✉ 139 Calhoun St., ☎ 843/965–5333) Wednesday through Saturday. The **Windjammer** (✉ 1000 Ocean Blvd., ☎ 843/886–8596), on the Isle of Palms, is an oceanfront spot with live rock.

DINNER CRUISES

For an evening of dining and dancing, climb aboard the luxury yacht, ***Spirit of Carolina*** (☎ 843/722–2628). Reservations are essential; there are no cruises Sunday and Monday.

Breakfast, brunch, deli, and hot luncheons are prepared on board the ***Charlestowne Princess*** (☎ 843/722–1112), which also offers its Harborlites Dinner with live entertainment and dancing while cruising the harbor and rivers.

HOTEL AND JAZZ BARS

The **Best Friend Lounge** (✉ 115 Meeting St., ☎ 843/577–2400), in the Mills House Hotel, has a guitarist playing light tunes most nights. The elegant **Charleston Grill** (✉ 224 King St., ☎ 843/577–4522), in Charleston Place, offers live jazz nightly. In the **Lobby Lounge** (✉ 130 Market St., ☎ 843/722–4900) in Charleston Place, cocktails and appetizers are accompanied by piano. At **Mistral Restaurant** (✉ 99 S. Market St., ☎ 843/722–5709) there's a regular four-piece jazz band on weekends. **Mitchell's** (✉ 102 N. Market St., ☎ 843/722–0732) has nightly, changing acts, from jazz pianists to bands.

LOUNGES AND BARS/BREWERIES

Charlie's Little Bar (✉ 141 E. Bay St., ☎ 843/723–6242), above Saracen Restaurant, is intimate, cozy, and popular with young professionals. **Club Habana** (✉ 177 Meeting St., ☎ 843/853–5900) is a chic, wood-paneled martini bar (open late) with a cigar shop downstairs. **Southend Brewery** (✉ 161 E. Bay St., ☎ 843/853–4677) has a lively bar with beer brewed on the premises; the food is good, especially soups. You'll find authentic Irish music at **Tommy Condon's Irish Pub & Restaurant** (✉ 160 Church St., ☎ 843/577–3818). **Vickery's Bar & Grill** (✉ 139 Calhoun St., ☎ 843/723–1558) is a festive nightspot with a spacious outdoor patio and good, late-night food. There's another equally popular location in Mount Pleasant (✉ 1205 Shrimp Boat La., ☎ 843/849–6770). **Zebo** (✉ 275 King St., ☎ 843/577–7600) brews its beer here and offers tasty meals.

Outdoor Activities and Sports

Beaches

The Charleston area's mild climate generally is conducive to swimming from April through October. This is definitely not a "swingles" area; all public and private beaches are family oriented, providing a choice of water sports, sunbathing, shelling, fishing, or quiet moonlight strolling. The **Charleston County Parks and Recreation Commission** (☎ 843/762–2172) operates several public beach facilities.

Beachwalker Park on the west end of Kiawah Island (which is otherwise a private resort) has 300 ft of beach frontage, seasonal lifeguard service, rest rooms, outdoor showers, a picnic area, snack bar, and a 150-car parking lot. ✉ *Kiawah Island,* ☎ *843/762–2172.* 🎫 *$4 per car (up to 8 passengers).* ⏲ *June–Aug., daily 10–7; May and Sept., daily 10–6; Apr. and Oct., weekends 10–6.*

Folly Beach County Park, 12 mi south of Charleston via U.S. 17 and SC 171 (Folly Road), has 4,000 ft of ocean frontage and 2,000 ft of river frontage. Lifeguards are on duty seasonally along a 600-ft section of the beach. Facilities include dressing areas, outdoor showers, rest rooms, and picnicking areas; beach chairs, raft, and umbrella rentals; and a 400-vehicle parking lot. Pelican Watch shelter is available year-round for group picnics and day or night oyster roasts. ✉ *Folly Island,* ☎ *843/588–2426.* 💵 *$5 per car (up to 8 passengers).* ⏲ *May–Aug., daily 9–7; Apr. and Sept.–Oct., daily 10–6; Nov.–Mar., daily 10–5.*

Isle of Palms County Park is on the Isle of Palms at the foot of the Isle of Palms connector. Lifeguards are on duty seasonally along a 600-ft section of the beach. Facilities include dressing areas, outdoor showers, rest rooms, picnicking areas, beach chair and raft rentals, and a 350-vehicle parking lot. ✉ *1 14th Ave., Isle of Palms,* ☎ *843/886–3863.* 💵 *$5 per car (up to 8 passengers).* ⏲ *May–Aug., daily 9–7; Apr. and Sept.–Oct., daily 10–6; Nov.–Mar., daily 10–5.*

Private resorts with extensive beaches and amenities include **Fairfield Ocean Ridge** (☎ 843/869–2561), on Edisto Island; **Kiawah Island** (☎ 903/768–2121 or 800/654–2924); **Seabrook Island** (☎ 843/768–1000 or 800/845–5531); and **Wild Dunes** (☎ 843/886–6000 or 800/845–8880), on the Isle of Palms.

Participant Sports

BIKING

The historic district is ideal for bicycling, and many city parks have biking trails. Palmetto Islands County Park (☞ Mount Pleasant and Vicinity, *above*) also has trails. Bikes can be rented at the **Bicycle Shoppe** (✉ 280 Meeting St., ☎ 843/722–8168; Kiawah Island, ☎ 843/768–9122). **Island Bike and Surf Shop** (✉ Kiawah Island, ☎ 843/768–1158) has bikes, surfboards, and Rollerblades for rent. **Sea Island Cycle** (✉ 4053 Rhett Ave., North Charleston, ☎ 843/747–2453) serves all the local islands.

GOLF

One of the most appealing aspects of golfing in the Charleston area is the relaxing pace. With fewer golfers playing the courses than in destinations that are primarily golf oriented, golfers find choice starting times and an unhurried atmosphere. For a listing of area golf packages, contact **Charleston Golf Inc.** (✉ Box 975, 29402, ☎ 843/853–8000 or 800/774–4444).

Nonguests may play on a space-available basis at **private island resorts** such as Kiawah Island, Seabrook Island, and Wild Dunes. The prestigious Pete Dye–designed **Ocean Course at Kiawah Island Resort** (✉ 1000 Ocean Course Dr., Kiawah Island, ☎ 843/768–7272) is an 18-hole, par-72 course that was the site of the 1991 Ryder Cup. Other championship **Kiawah courses,** all 18-hole and par 72, are the Gary Player–designed Marsh Point; Osprey Point, by Tom Fazio; and Turtle Point, a Jack Nicklaus layout (for all three: ✉ 12 Kiawah Beach Dr., ☎ 843/768–2121). **Seabrook Island Resort,** a secluded hideaway on Johns Island, offers two more 18-hole, par-72 championship courses: Crooked Oaks, by Robert Trent Jones Sr., and Ocean Winds, designed by William Byrd (for both: ✉ Seabrook Island Rd., ☎ 843/768–2529). **Wild Dunes Resort,** on the Isle of Palms, is home to two 18-hole, par-72 Tom Fazio designs: the Links (✉ 10001 Back Bay Dr., ☎ 843/886–2180) and Harbor Course (✉ 5881 Palmetto Dr., ☎ 843/886–2301).

Top **public courses** in the area include **Charleston Municipal** (✉ 2110 Maybank Hwy., ☎ 843/795–6517), **Charleston National Country Club** (✉ 1360 National Dr., Mount Pleasant, ☎ 843/884–7799), the **Dunes West Golf Club** (✉ 3535 Wando Plantation Way, Mount Pleasant, ☎ 843/856–9000), **Links at Stono Ferry** (✉ 5365 Forest Oaks Dr., Hollywood, ☎ 843/763–1817), **Oak Point Golf Course** (✉ 4255 Bohicket

Rd., Johns Island, ☎ 843/768–7431), **Patriots Point** (✉ 1 Patriots Point Rd., Mount Pleasant, ☎ 843/881–0042), and **Shadowmoss Golf Club** (✉ 20 Dunvegan Dr., ☎ 843/556–8251). All the above are 18-hole, par-72 courses.

SCUBA DIVING

The **Cooper River Underwater Heritage Diving Trail** is more than 2 mi long and consists of six submerged sites including ships that date to the Revolutionary War. Contact the **East Coast Dive Connection** (✉ 206B E. 5th North St., Summerville, ☎ 843/821–0001) or **Charleston Scuba** (✉ 335 Savannah Hwy., ☎ 843/763–3483) for maps, rentals, and excursion information.

TENNIS

Courts are open to the public at **Kiawah Island** (☎ 843/768–2121), **Shadowmoss Plantation** (☎ 843/556–8251), and **Wild Dunes** (☎ 843/886–6000).

Spectator Sports

BASEBALL AND BASKETBALL

The minor-league **RiverDogs** (✉ 360 Fishburne St., ☎ 843/723–7241), a Class-A affiliate of the Tampa Bay Devil Rays, play at the Joseph P. Riley Jr. Ballpark from April through August.

The College of Charleston **Cougars** (✉ Johnson Gym, 30 George St., ☎ 843/953–5556) basketball team is consistently a top contender in the Southern Conference.

HOCKEY

The Charleston **Stingrays** (✉ North Charleston Coliseum, 3107 Firestone Rd., North Charleston, ☎ 843/744–2248) are a minor-league team affiliated with the NHL's Buffalo Sabres. They attract record-breaking crowds from October through March.

Shopping

Shopping Districts

The Market is a complex of specialty shops and restaurants. Don't miss the colorful produce market in the three-block **Old City Market** (✉ E. Bay and Market Sts.) and, adjacent to it, the open-air flea market, with crafts, antiques, and memorabilia. You'll find locally produced sweetgrass and other baskets here. Shopping complexes in the historic district are **Market Square** (Market St.); **Rainbow Market** (✉ 40 N. Market St.), in two interconnected 150-year-old buildings (don't miss the filled-to-the-hilt Good Scents in Rainbow Market, known for its perfume oils and lotions); **Shops at Charleston Place** (✉ 130 Market St.), with Gucci, Gap, and Brookstone; and **State Street Market** (✉ Market St.). **King Street** has some of Charleston's oldest and finest shops, including **Saks Fifth Avenue** (✉ 211 King St., ☎ 843/853–9888). From May until September, the festive **farmers' market** takes place each Saturday morning in Marion Square.

Antiques

King Street is the center for antiques shopping. **Birlant & Co.** (✉ 191 King St., ☎ 843/722–3842) presents fine 18th- and 19th-century English antiques, as well as the famous Charleston Battery bench, identical to those on Charleston Green. **Period Antiques** (✉ 194 King St., ☎ 843/723–2724) has 18th- and 19th-century pieces. **Petterson Antiques** (✉ 201 King St., ☎ 843/723–5714) offers curious objets d'art, books, furniture, porcelain, and glass. **Livingston & Sons Antiques,** dealers in 18th- and 19th-century English and Continental furniture, clocks, and bric-a-brac, has a large shop west of the Ashley River (✉ 2137

Savannah Hwy., ☎ 843/556–6162) and a smaller one on King Street (✉ 163 King St., ☎ 843/723–9697).

On James Island, a 10-minute drive from downtown, **Carolopolis Antiques** (✉ 2000 Wappoo Dr., ☎ 843/795–7724) has good bargains on country pieces, many of which are bought by downtown stores. On U.S. 17 in Mount Pleasant, **Hungryneck Mall** (✉ 401 Johnnie Dodds Blvd., ☎ 843/849–1744) has more than 60 dealers hawking sterling silver, oak and mahogany furnishings, linens, and Civil War memorabilia. In Mount Pleasant, **Page's Thieves Market** (✉ 1460 Ben Sawyer Blvd., ☎ 843/884–9672) has furniture, glassware, and "junque."

Art and Crafts Galleries

The **Birds I View Gallery** (✉ 119A Church St., ☎ 843/723–1276) sells bird paintings and prints by Anne Worsham Richardson. **Blink** (✉ 62B Queen St., ☎ 843/577–5688) has regionally and locally produced paintings, photos, pottery, jewelry, and garden art. **Charleston Crafts** (✉ 87 Hasell St., ☎ 843/723–2938) has a fine selection of pottery, quilts, weavings, sculptures, and jewelry fashioned mostly by local artists. **Charleston Gardens** (✉ 61 Queen St., ☎ 843/723–0252) has garden ornamentations and home accessories including English pottery, Charleston-style iron gates, urns, and contemporary lighting. The **Elizabeth O'Neill Verner Studio & Museum** (✉ 79 Church St., ☎ 843/722–4246), in a 17th-century house, is open to the public. Prints of Elizabeth O'Neill Verner's pastels and etchings are on sale at **Tradd Street Press** (✉ 38 Tradd St., ☎ 843/722–4246). The **Marty Whaley Adams Gallery** (✉ 2 Queen St., ☎ 843/853–8512) has original vivid watercolors and monotypes, plus prints and posters by this Charleston artist. At **Nina Liu and Friends** (✉ 24 State St., ☎ 843/722–2724), you'll find contemporary art objects including handblown glass, pottery, jewelry, and photographs. Famous for his Lowcountry beach scenes, local watercolorist Stephen Jordan displays his best at **Stephen Jordan Gallery** (✉ 192 King St., ☎ 843/722–8808). **Reflections South** (✉ 125 Meeting St., ☎ 843/577–9351) sells original paintings and limited-edition lithographs of Charleston and Lowcountry scenes.

Books

The independently owned **Chapter Two** (✉ 249 Meeting St., ☎ 843/722–4238), specializes in local and regional books; there's also a neat section for children. The **Preservation Society of Charleston** (✉ corner of King and Queen Sts., ☎ 843/722–4630) has books and tapes of historic and local interest, sweet-grass baskets, prints, and posters.

Gifts

Charleston's and London's own **Ben Silver** (✉ 149 King St., ☎ 843/577–4556), premier purveyor of blazer buttons, has more than 800 designs, including college and British regimental motifs. He also sells British neckties, embroidered polo shirts, and blazers. **Charleston Collections** (✉ Straw Market, Kiawah Island Resort, ☎ 843/768–7487; Quadrangle Center, ☎ 843/556–8911) has Charleston chimes, prints, candies, T-shirts, and more. **The Sugar Plantation** (✉ 48 N. Market St., ☎ 843/853–3924) has melt-in-your mouth pralines, fudge, Charleston chews, and Olde Colony Bakery benne-seed wafers. You can find Charleston foods, including peach leather, pepper jelly, and pickled okra, at area **Piggly Wiggly** grocery stores (two locations: ✉ 1501 U.S. 17N, Mount Pleasant, ☎ 843/881–7921; IOP Connector, Mount Pleasant, ☎ 843/881–8939).

Period Reproductions

Historic Charleston Reproductions (✉ 105 Broad St., ☎ 843/723–8292) has superb replicas of Charleston furniture and accessories, all authorized by the Historic Charleston Foundation. Royalties from sales contribute to restoration projects. At the **Old Charleston Joggling Board Co.** (✉ 652 King St., ☎ 843/723–4331), these Lowcountry oddities (on which people bounce) can be purchased.

Side Trips from Charleston

Gardens, parks, and the charming town of Summerville are good reasons to travel a bit farther afield for some day trips.

Moncks Corner

30 mi north of Charleston on U.S. 52.

This town is a gateway to a number of attractions in Santee Cooper Country. Named for the two rivers that form a 171,000-acre basin, the area brims with outdoor pleasures centered on the basin and nearby Lakes Marion and Moultrie.

Cypress Gardens, a swamp garden created from what was once the freshwater reserve of the vast Dean Hall rice plantation, is about 24 mi north of Charleston via U.S. 52, between Goose Creek and Moncks Corner. You can explore the inky waters by boat or walk along paths lined with moss-draped cypress trees, azaleas, camellias, daffodils, wisteria, and dogwood. ✉ *3030 Cypress Gardens Rd.,* ☎ *843/553–0515.* *$7.* *Daily 9–5.*

On the banks of the Old Santee Canal is the **Old Santee Canal State Park,** reached via I–26 and U.S. 52. You can explore on foot or take a canoe. There's also an interpretive center. ✉ *Rembert C. Dennis Blvd.,* ☎ *843/899–5200.* *$3 per car.* *Daily 9–5.*

Francis Marion National Forest consists of 250,000 acres of swamps, vast oaks and pines, and little lakes thought to have been formed by falling meteors. It's a good place for picnicking, camping, boating, and swimming. At the park's Rembert Dennis Wildlife Center (✉ off U.S. 52 in Bonneau, north of Moncks Corner, ☎ 843/825–3387) deer, wild turkey, and striped bass are reared and studied. ✉ *35 mi north of Charleston via U.S. 52,* ☎ *843/336–3248.* *Free.* *Daily 9–5.*

LODGING

$-$$ **Rice Hope Plantation.** A former rice plantation in Moncks Corner, it consists of 11 acres of live oaks and gardens overlooking the Cooper River. The house has six working fireplaces and antiques and reproductions. Guest rooms have four-poster beds, comfortable seating, and private baths; the suite has a porch overlooking the river. ✉ *206 Rice Hope Dr., 29461,* ☎ *843/761–4832 or 800/331–0510, FAX 843/884–5020. 4 rooms, 1 suite. Hot tub, tennis court, fishing, basketball. AE, MC, V. CP.*

OUTDOOR ACTIVITIES AND SPORTS

Two good fishing spots are **Lakes Marion** and **Moultrie,** both full of bream, striped bass, catfish, and large- and smallmouth bass. For information, contact **Santee Cooper Counties Promotion Commission** (✉ Drawer 40, Santee 29142, ☎ 843/854–2131; 800/227–8510 outside South Carolina).

Summerville

25 mi northwest of Charleston via I–26 (Exit 199), SC 78, or SC 61 and SC 165.

Built by wealthy planters, this picturesque town is a treasure trove of Victorian buildings, many of which are listed in the National Register of Historic Places. Colorful gardens of camellias, azaleas, and wisteria abound, and many streets curve around tall pines, as a local ordinance prohibits cutting them down. This is a good place for a bit of antiquing. To get oriented, stop by the **Summerville Chamber of Commerce** (✉ 106 E. Doty Ave., Box 670, 29483, ☎ 843/873–2931). It's open weekdays 8:30–12:30 and 1:30–5, Saturday 10–3.

DINING AND LODGING

$$$$ ★ ✕🏨 **Woodlands Inn.** People drive from Charleston for superb meals ($$$–$$$$) at this luxury inn, part of the prestigious Relais & Châteaux group. A four-course menu and a five-course menu with wine are available at the restaurant. Delicate sauces and subtle touches are key in entrées such as Angus beef with Barolo wine reduction, potato-encrusted crabcakes, and Asian spiced lobster. Though the inn, built in 1906 as a winter home, backs up to a suburb, it's a first-rate getaway, with such niceties as fireplaces, whirlpool or claw-foot tubs, and heated towel racks. Rates include a split of champagne at arrival and afternoon tea. *✉ 125 Parsons Rd., 29483, ☎ 843/875–2600 or 800/774–9999, FAX 843/875–2603. 15 rooms, 4 suites. Restaurant, lounge, pool, spa, 2 tennis courts, croquet, bicycles. AE, D, DC, MC, V.*

Charleston A to Z

Arriving and Departing

BY BOAT

Boaters on the Intracoastal Waterway may dock at **Ashley Marina** (✉ Lockwood Blvd., ☎ 843/722–1996) and **City Marina** (✉ Lockwood Blvd., ☎ 843/723–5098) in Charleston Harbor, or at **Wild Dunes Yacht Harbor** (☎ 843/886–5100) on the Isle of Palms.

BY BUS

Greyhound (✉ 3610 Dorchester Rd., N. Charleston, ☎ 800/231–2222 or 843/744–4247).

BY CAR

I–26 traverses the state from northwest to southeast and terminates at Charleston. U.S. 17, the coast road, passes through Charleston.

BY PLANE

Charleston International Airport (✉ 5500 International Blvd., ☎ 843/767–1100) on I–26, 12 mi west of downtown, is served by Continental, Comair, Delta, Midway Express, United Express, Northwest, TWA, and US Airways. For airline telephone numbers, *see* Air Travel *in* Smart Travel Tips A to Z.

Lowcountry Limousine Service (☎ 843/767–7111 or 800/222–4771) charges $15 per person (or $10 per person for two or more) to downtown. If you're traveling from the airport by **car,** take I–26S into the city.

BY TRAIN

Amtrak (✉ 4565 Gaynor Ave., N. Charleston, ☎ 843/744–8264 or 800/872–7245).

Getting Around

BY BOAT

CHARTS (✉ 196A Concord, ☎ 843/853–4700) is the only full-service water taxi providing transportation to and from Patriots Point naval and maritime museum. It also offers harbor cruises.

BY BUS

Regular buses run in most of Charleston from 5:35 AM until 10 PM and to North Charleston until 1 AM. The cost is 75¢ exact change (free transfers). DASH (Downtown Area Shuttle) trolley-style buses provide fast service in the main downtown areas. The fare is 75¢, $2 for an all-day pass. For **schedule information,** call ☎ 843/747–0922.

BY TAXI

Fares within the city average $3–$4 per trip. Companies include **Lowcountry Limousine Service** (☞ Arriving and Departing, *above*), **Safety Cab** (☎ 843/722–4066), and **Yellow Cab** (☎ 843/577–6565).

Contacts and Resources

EMERGENCIES

Ambulance, police (☎ 911). The emergency rooms are open all night at **Charleston Memorial Hospital** (✉ 326 Calhoun St., ☎ 843/577–0600) and **Roper Hospital** (✉ 316 Calhoun St., ☎ 843/724–2000).

GUIDED TOURS

Charleston Harbor Tour (☎ 843/722–1691) and **Princess Gray Line Harbor Tours** (☎ 843/722–1112 or 800/344–4483) ply the harbor. **Fort Sumter Tours** (☎ 843/722–1691) includes a stop at Fort Sumter and also offers Starlight dinner cruises aboard a luxury yacht. **Flying High over Charleston** (☎ 843/569–6148) provides aerial tours. **Adventure Sightseeing** (☎ 843/762–0088 or 800/722–5394) and **Colonial Coach and Trolley Company** (☎ 843/795–3000) give motor-coach tours of the historic district. **Gray Line** (☎ 843/722–4444) has tours of the historic district, plus seasonal trips to gardens and plantations.

Lowcountry Carriage Co. (☎ 843/577–0042), **Old South Carriage Company** (☎ 843/723–9712), and **Palmetto Carriage Tours** (☎ 843/723–8145) run approximately one-hour horse- and mule-drawn carriage tours of the historic district, some conducted by guides in Confederate uniforms. Carriage tours have a set itinerary and cover one of four zones in the historic district; after the carriages have passengers, the drivers draw from a lottery to decide which zone each carriage will cover. **Doin' the Charleston** (☎ 843/763–1233 or 800/647–4487), a van tour, combines its narration with audiovisuals and makes a stop at the Battery.

Chai Y'All (☎ 843/556–0664) shares stories and sites of Jewish interest. **Gullah Tours** (☎ 843/763–7551) is an expert on local African-American culture. **Sweetgrass Tours** (☎ 843/556–0664 for groups) focus on African-American influences on Charleston architecture, history, and culture.

Walking tours are given by **Charleston Strolls** (☎ 843/766–2080); **Charleston Tea Party Walking Tour** (☎ 843/577–5896 or 843/722–1779), which includes tea in a private garden; **On the Market Get Set, Tour!** (☎ 843/853–8687); and the **Original Charleston Walks** (☎ 843/577–3800 or 800/729–3420). For a spookier view of the city, take the **Ghosts of Charleston** (☎ 843/723–1670 or 800/854–1670) walking tour. The same guides also celebrate the city in the Story of Charleston walking tour. The unique **Watercolors About Charleston** (☎ 843/889–6978 or 888/295–3574) combines a walking tour with a watercolor class and lunch.

LATE-NIGHT PHARMACIES

Eckerds (✉ 466 Savannah Hwy., ☎ 843/766–5593). **Henry's Conway Drug Store** (✉ 517 King St., ☎ 843/577–5123). **Tellis Pharmacy** (✉ 125 King St., ☎ 843/723–0682).

LODGING ASSISTANCE

Rates tend to increase during the Spring Festival of Houses and Spoleto, when reservations are essential. For historic home rentals in Charleston, contact **Charleston Carriage Houses–Oceanfront Realty** (✉ Box 6151, Hilton Head 29938, ☎ 843/785–8161). To find rooms in homes, cottages, and carriage houses, try **Historic Charleston Bed and Breakfast** (✉ 60 Broad St., Charleston 29401, ☎ 843/722–6606). For condo and house rentals on the Isle of Palms—some with private pools and tennis courts—try **Island Realty** (✉ Box 157, Isle of Palms 29451, ☎ 843/886–8144). **Southern Hospitality B&B Reservations** (✉ 110 Amelia Dr., Lexington 29072, ☎ 843/356–6238 or 800/374–7422) handles rooms in homes and carriage houses.

PERSONAL GUIDES

Contact **Associated Guides of Historic Charleston** (☎ 843/724–6419); **Cary Parker Limousine Service** (☎ 843/723–7601), which offers chauffeur-driven luxury limousine tours; or **Charleston Guide Service** (☎ 843/722–8240), the city's oldest guide service. **Janice Kahn** (☎ 843/556–0664) has done individualized guiding for more than 25 years.

RADIO STATIONS

AM: WQIZ 810, gospel; WTMA 1250, talk radio; WXTC 1390, sports. **FM:** WBUB 107.5, country; WXLY 102.5, oldies; WALC 100.5 contemporary rock; WJZK 96.9, smooth jazz; WSCI 89.3, news, classical, jazz, information line; WWWZ 93.4, urban contemporary; WYBB 98.1, classic rock.

VISITOR INFORMATION

You can pick up a schedule of events at the **visitor center** (✉ 375 Meeting St.) or at area hotels, inns, and restaurants. Also see "Tips for Tourists" each Saturday in the *Post & Courier.* **Charleston Area Convention and Visitors Bureau** (✉ Box 975, Charleston 29402, ☎ 843/853–8000 or 800/868–8118) has information on the city and also on Kiawah Island, Seabrook Island, Mount Pleasant, North Charleston, Edisto Island, Summerville, and the Isle of Palms. **Historic Charleston Foundation** (✉ Box 1120, Charleston 29402, ☎ 843/723–1623) and the **Preservation Society of Charleston** (✉ Box 521, 29402, ☎ 843/722–4630) have information on house tours.

MYRTLE BEACH AND THE GRAND STRAND

The lively, family-oriented Grand Strand, a booming resort area along the South Carolina coast, is one of the eastern seaboard's megavacation centers. Myrtle Beach alone accounts for about 40% of the state's tourism revenue. The main attraction, of course, is the broad, beckoning beach—60 mi of white sand, stretching from the North Carolina border south to Georgetown, with Myrtle Beach as the hub. All along the Strand you can enjoy shell hunting, fishing, swimming, sunbathing, sailing, surfing, jogging, or just strolling on the beach. And the Strand has something for everyone: more than 100 championship golf courses, designed by Arnold Palmer, Robert Trent Jones, Jack Nicklaus, and Tom and George Fazio, among others; excellent seafood restaurants; giant shopping malls and factory outlets; amusement parks, water slides, and arcades; a dozen shipwrecks for divers to explore; fine fishing; campgrounds, most of which are on the beach; plus antique-car and wax museums, the world's largest outdoor sculpture garden, an antique pipe organ and merry-go-round, and a museum dedicated entirely to rice. It has also emerged as a major center for country music, with an expanding number of theaters.

Myrtle Beach—whose population of 26,000 explodes to about 350,000 in summer—is the center of activity on the Grand Strand. It is here that you find the amusement parks and other children's activities that make the area so popular with families, as well as most of the nightlife that keeps parents and teenagers happy. On the North Strand, there is Little River, with a thriving fishing and charter industry, and the several communities that make up North Myrtle Beach. On the South Strand, the family retreats of Surfside Beach and Garden City offer more summer homes and condominiums. Farther south are towns as alluring to visit as are the sights along the way: Murrells Inlet, once a pirate's haven and now a scenic fishing village and port; and Pawleys Island, one of the East Coast's oldest resorts, which prides itself on being "arrogantly shabby." Historic Georgetown forms the southern tip.

Myrtle Beach

94 mi northeast of Charleston, 201 mi east of Columbia.

Myrtle Beach, with its high-rises and hyperdevelopment, is a swirl of seaside activity. To capture its flavor, start at the Myrtle Beach Pavilion Amusement Park and wind your way north on Ocean Boulevard. Here's where you'll find an eclectic assortment of gift and novelty shops—everything from T-shirts to perfect shells—a wax museum, and a museum of oddities. Turn east when it suits your fancy and make your way back on the beach amid children building sand castles and kids-at-heart flying kites. The sights included here are in Myrtle Beach and north to North Myrtle Beach, with a couple to the south.

Dozens of colorful streetlight displays around major intersections add yet a few more volts of energy to the already pulsating scene, and at Christmas, Myrtle Beach stages one of the largest, most colorful light shows in the South.

Myrtle Beach Pavilion Amusement Park has thrill and children's rides, the Carolinas' largest flume, a new wooden roller coaster, video games, a teen nightclub, specialty shops, antique cars, and sidewalk cafés. ✉ *9th Ave. N and Ocean Blvd.,* ☎ *843/448–6456.* *Fees for individual attractions; 1-day pass for unlimited access to most rides $23.60.* *Mid-Mar.–May and mid-Aug.–Sept., weekdays 6 PM–10 PM, Sat. 1–10, Sun. 1–8; June–mid-Aug., daily 1 PM–midnight. Operating hrs can vary, so call ahead.*

Ripley's Believe It or Not Museum is based on the drawings that adults used to see in the newspaper, translated into lively displays of odd facts and figures. Among the more than 750 exhibits is an 8-ft, 11-inch wax replica of the world's tallest man. ✉ *901 N. Ocean Blvd.,* ☎ *843/448–2331.* *$8.95.* *Daily 10–9.*

Myrtle Beach National Wax Museum offers drama, sound, and animation in sections highlighting religious, historical, and entertainment people and events. ✉ *1000 N. Ocean Blvd.,* ☎ *843/448–9921.* *$5.* *Late Feb.–May and Sept.–mid-Oct., daily 9 AM–11 PM; June–August, daily 9 AM–2 AM.*

Hawaiian Rumble is the crown jewel of Myrtle Beach, the minigolf capital of the world (other courses mimic Jurassic Park and Never-Never Land). The course has a smoking mountain that erupts fire and rumbles at timed intervals. ✉ *3210 33rd Ave. S, U.S. 17,* ☎ *843/272–7812.* *$8 all day (9–5), $6 per round after 5 PM.* *Mar.–Dec., daily 9 AM–10 PM.*

Dragon's Lair has a fire-breathing dragon and two 18-hole courses. ✉ *U.S. 17 at Broadway at the Beach,* ☎ *843/444–3215.* *$8.50 all day (10 AM–6 PM), $6.50 per round after 6 PM.* *Mar.–Dec., daily 9 AM–10 PM.*

★ **Alligator Adventure** has exciting interactive reptile shows, including an alligator-feeding demonstration. The boardwalks go through marshes and swamps on the 15-acre property, where you'll see wildlife of the wetlands, including the only known collection of rare white albino alligators; the gharial, an exotic crocodilian from Asia; giant Galápagos tortoises; and all manner of other reptiles, including boas, pythons, and anacondas. Unusual plants and exotic birds also thrive here. ✉ *U.S. 17S at Barefoot Landing, North Myrtle Beach,* ☎ *843/361–0789,* FAX *843/361–0742.* 🎫 *$10.95.* ⏲ *Daily 10–9.*

Myrtle Beach Grand Prix is auto-mania heaven with Formula 1 race cars, go-carts, bumper boats, mini-go-carts, kids' cars, and mini-bumper boats for adults and children ages three and up. ✉ *3201 U.S. 17,* ☎ *843/238–2421; Windy Hill, 3900 U.S. 17S, North Myrtle Beach,* ☎ *843/272–6010.* 🎫 *Rides $3–$5 each.* ⏲ *Mar.–Oct., daily 10 AM–11 PM.*

At **NASCAR Speedpark,** you can drive on seven different NASCAR-replica tracks; the 26-acre facility also has racing memorabilia, an arcade, and miniature golf. ✉ *U.S. 17 Bypass and 21st Ave. N,* ☎ *843/626–8725.* 🎫 *$5 general admission, drives $3–$6 each.* ⏲ *Mar.–Oct., weekdays 5 PM–midnight, weekends 12 PM–midnight; hrs vary, so call to confirm.*

One of Myrtle Beach's newer attractions, **Ripley's Aquarium** has an underwater tunnel exhibit longer than a football field and exotic marine creatures from poisonous lionfish to moray eels and an octopus. Children can examine horseshoe crabs and eels in touch tanks. ✉ *9th Ave. N and U.S. 17N Bypass,* ☎ *843/916–0888 or 800/734–8888.* 🎫 *$13.95.* ⏲ *Sun.–Thurs. 9 AM–9 PM, Fri.–Sat. 9 AM–10 PM.*

South of Myrtle Beach, **Wild Water** provides splashy family fun for all ages in 25 rides and activities. ✉ *910 U.S. 17S, Surfside Beach,* ☎ *843/238–9453.* 🎫 *$17, $12 after 3 PM.* ⏲ *Memorial Day weekend–Labor Day, daily 10–7.*

Dining and Lodging

MYRTLE BEACH

$$–$$$ ★ ✕ **Collectors Cafe.** A successful restaurant, art gallery, and coffeehouse rolled into one, this unpretentious arty spot has bright, funky paintings and tile work covering its walls and tabletops. You can shop for a painting while enjoying the veal-stuffed ravioli or barbecued duck over polenta cake with goat-cheese cream. ✉ *7726 N. Kings Hwy.,* ☎ *843/449–9370. AE, D, DC, MC, V. Closed Sun.*

$$–$$$ ✕ **Villa Katrina's Underground Cantina.** Head downstairs into a fun, tavern-like space for Mexican fare of the elegant variety, including flaming coffees and desserts. ✉ *821 Main St.,* ☎ *843/946–6216. AE, D, MC, V. Closed Sun.*

$$ ✕ **Sea Captain's House.** At this picturesque restaurant with nautical decor, the best seats are in the windowed porch room, which overlooks the ocean. The fireplace in the wood-paneled dining room inside is warmly welcoming on cool off-season evenings. Menu highlights include Lowcountry crab casserole and avocado-seafood salad. The breads and desserts are baked here. ✉ *3000 N. Ocean Blvd.,* ☎ *843/448–8082. AE, D, MC, V.*

$–$$ ✕ **Croissants Bakery & Café.** The lunch crowd loves this spot, which has an on-site bakery. Try the chicken or broccoli salad, and the peanut butter cheesecake. ✉ *504A 27th Ave. N,* ☎ *843/448–2253. D, MC, V. Closed Sun. No dinner.*

$–$$ ✕ **Vintage House Café.** Locals dine here on beef tips, smoked chicken ravioli, and homemade bananas Foster cheesecake. ✉ *1210 N. Kings Hwy.,* ☎ *843/626–3918. AE, D, DC, MC, V. Closed Sun. No dinner Mon.*

$$$–$$$$ ★ **Kingston Plantation.** The Grand Strand's most luxurious property, the 20-story glass-sheathed tower is part of a complex of shops, restaurants, hotels, and one- to three-bedroom condominiums set amid 145 acres of oceanside woodlands. Guest rooms are highlighted by bleached-wood furnishings and an Art Deco theme; all have kitchenettes. ✉ *9800 Lake Dr., 29572,* ☎ *843/449–0006 or 800/876–0010,* FAX *843/497–1110. 255 suites; 510 villas and condos. 2 restaurants, lounge, indoor pool, 7 outdoor pools, sauna, tennis court, aerobics, health club, racquetball. AE, D, DC, MC, V.*

$$$ **Breakers Resort Hotel.** The rooms in this oceanfront hotel are airy and spacious, with contemporary decor. Many have balconies and refrigerators. ✉ *2006 N. Ocean Blvd., Box 485, 29578,* ☎ *843/444–4444 or 800/845–0688,* FAX *843/626–5001. 204 rooms, 186 suites. 2 restaurants, lounge, indoor pool, 3 outdoor pools, 4 hot tubs, 3 saunas, exercise room, children's programs, laundry service. AE, D, DC, MC, V.*

$$–$$$ **Holiday Inn Oceanfront.** This oceanfront inn is right at the heart of the action, and rates vary according to the season. The spacious rooms are done in cool sea tones. After beach basking, you can prolong the mood in the inn's spacious, plant-bedecked indoor recreation center. ✉ *415 S. Ocean Blvd., 29577,* ☎ *843/448–4481 or 800/845–0313,* FAX *843/448–0086. 306 rooms. 2 restaurants, lounge, snack bar, indoor pool, outdoor pool, hot tub, sauna, recreation room. AE, D, DC, MC, V.*

$$–$$$ **Sheraton Myrtle Beach Resort.** All rooms and suites have a fresh, contemporary look. Oceanfront Lounge, highlighted by tropical colors and rattan furnishings, is a lively evening gathering spot. There are a lazy river (artificial stream) and an arcade nearby. ✉ *2701 S. Ocean Blvd., 29577,* ☎ *843/448–2518 or 800/992–1055,* FAX *843/449–1879. 211 rooms, 8 suites. Restaurant, indoor pool, outdoor pool, health club. AE, D, DC, MC, V.*

$–$$ **Chesterfield Inn.** A remnant from the past, this oceanfront brick inn, hidden beneath the towers of Myrtle Beach's glitzier hotels, has been in operation for more than a half century. The rooms in the original building are plain and a bit worn, but many guests prefer them to those in the newer wing. The highlight: family-style meals are served on white tablecloths in the seafront dining room. ✉ *700 N. Ocean Blvd., 29578,* ☎ *843/448–3177,* FAX *843/626–4736. 57 rooms, 6 kitchenette units. Restaurant, pool, shuffleboard. AE, D, DC, MC, V.*

$ **Days Inn at Waccamaw.** Relax by the pool or in the gazebo after a day of shopping at the nearby Waccamaw Pottery and Factory Shoppes. The theaters of the Fantasy Harbor complex are also close at hand. Rooms here are clean and functional, filled with contemporary furnishings, and most are equipped with a refrigerator. ✉ *3650 U.S. 501, 29577,* ☎ *843/236–1950 or 800/325–2525,* FAX *843/236–9415. 160 rooms. Restaurant, pool, hot tub. AE, D, DC, MC, V.*

$ **Driftwood on the Oceanfront.** Under one ownership for more than 60 years, the Driftwood is popular with families. Some rooms are oceanfront; all are decorated in sea, sky, or earth tones. ✉ *1600 N. Ocean Blvd., Box 275, 29578,* ☎ *843/448–1544 or 800/942–3456,* FAX *843/448–2917. 90 rooms. 2 pools, exercise room. AE, D, DC, MC, V.*

$ **Landmark Resort Hotel.** This high-rise oceanfront resort hotel, with a rooftop sundeck and artificial "lazy rivers" indoors and out, also has a building across the street. Rooms are colorfully decorated in a Caribbean motif, and some in the oceanfront building have balconies and refrigerators. ✉ *1501 S. Ocean Blvd., 29577,* ☎ *843/448–9441 or 800/845–0658,* FAX *843/448–6701. 313 rooms, 257 suites. Restaurant, pub, 2 pools. AE, D, DC, MC, V.*

NORTH MYRTLE BEACH

Dinner cruises are one dining option here. The cruise ship **Hurricane** and yachts of the Hurricane pleasure fleet (☎ 843/249–3571) depart from Vereen's Marina (✉ U.S. 17N and 11th Ave.). The **Barefoot Princess** (☎ 843/272–7743 or 800/685–6601), a replica of a side-wheel riverboat, offers dinner, sunset, and sightseeing cruises along the Intracoastal Waterway from Barefoot Landing (✉ 4898 U.S. 17S).

$$–$$$$ ✕ **Greg Norman's Australian Grille.** Overlooking the Intracoastal Waterway, this large restaurant in Barefoot Landing has leather booths, handpainted walls, an extensive wine list, outdoor seating, and even a piano bar. Much of the menu has an Asian flair; try the lobster dumplings or crispy duck. ✉ *4930 Hwy. 17S,* ☎ *843/361–0000. Reservations essential. AE, D, DC, MC, V.*

$–$$ ✕ **Horst Gasthaus.** Dine on knockwurst, bratwurst, sauerbraten, and other traditional German foods at this Bavarian-style restaurant, where there's music every night but Sunday. ✉ *802 37th Ave. S,* ☎ *843/272–3351. AE, D, MC, V.*

$$ **Sea Island Inn.** In the quiet residential end of Myrtle Beach, this inn has oceanfront rooms with comfortable, standard decor plus several social areas. Meals are served in the elegant oceanfront dining room. ✉ *6000 N. Ocean Blvd., 29577,* ☎ *843/449–6406 or 800-548–0767,* FAX *843/449–4102. 113 rooms, 1 suite, 1 penthouse. Restaurant, 2 pools, Ping-Pong, children's programs. AE, D, MC, V. MAP.*

Nightlife and the Arts

CLUBS AND LOUNGES

Clubs offer varying fare, including beach music, the Grand Strand's unique '50s-style sound. Some clubs and resorts have sophisticated live entertainment during summer. Some hotels and resorts also have piano bars or lounges with easy-listening music.

South Carolina's only Hard Rock Cafe, Planet Hollywood, and NASCAR Cafe are just a few of the hot spots in **Broadway at the Beach** (✉ U.S. 17 Bypass between 21st and 29th Aves. N, ☎ 843/444–3200), which also has shopping. You can dance the shag (the state dance) at **Duck's** (✉ 229 Main St., North Myrtle Beach, ☎ 843/249–3858). **Gypsy's** (✉ 501 8th. Ave N, ☎ 843/916–2244) is great for late-night blues music and has a nice wine selection. **Sandals** (✉ 500 Shore Dr., ☎ 843/449–6461) is an intimate lounge with live entertainment. The shag is popular at **Studebaker's** (✉ 2000 N. Kings Hwy., ☎ 843/448–9747 or 843/626–3855).

FILM

The **IMAX Discovery Theater** at Broadway at the Beach (✉ U.S. 17 Bypass between 21st and 29th Aves. N, ☎ 843/448–4629) shows educational films on a six-story-high screen.

MUSIC AND LIVE SHOWS

Live acts, and country-and-western shows in particular, are a big draw at the Grand Strand. Music lovers have many family-oriented shows to choose from: the 2,250-seat **Alabama Theater** (✉ Barefoot Landing, 4750 U.S. 17, North Myrtle Beach, ☎ 843/272–1111); **Carolina Opry** (✉ 82nd Ave. N, Myrtle Beach, ☎ 843/238–8888 or 800/843–6779); **Dolly Parton's Dixie Stampede** (✉ 8901B U.S. 17 Business, next door to Carolina Opry, Myrtle Beach, ☎ 843/497–9700); **Legends in Concert** (✉ 301 U.S. 17 Business, Surfside Beach, ☎ 843/238–7827 or 800/843–6779). The elegant **Palace Theater** (✉ Broadway at the Beach, U.S. 17 Bypass between 21st and 29th Aves. N, ☎ 843/448–0588 or 800/905–4228) hosts performances by the likes of Aretha Franklin, Kenny Rogers, and the Radio City Rockettes.

The **Fantasy Harbor** complex (☒ SC 51, across from Waccamaw Factory Shoppes) includes several theaters: the 2,000-seat Crook and Chase Theater (☎ 843/236–8500 or 800/681–5209), The Savoy (☎ 843/236–2200 or 800/681–5209), Medieval Times Dinner & Tournament (☎ 843/236–8080 or 800/436–4386), and the 2,000-seat Forum Theater (☎ 843/236–8500).

The **House of Blues** (☒ 4640 U.S. 17S, North Myrtle Beach, ☎ 843/272–3000 for tickets), adjacent to Barefoot Landing, showcases big names and up-and-coming talent in blues, rock, jazz, country, and R&B on stages in its Southern-style restaurant and patio as well as in its 2,000-seat concert hall.

PERFORMING ARTS

Theater productions, concerts, art exhibits, and other cultural events are regularly offered at the **Myrtle Beach Convention Center** (☒ Oak and 21st Ave. N, ☎ 843/448–7166).

Outdoor Activities and Sports

BEACHES

All the region's beaches are family oriented, and most are public. The widest expanses are in North Myrtle Beach, where, at low tide, the sand stretches up to ⅛ mi from the dunes to the water. Those who wish to combine their sunning with enjoying nightlife and amusement-park attractions can enjoy it all at Myrtle Beach, the Strand's longtime hub. Vacationers seeking a quieter day in the sun head for the South Strand communities of Surfside Beach and Garden City.

Besides ocean swimming, **Myrtle Beach State Park** has surf fishing, a nature trail, and a pool; there's camping, too, but book in advance. ☒ *U.S. 17, 3 mi south of Myrtle Beach,* ☎ *843/238–5325.* *$3 per car.*

FISHING

The Gulf Stream makes fishing usually good from early spring through December. Anglers can fish from 10 piers and jetties for amberjack, sea trout, and king mackerel. Surfcasters may snare bluefish, whiting, flounder, pompano, and channel bass. In the South Strand, salt marshes, inlets, and tidal creeks yield flounder, blues, croakers, spots, shrimp, clams, oysters, and blue crabs. The annual **Grand Strand Fishing Rodeo** (☎ 843/626–7444 Apr.–Oct.) hosts a "fish of the month" contest, with prizes for the largest catch of a designated species.

GOLF

Many of the Grand Strand's 91 courses are championship layouts; most are public. **Tee Times Central** (☎ 843/347–4653 or 800/344–5590) books tee times for eight courses, including 18-hole, par-72 **Long Bay** (☒ 350 Foxtail Dr., Longs, ☎ 843/399–2222); 18-hole, par-72 **Myrtle Beach National Golf Club** (☒ 4900 National Dr., ☎ 843/448–2308); and 9-hole, par-36 **Waterway Hills** (☒ U.S. 17N, ☎ 843/449–6488). Some popular courses include in Myrtle Beach, the 18-hole, par-72 **Arcadian Shores Golf Club** (☒ 701 Hilton Rd., ☎ 843/449–5217) and the three 18-hole, par-72 courses of the **Legends** (☒ U.S. 501, ☎ 843/236–9318); in North Myrtle Beach, the 18-hole, par-72 **Bay Tree Golf Plantation** (☒ SC 9, ☎ 843/249–1487 or 800/845–6191), **Gator Hole** (☒ 700 U.S. 17N, ☎ 843/249–3543 or 800/447–2668), **Heather Glen Golf Links** (☒ U.S. 17N, Little River, ☎ 843/249–9000), and **Robbers Roost Golf Club** (☒ 1400 U.S. 17N, North Myrtle Beach, ☎ 843/249–1471 or 800/352–2384); near Surfside Beach, the 18-hole, par-72 **Blackmoor Golf Club** (☒ SC 707, Murrells Inlet, ☎ 843/650–5555), one of the country's top female-friendly courses; and in Cherry Grove Beach, the much-touted 18-hole, par-72 **Tidewater** (☒ 4901 Little River Neck Rd., North Myrtle Beach, ☎ 800/446–5363).

SCUBA DIVING

In summer, a wide variety of warm-water tropical fish travel to the area from the Gulf Stream. Off the coast of Little River, near the North Carolina border, rock and coral ledges teem with coral, sea fans, sponges, reef fish, anemones, urchins, and crabs. Several outlying shipwrecks are home to schools of spadefish, amberjack, grouper, and barracuda. Instruction and equipment rentals are available from **Scuba Syndrome** (✉ 2718 U.S. 501, ☎ 843/626–6740).

SPECTATOR SPORTS

The **Pelicans,** a single-A baseball team affiliated with the Atlanta Braves, play at the Coastal Federal Field (✉ U.S. 17 Bypass, ☎ 843/918–6000) at Broadway at the Beach.

TENNIS

There are more than 200 courts on the Grand Strand. Facilities include hotel and resort courts, as well as free municipal courts in Myrtle Beach, North Myrtle Beach, and Surfside Beach. Among tennis clubs offering court time, rental equipment, and instruction are **Myrtle Beach Racquet Club** (☎ 843/449–4031) and **Myrtle Beach Tennis and Swim Club** (☎ 843/449–4486).

WATER SPORTS

Surfboards, Hobie Cats, Jet Skis, Windsurfers, and sailboats are available for rent at **Downwind Sails** (✉ Ocean Blvd. at 29th Ave. S, ☎ 843/448–7245) and **Myrtle Beach Yacht Club** (✉ Coquina Harbor, North Myrtle Beach, ☎ 843/249–5376).

Shopping

DISCOUNT OUTLETS

The **Factory Shoppes** (✉ U.S. 501, ☎ 843/236–6152) is a large outlet center with Gap, Nike, Polo, and Off 5th (a division of Saks Fifth Avenue). In North Myrtle Beach head for the **Myrtle Beach Factory Stores** (✉ Hwy. 501 and Waccamaw Pines Drive, ☎ 843/903–1614) for Brooks Brothers, Donna Karan, Banana Republic, and Eddie Bauer. At **Waccamaw Pottery and Linen** (✉ U.S. 501 at the Waterway, ☎ 843/236–1100) more than 3 mi of shelves in several buildings are stocked with china, glassware, brass, pewter, and other items, and about 50 factory outlets sell clothing, furniture, books, jewelry, and more.

MALLS

Malls are generally open Monday–Saturday 10–9, Sunday 1–6. **Barefoot Landing** in North Myrtle Beach (✉ 4898 S. Kings Hwy., ☎ 843/272–8349), built over marshland and water, has scores of shops and restaurants. There are 100 specialty shops at **Briarcliffe Mall** (✉ 10177 N. Kings Hwy., ☎ 843/272–4040). **Broadway at the Beach** (✉ U.S. 17 Bypass, ☎ 843/444–3200 or 800/819–2282) offers 75 shops with restaurants and nightlife venues. **Myrtle Square Mall** (✉ 2501 N. Kings Hwy., ☎ 843/448–2513) has 71 upscale stores and restaurants, and a food court.

Murrells Inlet

15 mi south of Myrtle Beach on U.S. 17.

Murrells Inlet, a fishing village with some popular seafood restaurants, is a perfect place to rent a fishing boat or join an excursion. A notable garden and state park provide other diversions from the beach.

★ **Brookgreen Gardens,** begun in 1931 by railroad magnate–philanthropist Archer Huntington and his wife, Anna (herself a sculptor), displays more than 500 sculptures by such artists as Frederic Remington and Daniel Chester French. The works are set amid beautifully landscaped grounds, with avenues of live oaks, reflecting pools, and more than 2,000 plant species. Also on the site are a wildlife park, an aviary, a cypress swamp, nature trails, and an education center. Summer nights sculptures are illuminated. ✉ *West of U.S. 17, 3 mi south of Murrells Inlet,* ☎ *843/237–4218 or 800/849–1931.* *$8.50.* ⏲ *Oct.–May, daily 9:30–5; June–Sept., Wed.–Fri. 9:30–9:30.*

Huntington Beach State Park, the 2,500-acre former estate of Archer and Anna Huntington, lies east of U.S. 17, across from the couple's Brookgreen Gardens (☞ *above*). The park's focal point is **Atalaya** (circa 1933), their Moorish-style, 30-room home, open to visitors in season. In addition to the splendid beach, there are nature trails, fishing, an interpretive center, a marsh boardwalk, picnic areas, a playground, concessions, and a campground. ✉ *Off U.S. 17, 3 mi south of Murrells Inlet,* ☎ *843/237–4440.* *$4.* ⏲ *Nov.–mid-Mar., daily 6 AM–6 PM; mid-Mar.–Oct., daily 6 AM–10 PM.*

Nightlife and the Arts

THE ARTS

In the fall, the **Atalaya Arts Festival** (☎ 843/237–4440) at Huntington Beach State Park is a big draw.

NIGHTLIFE

Drunken Jack's (✉ U.S. 17 Business, ☎ 843/651–2044 or 843/651–3232) is a popular restaurant with a lounge overlooking the docks.

Outdoor Activities and Sports

Capt. Dick's (✉ U.S. 17 Business, ☎ 843/651–3676) offers half- and full-day fishing and sightseeing trips.

Pawleys Island

10 mi south of Murrells Inlet.

About 4 mi long and ½ mi wide, this island, referred to as "arrogantly shabby" by locals, began as a resort before the Civil War, when wealthy planters and their families summered here. It's mostly made up of weathered old summer cottages nestled in groves of oleander and oak trees. You can watch the famous Pawleys Island hammocks being made and bicycle around admiring the beach houses, many dating to the early 1800s. Golf and tennis are nearby.

Dining and Lodging

$$–$$$ ✕ **Frank's.** Seasonal ingredients make this a local favorite. In a former 1930s grocery store with wood floors, framed French posters, and cozy fireside seating, diners indulge in large portions of fish, seafood, beef, and lamb cooked over an oak-burning grill. The roasted asparagus with prosciutto in phyllo and pork tenderloin with shiitake mushrooms and a Dijon cream sauce are just two highlights. Behind Frank's is the casual Outback at Frank's, specializing in rotisserie chicken, salads, and lighter fare. ✉ *10434 Ocean Hwy. (U.S. 17),* ☎ *843/237–3030. Reservations essential. D, MC, V. Closed Sun.*

$–$$ ✕ **Island Country Store.** This little eatery has terrific crab cakes, hickory-smoked barbecue, roasted chicken, and pizza (they deliver). Summer nights, tiki torches outside blaze and live music rocks the place. ✉ *The Island Shops, U.S. 17,* ☎ *843/237–8465. AE, MC, V.*

$$$–$$$$ ✕🏨 **Litchfield Plantation.** Period furnishings adorn four spacious suites of this impeccably restored 1750 rice-plantation manor house turned country inn. A beach-house club a short drive away is part of the package. After entrées of grouper or steak at the elegant Carriage House Club ($$–$$$), you can retire to the restaurant's book-lined library. The resort is approximately 2 mi south of Brookgreen Gardens on U.S.

17 (turn right at the Litchfield Country Club entrance and follow the signs). ✉ *River Rd., Box 290, 29585,* ☎ *843/237–9121 or 800/869–1410,* FAX *843/237–8558. 26 rooms, 4 suites, 7 2- and 3-bedroom cottages. Restaurant, pool, 2 tennis courts, horseback riding, boating, concierge. AE, D, MC, V. CP.*

$$$$ **Litchfield Beach and Golf Resort.** Rentals from one-bedroom condos to four-bedroom villas are within the resort's expansive garden-like grounds, which include three private golf clubs and a racquet club open to guests. Suites are tastefully decorated in pastel tones and light woods, with marble baths, wet bars, refrigerators, and microwave ovens. The Country Club cottages and marsh-side villas are ideal for families or couples seeking extra privacy. The beachfront Litchfield Inn has standard motel-style rooms. ✉ *U.S. 17, 2 mi north of Pawleys Island (Drawer 320, 29585),* ☎ *843/237–3000 or 800/845–1897,* FAX *843/237–4282. 124 rooms; 112 suites; 254 condominiums, cottages, and villas. Restaurant, 2 indoor pools, 12 outdoor pools, 3 18-hole golf courses, 4 tennis courts, health club. AE, D, DC, MC, V.*

$$$ **Pelican Inn.** This unique inn, with the beach out back and creek out front, gives you a look at how families have idled away the summer at Pawleys for years. Rooms are no-fuss (some share baths) with hardwood floors and throw rugs. There's no air-conditioning, but with the breezes, ceiling fans, and relaxed lifestyle, you'll barely miss it. ✉ *500 Myrtle Ave., Box 15, 29585,* ☎ *843/237–2295 or 843/288–8255. 6 rooms. Dining room. 2-night minimum. Closed Nov.–Mar. No credit cards. MAP.*

$$–$$$ **Sea View Inn.** A "barefoot paradise," Sea View is a no-frills beachside boardinghouse with long porches. Rooms, with views of the ocean or marsh, have half baths; showers are down the hall and outside. Three meals, served family style—with grits, gumbo, crab salad, pecan pie, and oyster pie—make this an unbeatable deal. ✉ *Myrtle Avenue, 29585,* ☎ *843/237–4253,* FAX *843/237–7909. 20 rooms. Dining room. 2-night minimum May and Sept.; 1-wk minimum June–Aug. Closed Nov.–Mar. No credit cards. FAP.*

$ **Ramada Inn Seagull.** This is a well-maintained inn on a golf course (excellent golf packages are available). Outfitted with motel-modern furnishings, the rooms are spacious, bright, and airy. ✉ *U.S. 17S, Box 2217, 29585,* ☎ *843/237–4261 or 800/272–6232,* FAX *843/237–9703. 99 rooms. Dining room, lounge, pool. AE, D, DC, MC, V.*

Outdoor Activities and Sports

GOLF

Popular 18-hole, par-72 courses include **Litchfield Beach and Golf Resort** (✉ U.S. 17S, Litchfield Beach, ☎ 843/237–3000 or 800/845–1897), **Litchfield Plantation** (✉ U.S. 17S, Litchfield Beach, ☎ 843/237–9121 or 800/869–1410), and **Pawleys Plantation Golf & Country Club** (✉ U.S. 17S, Pawleys Island, ☎ 843/237–8497 or 800/367–9959). **Tee Times Central** (☎ 843/347–4653 or 800/344–5590) books tee times for **Litchfield Country Club** (✉ U.S. 17S, Pawleys Island, ☎ 843/237–3411), **River Club** (✉ U.S. 17S, Pawleys Island, ☎ 843/626–9069), and **Willbrook** (✉ U.S. 17S, Pawleys Island, ☎ 843/247–4900).

TENNIS

You can get court time, rental equipment, and instruction at **Litchfield Country Club** (☎ 843/237–3411).

Shopping

The **Hammock Shops at Pawleys Island** (✉ 10880 Ocean Hwy., ☎ 843/237–8448) is a complex of two dozen boutiques, gift shops, and restaurants built with old beams, timber, and ballast brick. Outside the Original Hammock Shop, in the Hammock Weavers' Pavilion, craftspeople demonstrate the more than 100-year-old art of weaving the famous cotton-rope Pawleys Island hammocks. Also look for jewelry, toys, antiques, and designer fashions.

Georgetown

10 mi south of Pawleys Island.

Founded on Winyah Bay in 1729, Georgetown became the center of America's colonial rice empire. A rich plantation culture developed on a scale comparable to Charleston's, and the historic district, which can be walked in a couple of hours, is among the prettiest in the state. Today, oceangoing vessels still come to Georgetown's busy port, and the **Harbor Walk,** the restored waterfront, hums with activity. For information on tours, *see* Contacts and Resources *in* Myrtle Beach and the Grand Strand A to Z, *below.*

The graceful market and meeting building in the heart of Georgetown, topped by an 1842 clock and tower, has been converted into the **Rice Museum,** with maps, tools, and dioramas. At the museum's Prevost Gallery next door, you can buy glass, jewelry, home accessories, and art made by South Carolina artisans. ✉ *Front and Screven Sts.,* ☎ *843/546–7423.* *$2; combination ticket for Rice Museum, Harold Kaminski House (☞ below), and tour of Georgetown $13.50.* ⌚ *Mon.–Sat. 9:30–4:30.*

Prince George Winyah Episcopal Church (named after King George II) still serves the parish established in 1721. It was built in 1737 with bricks brought from England. ✉ *Broad and Highmarket Sts., Georgetown,* ☎ *843/546–4358.* *Donation suggested.* ⌚ *Mar.–Oct., weekdays 11:30–4:30.*

Overlooking the Sampit River from a bluff is the **Harold Kaminski House** (circa 1769). It's especially notable for its collections of regional antiques and furnishings, its Chippendale and Duncan Phyfe furniture, Royal Doulton vases, and silver. ✉ *1003 Front St.,* ☎ *843/546–7706.* *$4; combination ticket for Rice Museum (☞ above), Harold Kaminski House, and tour of Georgetown $13.50.* ⌚ *Mon.–Sat. 10–5, Sun. 1–4.*

Bellefield Nature Center is at the entrance of Hobcaw Barony, on the vast estate of the late Bernard M. Baruch; Franklin D. Roosevelt and Winston Churchill came here to confer with him. The nature center is used for teaching and research in forestry and marine biology. There are aquariums, touch tanks, and video presentations. ✉ *On U.S. 17, 2 mi north of Georgetown,* ☎ *843/546–4623.* *Nature center free, estate $15.* ⌚ *Variety of nature tours and estate tours given yr-round; call at least 1 month in advance for schedules and fees.*

Hopsewee Plantation, surrounded by moss-draped live oaks, magnolias, and tree-size camellias, overlooks the North Santee River. The circa-1740 mansion has a fine Georgian staircase and hand-carved Adam lighted-candle moldings. ✉ *U.S. 17, 12 mi south of Georgetown,* ☎ *843/546–7891.* *Mansion $6; grounds $2 per car; parking fees apply toward the tour if taken.* ⌚ *Mansion Mar.–Nov., Tues.–Fri. 10–4; Dec.–Feb., by chance or appointment. Grounds, including nature trail, yr-round, daily dawn–dusk.*

Hampton Plantation State Park preserves the home of Archibald Rutledge, poet laureate of South Carolina for 39 years until his death in 1973. The 18th-century plantation house is a fine example of a Low-country mansion. The exterior has been restored; cutaway sections in the finely crafted interior show the changes made through the centuries. The grounds are landscaped, and there are picnic areas. ✉ *Off U.S.*

17, at edge of Francis Marion National Forest, 16 mi south of Georgetown, ☎ 843/546–9361. Mansion $2, grounds free. Mansion Thurs.–Mon. 1–4, grounds Thurs.–Mon. 9–6.

Dining and Lodging

$$$ ★ ✕ **Rice Paddy.** This riverfront Lowcountry restaurant can be crowded at lunch, when locals flock in for vegetable soup, garden-fresh salads, and sandwiches. Dinner is more relaxed, and the menu might have broiled seafood, crabmeat casserole, or quail with ham cream grits. ✉ *819 Front St., ☎ 843/546–2021. AE, D, MC, V. Closed Sun.*

$–$$ ✕ **River Room.** This restaurant on the Sampit River specializes in chargrilled fish, seafood pastas, and steaks. For lunch you can have shrimp and grits or a variety of sandwiches and salads. The dining room has river views from most tables. It's especially romantic at night, when the oil lamps and brass fixtures cast a warm glow on the dark wood and brick interior of the early 20th-century building. ✉ *801 Front St., ☎ 843/527–4110. Reservations not accepted. AE, MC, V. Closed Sun.*

$ ✕ **Kudzu Bakery.** Here are some of the best desserts in town (including deep-dish pecan pie and Red Velvet cake), fresh bread and deli items, plus jams and jellies. There's a small counter space for a quick bite. ✉ *714 Front St., ☎ 843/546–1847. MC, V. Closed Sun. No dinner.*

$$$$ **Lodge at Lofton Landing.** You rent the entire lodge, a modern facility overlooking the marshland of Cape Romain National Wildlife Refuge. It has a furnished kitchen, wraparound porch, and dock for fishing and crabbing. ✉ *8889 U.S. 17, McClellanville 29458, ☎ 843/720–7332, FAX 843/856–8468. 3 rooms, 1 loft. Boating, fishing. AE, D, DC, MC, V.*

$–$$ **Laurel Hill Plantation.** This plantation bed-and-breakfast home overlooks the marsh near the Intracoastal Waterway, near the quaint shrimping village of McClellanville. It's furnished with country antiques and folk art. Guests can read in the hammock, go fishing or crabbing, take a boat ride, or watch the birds. ✉ *8913 U.S. 17N (22 mi south of Georgetown), Box 190, McClellanville 29458, ☎ 843/887–3708. 4 rooms. Fishing. AE, D, DC, MC, V. BP.*

$–$$ **1790 House.** Built in the center of town after the Revolution, at the peak of Georgetown's rice culture, this lovely restored white Georgian house with a wraparound porch contains colonial antique and reproduction furnishings suitable to its age. A (very) full breakfast and evening refreshments are included in the rate. Guest rooms downstairs in the former slave quarters have exposed brick walls. ✉ *630 Highmarket St., 29440, ☎ 843/546–4821 or 800/890–7432. 4 rooms, 1 suite, 1 cottage. Bicycles. AE, D, MC, V. BP.*

$ **Mansfield Plantation.** As you drive up the unpaved road to the 760-acre plantation, past slave quarters and under the requisite canopy of moss-draped oaks, you'll sense what a plantation must have looked like 200 years ago. Guests stay in three historic redbrick outbuildings—the old kitchen, the former schoolhouse, and the 1930s guest house—which overlook the Black River. Rooms have hardwood pine floors, reproduction period antiques, and coal or wood-burning fireplaces. Both children and pets are welcome; guests can roam freely on the plantation grounds. ✉ *U.S. 701N, (Rte. 8, Box 590), 29440, ☎ 843/546–6961 or 800/355–3223, FAX 843/546–5235. 8 rooms. In-room VCRs, boating, fishing, bicycles. No credit cards.*

Myrtle Beach and the Grand Strand A to Z

Arriving and Departing

BY BOAT

Boaters traveling the Intracoastal Waterway may dock at **Hague Marina** (✉ Myrtle Beach, ☎ 843/293–2141), **Harbor Gate** (✉ North Myrtle Beach, ☏ 843/249–8888), and **Marlin Quay** (✉ Murrells Inlet, ☏ 843/651–4444).

BY BUS

Greyhound Bus Lines (☏ 800/231–2222) serves Myrtle Beach.

BY CAR

Midway between New York and Miami, the Grand Strand can be reached from all directions via Interstates 20, 26, 40, 77, 85, and 95, which connect by other routes to U.S. 17, the major north–south coastal route through the Strand.

BY PLANE

The **Myrtle Beach International Airport** (✉ 1100 Jetport Rd., ☏ 843/448–1580) is served by Air Canada, AirTran, ASA/Delta/Comair, Continental, Midway/Corporate, Spirit, Vanguard, and US Airways. For airline telephone numbers, *see* Air Travel *in* Smart Travel Tips A to Z.

BY TRAIN

Amtrak (☏ 800/872–7245) service for the Grand Strand is available through a terminal in Florence. Buses connect with Amtrak there for the 65-mi drive to Myrtle Beach.

Getting Around

BY TAXI

Service in Myrtle Beach is provided by **Coastal Cab Service** (☏ 843/448–3360 or 843/448–4444) and **Orange Cab** (☏ 843/448–2941).

Contacts and Resources

EMERGENCIES

Dial **911** for emergency assistance. The emergency room is open 24 hours a day at the **Columbia Grand Strand Regional Medical Center** (✉ 809 82nd Pkwy., off U.S. 17, Myrtle Beach, ☏ 843/692–1000) and the **Georgetown Memorial Hospital** (✉ 606 Black River Rd., Georgetown, ☏ 843/527–7000).

GOLF

Spring and fall, with off-season rates, are the busiest seasons, and there are many packages available in the area; call **Golf Holiday** (☏ 843/448–5942 or 800/845–4653). **Tee Times Central** (☏ 843/347–4653 or 800/344–5590) books tee times at a number of area courses.

GUIDED TOURS

At the **Georgetown County Chamber of Commerce and Information Center** (✉ 1005 Front St., Georgetown, ☏ 843/546–8436 or 800/777–7705), you can arrange to tour historic areas March–October by tram, by 1840 horse-drawn carriage, or by boat. You can also pick up free driving- and walking-tour maps. **Georgetown Tour Company** (✉ 627 Front St., Georgetown, ☏ 843/546–6827) offers tram tours of the historic district, a Ghostbusting Tour, and an afternoon Tea 'n Tour. For an insider's view, hire Georgetown native Miss Nell to take you on one of **Miss Nell's "Real South" Tours** (✉ 308 Front St., Georgetown, ☏ 843/546–3975). **Palmetto Tour & Travel** (☏ 843/626–2660) and **Leisure Time Unlimited/Gray Line** (☏ 843/448–9483), both in Myrtle Beach, offer tour packages and guide services.

LODGING ASSISTANCE

With about 60,000 rooms available along the Grand Strand, it's seldom difficult to find a place to stay, and discounting is rampant. Package deals are offered year-round, the most attractive of them between Labor Day and spring break. You can choose among cottages, villas, condominiums, and hotel-style high-rise units. For the free directory *Where to Stay and Play* write to the **Myrtle Beach Area Convention Bu-**

reau (✉ 710 21st Ave. N, Suite J, Myrtle Beach 29577, ☎ 843/448–1629 or 800/356–3016). For Pawleys Island and Litchfield Beach, try **Pawleys Island Realty** (✉ Box 306, Pawleys Island 29585, ☎ 843/237–4257 or 800/937–7352).

RADIO STATIONS

FM: WDAI 98.5, urban contemporary; WJXY 93.9, country; WJYR 92.1, easy listening; WKZQ 101.7, rock and roll; WNMB 105.9, best of the '60s–'80s; WRNN 94.5, talk; WSYN 106.5, oldies.

24-HOUR PHARMACY

The only all-night pharmacy in the area is at the **Columbia Grand Strand Regional Medical Center** (☞ Emergencies, *above*).

VISITOR INFORMATION

Georgetown County Chamber of Commerce and Information Center (☞ Guided Tours, *above*). **Myrtle Beach Area Chamber of Commerce and Information Center** (✉ 1200 N. Oak St., Box 2115, Myrtle Beach 29578, ☎ 843/626–7444; 800/356–3016 brochures only). **Pawleys Island Chamber of Commerce** (✉ U.S. 17, Box 569, Pawleys Island 29585, ☎ 843/237–1921).

HILTON HEAD AND BEYOND

Anchoring the southern tip of South Carolina's coastline is Hilton Head Island, named after English sea captain William Hilton, who claimed the 42 square mi for England in 1663. It was settled by planters in the 1700s and flourished until the Civil War. Thereafter, the economy declined and the island languished until Charles E. Fraser, a visionary South Carolina attorney, began developing the Sea Pines resort in 1956. Other developments followed, and today Hilton Head's casual pace, broad beaches, myriad activities, and genteel good life make it one of the East Coast's most popular vacation getaways.

Beaufort, some 40 mi north of Hilton Head, is a graceful antebellum town with a compact historic district preserving lavish 18th- and 19th-century homes from an era of immense prosperity, based on silky-textured Sea Island cotton. The *beau* in Beaufort is pronounced as in "beautiful," and Beaufort certainly is. Southeast, on the ocean, lies Fripp Island, a self-contained resort with controlled access. And midway between Beaufort and Charleston is Edisto (pronounced *ed*-is-toh) Island, settled in 1690, also once notable for its Sea Island cotton. Some of its elaborate mansions have been restored; others brood in disrepair.

Hilton Head Island

108 mi southwest of Charleston, 164 mi southeast of Columbia, over bridge on U.S. 278.

Lined by towering pines, palmetto trees, and wind-sculpted live oaks, Hilton Head's 12 mi of beaches are a major attraction, and the semitropical barrier island also has oak and pine woodlands and meandering lagoons. Choice stretches are occupied by various resorts, called "plantations," among them Sea Pines, Shipyard, Palmetto Dunes, and Port Royal. In these areas, accommodations range from rental villas and lavish private houses to luxury hotels. The resorts are also private residential communities, although many have public restaurants, marinas, shopping areas, and recreational facilities. All are secured, and visitors cannot tour them unless arrangements are made at the visitor office near the main gate of each plantation. A 5¾-mi Cross Island Parkway toll bridge ($1) makes it easy to bypass traffic and reach the south end of the island, where most of the resort areas and hotels are.

Hilton Head prides itself on its strict regulations that keep "light pollution" to a minimum; the lack of neon and streetlights also makes it difficult to find your way at night, so be sure to get good directions.

Audubon-Newhall Preserve, in the south of the island, is 50 acres of pristine forest, where you'll find native plant life identified and tagged. There are trails, a self-guided tour, and seasonal plant walks. ✉ *Palmetto Bay Rd.,* ☎ *843/785–5775.* *Free.* *Daily dawn–dusk.*

Sea Pines Forest Preserve is a 605-acre public wilderness tract with walking trails, a well-stocked fishing pond, a waterfowl pond, and a 3,400-year-old Indian shell ring. Both guided and self-guided tours are available. ✉ *At the southwest tip of the island, accessible via U.S. 278 (William Hilton Pkwy.),* ☎ *843/785–3333.* *Sea Pines Plantation $3 per car for nonguests, includes access to preserve.* *Daily dawn–dusk; closed during Heritage Golf Classic in Apr.*

The **Museum of Hilton Head Island** has a permanent collection depicting Native American life and hosts changing exhibits. Beach walks are conducted on weekdays, and tours of Native American sites, forts, and plantations are given randomly in season. ✉ *100 William Hilton Pkwy.,* ☎ *843/689–6767.* *Free.* *Mon.–Sat. 10–5, Sun. noon–4.*

At the **James M. Waddell Jr. Mariculture Research & Development Center,** 3 mi west of Hilton Head Island, visitors may tour the 24 ponds and the research building to see how methods of raising seafood commercially are studied. ✉ *Sawmill Creek Rd. near intersection of U.S. 278 and SC 46,* ☎ *843/837–3795.* *Free.* *Tours weekdays at 10 AM and by appointment.*

OFF THE BEATEN PATH

DAUFUSKIE ISLAND – From Hilton Head, you can go by boat to nearby Daufuskie Island, the setting for Pat Conroy's novel *The Water Is Wide,* which was made into the movie *Conrack*. The Dafuskie Island Club & Resort—with an oceanfront inn, cottages, golf courses, tennis, pools, water sports, and several restaurants—is a wonderful getaway (☎ 843/341–4820 or ☎ 800/648–6778). Despite increasing development on the island, many inhabitants, descendants of former slaves, live on small farms among remnants of churches, homes, and schools—reminders of antebellum times. Excursions to Daufuskie are run out of Hilton Head by Adventure Cruises (✉ Shelter Cove Marina, ☎ 843/785–4558), Calibogue Cruises (✉ 164B Palmetto Bay Rd., ☎ 843/785–8242), and Vagabond Cruises (✉ Harbour Town Marina, ☎ 843/842–4155).

Dining

$$$–$$$$ ★ ✕ **Barony Grill.** This sophisticated yet unpretentious restaurant has a high-beamed ceiling, high-back chairs, and French doors. Diners can try different wines in the Tasting Room before choosing a bottle or glass. The oak-smoked rack of lamb, seared tuna with shiitake mushroom risotto, and prime rib with bourbon jus are supreme; desserts are fantastic, too. ✉ *Westin Resort, 135 S. Port Royal Dr.,* ☎ *843/681–4000. Reservations essential. AE, D, DC, MC, V. Closed Sun.–Mon. No lunch.*

$$–$$$$ ✕ **Old Fort Pub.** Tucked away on a quiet site overlooking the marshlands of the Intracoastal Waterway and beside the Civil War ruins of Fort Mitchell, this rustic restaurant specializes in such dishes as oyster stew, corn-crusted pork chops, and mesquite-smoked filet mignon with mushroom cabernet sauce. The ambience is publike casual, but the service is not. Sunday brunch is wonderful. ✉ *65 Skull Creek Dr.,* ☎ *843/681–2386. AE, D, DC, MC, V.*

$$–$$$$ ✕ **Starfire Contemporary Bistro.** Ultrafresh ingredients are served in a pleasingly unique way at this small bistro with a somewhat formal yet pleasant atmosphere. Try the wild mushroom soup with roasted rosemary; salmon with spiced seed crust atop a crunchy cucumber salad; and the intense chocolate sorbet with homemade biscotti. ✉ *37 New Orleans Rd.,* ☎ *843/785–3434. AE, DC, MC, V. No lunch.*

$–$$$ ✕ **Two Eleven Park.** Choose from 75 wines by the glass and more than 200 by the bottle at this lively wine bar–bistro. Fans come here for the convivial atmosphere and specials like smothered shrimp over grits and beer-battered lobster tails. ✉ *211 Park, Park Plaza,* ☎ *843/686–5212. AE, D, DC, MC, V. No lunch. Closed Sun.*

$–$$ ✕ **Brick Oven Café.** Velvet drapes, chandeliers, booths, and '40s lounge-style entertainment, on top of good, reasonably priced food served late, make this the trendy place to be. There's a nice wine selection. ✉ *Park Plaza,* ☎ *843/686–2233. Reservations essential. No lunch. AE, D, DC, MC, V.*

$ ✕ **Antojitos.** At this basic little joint, you get the real taste of Mexico; try the *carne asada* (roasted meat). ✉ *Suite 302A, Pineland Station, Hwy. 278,* ☎ *843/681–2233. Reservations essential. No lunch. AE, D, DC, MC, V.*

Lodging

Sea Pines, the oldest and best known of Hilton Head's resort developments, or plantations, occupies 4,500 thickly wooded acres with three golf courses, a fine beach, tennis clubs, stables, and shopping plazas. The focus of Sea Pines is **Harbour Town,** built around the charming marina, which has shops, restaurants, some condominiums, and the landmark Hilton Head Lighthouse. Accommodations are in luxurious houses and villas facing the ocean or the golf courses.

The Crowne Plaza Resort is the oceanfront centerpiece of **Shipyard Plantation,** which also has villa condominiums, three nine-hole golf courses, a tennis club, and a small beach club. **Palmetto Dunes Resort** has the oceanfront Hyatt Regency Hilton Head, Hilton Resort, and other accommodations, along with the renowned Rod Laver Tennis Center, a good stretch of beach, three golf courses, and several oceanfront rental villa complexes. At **Port Royal Plantation** there's the posh Westin Resort, which is on the beach and has three golf courses and a tennis club.

Hilton Head Central Reservations (✉ Box 5312, Hilton Head Island 29938, ☎ 843/785–9050 or 800/845–7018, FAX 843/686–3255) represents almost every hotel, motel, and rental agency on the island. Other options are available through the **Hilton Head Condo Hotline** (☎ 843/785–2939), **Hilton Head Reservations and Golf Line** (☎ 843/444–4772), and **Island Rentals** (☎ 800/845–6134).

$$$$ **Crowne Plaza Resort.** Holiday Inn Worldwide's first property of this caliber in the United States, the oceanfront resort glimmers with brass railings and accents, and shiny wood floors and trim. Decorated in a nautical theme and set in a luxuriant garden, the Crowne Plaza has access to all the amenities of Shipyard Plantation. ✉ *130 Shipyard Dr., 29928,* ☎ *843/842–2400 or 800/465–4329,* FAX *843/785–8463. 315 rooms, 25 suites. 2 restaurants, lounge, indoor pool, outdoor pool, sauna, 3 18-hole golf courses, health club, racquetball, business services, meeting rooms. AE, D, DC, MC, V.*

$$$$ **Hilton Oceanfront Resort.** There's a Caribbean feel to this five-story resort hotel, part of the Hilton chain. The grounds are beautifully landscaped, and the spacious rooms, all ocean side, are spacious and decorated with contemporary wood furniture and warm colors; all have kitchenettes. ✉ *23 Ocean La., Box 6165, 29938,* ☎ *843/842–8000 or 800/845–8001,* FAX *843/842–4988. 303 rooms, 20 suites. 2 restau-*

rants, deli, lounge, 2 pools, hot tubs, sauna, 3 18-hole golf courses, health club, Ping-Pong, volleyball, boating, fishing, bicycles, children's programs. AE, D, DC, MC, V.

$$$$ **Holiday Inn Oceanfront Resort.** A handsome high-rise motor hotel, the Holiday Inn is on a broad, quiet stretch of beach. The rooms are spacious and well furnished in a contemporary style. The outdoor Tiki Hut lounge (☞ Nightlife, *below*) is hugely popular. ✉ *S. Forest Beach Dr., Box 5728, 29938,* ☎ *843/785–5126 or 800/465–4329,* FAX *843/785–6678. 202 rooms. Restaurant, lounge, pool. AE, D, DC, MC, V.*

$$$$ ★ **Main Street Inn.** The outside of this inn looks like an Italianate villa or a Charleston Battery home, with gardens, shuttered French doors, and iron railings. Luxury abounds inside, too, in the antique furnishings and the heart-pine floors covered in Turkish and sisal rugs. Guest rooms have velvet and silk brocade linens, feather duvets, and porcelain and brass sinks. Included in the rate are a European breakfast of imported meats, cheeses, quiches, breads, and pastries, and afternoon tea with homemade scones and tea sandwiches. ✉ *2200 Main St., 29926,* ☎ *843/681–3001 or 800/471–3001,* FAX *843/681–5541. 34 rooms. Bar, breakfast room, pool, hot tub, spa, concierge. AE, MC, V. BP.*

$$$$ **Marriott's Grande Ocean Resort.** It was built as a time-share property, but this beautiful oceanfront condo development, within walking distance of shops and restaurants, has a limited number of rentals. The luxurious, fully furnished two-bedroom, two-bath villas come with kitchens, whirlpool tubs, and maid service. ✉ *51 S. Forest Beach Dr., 29929,* ☎ *843/785–2000 or 800/527–3490,* FAX *843/842–3413. 140 villas. Deli, lounge, indoor pool, outdoor pool, exercise room. AE, D, DC, MC, V.*

$$$–$$$$ ★ **Disney's Hilton Head Island Resort.** More than 100 villas have fully furnished kitchen, dining, living, and sleeping areas. The smallest is a studio villa, and the largest has three bedrooms and four baths and sleeping accommodations for up to 12; all have marsh or marina views. Decorated in blues, greens, and deep reds, villas have porches with rocking chairs and picnic tables and suggest the rusticity of Adirondack cabins. The resort offers golf, tennis, and romance packages, beach shuttle service, and access to a fishing pier. The resort's 13,000-square-ft beach house has a fireplace in the living room, a heated pool, and an arcade. ✉ *22 Harbourside La., 29928,* ☎ *843/341–4100 or 800/453–4911,* FAX *843/341–4130. 102 units. Restaurant, pool, boating, fishing, bicycles, children's programs. AE, MC, V.*

$$$–$$$$ ★ **Westin Resort, Hilton Head Island.** One of the area's most luxurious properties, the horseshoe-shape Westin sprawls in a lushly landscaped oceanfront setting. The guest rooms, most with ocean views, are decorated with a residential feel: down pillows, rich colors, and comfortable wicker and contemporary furniture. All have seating areas and desks, and baths have marble flooring and distinctive lighting. Public areas display fine Asian porcelains and paintings. ✉ *2 Grass Lawn Ave., 29928,* ☎ *843/681–4000 or 800/228–3000,* FAX *843/681–1087. 412 rooms, 38 suites. 3 restaurants, 2 lounges, indoor pool, 2 outdoor pools, health club, children's programs. AE, D, DC, MC, V.*

$ **Best Western Inn.** Just a five-minute walk from the beach, it's a front-runner in the budget category; rooms are clean with standard decor. ✉ *40 Waterside Dr., 29928,* ☎ *843/842–8888,* FAX *843/842–5948. 120 rooms. Pool. AE, D, DC, MC, V.*

$ **Hampton Inn.** A short drive from the public beaches, it is clean, nicely landscaped, and sheltered from the noise and traffic; suites have kitchenettes. ✉ *1 Dillon Rd., 29926,* ☎ *843/681–7900,* FAX *843/681–4330. 124 rooms. Pool. AE, D, DC, MC, V.*

$ 🏨 **Red Roof Inn.** This two-story inn is popular with families. Clean and functional rooms are just a short drive from the public beaches. ✉ *5 Regency Pkwy., 29928, ☎ 843/686–6808 or 800/843–7663, FAX 843/842–3352. 112 rooms. Pool. AE, D, DC, MC, V.* 🚭

Nightlife and the Arts

THE ARTS

The **Self Family Arts Center** (✉ Shelter Cove La., ☎ 843/686–3945) has details on Hilton Head arts events; it includes an art gallery, a theater, and a theater program for youth. In warm weather, free **outdoor concerts** are held at Harbour Town and Shelter Cove. Concerts, plays, films, art shows, theater, sporting events, food fairs, and minitournaments make up Hilton Head's **SpringFest** (☎ 843/686–4944 or 800/424–3387), which runs for the month of March. A Winter Carnival and Winefest are held each year.

NIGHTLIFE

Bars, much like everything in Hilton Head, are often in strip malls. Try the **Blue Nite** (✉ 4 Target Rd., ☎ 843/842–6683) for live music or **Hilton Head Brewing Co.** (✉ Hilton Head Plaza, ☎ 843/785–2739) for late-night disco every Wednesday. The **Lodge** (✉ Hilton Head Plaza, ☎ 843/842–8966) has pool tables and roaring fires in the stone fireplaces. **Moneypenny's** (✉ Palmetto Bay Rd., Village Exchange, ☎ 843/785–7878) is a cozy spot with acoustic music. **Monkey Business** (✉ Park Plaza, ☎ 843/686–3545) is a dance club popular with young professionals.

The **Pelican Poolside** (☎ 843/681–4000), an oceanfront lounge at the Westin Resort, offers informal entertainment every night but Sunday. **Regatta** (✉ 23 Ocean La., ☎ 843/842–8000), a sophisticated oceanfront nightspot in the Hilton Resort, features live beach and jazz music nightly. **Tiki Hut** (✉ S. Forest Beach Dr., ☎ 843/785–5126), a locally popular beachside bar at the Holiday Inn Oceanfront Resort, has live music during the season.

Outdoor Activities and Sports

BEACHES

Although the resort beaches are reserved for guests and residents, there are four public entrances to Hilton Head's 12 mi of ocean beach. Two main parking and changing areas are at Coligny Circle, near the Holiday Inn, and on Folly Field Road, off U.S. 278. Signs along U.S. 278 point the way to Bradley and Singleton beaches, where parking space is limited.

BIKING

There are pathways in several areas of Hilton Head (many in the resorts), and pedaling is popular along the firmly packed beach. Bicycles can be rented at most hotels and resorts and at **Hilton Head Bicycle Company** (✉ 11B Archer Rd., ☎ 843/686–6888), **Harbour Town Bicycles** (✉ Heritage Plaza, ☎ 843/785–3546), and **South Beach Cycles** (✉ Sea Pines Plantation, ☎ 843/671–2453).

CANOEING AND KAYAKING

Outside Hilton Head (✉ South Beach Marina, ☎ 843/671–2643; Shelter Cove Plaza, ☎ 843/686–6996) is an ecologically sensitive company that rents canoes, kayaks, bikes, and Rollerblades; it also has nature tours.

FISHING

On Hilton Head, you can pick oysters, dig for clams, or cast for shrimp; supplies are available at **Shelter Cove Marina** at Palmetto Dunes (☎ 843/842–7001). Local marinas offer in-shore and deep-sea fishing charters. Each year a billfishing tournament and two king mackerel tournaments attract anglers.

GOLF

Many of Hilton Head's 29 championship courses are open to the public, including 18-hole, par-72 **Island West Golf Course** (✉ U.S. 278, 8 mi before the bridge to Hilton Head, ☎ 843/689–6660); 18-hole, par-72 **Old South Golf Links** (✉ U.S. 278, ☎ 843/785–5353); 18-hole, par-72 **Palmetto Dunes** (✉ Ocean La., ☎ 843/785–1138); 18-hole, par-72 and 9-hole, par-36 **Port Royal** (✉ Grass Lawn Ave., ☎ 843/689–5600); and 18-hole, par-72 **Sea Pines** (✉ William Hilton Pkwy., ☎ 843/842–8484). **Harbour Town Golf Links at Sea Pines** (✉ 11 Lighthouse La., ☎ 843/671–2448 or 800/955–8337), 18 holes and par 71, hosts the MCI Classic every spring.

HORSEBACK RIDING

Many trails wind through woods and nature preserves. Some stables in and near Hilton Head are **Lawton Stables** (✉ Sea Pines, ☎ 843/671–2586) and **Sandy Creek Stables** (✉ Near Spanish Wells, ☎ 843/689–3423). At **Sea Horse Farms** (✉ 34 Mitchellville Rd., ☎ 843/681–7749), you can ride on the beach. **Old South** (✉ Fording Island Rd., Bluffton, ☎ 843/842–7433) offers landscape riding. Rates are generally per person by the hour. **Rose Hill Plantation** (✉ 1 Equestrian Way, Bluffton, ☎ 843/757–3082) welcomes experienced riders only.

SUMMER CAMP

On Hilton Head Island, all major hotels offer summer youth activities; some have full-scale youth programs. The **Island Recreation Center** runs a summer camp that visiting youngsters can join. ✉ *Hilton Head Island Recreation Association, Wilborn Rd., Box 22593, Hilton Head Island 29925,* ☎ *843/681–7273.* ⏲ *Camp mid-June–late Aug., weekdays.*

TENNIS

There are more than 300 courts on Hilton Head. **Port Royal** (✉ 15 Wimbledon Ct., ☎ 843/686–8803); **Sea Pines Racquet Club** (✉ 32 Greenwood Dr., ☎ 843/842–8484), home of the Family Circle Tournament; and **Shipyard** (✉ Shipyard Dr. next to Crowne Plaza Resort, ☎ 843/686–8804) are highly rated. Other clubs that welcome guests include **Palmetto Dunes** (✉ 6 Trent Jones La., ☎ 843/785–1151) and **Van der Meer Tennis Center** (✉ 19 deAllyon Rd., ☎ 843/785–8388).

WINDSURFING

Lessons and rentals are available from **Outside Hilton Head** (☞ Canoeing and Kayaking, *above*).

Shopping

MALLS AND OUTLETS

Coligny Plaza (✉ Coligny Plaza, off Coligny Circle, ☎ 843/842–6050) has 60-plus shops, restaurants, a movie theater, and a supermarket. **Hilton Head Factory Stores 1 & 2** (✉ U.S. 278 at the island gateway, ☎ 843/837–4339 or 888/746–7333) has more than 80 outlets, including J. Crew, Gap, Brooks Brothers, Harry & David, and Coach, selling clothing and housewares. The **Mall at Shelter Cove** (✉ U.S. 278, ½ mi north of Palmetto Dunes Resort, ☎ 843/686–3090) has 55 shops and four restaurants. **Shoppes on the Parkway** (✉ U.S. 278, 1 mi south of Palmetto Dunes Resort, ☎ 843/686–6233) comprises 30 outlets, including Dansk, Gorham, and Van Heusen.

ART GALLERIES

The **Red Piano Art Gallery** (✉ 220 Cordillo Pkwy., ☎ 843/785–2318) showcases 19th- and 20th-century works by regional and national contemporary artists.

BOOKS

Authors Bookstore (✉ The Village at Wexford, ☎ 843/686–5020) carries a good selection of books focusing on local history and culture.

JEWELRY

The **Bird's Nest** (✉ Coligny Plaza, ☎ 843/785–3737) sells locally made shell and sand-dollar jewelry. The **Goldsmith Shop** (✉ 3 Lagoon Rd., ☎ 843/785–2538) carries classic jewelry and island charms.

NATURE

The **Audubon Nature Store** (✉ The Village at Wexford, ☎ 843/785–4311) has items with a nature theme. The **Hammock Company** (✉ Coligny Plaza, ☎ 843/686–3636 or 800/344–4264) sells gifts and other items with an emphasis on nature.

Beaufort

43 mi north of Hilton Head.

Charming homes and churches from Beaufort's prosperous antebellum days as a cotton center grace this historic town on Port Royal Island. Although many private houses in **Old Point,** the historic district, are not usually open to visitors, some may be on the annual Fall House Tour in mid-October and the Spring Tour of Homes and Gardens in April or May. The **Greater Beaufort Chamber of Commerce** (☎ 843/524–3163) can provide more information about house-tour schedules. The Gullah Festival, which takes place Memorial Day weekend, celebrates Lowcountry and West African culture.

The **John Mark Verdier House Museum,** built about 1790 in the Federal style, has been restored and furnished as it would have been between 1790 and the visit of Lafayette in 1825. It was the headquarters for Union forces during the Civil War. *✉ 801 Bay St., ☎ 843/524–6334. 🎫 $4. ⏲ Mon.–Sat. 10–4:30.*

Built in 1795 and remodeled in 1852, the Gothic-style arsenal that was home of the Beaufort Volunteer Artillery now houses the **Beaufort Museum,** with prehistoric relics, native pottery, and Revolutionary War and Civil War exhibits. *✉ 713 Craven St., ☎ 843/525–7077. 🎫 $2. ⏲ Mon.–Tues. and Thurs.–Sat. 10–5.*

St. Helena's Episcopal Church (1724) was turned into a hospital during the Civil War, and gravestones were brought inside to serve as operating tables. *✉ 501 Church St., ☎ 843/522–1712. ⏲ Mon.–Sat. 10–4.*

Henry C. Chambers Waterfront Park, off Bay Street, is a great place to survey the scene. Barbra Streisand filmed *Prince of Tides* here. Its 7 landscaped acres along the Beaufort River, part of the Intracoastal Waterway, include a seawall promenade, a crafts market, gardens, and a marina. Some events of the popular mid-July Beaufort Water Festival, as well as a seasonal farmers' and crafts market, take place here.

At **Parris Island,** 10 mi south of Beaufort via SC 802, you can observe U.S. Marine Corps recruit training and either take a guided tour or drive through the base on your own. There's a replica of the Iwo Jima flag-raising monument on the base. The **Parris Island Museum** exhibits uniforms, photographs, and weapons chronicling military history since 1562, when the French Huguenots built a fort on St. Helena. *☎ 843/525–2951. 🎫 Free. ⏲ Fri.–Wed. 10–4:30, Thurs. 10–7.*

Close-Up

THE WORLD OF GULLAH

IN THE LOWCOUNTRY, Gullah refers to several things: language, people, and a culture. Gullah (the word itself is believed to be a version of Angola), an English-based dialect rooted in African languages, is the unique language of the African-Americans of the Sea Islands of South Carolina and Georgia. More than 300 years old, this rhythmic language has survived, in part, because of the geographic isolation of the people who speak it; most locally born African-Americans of the area can understand, if not speak, Gullah.

Descended from thousands of slaves who were imported by planters in the Carolinas during the 18th century, the Gullah people have maintained not only their dialect but also their heritage. Much of Gullah culture traces back to the African rice-coast culture and survives today in the art forms and skills, including sweet-grass basket making, of Sea Islanders. During the colonial period, when rice was king, Africans from the West African rice kingdoms drew high premiums as slaves. Those with basket-making skills were extremely valuable because baskets were needed for agricultural and household use. Still made by hand, sweet-grass baskets are intricate coils of a marsh grass called sweet grass. Highly prized by residents and visitors alike, the baskets are named for the sweet, haylike aroma of the sweet grass. Other Gullah art forms can be seen in hand-carved bateaus and gourds and in hand-tied nets used to catch shrimp in local creeks and rivers.

Nowhere is Gullah culture more evident than in the foods of the region. Rice, of course, appears at nearly every meal. Africans taught planters how to grow rice and how to cook and serve it as well. Like many African dishes, Lowcountry dishes use okra, peanuts, benne (the African word for sesame seeds), field peas, and hot peppers. Gullah food reflects the bounty of the islands: shrimp, crabs, oysters, fish, and vegetables such as greens, tomatoes, and corn. Watermelons, indigenous to West Africa, are grown all over the Lowcountry.

Many dishes are prepared in one pot, similar to the stew-pot cooking of West Africa. Frogmore stew calls for cooking shrimp, potatoes, sausage, and corn together in one large pot. Hoppin' John—a one-pot mixture of rice and field peas traditionally served on New Year's Day—is similar to rice and pigeon peas, a mainstay in West Africa.

The practices of plantation owners unknowingly helped the Gullah culture survive: from praise houses—one-room houses of worship where Christianity was introduced to keep slaves from running away—came plantation melodies. These songs live on in performances by groups including the Hallelujah Singers, Sea Island Singers, Mt. Zion Spiritual Singers, and Ron and Natalie Daise, all of whom perform regularly in Charleston and Beaufort.

The Penn Center on St. Helena Island near Beaufort is the unofficial Gullah headquarters, preserving the culture and developing opportunities for Gullahs. Until 1927 or so, St. Helena felt little influence from the outside world. Blacks retained the land, their language, and their unique culture. Many still go shrimping with hand-tied nets, harvest oysters, and grow their own vegetables. Nearby on Daufuskie Island, as well as on Edisto, Wadmalaw and Johns islands near Charleston, Gullah communities can still be found, though development continues to encroach. A number of companies can help visitors explore this world (☞ Guided Tours *in* Charleston A to Z, *above*).

A famous Gullah proverb says: *If oonuh ent kno weh oonuh dah gwine, oonuh should kno weh oonuh come f'um.* Translation: If you don't know where you're going, you should know where you come from.

St. Helena Island, 9 mi southeast of Beaufort via U.S. 21, is the site of the **Penn Center Historic District** and **York W. Bailey Museum.** Penn Center, established in the middle of the Civil War as the South's first school for freed slaves, today provides community services and has cottages for rent. The **York W. Bailey Museum** (formerly a clinic) has displays reflecting the heritage of Sea Island blacks. These islands are where Gullah, a musical language that combines English and African languages, developed. ✉ *Land's End Rd., St. Helena Island,* ☎ *843/838–2432.* *Donation suggested.* *Tues.–Fri. 11–4 and by appointment.*

OFF THE BEATEN PATH

HUNTING ISLAND STATE PARK – This secluded domain of beach, nature trails, and varied fishing has about 3 mi of public beaches. The 1,120-ft fishing pier is among the longest on the East Coast. You can climb the 181 steps of the 140-ft **Hunting Island Lighthouse** (built in 1859 and abandoned in 1933) for sweeping views. The park is 18 mi southeast of Beaufort via U.S. 21; write for cabin and camping reservations. ✉ *1775 Sea Island Pkwy., St. Helena 29920,* ☎ *843/838–2011.* *$3 per car Mar.–Oct.; free rest of yr; $2 to climb lighthouse.* *Lighthouse daily 10–5.*

Dining and Lodging

$–$$$ ✕ **Emily's.** Long, narrow, and wood-paneled, Emily's is a lively restaurant and tapas bar that serves until 11. The crowds linger over tapas including chicken spring rolls, lamb chops, and crab wontons. This is definitely *not* a no-smoking haven. ✉ *906 Port Republic St.,* ☎ *843/522–1866. AE, MC, V.*

$–$$ ✕ **Bistro de Jong.** This light-filled spot, with a comfortable counter bar and indoor courtyard motif, is popular with the lunch crowd. The Belgian chef, originally with the Beaufort Inn, blends European styles with local ingredients; the result is peanut-and-cilantro fried shrimp with Cajun rémoulade (a mayonnaise-based sauce), chicken pecan salad on focaccia bread, or the yummy Peter's pasta with sun-dried tomatoes, artichokes, and Portobello mushrooms. The apple belly pastries are a must. ✉ *205 West St.,* ☎ *843/524–4994. AE, D, MC, V. Closed Mon. No dinner Sun.*

$–$$ ✕ **11th Street Dockside.** The succulent fried oysters, shrimp, and fish here are some of the best around. Other seafood specialties are steamed seafood pot and, by request only, Frogmore stew (consisting of shrimp, potatoes, sausage, and corn). It's all served in a classic wharf-side environment with screened porch and water views from nearly every table. ✉ *11th St. W, Port Royal,* ☎ *843/524–7433. AE, D, DC, MC, V. No lunch.*

$$–$$$ ✕ **Beaufort Inn and Restaurant.** This peach-color 1897 Victorian inn, with its many gables and porches, has a superb restaurant with two mahogany-paneled dining rooms, porch dining, and a wine bar. Among the classy seafood dishes are crispy flounder with yucca chips and sashimi tuna in peanut sauce. Guest rooms are decorated with period reproductions, tasteful florals and plaids, and comfortable chairs. All have pine floors; several have fireplaces and four-poster beds. Reservations are required for afternoon tea, complimentary for guests. ✉ *809 Port Republic St., 29902,* ☎ *843/521–9000,* FAX *843/521–9500. 11 rooms. Restaurant. AE, MC, V. BP.*

$$$–$$$$ ★ **Rhett House Inn.** A storybook inn (circa 1820) in the heart of the historic district is filled with art and antiques and abounds in such luxuries as down pillows and duvets, cotton linens, CD players in each room, and fresh flowers. Breakfast, afternoon tea, evening hors d'oeuvres, and dessert are included in the rate. Celebrity visitors have included Barbra Streisand, Jeff Bridges, and Dennis Quaid. The remodeled house across the street has six rooms, each with gas fireplace, whirlpool tub, private entrance, and porch. ✉ *1009 Craven St., 29902,* ☎

843/524–9030, FAX 843/524–1310. 15 rooms, 1 suite. Bicycles. AE, MC, V. BP.

$$–$$$ **Craven Street Inn.** This double-piazzaed 1870 inn is decorated in clean, Pottery Barn–style, with olive and neutral tones, hand-crafted cabinets, wreaths and baskets. Spacious guest rooms in the main house have pine floors, high ceilings, and fireplaces; those in the 1920s garden house are small but cozy and comfortable. Breakfast might be stuffed French toast or ham and cheese omelette with homemade crumpets. *1103 Craven St., 29902, 888/522–0250 or 843/522–1668, FAX 843/522–9975. 7 rooms, 2 suites, 1 cottage. AE, D, MC, V. BP.*

$$–$$$ **Cuthbert House Inn.** Overlooking the bay, this pillared 1790 home has original Federal fireplaces and crown and rope molding. The owners have filled it with 18th- and 19th-century heirlooms; rooms are elegant yet comfortable, with Oriental rugs on pine floors, commanding beds, quilts, and books. *1203 Bay St., 29902, 843/521–1315 or 800/327–9275, FAX 843/521–1314. 7 rooms, 1 suite. Bicycles. AE, D, MC, V. BP.*

$$–$$$ **Fripp Island Resort.** The resort encompasses the entire island; access is limited to guests only. Two- and three-bedroom villas and homes are contemporary in decor. The island is 19 mi south of Beaufort via U.S. 21, just beyond Hunting Island State Park. There's a pavilion with shops, restaurants, and a marina. *1 Tarpon Blvd., 29920, 843/838–3535 or 800/845–4100, FAX 843/838–9079. 240 units. 5 restaurants, 4 pools, 2 18-hole golf courses, 10 tennis courts, jogging, boating, bicycles, children's programs. AE, D, DC, MC, V.*

$–$$ **Best Western Sea Island Inn.** At this well-maintained but standard inn in the downtown historic district, rooms are basic. *1015 Bay St., Box 532, 29902, 843/522–2090 or 800/528–1234, FAX 843/521–4858. 43 rooms. Pool. AE, D, DC, MC, V. CP.*

$ **Howard Johnson.** This clean and cheerfully staffed hotel sits on the edge of the marsh a few miles from the historic district. Rooms are spacious and have desks; many have views of the river and marsh. *3651 Trask Pkwy. (U.S. 21), 29902, 843/524–6020 or 800/528–1234, FAX 843/521–4858. 43 rooms. Pool. AE, D, DC, MC, V. CP.*

Nightlife and the Arts

Bananas (910 Bay St., 843/522–0910) has a late-night bar and live music on weekends. **Plum's** (904½ Bay St., 843/525–1946) is good for a late drink and has live bands during the weekend.

Outdoor Activities and Sports

BIKING

Beaufort is great for bicycling. Rentals are available from **Lowcountry Bicycles** (904 Port Republic St., 843/524–9585).

GOLF

Most golf courses are about a 10- to 20-minute drive from Beaufort. Try the 27 holes designed by Tom Fazio at **Callawassie Island Club** (SC 170, Callawassie Island, 800/221–8431); the challenging and beautiful 18-hole, par-72 **Cat Island Golf Club** (8 Waveland Ave., Port Royal, 843/524–0300); or **Dataw Island**'s two 18-hole, par-72 courses (Dataw Club Rd., 6 mi east of Beaufort off U.S. 21, Dataw Island, 843/838–8250).

Shopping

ANTIQUES

Den of Antiquity (SC 170W, 843/521–9990), the area's largest antiques shop, carries a wide assortment of Lowcountry and nautical pieces.

ART GALLERIES

On canvas and sculpture as well as on bits of tin roofing, rugs, frames, and furniture, the colorful, whimsical designs of Suzanne and Eric Longo decorate their **Longo Gallery** (✉ 407 Carteret St.; 103 Charles St.; ☎ 843/522–8933 for both). The **Rhett Gallery** (✉ 901 Bay St., ☎ 843/524–3339) sells Lowcountry art by members of the Rhett family and antique maps and prints, including Audubons. On nearby St. Helena Island, the **Red Piano Too Art Gallery** (✉ 853 Sea Island Pkwy., ☎ 843/838–2241), in a huge old wooden building, is filled with quirky folk and Southern art, beads, and pottery.

JEWELRY

The **Craftseller** (✉ 818 Bay St., ☎ 843/525–6104) displays jewelry and other items by Southern craftspeople.

En Route The ruins of **Sheldon Church,** built in 1753, make an interesting stop en route from Beaufort to Edisto Island. The church was burned in 1779 and again in 1865. Only the brick walls and columns remain beside the old cemetery. Get here from Beaufort on U.S. 21 to Gardens Corner; then go west on U.S. 17 and north on SC 21.

Edisto Island

80 mi northeast of Beaufort; take U.S. 17N and then follow SC 174.

On this rural island, magnificent stands of age-old oaks festooned with Spanish moss border quiet streams and side roads; wild turkeys may still be spotted on open grasslands and amid palmetto palms. Many of the island's inhabitants are descendants of former slaves. **Edisto Beach State Park** has 3 mi of beach with excellent shelling, housekeeping cabins by the marsh, and campsites by the ocean (though severe erosion is limiting availability). Luxury resort development has begun to encroach around the edges of the park. For camping reservations, call ☎ 843/869–2156 or 843/869–3396.

OFF THE BEATEN PATH **CAW CAW INTERPRETIVE CENTER** – If you're heading toward Charleston, you might consider stopping at this 654-acre tract, once part of an old rice plantation. The 250 acres of rice fields are home to as many as 60 species of migratory birds, including long-legged wader birds such as blue herons. Eight miles of nature trails extend along cypress swamp, oak forest, and salt and fresh water marsh. ✉ *5200 Savannah Hwy. (U.S. 17S), 15 mi from Charleston,* ☎ *843/889–8898 or 843/762–2172.* *Free.* *May–Aug., Tues.–Sun. 8–7; Mar.–Apr. and Sept.–Oct., Tues.–Sun. 9–6; Nov.–Feb., Tues.–Sun. 9–5.*

Dining and Lodging

$$–$$$ ★ ✕ **Old Post Office.** Try the fussed-over pork chop or the blue-crab-and-asparagus pie, served with the house salad, vegetables, and fresh-baked bread. The house specialty at this restaurant on Store Creek is shrimp and grits and, well, *anything* with grits, rumored to be the best around these parts. Once Bailey's General Store and U.S. Post Office, the building contains the original post office boxes. ✉ *1442 SC 174, 5 mi from Edisto Beach,* ☎ *843/869–2339. MC, V. Closed Sun. June–Sept., Sun.–Mon. Oct.–May. No lunch.*

$$ **Seaside Plantation.** This Federal-style plantation house, built around 1810, has 12-ft ceilings, intricate crown molding, pine floors, and family antiques. Nestled among shady live oaks on 245 acres where cotton once grew, Seaside is about 1 mi from the beach. A full breakfast of French toast or egg, cheese, and ham casserole with fruit is included. ✉ *400 Hwy. 174, 29438,* ☎ *843/869–0971. 4 rooms. No credit cards. BP.*

$$ 🏨 **Fairfield Ocean Ridge Resort.** Although not on the beach, most accommodations are a short walk away and combine resort amenities with a get-away-from-it-all setting. Well-furnished one- to five-bedroom villas and homes tastefully decorated in contemporary style are available. A trolley transports guests to the resort's beach shelter. ✉ *1 King Cotton Rd., Box 27, 29438,* ☎ *843/869–2561,* FAX *843/869–2384. 100 units. Restaurant, lounge, pool, wading pool, 18-hole golf course, miniature golf, 4 tennis courts, hiking, beach, boating, fishing. AE, D, MC, V.*

Hilton Head and Beyond A to Z

Arriving and Departing

BY BOAT

Hilton Head is accessible via the Intracoastal Waterway, with docking available at **Harbour Town Marina** (☎ 843/671–2704), **Schilling Boathouse** (☎ 843/681–2628), and **Shelter Cove Marina** (☎ 843/842–7001).

BY CAR

Hilton Head Island is 40 mi east of I–95 (✉ Exit 28 off I–95S, Exit 5 off I–95N). Beaufort is 25 mi east of I–95, on U.S. 21.

BY PLANE

Hilton Head Island Airport (☎ 843/681–6386) is served by US Airways Express and Midway. Most travelers use the **Savannah International Airport** (✉ 400 Airways Ave., ☎ 912/964–0514), about an hour from Hilton Head, which is served by US Airways and Colgan-Air. For airline telephone numbers, *see* Air Travel *in* Smart Travel Tips A to Z.

Getting Around

BY TAXI

Lowcountry Taxi and Limousine Service (☎ 843/681–8294) and **Yellow Cab** (☎ 843/686–6666) provide service in Hilton Head; other options include **At Your Service** (☎ 843/837–3783) and **Lowcountry Adventures** (☎ 843/681–8212). In Beaufort, the **Point** (☎ 843/522–3576) and **Yellow Cab** (☎ 843/522–1121) provide service.

Contacts and Resources

EMERGENCIES

Ambulance, fire, police (☎ 911). Emergency medical service is available at the **Hilton Head Medical Center and Clinics** (✉ Hospital Center Blvd., ☎ 843/681–6122).

GUIDED TOURS

Hilton Head's **Adventure Cruises** (☎ 843/785–4558) offers dinner, sightseeing, and murder-mystery cruises. Several companies, including **Harbour Town Charters** in Hilton Head (☎ 843/363–2628), run dolphin sightseeing and environmental trips. **Lowcountry Adventures** (☎ 843/681–8212) offers tours of Hilton Head, Beaufort, and Charleston. **Steel Horse Helicopters** (☎ 843/689–6747) gives tours of Hilton Head with a bird's-eye view, starting at $20 for five minutes.

Carolina Buggy Tours (☎ 843/525–1300) will show you Beaufort's historic district. **Carriage Tours of Beaufort** (☎ 843/221–1651) has tours of the historic district by horse-drawn carriage. **Gullah 'n' Geechie Mahn Tours** (☎ 843/838–7516) provides tours of Beaufort and Sea Islands such as St. Helena that focus on the traditions of African-American culture. Costumed guides sing and act out history during walking tours by the **Spirit of Old Beaufort** (☎ 843/525–0459). Call the **Greater Beaufort Chamber of Commerce** (☎ 843/524–3163) to find out about self-guided walking or driving tours of Beaufort.

LATE-NIGHT PHARMACIES

CVS (✉ 95 Matthews, Hilton Head, ☎ 843/681–8363) is open until 9.

RADIO STATIONS

AM: WFXH 1130, sports talk. **FM:** WFXH 106.1, classic rock; WAEV 97.3, adult contemporary; WHVZ 99.7, beach, boogie, and blues; WLVH 101.1, soft soul; WJCL 96.5, country; WOCW 92.1, oldies.

VISITOR INFORMATION

For information on Edisto, call **Edisto Island Chamber of Commerce** (✉ Box 206, Edisto Island 29438, ☎ 843/869–3867 or 888/333–2781). **Greater Beaufort Chamber of Commerce** (✉ 1006 Bay St., Box 910, Beaufort 29901, ☎ 843/524–3163) has information about Beaufort and the surrounding area. You can call the **Hilton Head Island Chamber of Commerce** (✉ Box 5647, Hilton Head 29938, ☎ 843/785–3673) for information. Two **Hilton Head welcome centers,** run by a private real-estate firm, are on U.S. 278 next to the bridge to Hilton Head and at 6 Lagoon Road at the island's south end. The centers provide visitor information and also attempt to entice you into purchasing real estate. In Hilton Head, your best bet is to stop by the **Welcome Center and Museum of Hilton Head** (✉ 100 William Hilton Pkwy.).

COLUMBIA AND THE HEARTLAND

Camden, Aiken, Abbeville

South Carolina's Heartland, between the coastal Lowcountry and the mountains, is a varied region of swamps and flowing rivers, fertile farmland, and vast forests of pines and hardwoods. Lakes Murray, Marion, and Moultrie have wonderful fishing, and the many state parks are popular for hiking, swimming, and camping. At the center of the region is the state capital, Columbia, an engaging contemporary city superimposed on cherished historic remnants. It has restored mansions, several museums, a university, a variety of restaurants, a lively arts scene, and a fine zoo and botanical garden.

In Aiken, the center of South Carolina's Thoroughbred Country, such champions as Sea Hero and Pleasant Colony were trained. The beautiful landscape is studded with the fine mansions of wealthy Northerners such as the Vanderbilts and Whitneys. Throughout the region, such towns as Ninety Six, Sumter, and Camden preserve and interpret the past, with historic re-creations, exhibits, and restorations. Several public gardens provide islands of color during most of the year.

Columbia

112 mi northwest of Charleston, 101 mi southeast of Greenville.

In 1786 South Carolina's capital was moved from Charleston to Columbia, in the center of the state along the banks of the Congaree River. One of the nation's first planned cities, Columbia has streets that are among the widest in America—because it was then thought that stagnant air in narrow streets fostered the spread of malaria. The city soon grew into a center of political, commercial, cultural, and social activity, but in early 1865 General William Tecumseh Sherman invaded South Carolina and incinerated two-thirds of Columbia. A few homes and public buildings were spared—as was the First Baptist Church, where secession was declared, because a janitor directed Sherman's troops to a Methodist church when asked directions. Today the city is a sprawling blend of modern office blocks, suburban neighborhoods, and the occasional antebellum home. Here, too, is the expansive main campus of the University of South Carolina, including the historic and scenic Horseshoe.

The **Columbia Museum of Art** contains the Kress Foundation Collection of Renaissance and Baroque treasures, sculpture, decorative arts including art glass, and European and American paintings; there are also changing exhibitions. Children may enjoy the museum's doll collection. ☒ *Main and Hampton Sts.,* ☏ *803/799–2810.* *$4.* *Tues. and Thurs.–Sat. 10–5, Wed. 10–9, Sun. 1–5.*

Stop by the **Museum Shop** of the Historic Columbia Foundation in the Robert Mills House (☒ 1616 Blanding St., ☏ 803/252–1770) in the historic district to get a map and buy tickets to tour four Columbia houses: the Hampton-Preston Mansion, the Robert Mills House, the Mann-Simons Cottage, and the Woodrow Wilson Boyhood Home. *Each house $4.* *All houses Tues.–Sat. 10:15–3:15, Sun. 1:15–4:15.*

The **Hampton-Preston Mansion** (☒ 1615 Blanding St., ☏ 803/252–1770), dating from 1818, is filled with lavish furnishings collected by three generations of two influential families (☞ Museum Shop, *above*). The classic, columned 1823 **Robert Mills House** (☒ 1616 Blanding St., ☏ 803/252–1770) was named for its architect, who later designed the Washington Monument. It has opulent Regency furniture, marble mantels, and spacious grounds (☞ Museum Shop, *above*). The **Mann-Simons Cottage** (☒ 1403 Richland St., ☏ 803/252–1770) was the home of Celia Mann, one of only 200 free African-Americans in Columbia in the mid-1800s (☞ Museum Shop, *above*). The **Woodrow Wilson Boyhood Home** (☒ 1705 Hampton St., ☏ 803/252–1770) displays the gaslights, arched doorways, and ornate furnishings of the Victorian period (☞ Museum Shop, *above*).

The **Fort Jackson Museum,** on the grounds of the U.S. Army Training Center, displays heavy equipment from the two world wars and has exhibits on the history of the fort from 1917 to the present. ☒ *Bldg. 4442, Jackson Blvd.,* ☏ *803/751–7419.* *Free.* *Tues.–Fri. 10–4, Sat. 1–4.*

Exhibits at the **South Carolina State Museum,** in a large, refurbished textile mill, interpret the state's natural history, archaeology, historical development, and technological and artistic accomplishments. One exhibit portrays noted black astronauts (dedicated to South Carolina native Dr. Ronald McNair, who died on the *Challenger*), and another focuses on the cotton industry and slavery. An iron gate made for the museum by Phillip Simmons, the "dean of Charleston blacksmiths," is on display, as is the surfboard that physicist Kary Mullis was riding when he heard he'd won the Nobel Prize. In the Stringer Discovery Center, an interactive display, children can check out microorganisms under a microscope and climb trees to observe the animals who live in the branches. ☒ *301 Gervais St.,* ☏ *803/737–4921.* *$4.* *Mon.–Sat. 10–5, Sun. 1–5.*

South Carolina's capitol, the **State House,** started in 1855 and completed in 1950, is made of native blue granite in the Italian Renaissance style. Six bronze stars on the outer western wall mark direct hits by Sherman's cannons. The interior is richly appointed with brass, marble, mahogany, and artwork. A replica of Jean-Antoine Houdon's statue of George Washington is on the grounds. ☒ *Main and Gervais Sts.,* ☏ *803/734–9818.* *Free.* *Weekdays 9–5, Sat. 10–5, 1st Sun. of month 1–5.*

Make sure it's dark out when you drive by **Tunnelvision,** an optical illusion painted on the wall of the Federal Land Bank Building by local artist Blue Sky. ☒ *Taylor and Marion Sts.*

A highlight of the sprawling **University of South Carolina,** near the State House, is its original campus—the scenic, tree-lined **Horseshoe**—dating to 1801, when the school was first established. Researchers explore the special collections on state history and genealogy at the **South Caroliniana Library,** established in 1840 (✉ Sumter St., ☎ 803/777–3131). It's free and open Monday, Wednesday, and Friday 8:30 to 5, Tuesday and Thursday 8:30 to 8, Saturday 9 to 5 (9 to 1 mid-May through mid-August). Here, too, is the **McKissick Museum,** with geology and gemstone exhibits and a fine display of silver (✉ Sumter St., ☎ 803/777–7251). It's free and open weekdays 9–4, weekends 1–5.

Riverfront Park and Historic Columbia Canal, where the Broad and Saluda rivers meet to form the Congaree River, was created around the city's original waterworks and hydroelectric plant. Interpretive markers describe the area's plant and animal life and tell the history of the buildings. ✉ *312 Laurel St.,* ☎ *803/733–8613.* *Free.* *Daily dawn–dusk.*

★ **Riverbanks Zoological Park and Botanical Garden** contains more than 2,000 animals and birds, some endangered, in natural habitats. Walk along pathways and through landscaped gardens to see sea lions, polar bears, Siberian tigers, and black rhinos. The South American primate collection has won international acclaim, and the park is noted for its success in breeding endangered and fragile species. The aquarium-reptile complex has South Carolina, desert, tropical, and marine specimens. A 70-acre botanical garden on the west bank of the Saluda River includes a forested section with trails past historic ruins and spectacular views of the river. At the Bird Pavilion, you can view birds and wildlife from a safarilike tent. ✉ *I–126 and U.S. 76 at Greystone Riverbanks exit,* ☎ *803/779–8717.* *$6.25.* *Apr.–Oct. weekdays 9–4, weekends 9–5; Nov.–Mar. daily 9–4.*

Dining and Lodging

$$–$$$ ✕ **Motor Supply Co. Bistro.** Dine on cuisine from around the world at a restaurant in the heart of town. Fresh seafood and homemade desserts are among the many offerings; on Sunday there's a bountiful brunch. ✉ *920 Gervais St.,* ☎ *803/256–6687. AE, DC, MC, V.*

$–$$$ ★ ✕ **Mangia! Mangia!** Earth tones, hammered copper, and mosaic tiles transform an early 20th-century building into an elegant place to dine. Window-side tables have a view of the Columbia skyline across the Congaree River; there's a lively outdoor patio, too, with heaters for chilly nights. Try the mussels steamed in wine-garlic sauce, followed by wild mushroom pizza baked in the wood-burning oven. The Tuscan-influenced menu also includes lamb shank roasted in red wine with herbs. The entire restaurant, except for the bar, is no-smoking. ✉ *100 State St., West Columbia,* ☎ *803/791–3443. AE, MC, V.*

$–$$ ✕ **Blue Marlin.** With polished wood, lines of booths, artsy light fixtures, and an oceanic mural over the bar, this restaurant speaks of bygone years—fitting for an eatery that was once a train station. Start with deviled crab or oyster shooters (raw oysters with jalapeño peppers, each in its own shot glass). Seafood and pasta dishes, always served with steaming collard greens and grits, are the staples here. Fruit cobblers with liqueur-laced whipped cream are popular dessert items. ✉ *1200 Lincoln St.,* ☎ *803/799–3838. Reservations not accepted. AE, DC, MC, V.*

$–$$ ✕ **California Dreaming.** This airy, greenery-bedecked space is the renovated old Union Train Station. The only drawback: an echo that's noticeable when it's crowded. Specialties include prime rib, barbecued baby-back ribs, Mexican dishes, and homemade pasta. ✉ *401 S. Main St.,* ☎ *803/254–6767. AE, MC, V.*

$ ✕ **Maurice Gourmet Barbecue–Piggie Park.** One of the South's best-known barbecue chefs, Maurice Bessinger has a fervent national following for his mustard-sauce-based, pit-cooked ham barbecue. Fans also love the chicken, ribs, hash over rice, and thick-battered onion rings. ✉ *1600 Charleston Hwy.,* ☎ *803/796–0220; 800 Elmwood Ave.,* ☎ *803/256–4377; 1141 Lake Murray Blvd., Irmo,* ☎ *803/732–5555. Reservations not accepted. AE, D, MC, V.*

$$$–$$$$ **Embassy Suites Hotel Columbia.** In the spacious seven-story atrium lobby with skylights, fountains, pools, and live plants, overnight guests enjoy sumptuous breakfasts and evening cocktails. The pleasing staff caters to a mostly business clientele. ✉ *200 Stoneridge Dr., 29210,* ☎ *803/252–8700 or 800/362–2779,* FAX *803/256–8749. 214 suites. Indoor pool, health club, billiards. AE, D, DC, MC, V. BP.*

$$$ **Claussen's Inn.** A small hotel in a converted bakery warehouse in the attractive Five Points neighborhood, the inn is near lively nightlife and specialty shops. Claussen's has an open, airy lobby with a Mexican-tile floor; the rooms, some two-story, are arranged around the lobby. The eight loft suites have downstairs sitting rooms, period reproductions, and four-poster beds. ✉ *2003 Greene St., 29205,* ☎ *803/765–0440 or 800/622–3382,* FAX *803/799–7924. 21 rooms, 8 suites. Hot tub, meeting rooms. AE, D, MC, V. CP.*

$$–$$$ **Adam's Mark.** This upscale downtown hotel is near state offices and the University of South Carolina. It has leather armchairs, suspended lights, and brass accents in public areas. Guest rooms are contemporary, with armoires and desks. Finlay's Restaurant, in a spectacular atrium with wood-wrapped columns, serves American fare; Players Sports Bar is also an option. ✉ *1200 Hampton St., 29201,* ☎ *803/771–7000 or 800/444–2326,* FAX *803/254–8307. 296 rooms, 4 suites. Restaurant, lounge, sports bar, indoor pool, hot tub, health club, business services. AE, D, DC, MC, V.*

$$–$$$ ★ **Richland Street B&B.** Relax on the front porch or in the spacious common area of this no-smoking inn in the heart of Columbia's historic district. Each antiques-furnished room has its own personality; the suite has a whirlpool tub. The complimentary breakfast includes fresh fruit and Belgian waffles or French toast; there are also afternoon refreshments. ✉ *1425 Richland St., 29201,* ☎ *803/779–7001,* FAX *803/765–0370. 7 rooms, 1 suite. Library. AE, MC, V. CP.*

$ **Best Western Riverside Inn.** Close to the University of South Carolina's Williams-Brice Stadium and Coliseum, this inn has comfortable rooms and a cheerful staff. Rates include a complimentary Continental breakfast of breads, fruit, yogurt, grits, and oatmeal. Golf packages are available. ✉ *111 Knox Abbott Dr., 29033,* ☎ *803/939–4688 or 800/528–1234,* FAX *803/926–5547. 64 rooms. Pool, putting green. AE, D, DC, MC, V. CP.*

$ **La Quinta Motor Inn.** At this three-story inn on a quiet street near the zoo, the rooms are spacious and well lighted, with large working areas. ✉ *1335 Garner La., 29210,* ☎ *803/798–9590 or 800/531–5900,* FAX *803/731–5574. 122 rooms. Pool. AE, D, DC, MC, V.*

Nightlife and the Arts

THE ARTS

The **Columbia Music Festival Association** (☎ 803/771–6303) can inform callers about events of the Choral Society, the Opera, Opera Guild, Dance Theatre, Brass Band, Caroliers, and Cabaret Company. The **Koger Center for the Arts** (✉ Assembly St., ☎ 803/777–7500) presents national and international theater, ballet, and musical groups as well as individual performers. Call the **South Carolina Philharmonic** (☎ 803/254–7445) for information about scheduled concerts of the Philharmonic, the Chamber Orchestra, and the Youth Orchestra.

The **Town Theatre** (✉ 1012 Sumter St., ☎ 803/799–2510), founded in 1919, stages six plays a year from September to late May, plus a special summer show. The **Workshop Theatre of South Carolina** (✉ 1136 Bull St., ☎ 803/799–4876) produces a number of plays.

NIGHTLIFE

In the hopping Vista neighborhood, the **Art Bar** (✉ 1211 Park St., ☎ 803/254–4792) is funky, with splash-painted walls, lighted lunch boxes, and dancing to world music. At **Billy G's** (✉ 828 Gervais Rd., ☎ 803/806–8870) you'll find live bands. **Willy's Bar & Grill** (✉ 1200B Lincoln St., ☎ 803/799–3111), in a former train station waiting room, has live music and an outdoor patio. In Five Points, **Goatfeathers** (✉ 2017 Devine St., ☎ 803/256–3325 or 803/256–8133), popular with university and law school students, is a tradition; its bohemian atmosphere draws the late-night coffee and dessert seekers.

Outdoor Activities and Sports

BASEBALL

The **Capital City Bombers** (☎ 803/256–4110), a Class-A affiliate of the New York Mets, play from mid-April through August at Capital City Stadium (✉ 301 S. Assembly St.) downtown.

CANOEING, KAYAKING, RAFTING

Self-guided canoe trails traverse an alluvial floodplain bordered by high bluffs at the 22,200-acre **Congaree Swamp National Monument** (✉ 20 mi southeast of Columbia, off SC 48, ☎ 803/776–4396). The water and trees here, including many old-growth bottomland hardwoods, are full of wildlife. Canoe rentals are available in Columbia at **Adventure Carolina** (☎ 803/796–4505) and the **River Runner Outdoor Center** (☎ 803/771–0353).

Rafting, kayaking, and canoeing on the **Saluda River** near Columbia offer challenging Class III and Class IV rapids. Guided river and swamp excursions can be arranged through Adventure Carolina and River Runner Outdoor Center (☞ *above*).

GOLF

Sedgewood (✉ Sumter Hwy., ☎ 803/776–2177), 18-hole, par-72, is among the many fine area courses. Call **Golf Vacations of Columbia** (☎ 888/501–0954) for tee times.

HIKING

Congaree Swamp National Monument (☞ Canoeing, *above*) has 22 mi of trails for hikers and nature lovers and a ¾-mi boardwalk for visitors with disabilities. Guided nature walks leave Saturday at 1:30.

Shopping

ANTIQUES AND FLEA MARKETS

Many of Columbia's antiques outlets (as well as boutique shops) are in the **Congaree Vista** around Huger and Gervais streets, between the State House and the river. A number of intriguing shops and cafés are in **Five Points,** around the intersection of Blossom and Harden streets. There are antiques shops across the river on Meeting and State streets in **West Columbia.** The **Old Mill Antique Mall** (✉ 310 State St., West Columbia, ☎ 803/796–4229) has items from many dealers. The **Thieves Market Antique Flea Mall** (✉ 502 Gadsden St., ☎ 803/254–4997) shows off the wares of dozens of antiques and collectibles dealers.

FARMERS' MARKET

The **State Farmers' Market** (✉ Bluff Rd., ☎ 803/253–4664) is one of the 10 largest in the country. Fresh vegetables are sold each weekday, along with flowers, plants, seafood, and more, from 6 AM to 9 PM.

Camden

32 mi northeast of Columbia via I–20.

Charming Camden, a town with a horsey history and grand Southern colonial homes, has never paved its fanciest roads for the sake of the hooves of the horses who regularly trot over them. The Carolina Cup and Colonial Cup are run here; in addition to the horse races, you'll see champagne tailgate parties with elegant crystal and china.

Camden is South Carolina's oldest inland town, dating from 1732. British general Lord Cornwallis established a garrison here during the Revolutionary War and burned most of Camden before evacuating it. A center of textile trade from the late 19th century through the 1940s, Camden attracted Northerners escaping the cold winters; the DuPont family is today one of Camden's major employers. Because General Sherman spared the town during the Civil War, most of its antebellum homes still stand.

The **Historic Camden Revolutionary War Site** re-creates the British occupation of 1780 on the site of the early 19th-century village. Several house restorations display period furnishings, including Cornwallis's headquarters, the **Kershaw-Cornwallis House** (circa 1770). Nature trails, fortifications, a powder magazine, a picnic area, and a crafts shop are also here. ✉ *U.S. 521, 1½ mi north of I–20,* ☎ *803/432–9841.* *$5.* *Guided tours Mon.–Sat. 10–4, Sun. 1–4; museum shop daily 10–5.*

Dining and Lodging

$$$–$$$$ ★ ✕ **Mill Pond Restaurant.** In a historic building overlooking a sprawling millpond, this restaurant, about a 10-minute drive south of Camden, specializes in Mediterranean-influenced dishes. Try the wild boar on grits, bacon-wrapped scallops, or garlic toast and crab cakes with shrimp tartar sauce. ✉ *84 Boykin Mill Rd., Rembert,* ☎ *803/424–0261. Jacket and tie. MC, V. Closed Sun.–Mon. No lunch.*

$–$$ ✕ **Avanti's Restaurant.** Cane-back chairs, fox-hunting prints, and elaborately tiled fireplaces set the tone for an elegant meal in the Victorian Greenleaf Inn (☞ *below*), the site of this restaurant. Avanti's serves wonderful pastas and pork with Italian family-style side dishes, plus great cannoli. ✉ *1308 Broad St.,* ☎ *803/713–0089. AE, D, MC, V. Closed Sun. No lunch.*

$–$$$ ★ ✕ **Greenleaf Inn.** Alice Boykin, whose name is to Camden what Carnegie's is to Pittsburgh, opened the Greenleaf in 1993. The inn consists of three buildings: the main inn, with four rooms on the second floor above Avanti's Restaurant (☞ *above*); a nearby carriage house with seven rooms; and a guest cottage, which is particularly good for families. The spacious rooms have classic Victorian furniture and floral wallpaper; all baths are modern. You won't find a nicer or better-value lodging in the region. ✉ *1308 Broad St., 29020,* ☎ *803/425–1806 or 800/437–5874,* FAX *803/425–5853. 8 rooms, 3 suites, 1 cottage. Restaurant. AE, MC, V. BP.*

$–$$$ ★ **A Camden Bed & Breakfast.** This Federal-style 1920s home in Camden's historic district has wood-burning fireplaces in every room, antiques, and Persian rugs. The full breakfast might include a Canadian ham casserole or French toast. ✉ *127 Union St., 29020,* ☎ *803/432–2366. 2 rooms, 1 cottage. AE, MC, V. BP.*

$–$$ **Holiday Inn.** This well-maintained chain offering is 3 mi west of downtown Camden. The restaurant is excellent. ✉ *U.S. 1/601S, Box 96, Lugoff 29078,* ☎ *803/438–9441 or 800/465–4329,* FAX *803/438–9441. 117 rooms. Restaurant, lounge, pool. AE, D, DC, MC, V.*

Nightlife and the Arts

The **Paddock Restaurant & Pub** (⊠ 514 Rutledge St., ☎ 803/432–3222) has music and dancing weekends.

Outdoor Activities and Sports

EQUESTRIAN EVENTS

Camden puts on two steeplechase events at **Springdale Race Course** (⊠ 200 Knights Hill Rd., ☎ 803/432–6513): the Carolina Cup in late March or early April and the Colonial Cup in November.

GOLF

White Pines Golf Club (⊠ 615 Mary La., ☎ 803/432–7442) is an 18-hole, par-72 course.

OFF THE BEATEN PATH

CHERAW – The town's well-preserved, 213-acre historic district holds the Town Green, part of the original 1768 plan. The district encompasses more than 50 antebellum public buildings and houses, as well as later structures, including the Market Hall, Town Hall, Lyceum Museum, and Inglis-McIver law office. Stop by the Greater Cheraw Chamber of Commerce (⊠ 221 Market St., ☎ 803/537–7681) for a brochure about the area. Cheraw is 55 mi northeast of Camden on U.S. 1; you pass the Carolina Sandhills National Wildlife Refuge en route.

Sumter

30 mi southeast of Camden on U.S. 521; 44 mi east of Columbia on U.S. 378.

Sumter—named for the Revolutionary War hero and statesman General Thomas Sumter—was settled about 1740 as the center of a cultivated plantation district. Today it is home to varied industries, lumbering, agricultural marketing, and nearby Shaw Air Force Base.

The **Sumter County Museum** (headquarters of the Sumter County Historical Society), in a lovely 1845 Victorian Gothic house, exhibits fine period furnishings, Oriental carpets, vintage carriages, dolls, and various memorabilia. ⊠ *122 N. Washington St.,* ☎ *803/775–0908.* *Free.* *Tues.–Sat. 10–1 and 2–5.*

Swan Lake Iris Gardens is like Eden when its 6 million irises are in bloom. Coscoroba, whooper, trumpeter, and black Australian swans paddle leisurely around the 45-acre lake. The 150-acre park also includes walking trails, picnic areas, tennis courts, a playground, and concessions. ⊠ *W. Liberty St.,* ☎ *803/775–1231.* *Free.* *Daily 8–sunset.*

Lodging

$$–$$$ **Magnolia House.** In Sumter's historic district, this four-column Greek Revival structure is a nice alternative to the region's generic chain motels. Antiques, many of them French, furnish the rooms; there are also stained-glass windows, inlaid oak floors, and five fireplaces. ⊠ *230 Church St., 29150,* ☎ *803/775–6694. 3 rooms, 1 suite. AE, MC, V. BP.*

$–$$ **Holiday Inn.** This well-maintained motor inn is 4 mi west of town, near Shaw Air Force Base. Simple, clean rooms are as you would expect from this chain. ⊠ *2390 Broad St. Extension, 29150,* ☎ *803/469–9001 or 800/465–4329,* FAX *803/469–7001. 124 rooms. Café, pool, exercise room. AE, D, DC, MC, V.*

Outdoor Activities and Sports

About 30 mi from Sumter, a mysterious canoe trail leads into a remote swampy depression at **Woods Bay State Park** (⊠ from Sumter, take

U.S. 378E to U.S. 301N, ☎ 803/659–4445), where rentals are available for $3 per hour or $10 for a full day.

Aiken

64 mi south of Sumter via U.S. 301/601 and U.S. 78, 56 mi southwest of Columbia via I–20.

Aiken, in Thoroughbred Country, first earned its fame in the 1890s, when wealthy Northerners wintering here built stately mansions and entertained one another with lavish parties, horse shows, and hunts. Many of the mansions—some with up to 90 rooms—remain as a testament to this era of opulence. The town is still a center for all kinds of outdoor activity, including the equestrian events of the Triple Crown, as well as tennis and golf.

The area's horse farms have produced many national champions, which are commemorated at the **Aiken Thoroughbred Hall of Fame** with exhibitions of horse-related decorations, paintings, and sculptures, plus racing silks and trophies. The Hall of Fame is on the grounds of the 14-acre Hopeland Gardens, with winding paths, quiet terraces, and reflecting pools. There's a Touch and Scent Trail with Braille plaques. Open-air free concerts and plays are presented on Monday evening mid-July through August. ✉ *Corner of Dupree Pl. and Whiskey Rd.,* ☎ *803/642–7630.* *Free.* ⏲ *Museum Oct.–May, Tues.–Sun. 2–5; grounds daily dawn–dusk.*

The **Aiken County Historical Museum,** in one wing of an 1860 estate, is devoted to early regional culture. It has Native American artifacts, firearms, an authentically furnished 1808 log cabin, and a one-room schoolhouse. ✉ *433 Newberry St. SW,* ☎ *803/642–2015.* *Donations accepted.* ⏲ *Tues.–Fri. 9:30–4:30, weekends 2–5.*

Aiken surrounds the serene and wild **Hitchcock Woods** (✉ enter from junction of Clark Rd. and Whitney Dr., Berrie Rd., and Dibble Rd.), 2,000 acres of Southern forest with hiking trails and bridal paths.

Stop for a wine tasting at **Montmorenci Vineyards** (✉ U.S. 78, 2½ mi east of Aiken, ☎ 803/649–4870). Montmorenci wines are made from French-American hybrid grapes, many typical of the Southeast, and include rosés, blushes, whites, and reds. Tours are by appointment during February and March.

Dining and Lodging

$–$$ ✕ **Malia's.** At this busy lunch and dinner spot, you get international cuisine, including lamb soup with curry; veal with shiitake mushrooms and brandy demi-glace; and a baked ham, Brie, and Portobello mushroom sandwich. ✉ *120 Laurens St.,* ☎ *803/643–3086. D, MC, V. No lunch weekends, no dinner weekdays.*

$–$$ ★ ✕ **No. 10 Downing Street.** This stately Southern colonial dates from 1837 and serves some of the best—and most diverse—food in town. The menu changes regularly: one month might focus on such Italian fare as *pollo al prosciutto* (chicken wrapped in prosciutto and fresh herbs with fettuccine Alfredo) and baked beef tenderloin with tomatoes, garlic, and oregano; another month may salute country French or regional cuisine. The bakery here sells fantastic breads. ✉ *241 Laurens St.,* ☎ *803/642–9062. AE, D, DC, MC, V. Closed Sun.–Mon.*

$ ✕ **Track Kitchen.** The who's who of Aiken's horsey set can be found here most mornings, feasting on the heavy and hearty cooking of Carol and Pockets Curtis. The small dining room is unpretentious, with walls of mint-green cinder block and simple Formica counters. ✉ *420 Mead Ave.,* ☎ *803/641–9628. No credit cards. No dinner.*

$$–$$$ **Willcox Inn.** Winston Churchill, Franklin D. Roosevelt, and the Astors have slept at this elegant inn, built in grand style in the early 1900s. The lobby is graced with massive stone fireplaces, rosewood woodwork, heart-pine floors, and Oriental rugs. Though rooms have fine furnishings such as high four-poster beds, the decor could use a touch-up. ✉ *100 Colleton Ave., 29801,* ☎ *803/649–1377 or 800/368–1047,* FAX *803/643–0971. 24 rooms, 6 suites. Bar, dining room. AE, D, DC, MC, V. CP.*

$ ★ **Briar Patch.** You can learn plenty about both the Old and New South from the knowledgeable innkeepers of this terrific B&B, which was formerly tack rooms in Aiken's stable district. Choose either the frilly room with French provincial furniture or the less dramatic one with pine antiques and a weather vane. ✉ *544 Magnolia La. SE, 29801,* ☎ *803/649–2010. 2 rooms. Tennis court. No credit cards. CP.*

Outdoor Activities and Sports

EQUESTRIAN EVENTS

In Aiken, **polo matches** are played at Whitney Field (☎ 803/648–7874) on Sunday afternoon September through November and March through July. Three weekends in late March and early April are set aside for the famed **Triple Crown** (☎ 803/641–1111)—Thoroughbred trials of promising yearlings, a steeplechase, and harness races by young horses making their debut.

GOLF

The many fine 18-hole, par-70 courses in the area include **Highland Park Country Club** (✉ 555 Highland Park Ave., ☎ 803/649–6029).

Greenwood

55 mi northwest of Aiken via SC 19, U.S. 25, and SC 72; 75 mi west of Columbia via U.S. 378, U.S. 178, and SC 72.

Founded by Irish settlers in 1802, Greenwood received its name from the site's gently rolling landscape and dense forests. Andrew Johnson, the 17th U.S. president, operated a tailor shop at Courthouse Square before migrating to East Tennessee. Anglers, swimmers, and boaters head for nearby Lake Greenwood's 200-mi shore. Two sections of Sumter National Forest are nearby.

The **Greenwood Museum** has more than 7,000 items in eclectic displays: Native American artifacts, natural history and geology exhibits, and a replicated village street including a one-room school and a general store. ✉ *106 Main St.,* ☎ *864/229–7093.* *$2.* ⏲ *Wed.–Sat. 10–5.*

The **Gardens of Park Seed Co.,** one of the nation's largest seed supply houses, maintains colorful experimental gardens and greenhouses 6 mi north on U.S. 178 at Hodges. The flower beds are especially vivid June 15 through July, and seeds and bulbs are for sale in the company's store. The South Carolina Festival of Flowers—with a performing-artists contest, a beauty pageant, private house and garden tours, and live entertainment—is held at Park's headquarters annually at the end of June. ✉ *On SC 254, 7 mi north of town,* ☎ *864/941–4213 or 800/845–3369.* *Free.* ⏲ *Gardens daily dawn–dusk; store Mon.–Sat. 9–5.*

Lodging

$ **Inn on the Square.** This inn was fashioned out of a warehouse in the heart of town. Though the rooms suffer from rather unremarkable views, they're bright and spacious, with reproduction 18th-century antiques, four-poster beds, writing desks, and such thoughtful touches as turndown service and complimentary morning newspapers. The staff is attuned to the needs of business travelers and vacationers alike. ✉

104 Court St., 29648, ☎ 864/223–4488, FAX 864/223–7067. 48 rooms. Restaurant, lounge, pool. AE, D, DC, MC, V.

Ninety Six

10 mi east of Greenwood on SC 248.

The town of Ninety Six, on an old Native American trade route, is so named for being 96 mi from the Cherokee village of Keowee in the Blue Ridge Mountains—the distance a young Cherokee maiden, Cateechee, is supposed to have ridden to warn her English lover of a threatened Native American massacre. The **Ninety Six National Historic Site** commemorates two Revolutionary War battles. The visitor center's museum has descriptive displays, and there are remnants of the old village, a reconstructed French and Indian War stockade, and Revolutionary-era fortifications. ✉ *SC 248,* ☎ *864/543–4068.* *Free.* *Daily 8–5.*

Abbeville

14 mi west of Greenwood on SC 72.

★ **Abbeville** may well be one of inland South Carolina's most satisfying, though lesser-known, small towns. An appealing historic district includes the old business district, early churches, and residential areas. The "Southern cause" was born and died here, where the first organized secession meeting was held and where, on May 2, 1865, Confederate president Jefferson Davis officially disbanded the defeated armies of the South in the last meeting of his war council. The 1830 house where the Confederate council met is the **Burt-Stark House.** ✉ *306 N. Main St.,* ☎ *864/459–4297 or 864/459–2181.* *$3.* *Sept.–May, Fri.–Sat. 1–5 or by appointment; June–Aug., Tues.–Sat. 1–5 or by appointment.*

An 1850s jail houses the **Abbeville County Museum,** which contains area memorabilia. It's adjacent to the 1837 log-cabin home of Marie Cromer Siegler, founder of 4-H clubs, and an educational garden. ✉ *Poplar and Cherry Sts.,* ☎ *864/459–4600.* *Free.* *Wed. and Sun. 3–5 or by appointment.*

The **Abbeville Opera House** (✉ Town Sq., ☎ 864/459–2157) faces the historic town square. Built in 1908, it has been renovated to reflect the grandeur of the days when lavish road shows and stellar entertainers came center stage. Current productions range from light, contemporary comedies to Broadway-style musicals. Call about tours.

OFF THE BEATEN PATH

HICKORY KNOB STATE RESORT PARK – This park on the shore of Strom Thurmond Lake, about 20 mi south of Abbeville, has everything for a complete vacation: fishing, waterskiing, sailing, motorboating, a swimming pool, a tackle shop, nature trails, an 18-hole championship golf course, a pro shop, and tennis courts. A 1770s log cabin, an 80-room lodge, nine duplex lakeside cottages, campgrounds, and a restaurant round out Hickory Knob's offerings. You're also near a stretch of the **Savannah River Scenic Highway,** which follows the Savannah River along the Georgia border, winding 100 mi and past three lakes. ✉ *Rte. 1, Box 199B, McCormick 29835,* ☎ *864/391–2450 or 800/491–1764.* *Free; fees for some activities.* *Office daily 7 AM–11 PM.*

Dining and Lodging

$–$$ ★ ✕ **Village Grille.** Locals come to this high-ceiling room with pomegranate-color walls and antique mirrors for the herb rotisserie chicken. Other choices are the ribs, homemade pastas, and cordial-laced desserts. The atmosphere is trendy and friendly; the staff bends over backward to please. ✉ *114 Trinity St.,* ☎ *864/459–2500. AE, D, MC, V. Closed Sun.–Mon.*

$ ✕ **Yoder's Dutch Kitchen.** You'll find authentic Pennsylvania Dutch home cooking in an unassuming redbrick building with a mansard roof. There are a lunch buffet and evening smorgasbord with fried chicken, stuffed cabbage, Dutch meat loaf, breaded veal Parmesan, and plenty of vegetables. Shoofly pie, Dutch bread, and apple butter can be purchased to go. ✉ *U.S. 72,* ☎ *864/459–5556. No credit cards. Closed Sun.–Tues. No dinner Wed.*

$–$$ **Belmont Inn.** Built in the early 1900s, this restored Spanish-style structure is a popular overnight stop with Opera House visitors. Guest rooms are spacious, with high ceilings and pine floors. Theater-and-dining package plans are offered. ✉ *106 E. Pickens St., 29620,* ☎ *864/459–9625 or 888/251–2000. 25 rooms. Restaurant, lounge, meeting rooms. AE, D, MC, V.*

Nightlife and the Arts

The **Abbeville Opera House** (✉ Town Sq., ☎ 864/459–2157) stages high-caliber productions in an early 20th-century setting. Reservations are taken weekdays 10–5.

Shopping

Abbeville's **Town Square** is lined with attractive gift and specialty shops in restored historic buildings dating from the late 1800s.

Columbia and the Heartland A to Z

Arriving and Departing

BY BUS

Greyhound (☎ 800/231–2222) serves all of South Carolina.

BY CAR

I–77 leads into Columbia from the north. I–26, I–20, and U.S. 1 intersect at Columbia.

BY PLANE

Columbia Metro Airport (✉ 3000 Aviation Way, ☎ 803/822–5000), 10 mi west of downtown, is served by American Eagle, ComAir/Delta, and US Airways. For airline telephone numbers, *see* Air Travel *in* Smart Travel Tips A to Z.

BY TRAIN

Amtrak (☎ 800/872–7245) makes stops at Camden, Columbia, Denmark, Dillon, Florence, and Kingstree in the Heartland.

Getting Around

BY BUS

A local utility provides city bus service in and around **Columbia** (☎ 803/748–3019).

BY TAXI

Companies providing service in Columbia include **AAA Airport Shuttle Service** (☎ 803/796–3626), **Blue Ribbon** (☎ 803/754–8163), and **Checker-Yellow** (☎ 803/799–3311). **Gamecock Cab Co.** (☎ 803/796–7700) offers service from Columbia to other cities statewide.

Contacts and Resources

EMERGENCIES

Ambulance, fire, police (☎ 911). Emergency room services are available at **Richland Memorial Hospital** (✉ 5 Richland Medical Park, Columbia, ☎ 803/765–7561).

GUIDED TOURS

The **Aiken Chamber of Commerce** runs a 90-minute tour of the historic district and will customize tours to suit individual interests. In Sumter, the charismatic former mayor **"Bubba" McElveen** (☎ 803/775–2851) gives walking, bus, and auto tours of the area. Customized tours of Camden are available from **Greenleaf Tours** (contact Louise Burns, ☎ 803/432–1515) or through **Kershaw County Chamber of Commerce** (☎ 803/432–2525). **Richland County Historic Preservation Commission** (☎ 803/252–1770) runs guided tours and rents out historic properties.

LATE-NIGHT PHARMACIES

CVS (✉ 3595 Harden St., ☎ 803/779–1217) and **Kroger Sav-On** (✉ 817 St. Andrews Rd. and 6 other locations, ☎ 803/551–1145) are open 24 hours.

OUTDOOR ACTIVITIES AND SPORTS

The 41-mi-long **Lake Murray,** just 15 mi west of Columbia via I–26 (Irmo exit), has swimming, boating, picnicking, and superb fishing. There are many marinas and campgrounds in the area. For information, contact the **Lake Murray Tourism and Recreation Association** (✉ 2184 N. Lake Dr., Irmo 29063, ☎ 803/781–5940).

For **fishing,** Lakes Marion and Moultrie attract anglers after bream, crappie, catfish, and several kinds of bass. Supplies, camps, guides, rentals, and accommodations abound. For information, contact **Santee Cooper Counties Promotion Commission** (✉ Drawer 40, Santee 29142, ☎ 803/854–2131, 800/227–8510 outside SC).

For information on **hiking** trails in the Francis Marion National Forest and the Sumter National Forest, contact the **National Forest Service** (✉ 4931 Broad River Rd., Columbia 29210-4021, ☎ 803/561–4000).

RADIO STATIONS

In Columbia: **AM:** WCOS 1400, country; WOMG 1320, oldies; WVOC 560, news/talk. **FM:** WLTR 91.3, classical; WMFX 102.3, classic rock; WNOK 104, Top 40 hits; WTCB 106.7, adult contemporary; WUSC 90.5, alternative (jazz, blues, folk, reggae); WWDM 101.3, urban hits.

VISITOR INFORMATION

The **Columbia Metropolitan Convention and Visitors Bureau** (✉ Box 15, 29202; visitor center: ✉ 1012 Gervais St., ☎ 803/254–0479 or 800/264–4884) has brochures, maps, and advice for travelers; the center also presents a short film on area history. In Abbeville, contact the **Greater Abbeville Chamber of Commerce** (✉ 104 Pickens St., Abbeville 29620, ☎ 864/459–4600). **Greater Aiken Chamber of Commerce** (✉ 400 Laurens St. NW, Box 892, Aiken 29802, ☎ 803/641–1111) serves the Aiken area. **Kershaw County Chamber of Commerce** (✉ 724 S. Broad St., Box 605, Camden 29020, ☎ 803/432–2525) has information and advice on where to go in Camden. **Ninety Six Chamber of Commerce** (✉ Box 8, 29666, ☎ 803/543–2900) provides information on the town and district of Ninety Six.

THE UPCOUNTRY

The Upcountry, in the northwest corner of the state, has long been a favorite for family vacations because of its temperate climate and natural beauty. The abundant lakes and waterfalls and several state parks (including Caesar's Head, Keowee-Toxaway, Oconee, Table Rock, and the Chattooga National Wild and Scenic River) provide all manner of recreational activities. Beautiful anytime, the 130-mi Cherokee Foothills Scenic Highway (SC 11), which goes through the Blue Ridge

Mountains, is especially delightful in spring (when the peach trees are in bloom) and autumn.

Greenville is growing fast and attracting lots of industry, much of it textile-related, in keeping with the area's history. Clemson, home of Clemson University and the "Orange Wave," is pretty much a university town. Pendleton, just a few miles away, has one of the nation's largest historic districts. With its village green, surrounded by shops and restaurants, it's a lovely step back in time. The comfortable communities of Spartanburg and Anderson are beginning to rejuvenate their downtown areas.

Greenville

100 mi northwest of Columbia.

Although known for its textile and other manufacturing plants, Greenville has many tree-lined streets and a number of attractions including a zoo and nearby state parks such as Caesar's Head and Table Rock. It's also home to Bob Jones University, which has a gallery of religious art and antiquities.

The renowned international collection of religious art at **Bob Jones University Art Gallery and Museum** includes works by Boticelli, Rembrandt, Rubens, and Titian. ⊠ *Bob Jones University, 1700 Wade Hampton Blvd.,* ☎ *864/242–1050.* *Free.* ⏲ *Tues.–Sun. 2–5.*

Housed in an innovative modern building, the **Greenville County Museum of Art** displays American art dating from the colonial era. Exhibited are works by Paul Jenkins, Jamie Wyeth, Jasper Johns, and noted Southern artists. ⊠ *420 College St.,* ☎ *864/271–7570.* *Free.* ⏲ *Tues.–Sat. 10–5, Sun. 1–5.*

★ Modeled after a 14th-century Japanese mansion, the **Nippon Center** is a cultural center with a rock garden and exquisite Japanese furnishings. It has an authentic Japanese restaurant and tea ceremony. ⊠ *500 Congaree Rd.,* ☎ *864/288–8471.* *Tours $3, tea ceremony $5.* ⏲ *Mon.–Sat. 10–3 or by appointment; tea ceremony 3rd Wed. of the month.*

Dining and Lodging

$$$–$$$$ ✕ **Palms Restaurant.** This restaurant, probably Greenville's best, is in the Phoenix–Greenville's Inn (☞ *below*). The modest dining room serves up sophisticated dishes including galantine of duck, sesame-crusted mahimahi, and chocolate truffle cake with espresso sauce. The dark, cozy piano bar with a fireplace and wing chairs is a great place to wait for your made-to-order hot apple tart with cinnamon ice cream. ⊠ *246 N. Pleasantburg Dr.,* ☎ *864/233–4651. AE, D, DC, MC, V.*

$$–$$$ ✕ **Seven Oaks.** The seven oaks on the property gave this 1895 home its name. Now a restaurant, it has seven dining rooms with 14-ft curved ceilings, stained glass, and parquet floors. The dinner selections are as elegant as the decor: veal scallopini, mustard-crusted rack of lamb, and sweet-potato bread pudding. ⊠ *104 Broadus Ave.,* ☎ *864/232–1895. AE, D, MC, V. Closed Sun. No lunch.*

$–$$ ✕ **Stax Omega Diner.** A contemporary diner with booths and a half-circle counter with stools serves everything from bacon and eggs and burgers to souvlaki, Greek-style chicken, and shrimp and grits. It's all good, and it's open almost around-the-clock. ⊠ *72 Orchard Park Dr.,* ☎ *864/297–6639. AE, MC, V.*

$$$$ ✕🏨 **La Bastide Inn & Restaurant.** About 19 mi northwest (30 minutes) from Greenville in the sloping Piedmont hills, this French provincial-style inn with surrounding vineyard re-creates the French countryside experience. A winery opens in fall 2001, and an entire petite village

with a 300-year-old chapel is planned for 2002. Rooms have European linens, French antiques and reproductions, elaborate chandeliers, wrought iron, gas fireplaces, and hillside views. Elegant French country meals and wine are available at the restaurant ($$$–$$$$). ✉ *10 Road of Vines, Travelers Rest 29690,* ☎ *864/836–8463 or 877/836–8463,* FAX *864/836–4820. 12 rooms, 2 suites. Restaurant, croquet. AE, D, MC. BP.*

$$–$$$ ✕ **Phoenix–Greenville's Inn.** Plantation shutters and four-poster beds adorn this transformed and renovated property, the former Thunderbird Motel. You'll enjoy the residential feel and hospitality of a Southern inn; the service is excellent. Ask for a room overlooking the courtyard pool area. Palms Restaurant (☞ *above*) serves Continental cuisine. ✉ *246 N. Pleasantburg Dr., 29607,* ☎ *800/257–3529,* ☎ FAX *864/233–4651. 185 rooms. Restaurant, pool. AE, D, DC, MC, V.*

$$$–$$$$ **Hyatt Regency Hotel.** This standard chain offering's best feature is its central location in the midst of the small, revitalized downtown area of shops and restaurants. Rooms overlooking the atrium are a must. Airport shuttle service is complimentary. ✉ *220 N. Main St., 29601,* ☎ *864/235–1234,* FAX *864/232–7584. 327 rooms. Restaurant, lounge, pool, hot tub, health club. AE, D, DC, MC, V.*

$$–$$$ **Westin Poinsett Hotel.** After years of being closed, this historic 12-story hotel, dating to 1925, reopened in fall 2000. The large guest rooms have down comforters, marble baths, and high ceilings. All public spaces are back in their original opulence, including ornate plaster details and mosaic tilework. ✉ *120 South Main St., 29601,* ☎ *864/421–9700,* FAX *864/421–9719. 181 rooms, 9 suites. Restaurant, coffee shop, lounge, health club, concierge. AE, D, DC, MC, V.*

Nightlife and the Arts

The **Peace Center for the Arts** (✉ 101 W. Broad St., ☎ 864/467–3030), which sits along the Reedy River, presents star performers, touring Broadway shows, dance companies, chamber music, and local groups.

Outdoor Activities and Sports

GOLF

South Carolinians sometimes prefer Upcountry courses to those on the coast, as they're less crowded and have the slightly cooler climate of the state's northwestern region. The area's rolling hills provide challenging courses. **Discover Upcountry Carolina** (☎ 800/949–6576 or 800/344–5590) has information on golf and other recreation in the area. Upcountry courses include **Links O'Tryon** (✉ 11250 New Cut Rd., Campobello, ☎ 864/468–4995) and **Table Rock Golf Club** (✉ 171 Sliding Rock Rd., Pickens, ☎ 864/878–2030).

ICE-SKATING

The **Greenville Pavilion Ice Rink** (☎ 864/322–7529) is a public indoor rink.

Spartanburg

31 mi east of Greenville.

Spartanburg once produced the state's largest peach crop. Lovely country drives in the area meander through peach orchards, which delight with fragrant, papery blossoms each spring and juicy treats at roadside stands each summer. While it's still part of the state's largest peach-producing area, today the town is better known as an international business center. So many foreign corporations have plants here that some local attractions provide brochures in German, French, and Spanish. In Spartanburg county, 20 German (including the new BMW plant), Swiss, or Austrian companies are visible from I–85. The town's early 20th-century downtown is slowly being revitalized with trendy shops and cafés. The NFL's Carolina Panthers train here each summer; their practice sessions at Wofford College (☎ 704/358–7000) are free and open to the public.

The **BMW Zentrum** plant, the company's only one in North America, exhibits BMW engineering in the auto, motorcycle, and aviation industries. On display is the Z3 James Bond drove in the film *Golden Eye,* classics from the past 80 years, and BMWs painted by artists including Warhol and Lichtenstein. The video about the making of the BMW Z3 roadster takes visitors down the factory line. ☒ *Exit 60 off I–85 on SC 101S, Greer,* ☎ *888/868–7269.* *Free, factory tour $5.* *Tues.–Sat. 9:30–5:30; factory tours by appointment.*

More than 10,000 plants make **Hatcher Gardens** a refuge for birds and wildlife. It also has walking trails and ponds. ☒ *Reidville Rd., Spartanburg,* ☎ *864/574–7724.* *Free.* *Daily dawn–dusk.*

Dining and Lodging

$$–$$$ ✕ **Abby's Grill.** A classy addition to downtown, it has a lounge and live jazz most evenings. High ceilings make the dining room open and airy. Try the calamari or pork chop with mashed potatoes. ☒ *149 W. Main St.,* ☎ *864/583–4660. AE, DC, MC, V. Closed Sun.*

$$–$$$ ✕ **Harry's on Morgan.** An old-city atmosphere reigns at this elegantly restored barbershop and pool hall. The ambience is upscale but relaxed. Specialties include steaks and seafood. ☒ *116 Magnolia St.,* ☎ *864/583–8121. AE, DC, MC, V. Closed Sun.*

$ ✕ **Beacon Drive-In.** This Spartanburg institution—and some of its staff—has been around for 50 years. They'll serve you curbside, but the action is inside at the counter. Locals come for the Beacon burgers (hamburgers with all the fixins'), onion rings, hot dogs, fried fish sandwiches, and sundaes. ☒ *255 Reidville Rd.,* ☎ *864/585–9387. AE, DC, MC, V. Closed Sun.*

$$ **Hampton Inn.** You'll find comfort and simple style here. It's at the intersection of I–26 and I–85 Business. ☒ *4930 College Dr., 29301,* ☎ *864/576–6080,* FAX *864/587–8901. 112 rooms. Pool, business services, meeting room. AE, D, DC, MC, V. CP.*

$$ **Inn at Merridun.** This antebellum 1855 home in Union, about 27 mi from Spartanburg, has country style and cozy floral rooms. Rates include a complimentary full breakfast and evening dessert; picnic lunches and dinners are available. ☒ *100 Merridun Pl., off U.S. 176, Union 29379,* ☎ *864/427–7052 or 888/892–6020,* FAX *864/429–0373. 5 rooms. AE, MC, V. BP.*

$$ **Red Horse Inn.** Victorian-style cottages with porches and hand-painted murals are scattered on 190 acres about 25 mi from Greenville. Each cottage has a sitting area and fireplace; some have lofts and whirlpools. In the small kitchen you'll find a basket of breakfast items. ☒ *4930 College Dr., Landrum 29301,* ☎ *864/895–4968,* FAX *864/587–8901. 9 cottages. AE, D, DC, MC, V. BP.*

Shopping

The more than 90 outlets at the **Prime Outlets of Gaffney** include the Gap, Nike, Levi's, and Donna Karan. The playground will keep older kids busy while you shop. Gaffney is about 20 minutes from Spartanburg via I–85N. ☒ *I–85, Exit 90, Gaffney,* ☎ *864/902–9900 information center.*

Pendleton

25 mi southwest of Greenville.

Charming Pendleton, a few miles from Clemson University, has a historic district and interesting architecture. The Farmers Hall, built in 1826, was originally a courthouse. The Square, a district of restaurants and shops, faces the Village Green.

The **South Carolina State Botanical Garden,** on the Clemson University campus in nearby Clemson, holds more than 2,000 varieties of plants on more than 256 acres, including wildflower, fern, and bog gardens as well as nature trails. The **Fran Hanson Discovery Center**, which opened in 2000, has information on regional history and cultural heritage. ☎ *864/656–3405.* *Free.* *Daily dawn–dusk.*

Lodging

$$ **Liberty Hall Inn.** There's great food and lodging at this country inn in the heart of town. The inn, built in the 1840s, caters to business travelers and vacationers. Rooms are furnished with antiques and family heirlooms; a breakfast of waffles, breads, fruit, and yogurt is included. ✉ *621 S. Mechanic St., 29670,* ☎ *800/643–7944,* ☎ FAX *864/646–7500. 10 rooms. Restaurant. AE, D, DC, MC, V. BP.*

Kings Mountain National Military and State Park

70 mi northeast of Greenville.

A Revolutionary War battle considered an important turning point was fought here on October 7, 1780. Colonial Tories commanded by British major Patrick Ferguson were soundly defeated by ragtag patriot forces from the southern Appalachians. Visitor center exhibits, dioramas, and an orientation film describe the action. A paved self-guided trail leads through the battlefield. ✉ *20 mi northeast of Gaffney, SC, off I–85 via a marked side road in NC,* ☎ *864/936–7921.* *Free.* *Labor Day–Memorial Day, daily 9–5; Memorial Day–Labor Day, daily 9–6.*

The 6,000-acre **Kings Mountain State Park** (☎ 864/222–3209), adjacent to the national military park, has camping, swimming, fishing, boating, and nature and hiking trails.

Upcountry A to Z

Arriving and Departing

BY BUS

Greyhound (☎ 800/231–2222) serves all of South Carolina.

BY CAR

I–85 provides access to Greenville, Spartanburg, Pendleton, and Anderson. I–26 runs from Charleston through Columbia to the Upcountry, connecting with I–385 into Greenville.

BY PLANE

Greenville-Spartanburg Airport (✉ 2000 G.S.P. Dr., ☎ 864/867–7426), off I–85 between the two cities, is served by US Airways, Delta, Northwest, American Eagle, Continental, and Midway. For airline telephone numbers, *see* Air Travel *in* Smart Travel Tips A to Z.

BY TRAIN

Amtrak (☎ 800/872–7245) stops in Greenville.

Contacts and Resources

OUTDOOR ACTIVITIES AND SPORTS

The **Chattooga National Wild and Scenic River,** on the border of South Carolina and Georgia, is excellent for guided rafting, canoeing, and kayaking trips. Contact **Nantahala Outdoor Center** (☎ 864/647–9014 or 800/232–7238), **Southeastern Expeditions** (☎ 800/868–7238), or **Wildwater Ltd.** (☎ 864/647–9587 or 800/451–9972).

STATE PARKS

For information about state parks in the area, contact the **South Carolina Division of Tourism** (✉ 1205 Pendleton St., Columbia 29201, ☎ 843/734–0122 or 800/872–3505). **Devils Fork State Park** (✉ 161 Holcombe Circle, Salem 29676, ☎ 864/944–2639), on Lake Jocassee, has luxurious new villas and facilities.

VISITOR INFORMATION

Contact **Discover Upcountry Carolina Association** (✉ Box 3116, Greenville 29602, ☎ 864/233–2690 or 800/849–4766). The **Greater Greenville Convention and Visitors Bureau** (✉ 206 S. Main St., Box 10527, 29603, ☎ 864/421–0000 or 800/717–0023) can provide information on accommodations, restaurants, and attractions in the Greenville area specifically.

SOUTH CAROLINA A TO Z

Arriving and Departing

By Boat

Boaters can reach most of South Carolina's coastal cities and towns by the Intracoastal Waterway.

By Bus

Greyhound (☎ 800/231–2222) serves all of South Carolina.

By Car

I–26 traverses the state from northwest to southeast and terminates at Charleston. I–77 leads into Columbia from the north. I–26, I–20, and U.S. 1 intersect at Columbia. I–85 provides access to Greenville, Spartanburg, Pendleton, and Anderson. U.S. 17, a north–south coastal route, runs along the coastal edge of the entire state.

By Plane

Major airports are **Charleston International Airport** (✉ 5500 International Blvd., ☎ 843/767–1100); **Columbia Metro Airport** (✉ 3000 Aviation Way, ☎ 803/822–5000); **Greenville-Spartanburg Airport** (✉ 2000 G.S.P. Dr., ☎ 864/867–7426); **Hilton Head Island Airport** (☎ 843/681–6386), served by US Airways Express; **Myrtle Beach International Airport** (✉ 1100 Jetport Rd., ☎ 843/448–1589); and **Savannah International Airport** (✉ 400 Airways Ave., ☎ 912/964–0514), about an hour's drive from Hilton Head.

By Train

Amtrak (☎ 800/872–7245) stops in Charleston, Camden, Columbia, Denmark, Dillon, Florence, Greenville, Kingstree, and Yemassee (near Beaufort).

Getting Around

By Bus

Greyhound (☎ 800/231–2222) links several cities and towns throughout South Carolina.

By Car

The speed limit on interstates is 65 mph. You can turn right at a red light unless otherwise noted by street signs.

Contacts and Resources

B&Bs

For reservation agencies in **Charleston,** *see* Contacts and Resources *in* Charleston A to Z, *above*. Write to the **South Carolina Bed and Breakfast Association** (✉ Box 1275, Sumter 29150-1275, ☎ 888/599–1234) for a current state directory of member B&Bs. For a complete list of B&Bs, write to the **South Carolina Division of Tourism** (✉ 1205 Pendleton St., Columbia 29201, ☎ 803/734–0122 or 800/872–3505) and ask for the pamphlet *Bed & Breakfasts of South Carolina.*

Emergencies

Ambulance, fire, police (☎ 911).

Guided Tours

Lowcountry Adventures (☎ 843/681–8212) offers tours of Hilton Head, Beaufort, and Charleston. For information about other specific tours, contact the **South Carolina Division of Tourism** (☞ Visitor Information, *below*).

National and State Parks

For information about South Carolina's national park areas, contact the **U.S. Forest Service** (✉ 4931 Broad River Rd., Columbia 29210, ☎ 803/561–4000). Several of South Carolina's 48 state parks operate like resort communities, with everything from deluxe accommodations to golf. For information, contact the **South Carolina Division of Tourism** (☞ Visitor Information, *below*).

Visitor Information

South Carolina Division of Tourism (✉ 1205 Pendleton St., Columbia 29201, ☎ 803/734–0122 or 800/872–3505) has information about the entire state.

Welcome centers: ✉ U.S. 17, near Little River; I–95, near Dillon, Santee and Lake Marion, and Hardeeville; I–77, near Fort Mill; I–85, near Blacksburg and Fair Play; I–26, near Landrum; I–20, at North Augusta; and U.S. 301, near Allendale.

5 COLD MOUNTAIN

by Charles Frazier
Excerpts from the novel

THEY WORKED AMONG THE PLANTS for some time that afternoon, and then they heard the sound of wheels, a horse, a metal pail banging against a sideboard with a ring that filled the cove. A pair of ancient mules and then a wagon rounded the curve of the road and stopped by the fence. The wagon bed was piled full with satchels and boxes to such extent that the people all walked. Ada and Ruby went to the fence and found the group to be made of pilgrims from Tennessee on their way to South Carolina. They had taken a number of wrong turnings along the river, had missed the way to Wagon Road Gap, and were now fetched up at this dead end. The party was composed of three broken women and a half dozen young children. They were tended by a pair of kind slaves, a man and wife, who hovered about the women as close as shadows, even though they might just as easily have cut every throat in the family any night as they slept.

The women said their husbands were off at the fighting, and they were fleeing the Federals in Tennessee, aiming for Camden in South Carolina where one of the women had a sister. They asked leave to sleep in the hayloft, and while they were making up their nests in the hay, Ada and Ruby went to work cooking. Ruby cut the heads off three chickens, for the yard was now so full of chicks they could hardly walk to the springhouse without stepping on one, and the population was such that they could anticipate a sufficiency of capons soon. They cut the chickens up and fried them, cooked pole beans, boiled potatoes and stewed squash. Ruby made a triple recipe of biscuits, and when supper was ready they called in the visitors and sat them at the dining-room table. The slaves had the same fare, but ate out under the pear tree.

The travelers dined hard for quite some time, and when they were done eating, there were but two wings and a thigh left on the chicken platter, and they had gone through more than a pound of butter and a pint pitcher of sorghum. One woman said, My, that was good. It's been two weeks now that we've had little to eat but dry corn bread, without butter or bacon drippings or molasses to wetten it up a little. Choky food.

—How do you come to be on the road? Ada said.

—The Federals rode down on us and robbed even the niggers, the woman said. They took every bit of food we had been able to raise this year. I even saw one man filling his coat pockets with our lard. Dipping it by the handful. Then we were tetotally stripped and searched right down to our very persons by a Federal we were told was a woman in uniform. But it was not. It had an Adam's apple. It took from us every article of jewelry we had hidden. Then they burnt our house down in the rain and rode away. Shortly it was only a chimney standing sentry over a cellar hole full of bitter-smelling black water. We had nothing, but we stayed awhile from lack of will to part from home. On the third day I stood with my least little girl looking down into that hole where was the wreckage of everything we had. She picked up a shard of a broken dinner plate and said, Mama, I expect we'll soon be eating off leaves. Then it was that I knew we had to go.

—That is the way of the Federals, another of the women said. They have come up with a fresh idea in warfare. Make the women and children atone for the deaths of soldiers.

—This is a time that carves the heart down to a bitter nub, the third woman said. You are luckier than you know, hid in this cove.

Ada and Ruby saw the travelers off to bed, and the next morning they cooked nearly all the eggs they had and made a pot of grits and more biscuits. After breakfast, they drew a map of the way to the gap and set them on the next leg of their journey.

That noon, Ruby said she wanted to walk up and check on the apple orchard, so Ada suggested they have their lunch there. They made a picnic of the leftover pieces of last night's fried chicken, a small bowl of potato salad for which Ruby had whipped up the mayonnaise, and some vinegared cucumber slices. They carried the dinner up to the apple orchard in a wooden bucket and ate it under the trees on a quilt spread in the grass.

It was an afternoon of bright haze, the sunlight sourceless and uniform. Ruby examined the trees and judged solemnly that the apples were making tolerably well. Then, out of the blue, she looked at Ada and said, Point north. She grinned at the long delay as Ada worked out the cardinal directions from her recollection of where the sun set. Such questions were a recent habit Ruby had developed. She seemed to delight in demonstrating how disoriented Ada was in the world. As they walked by the creek one day she had asked, What's the course of that water? Where does it come from and what does it run into? Another day she had said, Name me four plants on that hillside that in a pinch you could eat. How many days to the next new moon? Name two things blooming now and two things fruiting.

Ada did not yet have those answers, but she could feel them coming, and Ruby was her principal text. During the daily rounds of work, Ada had soon noted that Ruby's lore included many impracticalities beyond the raising of crops. The names of useless beings—both animal and vegetable—and the custom of their lives apparently occupied much of Ruby's thinking, for she was constantly pointing out the little creatures that occupy the nooks of the world. Her mind marked every mantis in a stand of ragweed, the corn borers in the little tents they folded out of milkweed leaves, striped and spotted salamanders with their friendly smiling faces under rocks in the creek. Ruby noted little hairy liverish poisonous-looking plants and fungi growing on the damp bark of dying trees, all the larvae and bugs and worms that live alone inside a case of sticks or grit or leaves. Each life with a story behind it. Every little gesture nature made to suggest a mind marking its life as its own caught Ruby's interest.

* * *

STILL, HE DID NOT MUCH FAVOR HIS CURRENT POSITION, backed up against the brow of the rocky ledge, the heath knotted up before him, and the sow nervous with a cub born out of season. In his favor was this: he knew a bear was much more likely to run than attack, that she might at most make a false charge, rushing forward fifteen feet or so, bouncing as she came on her front legs and snorting out air. The purpose would be to scare him off, not to hurt him. But he had nowhere to run. He wanted her to know where he was, so he spoke to her, saying, I've no aim to trouble you. I'll walk on from here and never be back. I'm just asking for clear passage. He spoke calm and straight and he wanted his voice to carry respect.

The bear sniffed more. She shifted from foot to foot, rocked from side to side. Inman slowly rolled up his bedding and slipped on his sacks.

—I'll be going, he said.

He moved two steps and the bear false-charged.

Inman could figure in his mind as it happened that none of the measurements would work out. Like a problem of carpentry where none of the dimensions match up. He had only three feet to back up. She had all the momentum of her bulk and only ten feet ahead of her before the lip of the cliff.

Inman took a step to the side and the bear rushed by him and plunged over the high ledge that she never saw in the gloom. He could smell her strong as she went by. Wet dog, black dirt.

He looked over and saw her break open on the rocks far below like a great red blossom in the dawn light. Black pelt scraps littering the rocks.

Shit, he thought. Even my best intentions come to naught, and hope itself is but an obstacle.

The cub in the fir bawled out in its anguish. It was not even yet a weanling and would wither and die without a mother. It would wail away for days until it starved or was eaten by wolf or panther.

Inman walked to the tree and looked into the little bear's face. It blinked its black eyes at him and opened its mouth and cried like a human baby.

To his credit, Inman could imagine reaching up and grabbing the cub by the scruff of its neck and saying, We're kin. Then taking his knapsack off and thrusting the cub in with only its head sticking out. Then putting the pack back on and walking away, the bear looking about from this new perspective as bright-eyed as a papoose. Give it to Ada as a pet. Or if she turned him away, he might raise it to be a part-tame bear, and when full grown it might stop by his hermit cabin on Cold Mountain now and again for company. Bring its wife and children so that in years to come Inman could have an animal family if no other. That would be one way this dead bear calamity might be rectified.

What Inman did, though, was all he could do. He picked up the LeMat's and shot the cub in the head and watched it pause as its grip on the tree failed and it fell to ground.

So as not to waste the meat, Inman built a fire and skinned out the cub and cut it in pieces and parboiled it. He laid the black pelt out on a rock and it was no bigger than a coon's. While the bear cooked he sat and waited at the scarp as morning came on. The mists broke and he could see mountains and rivers ranked to the earth's far verge. Shadows slid down the slopes of the nearest line of ridges, falling into the valley as if draining into a vast pool of dark under the ground. Rags of cloud hung in the valleys below Inman's feet, but in all that vista there was not a rooftop or plume of smoke or cleared field to mark a place where man had settled. You could look out across that folded landscape and every sense you had told only that this was all the world there was.

The wind sweeping up the mountain carried away the smell of the bear boiling and left only the odor of wet stone. Inman could see west for scores of miles. Crest and scarp and crag, stacked and grey, to the long horizon. Cataloochee, the Cherokee word was. Meaning waves of mountains in fading rows. And this day the waves could hardly be differed from the raw winter sky. Both were barred and marbled with the same shades of grey only, so the outlook stretched high and low like a great slab of streaked meat. Inman himself could not have been better dressed to conceal himself amid this world, for all he wore was grey and black and dirty white.

Bleak as the scene was, though, there was growing joy in Inman's heart. He was nearing home; he could feel it in the touch of thin air on skin, in his longing to see the leap of hearth smoke from the houses of people he had known all his life. People he would not be called upon to hate or fear. He rose and took a wide stance on the rock and stood and pinched down his eyes to sharpen the view across the vast prospect to one far mountain. It stood apart from the sky only as the stroke of a poorly inked pen, a line thin and quick and gestural. But the shape slowly grew plain and unmistakable. It was to Cold Mountain he looked. He had achieved a vista of what for him was homeland.

Cold Mountain *is available in paperback from Vintage Books and as a Random House Audiobook. The unabridged version is read by the author; the abridged version is read by Dylan Baker.*

INDEX

Icons and Symbols

★ Our special recommendations
✕ Restaurant
Lodging establishment
Lodging establishment whose restaurant warrants a special trip
Good for kids (rubber duck)
☞ Sends you to another section of the guide for more information
✉ Address
☎ Telephone number
Opening and closing times
Admission prices
Sends you to www.fodors.com/urls for up-to-date links to the property's Web site

Numbers in white and black circles ③❸ that appear on the maps, in the margins, and within the tours correspond to one another.

A

Abbeville, SC, *255, 264–265*
Abbeville County Museum, *264*
Abbeville Opera House, *264*
Aberdeen, NC, *152–153*
Ackland Art Museum, *145*
Aerobics, *47*
African-American Panoramic Experience (APEX), *23, 25*
African American Trail, *3–4*
Afro-American Cultural Center, *115*
Aiken, SC, *201, 255, 262–263*
Aiken County Historical Museum, *262*
Aiken-Rhett House, *202, 204*
Aiken Thoroughbred Hall of Fame, *262*
Air travel, *x–xi*
Atlanta, 51–52
Charleston, 229
Charlotte, 121–122
and children, xv
Coastal Isles and the Okefenokee, 86
Columbia and the Heartland, 265
Georgia, 94, 104
Hilton Head area, 254
luggage, xxvi
the mountains (NC), 191
Myrtle Beach and the Grand Strand, 242
New Bern and the Central Coast, 167
North Carolina, 193
Outer Banks, 162
Sandhills, 153
Savannah, 73
South Carolina, 271
the Triad (Greensboro/Winston-Salem/High Point), 132–133
the Triangle (Raleigh/Durham/Chapel Hill), 147
Upcountry (SC), 270
Wilmington and the Cape Fear Coast, 174
Airports, *xi*
Alliance Theatre, *29, 44*
Alligator Adventure, *232–233*
American Classic Motorcycle Museum, *153*
American Classic Tea Plantation, *213*
American Express (credit card), *xxiv*
American Military Museum, *204*
Amicalola Falls, *96*
Amusement parks
Georgia, 33, 82
North Carolina, 116, 183, 188
South Carolina, 232
Andersonville National Historic Site, *102–103*
Andrew Low House, *55, 56–57*
Angel Oak, *213–214*
Angela Peterson Doll and Miniature Museum, *131*
Apartment and villa rentals, *xxii, 82*
Apothecary Shop and Doctor's Office, *166*
Appalachian Cultural Museum, *189*
Aquariums
Charleston, 209, 210
Charlotte, 114
Myrtle Beach and the Grand Strand, 233
New Bern and the Central Coast, 165
Outer Banks, 3, 159
Savannah, 64
Wilmington and the Cape Fear Coast, 159
Armstrong House, *61, 62*
ArtQuest (gallery), *123*
ArtsCenter (Chapel Hill), *145*
Artspace (Raleigh), *134, 135*
Asheboro, NC, *153*
Asheville, NC, *6, 7, 111, 175, 179–185*
Asheville Art Museum, *179*
Atalaya, *238*
Athens, GA, *86–88*
Atlanta, GA, *6, 7, 16, 17–53*
Atlanta Botanical Garden, *28*
Atlanta Cyclorama and Civil War Museum, *19*
Atlanta Daily World Building, *23, 25*
Atlanta-Fulton Public Library, *18, 19*
Atlanta History Center, *30*
Atlanta International Museum of Art and Design, *18, 19*
Atlanta Journal and Constitution **building,** *18, 19*
Atlanta Life Insurance Company, *21, 23, 25*
Atlanta Market Center, *22*
Atlanta Marriott Marquis, *22*
Atlanta Symphony Orchestra, *29, 43*
Auburn Avenue Research Library on African-American Culture and History, *23, 25*
Audubon-Newell Preserve, *244*
Audubon Swamp Garden, *213*
Augusta, GA, *16, 93–94*
Auto racing, *116, 120*
Ava Gardner Museum, *136*
Avery Research Center for African American History and Culture, *205*

B

Babyland General Hospital, *97*
Balsam Mountain Inn, *184*
Bank of America Building, *18, 19*
Bank of America Corporate Center, *112, 114*
Bank of America Plaza Tower, *26, 28*
Banner Elk, NC, *190–191*
Baptist Student Center, *23, 25*
Bars, *45–46, 70, 130, 139, 171, 223–224, 252*
Baseball
Atlanta, 48
North Carolina, 120, 126, 130, 139, 144
South Carolina, 226, 237, 259
Basilica of St. Lawrence, *179*
Basketball
Atlanta, 48
North Carolina, 120, 130, 139, 144, 146
South Carolina, 226
Battery (Charleston), *209*
Battery Park Hotel, *179*
Beach Institute African-American Cultural Center, *57, 75*

Beaches
Georgia, 64, 79–80, 82–83
North Carolina, 109, 111, 157, 159, 160–161, 165, 167, 174
South Carolina, 197, 224–225, 236, 238, 247
Beaufort, NC, *164*
Beaufort, SC, *201, 249–253*
Beaufort Museum, *249*
Bellefield Nature Center Museum, *240*
Bennett Place State Historic Site, *143*
Bethesda Presbyterian Church, *152*
Bicycling, *xi*
Georgia, 47, 105
North Carolina, 139, 146, 193
South Carolina, 225, 247, 252
Biltmore Estate, *7, 179–180*
Blandwood Mansion, *124*
Blowing Rock, NC, *111, 187–189*
Blue Ridge Mountain Frescoes, *190*
Blue Ridge Parkway, *111, 186–187*
BMW Zentrum plant, *269*
Board sailing, *175*
Boat travel
Charleston, 229
Coastal Isles and the Okefenokee, 86
Hilton Head area, 254
Myrtle Beach and the Grand Strand, 241–242
New Bern and the Central Coast, 166–167
North Carolina, 193
Outer Banks, 162
South Carolina, 271
Wilmington and the Cape Fear Coast, 172, 173
Boating, *71, 237, 266*
Bob Jones University Art Gallery and Museum, *267*
Bonaventure Cemetery, *62*
Books and videos, *xii*
Boone, NC, *111, 189–190*
Boone Hall Plantation, *211*
Brasstown Bald, *98*
Brevard, NC, *183*
Breweries, *224*
Brookgreen Gardens, *237–238*
Brunswick Town State Historic Site, *173*
Buckhead, GA, *6, 29–31, 49*
Burgwin-Wright Museum House, *169*
Burt-Stark House, *264*
Bus travel, *xii–xiii*
Atlanta, 51, 52
Charleston, 229–230
Charlotte, 121, 122
Columbia and the Heartland, 265
Georgia, 103, 104
the mountains (NC), 191
Myrtle Beach and the Grand Strand, 242
New Bern and the Central Coast, 167
North Carolina, 192, 193
Savannah, 73, 74
South Carolina, 271
the Triad (Greensboro/Winston-Salem/High Point), 132
the Triangle (Raleigh/Durham/Chapel Hill), 147, 148
Upcountry (SC), 270
Wilmington and the Cape Fear Coast, 173–174
Business hours, *xiii*

C

Calhoun Mansion, *207, 209*
Callaway Gardens, *7, 103*
Callaway Plantation, *92*
Camden, SC, *201, 260–261*
Cameras and photography, *xiii*
Cameron, NC, *149*
Camping, *xxiii*
Charlotte, 119
Cumberland Island, 83
Durham, 144
Greensboro, 126
the mountains (NC), 192
Okefenokee National Wildlife Refuge, 85
Outer Banks, 163
Raleigh, 139
Sapelo Island, 76
Candler Building, *18, 20*
Canoeing
North Carolina, 119, 190, 191, 192
South Carolina, 247, 259, 261–262, 270–271
Cape Fear Coast. ☞ *Wilmington and the Cape Fear Coast*
Cape Fear Museum, *169*
Cape Hatteras Lighthouse, *160*
Cape Hatteras National Seashore, *6, 111, 154, 159–160*
Cape Lookout National Seashore, *154, 161–162*
Cape Romain National Wildlife Refuge, *211*
Capitol Area Visitor Center, *134, 135*
Car rental, *xiii–xiv*
Car travel, *xiv–xv*
Atlanta, 51, 52
Charleston, 229
Charlotte, 121
Coastal Isles and the Okefenokee, 85–86
Columbia and the Heartland, 265
Georgia, 3, 104
Hilton Head area, 254
the mountains (NC), 191
Myrtle Beach and the Grand Strand, 4, 242
New Bern and the Central Coast, 167
North Carolina, 193
Outer Banks, 162
Sandhills, 153
Savannah, 73
South Carolina, 271
the Triad (Greensboro/Winston-Salem/High Point), 132
the Triangle (Raleigh/Durham/Chapel Hill), 147
Upcountry (SC), 270
Wilmington and the Cape Fear Coast, 174
Carl Sandburg Home National Historic Site, *183*
Carriage rides, *152*
Carter Presidential Center, *7, 31*
Carteret County Courthouse, *166*
Cathedral of St. John the Baptist, *55, 57*
Caw Caw Interpretive Center, *253*
Centennial Olympic Park, *18, 20*
Center for Puppetry Arts, *28*
Chandler's Wharf (Wilmington), *169*
Chapel Hill, NC, *111, 133, 145–147*
Charles Pinckney National Historic Site, *211*
Charles Towne Landing State Park, *212, 213*
Charleston, SC, *6, 7, 200, 201–231*
Charleston Museum, *202, 204*
Charleston Place, *204, 205*
Charlotte, NC, *6, 111, 112–122*
Charlotte Hawkins Brown Memorial State Historic Site, *126–127*
Charlotte Nature Museum, *115*
Château Élan, *32*
Chatham County Courthouse, *61, 62*
Chattahoochee Nature Center, *32*
Cheraw, SC, *261*
Cherokee, NC, *175–177*
Chesnee, SC, *4*
Chicamacomico Lifesaving Station, *160*
Chickamauga and Chattanooga National Military Park, *16, 101*
Chief Vann House, *100*
Children, traveling with, *xv*
Chimney Rock, NC, *111, 183*
Chimney Rock Park, *183*

Chinqua-Penn Plantation, *127*
Chippewa Square (Savannah), *55, 57*
Christ Episcopal Church, *79*
Circular Congregational Church, *204, 205*
City Hall (Atlanta), *19, 20*
City Hall (Charleston), *207, 209*
City Hall (Savannah), *55, 57*
City Market (Raleigh), *134, 135*
City Market (Savannah), *55, 57*
Clayton, GA, *16, 99*
Cleveland, GA, *97*
Climate, *xxx*
Clothing for the trip, *xv–xvi*
CNN Center, *18, 20*
Coastal Encounters Nature Center, *82*
Coastal Isles and the Okefenokee, GA, *7, 75–86*
Cumberland Island, 82–83
Jekyll Island, 7, 80–82
Little St. Simons Island, 76–78
St. Simons Island, 79–80
Sapelo Island, 76
Sea Island, 78–79
Coffeehouses, 71
Colburn Gem & Mineral Museum, *179*
Cold Mountain, *178–179*
College of Charleston, *202, 205*
Colonial Heritage Center, *123*
Colonial Lake, *209*
Colonial Park Cemetery, *55, 57*
Columbia and the Heartland, SC, *201, 255–266*
Columbia Museum of Art, *256*
Columbia Square (Savannah), *57*
Concerts
Atlanta, 43
Charleston, 222
Columbia, 58
Raleigh, 138–139
Confederate Museum, *206*
Congregation Beth Elohim, *202, 205*
Consolidated Gold Mine, *96*
Consumer protection, *xv–xvi*
Coquina Beach, *157*
Corolla, NC, *111, 154–156*
Cotton Exchange, *169*
Crabbing, *167–168*
Cradle of Forestry in America National Historic Site, *183*
Credit card abbreviations, *xxiv*
Creek Lake, *103*
Crossnore School's Weaving Room, *184*
Cuisine, *36*
Cumberland Island, GA, *82–83*
Cumberland Island National Seashore, *82*
Currency exchange, *xviii*
Customs and duties, *xviii–xix*
Cypress Gardens, *6, 228*

D

Dahlonega, GA, *16, 96–97*
Dance, *43, 46, 138, 222*
Daufuskie Island, *244*
Day Butterfly Center, *103*
Diana Wortham Theatre, *179*
Dillsboro, NC, *178*
Diner's Club (credit card), *xxiv*
Dinner cruises, *224*
Disabilities and accessibility, *xvi–xvii*
Discounts and deals, *xvii*
Discover (credit card), *xxiv*
Discovery Place, *114*
Dixon-Stevenson House, *164*
Dock Street Theatre, *204, 205*
Douglass Theatre, *91*
Dragon's Lair (minigolf course), *232*
Drayton Hall, *7, 201, 212, 213*
Duck, NC, *154–156*
Duke Chapel, *141, 142*
Duke Homestead, *141, 142*
Duke University, *141, 142*
Dungeness (estate), *83*
Durham, NC, *7, 111, 140–144*

E

Eatonton, GA, *89*
Ebenezer (settlement), *63*
Ebenezer Baptist Church, *23, 25*
Edenton, NC, *159*
Edisto Island, SC, *253–254*
Edmondston-Alston House, *209*
82nd Airborne Division War Memorial Museum, *152*
Electricity, *xix*
Elizabeth City, *156*
***Elizabeth II* State Historic Site,** *158*
Elizabethan Gardens, *158*
Ellijay, GA, *99–100*
Emanuel African Methodist Episcopal Church, *202, 205*
Emerald Village, *186*
Emergencies, *xix*
Atlanta, 53
Charleston, 230
Charlotte, 122
Columbia and the Heartland, 265
Georgia, 95, 102, 105
Hilton Head area, 254
the mountains (NC), 191
Myrtle Beach and the Grand Strand, 242
New Bern and the Central Coast, 167
North Carolina, 193
Outer Banks, 162
Sandhills, 153
Savannah, 74
South Carolina, 272
the Triad (Greensboro/Winston-Salem/High Point), 133
the Triangle (Raleigh/Durham/Chapel Hill), 148
Wilmington and the Cape Fear Coast, 174
Emmet Park (Savannah), *56, 57*
Eno River State Park, *143*
Equestrian events, *261, 263*
Executive Mansion (Raleigh), *134, 135*
Exploris (children's museum), *134, 135*
Ezekiel Harris House, *93*

F

Factors Walk (Savannah), *55, 57*
Fayetteville Street Mall (Raleigh), *134, 135*
Federal Reserve Bank, *18, 20*
Fernbank Museum of Natural History, *32*
Fernbank Science Center, *31, 32*
Ferries. ☞ Boat travel
Festivals, *8–9*
Atlanta, 43
Charleston, 222–223
Myrtle Beach, 238
Film, *223, 235*
First Presbyterian Church, *112, 114*
Fishing
Charleston, 228
Charlotte, 119
Columbia and the Heartland, 266
Georgia, 105
Hilton Head area, 247–248
the mountains, 177
Myrtle Beach and the Grand Strand, 236, 238
New Bern and the Central Coast, 167–168
North Carolina, 193–194
Outer Banks, 163
Raleigh, 139
Wilmington and the Cape Fear Coast, 174
Five Points MARTA station, *18, 20*
Flannery O'Connor Room, *90*
Flat Rock, NC, *111, 183*
Flat Rock Playhouse, *183*
Flatiron Building (Asheville), *179*
Flatiron Building (Atlanta), *18, 20*
Folk Art Center (Blue Ridge Parkway), *186*

Folk Art Park (Atlanta), *18, 20–21*
Football, *48, 120*
Forsyth Park (Savannah), *55, 57–58*
Forsyth Park Apartments, *61, 62*
Fort Bragg/Pope Air Force Base, *152*
Fort Discovery, *93*
Fort Fisher State Historic Site, *172*
Fort Frederica National Monument, *79*
Ft. Jackson, *63*
Fort Jackson Museum, *256*
Fort Morris, *64*
Fort Moultrie, *211–212*
Fort Pulaski National Monument, *63*
Fort Raleigh National Historic Site, *158*
Fort Sumter National Monument, *210, 212*
Foundation for Aircraft Conservation Flying Museum, *153*
Founders Hall, *114*
Fourth Ward (Charlotte), *112, 114*
Fourth Ward Park (Charlotte), *114*
Fox Theatre, *26, 28, 44*
Fran Hanson Discovery Center, *270*
Francis Marion National Forest, *228*
Franklin, NC, *178*
Franklin House, *87*
Franklin Street (Chapel Hill), *145*
French Protestant (Huguenot) **Church**, *204, 205*
Furniture Discovery Center, *131*

G

Gardens, *7*
Georgia, 28, 87, 103
North Carolina, 116, 142, 145, 149, 158, 169, 173, 180
South Carolina, 197, 210, 213, 228, 237–238, 257, 261, 262, 263, 269, 270
tours, 75
Gardens of Park Seed Company, *263*
Gay and lesbian travelers, tips for, *xx–xxi*
Georgetown, SC, *240–241*
Georgia, *3, 4, 11–105.* ☞ *Also* Atlanta; Coastal Isles and the Okefenokee; Savannah
emergencies, 105
gardens, 7
historic sites, 14
itinerary recommendations, 16
lodging, 6–7, 14–15
nightlife, 15
restaurants, 3, 6, 14
road conditions, 105
sports and outdoor activities, 15
state parks, 33, 85, 105
timing the visit, 16
transportation, 103–104
visitor information, 105
Georgia Capitol Museum, *21*
Georgia Dome, *18, 21*
Georgia Governor's Mansion, *30*
Georgia Historical Society, *57–58*
Georgia Music Hall of Fame, *90–91*
Georgia-Pacific Center, *18, 21*
Georgia Railroad Freight Depot, *19, 21*
Georgia Sports Hall of Fame, *91*
Georgia State Capitol, *19, 21*
Georgia Trust for Historic Preservation, *29*
Georgian Terrace, *26, 28–29*
Gibbes Museum of Art, *204, 205–206*
Gold Museum, *96*
Golf
Aberdeen, 152
Atlanta, 47
Chapel Hill, 147
Charleston, 225–226
Charlotte, 119–120
Columbia and the Heartland, 259, 261, 263
Durham, 144
Greensboro, 126
High Point, 132
Hilton Head area, 248, 252
Jekyll Island, 82
the mountains (NC), 182, 190, 192
Myrtle Beach and the Grand Strand, 236, 239, 242
New Bern and the Central Coast, 168
Outer Banks, 156, 158
Pinehurst, 152
Raleigh, 139–140
Savannah, 71
Southern Pines, 150
Upcountry (SC), 268
Wilmington and the Cape Fear Coast, 171, 173, 174
Winston-Salem, 130
Gordon-Lee Mansion, *101*
Grady, Henry, statue, *18, 22*
Grand Strand, SC. ☞ Myrtle Beach and the Grand Strand
Grandfather Mountain, *186*
Great Smoky Mountains National Park, *177–178*
Great Smoky Mountains Railway, *178*
Greenfield Lake and Gardens, *169*
Green-Meldrim House, *55, 58*
Greensboro, NC, *123–127*
Greensboro Children's Museum, *124*
Greensboro Cultural Center at Festival Park, *123*
Greensboro Historical Museum, *123*
Greenville, SC, *201, 267–268*
Greenville County Museum of Art, *267*
Greenwood, SC, *263–264*
Greenwood Museum, *263*
Grove Park Inn Resort, *7*
Guilford Courthouse National Military Park, *123*
Gullah, *250*

H

Hamilton-Turner House, *61, 62*
Hammonds House Galleries and Resource Center, *21*
Hampton Plantation State Park, *240–241*
Hampton-Preston Mansion, *256*
Hang gliding, *158*
Harold Kaminski House, *240*
Hatcher Gardens, *269*
Hatteras Island, *111, 160*
Hawaiian Rumble (minigolf course), *232*
Hay House, *91*
Hayti Heritage Center, *141, 142*
Health Adventure, *179*
Health clubs, *48, 71, 139*
Health matters, *xxi*
Helen, GA, *97–98*
Henderson Village, *6*
Henry C. Chambers Waterfront Park (Beaufort), *249*
Heritage Hall, *88*
Herndon House, *21*
Heyward-Washington House, *207, 209*
Hezekiah Alexander Homesite and Charlotte History Museum, *115*
Hickory Knob State Resort Park, *264*
High Country, NC, *175*
High Museum of Art, *28, 29*
High Museum of Art, Folk Art and Photography Galleries, *21*
High Point, NC, *130–132*
High Point Museum/Historical Park, *131*
Hiking
Columbia and the Heartland, 259, 266
Greensboro, 126
High Point, 132

the mountains (NC), 177, 187, 192
Hilton Head area, SC, *201, 243–255*
Hillcrest Orchards, *99–100*
Historic Bethabara Park (Winston-Salem), *128*
Historic Camden Revolutionary War Site, *260*
Hitchcock Woods, *262*
Hockey, *48, 120, 140, 226*
Hodgson Hall, *57*
Hog Hammock Community, *76*
Holidays, *xxi*
Home exchanges, *xxiii*
Homes and garden tours, *75*
Hopeland Gardens, *262*
Hopsewee Plantation State Park, *240–241*
Horn in the West (outdoor drama), *189*
Horseback riding, *152, 182, 188, 191, 248*
Horseshoe, SC, *257*
Hoskins House, *123*
Hostels, *xxiii*
Hot Springs, NC, *185–186*
Hotels and other lodging, *xxii–xxiv.* ☞ Also Camping
Aberdeen, 152
Asheville, 7, 181–182
Atlanta, 6, 40–42,
bed-and-breakfasts, xxii, 53, 74, 94, 101, 105, 118–119, 272
Buckhead, 42
Chapel Hill, 7, 146
Charleston, 7, 218–222, 230–231
Charlotte, 117–119
Columbia and the Heartland, 258, 260, 261, 263, 265
Cumberland Island, 83
Durham, 143–144
Georgia, 6–7, 87–88, 89, 90, 92, 93–94, 97, 98, 99, 100, 101, 103
Greensboro, 125
High Point, 131–132
Hilton Head area, 7, 245–247, 251–252, 253–254
inns and guest houses, xxii, 68–69, 219–221
Jekyll Island, 7, 81–82
Little St. Simons Island, 78
motels, xxiv, 69–70, 117–118, 218–219
the mountains (NC), 176, 179, 185, 186, 187, 188, 189–190, 191
Myrtle Beach and the Grand Strand, 7, 234–235, 238–239, 241, 242–243
New Bern and the Central Coast, 165, 166
North Carolina, 7, 110
Okefenokee National Wildlife Refuge, 85
Outer Banks, 7, 156, 157, 158, 159, 161
Pinehurst, 7, 151
Raleigh, 137–138
rental cottages and condos, 80
resorts, 221–222
St. Simons Island, 80
Sapelo Island, 76
Savannah, 6, 68–70
Sea Island, 78–79
South Carolina, 7, 228, 229
Southern Pines, 150
Summerville, 229
Upcountry (SC), 267–268, 269, 270
Wilmington and the Cape Fear Coast, 170, 172, 173
Winston-Salem, 129
Hunting Island State Park, *251*
Huntington Beach State Park, *238*
Hurt Building, *18, 21–22*
Hyatt Regency Hotel, *22*

I

IBM Tower, *29*
Ice-skating, *268*
Icons and symbols, *xxix–xxx, 15, 110, 200, 278*
Ina Russell Library, *90*
Insurance, *xiv, xix, xxi–xxii*
International travelers, *xvii–xx*
Isaiah Davenport House, *56, 58*

J

James K. Polk Memorial, *116*
James M. Waddell Jr. Mariculture Research & Development Center, *244*
Jekyll Island, GA, *80–82*
Jekyll Island Museum Visitor Center, *81*
Jockey's Ridge State Park, *157*
Joe Odom's First House, *61, 62*
Joel Lane House, *136*
Jogging, *47, 72, 140*
John Mark Verdier House Museum, *249*
John Wesley Dobbs Plaza, *23, 25*
John Wright Stanly House, *164*
Johnson Square (Savannah), *58*
Joseph Manigault Mansion, *202, 206*
Julian Price Park, *187*
Juliette Gordon Low Birthplace/Girl Scout National Center, *55, 58*

K

Kayaking, *247, 259, 270–271*
Kelly Space Voyager Planetarium, *114*
Kennesaw Mountain National Battlefield, *32*
Kershaw-Cornwallis House, *260*
Kill Devil Hills, NC, *111, 156–157*
King Jr., Dr. Martin Luther, *6, 23, 25–26*
Kings Mountain National Military and State Park, *270*
King-Tisdell Cottage (museum), *58*
Kitty Hawk, NC, *111, 154–156*
Kure Beach, NC, *172*

L

Lafayette Square (Savannah), *59*
Lake Toxaway, *185*
Lee Adler's Home, *61, 62–63*
Lenox Square, *30, 49*
Lighthouses, *76, 79, 160, 251*
Linville Caverns, *186*
Linville Falls Visitor Center, *186*
Little St. Simons Island, GA, *76–78*
Little White House Historic Site, *103*
Llama treks, *182*
Lodging, *xxii–xxiv.* ☞ *Also* Hotels and other lodging
Lost Colony (historical drama), *159*
Louis Round Wilson Library, *145*
Lowe's Motor Speedway, *116*
Luggage, *xxvi*

M

Macon, GA, *16, 90–92*
Macon Convention and Visitors Bureau, *90*
Macon Museum of Arts and Sciences and Mark Smith Planetarium, *91*
Madison, GA, *88–89*
Madison-Morgan Cultural Center, *88*
Madison Square (Savannah), *59*
Magic Wings Butterfly House, *142*
Magnolia Plantation and Gardens, *7, 212, 213*
Mail and shipping, *xix*
Main Street Gallery, *99*
Malcolm Blue Farm, *152*
Mann-Simons Cottage, *256*
Manteo, NC, *158*
Margaret Mitchell House, *26, 29*

Margaret Mitchell Park (Atlanta), *18, 22*
Market Hall, Charleston, *204, 206*
Martin Luther King Jr. Birth Home, *23, 25–26*
Martin Luther King Jr. Center for Nonviolent Social Change, *6, 23, 26*
Mast General Store, *189, 190*
MasterCard (credit card), *xxiv*
McElreath Hall, *30*
McKissick Museum, *257*
McNinch House, *114*
Meadow Garden, *93*
Media, *xxiv*
Medicine Man Crafts, *184*
Melon Bluff, *64*
Mendenhall Plantation, *131*
Mercer House, *61, 63*
Merchants Millpond State Park, *156*
Michael C. Carlos Museum, *31, 32*
Middleton Gardens, *7, 212*
Middleton Place, *201, 213*
Midway, *64*
Mighty Eighth Air Force Heritage Museum, *64*
Milledgeville, GA, *90*
Mint Museum of Art, *115–116*
Mint Museum of Craft, *114–115*
Moncks Corner, SC, *6, 228*
Money matters, *xxiv*
Monterey Square (Savannah), *55, 59*
Montmorenci Vineyards, *262*
Moore's Creek National Battlefield, *170*
Mordecai Historic Park (Raleigh), *136*
Morehead City, *165–166*
Morehead Planetarium, *145*
Morris Museum of Southern Art, *93*
Moses H. Cone Park, *187*
Mountain Farm Museum, *178*
The Mountains (NC), *175–192*
Murrells Inlet, SC, *237–238*
Museum of Anthropology, *128*
Museum of Aviation, *91*
Museum of Coastal History, *79*
Museum of Early Southern Decorative Arts, *127*
Museum of Hilton Head Island, *244*
Museum of North Carolina Handicrafts, *178*
Museum of the Albemarle, *156*
Museum of the Cherokee Indian, *176*
Museum of the Hills, *98*
Museum on the Common, *210, 212*
Museum Shop of the Historic Columbia Foundation, *256*
Museums
African-American heritage, 25, 30, 58, 59, 91, 251
Air Force, 64, 152
anthropology, 128
Appalachian culture, 189
art, 19, 21, 22, 32, 60, 91, 93, 115–116, 127, 128, 136, 142, 145, 169, 179, 205–206, 256, 267
Ava Gardner, 136
aviation, 91, 153
children's, 124, 135
Coca-Cola, 19, 23
Confederacy, 19, 30, 32, 206, 212
crafts, 114–115, 178
dolls, 131
furniture, 131
gem and mineral, 179, 257
gold, 96
history, 21, 30, 32, 59–60, 79, 92, 98, 115, 123, 131, 135, 156, 169, 189, 204, 212, 249, 256, 261, 262, 263, 264
horses, 262
Hurricane Hugo, 212
Japanese culture, 267
lifesaving, 160
maritime, 166, 212
military, 152, 204, 249, 256
motorcycle, 153
music, 90–91
Native American heritage, 176, 244, 263
natural history, 32, 186, 263
natural sciences, 3, 135
nature, 115
pottery, 153
puppets, 28
railroads, 178
rice, 240
science and technology, 29, 32, 91, 93, 114, 142
ships, 60
sports, 91
tartans, 178
tobacco, 142
Uncle Remus, 89
the unusual, 232
wax, 232
Myrtle Beach and the Grand Strand, SC, *4, 6, 201, 231–243*
Myrtle Beach Grand Prix, *233*
Myrtle Beach National Wax Museum, *232*
Myrtle Beach Pavilion Amusement Park, *232*

N

Nags Head, NC, *111, 157–158*
NASCAR Speedpark, *233*
Nathaniel Russell House, *207, 209–210*
National parks, *xxiv, xxv*
Natural History Museum (Blue Ridge Parkway), *186*
Natural Science Center of Greensboro, *123*
Neptune Park (St. Simons Island), *79*
Neptune Park Casino, *79*
New Bern Academy, *164*
New Bern and the Central Coast, *164–168*
New Echota State Historic Site, *100*
New Hanover County Arboretum, *169*
Ninety Six, SC, *264*
Ninety Six National Historic Site, *264*
Nippon Center, *267*
North Carolina, *3, 4, 107–194.* ☞ *Also* Chapel Hill; Charlotte; Durham; Greensboro; the Mountains; Outer Banks; Raleigh; Sandhills; Wilmington and the Cape Fear Coast; Winston-Salem
arts and crafts, 184
beaches, 109
emergencies, 193
gardens, 7
historic places, 109–110
itinerary recommendations, 111
lodging, 7, 110
restaurants, 6, 109
sports and outdoor activities, 110
timing the visit, 112
transportation, 192–193
visitor information, 194
North Carolina Aquarium at Fort Fisher, *159*
North Carolina Aquarium at Pine Knoll Shores, *165*
North Carolina Aquarium at Roanoke Island, *3*
North Carolina Arboretum, *180*
North Carolina Blumenthal Performing Arts Center, *114, 119*
North Carolina Botanical Garden, *145*
North Carolina Central University Art Museum, *141, 142*
North Carolina Maritime Museum, *166*
North Carolina Museum of Art, *136*
North Carolina Museum of History, *134, 135*
North Carolina Museum of Life and Science, *141, 142*
North Carolina Museum of Natural Sciences, *3, 134, 135*
North Carolina Pottery Center, *153*

North Carolina Zoological Park, *153*

O

Oakwood Cemetery, *135*
Oakwood Historic District, *134, 135–136*
Ocmulgee National Monument, *91*
Oconaluftee Indian Village, *176*
Ocracoke Island, NC, *111, 160–161*
Ocracoke Pony Pen, *161*
Odd Fellows Building, *23, 26*
Okefenokee National Wildlife Refuge, *6, 84–85*
Okefenokee Swamp Park, *84*
Old Burying Grounds, *166*
Old Citadel Building, *202, 206*
Old City Market (Charleston), *204, 206*
Old Exchange Building/Provost Dungeon, *207, 210*
Old Governor's Mansion, *90*
Old Greensborough, *124*
Old Powder Magazine, *204, 206*
Old Salem (historic site), *6, 127*
Old Santee Canal State Park, *228*
Old Settlers Cemetery, *114*
Old Sunbury, *64*
Old White County Courthouse, *97*
Olde Pink House, *59*
Omnimax theater, *114*
One Atlantic Center, *27–28, 29*
One Ninety One Peachtree Tower, *18, 22*
Opera, *44, 125, 264*
Orton Plantation Gardens, *7, 173*
Outer Banks, NC, *154–164*
Owens-Thomas House and Museum, *55, 59*

P

Pack Place Education, Arts & Science Center, *179*
Packing for the trip, *xxv–xxvi*
Palmetto Islands Country Park, *211, 212*
Palmyra Plantation, *64*
Paramount's Carowinds (amusement park), *116*
Parkway Craft Center, *187*
Parris Island, SC, *249*
Parris Island Museum, *249*
Passports and visas, *xix–x*
Patriots Point, *210, 212*
Pawleys Island, SC, *201, 238–240*
Peachtree Center, *18, 22*
Pea Island National Wildlife Refuge, *160*
Pendleton, SC, *270*
Penland School of Crafts, *180*
Penn Center Historic District, *251*
Perry, GA, *6*
Philips Arena, *3*
Phipps Plaza, *30, 49*
Photo help, *xiii*
Piedmont Park (Atlanta), *28, 29*
Pinehurst, NC, *111, 150–152*
Pirates, *161*
Planetariums, *91, 114, 123, 127–128, 145*
Poplar Grove Historic Plantation, *169*
Price categories
Georgia, 14, 15
North Carolina, 109, 110
South Carolina, 197, 200
Prince George Winjah Episcopal Church, *240*
Public library (Charlotte), *114*
Pullen Park (Raleigh), *136*

Q

Qualla Arts and Crafts Mutual, *176*

R

R. J. Reynolds Whitaker Park, *128*
Rain forest (exhibit), *114*
Raleigh, NC, *6, 111, 133–140*
Ralph Mark Gilbert Civil Rights Museum, *59*
Reed Gold Mine State Historic Site, *116*
Rembert Dennis Wildlife Center, *228*
Restaurants, *xvi, 4–5, 6, 36*
Asheville, 180–181
Atlanta, 33–40
Buckhead, 39–40
Chapel Hill, 145–146
Charleston, 214–218
Charlotte, 116–117
Columbia and the Heartland, 257–258, 260, 262, 264–265
Cumberland Island, 83
Durham, 143
Georgia, 87, 89, 90, 91–92, 93, 96, 98, 99, 100, 103
Greensboro, 124
High Point, 131
Hilton Head area, 244–245, 251, 253
Jekyll Island, 81
Little St. Simons Island, 78
the mountains (NC), 176, 187, 189, 190
Myrtle Beach and the Grand Strand, 233, 238–239, 241
New Bern and the Central Islands, 165, 166
North Carolina, 109
Outer Banks, 156, 157, 159, 160, 161
Pinehurst, 151
Raleigh, 137
St. Simons Island, 79–80
Sapelo Island, 76
Savannah 64–67
South Carolina, 197
Southern Pines, 150
Summerville, 229
Upcountry (SC), 267–268, 269
Wilmington and the Cape Fear Coast, 170, 171
Winston-Salem, 128–129
Reynolda House Museum of American Art, *128*
Reynolds Mansion, *76*
Reynolds Square (Savannah), *59*
Rhodes Memorial Hall, *28, 29*
Rice Museum, *240*
Ripley Farmhouse, *64*
Ripley's Aquarium, *233*
Ripley's Believe It or Not Museum, *232*
Ritz-Carlton, Atlanta, *18, 22*
Ritz-Carlton, Buckhead, *6, 30–31*
Riverbanks Zoological Park and Botanical Gardens, *257*
Riverfront Park and Historic Columbia Canal, *257*
Riverfront Plaza (Savannah), *55, 59*
Roanoke Island, NC, *111, 158–159*
Roanoke Island Festival Park, *158*
Robert Mills House, *256*
Robert Toombs House, *7, 92*
Rock climbing, *187*
Rollerblading, *47*
Roosevelt, Franklin Delano, *103*
Running, *47, 72*

S

Safety, *xxvi*
St. Helena Island, *251*
St. Helena's Episcopal Church, *249*
St. John's Episcopal Church, *58*
St. John's Lutheran Church, *204, 206*
St. John's Museum of Art, *169*
St. Michael's Episcopal Church, *207, 210*
St. Philip's Episcopal Church, *204, 206–207*
St. Simons Island, GA, *79–80*
St. Simons Lighthouse, *79*
Saluda, NC, *183*
Sandhills, NC, *149–154*
Sandhills Horticultural Gardens, *149*

Sapelo Island, GA, *76*
Sapelo Island Visitors Center, *76*
Sapelo Lighthouse, *76*
Sarah P. Duke Gardens, *7, 141, 142*
Savannah, GA, *6, 16, 54–75*
Savannah History Museum, *55, 59–60*
Savannah Theatre, *57*
Savannah Visitors Center, *55, 60*
Scarbrough House, *55, 60*
Science Museum (Charlotte), *114*
SciTrek (museum), *26, 29*
SciWorks, *127–128*
Scottish Tartans Museum, *178*
Scuba diving, *163, 168, 174, 226, 237*
Sea Island, GA, *78–79*
Sea Pines Forest Preserve, *244*
Seabrook Village, *64*
Seagrove, NC, *153*
Senior citizens, tips for, *xxvi*
Serena Dawes's House, *61, 63*
Shaw House, *149*
Sheldon Church (ruins), *253*
Ships of the Sea Museum, *60*
Shopping
antiques, 50, 72, 97, 100, 121, 140, 149, 226–227, 252, 259
art galleries, 50–51, 72–73, 123, 124, 132, 134, 140, 227, 249, 253
Atlanta, 49–51
baskets, 211
benne wafers, 73
books, 51, 73, 97, 114, 120, 147, 227, 249
Chapel Hill, 147
Charleston, 226–228
Charlotte, 120–121
Columbia and the Heartland, 259, 265
crafts, 73, 121, 130, 144, 183, 186, 227
Durham, 144
farmers' market, 140, 259
flea markets, 259
food, 51, 121, 140, 144, 147
furniture, 132, 183
general stores, 189, 190
gifts, 97, 98, 227
Greensboro, 126
High Point, 132
Hilton Head, 248–249, 252–253
jewelry, 249, 253
the mountains (NC), 182–183, 189
Myrtle Beach and the Grand Strand, 237, 239–240
nature, 249
outlets, 49–50, 126, 237, 269
period reproductions, 227–228
plants, 121
pottery, 97, 100, 153, 189
Raleigh, 140
Savannah, 72–73
Seagrove, 153
Southern Pines, 150
toys, 98
Upcountry (SC), 269
Wilmington and the Cape Fear Coast, 171
Winston-Salem, 130
Shrine of the Immaculate Conception, *19, 22*
Siege of Savannah site, *59*
Six Flags Over Georgia (amusement park), *33*
Skidaway Marine Science Complex, *64*
Skiing, *182, 187, 189, 191*
Sliding Rock (water slide), *183*
Smoky Mountain Gold and Ruby Mine, *176*
Soccer, *132, 140*
South Carolina, *3–4, 195–272.* ☞ *Also* Charleston; Columbia and the Heartland; Hilton Head area; Myrtle Beach and the Grand Strand; Upcountry
beaches, 197
emergencies, 272
gardens, 7, 197
guided tours, 272
itinerary recommendations, 200–201
lodging, 7, 197, 200
national and state parks, 271, 272
outdoor activities and sports, 200
restaurants, 6, 197
timing the visit, 201
transportation, 271
visitor information, 272
South Carolina Aquarium, *209, 210*
South Carolina Festival of Flowers, *263*
South Carolina State Botanical Garden, *270*
South Carolina State Museum, *256*
South Caroliniana Library, *257*
Southeastern Center for Contemporary Art (SECCA), *128*
Southern Pines, NC, *149–150*
Southport, NC, *172–173*
Southport-Fort Fisher Ferry, *172–173*
Spartanburg, *268–270*
Spas, *185*
Spirit Square, *114, 119*
Sports and outdoor activities, *xxv, 5.* ☞ *Also* specific sports
State Botanical Gardens of Georgia, *87*
State Capitol (Raleigh), *134, 136*
State House (SC), *256*
State Legislative Building (Raleigh), *134, 136*
State parks, *xxiv*
Stephen C. Foster State Park, *85*
Stone Mountain Park (Atlanta), *33*
Students, tips for, *xxvi*
Studio Theater, *29*
Subways, *52*
Sullivan's Island, SC, *212*
Summer camp, *248*
Summerville, SC, *6, 228–229*
Sumter, SC, *261–262*
Sumter County Museum, *261*
Surfing, *163, 175*
Suwanee Canal Recreation Area, *85*
Swan House, *30*
Swan Lake Iris Gardens, *261*
Sweet Auburn Curb Market, *23, 26*
Swimming, *47, 120, 266*
Symbols and icons, *xxix–xxx, 15, 110, 200, 278*
Synagogues, *60, 202, 205*

T

Tanglewood Park (Winston-Salem), *128*
Tannenbaum Park (Greensboro), *123*
Taxes, *xxvi*
Taxis
Georgia, 53, 74, 94, 101
North Carolina, 122, 148, 162, 167
South Carolina, 230, 242, 254, 265
Taylor-Grady House, *87*
Telephones, *xx, xxvi–xxvii*
Telfair Mansion and Art Museum, *55, 60*
Temple Mickve Israel, *60*
Tennis
Atlanta, 47
Chapel Hill, 147
Charleston, 4, 226
Charlotte, 120
Durham, 144
Greensboro, 126
High Point, 132
Hilton Head, 248
Jekyll Island, 82
Myrtle Beach and the Grand Strand, 237, 239
Pinehurst, 152
Raleigh, 140
Savannah, 72
Theater

Atlanta, 29, 44–45
Chapel Hill, 146
Charleston, 223
Columbia, 258–259
Durham, 144
Greensboro, 125
High Point, 132
the mountains (NC), 177, 179, 183
Outer Banks, 159
Raleigh, 138
Wilmington, 171
Winston-Salem, 130
Thomas Wolfe Memorial, *179*
Timing the trip, *xxx*
Tours and packages, *xxvii–xxviii*
Train travel, *xxviii*
Atlanta, 52
Charleston, 229
Charlotte, 122
Columbia and the Heartland, 265
Georgia, 104
Myrtle Beach and the Grand Strand, 242
North Carolina, 193
Outer Banks, 162
Sandhills, 153
Savannah, 73
South Carolina, 271
the Triad (Greensboro/Winston-Salem/High Point), 133
the Triangle (Raleigh/Durham/Chapel Hill), 147–148
Upcountry, 270
Transportation, *xxviii–xxix*
Travel agencies, *xxix*
The Triad, NC, *122–133.* ☞ *Also* Greensboro; Winston-Salem; High Point
The Triangle, NC, *133–148.* ☞ *Also* Raleigh; Durham; Chapel Hill
Tryon Palace, *164*
Tubman African American Museum, *91*
Tufts Archives, *150*
Tullie Smith Farm, *30*
Tunnelvision, *256*
Tweetsie Railroad, *188*
Tybee Island, GA, *64*

U

Uncle Remus Museum, *89*
Underground Atlanta, *18, 22, 49*
Unitarian Church, *204, 207*
University of North Carolina, *145*
University of South Carolina, *257*
University president's house, *87*
Upcountry, SC, *266–271*
USS *North Carolina* Battleship Memorial, *169*

V

Valle Crucis, NC, *190*
Visitor information, *xxix.* ☞ *Also under specific areas*
Visitor Information Center (Charleston), *207*

W

Warm Springs, GA, *103*
Washington, GA, *7, 92–93*
Washington Historical Museum, *92*
Water parks, *82, 233*
Water sports, *237*
Waterfront Park (Charleston), *204, 207*
Waynesville, NC, *178–179*
Weatherspoon Art Gallery, *124*
Weaverville, NC, *183, 185*
Web sites, *xxix–xxx*
Gerogia, 15
North Carolina, 110
South Carolina, 200
Wesley Monumental Church, *55, 60*
West Point on the Eno, *141, 142*
Weymouth Center, *149*
Weymouth Woods Nature Preserve, *149*
White Point Gardens, *209, 210*
Whitewater rafting, *190, 191, 192, 259, 270–271*
Wild Water (water park), *233*
William-Oliver Building, *18, 22*
Wilmington and the Cape Fear Coast, NC, *111, 168–175*
Windsurfing, *163, 248*
Wineries, *32, 262*
Wing Haven Gardens and Bird Sanctuary, *115, 116*
Winnabow, NC, *7, 173*
Winston-Salem, NC, *6, 111, 127–130*
Winston-Salem Visitor Center, *127*
Woodrow Wilson Boyhood Home, *256*
Woodruff Arts Center, *28, 29, 44*
Woodruff Park (Atlanta), *18, 22–23*
World of Coca-Cola, *19, 23*
Wright Brothers National Memorial, *156–157*
Wright Square (Savannah), *55, 60*
Wrightsville Beach, NC, *171–172*

Y

YMI Cultural Center, *179*
York W. Bailey Museum, *251*

Z

Zebulon B. Vance Birthplace, *183, 185*
Zebulon Latimer House, *169*
Zoo Atlanta, *23*
Zoos, *23, 123, 153, 257*

NOTES

NOTES

NOTES

NOTES